More praise for *Into the American Woods*

"[A] deeply researched and beautifully written study . . . [with] a colorful cast of characters."
—John Mack Faragher, Yale University, *Raleigh News & Observer*

"Greatly enlarge[s] our understanding of life on the colonial frontier."
—Michael Kenney, *Boston Globe*

"Impressively researched and thickly annotated. [Merrell's] prose is vibrant and clear, and he brings the individual go-betweens to vivid life. It is obvious that he sympathizes with his subjects, and he does a splendid job of making the reader feel their triumphs, privations, and aspirations. In giving breath to these forgotten ones, James Merrell has done a great service to anyone who values American colonial history."
—Floyd Largent, *American History Magazine*

"A fascinating, perceptive look at professional negotiators, a group little known even to scholars."
—Bruce Clayton, *Pittsburgh Post-Gazette*

"[An] original and illuminating 'chronicle of contact.' Expressive and imaginative, Merrell vividly recounts the adventures of key individuals . . . all the while taking care to reveal the 'rough reality' behind official accounts."
—*Booklist*

"A pathbreaking scholarly work by one of the nation's leading historians. . . . Anthropologists, ethnographers, even naturalists and linguists, as well as historians, will welcome and mine the book for years. . . . A stunning achievement."
—*Kirkus Reviews* (starred review)

"A stunningly original and exceedingly well-written account of diplomacy on the edge of the Pennsylvania wilderness."
—*Publishers Weekly*

ALSO BY JAMES H. MERRELL

*The Indians' New World: Catawbas and Their Neighbors
from European Contact through the Era of Removal*

NEGOTIATORS ON THE
PENNSYLVANIA FRONTIER

Into the
American Woods

JAMES H. MERRELL

W. W. NORTON & COMPANY
New York · London

For information about permission to reproduce selections from this book,
write to Permissions, W. W. Norton & Company, Inc., 500 Fifth Avenue,
New York, NY 10110.

The text and display of this book is composed in Perpetua with Perpetua Italic
Composition and manufacturing by the Haddon Craftsmen, Inc.
Book design by Charlotte Staub
Cartography by Jacques Chazaud

Library of Congress Cataloging-in-Publication Data

Merrell, James Hart, 1953–

   Into the American woods : negotiators on the Pennsylvania frontier
   / James H. Merrell.
      p.   cm.
   Includes bibliographical references and index.
   ISBN 0-393-04676-1
1. Frontier and pioneer life—Pennsylvania. 2. Pennsylvania—History—
Colonial period, ca. 1600–1775. 3. Pioneers—Pennsylvania—History—
17th century. 4. Pioneers—Pennsylvania—History—18th century.
5. Negotiation—Pennsylvania—History—17th century. 6. Negotiation—
Pennsylvania—History—18th century. 7. Indians of North America—
Pennsylvania—Government relations—History—17th century. 8. Indians
of North America—Pennsylvania—Government relations—History—18th
century. 9. Intercultural communication—Pennsylvania—History—17th
century. 10. Intercultural communication—Pennsylvania—History—18th
century. I. Title.
F152.M48   1999
974.8'02—dc21   98-24835
                                                  CIP

ISBN 0-393-31976-8 pbk.

W. W. Norton & Company, Inc.
500 Fifth Avenue, New York, N.Y. 10110
www.wwnorton.com

W. W. Norton & Company Ltd.
Castle House, 75/76 Wells Street, London W1T 3QT

4 5 6 7 8 9 0

TO THE MEMORY OF
JOHN NEMOTO MERRELL

Contents

List of Figures

List of Maps

—≈≫≈—

Chronology

1630s– Dutch, Swedish, and English colonists migrate to the Dela-
1670s   ware River Valley.

1681   King Charles II grants William Penn a charter to lands in
       America called *Pennsylvania,* making Penn and his heirs "true
       and absolute Proprietaries."

1682 or According to legend, Penn convenes a treaty council with
1683   Delaware Indians at Shackamaxon, near Philadelphia.

1690s Shawnees and Conoys migrate to the lower Susquehanna
       River Valley, joining Delaware migrants and the native
       Susquehannocks (now called Conestogas) there.

1701   Penn holds a council in Philadelphia with Conestogas,
       Shawnees, Conoys, and an Iroquois observer, shortly before
       his final departure from the province. The treaty confirms
       friendship, trade agreements, and sale to the proprietor of
       lands on the lower Susquehanna.

1720s Delawares and Shawnees, pressed by Pennsylvania farmers,
       begin migrations farther up the Susquehanna and across the
       mountains into the Ohio country.

1722   The Five Nations Iroquois adopt Tuscarora refugees from Car-
       olina, becoming the Six Nations.

       August–September.   Pennsylvania ambassadors visit Albany for
       a council with the Iroquois and representatives from New
       York and Virginia, an important stage in the shift in Pennsyl-
       vania's Indian relations from nearby Shawnees, Delawares,
       and Conestogas to the more distant Iroquois.

1732   Six Nations ambassadors treat with William Penn's son Thomas in Philadelphia, conclude a formal "Chain of Friendship" with the province, and agree that the Oneida leader Shickellamy and the German colonist Conrad Weiser will manage relations between Pennsylvania and Iroquoia.

1736   An Iroquois-Pennsylvania treaty in Philadelphia renews friendship, cedes Six Nations' claims to lower Susquehanna lands, and secretly agrees that the Iroquois shall speak for Delawares and all of the other Indians on the colony's borders.

1737   Thomas Penn and his brother John arrange the "Walking Purchase," a land cession by which Pennsylvania acquires far more territory in the Delaware Valley than Indians intended to grant; angry Delawares later call this "ye Running Walk."

1742   Pennsylvania council in Philadelphia with Iroquois, Delawares, Shawnees, and Conestogas. The Onondaga headman Canasatego supports Pennsylvania's "Walking Purchase" and chastises Delaware protesters.

1744   *January.* Britain declares war on France, beginning the War of Austrian Succession (known in America as King George's War).

        June–July. Treaty at the Pennsylvania frontier town of Lancaster between the Iroquois and representatives from Pennsylvania, Maryland, and Virginia. The Iroquois surrender their land claims in the two Chesapeake provinces. Colonists write this cession in a way that, read by Virginia expansionists, stretches westward to include the Ohio country.

1747   *October.* Virginia land speculators, acting on that expansive reading of the 1744 Lancaster agreement, form the Ohio Company of Virginia with plans to settle the Ohio region with colonists.

        November. Ohio Iroquois visit Philadelphia to seek trade and allies against the French. This first formal contact between Pennsylvania and the Iroquois, Delawares, Shawnees, and other Indians in the Ohio country opens a new chapter in Pennsylvania's Indian affairs.

1748   Britain and France conclude peace.

1749   A large French force travels down the Ohio Valley to reassert claims to the region and demand that Indians there break off relations with English colonies.

1750–   Christopher Gist, agent of the Ohio Company of Virginia, 1751   arouses native suspicion about land encroachment when he travels through the Ohio country to scout prospects for colonial settlement.

1752   Virginia and Pennsylvania treat with Ohio Indians at Logstown. Without telling the Six Nations or the Delawares living in Ohio, colonists get Indian assent to a broad interpretation of the 1744 deed of cession.

1752–   The French presence in Ohio grows, including attacks on 1753   pro-British Indians, banishment or capture of Pennsylvania fur traders, and construction of forts. Ohio Indians and go-betweens press British colonial officials to respond in kind, with little success.

1754   *June–July.*   Albany Congress between the Six Nations and representatives from seven English colonies, including Pennsylvania, to renew friendship and discuss response to French actions. Outside of the formal proceedings, Conrad Weiser engineers a large land purchase for Pennsylvania.

         July.   George Washington, commander of a Virginia force sent to counter the French, surrenders to the French at Great Meadows on the Pennsylvania-Ohio-Virginia border. Opening of the French and Indian War, also known as the Seven Years' War.

1755   *April.*   William Johnson is commissioned Crown superintendent of Indian affairs for the Northern Department, adding another powerful voice to British colonial arguments over Indian policy.

         July.   Approaching Fort Duquesne at the Forks of the Ohio, British General Edward Braddock is killed and his army nearly destroyed by French troops and their native American allies. Indian raids on Pennsylvania frontier farms begin soon thereafter.

1756   *May.*   Britain declares war on France.

July and November.   Councils at the Pennsylvania frontier town of Easton open peace talks with Teedyuscung and other Delawares from the upper Susquehanna. The Indians' assertion that land fraud was one cause of their war on the province ignites a political firestorm between Quakers and proprietary officials in Pennsylvania.

December.   Quaker leaders establish the Friendly Association for Regaining and Preserving Peace with the Indians by Pacific Measures.

1758   *October.*   Treaty at Easton to further peace with Ohio Indians, renew friendship with the Iroquois, settle land disputes, and return some of the disputed 1754 purchase to the Six Nations.

November.   Assured that the British will not settle west of the mountains, Ohio Indians withdraw from the French and Fort Duquesne falls to General John Forbes's army. Raids on Pennsylvania diminish, though mistrust and hatred linger on both sides.

1762   *June.*   Treaty at Easton, attended by Superintendent William Johnson, formally settles Delaware complaints about the Walking Purchase.

August.   Council at Lancaster formally concludes peace with Ohio Indians. Iroquois protest continued land encroachment.

1763   *February.*   Britain and France make peace.

May.   Outbreak of the so-called Pontiac's War; Indian raiding parties again strike the Pennsylvania frontier.

December.   Frontier Pennsylvanians called the "Paxton Boys" massacre the Conestoga Indians.

1768   Treaty at Fort Stanwix on the Mohawk River. The Iroquois sell much of the Susquehanna Valley, along with vast tracts of land in the Ohio country.

INTO THE AMERICAN WOODS

"I Have a Large Intriestt in ye Woods"

"The Woods"
Indians, Colonists, and the Lay of the American Land

On September 12, 1748, the Pennsylvania colonists Conrad Weiser and George Croghan sat in the open air at Logstown, an Indian village on the banks of the Ohio River. Bearing gifts and greetings from officials in Philadelphia, the two men had crossed the frontier between "english ground" and "the Indian countries" to open diplomatic relations with the native peoples west of the Allegheny Mountains.[1]

The meeting that fall day began a new chapter in a much longer chronicle of contact. For almost seventy years, people like Weiser and Croghan had helped Pennsylvania carry on negotiations with its Iroquois, Delaware, Shawnee, and other native neighbors (Map 1). And long before William Penn's colonists first arrived in 1682, North American Indian nations were deep in conversation with other colonists—Dutch and Swedes along the Delaware and Hudson rivers, English to the north and south, Spanish and French planted still farther away. In a still larger sense, the conversational thread can be followed back across the centuries, across the Atlantic Ocean, and across Indian country, for wherever and whenever different peoples have met, there one finds a go-between. Ever since the mythic past, when Hermes carried messages from the gods to the Greeks and Deganawidah (with his disciple, Hiawatha) went from one Iroquois Indian nation to another building the Great League of Peace—indeed, ever since human beings thought in terms of *us* and *them*—figures like Croghan and Weiser have been a familiar sight.[2]

Across the vast reaches of time and space, each set of encounters between peoples has had its own vocabulary, its own protocol, its own pace and rhythm. At Logstown in 1748, as throughout much of British colonial America, the idiom drew its power from notions of *the woods*. Before talks on Pennsylvania's latest diplomatic initiative could begin, Croghan and Weiser had to be cured of the afflictions they had suffered on their passage through those woods. So Tanaghrisson, an Iroquois leader, stood amid the crowd—besides the Pennsylvania emissaries and assorted other colonists there were "Deputies" of nine Indian nations present—and faced the two men. "Brethren," he began, holding a string of wampum, the beads made from seashells that were Indians' customary means of giving words weight, "You came a great way to visit us, and many sorts of Evils might have befallen you by the way which might have been hurtful to your Eyes & your inward parts, for the Woods are full of Evil Spirits. We give You this String of Wampum," the Iroquois went on, "to clear up your Eyes & Minds & to remove all bitterness of your Spirit, that you may hear us speak in good Chear."[3]

Tanaghrisson, Croghan, Weiser, and the rest that day were following the old script of an "At the Woods' Edge Ceremony," a script that acknowledged, and worked to counter, the power of "the woods" to afflict those traveling through them. Adopting a tone and cadence closer to song than speech, pacing back and forth with a wampum string in hand, the speaker would rehearse for the traveler the difficulties of a journey "thro' dangerous places, where evil Spirits reign, who might have put several things in your way to obstruct your Business." Accidents of all sorts could happen on the road, from broken bones to empty bellies, from briars that tore at legs and feet to rumors that twisted mind and heart.

To repair the damage, a host metaphorically wiped sweat from the sojourner's body and pulled thorns from his feet; but most of the attention went to the ears, eyes, and mouth, the avenues of communication. For a traveler to hear properly, ears had to be cleared "from any evil Matter that on Your Journey might have settled there." To "make You look clearer about You, and see Us your Brethren without anything between Us," eyes had to be wiped clean of tears and dust. And to "make you speak freely to us in what You have to say to us," the visitor's mouth and throat, his "Heart and mind," had to be freed of "all Grief & Uneasiness."[4]

The At the Woods' Edge Ceremony apparently began among the Five Nations Iroquois before European contact. Tradition has it that the founding of their famous League—which united the Mohawk, Oneida,

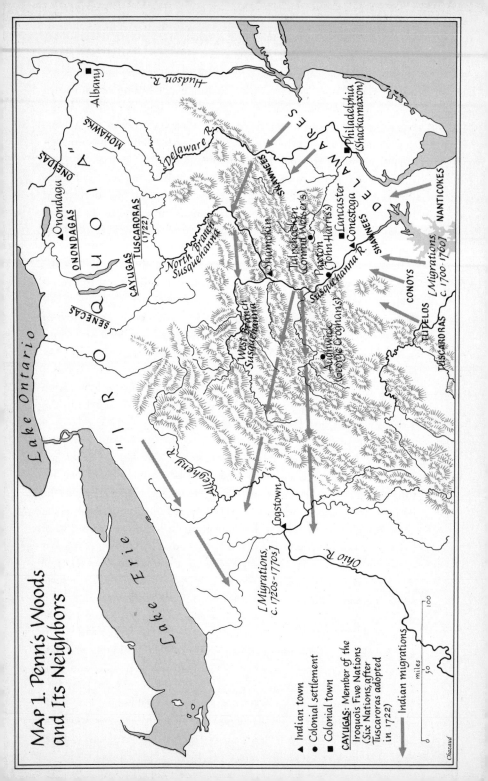

Map 1. Penn's Woods and Its Neighbors

Lake Ontario

Lake Erie

Albany

Hudson R.

MOHAWKS

ONEIDAS

Onondaga

ONONDAGAS

CAYUGAS

TUSCARORAS (1722)

SENECAS

"I R O Q U O I S"

Delaware

North Branch Susquehanna

West Branch Susquehanna

Allegheny R.

Logstown

Ohio R.

SHAWNEES

Shamokin

Tulpehocken (Conrad Weiser)

Paxton (John Harris)

Aughwick (George Croghan)

Lancaster

Conestoga

Susquehanna R.

Philadelphia (Shackamaxon)

D E L A W A R E S

SHAWNEES

NANTICOKES

CONOYS

TUTELOS

TUSCARORAS

[Migrations, c. 1700-1760]

[Migrations, c. 1720s-1770s]

miles

0   50   100

▲ Indian town
● Colonial settlement
■ Colonial town

CAYUGAS: Member of the Iroquois Five Nations (Six Nations, after Tuscaroras adopted in 1722)

→ Indian migrations

Chazaud

Onondaga, Cayuga, and Seneca peoples living west of the Hudson River in what is now upstate New York—included a gathering around a fire *"at the edge of the woods,"* between "the thorny underbrush" and "the cleared land."[5] Whatever the rite's origin, during the colonial era it became common among the peoples bordering the land of Iroquoia. In 1707 Shawnees welcomed a Philadelphia delegation to their Susquehanna River town by noting that "the ways are bad, and . . . the Bushes ware out your Cloths." Fifty years later, Delawares not only performed the Woods' Edge with Pennsylvania colonists but called it "an ancient and good Custom" that "Your Forefathers used to do with Ours when they met together."[6]

By then Pennsylvanians, too, had learned the language of the Woods' Edge. Provincial officials, coming to see that Indians wanted to be "spoke to in their own way," met arriving natives with "the usual addresses of clearing their throat, Ears and Eyes, and healing the Hurt of their Legs." "Brothers," Governor William Denny, holding four strings of wampum, said to Indians visiting Philadelphia in August 1758, "As you are Messengers, and have come a great way through the Woods, I Brush the Briers from your legs; I anoint the Bottom of your feet; I wipe the Dust out of your Eyes and Throat; I clear your Bodies from the Sweat and Dust, and I heartily bid you welcome."[7]

It is an image to cherish: the imperious Denny, decked out in wig and lace cuffs, standing there in the Pennsylvania State House (nowadays known as Independence Hall) with shell beads in his hand, on his tongue the talk of briars, sweat, and dust. In fact, however, while the Indian version certainly was new to Denny and the other colonists, the assumptions behind it were familiar enough, for these people were heirs of a tradition that considered the woods a forbidding place. For centuries, Europeans had drawn maps in their minds that set field against forest, order against disorder, light against darkness. To be sure, some threads of European thought depicted the wilderness as a realm of refuge, of spiritual testing, and some nations found in wild places the seed of their identity.[8] But it was more common to think of the wilds as what the Pilgrim leader William Bradford called "hideous and desolate" lands.[9] Lurking in those trackless wastes were peoples and creatures to be shunned lest one lose one's cultural bearings and lapse into the savagery Europeans proudly claimed they had left behind long ago.[10]

Little of this feel for the woods survives today. Whether resource to be harvested or refuge to be treasured, the woods are now so thoroughly bounded, mapped, and tamed that meanings once found there have faded. But some of the woods' ancient power remains, buried in our everyday speech. We talk of being *bewildered;* we call a neophyte *a babe in the woods;* we worry that someone is *not yet out of the woods.* The forest holds us in its grip still.

In colonial times that grip was almost unimaginably more powerful than it is in our day. Sailing from lands where people had beaten the forest back, perched on the edge of a vast and unknown continent, European immigrants cringed before America's shaggy countenance. Every colony founder, keen to see his province thickly settled, faced a formidable task in overcoming people's deep-seated fears of the wildwood; and none worked harder to banish those fears than Pennsylvania's proprietor, the great Quaker leader William Penn (Figure 1).

Like all advertisers, Penn tried to spin gold from straw by putting even the least appealing features of his product in a favorable light.

Figure 1. William Penn, by Francis Place, c. 1698.
Courtesy of the Historical Society of Pennsylvania.

Hence he called the American land grant he obtained from King Charles II "Pennsylvania," *Penn's Wood,* hoping that *sylvan* would banish dread from a prospective colonist's mind, conjuring up instead bright visions of sun-dappled groves.

Soon after arriving in his new land in October 1682, Penn set about reinforcing this message. He carefully listed all of "the Fruits that I find in the Woods" and exclaimed that "[t]he Woods are adorned with lovely Flowers, for colour, greatness, figure, and variety" superior even to the best garden in London. Are you frightened by all those trees crowding the very shore? Not to worry: "there is plenty for the use of man." And "the Beasts of the Woods"? Not terrible at all, the proprietor announced cheerfully, but rather furry or feathered natural resources, "some for Food and Profit, and some for Profit only."[11]

Other inhabitants of Penn's Woods were less inclined to celebrate its fruits, flowers, and creatures. This place would be "a fine country if it were not so overgrown with woods," grumbled Penn's cousin and advance man, William Markham, in 1681. An early German immigrant agreed, sighing: *Es ist alles nur Wald* ("But all of it is only forest"). And in 1734 the Founder's own son, John, less than a month after arriving in the province, shuddered that "the Woods are dark and thick."[12] So imposing was the forest that Pennsylvanians came to divide their world into two domains: "the Woods" and "the Inhabited Part of the Country."

The distinction here was artificial, a figment of the colonial imagination. Throughout the eighteenth century there still were forests within an afternoon's walk of Philadelphia, and plenty of clearings (as well as plenty of inhabitants) in "the woods."[13] But wilderness is a state of mind, not a state of nature; like beauty, it is in the eye of the beholder.[14] That is why transplanted Europeans living in *Penn's Woods,* the (steadily expanding) domain under English control, could talk fearfully of *the Woods,* the Indian countries lying beyond the limits of colonial settlement. And that is how these newcomers could construct a landscape of light and shadow that in the 1720s left Conestoga, a major Indian village just sixty miles west of Philadelphia, "far back in the Woods."[15]

This conceit was common not just with ignorant urbanites in the provincial capital but among colonists thoroughly acquainted with the lay of the American land. "I have a Large Intriestt in ye woods," observed one colonial fur trader in 1731, thinking of the Indian customers

awaiting him; though bound for native settlements, in his mind he was
heading "Back into ye Woods." Even a veteran go-between like Conrad
Weiser, who knew Indian clearings and communities well, so con-
formed to European habits of thought that he wrote of leaving "the inhabited part of Pennsylvania" and arriving three days later at Shamokin,
a native town on the Susquehanna River whose several hundred inhabitants made it among the largest urban areas, colonial or Indian, in the
region. In 1755 Lewis Evans, a Pennsylvania cartographer and sometime traveling companion of Weiser's, announced that "all America,
East of the Mississippi . . . , is every where covered with Woods, except
some interval Spots of no great Extent, cleared by the European
Colonets."[16]

These and other colonists bequeathed to future generations this
reading of the early American landscape, this delusion that dumped
Indians into what Evans called an "Ocean of Woods." The land in colonial times was "an ocean of leaves . . . ," remarked James Fenimore
Cooper, "one broad and seemingly interminable carpet of foliage."
"One vast, continuous forest shadowed the fertile soil," the great
nineteenth-century historian Francis Parkman agreed, "covering the
land as the grass covers a garden lawn, sweeping over hill and hollow
in endless undulation."[17] The paradigm lives on even today: when we
call natives living east of the Mississippi River *Woodland Indians* and
their negotiations *forest diplomacy,* we betray a habit of thought centuries old.[18]

As the At the Woods' Edge Ceremony suggests, native diplomats
would no more have practiced their craft in a forest than the United Nations would convene in an alley; the woods was simply the wrong place
for such work. Overlooked by colonists busy learning the At the
Woods' Edge rite was the obvious inference that the Indians teaching
them must also have mental maps setting off light from shadow, familiar from foreign, "the clearing" from "the Woods," "the Wilderness," or
"the Bushes," from what Delawares called *Tékene* and Iroquois termed
Garhàcu.[19] In the native Americans' clearing, with its houses and fields,
lay safety: here people were known and trusted; here the landscape
was ordered and subject to human control; and here, native storytellers
said, is where a cannibal, once cured, came to live, to bask in the sunlight of human society.[20]

But those storytellers also related how it was the forest that created cannibals in the first place. Not every corner of the Indians' woods was alien, dangerous territory, of course: natives left the clearing to hunt and fish, to collect everything from firewood and maple sap to berries and nuts. Nonetheless, Iroquois believed, ever since the day "Hiawatha plunged into the forest" on his sacred quest to found the Iroquois League and experienced "some occurrences of a marvelous cast," the woods had been an enchanted realm, a land of opportunity but also of peril. In the woods one might learn magical songs and dances or locate new sources of spiritual power. In the woods one could gain renown by killing deer or enemies. But in the woods, too, lurked stone giants and men with no heads, sorcerers and witches, mysterious forces that led the unsuspecting or the careless astray.[21]

And in the Indians' woods were Europeans. "There are . . . ," a French missionary observed, "tribes which the Iroquois call Garr hagon-ronnon, that is, 'inhabitants of the forests' or (remote lands)."[22] Whether colonists were included in this category is unclear, but there were suggestive parallels between Europeans and the other beings an Indian traveler encountered in his woods. Both were strange, unpredictable, and powerful. Both could win you status through acquisition of new goods or skills. And both could kill you. Certainly there are hints that a native venturing into what colonial Americans termed "the inhabited Parts" thought he was in woods. "Indians [are] ever Suspicious & cautious to go among white people . . . ," wrote one colonist; they did so only with "great . . . Mistrust & Apprehension."[23]

For Indians, too, the woods could be any spot one felt bewildered. In times of trouble, the woods threatened to invade the clearing itself, bringing "darkness" and "great noise" to towns like Shamokin. Even in Onondaga—the capital, the spiritual heart, of the Iroquois League— strife helped "evil Spirits" to "reign and bring forth Thorns and Briars out of the Earth."[24]

Thorns and briars, darkness and noise—Indians spoke in terms a colonist could grasp, for these folk, too, knew about woods. Both sides thought those territories a scary place, a domain of transformative power whether it turned medieval knights into wild men or Indian hunters into cannibals.[25] Ideas about where the woods could be found also overlapped: both counted as *woods* many of the same lonely stretches of forest and mountain in the interior. Such shared feelings and fears were vital in early America; they helped peoples construct what Richard White, studying the Great Lakes region in those times, has called a *middle ground,* a place where strangers found ways past their differences in order to gather and to talk.[26] *Woods* and *Woods' Edge* were, then, essential ingredients in the unlikely bond between men as different as William Denny and Tanaghrisson.

At the same time, however, *the woods* also marked the limits of that connection. After all, though Indian and colonial maps of America's wilderness overlapped, they were by no means identical. Gazing upon the landscape, each thought that the *other* inhabited those forbidding recesses: Philadelphia is in the woods, natives insisted, and Europeans are akin to stone giants or sorcerers; no, colonists countered, Onondaga—like Conestoga or Shamokin—is "far back in the Woods," and Indians are closer to bears or wolves than to people.

Moreover, the talk of woods masked a profound difference in cosmology. Indians believed that the woods ought to last forever. "[W]hole forests of standing trees . . . will be a source of happiness in the families," a modern Iroquois account has it. Native Americans were no tree huggers: they burned, felled, and tapped these forest giants as needed. But to them the dynamic, creative balance between order and disorder—a balance, a tension, represented by clearings and trees— was in the very nature of things. Indians could not imagine, and did not want, a world without woods.[27]

Colonists could, however, and they did. Fresh from European wars on the woods, veterans armed with axes and torches came to the New World ready to carry forward the Biblical injunction to subdue the earth. From John Smith at the beginning of the English colonial enterprise in eastern North America to J. Hector St. John de Crèvecoeur at its end, transplanted Europeans hacked away at the forest, dreaming of the day when the trees would be gone, the land cleared, the very climate and air forever changed.[28]

If colonists and Indians were ever to look past such fundamentally antithetical ideas of the American woods, if they were to get along at all, someone had to step in in order to downplay differences and play up— or, if need be, make up—areas of common ideology, common interest, and common experience. Locating (or constructing) consonance required people willing to go between "Indian ground" and "the English Country," to venture into foreign lands where the *other* dwelled—required, that is, someone "well vers'd in the Woods."[29]

"Wood's Men"
The Go-Betweens

Such "Wood's Men" were indispensable to the dialogue between cultures.[30] In dealing with Indians "[we] cannot do without you," wrote one colonial official to Conrad Weiser in 1751. Three years later an anxious George Washington sent word from western Pennsylvania that a go-between "would be of singular use to me here . . . in conversing with the Indians . . . . [F]or want of a better acquaintance with their Customs I am often at a loss how to behave." Young Washington was not alone: the collision of cultures in early America left Indian and European alike at sea, in need of the "Sheet Anchor" that a good negotiator was. With so many peoples, so many customs, so many languages, those who knew their way around the woods were "an invaluable Treasure."[31]

Given their importance, it is astonishing how far these figures remain cloaked in obscurity. From James Fenimore Cooper's Leatherstocking saga to Kevin Costner's *Dances with Wolves,* Americans have been fascinated by people who *lived* between Indian and white worlds. But few have noticed the many who *went* back and forth between those two worlds to carry messages, check out rumors, and settle disputes—who kept clear, as Indians put it, the path between peoples.

In Pennsylvania, the historical amnesia began almost at once, nurtured by the mythology that came to surround William Penn's relations with natives. Beginning shortly after the Founder's death in 1718, medals struck in England depicted Penn shaking hands with some Indian or, seated beneath a tree on a sunny day, passing the native a peace pipe across a cheerful fire; none of these tableaux included an interpreter (Figure 2).[32] Thus when Benjamin West, the Pennsylvania-born artist who won fame and fortune in London, began in 1771 to paint his own version of the Founder's benevolence, it is no surprise that he, too, omitted a translator. Choosing as his inspiration Penn's legendary 1682 treaty with the Indians beneath a majestic elm at Shackamaxon (near the site of Philadelphia), West depicted natives, emerging from the gloom of the woods, being drawn into the light brought by Penn and his people (Figure 3).[33]

In all of the attention to the painting's historical inaccuracies—Penn was not that fat in 1682; the colonial clothing and brick buildings re-

Figure 2. Peace Medal, 1757.

One of many medals struck during the eighteenth century to commemorate William Penn's friendship with Indians. Courtesy of the Historical Society of Pennsylvania.

Figure 3. William Penn's Treaty with the Indians, by Benjamin West, 1771.

Courtesy of the Pennsylvania Academy of Fine Arts, Philadelphia.

semble Philadelphia in the 1750s, not the 1680s; the natives' poses and postures owe more to classical Greece or Renaissance Italy than Indian America—no one has noticed the interpreter's absence. The mistake has since been compounded many times, because during the past two centuries Americans have embraced West's masterpiece and made his scene as central an icon of the American experience as Emmanuel Leutze's *George Washington Crossing the Delaware*.[34] West's *Treaty* has found its way onto everything from curtains and quilts to gravy boats and vegetable dishes, from jigsaw puzzles and banknotes to whiskey glasses and tavern signs, from Christmas cards and children's toys to an insurance company calendar and an advertisement for cough medicine.[35]

Closer to Shackamaxon, meanwhile, pride in the West version of Pennsylvania's birth grew apace. When the mythic "treaty elm" blew down in 1812, Philadelphians scurried off with the sacred wood to keep as mementos or carve into inkstands, armchairs, and snuffboxes.[36] A decade later another Pennsylvania painter, Edward Hicks, made the treaty a central motif of his life's work, both as a subject in itself and as a backdrop for his series of paintings on Isaiah, 11:6, *The Peaceable Kingdom* (Figure 4).[37] Like the West painting and its vast progeny, none of Hicks's many renderings of the treaty included a go-between. Looking toward the promised day when the lion would lie down with the lamb and the leopard keep company with the kid and calf, the Quaker artist clearly believed that on that glorious morn the barriers between Indians and Europeans, too, would come crashing down. Perhaps Hicks was right; but in early America, when these peoples did meet, they needed an interpreter.

A similar amnesia afflicts modern chronicles of those meetings and those interpreters. For all the recent attention to relations between Indian and European in colonial times, few scholars have ventured very far into the shadowy realm where negotiators operated. What work there is largely confines itself to biographies of major figures like Weiser and Croghan, then confines itself further by lauding them as pioneers in the opening of America to European settlement rather than as stage managers of a lively multicultural theater.[38] Nor has the imaginative use of the voluminous colonial treaty minutes given go-betweens their due.[39] Valuable as these works are in recovering native protocol and chronicling the Indians' diplomatic minuet with colonists, the account of formal proceedings is only part of the story.

Figure 4. The Peaceable Kingdom, by Edward Hicks.
Courtesy of the Abby Aldrich Rockefeller Folk Art Center, Williamsburg, Virginia.

Even as indifferent and inept a student of natives as Governor Denny knew that the official record did not do the formal treaty councils justice. "The private history of this very extraordinary Treaty . . . would afford good Entertainment had I time to go into the particulars," Denny remarked after one congress. The go-betweens on whom Denny and other Indian and colonial leaders relied so heavily offer an avenue into that entertaining—and illuminating—"private history," for it was their job "to go into the particulars." Equally important, they knew what Denny did not: the frontier's full story cannot even be found in a treaty's proceedings, public or private, but lay farther afield, in the day-to-day "drudgery" of what natives and colonists both termed "Indian Business."[40] Before a speaker could rise, wampum in hand, to open a treaty session, before a scribe's pen even began to scratch its way down a page, there was a vital round of journeys taken, meals shared, letters scribbled, beads strung, speeches drafted, and squabbles settled.

This work, and the famous council orations it framed, was as magical as it was mysterious, as powerful as it was perilous. Go-betweens transformed gibberish (whether English or Iroquois, Delaware or Shawnee) into words. They gave mute strings of shells and black marks on paper the power of speech. They took men with alarming scalplocks and tattoos or with curious wigs and odd shoes and, explaining them one to another, made these men less strange. Yet the alchemy of interpretation, the very essence of the American encounter, has been all but forgotten.[41]

The causes of this forgetfulness are easy enough to find. Colonial leaders who left most of the records tended to mistrust and despise the intermediary, uncomfortable with his importance and uncertain of his loyalties. "Rogue," "impudent felow," "vile . . . wretch" and worse epithets came easily to the tongues and pens of Pennsylvanians, reinforcing an inclination to dismiss or downplay the role of these people. Moreover, colonial devotion to the tidy *product* of frontier diplomacy— treaties with seals and signatures—led scribes to pay less attention to the messy *process* behind these documents. And historians, drawn to the copious council minutes, have tended to linger at the council ground, overlooking those who brought everyone together in the first place.

Perhaps another reason scholars avoid negotiators is the sheer difficulty of defining them, of picking them out of the crowd of peoples in America's border country. Not everyone there—not every colonial or Indian trader, not every missionary or Christian convert—was a go-between. What distinguished the fur trader George Croghan from the fur trader George Gabriel or the Conestoga Tagotolessa (Civility) from the Conestoga Tawenna was that now and then Croghan and Civility took on "a sort of publick Character," becoming a person "charged" with the "Publick Business" of "State affairs." This special status comes through powerfully in a later Iroquois story of one Hatondas who, en route to a foreign land, lost the wampum that served as his credentials, a calamity which "meant that when Hatondas should enter the strange country, it should be without honor and . . . as a common man."[42]

Nor was everyone who had a hand in state affairs a go-between. William Penn, the Penn family's secretaries James Logan and Richard Peters, and governors like William Denny devoted considerable time to Indian business, as did Tanaghrisson and other native leaders. But men such as Croghan and Weiser or the Oneida Iroquois Shickellamy and Scarouyady had a deeper, more intimate involvement. An Onondaga named Canasatego understood the difference. In 1742, half in jest, he told Pennsylvania officials that Weiser "has had a great Deal of Trouble with Us, wore out his Shoes in our Messages, and dirty'd his Clothes by being amongst Us, so that he is as nasty as an Indian."[43] However sarcastic, Canasatego caught something essential about go-betweens: they got dirty, both literally and figuratively. Negotiation entailed a weary round of trips across unforgiving terrain to reach the far side of the frontier and, once there, a journey of a different (if no less difficult) sort into another culture.

To come at these sojourners another way, it might be said that they were the ones who carried the letters, but did not sign and seal them; who memorized the speech on wampum belts, but did not draft it; who translated, but did not speak, at the grand councils; who stood between the tables crowded with colonial and Indian leaders at a treaty banquet to make sure that the liquor and talk flowed freely, but did not join the feast. If travel and translation left them considerable room for maneuver, if those drafts and speeches bore the imprint of their advice, nonetheless these people were operating on the borderlands in a particular and uniquely important fashion.

Sifting cultural interpreters from other frontier folk and from leaders on both sides still leaves a motley collection of people, from many walks of life, that resists easy generalization. Weiser was a German farmer, magistrate, and mystic, Croghan a hard-headed, hard-drinking Irish fur trader. Sometimes these two got along, as at Logstown in 1748; sometimes they did not. And in the course of their careers they worked with a varied cast of characters that included Shickellamy (on the Susquehanna), Scarouyady (an Ohio man), the *métis* Andrew Montour, the Delaware Presbyterian Tunda (Moses) Tatamy, and the former Indian captive Gersham Hicks.

To make it harder still to define go-betweens, there were vast differences in the extent to which people joined the cross-cultural conversation. Weiser, Croghan, Shickellamy, and Montour practically made a career of Indian business. But many others—Elizabeth Cornish and Barefoot (or Bearefoot) Brunsden, James Narrows and Conoy Sam—suddenly showed up to interpret a speech or deliver a message, then vanished as abruptly as they had appeared.

The bit players expose the risks of conventional biography or proso-pography to get at the go-between; too many people, too much of the discourse, can be lost in the attention to the Weisers and Shickellamys. Hence the approach here has a studied vagueness. Rather than hammering out hard and fast rules or concocting categories into which every "true" intermediary must fit, I have examined what everyone taking part in these discussions had to say, and how they said it.

My terminology is equally eclectic. Indians and colonists called these people by many names: *agent, messenger, ambassador, Mr. Interpreter, Manager, Province Interpreter, mediator, ne horrichwìsax, n'donasĩt, friend, a person to do Indian Business, thuwawœnachquáta, Anhuktõnheet, Guardian of all the Indians, a person to go between Us.* The pages ahead employ many of these terms, along with *negotiator,* because that word so aptly conveys what these people were about. *Negotiation*—what George Croghan once called "Nogeaucating Maters"—entails compromise, give-and-take, a need to get over, through, or around obstacles "by skill or dexterity." The word's Latin roots—*not easy* (or *quiet*)—are also telling.[44] Compromise, dexterity, difficulty, noise—these capture nicely what a woodsman faced.

⸻❧⸻

"That They Might the Better Be as ye Same"
Approaching the Woods and Woodsmen

Though long ignored, negotiators are not particularly hard to find. Pocahontas and the Pilgrims' friend Squanto are only the most famous of the many intermediaries in colonial times. When read between the lines or with an eye for asides and afterthoughts, for slips of tongue and pen, the usual sources on Indians in early America—treaty minutes and other official documents, accounts by travelers, missionaries, and fur traders—have many tales to tell of go-betweens' adventures and misadventures. Rather than try to recount all of those tales, I consider in depth one stretch of the colonial borderland, for the frontier's human face is easiest to see, I think, in a narrower compass.

But not too narrow. Indeed, I explore the Pennsylvania frontier because the scale there is just right. William Penn's vision of harmony and its enduring hold on the colonial and Indian imagination lend the story coherence; it is possible to trace how peoples from Pennsylvania's founding in the early 1680s to the late 1760s tried to realize, and how they ultimately abandoned, that bright dream. At the same time, the Pennsylvania frontier offers a substantially larger canvas than Benjamin West and Edward Hicks used—or, rather, four canvases, four stages, each larger than the last.

The story starts small, with Penn's first settlers perched beside the Delaware River, dealing primarily with local natives. After 1700, however, the colony's expanding horizons carried its frontier farther afield, first to the Susquehanna Valley, then north into Iroquoia, and ultimately, by midcentury, west toward the heart of the continent. Picking up the go-between's trail along the Delaware in Pennsylvania's infancy, then following that trail up the Susquehanna and over the mountains in the eighteenth century, weds a tight focus to a wide geographical and chronological range.

Thanks to an abundance of fine modern scholarship, the four phases of Pennsylvania's frontier history are familiar. In some ways, Edward Hicks was right: the Quaker province was a remarkably peaceable kingdom, a place unusual, even unique, in the annals of colonial British America. Virginians had their battles with Powhatan and Opechancanough, New Englanders their wars against Pequots and King Philip, Carolinians their bloody conflicts with Tuscaroras and Yamasees. And Pennsylvanians? They had "the Long Peace," stretching from the colony's founding to the mid-1750s.

The secret of that peace lay in a happy conjunction of Penn's benevolent views on Indians with the conditions his settlers found on their arrival. The nearby Delawares were predisposed to get along with the newcomers. Fragmented in small bands, fearful of the Iroquois, accustomed to (yet wary of) Europeans after two generations of dealing with Dutch, Swedish, and English colonists, these natives were inclined to be friendly. Penn's talk of having "come to sit downe Lovingly among them," his hope that in time "we may more largely and freely confer & discourse," was welcome indeed, as was his willingness to pay for lands his people settled. It helped that the Susquehanna Valley just to the west sat virtually empty, Iroquois raiders having all but annihilated the natives there in the 1670s. Thus when Penn purchased large portions of the Delawares' ancestral territory, the sellers had someplace else to go.[45]

As Penn's people, their numbers growing rapidly, pushed west from their Delaware River beachhead after 1700, the borderlands became a more complicated, more contentious place. Settling the Susquehanna Valley, colonists crossed paths not just with those Delaware emigrants but also with Shawnees from remote lands to the south and west, Conoys and Nanticokes from Maryland, and other groups in retreat from skirmishes with Europeans elsewhere in eastern North America. Then, in the late 1720s, Pennsylvania's Indian relations entered a third phase as provincial leaders, partly to master those new (and sometimes unruly) Indian neighbors, looked farther up the Susquehanna in order to befriend the Iroquois, now called the Six Nations after the 1722 adoption of Tuscarora refugees from North Carolina. Together, men in the Iroquois capital of Onondaga and Philadelphia worked to control the native peoples living between them, control that included completing the Delawares' dispossession in a series of shady land deals, the most infamous of them the 1737 Walking Purchase that angry Delawares called "ye Running Walk."

Its neighbors thus subdued, in the late 1740s Pennsylvania's frontier saga began a fourth, and final, phase as the colony shifted its attention yet again, this time to Indians of the Ohio country. Those distant groups, many of them disgruntled Delaware and Shawnee migrants from Pennsylvania and Iroquoia with little love for either, came to preoccupy the province, even as officials in Philadelphia kept talking with the Six Nations and with what Indians still lived beside the Delaware and Susquehanna. As if longer and more tangled lines of communication were not enough to sow confusion, after 1750 Pennsylvania's relentless expansion (and its even greater territorial and trading appetites) collided in Ohio with the ambitions of Virginia and French Canada.

In the end, no amount of negotiation, however skilled, could satisfy so many competing interests. Nor could it subdue lingering native resentments about land fraud and other past wrongs or lay to rest fears of further colonial encroachment. With these pressures, and with French agents bent on turning Indians against Britain, in the mid-1750s the Long Peace ended when native warriors struck Pennsylvania and its neighbors, igniting a conflagration since known as the French and Indian War or the Seven Years' War. The bloodshed and anguish forever changed the face of the frontier, leaving Penn's peaceful vision little more than a memory. Shackamaxon's bright beginning had as its grim counterpart the slaughter in 1763 of friendly Conestoga Indians by Pennsylvania frontiersmen calling themselves the Paxton Boys.

The drama that unfolded—from the Delaware Valley in the 1680s to the Susquehanna a generation later and, a generation after that, to the Ohio—marked a sickening plummet from peace to war. By including go-betweens in this story, we may restore them to their proper place in America's past while also shedding new light on the frontier experience. The famous "Long Peace" looks less peaceful than legend would have it. Behind all the smiles, handshakes, and kind words was hard, sometimes dirty work. Rescuing that work from oblivion suggests how fragile peace was, how often misunderstanding and mistrust ruled. Using the emissary to recall the anxieties, insults, and threats helps, too, to chart how, after 1750, Penn's Woods became an abbatoir.

Just as setting Benjamin West and Edward Hicks aside in favor of Shickellamy and Conrad Weiser changes Pennsylvania from abstract icon to rough reality, so tuning out the eloquent rhetoric about ambassadors that Indians and colonists traded at public councils overturns powerful assumptions about negotiators. To hear the cheerful treaty talk tell it, the go-between was some real-life Natty Bumppo, one foot planted—like his famous fictional kinsman, Cooper's legendary Leatherstocking—in each world. Conrad Weiser (known as *Tarachiawagon* or *Siguras*) is "divided . . . into two equal Parts," the Iroquois once explained to colonists, "one we kept for our selves and one we left for you." Putting this exalted, liminal position to good use, the fine phrases went on, envoys choreograph relations between peoples so well that, as a Delaware headman named Sassoonan said, native and colonist "should be Joyn'd as one, that the Indians should be half English & the English make themselves as half Indians, that they might the better be as ye same."[46]

A closer look at go-betweens shatters the illusion. Negotiators were not, it turns out, denizens of some debatable land between native and newcomer; almost without exception, they were firmly anchored on one side of the cultural divide or the other. Moreover, the European and native American visions obscured by elegant oratory bore little resemblance to William Penn's benevolent blueprint or Sassoonan's ringing call for union. Weiser and other colonial mediators, never shedding prejudices that Europeans brought to America, embraced the idea that getting along with Indians was only a necessary step on the road to a brighter future, a time when those Indians would follow the forest into oblivion. For their part, Shickellamy, Scarouyady, and the other envoys from Indian country did pursue coexistence, but it was a coexistence designed to keep colonists at arm's length so that Indian peoples could remain masters of their own destiny. Here we approach the woods' harsh lesson: the ultimate incompatibility of colonial and native dreams about the continent they shared. Just as Indians envisioned a world of woods and clearings, so they could imagine a world shared by natives and Europeans. But just as colonists—even colonial negotiators—anticipated, someday, a world without woods, so they pictured a world without Indians.

Thus go-betweens, whose charge was to bring native Americans and Europeans into the clearing's sunlight, end up revealing how much darkness and noise reigned even there. While all sought harmony, while they played up similarities, they could not, they did not want to, erase the differences they saw between colonist and Indian. They, too, thought the existence of *English ground* and *Indian ground,* of *us* and *them,* was nonnegotiable.

Revealing the darkness at the heart of the frontier, negotiators also uncover that frontier's paradox. Over time, mediators actually got better at conducting the conversation between cultures; in 1748, when Weiser and Croghan set off for Logstown, Indians and colonists had more capable people to call on than ever before. But at the same time, the distance between those cultures, pushed by unhappy memories and continual friction, actually widened rather than closed. Familiarity bred people with the skill to bring strangers together in order to share ideas and solve problems; but familiarity also bred contempt, contempt so deep that by the end of the colonial era go-betweens were practically out of work, the time for talk was all but over.

"Enter In and Examine Every Part"
Telling of Woods and Woodsmen

Uncovering the go-between's story is one thing, telling it another. Though biographies of this negotiator or that are standard fare, the genre's limits are as obvious as the limits to one person's life: it is hard to tell if the fellow under the microscope is typical of the species. Collections containing short studies of various individuals remedy that defect, but what these volumes gain in breadth they lose in coherence. The whole is often less than the sum of its parts, for the attention to scattered, solitary actors risks losing the nuances of the world in which each lived.[47] A straightforward narrative that marched down the years from one treaty to the next seemed no more suited to my search for patterns in the tapestry of negotiation.

Not that I altogether leave the familiar behind. William Penn's vision; Delaware removal; historic treaties at Philadelphia, Lancaster, and Easton; frontier war; the Paxton Boys' rendezvous with infamy—these and other landmarks on the road from Shackamaxon to Paxton and beyond were all part of a go-between's business, and all find their place in the pages that follow. But that business itself is my central concern.

To make that business my business, to chronicle the life of this frontier, the book assumes an unconventional shape that is in keeping with these unconventional characters. Alternating with chapters of woodslore, which I describe below, four chapters analyze the essential ingredients of negotiation. The first, "Paths to the Woods," considers what Indians and colonists were looking for in an emissary, then explores the native villages, colonial trading posts, missionary stations, and other communities where they found performers to cast in the role. The next, "Passages through the Woods," finding significance in the way people crossed the borderlands, follows go-betweens into the woods in order to elucidate the meaning of such things as horses and insects, fords and foods, canoes and campsites. A third chapter, on "Conversations," then explores the lifeblood of coexistence, the talks negotiators carried on once they reached their destination; it contemplates the hazards of carrying and translating messages, and the changing fortunes of the wampum and paper that encoded those words. "Treaties," the final chapter, ventures at last onto the council ground to scrutinize these grand events—sometimes including thousands of people—as the go-between saw them. From drinking and dancing to threats and thefts, from haughty provincial officials and Indian leaders to angry farmers and warriors, this behind-the-scenes look explains why a congress was at once the intermediaries' finest hour and their worst nightmare.

That treaty ground, where all eyes were on the interpreter, is a long way from the isolated hut, lonely trail, and quiet chatter that occupied most of a go-between's days. But different as these four chapters are in subject, they share a common organization and argument. Each starts by laying out the challenges negotiators faced, then goes into how they sought to overcome these obstacles, only to return, at the end, to the enduring sense of difference that neither side could shake—a sense that, I argue, was even more pronounced at the end of the colony's history than the beginning.

Reconstructing these four dimensions of the interpreters' enterprise suggests the patterns of negotiation central to frontier life. To more fully evoke that life, to complement and explicate those patterns, I also include long-forgotten stories of the woods that might once have been told around a fire in Onondaga or Logstown, at Croghan's hearth or Weiser's. Retelling this old lore unveils the particulars that went into the patterns, and helps us to see the frontier as go-betweens did: one task, one trip, one crisis at a time.[48]

That retelling gives the book a contrapuntal rhythm. It opens with a murder mystery from 1744, which introduces go-betweens at the very height of their powers; it closes with another killing twenty-five years later that measures how much had changed in that short span. Between these two tales, interwoven with the chapters on recruitment, travel, talk, and treaties, are other chapters, full of woodslore, that help to recover the rough texture, the gritty feel of the colonial frontier.

Throughout, go-betweens provide a different angle of approach to the American encounter, fresh ways of seeing familiar sights like treaties while offering new vistas—life on the trail, the murmur of conversation—to contemplate. "Our Indian agents are a kind of Load Stone attracting the Indians," groused the British officer Henry Bouquet in 1762, fretting about the cost of presents for those crowds of natives. Bouquet's burden is our boon; in this very attraction lies the negotiator's value for obtaining a fuller, richer, more colorful picture of the early American scene.[49]

"Do not [just] Stand at the Doors of the Houses of the Six Nations," Pennsylvania's Governor Robert Hunter Morris advised Scarouyady as the Oneida man headed off to Iroquoia one winter; "Enter in and examine every part of them, and see exactly what they are doing. Things may look fair when viewed at the Door, that upon going in will look much otherwise," Morris explained. Therefore you must "Search their real Inclinations and return this Way and let us know them. . . . See for us Scarroyady; Hear for us; Speak for us."[50] So, too, shall we "enter in and examine" the frontier in order to learn more "exactly" what it was like. Trailing along behind Scarouyady and the rest, crowding in with them as they crossed the threshold, peering over their shoulders, picking up snatches of their conversation, we necessarily must spend, as they did, some time on the road, in the woods, and "in the bushes" (that is, behind the scenes) before emerging into the light of the great treaties. But the journey is worth it, for with the go-between as our guide we can make our way back to where Indian met colonist face to face. In taking us there, negotiators play a new (though familiar) role: not just explaining Old World to New, but also their world to our own.

The Killing of Jack Armstrong, 1744

"Give Me My Horse, I Tell You"
The Killing

The best way to become better acquainted with go-betweens—to appreciate the noise and darkness they contended with, to grasp how they muffled that noise and dispelled that darkness—is to watch them, at the apex of their abilities, handle a particular problem. No problem serves that purpose better than the one involving Jack Armstrong, Mushemeelin, and a horse.[1]

The version of the story that negotiators agreed to credit goes like this. One February morning in 1744, Mushemeelin, a Delaware from the Susquehanna River town of Shamokin, killed a Pennsylvania fur trader named John (Jack) Armstrong. The two men had known each other for some time, long enough at least for the Indian to run up a debt to the colonist. In the fall of 1743, Armstrong, rather than wait for that debt to be paid off in bear or beaver, had seized Mushemeelin's horse and gun. Then, with his servants James Smith and Woodward Arnold, Armstrong left his Susquehanna home to barter with Indians beyond the Allegheny Mountains (Map 2).

Mushemeelin, whose hunting cabin was near "the Allegheny Road" that followed the Juniata River west, wanted that horse back. His first chance came when he intercepted Armstrong close to the Juniata's junction with the Susquehanna. The Delaware "demanded his Horse"; Armstrong refused. Days later, as the colonial traders passed Mushemeelin's hut, his wife, too, asked for the animal, only to get the same answer. On returning from a hunt and hearing her story, Mushemeelin decided "to pursue and take Revenge of Armstrong." Collecting his

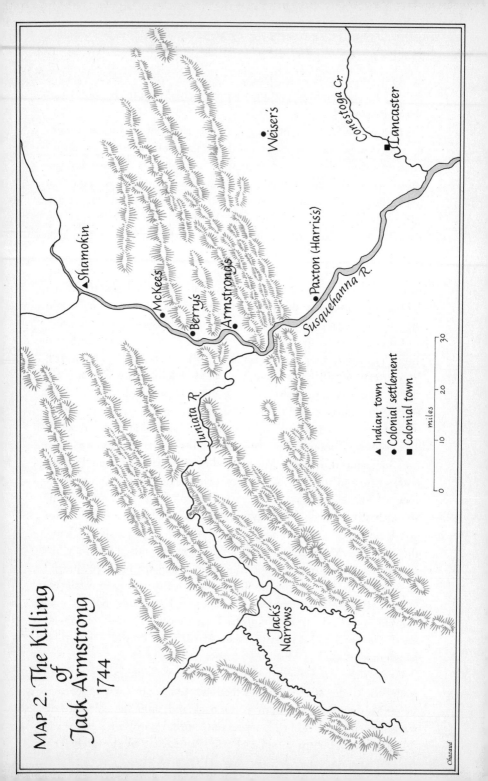

MAP 2. The Killing of Jack Armstrong 1744

Shamokin
McKee's
Berry's
Armstrong's
Weiser's
Paxton (Harris's)
Lancaster
Conestoga Cr.
Susquehanna R.
Juniata R.
Jack's Narrows

▲ Indian town
● Colonial settlement
■ Colonial town

miles
0   10   20   30

Chazaud

hunting companions, two young Delawares whom Pennsylvanians called John and Jemmey, the angry native headed west to (he told them) "Hunt Bears."[2]

Having traveled all night, soon after sunrise the three Indians caught up with Armstrong and his men at the Juniata Narrows, where mountains crowded close to the river. Before they approached the colonists' camp, Mushemeelin stopped to blacken his face like a warrior—in hopes, he said, of scaring Armstrong into surrendering the horse. If Jack still refuses, the Delaware laughed, "I will kill him." The two young men, their bear hunt turning into something quite different, "thought he Joaked as he used to do" and followed him nervously into the traders' bivouac. There they found James Smith sitting by a fire; Arnold was off in the trees someplace; Armstrong was ahead, breaking trail. While John and Jemmey joined Smith to plan breakfast, Mushemeelin, "laughing," went after the other two. He found Arnold, shot him in the head, and then returned to the campfire, where he discovered Smith still alive. "How will you do to kill Catabaws," bitter foes of the Delawares, "if you cannot kill white Men?" he scolded John. "You Coward, I'll shew you how you must do." Burying an axe in Smith's brain, he led his terrified companions off to find Jack Armstrong.

Armstrong, sitting on a log near the trail, looked up to see trouble. Two frightened young Delawares, hanging back. And here came Mushemeelin, painted for war; Mushemeelin, who had left their last encounter furious and on foot; Mushemeelin, asking again, "Where is my Horse?" The trader was conciliatory. "He will come by and by," Armstrong hastily assured the Delaware, "you shall have him." That was not good enough: "I want him now," came the reply. "[Y]ou shall have him," the colonist said again. Desperate, Armstrong proposed that they follow the Indian custom signaling friendship among travelers. "Come, let us go to that Fire" nearby, he urged, "and let us smoke and talk together." The Delaware seemed willing enough, but then neither man wanted to go first—and turn his back on the other. " 'Go along then,' say'd Mussemelin. 'I am coming,' said Armstrong, 'do you go before[.'] Mussemeelin [said,] [']do you go foremost.' "

Armstrong knew then that he was doomed: looking "like a Dead Man," the trader started toward the fire. He had gone but a few steps when Mushemeelin shot him in the back and, after the colonist fell, sank a hatchet into his head, asking once more: "Give me my Horse, I tell you." Next the three Indians buried Armstrong and tossed his servants' bodies into the Juniata. Then, with a warning that if they told anyone they would "fare like the White men," Mushemeelin led John and Jemmey back to his hunting cabin.

～～～

"A Great Noise Arose"
Go-betweens Get to Work

Jack Armstrong and his men were not the first Pennsylvanians killed by Indians. Ordinarily, their deaths would have attracted little attention, and Armstrong's name would live on only in "Jack's Narrows" on the Juniata, a reminder to all who passed that way not to push an Indian too far.[3] But the early months of 1744 were far from ordinary. Many of Pennsylvania's Delaware and Shawnee neighbors were said to be abandoning the English for the French, and this at a time when the two European powers were on the brink of another war. The Six Nations Iroquois, who could, perhaps, win back disaffected Indians and at least serve as a buffer against French Canada, were mysteriously quiet about the upcoming treaty conference at the Pennsylvania frontier town of Lancaster, called to cement an alliance with Pennsylvania, Maryland, and Virginia. Now, while people worried about the French and wondered about the silence from Iroquoia, came the news about Armstrong. If the Lancaster council was to go forward, if the Iroquois (and those Shawnees and Delawares) were to remain friends, if the French menace was to be met, this matter had to be handled in a way that mollified frontier settlers without provoking Indians. Improbable as it might appear to us, it seemed to some at the time that the fate of empires (not to mention colonial farms and Indian towns on Pennsylvania's border) might be decided by a squabble over a horse.[4] Go-betweens would have their work cut out for them.

That work began one morning in early April with a Tutelo Indian making his way through Shamokin toward the door of the prominent Oneida go-between, Shickellamy. Late last night, the Tutelo said, a drunken Delaware dropped by my house with "a piece of bad News" about what had happened on the Juniata. The Susquehanna country had been alive with rumors about foul play, but wild talk was common on the frontier. Now Shickellamy began to think it more than talk, and to fear the worst. Knowing how explosive this news was—but knowing, too, that it was Delaware business—he went straight to Sassoonan, the aged Delaware headman, "and pressed upon him to make Imediatly inquiry and find out the murderers." While Sassoonan gathered his councilors, Shickellamy quietly pursued his inquiries among Delawares said to know the details. One old man, confirming the story, "was a feared there would be Some Blood Shed about it before all was over."[5]

The Delaware council set out to prevent that. Its first step was to have a Tutelo write to Conrad Weiser at the colonist's farm in the Tulpehocken Valley, asking him to come quickly. Weiser, an Iroquois specialist, decided that he "did not care to medle with Delaware Indian affairs" and stayed put. But in the colonial trading community beside the Susquehanna, other Pennsylvanians were making it their business. Determined to learn Jack Armstrong's fate, his brother Alexander, along with Thomas McKee, James Berry, and six more fur traders, went upstream to Shamokin. There they met with Indian leaders and agreed to send a joint search party—eight Delawares would go with the colonists—up the Juniata.

Finding the bodies after two months would be as hard as it was grim. Close to Armstrong's last campsite, James Berry saw a tree with three notches cut in it; nearby was a human shoulder bone. Their worst fears confirmed, the men widened the search: up and down both banks of the Juniata they went, finding nothing until someone noticed "Some Bawld Eagles and Other Fowles" circling high overhead. The birds led them to the remains of James Smith and, on a rock just downstream, what was left of Woodward Arnold. Both had "Very Gastly and deep cuts on their Heads," as if a hatchet "had sunk into their Sculs & Brains." All that could be found of Armstrong was that shoulder bone; the rest, the colonial searchers concluded, his killers must have eaten.

As if these discoveries were not unnerving enough, the colonists began to fear that they were to meet the same gruesome fate, for the Indians accompanying them from Shamokin were behaving oddly. Three slipped away the first night out. One of the five remaining was, traders thought, a suspect, for when they handed him Armstrong's shoulder bone, "his Nose Gushed out with Blood," in European lore a sure sign of guilt. By day's end that Indian and his friends had also vanished. They may not have gone far, however: that night the traders' dog started barking at the darkness. Taking no chances, McKee, Berry, and the others hid behind trees until dawn, guns cocked. The next morning they quickly buried the bodies and took a different route home.

While Alexander Armstrong hunted for his brother, back at Shamokin Sassoonan and his council asked a conjurer to find out the killers' identity. Next morning the "Seer," having worked through the night, instructed them to question Jemmey and John. Jemmey talked, giving what became the accepted version of Armstrong's demise; John said nothing. After consulting Shickellamy, Delaware leaders decided to hand Mushemeelin and John over to Alexander Armstrong.[6]

"[A] great noise arose" in Shamokin when word of this plan got out. Many Delawares, including Sassoonan, were said to be drunk. Drunk or sober, they were so bitterly divided over the right course of action that some left town and Sassoonan, fearing for his life, took refuge with Shickellamy. None were keen to "medle with" the accused: Mushemeelin, a conjurer, was no fellow to cross; John, the son of a prominent man, may have been shielded by influential kinfolk.

At this point Shickellamy and his sons went to work, persuading some Delawares to tie up John and Mushemeelin. That was hard enough; harder still was getting anyone to take them downriver. For twenty-four hours the bound prisoners sat until Jack, Shickellamy's eldest son, approached the Delawares once more. If you will not deliver these two men to Alexander Armstrong, he said, I have an alternative: "separate their Heads from their Bodies and lay them in the Canoe, and carry them to Alexander to Roast and eat them; that would satisfy his Revenge, as he wants to eat Indians."[7] That threat, and the promise that Jack and one of his brothers would go along, convinced a few Delawares to load the prisoners into canoes and head off down the Susquehanna.

The trip proved eventful. When the party stopped at trader James Berry's house on the east bank, Berry told John: "I am sorry to see you in such a Condition. I have known you from a Boy, and always loved you." The kind words broke the young Delaware's silence, and he turned on Mushemeelin. "Now I am going to Dye for your Wickedness," he chided his old hunting companion. "You have killed all the three White men; I never did intend to kill any of them." Mushemeelin was furious. "It is true I have killed them," he retorted. "I am a Man, you are a Coward; it is a Great satisfaction to me to have killed them. I will Dye with Joy for having killed a Great Rogue and his Companions." Hearing this outburst, Shickellamy's sons abruptly pronounced John innocent and turned him loose. On April 22 Mushemeelin, suddenly alone, landed in the Lancaster jail.[8]

From his cell that conjurer, calmer now, gave his own version of events beside the Juniata, a tale sharply at odds with the story told in Shamokin.[9] I did approach Armstrong about the debt, the Delaware explained in "good English," and I did kill both "Jack" and Arnold, but it was self-defense. After talking things over for two hours, "Armstrong . . . grew angry and" hit me "with a Stick." When I defended myself with a hatchet, the Delaware went on, Arnold swung at me with an axe, so I grabbed my gun and shot him. Meanwhile "Little John," the Delaware even now heading home a free man, killed James Smith. "He thinks it very hard," wrote the colonist who listened to Mushemeelin's story, "that the other Indian shou'd be released."

While Mushemeelin pleaded his case with his colonial keepers, Jack Armstrong's grieving brother, who also thought "it very hard" that only one Indian was in jail, set about getting the other two in custody. On April 25 he sent angry letters to Sassoonan and Shickellamy promising more bloodshed if the Indians did not hand over all of the suspects. The threats "caused great Disturbance" at Shamokin, for it looked like "Friends of the Deceased intended to revenge themselves on the Indians."

The day Armstrong sent those letters, the governor and council in Philadelphia, having finally heard about what was going on, instructed Weiser to head for Shamokin at once in order "to make a peremptory demand in his Honor's Name" that the Delawares hand over John and Jemmey.[10] Weiser received his marching orders on the evening of April 27; grumbling that he had better things to do, complaining about the government's failure to send along the requisite belt of wampum, predicting that the two Delawares would be long gone by now, he set off, promising to do what he could.

The morning of May 2 found him sitting among Sassoonan and the Delaware councilors, with Shickellamy and a few more Iroquois looking on. Pennsylvania's man could not speak directly to the council, however; he had to give his message in Mohawk, which Andrew Montour, a multilingual man from a mixed family of Iroquois and French folk prominent in those parts, then translated into Delaware.[11] Sassoonan's reply, carried back over the same linguistic bridge, was conciliatory. "We the Delaware Indians . . . ," he said, did this terrible deed, and we have handed over the killer "to the Relations of the Deceased. . . . Our Hearts are in Mourning," the Delaware leader concluded, "and we are in a dismal condition and cannot say any thing [more] at present." There was no mention of John or Jemmey.

At this point Shickellamy took over, to settle what became the accepted version of the killings and to explain why Weiser would be returning home without Mushemeelin's alleged accomplices. "We desire . . . our Brother the Governor will not insist to have either of the two Young Men in Prison or Condemned to Dye," the Oneida said. These two are innocent, and "[i]t is not with Indians as with White people, to put People in Prison on Suspicion or for Triffles. Indians must first be found Guilty of a Crime, then Judgment is given and immediately Executed." Promising to give the governor a full report at the upcoming Lancaster treaty, he asked "in the mean time . . . that good friendship and Harmony may continue, and that we may live long together." The business done, Weiser joined one hundred Indians for a feast. "[A]fter we had in great Silence devoured a fat Bear," the emissary recalled two years later, "the oldest of the Chiefs made a Speech" giving thanks that the "small Cloud" blocking the sun "was now done away . . . , and thereupon began to sing with an awful Solemnity, but without expressing any Words; the others accompanied him with their Voices."[12]

Time's passage had colored Weiser's memory a rosy hue. In fact, he "left the delawares in great Confusion among themselves" that May; the elders favored peace at any cost, but young men resented Mushemeelin's arrest. Fearing "sat [sad] work" still to come, the Pennsylvanian wondered if the two factions "may perhaps agree in Nothing [more] then to do Mischief to the bake [back] Inhabitants of this province." To ensure that the Iroquois en route to Lancaster did not join in any of that mischief, Shickellamy sent a messenger to inform the approaching ambassadors "of this noise" and urge them to come anyway, ignoring whatever tales the Delawares were spreading.[13] Meanwhile Governor George Thomas, concerned that seeing Mushemeelin in a Lancaster cell "might give some uneasiness" to the Iroquois visitors, had the prisoner transferred to Philadelphia.

When the Six Nations delegation, some 250 strong, reached Lancaster in June, the Armstrong affair occupied only a small portion of the treaty business. Pennsylvania still insisted on trying all three men present at the traders' deaths. The Iroquois, having talked things over at Shamokin on their way south, would promise only to urge Delaware leaders to take John and Jemmey to Philadelphia for questioning, "but not as prisoners."[14]

Late that summer Shickellamy, Weiser, and about thirty Delawares (including the two suspects) reached the provincial capital.[15] There they found Mushemeelin unbowed by several months in a cell; this "Master of the Black Art" bragged to some of the young men in the party that he planned to escape that very night. Governor Thomas had enough respect for conjuring (he was partial to Indian medicines) to take no chances: he ordered the prisoner put in irons and closely watched. Then it was time for the colony's chief justice to examine John and Jemmey. On August 24 he pronounced himself convinced of their innocence, and the province was satisfied.

For Indians, satisfaction required something more. The Delaware speaker, Quidahickqunt, had to put formally to rest this "very unhappy Affair, something worse than any thing that ever happened before." To restore harmony, he invoked the time-honored ritual of clearing the road between peoples, wiping tears from colonists' eyes, and removing from their hearts the "Spirit of Resentment and Revenge against Us"—each action confirmed by a string of wampum or a bundle of skins. Three days later, armed with wampum belts and strings, Shickellamy, too, covered the wound, buried the hatchet, and cleared the "foul and Corrupted" air. "[T]he Sun which was darken'd now Shines again as clear as ever," he proclaimed.

The only darkness left was Mushemeelin. Explaining to his listeners that "I do not impute the Murders . . . to the whole Delaware Nation," Thomas, puzzled by such an outlandish idea, went on to say that English law required a trial. "Your Forms and ours differ widely," he pointed out, but have faith that "ours . . . are good . . . and it will be fore the Benefit of the Indians to be tryed in the same manner the white People are." Good or bad, those forms took time. The trial did not start until October; Mushemeelin did not hang until November 14. At last, the noise that had erupted a year before was silenced.[16]

～～～

"Wholly Unintelligible to Each Other"
Negotiating the Cultural Divide

The long train of events that followed from that fateful decision to snatch Mushemeelin's horse shows how negotiators—Conrad Weiser, Andrew Montour, and others, but in this case especially Shickellamy— worked the Pennsylvania frontier during the mid-eighteenth century. In coping with this crisis the Oneida had to make inquiries and sift ru-

mors, send and receive messages, sit with Delaware and colonial councils, and explain things to Iroquois ambassadors and provincial officials. Much was on his mind in the days and weeks after that Tutelo paid
him a visit. In Shamokin were angry (and sometimes intoxicated) Delawares, as well as Delaware leaders he could only hope to persuade,
never command. Somewhere up the Susquehanna was a delegation en
route from Iroquoia that might already have heard ugly rumors. Downriver was Alexander Armstrong, spoiling for a fight. Then there was
Conrad Weiser's reluctance to get involved and, when he did finally
show up, the demands he carried from Philadelphia, demands that
would only further enrage those Delawares.

It did not help that this corner of the frontier was a particularly
complicated place. Shickellamy and the other Iroquois in Shamokin
lived with Delaware emigrants from the east and Tutelo refugees from
the southern piedmont. Each group managed its own affairs; there was
no town council overseeing the settlement as a whole. "[T]hree different tribes of Indians; speaking three languages," sighed a colonial visitor in 1745, "wholly unintelligible to each other." A few years later
another bewildered colonist reported "so many Languages" being spoken in the village that "its rare to hear two Indians talking in one Language."[17]

The Mushemeelin-Armstrong fracas also reveals that in dealing with
this cacophonous, kaleidoscopic frontier, the go-between had a number
of tools at his disposal. One was the firm foundation of friendship between native and newcomer, a foundation laid by William Penn in the
early 1680s and carried on, with varying degrees of sincerity and success, by the men who came after him. Though metaphorical, talk of
concord between Delawares and their English "Brethren" was also genuine. Genuine, too, was James Berry's sadness at seeing young John, a
boy he had known for years, trussed up and bound for the gallows, sadness all the more remarkable because the fur trader had just buried the
men John allegedly had butchered. This tradition of peaceful contact
gave go-betweens some of the wherewithal they needed to cope with
crisis.

Out of that tradition, too, came a body of knowledge vital to a negotiator's work. Simply knowing whom to approach in an emer-
gency—as Shickellamy and the Delawares did when they sent word to
Weiser—was an important first step. So was having the means to get a
message across: that Tutelo who could pen a letter to Weiser had his

counterpart in the German negotiator, who knew that if the colony's words were to carry weight in Shamokin he needed a belt of "Blake wampum . . . to make use of to the Delawares." Neither beads nor paper would have done much good, however, had there been no one to speak the other's language. Mushemeelin was one of many Delawares who knew some English; for those who did not, translators like Andrew Montour were easily found.

Certain congruities between the two peoples made the negotiators' job easier still. Both Indians and colonists believed in what many today would call superstition. While a Delaware conjurer at Shamokin murmured secret incantations to identify the killers, along the Juniata Alexander Armstrong was settling the question of guilt by handing one suspect a bone. Similarly, in Philadelphia that August Governor Thomas heeded warnings about Mushemeelin's "Black Art" because he respected magic's power.

There was also a meeting of minds on the relative importance of truth in keeping the peace: neither side believed it essential. The story featured here, the one Shickellamy pressed upon men from Philadelphia and Onondaga, is probably not the whole truth. Weiser, introducing it, would say only that "[t]he following is what Shick Calamy declared to be the Truth."[18] Though in August everyone from the chief justice on down professed to believe the denials by John and Jemmey, John's behavior remains suspicious.[19] Perhaps the Delaware youth's kin connections combined with resentment against a feared conjurer like Mushemeelin to deflect suspicion from one to the other, resulting in an arranged marriage of man to deed, an arrangement all (except, of course, the condemned) could live with. In any case, the Delaware's fate holds a lesson about how negotiators, to defuse a volatile situation, might work not to get at the truth but to shade it, to twist it, and sometimes to bury it altogether.

But reconstructing how Shickellamy and the rest settled the Armstrong business to almost everyone's satisfaction should not obscure the obstacles in the way. After all, while some cross-cultural conjunctions in values or behavior might help a go-between, others might not. Delawares, for example, took seriously Alexander Armstrong's talk of personally avenging his brother's death—and might have contemplated a preemptive strike down the Susquehanna—because it was talk natives understood: the idea of kinfolk seeking revenge on those who had harmed one of their own was deeply embedded in native culture.

Perceived differences between colonist and Indian would cause more trouble still. Even as they tried to build bridges of understanding, both sides believed that a cultural chasm lay between them. When Shickellamy observed that "[i]t is not with Indians as with White people" and Governor Thomas told natives that "[y]our Forms and ours differ widely," both men were talking about legal culture: Thomas was looking for particular suspects when, to the Delawares' way of thinking, all of them were responsible; Thomas wanted those suspects in his custody, whereas Delawares, following native dictates, planned to turn Mushemeelin over "to the Relations of the Deceased." But the sense of difference reached well beyond legalities to embrace everything from war to peace, from trade to land, from travel to treaties. At bottom was not just that nagging sense of difference but assumptions about the savagery of people on the other side. Once again that business beside the Juniata, with its talk of cannibalism, illuminates the frontier's obscure corners. In fact, it was as likely that Mushemeelin and his companions had devoured Jack Armstrong as it was that Jack's brother would dine on Indian heads. But both stories were believed because each side thought the other capable of such horrors. Such notions at once made the go-between necessary and guaranteed that his task would be difficult.

CHAPTER I

"Fitt & Proper Persons to Goe Between": Paths to the Woods

The lead actors in the Armstrong affair—Shickellamy, Conrad Weiser, and Andrew Montour—make an unlikely ensemble of allies. Shickellamy, an aged Oneida sent to the Forks of the Susquehanna by the Six Nations to keep an eye on Iroquoia's southern frontier, had been Pennsylvania's friend ever since he showed up in Philadelphia sixteen years before. Weiser, close to fifty that spring of 1744, was born in Germany and brought over to New York as a boy before hard times there pushed him south, in the late 1720s, to the rich soil along Tulpehocken Creek. Montour, much the youngest of the three, came to Shamokin by still another route. Raised at Ostonwakin ("French Town") on the Susquehanna's West Branch, he was the son of an Oneida named Currundawanah and "the celebrated" Madame Montour, a woman well versed in French, English, and Iroquois ways. One of these men spoke Oneida and a little English; another had German as his first language, with Mohawk his second and English his third; the last, greeted in French, might reply in English, Delaware, Shawnee, or one of the Iroquois tongues.[1]

The different paths bringing the Iroquois leader, the stolid German farmer, and the colorful fellow from French Town to council houses at Shamokin and Philadelphia in 1744 only begin to suggest the range of people who managed contact on the Pennsylvania frontier. Just a year earlier, Thomas McKee, one of the fur traders in the Armstrong search party, had accompanied Weiser to Shamokin in order to negotiate with Indians there; in times to come McKee, like many in the peltry business, would be deeply involved in the negotiator's round of travels, translations, and treaties.[2] And a year after it debated Mushemeelin's fate, Shamokin greeted people who would become go-betweens of still another stripe: Christian missionaries like the Moravian David Zeisberger, along with the Presbyterian Delaware Tunda (Moses) Tatamy and other native converts.

The difficulty in sketching a group portrait of such a passel of humanity is compounded by the fact that go-betweens tended to be as obscure as they were diverse. Many who only joined the formal conversation between peoples once or twice left little trace in the records. But even more famous mediators remain shadowy figures. None of the prominent men who crossed paths with them—no proprietor or his governors and agents, no provincial councilor or assemblyman— paused to jot down their stories. Those few colonists curious enough to ask a question or two were stymied by go-betweens' tendency to remake themselves. None was more adept at this than Madame Montour. "[I]n mode of life a complete Indian," announced one colonist who met her; no, another insisted, she is "a handsome woman, genteel and of polite address."[3] Her son Andrew inherited this cultural agility. A missionary detected "signs of grace" in him, but another colonist found the man "[i]ll natured." Montour is, concluded one who saw a lot of him over the years, "really an unintelligible person."[4]

Nor did the Montours and other mediators write much for themselves. Most were at best semi-literate; lacking the skill, they also lacked the inclination or spare time to pen memoirs. The handful who did, like Weiser, could be maddeningly cryptic. The German gave a fascinating account of his early years, but after bringing the tale up to his arrival in Pennsylvania—and the start of his work as an interpreter there—he confined himself to listing the births (and, sometimes, deaths) of his children.[5]

Despite being highly visible public figures, then, go-betweens are an elusive lot. Shickellamy's life before 1728 is a blank, save for a remark he made, near the end of his days, about a long-ago Catholic baptism.[6] Weiser's reasons for leaving his Tulpehocken farm for weeks on end to join the Oneida in managing relations between Pennsylvania and Iroquoia are no more clear. Yet these two are an open book compared to the enigmatic Montour, as "unintelligible" now as he was then.

But to say that go-betweens are obscure is not to say they are invisible. To say that they are hard to read is not to say they are inscrutable. And to say that they came from many walks of life is not to say they were chosen at random. In fact, the negotiators who wound up on a

path into the woods were themselves a product of negotiations between colonists and Indians over who constituted "fitt & proper Persons
to goe between."[7] The way Weiser and the others simply came forward to handle the nasty business in 1744 masks the difficulties of casting people in this role. Getting to the point where everyone agreed that
a Shickellamy, a Conrad Weiser, or an Andrew Montour was right for
the part required peoples to overcome, or overlook, fundamental differences in their notions of a proper envoy.

A tour of the likeliest recruiting grounds—a look at Indian villages,
French Town, Pennsylvania fur trade settlements, mission posts, and,
near the end of the colonial period, at the ranks of Indian captives—reveals that no group, and no individual, was perfect for the part. People
like Andrew Montour were scarce and, with their French connections,
suspect. Traders like Thomas McKee were often rogues. Native leaders like Shickellamy tended to be as ignorant of colonial ways as they
were arrogant, while Christian Indians like Tatamy, humble folk well acquainted with provincial culture, knew too little about the finer points
of native American diplomatic protocol. Redeemed captives might
know that protocol, but colonists never quite trusted their loyalties.
Missionaries prayed too much, and almost everyone drank too much.

By the time Shickellamy, Weiser, and Montour gathered at Shamokin
that spring, however, Pennsylvania and its Indian neighbors had reached
a consensus on the criteria for go-betweens, and these specialists were,
at midcentury, both numerous and adept. Shickellamy and Weiser,
Montour and George Croghan were on hand, soon to be joined by
missionaries and their converts, and later still by some former prisoners of war.

But even then, even at this high-water mark of cultural communication—even with universal agreement that the best negotiator was "a
true good Man . . . [who] spoke their Words & our Words, and not his
own," someone "hearty & sincere"—problems plagued frontier concourse.[8] However skilled he was, chicanery was also part of the go-
between's repertoire. Moreover, for all the talk about these figures
standing squarely between native and newcomer, mediators themselves saw, and set, limits to their acquaintance with another world. A
good ear and a glib tongue could achieve a meeting of minds, as
Shickellamy and his partners did in 1744; a meeting of hearts proved
another matter.

"He Is as a Dumb Man to Us"
Philosophical Differences

On January 25, 1723, a Cayuga named Satcheecho, "the Indian Messenger," walked into Pennsylvania's provincial council chamber, in his hand a letter that a colonist had penned for some Susquehanna Indian leaders. Governor William Keith and his councilors were puzzled and, truth to tell, a little annoyed. *Why did you send only this fellow?* Keith asked the Indians in the letter he wrote back. The Cayuga could not "have further informed us of the Matter [mentioned in the letter] by Speech [,] for altho' Sacheechoe be a very honest good Man yet, as he can Speak nothing but Mingoe [Iroquois] and there is no person here who understands that Language he is as a dumb man to us."[9]

Back on the Susquehanna River, headmen of the Conestogas, Shawnees, and Conoys, listening as a colonist read Keith's answer, must have been equally perplexed. To their mind, linguistic skill was not essential to a go-between. True, some native envoys—the Conestoga Shawydoohungh (Indian Harry) in the early eighteenth century, the Delaware Pisquetomen later on—could speak English; but most, like Satcheecho, could not. As late as the 1750s, colonists in Philadelphia still fumed that Scarouyady and other Indian negotiators were "coming to Town without an Interpreter," then sitting around while frantic officials came up with one.[10]

Keith standing before a silent Cayuga, like councilors glumly going out to fetch a translator for Scarouyady, serves as an instructive counterpoint to the smooth diplomacy in the Armstrong business. Indians and colonists, operating under different assumptions, often worked at cross purposes, squabbling over what a go-between should be able to do—indeed, over who a go-between should be.

The men scurrying about in search of a translator might not have known it, but they were losers in a diplomatic contest where one side asserted its superiority by making the other use a foreign language.[11] The war of words was common among Indians. Six Nanticokes from Maryland's Eastern Shore once brought a message to Onondaga, even though "none [of the envoys] could speak a word of the Language of the united [Iroquois] Nations." Those Iroquois knew the game: in 1756 they sent two parties of messengers to Delaware towns, not caring that no one in either delegation knew Delaware. Though many Indians speak English, one colonist grumbled, they still "always expect to be treated with an Interpreter."[12]

Nowhere were the different priorities more evident than at Conestoga during the summer of 1721, when the Penn family's agent, James Logan, chatted with an Iroquois named Ghesaont. On learning that the Indian and his party planned to push on to Virginia, Logan at once "asked how they would get an Interpreter in Virginia where the [local] Indians knew nothing of their [Iroquois] Language." Not to worry, Ghesaont replied, declining the offer of a translator (and spy) from Pennsylvania. "[T]here would be no occasion for any Care of that kind, for they very well knew the Governor of Virginia had an Interpreter for their Language always with him." Not true, in fact, but that was not Ghesaont's problem.[13]

Colonists entering on formal talks with Indians thought first of the language barrier; Indians thought of it last (or not at all). Their battle stretched well beyond questions of English or Iroquois, Delaware or Nanticoke to a wider culture war, a conflict that Indians also won by insisting that their diplomatic customs hold sway. The famous negotiator William Johnson of New York, who followed the same native protocol prevailing in Pennsylvania, made a virtue of necessity. "I would deal with all people in their own way . . . ," he grandly told the Iroquois, observing that "your Ancestors have from the earliest time directed and recommended the observation of a Sett of Rules which they laid down for you to follow." The Indians replied that "We consider them as the cement of our Union."[14] At the Woods' Edge Ceremonies and wampum belts, gift exchanges and talk of paths cleared or fires kindled—native etiquette set the tone of frontier foreign relations.

This victory meant that instead of interpreters or people otherwise expert in the strange world of Anglo-America, natives recruiting go-betweens could look, as they customarily did, to people of stature. Younger men "of great endurance" being taught conciliar ways might be chosen, "to give them an opportunity to exercise themselves in public speaking." But usually those youths, still learning statecraft, would accompany more experienced hands, "old men whose talents and abilities are known." Young or old, a negotiator "must," to the Indian way of thinking, "be a sensible and reliable man," a man from "a great Family"— "a Man," as one Shawnee said of Scarouyady, "of Authority . . . , and of great Experience and Eloquence." Selection at once reflected and conferred status. In the Indian countries "Any one employed as a messenger," a Pennsylvanian remarked, "is held in high regard."[15]

A council dispatching such a man to Philadelphia neither expected nor encouraged him, once there, to go native. As the insistence on speaking to colonists in Delaware, Shawnee, or Iroquois suggests, Indian messengers did not try to fit in. If the Conestoga envoy Tagotolessa (Civility) earned his English name from polished colonial manners—and, since he spoke no English, that seems unlikely—he would have been almost alone in aping Pennsylvania ways. Most native negotiators were akin to a party of Iroquois, who "acc[oun]t themselves great men and are stiff," or a Delaware said to be "haughty, and very desireous of Respect and Command."[16]

That stiffness required colonists to meet native go-betweens more than halfway, to have on hand or dispatch on missions people who knew their way around Indians. Where a Delaware or Iroquois council looked for kin and standing, then, a colonial council sought someone "much versed in the Arts of Manageing" Indians. Conestogas sent the "dumb" Satcheecho, colonists people with "Skill in the *Indian* Languages and Methods of Business." At the core of "Indian Talents" was such intimate acquaintance with "the Disposition of Indians" that one knew how things sounded "in an Indian Ear" or looked "in the Indian Light," knew even how to get an Indian joke.[17]

The only way to learn all this, Conrad Weiser advised, was "to converse with the Indians, and study their Genius." Easier said than done, cautioned other experienced colonists. "To treat Indians with propriety and address is perhaps of all Tasks, the most difficult," George Croghan remarked, "and allowances must be made to those who are strangers to their customs and manners, should they not succeed in acquiring their good opinion."[18]

Croghan's superior in the British Indian service after 1755, the Crown's superintendent of Indian affairs, William Johnson, was less charitable about armchair experts. Everyone claims to know Indians, Johnson once complained; but no one gains expertise by sitting in some provincial capital or frontier garrison. "It is only to be acquired by a long residence amongst them, a daily intercourse with them, and a desire of information in these matters Superseding all other considerations."[19] Substitute *colonist* for *Indian* in these remarks—imagine an Iroquois or Delaware speaking of the need for "*colonial* Talents" and "a *colonial* Ear," or urge "long residence" in *Philadelphia* and "daily intercourse" with *Pennsylvanians*—and the gulf between native and colonial prescriptions becomes apparent.

Like Weiser, Croghan, and Johnson, then, a colonist had to go native, to let himself, as Croghan once put it, be "led a little into the mystery and Policy of the People of this Country." Part of "the mystery" involved simply figuring out who "the People of this Country" were, no easy task when Indians might be called, say, *Seneca* or *Oneida* (their particular nation) one day, *Iroquois* (their larger affiliation) the next. And sorting through the nomenclature was only the beginning. On a journey up the Susquehanna in 1760, one Pennsylvania messenger, John Hays, boasted that he and his colonial companion, the missionary Christian Frederick Post, "L[i]ved A Indien Life."[20] The casual aside obscures what could, for some, be severe culture shock. To a colonial visitor, Indian country looked different, from its bark houses and unkempt fields to its denizens' dress and tattoos (Figure 5). It sounded different, from its jangling beads and soft, guttural voices to its wailing mourners and warriors' whoops. It smelled different, the air thick with the scent of curing deerskins and tobacco smoke. It even tasted different, with its dishes of dog and bear, its array of corn soups and stews.

All this, and much more besides, a colonist found on reaching a native settlement. But a provincial negotiator had to be still more deeply immersed in Indian life, more closely in tune with its melodies and rhythms. On special occasions he might fire his gun with townsfolk to greet a visitor's arrival or help carry the corpse at a funeral; he might sit in on a council or drop by "a very extraordinary Kind of a Festival" that dissolved marriages and let a woman—singing *I am not afraid of my Husband, I will choose what Man I please*—grab her new mate and lead him into the dark. On a more ordinary day the colonist might climb out of the bed he shared with one of those native women and prepare to join a band of warriors or hunters, or stay in town to help torture a captive or drink with friends and kin deep into the night, "Singing and dancing with the indians after their manner."[21]

Indian country was a hard school, so hard that few colonists graduated. Weiser himself recalled how, during his first stay among the Mohawks, he "had to suffer much" from cold and hunger, and when the town got drunk he "often had to hide" from "very cruel" natives. Weiser recovered; others did not. One apprentice in the Indian trade farther north spent "the whole Winter . . . at the fire side with his Elbow on

Figure 5. Tishcohan, Delaware Leader,
by Gustavus Hesselius, 1735.

Tishcohan was among the headmen involved in the negotiations that
led to the infamous Walking Purchase. The blanket, the squirrel-skin
tobacco pouch, and the pipe of European manufacture typify Indian
dress of that era. Courtesy of the Historical Society of Pennsylvania.

his knee and Chin on his hand picking his nose," never "speaking a
Word" or changing his lice-infested clothes. How many Pennsylvanians
resembled the poor fellow is unknown, but alienation and anomie were
facts of life for every novitiate.[22]

Colonists enrolled in this native school usually turned out to be men
of modest standing in their own world, though this was not the initial
plan. At first, Pennsylvanians agreed with natives that the go-between
should be chosen from society's leaders. To prove the point, Penn himself tried out for the part. "I have made it my business to understand"

the local Delawares' language, he wrote in August 1683, ten months after arriving in his province, "that I might not want an Interpreter on any occasion." Apparently the proprietor was a quick study, for the following spring he was said to "speak their language fairly fluently," and his lively interest in Indians prompted frequent visits to their settlements.[23] But Penn had many distractions, and in August 1684 one of those, a boundary dispute with Maryland's proprietor, Lord Baltimore, compelled his return to England.[24]

Some of Penn's successors—Lars Pärsson (Lasse) Cocke before 1700, Edward Farmer and John French just after the turn of the century—were men of enough substance to have "Esquire," "Gent," or "Colonel" attached to their names.[25] But these three, themselves exceptional, had no successors, no men of their stature who got into the Indian business. Indeed, so unusual were they that soon after the Founder's second—and last—stay in his province from 1699 to 1701, colonial officials started to worry about the widening gap between the preference for men of quality and the reality that those actually entering the woods were no gentlemen. The proprietor's dream of converting and civilizing Indians "was a great motive" in founding this colony, the provincial assembly reminded everyone in 1706; therefore, the legislators went on, we expect that "the persons concerned from time to time in ye . . . negotiations . . . , may be such as Demonstrate their Christianity by a sober and virtuous Conversation." On Pennsylvania's frontier a half century later George Washington, facing the French foe and keen to end his reliance on lowly "Traders & Common Interpreters," yearned for "a Person of Distinction acquainted with their [Indians'] language." Find one, Washington pleaded, and pay him anything he asks; failing that, at least recruit "a Man of Sense and Character."[26]

Unfortunately for the assembly and for young Washington, few such people answered the call. James Logan, merchant, provincial secretary, Clerk of the Council, the Penn family's man in the province for much of the first half of the eighteenth century, was deeply involved in Indian affairs—shipping London goods to his stable of fur traders, sending messages to native headmen, running treaty councils (Figure 6). But he never added Iroquois, Shawnee, or Delaware to his Greek, Latin, and Hebrew. And though Logan sometimes visited Indian towns to talk to headmen or look after his business interests, come nightfall he retreated to a nearby trader's house.[27] Where his master, William Penn, left rich descriptions of Delaware life, Logan's prodigious cu-

Figure 6. James Logan, by Gustavus Hesselius, c. 1716.
Courtesy of the Historical Society of Pennsylvania.

riosity and voluminous correspondence betray little interest in Indians beyond trade and diplomacy.

His successor as proprietary agent, Richard Peters, was cut from the same cloth (Figure 7). Yet even though he never tried to sound out an Iroquois or Delaware sentence and never entered, much less stayed in, an Indian town, this Anglican clergyman fancied himself something of an expert. "[A]t no small Expense and with an unwearied assiduity [I have] endeavour'd to gain the Esteem of the Indians," he boasted in 1748. The hard work paid off: "I am told by Mr. Weiser that I have succeeded so far as to be consider'd as a Young Logan that does not want affection for the Indians, & *in time* may understand to do their business honestly for them." Weiser's flattery here is as transparent as his hint that Peters was no go-between. Indeed, the minister himself had learned

Figure 7. Richard Peters, attributed to John Wollaston, c. 1758.
Courtesy of the Pennsylvania Academy of Fine Arts,
Philadelphia. Gift of Mrs. Maria L. M. Peters.

enough to appreciate how little he truly knew. In the next breath he pleaded with William Penn's sons Thomas and John, the current proprietaries, for money to train Weiser's successor. Conrad had been sick, Peters explained, so sick he almost died; "if he had[,] what must have become of Indian Affairs"? Scarcely able to conceal panic, Peters begged the Penns to "think . . . of the dreadful Situation this Province will be in for want of an Indian Interpreter in case of his Death."[28]

The frontier war of the late 1750s only increased the elite's tendency to keep natives at a distance. Now a new breed of distinguished men—British officers on the western front—dropped even the pretense to the expertise of a Penn, a Logan, or a Peters. Indeed, calling the job of dealing with Indians "the greatest curse which Our Lord could pronounce against the greatest sinners," they bragged about their ignorance of native ways. "I am not Sufficiently acquainted with the Manner of Managing them," wrote one, so find somebody else "who can take that Care Upon himself." The curriculum Weiser and other old hands advocated, requiring deep engagement with Indian people, went against a gentleman's grain. "[Y]ou will soon be relieved from those Regions where you can experience no real Felicity," wrote one officer to another, "deprived of all agreeable Society & exposed to the Clamour of the Delaware, the Perfidy of the Shawnesse—the Noise of the Tawaw, and the Treachery of the Mingo, and in short—the Damnation that is attendant on the whole Race of Barbarions—a Plague & Pain that beggars all Imagination to those whom Experience has not given some faint Idea."[29]

Such outbursts were extreme, the product of war and the famous arrogance of the British officer. But they grew out of an older notion, long pervasive in the upper reaches of colonial society, that no gentleman got too close to Indians. As a result, native go-betweens sent by Indian peoples had a strikingly different profile from people recruited by provincial rulers: an Indian envoy might be as ignorant of foreigners (and as arrogant) as any British captain, but he had a position of high status and the respect of his tribe; a colonial emissary, fluent in foreign words and ways, had a menial job and his own people's contempt. It seemed an unlikely starting point for conversation across the frontier; yet from these opposites, peoples would find ways to meet and talk.

"Well Disposed to Accomodate Differences" *Finding Common Ground*

"He Is Everywhere Known" *The Ideal Negotiator*

On August 22, 1755, the Ohio Seneca go-between Kanuksusy (also called Kos Showweyha) stood in the Pennsylvania State House, facing Governor Robert Hunter Morris and the provincial council. At the Seneca's elbow were Scarouyady, Andrew Montour, Conrad Weiser, and other intermediaries who had recently arrived in the capital from the west. There was much to talk about: a force of French and Indians had destroyed General Edward Braddock's British army on the Pennsylvania frontier little more than a month before, and now the province was desperate to woo native allies. But that could wait. First, please "hearken," Morris told Kanuksusy; I shall bestow on you "an English name." Wampum string in hand, the governor proceeded. "Brother," he said, "In token of our Affection for your parents & in expectation of Your being a useful man in these perillous Times, I do in the most solemn manner adopt you by the name of Newcastle . . . , because in 1701 I am informed that your parents presented you to the late Mr William Penn at Newcastle," just downstream from Philadelphia.[30]

The Seneca had been through this before. Just a year earlier, Virginia had named him after its most distinguished inhabitant, "Colo Fairfax[,] which was told him signified the first of the Council." And just six months after tacking *Newcastle* onto his string of titles, Kanuksusy stood at yet another council with Governor Morris while another Iroquois informed Morris that, needing a colonial messenger, they had "adopted Thomas Græme" and "have given him the name Kos Showweyha (Newcastle's Indian name), and Newcastle we call Ah Knoyis, for the future."[31]

Kanuksusy. Kos Showweyha. Fairfax. Newcastle. Ah Knoyis. This name game was symptomatic of how far colonists and Indians had come in settling their differences over who a go-between should be. As they did with Thomas Græme, Indians forged tighter bonds with a colonial mediator by adopting him, complete with new name and high status. We "let you know," Ohio Iroquois told colonists at one meeting, that George Croghan *(Anaquarunda)* "is one of our People & shall help us . . . & be one of our Council." Weiser, too, renamed *Tarachiawagon* ("Holder of the Heavens," an Iroquois deity), is, Six Nations Iroquois said, "of our Nation and a Member of our Council."[32]

By going along with such constructions and reconstructions of identity, colonists signaled their readiness to obey Indian custom. They let natives adopt them. They accepted demands that a negotiator be "better acquainted with Indians," that in choosing a go-between Pennsylvania should avoid "such as Do nott understand us nor We Them."[33] They smiled and shook hands with Kanuksusy, Shickellamy, Scarouyady, and other envoys who were every bit as "dumb" as Satcheecho had been. For their part, natives, on finding a Weiser or Croghan, someone well-versed in Indian ways, added him to their ranks of prominent people who could be trusted to carry on the conversation with colonial America.

It helped that, from the first, Pennsylvanians and their native neighbors had plenty of reasons to get along. Delawares, Iroquois, Shawnees, and the rest coveted European tools, weapons, clothing—and allies. Colonists needed friends, too, not least because friends were more likely to sell peltry and land. Eager to talk, peoples looked for, and found, areas of agreement in the qualities deemed essential to those who would do the talking.

The first requirement of a mediator in this face-to-face world was to be known. Neither side trusted a stranger, however gifted he was in the diplomatic art. When Scarouyady brought a fur trader named John Davison into the provincial council chamber as his interpreter, wary Pennsylvania officials summoned "another Indian Trader who spoke the Indian Language, to attend the Council that he might assist in the Interpretation." Scarouyady might have been annoyed by the rebuff, but he understood; after all, the same principle guided Indians' choice of negotiators. "You are well known to us & a Man we can trust," the Oneida told William Johnson in 1755, a year after Pennsylvania rejected Davison. "We all know him," "he is everywhere known": the words ran like a refrain through Indian talk about their preferences in negotiators.[34]

Simply being known, of course, was not enough; one had to be known for having the right temperament, which Indian and colonist described as "Sober" and "quiet," someone "well disposed to accomodate differences." Mediators must also, both sides agreed, have "Sound hearts" that render them "faithful and honest."[35] "A European who wishes to stand well with" native Americans must, Weiser cautioned, "Speak the truth."[36] To go with sound heart and straight tongue, negotiators needed "strong heads." George Croghan once took this literally: "so You may See," he bragged after surviving a tomahawk blow, "a thick Scull is of Service on some Occasions." But most spoke metaphorically—a go-between must, as Weiser said, "Show himself not a coward, but courageous in all cases." Related to this was a certain stoicism. Indian or colonist, someone known to be (as Scarouyady once called John Davison) "foolish, and unguarded in his Cups," someone who "always speaks . . . as if he was drunk," made poor material from which to fashion a mediator. The best took self-control to great heights. Shickellamy, it was said, "had learned the art of concealing his sentiments," and Croghan had a similar ability to "appear highly pleased when most chagrined and show the greatest indifference when most pleased."[37]

For John Hays, with Post on a delicate mission up the Susquehanna in 1760, adopting this pose meant knowing when to laugh—and when not to. One day the two Pennsylvanians "had Sum Sport" watching the antics of drunken Indians, "but Dorst not Lauf at it." A few days later, though, Hays forced a laugh when a drunken Shawnee "came Be hind Me and Strock me and said that he Never would Love [The] White men any More." Hays nearly lost his composure—"My flesh creeped on My Back," he confided to his journal—but in the end the stoic mask held, as he "Laft and Said Nothing."[38] Indian and colonial negotiators alike, watching the performance, would have applauded.

"Foolish People and Women"
Silencing Women

Part of reaching consensus on what sort of person should be a negotiator was coming to some agreement about what sort of person should not be one. Both colonists and Indians, from the first, excluded one sort altogether: women. On the face of it this is surprising, for female go-betweens have been common in many parts of the world, and the Pennsylvania border country had no lack of qualified candidates.

Among colonists, a number of women had the standard tools of the mediator's trade. A visitor to Shamokin in the 1740s, for example, would have discovered that Anna Mack, one of the Moravian missionaries there, was a better linguist than her husband Martin, and had been able, with a Mohican woman, to construct ways over the language barrier. Just up the Susquehanna, that visitor would have found, during at least one winter, a colonial woman named Esther Harris running a trading post for Indians, some sixty miles from her husband John's store downstream. Harris might have been unusual in her isolation from husband and home, but many another Pennsylvania fur trader's wife, as an active partner in the family business, was well acquainted with Indian ways.[39]

While many colonial women had the skills provincial officials looked for in a go-between, many native women enjoyed the status Indian councils expected. As matrilineal societies, native peoples bordering Pennsylvania gave women prominent roles in everything from creating the cosmos to selecting headmen, from owning houses and fields to pressing for peace and war. Women, said one Oneida man in 1763, "have a Good Dale to say in our Nations"; sometimes they even spoke in council and held positions of political leadership. Newcastle's mother, a Seneca "Queen" named Aliquippa who lived on the upper

Ohio at midcentury, was important enough to chastise both Conrad Weiser and George Washington for failing to pay her proper respect when they passed through.[40]

But the woman most likely to be delegated a negotiator by Indians bordering Pennsylvania was Andrew Montour's mother. The trails Madame Montour took to reach the Pennsylvania frontier are as obscure as they were, apparently, convoluted. Just as people disagreed about her cultural persona, so they never got straight her story (perhaps because she wanted it that way): some said she was born of French parents in Canada, then captured and raised by Iroquois; others thought her a *métis* (of mixed parentage) who grew up in Iroquoia. But all agreed that she was fluent in frontier ways, having traveled throughout the Great Lakes and served as interpreter for a French commandant and a New York governor before coming south around 1720, with her husband, to the edge of Penn's Woods.[41]

From Montour to Esther Harris, the number of qualified female candidates makes their absence from the ranks of go-betweens all the more remarkable. Yet absent they were.[42] Neither Anna Mack nor that anonymous Mohican woman ever did public business, while Esther Harris's sole contribution to diplomatic discourse was to join two men "at the Council Door" in Philadelphia one day to report rumors of an Indian raid. Wives of other fur traders interpreted only rarely, and always under close supervision. In 1728 Elizabeth Cornish, who lived with her husband Andrew just a mile from Conestoga and "speaks the [local Indians'] language," was instructed to "privately" find out "what news" Civility had. Four years later provincial officials told Andrew Cornish to have "thy good Wife . . . interpret" another message to that Conestoga leader.[43]

"Mistress Montour," as "Interpretess" at an Iroquois council with Pennsylvania in 1727 and an important contact during troubles a year later, seems the exception to the lack of female voices in the conversation between cultures. But in the long run Montour proved unable or unwilling to transfer to Penn's Woods the prominent role she had played in Albany as a governor's confidant. Until her death around 1750 she remained a person of note, someone Pennsylvania officials thought "should be well treated," and she drew curious colonists out to the Indians' camp at councils; but after her brief stint as adviser and translator in the late 1720s, she rarely handled public affairs.[44]

What had happened? It is possible that age caught up with her—in

1733 one Pennsylvanian called Montour "ancient," and she later went blind—but she was well enough in 1744 to join Indians heading down the Susquehanna to council with colonists.[45] Though the death in 1729 of her husband might have undercut her prestige, in a matrilineal world that respected the aged neither of these should have been a liability.

It is easy, and tempting, to explain Montour's plunge from Interpretess at one treaty to curio at another—and the silence of Esther Harris and Elizabeth Cornish, too—by reference to the circumscribed lives of British colonial women. Their sphere largely confined to home and hearth, their participation in public life finding expression only in church, women in the colonies made unlikely candidates for the "Public Person" a negotiator was. If no man were available they might come forward, as Elizabeth Cornish did, to do a man's work, but man's work it remained. Even though she spoke Civility's language better than her husband did, it was Andrew, not Elizabeth, who was "to manage this affair."[46]

Such an explanation, while certainly true, is one-sided, for Indians debating with colonists over proper negotiators never insisted that women be candidates. In Indian country, too, custom was against a woman filling this role. Her place was in the clearing, her domain its houses and fields. Diplomacy, which like hunting and war involved travel through the woods, was by definition a man's realm.[47]

Indian men marked the boundary by tarring women with the same brush used on incompetent negotiators. When Newcastle had a falling out with another Iroquois messenger, he called his comrade not only a "silly fellow" but "a Woman." The epithets, closely linked, relegated women to the ranks of those unfit for public concourse. Your messages "have come to us by foolish people and women," an Onondaga chastised colonists in 1757, and later that year a second exasperated Iroquois urged them not to "believe every old woman that comes down and brings you News."[48]

One of those old women, Madame Montour, once drew a Seneca go-between's fire merely by offering an opinion on the credentials of Six Nations ambassadors who had come to Philadelphia.[49] "[A] certain Woman," one Hetaquantagechty pointedly told Pennsylvania leaders in 1734, in a thinly veiled attack on her, has been spreading "base Misrepresentations" about some Iroquois who had recently been in the capital; "old Age only," he threatened, "protects her from being punished for such Falshoods; . . . in the mean time they must resent it and hope to get rid of her." In fact, Hetaquantagechty had it wrong: someone else had questioned the visitors' legitimacy, and Montour had backed them. But what matters here is less Hetaquantagechty's misrepresentation of the story than his representation of Montour, which targeted her sex and her age.

Perhaps Madame Montour had been able to acquire influence in New York because she stuck close to Albany, a clearing where council fires blazed, where *woman negotiator* was not a contradiction in terms. But in Penn's Woods, her career was over. After Hetaquantagechty's tirade, Montour never again served as a translator, adviser, or messenger. If someone of her talents was silenced, it is less surprising to hear so little from Esther Harris, Elizabeth Cornish, and other frontier women, Indian or colonial.

⟶∞∞⟶

"No Doubt amongst So Many Thousands As There Are in the World One Such Man May Be Found" Negotiators' Proving Grounds

For all their differences over what sort of person was suitable, then, peoples managed to agree on roughly who a negotiator should be. Their "sufficient person" was a man, a man widely known, a man who could find his way around Indian America, a man natives could respect and colonists at least tolerate as a necessary evil.[50]

Drawing up such a profile is one thing, giving that composite sketch a human face quite another. The Onondaga Canasatego thought that recruiting negotiators with such qualities would be easy. Looking ahead to the day when Conrad Weiser *(Tarachiawagon)* was no more, Canasatego shrugged, saying that "When he is gone under Ground it will then be time enough to look for another; and no Doubt amongst so many Thousands as there are in the World one such Man may be found who will serve both Parties with the same Fidelity as Tarachawagon does."[51]

Perhaps. But most knew that a Weiser did not happen along every day; colonial and Indian councilors had to cast about among those many thousands in search of go-betweens. Sometimes recruiters tried formal apprenticeships in the negotiator's craft. When those experiments failed, the search came to target several sorts of communities—families like the Montours, towns in Indian country, fur trading centers, Christian missions, colonists redeemed from Indian captors—that proved fertile ground for mediators.

"The Indians Are Not Inclined
to Give Their Children Learning"
The Failure of Apprenticeships

In our modern age of aptitude tests and foreign service exams, of schools for translators and teams of experts on this country or that, it is hard to imagine how casually, how serendipitously, people on the early American frontier wound up as go-betweens. Consider Daniel Claus, a German immigrant of twenty-two, lured to America in the fall of 1749 by heady talk of the "Success and Advantage" awaiting him there. Finding disappointment instead, the forlorn Claus was in Philadelphia the next spring, looking for a ship headed home, when he crossed paths with Conrad Weiser. The older man, bound for Onondaga, persuaded the castaway to come along "as a Companion and [to] introduce him to the Natives of America & shew him the Curiosities &ca of their Country." And why not? No vessel was scheduled to leave before fall; it was easy to agree. Disappointment and home were soon forgotten as the young man was drawn deeper into this seductive new world. Sponsored by Pennsylvania and then by New York, before long he was in a Mohawk town, taking a crash course on the Iroquois from "his Indn. Tutor."[52]

Weiser, who encouraged Claus to take this path, had been down it himself. Some forty years earlier he spent the better part of a year in another Mohawk village undergoing a similar initiation into Iroquois society, sent there by his father so that Germans moving into Indian territory would have an interpreter of their own.[53] Adopted by the local headman, the youth formed an abiding attachment to the Iroquois. But Conrad was a farmer at heart. Back, in 1713, among his own people, he devoted himself more to crops than councils, and ultimately his quest for land took him away from Iroquoia to the Delawares' Tulpehocken territory. When the Six Nations' search for trade outlets and allies shifted south toward Pennsylvania at about the same time, Weiser brushed up on his Mohawk and ventured onto the path being cleared between Onondaga and Philadelphia.

These two German colonists, so typical in the way they practically fell into the role of negotiator, were exceptional in being formally trained for it. In other times and places, European colonial leaders would send a young man to be educated in Indian country, counting on him to repay the investment by returning to help with frontier diplomacy.[54] But on the Pennsylvania frontier, tentative steps in that direction came to nothing because each side was loathe to part with its young. Thanks but no thanks, Canasatego once replied when Virginians invited the Iroquois to send some children to school in Williamsburg. "[W]e love our Children too well to send them so great a way," the Onondaga said, "and the Indians are not inclined to give their Children learning"—at least not colonial learning.[55] When roles were reversed and Indians issued the invitation, colonists, too, usually declined. I "think it would strengthen the English Interest more in having many of their People living among" Indians, remarked a disappointed Scarouyady in 1756 when Pennsylvania said no.[56]

Those few who did agree to try this educational experiment found the results disappointing. One Iroquois named Kisheta (Kissity) sent his "little lad" to Philadelphia "in order to learn English, to be an Interpreter," but in 1762 Indians reclaimed the youth, still a "little Boy," and apparently never used his new skills.[57] Even Conrad Weiser's son Sammy—whom the agent left among his Mohawk kin in 1751 with the request that they teach him "your linguage, particularly in Council affair[s]"—returned home too soon to acquire the knowledge his father commanded or the trust the elder Weiser enjoyed. "Samuel has almost forgot what little he learned," lamented one provincial official some years later. When Conrad Weiser died in 1760 and the Iroquois tried to appoint Sammy his successor, Pennsylvania politely promised to "make Tryall of him," then ignored him.[58]

Negotiators were made, not born, but they proved hard to manufacture. As colonists and Indians "pitched upon" first this one, then that, as they tried to "think of a fit person to carry the Message," the search went on.[59]

"We Reckon Him One of Us"
Métis

The obvious place to look for go-betweens was among those people—the French called them *métis;* the English, mixed blood, half-breed, or worse—born and bred in the frontier's interstices. These places at the junction of peoples have produced mediators the world over.[60] In North America, denizens of such new communities had the very traits Indians cherished—kin ties, familiarity and the trust it inspired—while also boasting the linguistic gifts and other knowledge colonists wanted. On Pennsylvania's borders two men personified the possibilities, and the pitfalls, of having *métis* do the business of diplomacy.

The first, Peter Chartier, grew up on the lower Susquehanna River in the early eighteenth century, son of a Shawnee woman and a French fur trader named Martin Chartier. After his father's death in 1718, Peter carried on the trade with Philadelphia; when Shawnees, pressed by Pennsylvania farmers and seeking better hunting grounds, began to move across the Alleghenies during the 1720s, young Chartier followed his kin and customers.

Plenty of other Pennsylvania traders pursued these emigrants; what set Chartier apart from his competitors was not access to European goods and the sense to bestow them on Shawnee leaders in order to acquire "a great deal of influence"; it was his Shawnee mother, which by Indian reckoning made him, as the tribe told Pennsylvania in 1734, "one of us." At the same time, those colonists noted happily, the man "Stands firm by the Interestt of Pensylvania, & seems Very Ready on all acc[oun]tts to Do all the Service hee Can, and as hee has the Shawanise Tongue Very perfectt and [is] well Looktt upon among them, hee may Do a greatt Deale of Good."[61]

During the 1730s Chartier did just that, interpreting at councils and helping maintain the longer lines of commerce and communication between Philadelphia and Shawnee settlements in the west. In 1739, discouraged French authorities, after quizzing some Shawnees at Montreal, reported that Chartier, "much esteemed by the English," was still firmly in Pennsylvania's camp.[62]

The French had not lost all hope, however; the Shawnees here at Montreal advised, the French governor went on in his report, that I "induce Chartier to descend with them next spring, as they had reason to think that when I had spoken to him, he would change his mind."[63] Though it was not that easy, in 1745 Chartier and his band of Shawnees did break with the English when he led a raid on Pennsylvania traders in the Ohio country. The man's reasons, at this remove, are hard to recover, but they probably included unhappy memories of land encroachments by Penn's people, chicanery by James Logan that, among other things, robbed Chartier of his father's farm, and more recent, unnamed slights by Pennsylvania's governor.[64] Whatever the cause of his disaffection, outraged Iroquois and British colonial leaders, feeling betrayed, unleashed a fusillade of scorn Chartier's way. "[A] great Cowart," Shickellamy said. "[S]avage, treacherous," and "Brutish," provincial headmen agreed. Because the Shawnees' "perfidious Blood partly Runs in Chartier's Veins," he is, they concluded, "capable of any Villany." Shawnee leaders opposed to Chartier's rise, and to the direction he took his band, were no happier. One of us? No, they insisted, he is French, or *francois métis*.[65]

French? Shawnee? English? Who could tell? The versatility that made Chartier seem at home among French, English, and Shawnees alike also made him suspect to one and all. He can talk to us, can seem loyal to anyone when it suits him. But where does his heart truly lie?

The same doubts followed another *métis*, Andrew Montour, whose debut on the Pennsylvania diplomatic stage came in the early 1740s, just as Chartier was leaving it. For the next three decades Montour made a name for himself, traveling hundreds of miles on errands for Pennsylvania and her sister colonies.[66] But what sort of name? What sort of man? Montour never answered, and never eluded, the questions.

From beginning to end, Montour puzzled people. Richard Peters, the man who pronounced him "unintelligible," had plenty of company. Conrad Weiser, for one, "found him faithful, knowing, and prudent" in June 1748, but by summer's end was "at a lost what to say of him." Nor could Montour's acquaintances make up their minds about his identity. Peters considered him an Indian, but others called him "white," and Weiser referred to Montour as Indian on one page of a letter and white on another.[67]

Montour's impressive collection of names—*Andrew Montour, French Andrew, Henry Montour, Andrew* (or *Andreas*) *Sattelihu, Echnizera* (or *Oughsara*)—did not help fix his identity.[68] Nor did his appearance. "Andrew's cast of countenance is decidedly European," wrote the Moravian leader Count Nikolaus Ludwig von Zinzendorf after meeting Montour in September 1742,[69]

> and had not his face been encircled with a broad band of paint, applied with bear's fat, I would certainly have taken him for one. He wore a brown broadcloth coat, a scarlet damasken lappel-waist coat, breeches, over which his shirt hung, a black Cordovan neckerchief, decked with silver bugles, shoes and stockings, and a hat. His ears were hung with pendants of brass and other wires plaited together like the handle of a basket.

To people accustomed to European and native American badges of identity—color of skin and cut of hair, clothing and other adornments, literacy and kin ties—Montour broadcast mixed signals.[70]

Yet in that fashion statement lay the secret of Montour's success: his unmatched ability to negotiate the frontier's cultural terrain. At home in a longhouse and at a governor's table, able to perform the Iroquois Condolence Ceremony and explain Christian baptism to Indians, bearing a provincial captain's commission and a wampum belt with his credentials as an Iroquois leader, wearing a hat on his head and paint on his face—Montour became "a very useful Person" with "a good Character, both amongst White people and Indians."[71]

Connections were one source of Montour's good character. His father Currundawanah linked him to the Oneidas, and to a martyr whose death in 1729 at the hands of the hated Catawbas lived on in Iroquois memory for a generation. From his mother he received with his surname a far-flung network of kin, including a brother in Canada, cousins wed to Iroquois and living at various places in the Susquehanna Valley, an uncle tied by marriage to a Delaware family at the confluence of the Lehigh and Delaware Rivers, and, near Lake Erie, an aunt among the Miamis. Montour's own marriages—to the granddaughter of a Delaware leader at Shamokin and, later, to the kinswoman of a Conoy headman—spun additional strands in the human web that bound him to the Indian countries.[72]

At the same time, Montour fashioned connections with the Anglo-American world founded not on kinship but on patronage. Besides Count Zinzendorf, Montour cultivated Conrad Weiser, who in 1748 "presented Andrew to the Board [Pennsylvania Council] as a Person who might be of Service to the Province";[73] Virginia land speculators active in the west; George Croghan, another important figure out west; and, after 1755, Crown Superintendent of Indian Affairs William Johnson. Drawing strength from these friends and family, before long Montour was a familiar face everywhere from Williamsburg and Philadelphia to Onondaga and Logstown.

A familiar face, yes, but still hard to read. Whose side was this French Andrew from French Town on? The harder one studied the man, the harder it was to tell, for he was, in some alarming way, unfathomable. Perhaps that is why amid the testimonials to Montour there were tirades against him, sometimes by the very people singing his praises. A "dull stupid creature," raged Richard Peters, an "untractable," "extravagant," and "expensive man." "[A]n Impudent felow" with "great pride" who was "very hard to please," agreed Conrad Weiser. "I am Sorry that ever I recommended him . . . in the least thing." Some Indians, too, were sorry. "I cannot Trust . . . Montour," said one Delaware leader. Neither, sometimes, could the Iroquois, who once doubted the man enough to ask colonists, in his presence, for a second opinion on his translation of a message.[74]

If Montour never broke ranks with the English as Chartier did, neither did he ever shake off the shadow of doubt. The controversial careers of these two men suggest how perilous was the ground between Indian and colonial worlds. Montour and Chartier, endowed with precious skills, were handicapped by their own ambiguity; their gift, their blessing, was also a curse.

But the two men are important not just because their cultural ways catapulted them from obscurity to fame—and, some said, to infamy—but because so few people on the Pennsylvania borderlands resembled them. That uniqueness highlights the lines of force working against a mingling and mixing of peoples in Anglo-America. Sexual liaisons with Indians were relatively rare in Britain's provinces; it is telling that Chartier's father and (if one of the stories about her is true) Montour's mother were of French, not English, extraction. Certainly some Pennsylvanians had children by Indian women. But no *métis* community emerged from these unions, because the offspring of a Pennsylvania man and, say, a Delaware woman would, following native matrilineal rules, be brought up Delaware. Few fur traders stayed around an Indian town enough to teach a child colonial ways, and none brought a child back to the province for an education. That left no pool of *métis* to be tapped as go-betweens; Montour and Chartier were, in a sense, freaks of culture if not of nature. Indian and provincial councils, even as they employed Montour and Chartier, would have to continue the hunt for go-betweens.

"A Person of Consequence"
Men from the Indian Countries

That search, canvassing Indian countries and councils, yielded men who became fixtures of frontier culture. The Conestogas Shawydoohungh (Indian Harry) and Tagotolessa (Civility) in the early eighteenth century, the later Oneida ambassadors Shickellamy and Scarouyady—these and other natives were celebrities in their own day. But unlike

Chartier or Montour—who attracted attention because they stood out from the crowds of colonists and Indians—these native go-betweens remain relatively obscure. More obscure still are the deliberations at Conestoga, Onondaga, Logstown, and elsewhere that made them mediators. The formulae that an occasional colonist jotted down—distinguished men, either promising apprentices or past masters in the diplomatic arts—survived the colonial era; the personal and polit-ical variables Indians used to work out those formulae did not. How important was it that Shawydoohungh knew English? What won Shickellamy the Susquehanna Forks? What prompted Cayugas to ask Shickellamy's son Tachnechdorus (John Shickellamy) "to apply himself to public Business"?[75] Such questions meet only silence.

Nonetheless, some clues at once confirm and clarify the variables in the equation. The negotiator crossing into Pennsylvania from Indian country tended to be "a person of Consequence" among his own peo-ple, "a man of note" formally installed through ceremonies replete with talk of being "sure our Business will go on well, & Justice be done on both sides," talk sanctioned by belts or strings of wampum.[76] The Six Nations first deputed Shickellamy "to look after the" Susquehanna Shawnees; Scarouyady was to do the same for Shawnees in Ohio, and around 1750 a third Iroquois, Seneca George (Osternados), was given a similar charge for Conoys, Nanticokes, and other groups on Iroquoia's southern frontier.[77] From there it was a logical step for such men to open negotiations with other peoples in the vicinity, including colonists.

As with Montour and Chartier, kinship was important. In the Susquehanna country, Oneida go-betweens such as Shickellamy were prominent, probably because that "nation," as Conrad Weiser once ob-served, "pretents to have the greatest right to the land upon Susque-hana." Cayugas, too, claimed a say in Susquehanna affairs, and it probably strengthened Shickellamy's hand that his wife—and there-fore his children—came from that nation.[78]

Yet while certainly men of stature, few Indian negotiators were from the very pinnacle of their societies.[79] The Delaware "Kings" Sassoonan and Nutimus, like the Conestoga headman Tawenna—and like James Logan and Richard Peters, as well as the Penns and their governors—tended to remain above the fray. They sent and received messengers, but did not become messengers themselves. They attended treaties and sometimes spoke at them, but did not prepare the way for those grand conclaves or interpret at them.

Conrad Weiser, at Shamokin in September 1736 on the eve of an Iroquois treaty with Pennsylvania, learned the distinction. For several
years, Shickellamy and the Seneca Hetaquantagechty had gone back
and forth between Philadelphia and Onondaga in order to clear the way
for a council. Now, at last, here came the Iroquois delegation to the
town at the Susquehanna Forks, a party headed by "people of authority and the very chiefs." The Oneida and Seneca had brought the visitors there, yet for days, while the travelers rested and counciled at
Shamokin, those visitors "Keeps their buisnes Intirely Close from Het-
quantagechte and Shykelimo." At times the Iroquois dismissed not only
Weiser but the two Indian go-betweens from their discussions. "I ask
Hetqu:ty why he did not stay there," a puzzled Weiser wrote when he
"and Hetquanta gechte and Shykelemo," at the council's order, "went a
way to gether; . . . he told me he was not iet alowed to do so till the
Chiefs Send for him." While colonists tended to invest Indian go-
betweens with great authority, Weiser, taught by Hetaquantagechty
and Shickellamy, knew better, knew that whatever "Consequence" a
man like Shickellamy or Scarouyady might have, he was still the creature of a shadowy cadre of native leaders, more mouthpiece for an Indian council than master of it.[80]

> *"None Were Acquainted with the Indians or the*
> *Road to Them but the Indian Traders"*
> *Colonial Fur Peddlers*

The Indian towns that produced Shickellamy, Scarouyady, and the
rest were also training grounds for another sort of candidate: the colonial fur trader. From the Swede Lars Pärsson Cocke and the Frenchman
Jacques Le Tort before 1700 through Le Tort's fellow Frenchman Pierre
Bizaillon and the Quaker Edmond Cartlidge in the early part of the
eighteenth century to the Irishmen Thomas McKee and George
Croghan toward the close of the colonial era, commerce produced
more than its share of negotiators.

This crew might seem unlikely raw material out of which to construct a quiet, sober public figure, for traders had a terrible reputation
among Indians and colonists alike. "[L]ow, immoral people," "rascally
fellows" full of "lyes and treachery," men who were "worthless, expensive, dishonest, prey to the Indian women, and regardless of publick or private truth," "a set of abandoned Wretches"—an avalanche of
invective cascaded from colonial pens.[81]

Part of the officials' scorn was prejudice against men from the lower orders, especially men with bad accents and worse manners disinclined to respect their betters. "[I]nsolent," "very impudent," "very high and abusive" with a tendency to "talk high," the trader often refused to conform to British codes of deference, meeting rebukes from colonial leaders "in a laughing manner" punctuated by "ludicrous burlesque" or "Oaths and Imprecations."[82]

As if this were not bad enough, most traders were thought as unreliable as they were truculent. For all their knowledge of Indian ways, these men still, colonial leaders concluded, were "generally too ignorant" and "not observant" enough to be go-betweens. Their "Ideas," one official scoffed, "do not extend beyond the Circumference of a Beaver-Skin."[83]

The very preoccupation that gave the trader valuable negotiating tools—the traffic in peltry—might also hinder him when called to serve. Intent on satisfying the demands of his Indian and Philadelphia customers, with an eye always on "the sweet profits" to be made in trade, the fur peddler "can with eagerness go thro the greatest hardships and Difficaltyes for sake of Gaine."[84] Few, however, were eager to go through the same trials for king and country, or proprietor and province. In December 1731 the Susquehanna trader and sometime go-between Edmond Cartlidge found that diplomacy and trade pulled him in different directions. Authorities in Philadelphia summoned him to talk over French doings on the Allegheny River; at the same time, however, "my Affairs so Pressingly call mee Back into ye Woods," Cartlidge fretted, that "I Know not whatt to Do." In the end, the woods won: Cartlidge got word to Philadelphia that the French threat was exaggerated, then headed across the Susquehanna to join his packhorse train for the journey west.[85]

Men in Philadelphia were not the only ones disappointed by traders. Indians, too, added their voices to the chorus of condemnation. Though just one of what natives called "that vile Sort of Men, the Traders," was actually named Swindel, many more earned the title. These men overcharge us, native leaders complained; they add stones to their scales; they miscount matchcoats; they steal corn, skins, and horses; they promise to have a gun repaired, then sell it instead; they "make it their business to waylay . . . young men returning from hunting, making them drunk with rum, and then Cheat them of their Skins."[86] Nor were young men and old the only victims. Indians also said that a trader "would lie, cheat, and debauch their Women, and even their Wives, if their Husbands were not at Home." So troublesome were these men that some natives thought "traders . . . as bad as Oonasahroona, or the under ground inhabitant, which is the name they give the devil."[87]

The verdict, it would seem, was unanimous: colonial fur traders were as far from the sort of person Indians and colonists sought for a go-between as one could be. At the same time, however, even as native Americans drew up an indictment against the ruffians in their midst, they distinguished "Fair Traders," men "who furnish them with . . . necessarys," from "wicked Whiskey Sellers," "strangers," "Loose persons who have no fixt settlements."[88]

"Fair Traders" were more than good sources of coveted European goods; immersed in native life, they acquired skills a go-between needed. If few could match the claims of Jacques Le Tort's son, James, of "having from his Infancy been educated to no other business than to deal with the Indians for their Peltry," many could boast years of acquaintance with native peoples, an education that could be used in other sorts of bargaining. Many learned by lodging in Indian houses, as references to "Our Land Lady at the Cannois [Conoys]," "the Landlord where Edmond Cartlidge lodged," and "Teaffes Lanlord" testified. Many also bedded down with an Indian woman, an arrangement thought "necessary to a successful trade." Besides the obvious sexual advantages, this woman provided an outsider with the network of personal connections that gave shape and meaning to life in Indian country; she also taught him the language, prepared his meals, even helped him out in the store. At Shamokin in 1743, when some Indians roused a trader and "his squaw" at midnight, it was she who got out of bed and sold rum to the clamorous customers.[89]

Eating and sleeping with Indians, hunting and trading with Indians, the "Fair Trader" earned their affection and respect. Natives adopted a trader's name—there were Indians named *Thomas McKee* and *James Le Tort*—as "a seal of friendship." Further evidence of a close relationship lies in testimonials of trust and affection. Of all the colonists peddling European wares in our town, Conestogas announced in 1711, only Pierre Bizaillon is allowed to live among us. Delawares called Cartlidge "our fr[ien]d Edm[on]d," and Shawnees said that "[t]hey reckon [Thomas McKee] one of themselves."[90]

No colonial fur trader earned greater respect from Indians, or traveled farther on that respect, than George Croghan. Arriving in Pennsylvania in 1741 to escape famine in his native Ireland, Croghan in a few short years established himself as "King of the Traders," the foremost Pennsylvanian in the Ohio country. Courageous and quick-witted, glib and nimble, a boon companion to one and all, Croghan became "a meer Idol among his Countrymen the Irish Traders."[91] He also worked the crowd in Philadelphia, overcoming a brogue and a spotty education to charm polished merchants there into advancing him warehouses worth of European goods, which he then used, like Peter Chartier before him, to strengthen his ties to natives.

The results were impressive. Croghan and his partner "can do more with ye Indians yn all the other Traders put together," marveled Richard Peters in 1748. Waiting to hear of Croghan's efforts to entice Indians to peace talks a decade later, another colonist was "pretty Sure . . . that if he could not bring them in, no man on the Continent could do it." Indians agreed. In 1763, with war brewing once again, a Shawnee told one Pennsylvanian that Croghan was "the only Man amongst us [colonists] they regard'd & only for him it might be War again & that none of us knew how to please Indians but him."[92]

Like Conrad Weiser, Croghan was the right man in the right place at the right time, for in the 1740s the Ohio country became a cockpit of imperial ambitions, a hotbed of petty intrigues and grand schemes. Croghan—beloved by Indians, adept at petty intrigue, given to grand schemes himself—became the man Pennsylvania officials and western peoples looked to first as they opened diplomatic channels. In 1756 he brokered this pivotal role into a commission to become Britain's agent out there, winning from William Johnson a coveted Crown office as deputy superintendent of Indian affairs.

The Pennsylvania provincial council, "knowing Mr. Croghan's Circumstances[,] was not a little surprized" at this turn of events. The surprise stemmed not just from Croghan's mountain of debt to Philadelphia merchants but from prejudice against men like him. The fellow is "illiterate, impudent, and ill-bred," stormed one British officer forced to deal with the Irishman. A "vile Rascal," agreed Richard Peters, and Governor James Hamilton thought him "an Intriguing, Disaffected Person."[93]

Whatever their misgivings, Hamilton, Peters, and the rest were stuck with men like Croghan. Where else could they turn? "[N]one were acquainted with the Indians or the Road to them but the Indian Traders," moaned one leader after searching in vain for an alternative.

Who else was around Indians enough to, as Thomas McKee wrote of some Delawares he knew, "have an opportunity of hearing their sentiments both in sobriety & in their Cups"? To notice that they were buying suspiciously large amounts of arms and ammunition? That they were "more Sulky than usual" or "very reserved to their most Intimate Friends amongst the Traders"?[94]

Necessity made polished Philadelphia gentlemen depend on the hinterlands' scruffy denizens. In 1703 James Logan debated whether to bring James Le Tort in for questioning about the trader's suspicious trip to Canada—or send him as an envoy to the Shawnees. A generation later Logan faced the same dilemma: Logan the merchant, stern and righteous, was chasing down Edmond Cartlidge, trader, for overdue debts, while Logan the provincial official, oozing false flattery, enlisted the aid of Edmond Cartlidge, emissary, on Shawnee affairs.[95] Like it or not, authorities were yoked to a man not fit to sit at the same table with the gentlemen dispatching him into Indian country, gentlemen who later hung on his every accented or misspelled word.

"We Were . . . from Other White People Quite Different" Missionaries

Pennsylvania leaders reluctantly turning to Cartlidge, Le Tort, and Croghan wished that a different breed of colonist would make Indians their business. In 1706 the provincial assembly asked "that the Persons employed in such Treaties and Visits [with natives], be of sober Life, in order to induce the said *Indians* to civil Society, and the Christian Religion." Those natives, too, painfully aware that their friends the "Fair Traders" were a minority, welcomed colonists of a different stripe. The very year that the legislature issued its plaintive lament, a Conestoga leader embraced a band of Quakers out by the Susquehanna, noting how, unlike most Pennsylvanians, these visitors "did not come to buy, or sell, or get Gain, but came in Love and Respect to them, and desired their Well-doing both here and hereafter."[96]

Both the assemblymen and the Conestogas would have to wait a long time to see more of these people. For a generation no Quaker—indeed, no Christian missionary at all—followed that band to Conestoga or any other Indian town. When in 1744 a Presbyterian minister named David Brainerd, scouting fertile soil for sowing the gospel, preached to some Indians between the Delaware and Susquehanna Valleys, his native listeners pronounced themselves "somewhat surprised [by his message], having never before heard of these things."[97]

By then some colonial Christians were bestirring themselves to rescue pagan peoples from darkness. Brainerd himself occasionally left his native charges in New Jersey and at the Delaware Forks (where the Lehigh emptied into the Delaware) to tour the Susquehanna country, as did his brother John and a colleague, John Sergeant. None stayed long or returned to the Susquehanna to plant a mission, but Moravians did. Indeed, only months after this sect of German pietists founded Bethlehem at the Forks of the Delaware in 1741, their leader, Count Zinzendorf, was courting Iroquois headmen at Weiser's house, then heading off to visit Shamokin and other Susquehanna towns to gauge interest in Jesus Christ. Soon Zinzendorf's disciples, men and women of the *Unitas Fratrum,* had established near Bethlehem a village for Indians, Gnadenhütten, and built a house at Shamokin. In the years to come Christian Frederick Post, David Zeisberger, John Heckewelder, and others would fan out across the frontier, northward to Iroquoia, and ultimately over the western mountains into Ohio to spread their version of the good news and the good life.[98]

In many ways these pious souls were ideally suited to be gobetweens. Unlike most English missionaries, "well meaning but gloomy people" who (according to one critic) were reluctant "to sacrifice their friends[,] hopes, and Connections to bury themselves in an obscure Village Surrounded by a parcel of Indians," Moravians wanted to live among and learn from natives. Rather than badger their hosts about Christ, these folk counted on the force of Christian example to win hearts and souls, only bringing up the gospel if the moment seemed right. Most of the time they spent praying, planting, singing, and visiting; they fed the hungry, lodged the weary, and pitched in to harvest corn or chop wood, to help build a canoe or a cage for a pet bear. Their willingness to bleed ailing townsfolk further impressed natives, for it combined the roles of healer and spiritual leader in ways that made sense to Indians. The first Moravian missionaries at Shamokin, Martin and Anna Mack, are "especially held in high esteem" there, claimed one visitor, "as they . . . are always ready to assist in cases of sickness."[99]

The generosity and gentle ways combined to make some Indians agree with Moravian claims that "we were a separate people, and from other white people quite different." Acknowledging that difference, natives adopted several Moravians, making Martin Mack *Ganachragéjat* and Zeisberger *Anouserácheri*. One, Christian Frederick Post *(Wallangundowngen)*, even married a Wampanoag and a Delaware woman in turn.[100]

Wallangundowngen became an important negotiator during the darkest days of the frontier war that erupted in the 1750s. In the summer of 1758 he twice ventured with words of peace to the Indian town of Wyoming on the Susquehanna's North Branch, and that fall twice more to Ohio.[101] Reflecting on these adventures, Post captured the missionary's view on becoming an envoy. "I have been these fifteen years past a Messenger of the Gospel among the Indians," he explained. Though as "a man whose Caracter it is to bring Words of Goddely and immutable Truth to the Nations," I am "somewhat more cautious then others in carrying to the same People worldly messages," he continued, nonetheless I am "convinced" that carrying those secular words "will not be a hurt to my proper Call and destination viz to make known our Sacred Religion." Such work, far from "out of the way of a Minister of the Gospel," was in fact essential to that larger enterprise, since "bringing about a Peace with the Indians would," Post argued, "open the Way for the Servants of God to look for a future harvest."[102]

What is surprising, given this philosophy, is not that Post became a go-between but that none of his brethren did. For all their personal charm and their knowledge of Indians, missionaries rarely served as envoys on the Pennsylvania frontier. One reason for their absence lies in Post's own hesitation about "a Messenger of the Gospel" bearing "worldly messages." Post here was trying to get around missionaries' reluctance to become involved in "the Publick Affairs of the Indians," as Moravian leaders told Pennsylvania's governor in 1752. "[I]t had been an establish'd Maxim for many Years amongst us not to intermeddle in any Thing of that kind." Indeed, they went further, asking that the governor "vouchsafe for ever to exempt us from all Affairs of a civil Nature." Our devotion to interpreting God's word for the Indian leaves us no room, they declared, to do the same for messages from man to man. Though they never received official exemption, until Post's journeys in 1758 missionaries exempted themselves.[103]

Whether this was sound theology, it was certainly smart politics, for another reason Post had no company was Pennsylvania's suspicion of Moravians. These people were new to the colony; they were German, and the influx of Germans was already causing anxiety among Anglo-Pennsylvanians; why this sudden interest in Indians? Some colonists answered that these missionaries had tried to win the Iroquois for the French, had told natives to sell no more land to the English, had even asserted that henceforth they, not Conrad Weiser, were the proper channel of communication between Pennsylvania and Iroquoia. Moravians stoutly denied the charges, the authorities accepted their version—but doubts remained.[104]

Among Indians, meanwhile, colonial fur traders who thought missionaries bad for business tried to breed further suspicion. Not every encounter between colonists seeking souls and those seeking pelts was unfriendly, but many traders swore at, beat up, even "tried to excite the Indians to kill" missionaries.[105] No trader got his wish; no missionary on the Pennsylvania frontier died by an Indian's hand. But with or without traders' agitation, mistrust of Christ's servants—however humble they were, however attached some natives were to them—pervaded Indian country. Even in his own domain at the Delaware Forks, David Brainerd's sermons drew mixed reviews. While some natives listened attentively, others "refused to hear me preach, and have been enraged against those that have attended my preaching. But of late," Brainerd fretted, "they are more bitter than ever, scoffing at Christianity, and sometimes asking my [Indian] hearers how often they have cried, and whether they han't now cried enough to do the turn, etc."[106]

Bad as the Delaware Forks could be, Shamokin at the Susquehanna Forks, where Brainerd thought "the devil now reigns in the most eminent manner," was worse. Not even Moravians made much headway there. Tutelos "Ridiculed Us," the Moravian Martin Mack noted during his first stay at Shamokin in the fall of 1745, and some Delawares were "so buisy at Cards, that they had no Time to look at us." Another Susquehanna native "Spoke many Evill things of the Brethren. Said . . . yt the Brethren wanted to make them to Slaves." The Six Nations, too, were suspicious of "the Moravians coming to Susquhannah and Building Churches and learning some of the People to sing Psalms, which they said was only to steal their Lands."[107]

Sober, Indians talked; drunk, they acted, making "great Noise and Disturbance" around the missionary house that drowned out an evening's anthem or kept those inside awake. Other drunken natives were more direct. At Shamokin one woman, "Swaring Bitterly," pounded on the door at midnight and tried so hard to "break it Down" that she almost tore it off its hinges. Those who did manage to get inside "look'd very dismal and roar'd like the very Beasts." "During the four months we resided there," Martin Mack recalled of the Shamokin mission's early days, "we were in constant danger, and there was scarcely a night but we were compelled to leave our hut, and hide in the woods, from fear of the drunken savages."[108]

Brainerd, who stayed in Shamokin only a day or two and brusquely tried to herd the locals together so that he could preach to them, was easy for Indians to despise. So was the imperious Count Zinzendorf, who bossed natives around and openly detested their "repugnance to labor," their "indigestible Indian corn that . . . tends to stupefy their faculties," their disdain for clothes and hats. But Moravians who followed in the *reichscount*'s footsteps, neither as haughty nor as hotheaded, also drew Indians' ire because they were unable to hide the fact that they shared Zinzendorf's views on native life as "Gluttony, Drunkenness, whoredom, Theft, Murder, Lying, [and] Deceit."[109]

Nor could they keep such thoughts to themselves: their expressions and actions, if not their words, betrayed them. Why, Indians must have wondered, did only Post marry among us? Why did he and the others turn down an invitation to a festival, why refuse a drink, why decline a bite of cooked dog? There was, whether missionaries saw it or not, rebuke in refusal, in silence, in absence from a ceremony, a feast, a woman's bed. For all of the Moravians' determination to mingle with Indians, they admitted that they "are not at home in their [Indian] manners and modes of expression." One of their leaders, John Christian Frederick Cammerhoff, hoped that someday he would be. I "sometimes felt like saying to myself: [']I am dwelling among my own people,[']" he mused, "and when I shall be able to say that in its true meaning, my heart will rejoice." But Cammerhoff never saw that glorious day; indeed, just two weeks later he wrote that he and his Moravian companion "spent a very happy evening, and were especially glad to be alone and not to have any Indians with us."[110]

No wonder many natives, seeing or sensing all this, lumped these folk with other colonists. Beset by drunk and (in some ways, worse) sober Indians, cursed by traders, doubted by provincial officials, their eyes fixed not on this world but the next, missionaries had good reason to stay out of frontier diplomacy. Their gift of tongues and their humble ways recommended them, but widespread mistrust hurt their chances of becoming negotiators in any numbers.

"Much in the English Style"
Settlement Indians

But if, for all of these reasons, few missionaries became go-betweens, they did plant the seeds of a whole new crop of mediators, a crop that ripened with the coming of war to Pennsylvania in the mid-1750s: Christian Indians, most of them Delawares originally from both banks of that river, who to one degree or another accepted European ways. Just when war made colonists unwelcome in Indian country, Christian natives emerged as candidates for this calling.

The most famous of these folk was the Delaware Teedyuscung, a lapsed Moravian who, after moving from New Jersey to the Delaware Forks and then, in 1754, on to Wyoming, set himself up as a putative king and sometime peacemaker. But the attention the mercurial and bombastic Teedyuscung attracted has cast in shadow other Delaware negotiators, many of them disciples of the Presbyterian missionaries David and John Brainerd. These natives—Tunda (Moses) Tatamy, Isaac Stille, Joseph Peepy (Weholelahund), John Pumpshire (Cawkeeponen)—were quieter, calmer men; having stayed behind at the Delaware Forks or in their old Jersey haunts, when war came they mounted the public stage.[111]

These remnant groups—called "Settlement," "Neighbor," or "tame" Indians to distinguish them from "remote," "wild," or "far" natives beyond the frontier—were tiny islands in an alien, forbidding sea.[112] Only Tatamy, who in 1733 cultivated friends in high places in order to get title to three hundred acres near the Delaware Forks, escaped poverty. The rest eked out a bare existence farming small plots of land, hunting where they could, and making baskets, brooms, spoons, and bowls, then peddling these household items to nearby colonists.[113]

Beginning in the 1740s, the burdens of this hardscrabble life were eased, for some, by Christianity. The Moravian founding of Bethlehem, followed by David Brainerd's arrival in New Jersey, promised a brighter day. Some Delawares found in the new faith solace, hope, and an outlet for anger or frustration. In 1750 Moravians baptised Teedyuscung, after considerable hesitation. By then David Brainerd and his brother John had brought Tatamy and other Delawares into the Christian fold. At the Forks, at Jersey mission towns, the shepherds happily reported the weeping and ecstacy, the shrieks and prayers of Indian souls seeking salvation.[114]

"Oh, what a difference is there between these" Delawares in New

Jersey, exclaimed David Brainerd, "and the Indians I had lately treated with upon Susquehanna!" The contrast was indeed startling. Years of living among colonists, combined with missionary work that included schooling as well as sermons, had wrought tremendous change in the "conversation & deportment," the "countenance and conduct" of these folk. Not all of them had a thoroughly "English method of living"— Teedyuscung's English was worse than Tatamy's, Stille's, or Peepy's; Stille and Peepy, among others, could read and write, but Tatamy could not—yet all took their bearings from the colonial compass (Figure 8). Tatamy "spoke English well," remarked Count Zinzendorf after meeting the Delaware, "and had regulated his housekeeping much in the English style." Desperate for a translator to get his message across, David Brainerd thought Tatamy a godsend. The man is "well fitted for

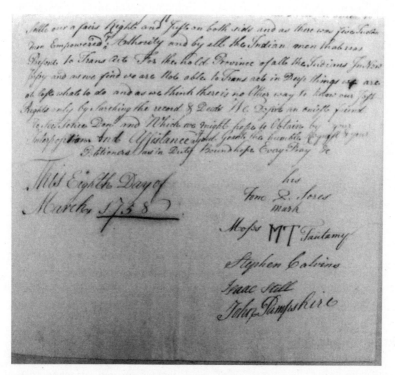

Figure 8. Delaware Indian Signatures.

The marks and signatures by these Delawares—including the go-betweens Isaac Stille, Moses Tatamy, and John Pumpshire—reveal the varying degrees of literacy in this group. Courtesy of Quaker Collection, Haverford College Library, Haverford, Pennsylvania.

the business of an Interpreter," the young Presbyterian clergyman rejoiced, "[i]n regard of his acquaintance with the Indian & English languages; & likewise with the manners of both nations." Tatamy's Christian name, Moses, may have reflected hopes that he, too, would lead his people out of the wilderness and into the promised land.[115]

Without losing his skills as hunter or weaver, without severing his ties to kin on the Susquehanna or the Ohio—without, always, removing the rings that dangled from his ears—a man like Stille or Pumpshire took on colonial trappings. Preparing for a trip, he donned shoes and stockings to go with his ruffled shirt and waistcoat, packing spare clothes in a portmanteau. In that bag he might also put a Bible and a treaty to read en route, along with pencil and paper so that he could write a letter back to his colonial sponsors.[116] On his return he might take tea with colonists in Reading or stop in Philadelphia to see his children, enrolled in school there. Enlisting in colonial armies, acting as "Indian Attorneys" for their people, these men came to bear a striking resemblance to their colonial neighbors.[117]

As striking as the fancy get-up was the humble demeanor that went with it, which differed dramatically from the ill-concealed arrogance of other Indian go-betweens. Tatamy, noted Zinzendorf, is "a man of remarkably quiet and honest deportment." Where Susquehanna Indians bridled at the Moravian leader's highhanded ways—at one town, men painted red and black and armed with knives "came in crowds about the tent" the *reichscount* had pitched "to keep an eye on him"—Tatamy "very well listened to the admonitions given him by the Count."[118] Adopting a low profile, when among European colonists Settlement Indians put up a placid, pleasant front as a form of protective coloration.

From hats to shoes, from pencils to prayers, these subdued folk looked to provincial officials like promising candidates for go-between. Pennsylvanians accepted Teedyuscung, the least placid of the bunch, because they had to: in 1756, when the man burst on the frontier scene from his new Susquehanna home, he was almost the only person from Indian country talking peace. But the province accepted other Delawares living closer to hand because it wanted to. More like humble missionaries than haughty fur traders, *métis,* or native headmen, these Indians were "known to be of good disposition well attached to the English." Better yet, they had the languages and other branches of knowledge provincial leaders sought. However far removed from their aboriginal cultural moorings, these Delawares had not altogether forgotten the world they grew up in. While squiring Zinzendorf around his farm, Tatamy knew enough traditional lore to explain "heathen" ceremonies, and at a treaty he knew enough diplomatic protocol to remind a governor that the Indian delegation would expect the At the Woods' Edge Ceremony. As another council opened, Joseph Peepy himself took wampum in hand and "went thro' the Ceremony of Condolence usual upon those occasions."[119]

Quite without planning it, colonial neighbors and Christian missionaries had created a cadre of men whose fingers knew both quill pen and wampum string, who could chat about the At the Woods' Edge rite with Indians or spend an evening with Quakers discussing baptism.[120] To Pennsylvanians groping about for negotiators, it seemed too good to be true—and it was. Like every other group Indians and colonists approached about joining the cross-cultural conversation, this pool of recruits had problems that diminished its appeal and its effectiveness.

Teedyuscung's flaws were glaring enough. The man is, Moravians despaired, as "unstable as water and like a reed shaken before the wind." One minute he boasted loudly to colonists of his greatness, the next, weeping and berating himself, he begged their forgiveness.[121] But temperate Delawares had handicaps of their own. For one thing, the very colonists recruiting them also despised them. "[Y]ou know what sort of People those are," wrote Richard Peters to Thomas Penn; like Teedyuscung, they were "Rascalls," "Riffraff," "straggling Indian[s]." Weiser, too, scoffed that Teedyuscung was merely "a Baskit and Broom-Maker by Trade," and "Jersey Basket makers" became a common epithet.[122]

Some of the colonial contempt arose from the conviction that, despite occasional evidence to the contrary, these people did not know enough about Indian ways to do business properly. "The Governor punctually observed all the Indian forms . . . ," Peters wrote after one meeting with Teedyuscung, which "pleased him vastly, . . . tho' he neither understood nor observed them himself"; he "knows," Peters concluded, "nothing of Business." Neither did the other "Natives of West Jersey"; having "lived there from their Infancy, . . . [they] are intirely unacquainted with foreign Indians and their Customs."[123]

"[F]oreign Indians," too, despised these messengers. If many in Indian country opposed the missionary, imagine their scorn for natives taken in by those preachy people. It did not help that Christian Indians, as if to show off their new creed, "carry a great deal of holiness in their Countenances & Exterior deportment." Striking a holier-than-thou

pose, they had a sanctimonious attitude likely to infuriate other natives.[124]

In fact, Settlement Indians were handicapped as go-betweens because
they looked as odd as Andrew Montour or Peter Chartier. *Christian Indians? Civilized Indians?* To most people—Indian and colonial—these
were oxymorons if not impossibilities, as two encounters beside the
Susquehanna suggest. In September 1745 David Brainerd, with six of
his Jersey Delaware disciples, was heading down the Susquehanna's
eastern shore from Shamokin. Tired, weak, soaked by a thunderstorm,
the sojourners found a roof and a meal with some "poor ignorant" colonial frontier folk. When, sitting down at the table, the family "saw my
Indians ask a blessing and give thanks," the hosts gaped, "much astonished" to see natives pray. Upstream at Shamokin itself a few years later,
it was local natives' turn to gawk when a Moravian Indian convert
named Jeremias visited his German brethren at the mission there. The
townspeople "wondered a lot about him," the brethren reported, "and
could not view him enough."[125] Like their stunned colonial neighbors
just downstream, Shamokin's inhabitants could not place the fellow,
could not fit him into the social categories they carried about in their
heads.

"So Much like an Indian"
Prisoners and Other White Indians

Whatever their liabilities, Christian missionaries and their Indian
charges substantially enlarged the pool of candidates for go-between at
midcentury. After the outbreak of frontier war, converts of a different
sort promised to further expand that pool: the so-called "White Indians" who forsook their natal culture and made a new life for themselves among natives.

The breed was not altogether new, of course. Philadelphians had
long considered the fur trader too close to Indians in appearance and
outlook. And according to one version of Madame Montour's story,
she, too, may have been a colonist captured and adopted by Indians,
who then translated what she learned into a position of prominence.
But the raids beginning in the mid-1750s brought unprecedented numbers of colonial people into Indian villages. Some were deserters from
imperial armies; most were captives, hundreds of them, torn by bloody
hands from all that was familiar and dragged off to an uncertain fate.[126]

If they survived the grueling trip and Indians elected to adopt them to replace dead kinfolk instead of kill them to ease the mourners' grief, these people had obvious potential as negotiators, for they straddled the cultural divide in ways that appealed to natives and colonists alike. With a new name and a new language, with new kin and new friends, the former captives became, Indians thought, "just the same as one of themselves." Redeemed by colonists as part of the peace agreement, many kept a "deep Attachment to the Indian life" and remained someone in whom "the Indians had great Confidence."[127]

That confidence appealed to European colonial officials. When war destroyed customary channels of frontier concourse, finding someone familiar with enemy territory was of incalculable value. Like the trader Lawrence Burke, who spent the first years of the war up the Susquehanna with his Delaware wife, these people knew the lay of the land beyond the frontier. As Burke boasted, they might even have "more influence over ye Delaware Indians, I think, then any other" colonist— and could put that influence to the service of "King & Country." Because they had priceless information, Burke and others who emerged from enemy territory faced a barrage of questions. Where did you live? What Indians do you know? Are any of them talking of peace? How many captives did you see, how many war parties, how many French? How much food do the Indians have? Ammunition?[128]

Such questions were often followed by assignments as go-betweens. Some, like Ooligasha (Owiligaska, Peter Spelman), a German and son-in-law to a Shawnee headman, surfaced once or twice.[129] Others took a more prominent role. In 1757 Philadelphia officials dispatched Burke to spy on the French, and a year later military officers consulted him about a push into Indian country. David Owens, son of a fur trader, who deserted from British forces—"several times," some said—appeared (several times, too) in Ohio and Iroquoia as a Delaware interpreter. So did Joseph Nickels, taken captive as a boy, later drawing a translator's salary from the Crown.[130]

It is no surprise that some wound up standing beside the speaker at a treaty or figuratively guiding officials through war-torn Indian country; but it is surprising that more did not do so. Considering their numbers and skills, colonial converts provided few recruits to the cross-cultural conversation, even when recruits were so desperately needed.

Perhaps a deserter was reluctant to become a go-between because he feared punishment if authorities learned his whereabouts. While those who applied for clemency often received it—indeed, in one case

the authorities actually wanted a deserter to stay among Indians in
hopes he would learn the language and become an interpreter!—many
more might never have heard of such clemency, or might not have
trusted it.[131]

Captives, too, proved unsuitable in a variety of ways. Many were
women, and therefore automatically excluded from such work. Many
more, taken as children, left their colonial home and hearth so early in
life and dwelled among Indians so long that they forgot their native
tongue, forgot their parents, forgot even their names. Others, faced
with repatriation to their birthplace, might well have feigned such ignorance, for they had grown so attached to Indian kin that they wanted
to forget, forever, their colonial roots. More than one colonial traveler
through Indian country found that upon his arrival in a town the captives, fearing he had come to take them "home," would flee at the very
sight of him.[132]

But even men who returned to the colonial world were not always
inclined to pursue the opportunity fate had handed them. With hatred
of Indians now sweeping Pennsylvania, it could be dangerous to be
thought too friendly with natives. To deflect colonial doubts or perhaps
to get revenge on their captors, some former prisoners used what they
had learned from Indians against those Indians. James Smith, five years
a captive in Ohio, was one of these. On his return to Pennsylvania,
Smith later recalled, his family "received me with great joy, but were
surprised to see me so much like an Indian, both in my gait and gesture." To wash off the stain of savagery, Smith joined two other former
captives to train colonial war parties. The plan, he explained, was to recruit likely men and "dress them uniformly in the Indian manner, with
breech-clouts, leggins, mockesons and green shrouds. . . . In place of
hats," Smith continued, "we wore red handkerchiefs, and painted our
faces red and black, like Indian warriors." With peace, Smith went on
to a distinguished career, a career that did not include serving as a go-
between. Significantly, though he kept a journal during the 1750s and
1760s, he did not publish it until 1799, by which time he was well out
of the woods and Indians, long since removed from Pennsylvania, were
solely of antiquarian interest.[133]

Smith was smart. Men like him were suspect, tainted in accent, body
language, and other ways by intimacy with people colonists now branded
savage foes. Ironically, just when they would have been most useful,

men with Smith's knowledge also elicited the greatest doubt and fear. The very source of their appeal as go-betweens—"always much attached to the Indians," with "many friends amongst them"—was a two-edged sword. They might, like Lawrence Burke, insist that they had "the Intrest of King & Country Intirely at heart," but who could get past biography and bearing to peer into that heart? With war raging, questions became interrogations, hope of help from them surrendered to doubt, and eventually to venom. Burke, colonial leaders concluded, is "a great rogue," David Owens a "shocking reprobate," Gersham Hicks "a most Notorious Villain." Owens, detained in Philadelphia so that authorities could check his story, and Hicks, in chains at Pittsburgh while colonists figured out what to do with him, had the leisure to ponder the perils of being thought "attached to the Indians."[134]

"I . . . Wish My Self out of Thire Contry"
Ideals and Realities

"Why Did We Wander Around in the Woods?"
Motivations

Hard as it is to piece together the general formula for choosing go-betweens, it is harder still to explain why certain men and not others stepped forward to become a public person charged with messages. Count Zinzendorf, who so thoroughly "made a complete mess of things" in Indian country, was not likely to be chosen. Neither was John Burt, a Susquehanna fur trader so lacking in self control that, drinking with some Delawares one night in 1727, he got into a fight with his companions, went to his chamber pot, "fill'd his hand with his own Dung[,] and threw it among the Indians."[135] But why did Christian Frederick Post *(Wallangundowngen)* end up carrying messages, and not Martin Mack *(Ganachragéjat)*? Why Thomas McKee, and not his neighbor and fellow trader James Berry? Why Moses Tatamy rather than Tom Sores or some other Settlement Indian? The chemistry that decided these questions, made up of such elements as character and circumstance, is forever lost, leaving us only to wonder at the process—or serendipity—of selection.

We might well wonder, too, why anyone came forward at all. Negotiation was always a time-consuming, often frustrating, sometimes perilous business. "Why did we wander around in the woods," asked one incredulous frontier farmer when two missionaries stopped at his house, "and not live like other Christians?" The Moravians had an easy answer: they were doing God's work. Others on earthly "Errands" went into the woods for a whole host of reasons ranging from service to a higher calling—God, crown and colony, town and tribe— to the status Indians accorded a negotiator and the payment provincial officials offered.[136] Doubtless coercion was sometimes involved. Colonial fur traders in debt to James Logan might have found it hard to refuse his invitation to carry a message, as would a Delaware living among colonists or a Lawrence Burke or Andrew Montour, whose loyalty to king or proprietor was suspect. But enough people declined the invitation—Edmond Cartlidge once turned his back on Logan and Philadelphia, as did Weiser a decade later, and Satcheecho became "the Indian Messenger" only because another Indian approached by native leaders "excused himself"—to suggest that not everyone was forced to accept.[137]

Whatever other reasons put people on a path to the woods, all— even the pious Post—had tangible incentives. "Indians always expect to be well rewarded for their Trouble" bearing messages, wrote one Pennsylvania governor. Colonists did, too, and the public record is littered with payments—cash and clothing, guns and powder—by grateful officials "for Services" that included trips to Shamokin and Onondaga, interpretation at councils, and "attendance" on Indians traversing the colony. Shawydoohungh leaving Philadelphia in 1711 with lead, a blanket, and shirts for himself and his two children, Newcastle leaving the same town in 1756 with ten pieces of eight in his pocket, Weiser coming in to collect £20 for a trip to Iroquoia—these and other men reaped benefits from public office.[138]

However, although one official dangled "a pension for life" before Weiser, no one was going to get rich.[139] Regular salaries came late, when Britain's creation of the Indian superintendency in 1755 put Croghan, Montour, and others on the Crown payroll. Most negotiators, most of the time, did what amounted to piece work, which was unpredictable at best, because the need for go-betweens followed no schedule. Satcheecho made two trips to Onondaga and another to Albany in 1722, but none in 1721 or 1723. Moreover, there was no set rate for services, and even negotiators promised a specific reward often had to wait for payment—sometimes for years, sometimes forever.[140]

Delay could fray tempers. One outburst by the Ohio Oneida Scarouyady not only measures the level of frustration but also suggests Indian motivations. "You think You perfectly well understand the Management of Indian Affairs," Scarouyady scolded provincial officials in 1755, "but I must tell You that it is not so, and that the French are more politick than You. They never employ an Indian on any Business, but they give him fine Cloathes, besides other Presents, and this makes the Indians their hearty Friends." The English, by contrast, are fools, the aged Oneida went on, to be so niggardly with "those large Pieces of Goods that your City is full of." If Indian negotiators return home from English colonies poorly clad, "they will be laughed at and made ashamed." The go-between was particularly concerned about the treatment men in his party would receive. He "made heavy Complaints that the Indians which he brought from the Country of the Six Nations in order to serve the Governmt were naked, and he should be ashamed to carry them with him to Aucgquick [Croghan's frontier farm, where many natives were then camped] in so miserable a Condition; and if they should be permitted to go so bare to Aucgquick it would prejudice the Indians there mightily against the People of Pennsylvania."[141]

Though colonists dismissed such carping as greed, proof of "Mercenary motive," it was more complicated than that. In Indian societies, European goods were status symbols, announcing a man's access to coveted merchandise from a magical, mysterious realm. Colorful cloth, ruffled shirts, fancy pistols—these marked their owner's prestige and power. So did a horse, a gift native messengers often requested. "I am now grown old," one Cayuga told Pennsylvania officials in a typical speech, "and have been employ'd as a Messenger, and am become stiff with Travelling, and I desire you will help me, and give me a Horse, that I may not be obliged to walk when I go home."[142]

A horse made a statement; a house spoke even louder. It was no coincidence that in September 1744, just after Shickellamy returned from settling the Armstrong affair in Philadelphia, Conrad Weiser showed up with a work crew to build the Oneida a log dwelling. The structure, seventeen by forty-nine feet, fit Iroquois notions of a longhouse even as it announced the Oneida's influence with foreign powers. When Weiser returned to Shamokin a decade later to put up another house for Shickellamy's kin, when in 1758 a small army of Pennsylvanians built an entire settlement for Teedyuscung's Delawares at Wyoming, the actions spoke louder than mere words.[143]

But Shickellamy and the other Indians pressing colonists for goods were not out only for themselves. That house was for guests, too, as were the bushels of meal Shickellamy and his sons hauled home from colonial mills. In Indian country prestige came less from what one owned or accumulated than what one shared, and a native negotiator was admirably situated to follow Peter Chartier's example, handing out goods in ways designed to enhance his status.[144]

For colonial go-betweens, too, the benefits of negotiation lay less with immediate payment than with such intangibles as contacts and connections. Few rose farther on Pennsylvania's pressing need for go-betweens than Conrad Weiser, who used his Iroquois skills to win a place on the county bench, a hand in founding the town of Reading, and a colonel's commission in the war. But many others did rise, their commercial ventures helped along by patrons in the upper reaches of both Indian and Pennsylvania societies. Trade was tricky, easy prey to unreliable suppliers, wars near and far, fickle Indians, and unforgiving Philadelphia merchants. It helped, if disaster struck, to have influential contacts. Powerful Indian friends could warn of trouble. Powerful colonial friends could forgive debts and fend off other, less patient creditors.

And then there was the prospect of getting land. Here the colonial go-between had many advantages. Knowing the territory, he knew the likeliest mill stream, roadbed, or river bottom. With the choicest spots selected, Weiser, Cartlidge, Croghan, McKee, and others could use their influence among Indians to arrange a personal grant. But most went at things from the colonial end, getting a sale to the province, then turning to grateful superiors for the best pickings.

Being a go-between was, then, no way to make a living, and no one did. Weiser and Tatamy farmed. Croghan traded. Civility, Montour, Stille, and Shickellamy hunted and traded. As a sideline, though, negotiation did offer an avenue of advancement. It brought prestige, status symbols, and—for some—hopes of much more, of fabulous wealth, empires of the air conjured up beside some flickering fire in the middle of nowhere.

"The Part He Shoud Act"
Brawls and Binges

Attention to more mundane concerns of land and an edge in trade, of finery and a fresh horse, has the salutary effect of pulling us down from the ringing rhetoric about go-betweens, with its talk of honest people faithfully carrying sacred messages. To suggest that a go-between pursued his own personal possibilities as well as (and, occasionally, instead of) some larger public good is only to point out that these frontier figures were akin to most everyone else in early America. All the pious treaty testimonials to truth mongers should be taken more as aspiration than observation, as rhetorical flourishes more than reflections of reality. Far from paragons, this tribe of people had its share of flaws and failings, moments of weakness when they strayed from the high road marked out in formal councils.

For one thing, despite all the talk, few negotiators managed to remain "sober" in either sense of the term. In Philadelphia on diplomatic business one summer, Seneca George "in a drunken fitt almost Kill'd himself." Scarouyady, who broke with his translator John Davison because the colonial trader was "unguarded in his cups," dropped his own guard from time to time. During Philadelphia strategy sessions on peace in April 1756, the Oneida went on a two-day binge, and he later missed peace talks at Lancaster because he and his wife got into a drunken brawl with some colonists. Another pivotal figure in peace negotiations, the Delaware Pisquetomen, was among those berating a native messenger for always talking as if he were intoxicated, yet Pisquetomen, like Scarouyady, could go on a spree that left him "lying on the ground very drunk."[145]

These three Indians were teetotallers compared to Teedyuscung. "[A] lusty, raw bon'd Man . . . ," wrote one awed colonist; "he can drink three Quarts or a Gallon of Rum a Day, without being drunk." The Delaware must often have gotten ahold of more than that, for time and again he fell "under the Force of Liquor." Though sometimes Teedyuscung might surprise everyone and stay sober, it was hard for colonists or Indians to shake the image of him with "a bottle of Rum in each of his coat Pockets."[146]

Andrew Montour could—and, probably, sometimes did—match the Delaware tippler glass for glass. During the course of his travels across colonial America Montour had a tendency to run up tavern debts, and in Indian country his drinking bouts were famous. At one treaty, a Delaware speaker asked colonists to continue selling Indians liquor because his people "loved" rum; Montour, concluding his interpretation of the speech, added that he "loves it too," an aside that "made the Indians laugh so hearty, that some of the young men could hardly stop." The fellow "Dose nott Drink att all" here, reported George Croghan from one council, as if Montour sober were news.[147]

Croghan was hardly one to talk; his own bouts with the bottle were legendary. Among his fellow colonists Croghan was the life of every party. Proud author of ribald toasts—"May We kiss whom we please & please whom we kiss"; "days of sport & Nights of transport"—he was widely known as a man who "Generally pushes About the Glass . . . copiously and briskly." Among Indians, his taste for rum sometimes landed him in trouble. One night he and Teedyuscung, both drunk, traded punches that left the Pennsylvanian to nurse a black eye the next day along with his hangover.[148]

Pondering that black eye and those Delawares laughing at Montour, picturing Pisquetomen sprawled beside a dusty road or a reeling Scarouyady grappling with farmers, it is tempting to conclude that the role of go-between either attracted or created men given to alcoholic excess. But heavy drinking was common in early America; Indian towns and fur trading communities alike were routinely awash in rum.[149] Nor did every negotiator go on binges. Croghan drank too much, but Thomas McKee did not; Scarouyady might disappear for a time into an alcoholic haze, but Shickellamy never did; and Moses Tatamy, for much of his life, was as famously sober as his fellow Delaware Teedyuscung was infamously drunk.

But if liquor was not peculiarly the province of go-betweens, the fondness some had for it reminds us that these people were not a breed apart; far from being strong heads impervious to all manner of temptation and criticism, those heads, those minds, were sometimes as addled as the next fellow's.[150] Sober as well as drunk, mediators could lose their composure, could let their trademark unruffled demeanor slip. Croghan, sober, stamped his foot and spewed "a great deal of foul & abuseful Language" at anyone thwarting his plans. Pisquetomen, too, resorted to "English oaths and curses" during fits of anger. Scarouyady lacked the English to match such verbal flights of fury, but—as those Pennsylvania officials slow to reward him in 1755 learned—he had a "fretting way" about him. Even Shickellamy, who boasted that "it is not his Custom to bear any Man Ill will," could be curt with Weiser when the German was slow to pick up the finer points of Indian protocol. Weiser, in turn, thought by all a model of temperance and even temper, had a grumpy side that came across as "imperiousness," "impatience," and "great vexation."[151]

But nowhere was the gap between high rhetoric and low reality more pronounced than in the commandment to tell the truth. Here lay a central paradox of the go-between's avowed creed. Everyone concurred that "speaking true" should be the compass point guiding negotiators through the woods. But everyone also believed that the best intermediaries were men known for hiding their thoughts and feelings. Disguise and honesty were in constant tension, leaving truth, often, a casualty of negotiation. Andrew Montour, with his quiver full of languages, his remarkable ability to smear on or wipe off paint, was only the most obvious of those who made a habit of shifting their stance. Many another go-between recast his countenance to suit "the part he shoud act" in his "public performances." Teedyuscung earned the derisive name "Honest John" for his habit of changing his mind about Christianity—and about Pennsylvania. Both Indians and colonists at one time or another thought Croghan a liar. And when "it was thought fit" that some Indians not learn who Weiser was, the German promptly forgot his advice about always telling the truth and ducked questions from curious Iroquois, making up a yarn about how "I lived at Shohary [on the New York frontier] and travelled up and down among the Indians, and so forth."[152]

On the council ground, Indians and colonists spoke of negotiators in reverent tones. But the frontier, where chaos was king, was a less refined place. There, stretching the truth—even abandoning it altogether—sometimes was, if not a virtue, at least a necessity. If negotiators did not always live up to the exacting standards set down for them in treaty talk, neither were they routinely or universally a pack of liars prone to tantrums and binges. The truth lies somewhere between the two caricatures.

> ### *"Such Message Required a Good Deal of Sermonies, Which No European Can Perform"*
> #### The Limits of Consonance

Measuring the gap between rhetoric and reality tends to homogenize go-betweens, to lump them all as prey to the same pressures, frustrations, and temptations of the woods. But another feature of that gap serves as a reminder that, for all they shared, negotiators—like the native American and European colonial societies they served—never shed prevailing ideas about the frontier that divided Indians from colonists, never came together as a distinct group between two worlds, two ways of life.

As with liquor and lies, the place to begin charting this dichotomy is the council speeches where the peoples of early America articulated the view of the world they shared. That talk made negotiators out to be men attached to both sides of the cultural divide. The new Conestoga leader "has an English heart," Civility announced in 1715, and some go-betweens went still farther. Pisquetomen once pronounced himself a Quaker, and Croghan, it was said, claimed to be an Indian. But the fullest expression of this idea came in the Iroquois assessment of Weiser and Shickellamy. Their "Bodies . . . [are] to be equally divided between them & us," colonists reported the Six Nations saying in 1736, "we to have one-half & they the other."[153]

Fine sentiments indeed, but a convenient fiction. In practically his next breath, that Iroquois speaker revealed that his words had been an attempt to bridge, using fabricated affection and attachment, what he saw as a cultural chasm. The Six Nations had given Weiser presents for his work, the speaker went on, and "as they had thus taken Care of *our* [Pennsylvania's] friend they must recommend *their's* (Shekallamy), to our Notice."[154] Talk of Weiser's adoption was also misleading: like Moravian missionaries, he was not thoroughly absorbed into Iroquois society. He did not shed his old identity, as Indians expected James Smith and other war captives to do. Rather, Weiser and the others were accorded a symbolic identity as a token of respect and a reflection of their importance. Indians neither wanted nor expected them to surrender their status as outsiders.[155]

Other colonial negotiators were even more disinclined than *Tarachi-awagon* to straddle the cultural divide, much less go native. John Hays, who once boasted that he and Post "L[i]ved A Indien Life" during that 1760 trek up the Susquehanna, meant it only in the narrowest sense. Though the two Pennsylvanians made soup and ate hominy, strung wampum and held councils, for the most part they were outside the charmed circle of daily life. When natives "were Dronk in Every corner," the visitors, cold sober, "were A[s] Still as Mis [mice]," watching the "Maney Raiging Divels" cavort. As dusk brought peace, Hays

"Hoped that w[e] might Never See the Like A Gean[,] . . . for it was So Strains A thing."[156]

And so it went, one "Strains" thing after another. The two emissaries looked on as "the Indians Began to Sacrifice to their Gods and Spent the Day in avery odd manner Howling and Danceing Raveling Like Wolves and Painted frightfull as Divels." They joined Indians for feasts where "Every one"—everyone, that is, except them—stood with a wampum string or a stick in hand, skins about shoulders, flowers in hair, bodies with "Snaks and Birdes & wonder full things Pented on them All colers," then circled the fire or house, "Joyned in coras," and "holoed" thanks to the spirits.[157]

The Pennsylvanians went so far as to throw bones into the flames as their hosts did, but the limits to Hays's Indian life were clear. One day the elders "went Rown [a gathering] With the Fat and they Did drink it," he wrote, "and When they came to Me I Would Not and they all Laft." Ten days later, when that drunk Shawnee struck Hays in the back, the colonial messenger kept his composure, but in his diary the wounded man again drew the boundary. "My flessh creeped on My Back to think that I Must Bear Such usige *of A Sevedges is Hand* . . . ," Hays wrote; "I . . . Wish My Self out of thire Contry."[158] Those elders might have said that, in some ways, the man had never been in their country in the first place.

Hays was no Weiser or Croghan, a veteran of Indian country. But even old hands, who bragged of their talents, never really wanted—and never were permitted—to unravel what Croghan had called the "mystery" of Indian ways. Indeed, as Richard Peters learned, the more a man knew about native America, the more he appreciated the depths of his ignorance. William Johnson, who unlike Hays did join Indian dances and even married an Iroquois woman, nonetheless always remained an outsider, and he knew it. In 1771, near the end of his long career, he admitted that, even living on the edge of Iroquoia so long, and with "the most diligent enquirys into these curious particulars" about Indian ways, still "I find all researches of that sort . . . involved in such difficulties & uncertainty as to afford but slender satisfaction." Similarly, Conrad Weiser, asked about Iroquois religion, had to look it up in "several Passages in their Treaties with the English" for the "best Account I could collect. . . . Their Form of Worship," he concluded feebly, "I have not learnt."[159]

Knowing his limits, *Tarachiawagon* routinely enlisted the aid of Iro-

quois friends when doing Indian business. At Onondaga in 1743, claiming ignorance, he "engaged" various Iroquois to take his part in council
speeches and rites. Thereafter Pennsylvania's Iroquois specialist routinely got someone "to serve him as his private Councellor, and direct
him what Measures to take." Weiser often went farther still, handing
over the whole business to an Iroquois because, he explained, "Such
Message required a good deal of Sermonies, which no European Can
perform."[160] Weiser here explicitly (and the natives he recruited implicitly) pointed to a barrier that colonists could never cross—not even
Weiser, *Tarachiawagon,* adopted Mohawk, honorary councilor, the man
Iroquois called half theirs.

That barrier blocked traffic in both directions. Shickellamy, the other
man Iroquois metaphorically shared with Pennsylvania, had no illu-
sions about any deeper significance of his bifurcated status. The Oneida
sternly set David Brainerd straight one day in 1745 when the missionary earnestly pressed him to become more than figuratively European.
"We are Indians," Shickellamy is said to have replied, "and don't wish to
be transformed into white men. The English are our Brethren, but we
never promised to become what they are."[161]

Even Settlement Indians well versed in colonial ways knew that they
needed a colonist to help them. In 1741, Delawares tried to get "an
honest [Pennsylvania] Man to Assist in anything that We Want, . . . to
take Our Parts in any Just Cause." In time, still greater felicity with
things colonial only made these natives appreciate how much they required guidance. "[S]ince we see that our brethren the English Manage
the Affairs which concern their Worldly Estates and Interests with
more Wisdom than the Indians do," one of those Delawares, Teedyuscung, asked during a council at Philadelphia in March 1758, please
"Support two honest Men amongst us to be our Councellors and In-
structors in temporal Affairs, and at the same to be the Guardians of
our Interest." That very spring, Moses Tatamy, Isaac Stille, John Pumpshire, and other Delawares far more familiar with English ways than
Teedyuscung—and having just, as "Indian Attorneys," finished negotiations with New Jersey—also knew their limited ability to make sense
of that world. "[W]e find we are Not able to Trans act in Deep Things
and are at lost what to do," they wrote to a prominent Pennsylvanian,
enlisting his help.[162]

Tarachiawagon asking Iroquois assistance, Indian attorneys seeking
colonial counsel "in Deep Things"—these mark the limits of coexis-

tence, even in and around Penn's Woods, a place famously tolerant of differences, and even in the hearts and heads of negotiators, the very men charged with promoting amity and understanding. Despite all the talk of sharing, few of these folk were lodged between cultures. More telling still, those few mixing Indian with colonial ways—Tatamy, Montour, Chartier, Stille—were branded freaks, historical accidents. The suspicions about Montour and Chartier, the stares a Christian Indian drew from native and colonist alike, the looks James Smith got as he strolled down a Pennsylvania street, the reluctance on both sides to send children to school beyond the frontier—these were symptomatic of an abiding distance between native and newcomer.

CHAPTER II

Finding Friends:
Woodslore, 1699–1723

However good at his craft, no go-between was above criticism by those who had dispatched him into the woods, and few negotiators escaped carping about dumb men or drunks, cheats or women, fools or knaves. But if no envoy was perfect, some were better than others. To appreciate just how much better, to gauge how hard it was to find good ones, consider the Pennsylvania frontier at the turn of the eighteenth century, when colonial and Indian peoples suddenly found themselves without any friends to go between them. Their desperate search for new friends is as painful to watch as it is, sometimes, amusing. Painful, too (though less amusing), is the discovery that, even when, during the 1710s, natives and Europeans did settle on a new cadre of men to do business, those men had no panacea for the borderlands' endemic confusion and contention.

That Pennsylvanians and their Indian neighbors were flying blind in the early eighteenth century was Lars Pärsson (Lasse) Cocke's fault: this indispensable man died in 1699. Son of a prominent Swedish colonist, married to an Englishwoman in 1669, Cocke had been a magistrate and fur trader before Pennsylvania's founding in 1682. When the English took over, he got his name placed atop a list of Swedes eager to be naturalized and soon changed that name to "Laurence Cox, Esq."[1] Such political astuteness and English ties, along with deep knowledge of the local natives, helped him become the principal—almost the *only*—go-between on that frontier in the late seventeenth century. Months before William Penn himself even set foot in his own province, Cocke/Cox was working with the proprietor's advance men to arrange Indian land sales; sometimes he even hosted the meetings at his house.

If Penn and the Delawares really did hold a treaty beneath an elm at Shackamaxon, Cocke would have been there (he probably lived on that spot, after all), standing in the middle.[2]

In the years to come Cocke was ubiquitous. He hurried to Philadelphia whenever natives showed up to talk. He headed up the Delaware with presents for peoples there and made his way to New York to buy more gifts. He ventured to the Susquehanna Valley to look into talk of a killing. So vital was the Swede to the early dialogue between native and English peoples that, more than a decade after his death, Indians still reckoned a past event by saying it was "formerly[,] when Captn. Cock was living."[3]

That such a dominant figure passed from the scene in 1699 was bad enough; worse, at that very moment the frontier was getting harder to fathom. Before 1700, Indian relations were simpler. Most of Pennsylvania's contacts were with small, pliable bands of nearby Delawares.[4] Few in number, politically fragmented, taught by Dutch and Swedes that Europeans were as unpredictable and dangerous as their goods were wondrous and powerful, these Delawares proved more than willing to sell pelts and lands to English newcomers. Cocke, who had spent his life among Delawares, was perfectly suited to the needs of the times. But by 1700 times were changing as the center of native gravity shifted from the lower Delaware to the lower Susquehanna. Iroquois from up north, Shawnees from the west and south, Conoys from the Potomac Valley—these emigrants joined the Susquehannock remnants (now called Conestogas) native to the area and Delawares retreating in the face of Pennsylvania's rapid expansion to people the Susquehanna country and reconfigure the face of the frontier.[5] Confronted with these swirling human currents, and now without Cocke to guide them, colonists and Indians had to cast about for suitable replacements. Those replacements proved hard to find.

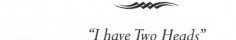

"I have Two Heads"
The Strange and Short Career of Sylvester Garland

In the fall of 1699 four travelers made their way down the east bank of the Susquehanna River, ending up among the Shawnees and Conestogas living there.[6] "[S]trange Indians," the locals concluded, guessing from the visitors' outfits that they had been servants of colonists. In fact, at least two were slaves, having been captured in a raid far to the south and then shipped by Carolina traders to New York.[7] Upon talking with them, Meealloua, the Shawnee leader, discovered that those two, a woman and her son, were kin to the "King of the Naked Indians," long-time enemies of Susquehanna River peoples.[8] Here was a chance to make peace with these foes. Meealloua took the two runaways to his house, thinking to buy their freedom and send them home as a good-will gesture. The other two strangers found shelter with Conodahto, headman at nearby Conestoga (Map 3).

That winter Sylvester Garland, a Pennsylvania fur trader, came to get them back. Armed with a paper bearing the proprietor's seal and ac-companied by another trader, Jonas Askew, Garland rode into the Shawnee town and, in the name of William Penn, ordered the fugitives' return.[9] When Meealloua refused, the two colonists tried their luck at Conestoga. Conodahto and the other townsmen were away, but the women there gave Penn's agent the same answer the Shawnees had. De-mands having failed, Garland resorted to threats, warning that "he would fetch Forty men and Carie them all a way and make Servants of them all." Then, "Rideing a way in great Furie," he took out his frus-trations by drawing pistols and shooting two of the natives' dogs.

Ten days later Garland did come back with reinforcements, though not with forty men. This time he and Askew brought another document (boasting a still larger seal) and James Read, a prominent landowner. Again Garland started with the Shawnees; again he demanded the run-aways' surrender. To bolster his case, he announced that Read was sec-ond only to Penn himself in authority. Read, apparently thinking to prove his importance, "putt of[f] his Wigg and said you may se[e] by this I am a great Man For that I have two heads." Meealloua, unimpressed, still declined. Only when the three colonists swore that they would re-turn with six hundred men and kill all the Indians did the headman fi-nally give in.

At Conestoga, Garland, starting with a different strategy, ended up with the same result. Claiming now that Read was actually the run-aways' owner, he had the new man lament how "he had payd mutch money for them" and set matchcoats on the ground as a reward for their capture. Read's ploy worked no better than had doffing his wig to Shawnees. The women hid their guests, only handing them over when Garland grabbed "one of the Cheife of the [Conestoga] women with vi-

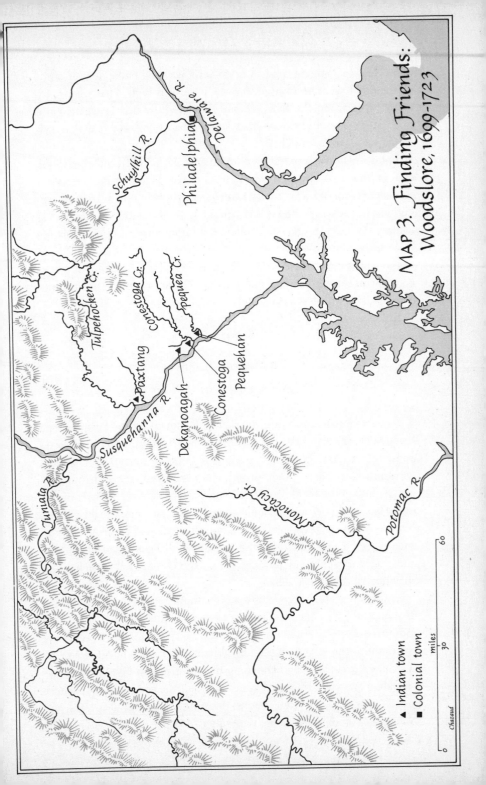

MAP 3. Finding Friends: Woodslore, 1699-1723

Juniata R.

Susquehanna R.

Tulpehocken Cr.

Schuylkill R.

Paxtang

Dekanoagah

Conestoga Cr.

Conestoga

Pequea Cr.

Pequehan

Philadelphia

Delaware R.

Monocacy Cr.

Potomac R.

▲ Indian town
■ Colonial town

miles

0   30   60

Chazaud

olent hands and threatned to Carrie her a way and make her servant."
Garland got what he wanted, but the price was high. That spring, Indian towns along the Susquehanna, still "wholy unsetled," had not
planted crops—always, colonists knew, a bad sign—for fear Pennsylvania was about to attack.[10]

Loud and bossy, impatient and petulant, Garland offered a textbook
case of how a go-between should not behave. Thinking Penn's orders
sufficient proof of his authority, he neglected to bring the wampum credentials Indians expected. Once among natives, he eschewed the customary councils, preferring to demand rather than discuss. Allowing
Read to join him was another mistake: Shawnees proved as indifferent
to the wig as Conestoga women were to the reward. Garland's clumsy
handling of the whole affair may explain why he was never again a mediator.[11] The search would go on.

<hr />

"Be Very Cautious"
Capturing Nicole Godin

Seven years after Sylvester Garland left Indians on the Susquehanna
"in such Feare," another, more distinguished band of colonists showed
up there. Heading the party was William Penn's governor, John Evans;
with him were three other prominent Pennsylvanians and four servants; guiding the lot through the woods was Michael (Michel) Bizaill-
lon. They came because Susquehanna natives had sent word to Evans
"that several strange Indians were amongst them, and Desired his presence there." Eager to please the colony's old friends and make new
ones, on the evening of June 28, 1707, the colonists approached the
Shawnee village of Pequehan.[12]

Evans was well coached: instead of simply barging in, he waited at
the house of fur trader Martin Chartier on the outskirts of town. There
some Shawnee leaders came to meet the party and formally escort the
visitors into the village, whose inhabitants fired guns into the air, the
customary greeting. Next morning the company pushed on to Dekanoagah, a Conoy settlement nine miles up the Susquehanna, where
more Indians (besides the Conoys, there were Senecas, Shawnees, and
Nanticokes) and more formalities waited. To open the proceedings the

natives pulled out "a large pipe with Tobacco, out of which every one smoakt" as a token of friendship and a means of cultivating good thoughts; then came speeches, complete with twenty wampum belts; at day's end Evans "treated ye Indian Chiefs at Dinner" before heading back to Pequehan for the night.

Penn's lieutenant must have been pleased with himself as he and his companions rode along in the gathering darkness. The natives seemed friendly enough, pronouncing themselves "extreamly glad" to see him. Yet Evans could not shed a certain unease. For one thing, "some ill Designing persons" were said to be spreading rumors through these towns that he planned "to destroy" the Indians. For another, while he was at Pequehan, several Shawnees from a village near Carolina showed up; Bizaillon whispered that these southerners had murdered colonists down there. When it came time, then, to ritually reaffirm Pennsylvania's friendship with the people of Pequehan on June 30, an anxious Evans remarked how "I have now (to let you see what confidence I have in you,) Trusted myself in the midst of you, with a very few of our great Queen's subjects, although"—he hastened to add—"I could easily have brought with me very great numbers."

Evans could be forgiven his anxiety; Pennsylvania's relations with Indians had gone steadily downhill since William Penn left his province for the second and last time in the fall of 1701. Over the next few years Philadelphia heard "Repeated Reports . . . of great uneasinesses among the Indians." Provincial officials openly admitted that "notwithstanding all his [Penn's] care things had not been so well managed as desired." So much in the dark were these colonial managers that they once spent hours quizzing Indians and debating each other in an attempt to decipher a wampum belt natives had given them.[13]

The problem was that the colony's leadership had no one it could trust to read the belts, or the peoples sending them. True, Shawydoohungh ("Indian Harry" or "Harry the Interpreter") was a talented man. Ever since the Susquehanna peoples' 1701 treaty with William Penn, this English-speaking Conestoga had crisscrossed the frontier, carrying Pennsylvania's words and wampum to the Iroquois capital of Onondaga and returning with packs of deerskins from Iroquoia, which he set on the floor of the provincial council chamber before proceeding to give the Indians' reply. But the men in that council chamber remained skeptics. This Harry was a useful fellow, certainly, but he was an Indian, and no Pennsylvania leader ever had relied, or ever would rely, solely on an Indian to steer the province through the frontier's treacherous waters.[14]

The only alternatives to Shawydoohungh in the early eighteenth century were people like Michael Bizaillon and Martin Chartier, the so-called "French Traders." This community traced its origins to Jacques Le Tort, a Protestant fleeing French Catholic persecution, who in 1686 arrived in Pennsylvania to run a trading post on the Schuylkill River. Business was good, and Le Tort's became a magnet for other Frenchmen. Before 1690 Pierre Bizaillon, Michael's brother, found his way there after a career as trader and explorer that took him from the far reaches of Canada to the mouth of the Mississippi. When the Bizaillons and Le Tort shifted their base of operations west to the Susquehanna around the turn of the century, they met Chartier, just arrived with his Shawnee friends and kin (including two wives and a daughter).[15]

These French folk were in many ways logical candidates to succeed Lasse Cocke. All, having "used the Woods" for years, boasted an unmatched acquaintance with the country and its peoples. Le Tort knew Delawares, Conoys, and Shawnees; Pierre Bizaillon had been "admitted into the Councell of the Indians"; and Chartier—called "Father" by some Shawnees, "MC" tattooed on his chest—had so completely adopted native ways that one colonist thought him "a Feather of the same Bird with the Indians."[16]

The problem for Pennsylvania officials seeking go-betweens was not that Chartier and the rest were too Indian; they were too, well, French. None rushed, as Lasse Cocke had, to change his name (at age eighty "Peter" Bizaillon, as most called him, was still signing himself "Pierre" in a shaky scrawl). Worse still, they arrived in Pennsylvania when England and France were almost continuously at war and anyone French—even if Protestant—was automatically considered "not right." Hence, while the provincial government, desperate for woodsmen, did enlist the aid of these "french men," that government was slow to trust them. "Allien," "Spie," "very dangerous Persons" who "Kept private correspondence with the Canida Indians and the French," who entertained "strange Indians" in "remote & obscure places" and who muttered "suspicious words," the French traders were followed, interrogated, fined, sometimes even jailed.[17]

No wonder Evans was uneasy that summer night in 1707. New to the woods, he needed help making his way through the tangle of towns and peoples along the Susquehanna, but he had to seek that help from men like Bizaillon and Chartier, men he neither understood nor trusted. The governor's doubts about these men would soon deepen, and his way through the woods become more tangled, for on the next leg of his journey he was going after Nicole Godin, one of their own.

Godin was among the lesser lights in the French constellation on the Susquehanna. Born in London, reared in France, after some twenty years in the colony this "bold active young fellow" remained, to Pennsylvania leaders, "a Frenchman in speech & extract." Godin lived in obscurity until, on the eve of Evans's departure for the Susquehanna in June 1707, word reached Philadelphia that this "french man . . . had been using endeavours to incense these People against the English . . . and to Joyn with our publick Enemy the French to our Destruction." With that, Evans added capturing Godin to his agenda.[18]

Shawnees at Pequehan, asked about Godin, pointed upstream to Paxtang. On the evening of July 2, with Martin Chartier in tow, Evans and his men camped three miles from that Shawnee-Delaware town.[19] At night he took "the Chief Indian of Peixtan" aside to tell him the plan. The headman's response was lukewarm: on the one hand, he "willingly agreed to it"; on the other, he "advised the Govr. to be very cautious in the manner [of taking Godin]: their being only young People at home, who perhaps might make some Resistance, if it were done without their first being told of it"—told, presumably, in formal council.

Evans decided to ignore the advice. At dawn he and his posse set off, dismounted near town, and hid behind some bushes. Now to bait the trap. Relying on traders' notorious thirst for liquor, Evans ordered Chartier to lure Godin out with news that two kegs of rum were stashed nearby; come with me, Chartier was to say, and have a taste. The ploy worked, sort of: out walked Chartier with two Pennsylvania traders eager to tap the imaginary kegs; Godin had declined the invitation. In the bushes, further deliberations. Back went Chartier "with Orders to bring down some of the Indians, and Nicole with them." Out again came Chartier, this time with two natives, but still no Godin. Again, hasty explanations to the bewildered Indians of what was going on. Again, mixed reviews: the two said that they were "contented" with the plot, but they also pointedly asked the colonists "how many we were and how armed," and, upon learning that the villagers were outnumbered, looked decidedly unhappy.

The day was growing old; so was crouching in the underbrush. Another consultation; they would try once more. In went Chartier, and out, this time, he came with the prize. But the bird was not yet in the hand, not even, quite, in the bush. Chartier, playing his assigned part to the bitter end, invited Godin to have a drink from the phantom keg, then seized him, only to have the quarry slip free and make a run for it. Instantly Evans and his men sprang from the bushes in pursuit. Grabbing Godin, they hauled him into Paxtang—"thro' which," Evans added uneasily, "we were obliged to pass" in order to get home.

There the governor met the risks of rejecting natives' advice in favor of lying in the bushes and tackling his prey. Indians stood about, "Guns in their hands," looking "much displeased" by this turn of events. The colonists' superior numbers and "readiness against any surprize"— were their guns in hand, too?—kept trouble at bay. Off the visitors rode for Philadelphia, their prisoner tied to a horse to preclude another escape.

The scene at Paxtang was so different from Pequehan or Dekanoagah that we are left to ponder the strange turn of events. In the early stops on his Susquehanna tour, Evans, puffing on a pipe and dining with the locals, resembled Lasse Cocke; at Paxtang, though, he matched Sylvester Garland in audacity and ineptitude. If the governor grabbed no women and shot no dogs, neither did he call a council or make a speech.

What had changed? That Evans was a young hothead with little political experience and less tact does not explain how he lost his touch somewhere between Pequehan and Paxtang.[20] Perhaps the man was suddenly in the dark because his guides put him there. He was, after all, asking men of French descent, who had felt the sting of English accusations, to help him capture another man of French descent who had come under the same cloud of suspicion. Chartier, for one, knew what the inside of the Philadelphia jail looked like; not wishing to see it again, he dared not openly defy Penn's man. At the same time, however, he may have had no wish to light the governor's way to Godin.

If the French did indeed try to sabotage the mission at Paxtang, they hid their tracks well; the evidence rests only in silence, absence, and assumption. Michael Bizaillon, at the governor's elbow through Dekanoagah and Pequehan, suddenly is missing in the account of adventures at Paxtang. Martin Chartier was there, but he was either inept—unlikely, given his knowledge of Indian ways—or unenthusiastic. Evans twice *ordered* him into town; that, along with the bungled efforts to entice

Godin out and Chartier's halfhearted attempt to seize the suspect, suggests a certain studied reluctance.

In the end, Evans got his man; the last glimpse of Godin has him sitting in jail while the authorities decided whether to try him as an Englishman or a Frenchman.[21] But his significance lies back at Paxtang, in the farce Evans put on that summer's day and the frowns on those Indian faces. The lack of finesse, the penchant to bully and bluff, again spells out how lost people were without a go-between.

∼∽∽∽∼

"His Friends Had Killed Him"
Burying Sawantaeny

Toward dusk one winter's day early in 1722 seven men on horseback approached an Indian hunting cabin on Monocacy Creek, a tributary of the upper Potomac River some three days' ride west of Conestoga.[22] In the lead were John Cartlidge and his younger brother Edmond, fur traders based near Conestoga; with them were two young servants, Jonathan Swindel and William Wilkins, and Ayaquachan, a Conoy guide; trailing behind were two Shawnee youths, Acquittanachke and Metheequeyta, dispatched by their headman to invite the Pennsylvanians to a trading session.[23] The Shawnees would have to wait, however; the colonists, having gone "into ye Woods with Design to trade," had business at this cabin by the creek, where a Seneca named Sawantaeny and his Shawnee wife, Weynepeeweyta, waited with a winter's peltry.

With night coming on, the visitors made a fire near the hut, gave Sawantaeny several helpings of punch and rum, then sold him another quart of the stuff. The Seneca and the Conoy apparently sat up all night drinking. Early in the morning John Cartlidge and Sawantaeny sat down at the fire to bargain, with John refilling Sawantaeny's rum pot and promising more after they were done. As agreed, once the Indian had hauled his leftover skins to the cabin and returned to the fire, John filled the pot, and did the same when Sawantaeny came back for more.

On the Seneca's third trip to the fire and the keg, things began to fall apart. Cartlidge now insisted that further refills required a skin or two. Puzzled by the change, convinced that the colonist still owed him, Sawantaeny retreated to his house to think it over. After a while he came back, only to be told that the cask would stay stoppered. Again a walk to the cabin. Then out Sawantaeny strode once more, one hand clutching the pot, the other clenched into a fist, and "his Countenance Seeming"—to the Pennsylvanians, at least—"very angary and Disturbed."[24] By now Cartlidge was mad, too. "Why do you come after this Manner?" he demanded, stepping up to the Indian. "Who do you think is afraid of you?" Snatching the container from the Seneca's hand, Cartlidge threw it aside. More "words past betwixt them"; then John knocked Sawantaeny down.

For several minutes Sawantaeny sat there, head between his legs. Whether he was recovering his senses or planning his next move is unclear; perhaps he was doing both. All at once he leaped to his feet, flung his cloak from his shoulders, and ran for his cabin—and his gun. He shook off his shrieking wife and, outside, wrestled Wilkins for the weapon. Up rushed Edmond Cartlidge: twisting the musket from Sawantaeny's grasp, the trader smashed the Indian's head with it so hard that the gunstock shattered. Sawantaeny, his skull fractured, fell "on his breech to the Ground."

Now it was John Cartlidge's turn. Having "stript off his Clothes" at the fireside, he joined the crowd at the cabin. "Were you going to shoot us?" he asked, kicking Sawantaeny in the face and splintering what was left of the gun against a tree.[25] The Seneca, blood gushing from nose and mouth, could make no reply, but only "rattled in the Throat." Enough. Ordering the servants to pack up and get the horses, the Cartlidges rode off, John calmly checking his watch.[26]

Back at the cabin, a mortally wounded Sawantaeny managed a few last words. "[H]is Friends had killed him," he told his wife after he had made it inside and collapsed onto a bearskin. The next morning he was dead. Weynepeeweyta left to get help burying him, but before she returned a Cayuga who came upon the corpse got two Conestogas to dig Sawantaeny's grave.

Burying Sawantaeny must have been hard work—the stench of decay, the grisly wounds, the frozen ground. But it was easier than burying Sawantaeny's death itself. No mere runaway woman or child from some remote nation, he was "a Warriour, a civil Man of very few Words," a kinsman of leading Iroquois and, not least, a Seneca, westernmost of the Iroquois nations, a powerful and dangerous people.[27]

Nor were the Cartlidge brothers Nicole Godin, some obscure youth who could be summarily dragged off to jail. Among the most important Pennsylvanians on the Susquehanna—Edmond was the tax collector, John a magistrate and one of the richest men around—they had powerful friends in the provincial capital.[28] Moreover, both Indians and colonists called John "our good Friend," and emissaries from Philadelphia and Onondaga alike stopped at his house on Conestoga Creek. Sitting at the walnut table in his parlor or arranging themselves on his couch and chairs, they sought his advice and asked him to interpret at their treaties.[29] So "Serviceable" was he that when Pennsylvania officials and Indian leaders agreed to run a line around Conestoga, he was the only colonist permitted to live "within those Lines."[30]

What happened to the Cartlidges and Sawantaeny mattered. They could not just disappear into the earth or into a Philadelphia cell. At first, though, with that cell looming, John and his brother did try to keep themselves out of jail by making the Seneca disappear. When, in early March, word of the bloodshed beside the Monocacy began to reach Indian and colonial settlements along the Susquehanna, the two traders decided to stage "A Councile" to bury Sawantaeny quickly and quietly.

To help pull off this charade they called on Tagotolessa (Civility). This Conestoga was a logical choice. For a decade he had been among the leading men in the region, speaking for Susquehanna Indians at treaties and, sometimes, joining John Cartlidge at those sessions to link English, Delaware, and Iroquois.[31] Better still, Civility was among those Susquehanna people who chafed at Iroquois claims to rule them. He never went so far as to assert publicly, as one Susquehanna headman did in 1718, that "those [five] nations have their own Lands and Countrey and these here [on the lower Susquehanna] have theirs, and each of them are to manage their own concerns." But in 1720 Civility did join other Susquehanna leaders to warn Pennsylvania that "the Sinnekaes . . . do not bear true affection to your Government, and Some of them are already very bold and impudent to the Christian Inhabitants and us also."[32]

A man the Cartlidges knew, a man with prestige and little love for Senecas—no wonder John and Edmond turned to Civility. He did not disappoint them at that spurious council on March 6. First he listened as the Cartlidges told their story, which featured innocent colonial traders who, set upon by a drunk and armed Seneca, somehow got "intangled wth ye Indian" and accidentally clobbered him "in Struggleing to gett the gun Loose." Then the Conestoga leader accepted the stroud and wampum string John Cartlidge offered by way of apology.

Next he found the colonists innocent by concluding that Sawantaeny had actually "Murthered himself." Finally he announced that he had heard enough. "[I]f ye Xtians were Sattisfied the Indians were Soe too," Civility went on; let there be "noe more noise About it."[33]

The noise, however, was just beginning. Even as the Cartlidges tried to engineer their exoneration on March 6, two colonists arrived in Philadelphia with the first news of the killing to reach the capital. Officials there knew at once that more had to be done.[34] The colony could not botch this business in the grand tradition of Sylvester Garland and John Evans. Not only were the men involved too important, the stakes were too high. Three years earlier James Logan had "found ye Noise about our Ind[ian]s [on the Susquehanna] thicken. . . . [They] Seem animated in a manner that has never been known here before." While colonists worked to quiet that noise, they made a breakthrough in their long campaign to win the favor (and the furs) of the almighty Iroquois. In 1721 Governor William Keith and six councilors had scurried off to Conestoga upon learning that, with Iroquois seeking better allies and trading partners than Albany or Montreal, for "the first time . . . the five Nations had thought fit to send any of their Chiefs to visit" Pennsylvania. With Susquehanna natives restless and the Iroquois interested, this was no time for trouble.[35]

Fortunately, by now colonists and Indians could turn to a number of experienced hands to head off that trouble. The day after getting word of "ye Murmur" on the Susquehanna, two councilors set out from the capital to look into things. Colonel John French had made the trip before. He was with Evans during the Godin escapade, and thereafter served Pennsylvania as occasional ambassador and troubleshooter. His companion, James Logan, was still better acquainted with the place. For the past two decades Logan's posts as secretary to the proprietor and to the Pennsylvania council, along with his interests in the fur trade, had often sent him to the Susquehanna "to look after our Traders" and tend to provincial business.[36]

Awaiting Logan and French at Conestoga was a group of colonial and Indian men, many of them Logan's client traders, who had the experience, trust, and stature needed to bury Sawantaeny properly. From forty miles upriver came Peter Bizaillon, at last—like James Le Tort, son of Jacques—free enough of suspicion to be counted on for "a just Interpretation." Closer to hand were Englishmen like John and Edmond Cartlidge, who at recent councils had stood with Le Tort and Bizaillon to translate speeches.[37]

Standing with those colonists, too, had been Indians like Civility and the remarkable "Capt. Smith" (Ousewayteichks), a linguistic prodigy said to know not only his native Conoy but also Iroquois, Shawnee, and Delaware.[38] The new breed was part of what Indians called "a younger Generation" of leaders in the Susquehanna towns, a cadre that had emerged during the past decade. Unlike their predecessors, these men never met William Penn, but they pledged to be true to his legacy of friendship. To that end, they began to work together, to speak to Penn's people "with one voice & mind."[39] By 1722 the grueling round of meetings—one town after another through the lower Susquehanna Valley—that had characterized earlier colonial diplomatic missions was a thing of the past. Logan and French could head straight for Conestoga and stay there.

The Philadelphians' inquiry was nothing if not thorough. Arriving at John Cartlidge's on March 9, the two summoned Bizaillon, told Indian leaders to collect their witnesses, and had John (now under house arrest) convince his brother to come in. At last all was ready, and a large company—Delaware, Shawnee, Conoy, and Conestoga leaders, as well as "divers English & Indians"—assembled in Conestoga on the morning of March 14. The talks that ensued were painfully slow, with pauses at the end of each sentence so that Bizaillon could turn English into Delaware, which Civility then made into Iroquois and Ousewayteichks into Shawnee.

The very pace of the proceedings reveals the Pennsylvanians' better grasp of Indian protocol than in 1700 or 1707. Knowing (and caring) that Indians could not negotiate until their loss had been acknowledged and their grief eased, Logan began by setting a wampum belt "on the Board before them" and took pains "first to condole with you, which we now do very heartily."[40] Then, toward the end of that long day (the talks lasted eight hours), he ordered punch, meat, and bread for the Indians. The following morning he took the next step, arranging to send the Cayuga Satcheecho, then living in Conestoga, to Iroquoia on Pennsylvania's behalf. With Satcheecho went two coats "to cover our dead Friend" and a wampum belt "to wipe away Tears."

Even as he used wampum to dry tears, Logan never forgot those "divers English," friends and kin of the accused who needed to be appeased (or intimidated) if this matter was to be settled. After offering Indians his condolences, "We judged it necessary," he reported, "that our Commission [from the governor] should be publicly read in the hearing and for the satisfaction of the English who were there." What followed the solemn show of authority was also designed to fit colonial notions of proper form. Sternly instructing Indians to tell the truth, Logan interrogated Civility and took depositions from the witnesses.

Juggling native and colonial protocol was tricky, and at the end of the second day the situation remained volatile. Colonists saw the commission and heard the testimony, but what did they think of Acquittanachke and Ayaquachan testifying against men like John and Edmond Cartlidge? Of Logan's plan to haul the two colonists off to Philadelphia? Indians were no happier. The wampum and the condolences were right, but the barrage of questions was all wrong. After the first Indian witness had testified, the rest, unacquainted with English ideas about testimony, resisted telling their story, "alledging it was to no purpose to repeat what others had already declared." "[G]reat Pains were taken and Endeavours used to perswade" these people to go along, the frustrated colonial agents wrote, "but the Indians could not be prevailed with."

Not until the morning of March 16, when Logan and French were at John Cartlidge's preparing to leave, did it look as if the visitors, guided by Bizaillon, Civility, and the others, had gotten their men without unduly offending Indians or colonists. Edmond was safely bound for the capital under guard. Civility, Satcheecho, and "divers of the old men" had come to see the rest of the party off, a promising sign of continued native goodwill. But now John and his family almost spoiled everything. "[V]ery much pressed . . . to hasten and go along with us," the man stalled as "His Wife grieved almost to Distraction, and would force herself and her child with him." To the rescue came Civility and the other natives. "The woman's sorrows being loud the Indians went in to comfort her," Logan wrote, "and so we departed."

Pennsylvania was not yet out of the woods, for the months to come were full of uncertainty. The accused killers bounced in and out of jail while the colony's legal minds debated bail, *habeas corpus,* and murder trials without a body.[41] Satcheecho, meanwhile, made two trips to Onondaga and came back each time with promising but disturbing messages. On the one hand, the Five Nations pronounced themselves "thus far well pleased in what is done," assuring Pennsylvania that they still "desire a good understanding may be preserved between them & us, . . . that there should be no Heart-burning." Iroquois eager to befriend the province and accustomed to settling murders with gifts rather than the gallows were ready to forgive and forget. Free the two men, they said; "one life is enough to be lost."[42]

But the Five Nations were less pleased with what they construed as Pennsylvania's failure to follow protocol. Two strouds? Two men, going only as far as Conestoga? This was not nearly enough. "They expect a greater number of People," Satcheecho reported Iroquois leaders saying, and not just any people: they "require the Governour" himself to come to Onondaga.[43]

Pennsylvania had intended the strouds and the visit to Conestoga as opening remarks, not the last word. Did something get lost in translation? In any case, Governor Keith was not about to go all the way to Onondaga, no matter how important the business. "I cannot travel unless it be upon a Horse or in a Ship, and I am just now very busie," he replied in May. But, Keith conceded, I could go to Albany, where England's colonial governors treating with the Iroquois had gone for decades. And to Albany, that August, the governor went, accompanied by four councilors—and by Satcheecho, James Le Tort, and Ousewayteichks. There Keith and the Iroquois formally laid the matter to rest; by fall the Cartlidges were free men.[44] The following spring Civility, still insisting on Susquehanna Indians' independence from Onondaga, was in Philadelphia to have the last word. We hope, he said, that this "Blood may not only be buried but wash'd away as it were by a swift runnin[g] Stream of Water never more to be seen or heard of."[45] Keith happily agreed. At long last, men sitting in council houses a world away from his grave had buried Sawataeny.

"The Fourth Generation Perhaps Would . . . Forget"
Doubt and Dissent

Civility, Keith, and the rest got their wish: Sawantaeny was forgotten. But retrieving him from oblivion, like recalling Nicole Godin and those nameless runaway slaves, measures how far negotiators had come since Lasse Cocke's death. Imagine Sylvester Garland creeping forward, sentence by sentence, toward his quarry; picture Governor Evans opting for a council at Paxtang instead of a ruse and a confrontation. Garland had arrived in the Susquehanna Valley with a warrant, a wig, and a pair of pistols; Evans with Frenchmen he did not trust and an imaginary cache of rum; Logan and French came with wampum and words to dry tears and enough sense to rely on the locals' considerable expertise. Where Garland left behind dead dogs and Evans angry young men, in March 1722 the curtain closed on a tender scene of Indians entering John Cartlidge's parlor to comfort his distraught wife and child.

Capable go-betweens were the difference. In 1700 and 1707 there were no Lasse Cockes, no one with the essential combination of intercultural skills and widespread trust; by 1722, there were plenty. Pennsylvania's fur trade provided many of the new recruits: Shawydoohungh probably learned English the same way John Cartlidge picked up Delaware, over the course of bartering beaver pelts and deerskins.[46] Many more negotiators came out of the lower Susquehanna's increasingly polyglot Indian population. Shawnees and Oneidas, Conestogas and Conoys, Delawares and Cayugas—the collection of cultures there tutored Civility and other Indians in native languages.

Among the tools this new generation of mediators brought to the diplomatic arena was, strangely enough, William Penn. Though no longer in Pennsylvania—having left in 1701, the proprietor suffered a devastating stroke in 1712 and died in 1718—Penn cast a long shadow. The capstone to his career in Indian affairs came just before his departure in 1701, when the proprietor held a treaty with Conestogas, Shawnees, and Conoys (and one Onondaga observer). At that council, good feelings reigned; all parties agreed to "forever hereafter be as one Head & One Heart, & live in true Friendship & Amity as one People." A decade or so later, the new negotiators—"to cultivate the ancient friendship between" Indian and colonist and make it "last from one Generation to another"—returned again and again in formal conversation to the Founder's shining example.[47]

Penn was no saint. His colonists had fought him on many fronts, and his Indian neighbors found that however genuine his hopes for peace, he assumed the superiority of English ways.[48] Along with the amity and union, after all, that 1701 treaty had clauses about Indians "Duly Owning & Acknowledging the Authority of the Crown of England and Government of this Province" as well as "Submitting to the Laws of this Province in all things."[49] But the new breed of envoys, whether they called him Penn, *Onas* (Iroquois for "feather," a play on "pen"), or *Miquon* (the Delaware cognate), were canny enough to see the benefits of playing up his sunnier side.

Neither capable middlemen nor Penn's legacy were enough to bring forth his peaceable kingdom, however. Indeed, the very frequency with which go-betweens trotted out old Penn can be read as a sign of trouble, of the discontent even accomplished mediators could not altogether remove. Ironically, better negotiators meant that colonists and Indians were becoming acquainted, more able to realize their oft-stated dream that "our Hearts should be open that we may perfectly see into one another's Breasts." Seeing so well, they discovered they did not always like what they saw.[50]

One source of trouble was trade. Around 1710 Susquehanna Indians began to pepper provincial authorities with complaints that went beyond the usual petty frauds to question the very purpose of exchange. Natives accustomed to thinking of trade as a tangible mark of friendship between peoples now were "wholly ignorant how they had been dealth with, or how they should Trade"; colonial prices varied so much that "they knew not what they were to Expect for their Goods." Pennsylvanians' usual response was to shrug that "all trade is uncertain," explain that this was how the economic world worked, and advise Indians to do as colonists did: "every man should bargain as well as he could for himself."[51]

Susquehanna natives confused by "Goods placed in the Dark" were no less in the dark about Pennsylvania farmers. Le Tort and the other French folk who arrived there around 1700 proved to be the advance guard of a colonial settlers' army.[52] By 1714 a mill perched on Conestoga Creek, with roads, wagons, and smithies not far behind.[53] Close behind, too, were the clashes common wherever native Americans and European colonists lived side by side, with "thievish" and "Troublesome" Indians killing livestock while colonists would steal corn, loose hogs or horses into native fields, and otherwise "straiten or pinch" Indians "to make them remove further off."[54]

Natives looking to Philadelphia for protection from sharp traders and quarrelsome settlers found William Penn's successors disappointing.[55] Provincial officials were often speculators deeply involved in surveying the very Susquehanna lands natives wanted them to protect. James Logan was the biggest player of all, but soon after arriving in Pennsylvania in May 1717 Governor William Keith joined the game, becoming the first to survey the territory over the Susquehanna. When anxious natives asked him about it—they had not sold the land—Keith assured them, ominously, that "It was not the Intention of the Government *as yet* to suffer that side of the River to be settled."[56]

Frontier farmers and ambitious Philadelphians doubtless disappointed Indians clinging to the fine words of *Onas.* But the biggest disappointment in the opening decades of the century were the colonial go-betweens on whom Susquehanna natives counted for help with the millers and smiths, the Keiths and Logans of their new world. It turned out that these people were more akin to Logan or Keith than to Satcheecho or Civility. To the natives' dismay, Peter Bizaillon, Martin Chartier, and James Le Tort went off prospecting in Indian territory without permission.[57] In 1718 Le Tort stood above even John Cartlidge on the local tax lists, and Martin Chartier, he of the same feather as Indians, left a sizable estate at his death that year. However Indian Chartier might look to Governor Evans, beneath that tattooed breast beat the heart of a colonial man on the make.[58]

Its ringing phrases of friendship unable to contain all this contention, the very treaty rhetoric that Chartier and the rest carried across the linguistic and cultural divide in the early eighteenth century also showed signs of weakening. Provincial officials, without abandoning talk of being the natives' own flesh and blood, started to take a more imperious tone in their speeches to Indians. When Civility happened to remark in 1718 that Indians were "like Children," Pennsylvanians pounced, turning an isolated, uncharacteristic metaphor into a powerful weapon.[59] Governor Keith was clever enough to wed this new trope to the old, telling a council at Conestoga that "I speak to my own Flesh and Blood, who, I expect, will look upon me even as a Child would respect and obey the Words of a tender Father." As fathers, James Logan informed another Susquehanna delegation, "the English have opportunities of seeing farther than you." Superior vision gave Logan and other Pennsylvania authorities license to offer Indians "Advice." If those "Children" ignored the counsel, Logan "demanded the Reason why," and Keith warned them to "take Care how you provoke me to be angry with your Follies."[60]

This did not sound much like *Onas;* led by Civility, Indians said so. *Colonists had better vision?* Hardly. "William Penn knew the Indians to be a discerning People, that had Eyes to see a far off," the Conestoga headman insisted. *Children? Brethren?* On the contrary: "when Governour Penn first held Councils with them," Civility said, time and again, "he promised . . . that he would not call them Brothers, because Brothers might differ, nor Children because these might offend and require Correction, but he would reckon them as one Body, one Blood, one Heart, and one Head; . . . *they* always remembered this," he concluded, implicitly wondering if colonists had forgotten.[61]

Even as he resurrected *Onas* to counter provincial assaults on Indian autonomy, Civility also revised Penn's legacy and put it to work in a new way, to convey Indians' doubts about their future with colonists. Would the bond forged in 1701 really endure forever, as both sides so often said? At a council in 1720, after Conoys mouthed the familiar phrases about friendship with Pennsylvania being "continued from Generation to Generation," a Conestoga—probably Civility again—stood to "say, That William Penn made a League with them to last for three or four Generations." It was only a whisper of doubt: in the next breath the speaker returned to the usual talk of eternity. But two years later Civility went a little farther: clutching a copy of the 1701 treaty, he informed colonists that Penn had "told them to preserve it carefully for three Generations, that their Children might see and know what then passed in Council as if He remained himself with them to repeat it, but," the Conestoga concluded, "that the fourth Generation perhaps would both forget him and it."[62]

When Keith, picking up the significance of this change, objected, Civility backed down, at least publicly; but doubts remained.[63] What did the Conestoga leader really fear: that his grandchildren would forget, or that Penn's would? His stress on Indians' determination *on their part* to keep the spirit of 1701 alive suggests that in his eyes the problem lay in Philadelphia, not Conestoga. Neither he nor other Susquehanna Indians had yet given up on Penn's dream of coexistence; they even claimed that *Onas* had intended the Susquehanna territory "should be in Common amongst them viz the English and the Indians."[64] But watching Le Tort, Chartier, and Bizaillon bend to the prevailing colonial winds, listening to lectures from Logan and Keith, squabbling with traders and with new neighbors from the east, Susquehanna Indians wondered what the future held.

Another ominous sign was contention over treaties themselves, the very vehicle for bringing Indians and colonists together, the forum for all that happy talk about friendship and unity. As with trade, the two sides proved to be far apart on a treaty's purpose. Colonists assumed that once friendship was made, only fresh trouble required another meeting. "[A]ny new Treaty . . . would be needless," James Logan told Conestogas on one visit, "those that have already been made being in full force & sufficiently strong." But Indians believed that peace demanded constant attention. "[T]ell the Govr.," Susquehanna leaders instructed Peter Bizaillon in May 1711, "that they would be glad to see him at Conestogo to renew the League formerly made betwixt them and the Propr[ietar]y." *Renew:* it was a constant refrain in Indian speeches, but during these years colonists never quite got it. You are "very welcome" here, a puzzled James Logan told another delegation from the Susquehanna Valley. However, since "the chain of friendship had been so often confirmed . . . , there remained very little now to say on that head."[65]

Indian frustration with colonial obtuseness grew as Pennsylvania leaders increasingly refused invitations like the one Bizaillon brought in 1711. Susquehanna Indians, well aware that a treaty's location reflected the status of those assembled, knew how to read those refusals, and once again they called on the Founder in an attempt to counter the disturbing trend. "The Shawannoes, Ganawese, Connestogoes & Delawares, shall never forget the words of William Penn," Civility pointedly told Keith and his council in Philadelphia in 1723, "but since that [1701] Treaty was made between Him & Them, they do not find that we [colonists] have been so careful to come as often to renew it with them at Conestogoe, as they have been to come to us at Philadelphia."[66] Intentionally or not, the go-between miscounted; before 1722, councils had met at Conestoga as often as in Philadelphia. But he caught the trend nonetheless, for over the rest of the colonial era only one treaty between Pennsylvanians and Indians convened in Conestoga or anywhere else in Indian country.

One reason Keith and his successors could turn a deaf ear to Indian complaints was Pennsylvania's growing sense of power over its native neighbors. Keith might rush to Conestoga and even to Albany to court Iroquois favor. But if not even the almighty Iroquois could lure him to Onondaga, lesser tribes on the lower Susquehanna were going to have a hard time getting him to visit their settlements. Another reason for the changing venue was that no provincial leader after William Penn was much interested in Indians. At a council with Civility, one scribe made a revealing slip of the pen when he wrote that, besides various leaders, the congress consisted of "many other People & Indians."[67] Given this attitude, what official in Philadelphia wanted to face the "Inconveniencies of so fatiguing a Journey," a trip "among such people without any manner of accommodation, but what must be carried with him"?[68] Logan and French, Evans and Keith went because they felt they had to; with time, fewer Pennsylvania authorities saw the need of it. To such men the idea of spending a night "at the king's palace" in Conestoga, as Penn and his councilors had done in 1701, came to seem odd, even grotesque.[69] For better or worse, the colony's Indian business would be left ever more in the hands of woodsmen. Joining them on their travels suggests why people in Philadelphia were so anxious never again to set foot in Conestoga or any other place in their woods.

CHAPTER III

"That Road between Us and You":
Passages through the Woods

A go-between spent much of his life on the road. Lasse Cocke's journeys up the Delaware and over to the Susquehanna before William Penn had even arrived in the province were typical of the mediator's lot, as were Satcheecho's two round trips to Onondaga in 1722. "You have shewn yourself a good Traveller," Governor Keith congratulated the Cayuga that summer. A generation later Andrew Montour proved himself better still, twice leaving his Susquehanna home to take messages from Williamsburg to Iroquoia and back again, with side trips to Philadelphia and other Pennsylvania towns—all in less than a year.[1]

Whether covering a few miles in the 1680s or a few hundred in the 1750s, an emissary's work began not when he arrived at Philadelphia or Onondaga, Lancaster or Logstown, but when he set off for those far-away places. Negotiating paths was at once a prelude to, and an integral part of, negotiating with peoples. Hence messengers' voyages through the woods shed light on their larger enterprise.

The ways people managed to make it through the woods teach three important lessons about the colonial frontier and its middlemen. The first is the sheer difficulty of getting from here to there, the imposing obstacles confronting those dispatched over the cultural divide—from bad roads and bad weather to bad food and bad luck. Understanding the go-between's craft, indeed understanding the frontier experience, requires appreciation of travel's backbreaking demands.

But it also requires that we see how travelers met those demands and crossed that divide by learning from one another, developing rules of the road that had colonists donning moccasins and the rest of an "Indian walking Dress" while natives in hat and riding boots mounted a horse to embark on a voyage. Such consonance, constructed from harsh necessity, helped reduce what one exhausted go-between called the routine "wear and tear lost and broke in the Journey."[2]

Ultimately, however, negotiators' fortunes (and misfortunes) in the woods uncover how no cross-cultural borrowing altogether closed the distance between colonist and Indian. Men sharing the rigors of the paths, wearing the same sorts of clothes, eating from the same pot, puffing on the same pipe, nonetheless did not shake their different ways of thinking about the landscape and the people who traveled across it. On fundamental issues such as the ethic of hospitality and the spiritual power of the land, native and newcomer remained far apart; more, perhaps threatened by the mingling and melding travel fostered, they were, near the end of the colonial era, at pains to point out just how far apart they were. As it turned out, the greatest obstacles in the way of intercultural understanding were not swollen streams, steep hills, or rotten weather but deeply-rooted perceptions that passage through the woods exposed rather than effaced.[3]

"The Difficulties . . . Encounter'd on Such Journeys"
Life on the Road

The most famous account of a journey across the Pennsylvania frontier is John Bartram's diary of his 1743 trip to Iroquoia and back. The great Quaker naturalist makes a trip through the woods sound easy. *We rode, we forded, we dined, we lodged,* he wrote day after day, as if all this took hardly more work than did setting pen to paper.

But Bartram's experience was as atypical as it is well known. His delight in the natural world lent his sketch of the trail a rosy hue. Moreover, tagging along with the experienced hands Conrad Weiser and Shickellamy freed this novice from fretting about which path to take or where his next meal would come from; he could devote himself instead to hunting fossils, checking soils, studying trees, and otherwise seeing the sights. Further benefiting from his companions' wisdom, Bartram set forth in mid-summer, the best time of year to go. Even the weather cooperated: what little rain there was fell at night or in brief showers.[4]

At the opposite extreme was another trip along the same route that Weiser and Shickellamy, with several others, had made six years before.

For these poor souls, nothing was easy—not riding, not fording, not dining, not lodging. The same "Dismal Wilderness" that temporarily darkened even Bartram's sunny disposition in July 1743 almost killed Weiser in March 1737. "It is such a desolate region that I often thought I must [die of oppression]. . . . [I]t seemed," he wrote upon emerging on the other side, "as if we had escaped from hell." More hell lay ahead, however, so much more that at one point an exhausted Weiser "sat down under a tree to die." Shickellamy convinced him to press on, but the path took such a toll that when Pennsylvania's Indian agent finally staggered into Onondaga, even his friends there did not recognize him. "[O]ne said it is he; another said no, it is another person altogether."[5]

The typical journey fell somewhere between Bartram's lark and Weiser's ordeal, but most were more ordeal than lark. Certainly Indians thought so. After all, their At the Woods' Edge ritual opened with a litany of the traveler's suffering. Their affinity for Weiser's take on travel rather than Bartram's was clear that summer of 1743. The German colonist, recounting for his Onondaga acquaintances the trip he and Bartram had just made, told a different story than the one the Quaker confided to his journal. When an Iroquois remarked happily that Weiser always came with "good News," Pennsylvania's ambassador "smil'd and told him it was enough to kill a Man to come such a Long and bad Road over Hills, Rocks, Old Trees, and Rivers, and to fight through a Cloud of Vermine, and all kinds of Poisen'd Worms and creeping things, besides being Loaded with a disagreeable Message, upon which they laugh'd." The laughter was genuine, but Weiser's audience knew, too, that he was only half-joking. However each defined the woods, Indian and colonist alike knew the same hard road. "The difficulties to be encounter'd on such Journeys," wrote Christian Frederick Post near the end of one trek, "are hardly to be described."[6] Perhaps. But in order to grasp what go-betweens like Weiser, Shickellamy, and the rest faced, it is worth attempting a description.

The story, like the journey, begins with the paths, which ranged from good to bad to impossible to nonexistent. It might have helped that Indian custom required go-betweens to stay on major routes. "Such men," Weiser once observed, "must travle not only the frequented Roads but the usual Road that ambassadors travle."[7] But if some thoroughfares offered "clear Woods and good Road," most were less inviting. As late as 1769 colonial highways like "the Great Road" running west from Philadelphia were "very crooked" and had stretches of "bad Ground."[8]

Indian trails, many a mere twelve to eighteen inches wide, were just as crooked. Even the better ones could "excite" in colonists "an Idea of Horror" as they discovered that natives' talk of overgrown paths where briars and thorns tore at clothes, hands, and faces was not just a figure of speech. Many a go-between "coming from the bush" must have resembled Daniel Claus, who on his arrival "still had some [leaves or twigs] hanging down from the bottom of my coat."[9] And bushes were only part of the problem. Bog, swamp, slough, mud hole, mire, marsh, *ganawàte, Maskéek*—by various names these blocked the road and held the traveler fast in their grip, while on other routes toppled trees left people "at a loss whether to turn to the right or to the left."[10]

"[I]t is an art to keep in the right direction," remarked one colonist after a day battling tree trunks, an art neither Indian nor colonial wayfarers ever thoroughly mastered.[11] Pennsylvanians on Indian ground often got lost, as did Indians making their way through the province. More surprisingly, some routes were so poorly marked that a colonial traveler lost his way even in "the inhabited parts," and Indians sometimes had trouble picking up the right path on the outskirts of their own towns. In 1753, Iroquois bound for the next village admitted that they "lose themselves almost every time." "[T]hey fared no better than we had formerly done," one colonial traveler reported from the Indian countries. "They ran here and there in the forest, till at length they found a path." Small wonder that the Moravian David Zeisberger, compiling a list of handy words and phrases in English, German, Onondaga, and Delaware, included "to Err in the road," "you have missed the road," and "I have miss'd the Way."[12]

On many routes, forbidding hills compounded a path's trials. Colonial travelers soon came to understand why Iroquois called the Susquehanna country's heights *Tyannuntasacta,* the "Endless hills" (or mountains). "You can scarce go a Mile any where, without very Steep ascents, and descents," moaned a Pennsylvanian. This was more than a complaint about uphill hiking—at least one traveler only made it across this rugged terrain on hands and knees; others formed a train by grabbing the coat of the person in front; still others, on horseback, went up or down slopes that "made both Man & Beast tremble." And trembling was the least of it. Horses slipped, "Got Maney a Dispert [desperate] Falle," even rolled "like a wheel" downhill to their death.[13]

Trying as paths might be, the prospect could worsen when a trail deposited the traveler on the bank of a stream. Crossing was usually a chore. Some creeks might be forded easily enough, but during the course of a day's journey one might splash again and again through a twisted run like the one Iroquois called "*Dia-dachlu* (the lost or bewildered)." Where the water was deeper, people wasted time hunting a ford.[14] If none could be found, they had a choice: spend a day or two building a raft, or try to find someone to ferry them across.[15] Getting somebody else to do the work only seemed easier; it often took longer, and fate always seemed to place candidates for ferryman on the far shore. There they might—or might not—be roused by travelers who "hallooed till we were tired" or depleted their ammunition firing into the air to attract attention.[16] The Iroquois called one stream en route to Pennsylvania "Dawantaa, (the fretful or tedious)"; no doubt many more earned that title, or worse, from people trying to get across.[17]

One solution to the peril of paths and fords was to abandon them and go by canoe. This craft, one Pennsylvanian exulted, "is by far the most pleasant and convenient mode of traveling." "I should have liked some of our friends to have seen us glide smoothly over the water," another gloated.[18] That Indian travelers, too, often boarded canoes is evident not from any native ode to canoeing but from their extensive use of the craft. Sites "where the canoes were made" lined the region's riverbanks, and an "Indian Fleet" of fifteen or eighteen vessels occasionally swept down the Susquehanna.[19]

The canoe's popularity is easy to explain. Quickly made by an experienced hand if conditions were right for gathering bark, readily repaired, it could carry heavy loads of packages and passengers.[20] Better still, the river did the work. Having paddled with the current all day, travelers would pull ashore at dusk, make dinner, then climb back into their vessels "and let them drive down all night and they lie themselves down to Sleep." Heading upstream was harder, of course, but ingenious Indian and colonial canoeists beat the current by hoisting a sail and going "as fast against the stream as if we were flying away."[21]

The canoe was popular but far from perfect. Building a good one required an expert, and even then the timing had to be right. Would-be sailors found themselves sitting on shore, waiting for warmer weather so that they could harvest bark.[22] Nor did getting the thing built guarantee a smooth trip. Merely boarding a craft might put a hole in it; standing up in one invited a bath.[23] And it was a good thing the bark vessels were easy to fix, because they often needed to be—they were "as tender as brown paper when the least snag, rock or any sharp thing touch'd them." One day a traveler might lose an entire morning making repairs; the next he might have to unload, patch, and reload several times. Ever helpful, Zeisberger's multilingual vocabulary instructed readers how to say "the Canoe is not tight" or "the Canoe leaks," adding the verb for "to throw the Water out of the Canoe."[24] At best, canoes were of limited use, because no rivers penetrated the Allegheny wall. One could canoe from Iroquoia to Chesapeake Bay and back via the Susquehanna; getting from that waterway to Logstown or Philadelphia was something else again. Sooner or later even the most devoted riverman had to stash his canoe and return to the path.[25]

Colonist or Indian, those picking their way down that path were often on horseback.[26] But, like a canoe, a horse could be more trouble than it was worth. The beast had to eat, and food could be hard to find. As late as May the grass might not yet be high enough to sustain the animal, and a rider loathe to risk losing his transport had to bring or buy fodder. Moreover, horses had an annoying habit of straying when turned loose to graze overnight. Many travelers wasted a morning, and some several days, tracking their mounts.[27]

Horses that were well fed and easily found could still be a nuisance, for they injured themselves with maddening ingenuity. One, hobbled to prevent its wandering off, tumbled into a river and drowned. Others ate poisonous plants or died from snake bite, broke a leg or came up lame. But the most common problem was exhaustion. Countless horses simply "failed" and had to be left behind or exchanged for a fresh mount—if one was around. In 1743 John Bartram's mare made it home, but upon reaching "the pasture, she stretched herself at full length and rose no more for 24 hours."[28]

Doubtless more than one traveler felt like doing the same after a trip across the borderlands. Those setting out in winter, as negotiators sometimes did, were especially likely candidates for collapse.[29] Frost-bitten feet, frozen clothes, long days and nights huddled around a fire waiting for a break in the weather—such was the fate in store for many during that season. The mountains on Pennsylvania's western flank were "impassible in the Winter if deep Snows happen"; the trick, of course, was predicting snow in a climate that, one credulous European visitor claimed, could have several different kinds of weather in a single day, including "cold spells which come so suddenly that human beings as well as the cattle and the birds in the air are in danger of freezing to death."[30]

A faulty forecast was Weiser's mistake in 1737 when, studying the bare ground before his front door on February 27, he decided that spring was near and headed north. He and his companions soon learned that winter still ruled the land—it "snowed at times as if it wished to bury us," the emissary reported—and there were several hundred miles yet to go.[31] Weiser made it, but he had learned his lesson. "I could seek nor Expect nothing from a Journey to Onontago now than my Grave," he protested in March 1754 when Pennsylvania officials asked him to make the same trip, "or feeding the Wolves and Bears with my Body."[32]

Weiser had plenty of company in his reluctance. Even colonial fur traders, famous for courting disaster in pursuit of profit, retreated before bitter cold and deep snow, as did Indian hunters and messengers.[33] Those brave, desperate, or foolish enough to push on found that snow buried paths or alternated with "almost incredible" rain showers that, freezing, made difficult terrain even more treacherous.[34]

Crossing streams, never easy, was a nightmare in winter. A traveler coming upon a river in that season sometimes found a sheet of ice that might—perhaps—support him. Many an anxious wayfarer knew how to ask, in several languages, "how thick is the Ice"? Often he would discover only part of the surface frozen, or a waterway thick with icebergs that, racing downstream, menaced canoes, horses, and men alike.[35] Open water presented problems of its own. "I had new reasons to praise the protection of God," wrote Weiser after crossing a stream where "the water flew between the trees like arrows from a bow." Lying awake some winter night in a camp on the bank, listening to the ice booming and cracking on the river he had to cross the next morning, more than one traveler must have questioned his sanity at undertaking the trip.[36]

While winter travel was hardest, other seasons posed problems of their own. Summer could bring either heat so oppressive that horses collapsed and people felt faint or torrential rains that soaked travelers to the skin.[37] Building, borrowing, or stealing a canoe was no sure solution, for rivers might be too shallow in summer. Indeed, the very day that smug canoeist had wished that his friends could see him "glide smoothly over the water," his companion had to "drag the canoes"— presumably less smoothly—"up over the rocks." Those fording streams found the water warmer but not necessarily safer, since some currents remained strong enough to sweep waders off their feet or relieve horses of their riders.[38]

Walking, riding, or canoeing, people crossing the frontier during the summer also had to contend with armies of insects. Weiser, already leery of winter and spring, cautioned against trips before late summer, in part because "of the Gnats, Muskeetoes, flies and other vermin which are intollerable in the Summer Season." Those who failed to hear (or to heed) Weiser's words paid a high price. "We could har[d]ly Live" because "the Nates [gnats] Was So Plenty," moaned one colonial ambassador; they "wase Lik[e] to Eate us up." Sleeping, eating, even walking became almost impossible because "the Misquiteis Bit us So bad" or the invisible *"ponkis"* struck with a bite as "burning hot as sparks of fire or hot ashes."[39]

Travelers battling bugs or bushes and cursing their horses or their luck also had to worry about finding something to eat. At first glance it might appear that food was no problem; surely America's bounty would provide? "[G]ame is always to be found," proclaimed David Zeisberger; as mealtime approaches, "the Indians plunge into the woods and shoot a deer, a turkey-cock, or something else." Hungry colonists plunged in, too. One summer Zeisberger and his companions filled their kettle with deer and ducks, pigeons and squirrels, fish and pheasant. "[A]ll . . . kinds of wild game, are extremely plenty," wrote a delighted George Croghan from the Ohio Valley in 1765. "A good hunter, without much fatigue to himself, could here supply daily one hundred men with meat." It was even less trouble to pick up a snack. One "fine day" en route back to Pennsylvania from Onondaga with Weiser in August 1743, John Bartram was pleased to report that "the gooseberries being now ripened, we were every now and then tempted to break off a bough and divert ourselves with picking them, tho' on horseback."[40]

Alas, it was not always so easy. However skilled at hunting or fishing, any traveler expecting to live off the land or his hosts courted disappointment, even death. While devouring those gooseberries in 1743, Weiser might have told Bartram of that trip six years before when his party, on the brink of starvation, was reduced to eating maple sap and corn meal mixed with lye. And amid his paeans to America's abundance Zeisberger, too, admitted that he sometimes "suffered much from hunger." Nor, the Moravian missionary discovered, were colonists the only ones haunted by famine. "Two traveling Nanticokes" he met on a 1753 trip were as famished as he was, and many another Indian sojourner came back empty-handed from a hunting trip or fishing expedition.[41]

Once again, winter was worst. So Weiser and his companions learned when they set off for Onondaga in February 1737, expecting to be resupplied for the next leg of the journey at an Indian town on the Susquehanna. The winter's hunt had been so poor, however, that instead of stocking up there, Weiser had to share with his hosts what little he had left. Already hungry, the travelers pushed on, only to find things worse farther up the path. At one village "some of the old mothers asked *us* for bread"; at another, children "stood before us in tears" while the visiting party ate what was left of its meager rations. "Hunger is a great tyrant," Weiser noted; "he does not spare the best of friends, much less strangers."[42]

The tyrant also stalked the land at other times of year; June and July were little better than March and April. A traveler in Indian country found paths drier and creeks lower, but he might also find the locals eating stewed grass, unripe grapes, and cornstalks. Weiser, ever the voice of experience, cautioned colonists not to attempt a crossing of the frontier until the corn ripened in August.[43]

As Weiser and other scarred veterans of the road knew, no season exactly invited a voyage through the woods. Winter? Sheer folly. Spring? Rivers were high, the food supply for horses and men low. Summer? Those same rivers were now dry, the heat intense, the mosquitoes hungry, the corn young.

Autumn? The best time, certainly, with fields ripe and insects in full retreat, but any unexpected delay in a fall trip spelled trouble (see above, winter). Usually, however, intermediaries had little choice. Indian business was not a seasonal occupation, as those burying Sawantaeny knew all too well. Hence while go-betweens might sometimes postpone a trip, as Weiser did in March 1754, most ventured forth when the need arose, and took their chances.

<hr />

"We Discoursed a Good Deal of the Night Together"
Sharing the Road

Not every day, not even every trip, brought stewed grass or icy trails, fierce gnats or raging torrents, lost horses or shredded canoes. But some days, and many trips, certainly did. Even the worst days had their reward, however. Then as now, misery loves company; the path's perils brought travelers together in a crucible of common experience, thereby producing a rich, mixed travel culture that went well beyond Indians mounting horses and colonists clambering aboard canoes.

Misery was not all that travelers shared. Rules of the road dictated that they also share provisions. "[I]f We had but one Loaf of Bread when we met each other in the Woods," a Conoy proudly reminded his Pennsylvania friends, "We would cut it in two and divide it one with another." Among natives the habit of sharing with other travelers was so deeply ingrained that, on crossing paths with someone, they "immediately" or "at once" offered food.[44]

The same rules held at Indian settlements. Hospitality, noted John Bartram during his stay in Shamokin, is "so punctually adhered to, that not only what is dressed is immediately set before a traveller, but the most pressing business is postponed to prepare the best they can get for him." Not only was a visitor entitled to the best, he earned a double portion of it, as hosts bustled about preparing what they had on hand or went out to fetch more.[45]

To hear some Indians tell it, many Pennsylvanians lived up to this ideal. Toward the end of the colonial era Delawares recalled how they often had stopped at one colonist's house in the course of their journeys, "and had Always been supplied with Proviss.s and what they wanted . . . without Ever Chargeing them Anything for it."[46]

Being offered foreign food was one thing, liking it another. True, most of the dishes placed before guests—whether colonial staples like beef, pork, mutton, butter, turnips, milk, and bread or the "Indn Diet" of venison, bear, corn, and melon—probably were edible enough to any stomach, even if one colonist missed having bread and salt to go with his meat and another thought Indian "apples, . . . like everything grown in the woods[,] did not have much taste."[47] But at first many another traveler, on sitting down to dinner, suddenly lost his appetite. Indians were appalled that colonists, "careless of cleanliness," used "dirty ashes" to bake bread and cook meat; Pennsylvanians recoiled from cooks who were "Neaxty [nasty]" or "dirty" and dishes that were "unclean" or, worse, "licked by the dogs in lieu of washing."[48] Natives refused salted meat; colonists watched wide-eyed as Iroquois cooks dumped lice or entrails into soup. One Seneca, discussing food with two Pennsylvanians, was surprised to hear that they "could eat Indian fare[.] [N]ot all Asseroni [*axemakers,* meaning Europeans] were able to."[49]

Those two *Asseroni* were graduates of a course all travelers had to pass. Some Indians, while in their colonial woods, insisted that they "must have the victuals raw and let the wimens [in their party] Boil it," but most native go-betweens, traveling without women, learned to suffer colonial cooking in silence, just as Pennsylvania travelers stomached Indian cuisine.[50] The difference between a novice and a veteran in culinary matters is made clear by an astonished Daniel Claus on his maiden voyage into the woods in 1750. A meal of "Ind.n Corn Squash & Entrails of Deer &ca, . . . no Hardship for Mr Weiser who experienced the like before, was a great one to Mr Claus who never saw Such eatables made Use of before by Mankind, and was pretty well pinched with Hunger before he could persuade himself to taste them."[51]

The hospitality ethic that brought travelers, however reluctantly, to a Shamokin cook fire or a Tulpehocken hearth also arranged where those visitors would bed down at day's end. Accommodations varied greatly from one stop to the next. Many a trip included nights of stretching out on rocky or damp ground, even standing around a fire in the rain.[52] One traveler desperate for a dry bed crawled into a hollow stump;[53] others slept beneath a canoe.[54] Weiser occasionally had a hammock, and some people, including Indians, brought their own tents.[55] A better way to escape the elements was to put up a rude hut by driving forked sticks into the ground and covering them with a roof of bark, hides, branches, or cloth. Easy as these were to cobble together, easier still was an abandoned cabin or "trail lodge" colonists nestled near springs and Indians located a day's journey apart. Though these might be near collapse—one Pennsylvanian could hardly believe that "a wretched hut" on the road to Shamokin was "supposed to be a hotel"—on a wet night they were better cover than the trees or sky.[56]

If possible, the wise traveler sought shelter with the local inhabitants. Many Indian towns had buildings set aside for visitors (a house at Onondaga was actually reserved for "the messengers & travelers from pensilvania"); if not, one might stay with the village headman or simply move in with a family.[57] Housing an outsider was natives' way of showing respect and, perhaps, keeping an eye on him. One of many reasons Shawnees on the Susquehanna so disliked the Moravian leader Count Nikolaus Ludwig von Zinzendorf when he visited them in 1742 was his decision to decline their invitation to stay in town, preferring to sleep in "his tent at a distance from them." At another Susquehanna village three years later, one of Zinzendorf's disciples knew enough to accept when the locals "urged" him to leave his tent folded up and lodge with them instead.[58] Similarly, native travelers among Penn's people took rooms in Philadelphia, at the frontier town of Carlisle they announced that William Blythe's would be the "proper House to come to when they came among the Inhabitants," and during the Seven Years' War they even stayed in the captain's quarters of a fort.[59]

Sleeping under one roof, dipping into one pot, colonial and Indian travelers developed a fellowship of the road, a rough fraternity encouraged not just by brutal conditions and common experiences but by congruent habits and assumptions. Both took dreams seriously enough that a nightmare made Indian messengers turn back and a dream about visitors from Bethlehem had Moravian missionaries at Shamokin rejoicing.[60] Both painted or carved trees with their exploits.[61] Both sought guidance and comfort from invisible forces, with colonial travelers spouting Scripture as they plunged down a wintry riverbank while beside another stream an Indian prayed for rain to float his canoe. Both made the woods echo with song, whether a Moravian "singing hour" or an Indian melody "sung in a solemn harmonious manner."[62]

And both knew how important were good companions. "Fellow travellers" could patch each other up, revive flagging spirits, and help pass the time. Indians loved to talk, whether about battles, hunting trips, "droll Adventures," "affairs of state[,] . . . or the news of the day."[63]

Just as natives "entertained each other with stories" and "discoursed and joked till midnight," so among mixed parties of colonists and natives the air often was thick with conversation. "We discoursed a good deal of the night together," wrote Christian Frederick Post during a trip with several Indians. Weiser, waiting in a Susquehanna town for the weather to break so that he could push on to Onondaga, had frequent invitations to different houses "for the purpose of talking . . . , and thus we passed the . . . hours away, in relating old or new events or traditions, and smoking tobacco."[64]

Passing pipes and swapping stories, stumbling down hills and inching out onto the ice, sleeping at a Philadelphia inn and an Onondaga longhouse—colonial and Indian travelers came, in some ways, to bear a striking resemblance to each other. Natives wearing shoes, stockings, breeches, coats, and hats guided horses through the streets of the provincial capital; colonists in moccasins and fringed buckskin leggings walked into an Indian clearing.[65] Delaware and English, Oneida and German, go-betweens fell in step, one with another.

"Their Own Way in Traveling"
A Parting of Ways

But even as Conrad Weiser and his amused Onondaga friends knew that go-betweens did indeed tread the same "Long and bad Road," they also knew that Indian and colonist did not do so in quite the same way. Their songs never became duets featuring, say, Weiser and Shickellamy. Their prayers were rarely if ever uttered in unison or directed toward the same deity. And while one colonial wood-carver claimed to be marking trees "after the Indian manner," in fact he was scrawling his initials or the date, scratching a new history onto the land, effacing earlier native signatures that told of scalps or skins taken.[66]

A closer look at life on the road suggests that the trail's cultural confluence, while genuine, was superficial; behind memorable images of Indians astride horses or colonists in moccasins lay deep disagreements about travel and travelers, disagreements that worked against bringing the two cultures together. Conrad Weiser knew this as early as the fall of 1736 when, accompanying Iroquois to Philadelphia, he sighed that "I must let them have their own way in traveling."[67] For all the miles he had covered, for all he had shared with native companions, the German colonist nonetheless believed that Indians had one way of traveling, colonists another. The differences reveal as much about negotiators, and about the frontier, as do the hardships and habits they shared.

Some differences surfaced before a journey even began. Indians, contemplating the road ahead, thought in terms of the number of days it would take to reach their destination; colonists tended to talk of the miles to be covered. Thus Pennsylvanians trying to gauge distances from an Indian informant had to be content to learn that one town was "three day's journey in a Canoe" above Shamokin, another so close that an "old woman may carry a heavy Pack of Skins from thence . . . and return . . . in two nights."[68]

The difference in perception applied to the trails to be taken as well as the distances to be covered. What colonists considered "a Wilderness where there was neither Road nor Path" offered experienced Indians several possible routes to choose from. "[W]e all know," wrote a bewildered George Washington trying to plot a route through the forest, "that a blaz'd path in the eyes of an Indian is a large road: for they do not distinguish between one track and another . . . ; i.e. between a track which will admit of carriages, and a road sufficient for them to march in."[69]

Whatever the path taken, however the distance was measured, provisioning for a journey further divided native from colonial travelers. Colonists liked to go well-supplied "with everything necessary for the Woods." Kegs filled with rum or wine, casks of bread, cheese, or butter, and packs holding beef, bacon, salt, or rice accompanied Weiser on his missions. Among these packages Weiser and other colonists usually managed to find room for such delicacies as "Chocolate and Tea and Sugar &c."[70] Indians, by contrast, tended to travel light, contenting themselves with a bundle, a weapon, a tobacco pouch and pipe, perhaps a kettle, and a bag of corn meal mixed with sugar, their staple food.[71]

The Indian's bundle and the colonist's packhorse hint at profoundly different perceptions of the journey ahead. Some sense of that difference became strikingly clear to Weiser one day in 1745 when, en route to Iroquoia, he met up with Anontagketa, an Onondaga returning home from war. Anontagketa was not just traveling light; the fellow was practically naked. Fleeing the enemy (and, later, buying liquor from frontier colonists) had left him with "neither Shoes, Stockings, Shirt, Gun, Knife, nor Hatchet; in a Word," Weiser reported, "he had nothing but an old torn Blanket, and some Rags." The colonist, amazed, "asked, how he could undertake to go a Journey of Three Hundred Miles so naked and unprovided, having no Provisions, nor any Arms to kill Creatures for his Sustenance?" Anontagketa's reply measured his distance from the packhorseman's mentality. "[H]e told me very chearfully . . . ," Weiser went on, "that God would . . . provide in such a Manner, that he should arrive at Onondago; . . . that it was visible God was with the *Indians* in the Wilderness, because they cast their Care upon him; but that, contrary, to this, the *Europeans* always carried Bread with them." Though Pennsylvanians and their native neighbors both viewed a trip through the woods with some trepidation, Indians trusted those woods to sustain them in a way that colonists did not. "[T]hey are," observed David Zeisberger of native travelers, "everywhere at home in the woods."[72]

In fact, however, in the *colonial* corners of those woods natives felt less at home, and Anontagketa's god was less likely to provide. If he did not discover this hard truth, other natives certainly did, for Pennsylvanians often left an Iroquois or Delaware wayfarer homeless and hungry. Despite the times natives did find a warm welcome, as a rule Penn's people tended to be reluctant hosts. "Indians from the Woods" are "troublesome Guests," colonists would grumble, at best an "Inconvenience," at worst "So unruly that there is no Liveing with them."[73] Hence Pennsylvanians tended to put native guests "in a house by themselves," preferably one "a Good Distance of[f]." Better still was placing them with Weiser, John Harris, George Croghan, or other colonists known to be "somewhat used to Indians."[74]

Many Pennsylvanians less "used to Indians" were as loathe to feed an Indian as they were to house him. The reluctance stemmed in part from the awesome amount of food a native could consume, especially one expecting the customary extra helping. Some thought a Delaware or Iroquois ate twice what a colonist did; others put the figure at ten times as much. All would have agreed that "[w]hat an Indian can eat is scarcely credible to those who have not seen it."[75]

Credibility was a concern among colonial cooks because few were willing to serve an Indian a free meal. Expecting payment from the government, they feared that Philadelphia officials keeping a sharp eye out for profiteers would reject their vouchers as exorbitant. "[W]hat must I do with these people," Weiser fretted in 1749 of some Indian guests, "it is impossible for me to Know what to do." If I feed them, "Can I get my money again without begging or answering a tousand questions"? Weiser, as usual, handed out food, but other Pennsylvanians refused, leaving Indian travelers "prodigious angry." Iroquois visiting Philadelphia in 1736 were more puzzled than annoyed. "[A]mongst them," they explained, "there is never any Victuals sold, the Indians give to each other freely what they can spare, but," the visitors continued, "if they come amongst our People [colonists] they can have none without paying. They admire we should take Money on this Score." So serious did natives consider the colonial breach of hospitality that some Delawares blamed it for their decision to attack Pennsylvania in the 1750s.[76]

Yet while they might reject colonial explanations for such behavior—"every Man lives by his own Labour & Industry, . . . all victuals cost money"—Indians grasped the inclination to keep strangers at arm's length. After all, even as natives drew a colonial traveler into the center of town they, too, often put him in designated houses, perhaps because people there were "somewhat used to" *colonists*. After all, those visitors could be a trial. Polishing off his dinner at an Indian cabin, for example, one Pennsylvanian, in his ignorance, tossed a bone to a dog, only to have it intercepted by his frantic host, who followed custom and "committed it to the fire, religiously covering it over with hot ashes."[77] Perhaps, too, the colonial penchant for lodging Indians by themselves was in part to grant native wishes.

Certainly while on the trail colonist and Indian sometimes observed an informal segregation. Mixed companies of travelers might build two huts, one for colonists, the other for Indians; if they erected only one, natives might sleep on one side of the fire, colonists on the other. Or if colonists brought a tent, the Indians might help them set it up, then retire to sleep in the open air nearby. This was by no means a hard-and-fast rule—travelers of all stripes often stretched out for the night side by side—but the tendency to put some ground between the bedrolls was there.[78]

~~~~~~~

"The Evil Spirits That Dwell among the White People"
The Perils of Penn's Woods

Alienation deepened as Indians discovered that the colonial corners of their woods were different from the rest, that in those precincts a native traveler faced risks his colonial counterpart nowhere confronted. Far more alarming than having a door slammed in one's face or an apple snatched from one's hand were "the evil Spirits that Dwell among the White People" and caused sickness. Colonists fell ill on the road, too—"fatigue in the Woods" brought on colds, fevers, and the like— but for them travel held none of the terrors it did for Indians bound for Pennsylvania. Terrible diseases such as smallpox could—and did—visit natives in their own towns, of course. But a sojourn among colonial settlements dramatically increased an Indian's chances of getting sick, and friendly advice from colonists to "keep out of ye way of ye Small pox" was hard to follow.[79] In 1738, six years after Shawnee messengers from the Ohio country had died of smallpox in Philadelphia, tribal leaders declined Pennsylvania's invitation to return to their Susquehanna River lands. "[T]he Loss of our two Brothers which Died in Philad[elphi]a is still in our Mindes," they replied; "we should when we see the English Settlements . . . be sorry."[80]

Many natives who did venture into those settlements were indeed sorry. Oneidas lost twenty men to disease during a trip to Philadelphia in 1749, and it was widely believed in Indian country that the capital was a pesthouse. These people "cou'd not be beat out of a Notion they had entertain'd of this City's being sickly," groaned George Croghan in 1748 after trying to coax a band of "extremely a-fraid" Indian messengers across the frontier.[81] Countless native travelers shared the fate of one Tokayiendisery, who left Pennsylvania on a litter and was, one colonist observed, certain "never [to] see his own Country again."[82]

After war broke out in the 1750s, native go-betweens worried about smallpox had reason to fear spirits of another sort that came to inhabit Penn's Woods: colonists bent on revenge against any Indians, even those making peace. Here again, native and colonial ways diverged sharply. Indians rarely assassinated a messenger, even in time of war; a few Pennsylvania envoys were roughed up between 1755 and 1765, but none were killed.[83] Safe, too, were negotiators who came into Pennsylvania from Indian country before the conflict started. But then, just when native intermediaries were most needed, they faced the most danger. "We are all ways in Dred & in fere of our Lifes," Indians told provincial officials in 1761. "Never the less, Brother, we venter Down to See you according to your Desier, But," they repeated, "we are all ways in Fear."[84]

Some of the danger came from the shattered nerves of Pennsylvanians. Men so frightened that they thought a flock of cranes standing on a riverbank was an Indian war party or mistook the call of wild geese for "the Voice of Indians all around them" were unlikely to distinguish friendly messengers from enemy warriors.[85] To protect go-betweens from such mistakes, provincial officials did what they could to equip them with passports and other, more visible signs distinguishing friend from foe. An Indian traveler approaching colonists during the war might sport a red cockade or a green bough in his hat, he might wrap a yellow streamer around his arm or head, and he might frantically wave anything from a Union Jack, a linen flag, or a matchcoat to a red handkerchief, a blanket, or a bush.[86]

Unfortunately, in the middle of a war no sign, however obvious, was of interest to many colonists, convinced as they were that all tribes had a hand in the death and destruction raining down on Pennsylvania. These folk suffered not from shot nerves or vivid imaginations but from hatred, and it put the native negotiator in terrible danger. People here "think it their duty to destroy every Indian they see on the road going to the Governor . . . ," wrote one frustrated official from John Harris's trading post on the Susquehanna River in June 1756. "[A]nd whenever one begins to reason with them, they immediately put their fingers into their ears." Shickellamy's son Tachnechdorus (John Shickellamy) was "often insulted by the fearful ignorant people who have Sometimes told [John] Shekallamy to his face, that they had a good mind to Scalp him."[87]

Tachnechdorus got through unscathed; others were not so lucky. In July 1757 William Tatamy, son of the Delaware go-between Moses Tatamy and a messenger in his own right, was heading to Easton to prepare for a peace treaty to be held there when a colonist shot him in the leg. For a month the wounded Indian lingered at a farmhouse near Bethlehem, tended by a colonial physician, ministered to by Moravians, treated to sweet cakes. At last, as the Easton treaty drew to a close and the Indians headed home, Tatamy died. Two hundred of those natives attended his funeral at a cemetery on the outskirts of Bethlehem. As they watched the coffin being lowered into the ground and listened to the Moravian service, the Indians were reminded not just of the governor's platitudes—conveyed, with his sympathies, at Easton—about "the uncertainty of life in times of war," but also of the particular perils lurking in Penn's Woods.[88]

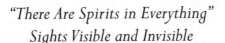

"There Are Spirits in Everything"
Sights Visible and Invisible

But for a traveler from the Indian countries, the perils of Penn's Woods ran deeper than "evil spirits" there, deeper than the lethal microbes and furious colonists those realms harbored, deeper even than the strangeness of Philadelphia's broad streets, towering brick houses, and throngs of people. Paradoxically, the real source of native alienation from that neck of their woods was not the crowd there but the emptiness, not the din but the silence. Appreciating just how empty, and how silent, requires a side trip into Indian territory in order to see the landscape as natives did.

Those districts were, for a trained eye, an open book. Graves, the "footsteps" of abandoned towns, conjurers' huts, posts to which warriors, camping en route home, had fastened captives for the night—each had a tale to tell. Other posts stood beside the trail, painted by a man eager to mark victory or defeat, scalps or captives, plunder taken

or comrades lost. Larger war parties worked so assiduously at recounting their deeds that one campground held "the whole chancery
court or archives of the Gajukas [Cayugas], painted or hanging in the
trees."[89]

Many other sites whispered stories to those who knew how to listen.
Near Great Island in the Susquehanna's West Branch was *Enda Mohàtink*
("where human flesh was eaten"); there, it was said, a woman crossing
the mountains with her children was snowbound and, desperate to save
some of her family, killed the youngest child in order to feed the rest.
At *Licking Pond,* on the road from Pennsylvania to Onondaga, two natives had fought and one had died, ruining this popular hunting ground
for years. Near the summit of a mountain north of Shamokin two skulls
perched atop poles, the remains of Iroquois warriors who, bound for
home with a brace of prisoners, had stopped there overnight. With
darkness the captives, untied by an evil spirit, pounced on their enemies
and left the heads behind to flaunt their deed. A cannibal's camp, a
bloody pond, a pair of skulls—travelers able to read them came away
with lessons to ponder.[90]

The grinning skulls, testimony to a malevolent spirit's power, hint at
the deeply spiritual nature of Indian travel through the woods. A native
who left his clearing entered an enchanted world, a world where geese
gathered on a lake each fall to set the date of their departure for warmer
climes, a world where snakes could turn into raccoons. "[T]here are,"
Indians believed, "spirits in everything, in stones, rivers, trees, mountains, roads, &c." As the skulls attested, some spirits sowed mischief and
mayhem. Anywhere in the woods, natives knew, "Wandering spirits
and ghosts . . . sometimes throw something into a public path and whoever goes over it is bewitched and becomes lame or ill." Indian travelers could point to such cursed spots, just as they could identify a place
on the Susquehanna where a hermit sorcerer had once preyed on
hunters or a cave where "evil spirits have their seats and hold their rev-
els." Sometimes that "*Otkon* (an evil spirit)" ruled an entire valley, brewing blizzards to bury travelers.[91]

Against such formidable foes the Indian traveler did what he could,
hurrying through haunted corners of the forest or calling on "magi-
cians" to appease an *Otkon.* A quest for protection against powerful
denizens of the invisible world might explain why one Iroquois, as he
paddled along, "Every now and then . . . would with a composed coun-

tenance utter somewhat pretty loud," probably a "magical incantation" or "prayer" to the invisible world, asking safe passage.[92]

The power of native belief in such forces was evident one evening when Conrad Weiser and Shickellamy stopped beside the path to build a hut. At first the rocky soil resisted the Oneida's efforts to drive in posts, so he tried another approach. "My Friend!" he said, speaking to the land beneath his feet. "I and my companion want to stay here to-night, and you must let me drive these stakes into the ground; so give way a little, or I will dig you out of the ground and throw you into the fire." Then Shickellamy went back to work, "every now and then speaking harshly, as if he were striving or fighting with some one." Indians "have it much easier," he explained to Weiser, "if we talk to the spirits, and call them friends, and mingle threats therewith, then we succeed."[93]

Such conversations, such sites, gave structure and meaning to the Indian lands a native passed through. In a snowstorm that sojourner saw *Otkon*'s hand. Rain was punishment for kicking stones down a hillside. A chorus of toads marked "*Tsquallutene,* i.e. Town of the Toads." And at one spot along the Susquehanna where insects ruled lay another village, "Ponks-utenink *i.e.* 'the town of the Ponkis.' " The word *ponkis*—living dust and ashes—accounted for the insects' tiny size and ferocious bite. Why did they plague this particular place? That hermit sorcerer, long dead, was at work yet. After terrorizing the area for years, the story went, he had finally been killed and his body cremated. But he tormented people still, for "the wind blew his ashes into the swamp and they became living things, and hence the *ponkis.*"[94]

Hearing or speaking with spirits did not transform an Indian's trip from an ordeal into a lark: flies still bit and rain still fell, the ground was just as rocky and the hills just as steep, the Endless Mountains still went on forever and the streams remained "fretful or tedious." But that these lands were inhabited by invisible beings "with which their old men can talk"—which they could explain and, sometimes, propitiate—made the domain beyond the woods' edge less intimidating, more easily endured, even if never completely controlled.[95]

An Indian venturing into Penn's Woods forsook this spiritual connection to the terrain. Here was a silent land, a territory with spirits the elders could not speak to.[96] Native imprints there—towns, graveyards, memorial stones, painted posts, even the giant ferryman who, "in ancient times," bore Indian travelers on his back across the Delaware

River—surrendered to the axe, the plow, the workings of wind and weather. The land remained, its hills and river courses much the same; but its older, faded signatures became harder for the native to read.[97]

Harder still for us to read, because colonists wrote little about it, is what Indians made of these changes. For some, the treaty council fires ritually kindled at Philadelphia, Lancaster, and Easton rendered those neighborhoods suitable for diplomatic negotiations. But natives' aversion even to these hallowed grounds was such that in 1744 and again in 1755 Iroquois leaders asked if Conodoguinet, an abandoned Indian town across the Susquehanna from John Harris's, could substitute for Philadelphia as the council site. Apparently an Indian ghost town was better than a place where the native presence had been reduced to the dim memories of aged hunters. Delawares, whose homeland included the site of that city, might have come to consider it *kwulakan,* a domain so tainted by conflict or dissonance that it was best avoided.[98]

So little survives of native sensibilities because colonists were largely oblivious to the disenchantment of America. The newcomers, having brought with them across the sea a rich cache of beliefs about landscape, soon were busily translating those habits of thought into the American vernacular.[99] The spot where William Penn first landed, the treaty elm at Shackamaxon—these and other sites acquired special significance, rendering Pennsylvania familiar, pregnant with meaning, able now to be read by colonial wayfarers even as it was, for Indians, increasingly indecipherable.

Indeed, legibility helped locate the enduring boundary between native and newcomer. Terrain that began to speak to Penn's people was becoming mute to their Delaware, Iroquois, or Shawnee neighbors. Meanwhile the Indian countries remained largely *terra incognita* to colonists, who could not "unfold the story or resolve on the meaning" of what they saw there.[100] To a Pennsylvania traveler, the skulls on that mountaintop said nothing, snow and rain simply fell, toads merely croaked, bugs just bit. Indian and colonist alike, men on the road always knew where the boundary was, where one world ended and another began. On one trip Post and his party, leaving "the last White Inhabitants" to head up the Susquehanna, paused and "committed our selves to the Care & protection of our heavenly Father to guide & provide for us on our Way." John Bartram, returning from Onondaga, marked the boundary in more secular fashion. "[W]e heartily congratulated our-selves," he wrote of Weiser and the other colonists with him, "on the enjoyment of good bread, butter and milk, in a comfortable house, and clean straw to sleep on, free from fleas."[101] The naturalist and his companions were out of their woods at last; an Indian coming to the same house would have just been entering the most alien and forbidding parts of his own.

~~~~~

"Silly Fancies"
Making, Marking, and Measuring Distances

Thus Indian and colonial travelers fell in step with each other yet remained always, somehow, out of step. Indeed, as time went on people on both sides of the frontier actually began to exaggerate the differences between them. Why they did so is unclear, but, paradoxically, the segregationist impulse probably grew out of closer acquaintance: even as they came to know each other better, even as travelers borrowed freely from one another, Indian and colonial peoples were coming to understand that they had contrary views of America's future, that while colonists looked toward the day when the forest and its native inhabitants would be gone, those natives were bent on preserving woodlands and on keeping newcomers at bay. Perhaps seeing the other's antithetical vision prompted both sides to continue drawing lines between them, even in the ways they got together.

Whatever the reason, distinguishing native from colonial travelers required amnesia. Forgetting men like Moses Tatamy, that Christian Delaware with a farm near Easton who was very much at home in Pennsylvania's inhabited parts, or Garrett Pendergrass, a fur trader who "knows the Woods Extreamely well," they mocked the travel customs of the other.[102]

Mockery had its roots in a selective blindness that pervaded assessments of life on the pathways. Instead of seeing that many "Travellers," whatever their background, "judge [distances] only from the Time taken up in Travelling," people stressed the dichotomy of miles and days.[103] Instead of appreciating that a Moses Tatamy might also have been spouting Scripture as his horse plunged down a riverbank, they contrasted Indian chants with Christian prayers. Eating customs were, for both sides, an important marker. Colonists "are not used [to dining] like us," Teedyuscung reminded Tatamy, Stille, and his other Delaware companions before one journey with Post; "they are regular & have their stated Times for eating & Drinking." Post, astonished by the Indians' ability to go for days without food, knew what the Delaware leader meant. "In regard to the Diet & Way of Life," he observed, "it is very Difficult for White People to come thro' among ye. Indians."[104]

Such distancing went on all the time. Instead of noticing that native messengers sometimes left Pennsylvania with packhorses groaning under a mountain of provisions, instead of admitting that more than one colonist had learned to make do with just a bundle of belongings, Indians scorned colonial travelers for carrying so much. "[T]he English," they laughed, "were a Parcel of old Women for that they could not travel without loaded Horses and Waggons full of Provisions and a great deal of Baggage."[105]

Indians, insisting that colonists did not know "how to behave on the Road," also heaped scorn on colonial woodcraft. Again exaggerating differences for added effect, natives would remark that they made pitching camp an art, carefully selecting the site, cutting bushes, branches, or ferns to lie on, and arranging these beds around a central fire.[106] Making themselves out to be experts, Indians then branded colonists rank amateurs, bumblers stupid enough to choose "any dirty and wet place, provided they are under large trees," never bothering to check those trees "to see whether there are not dead limbs that may fall on them while they are asleep." Having chosen the wrong site, Indian critics went on, colonists made things worse by building a fire with wet or rotten logs "so that they are involved during the whole night in a cloud of smoke"; others used green wood, "which throws sparks out to a great distance, so that their blanket, and clothes get holes burned in them, and sometimes the whole camp takes fire."[107]

Indians who did cross paths with a colonial novice could be merciless, as Count Zinzendorf discovered to his dismay during his 1742 tour of the Susquehanna Valley. The *reichscount* was hopelessly out of his depth. Added to his imperious manner and his indifference to local custom was his utter lack of experience in the woods. He toppled backwards off his horse into a stream, his saddle landing on top of him. He got lost on a path so easy to follow that it was said "nobody could have missed the Trail." The man even got hospitality wrong: after he gave natives everything he had, right down to his buttons and buckles, his disciples had "to fasten his under-clothes and tie his shoes with strings made of [bark]." So incompetent was Zinzendorf that his own Indian guides "showed no respect for his person," but "used to break wind in his presence in the tent, [and] were always making fun of him."[108]

Colonists had a different way of expressing their views, but they were just as quick to ridicule Indian travelers. John Bartram dismissed an Iroquois explanation of a sacred site as a "silly story" and called a guide who prayed "superstitious." The naturalist confined most of these opinions to his journal, but sometimes he found his companions' beliefs too outrageous to suffer in silence. One day he squabbled with Indians "much disturbed at" his rattling stones down a hill: "they said it would infallibly produce rain the next day," but the Pennsylvanian insisted that "I had sufficient experience, it signified nothing." Even Conrad Weiser, readier than most Pennsylvanians to appreciate Indian ways, laughed at Shickellamy's chat with stony ground and mocked natives' "silly fancies about spirits, about their dreams, and their sorceries."[109]

Drawing lines with a smirk or a chuckle, a sneer or, yes, a fart, travelers further divided native from newcomer by labeling Indians superior, even superhuman, woodsmen. The native's ability to negotiate the forests was legendary. A keen sense of direction "is a quality which seems born in them . . . ," wrote one colonist of the Iroquois. "In the thickest forests and at the darkest times, they do not lose, as they say, their star." "It is," agreed another, "as if Nature had fixed the compass in their heads."[110] But finding the way was only the beginning of Indian magic. It was said that a native could pick up a trail from a broken twig here, some torn moss there, a bit farther along some fallen leaves that had been disturbed. He could distinguish a wolf's step from a dog's, and "burst out into laughter" at colonists' "want of skill in so plain and common a matter." Those believing in an Indian's sharp eyesight and a sense of smell as keen as a hunting dog's were easily convinced that natives, "at first glance," could read in a footprint whether its maker was Delaware or Iroquois, man or woman, short or tall.[111]

In fact, the very colonists calling this craft natural also explained how it was anything but that. From their youth Indians made "constant application of the mind to observing the scenes and accidents which occur in the woods," wrote the Moravian missionary John Heckewelder, "together with an ardent desire to acquire an intimate knowledge of the various objects which surround them." This training gave them "practical acquaintance with the country that they inhabit," acquaintance they then expanded as hunting, diplomacy, and warfare took them farther afield. On their return from these long trips, travelers gave others "an account of their whole journey, and went into the most minute details of all that had happened to them," details sometimes including maps kept for future reference. The result was knowledge of the woods as intimate as it was extensive.[112]

However impressive, that education did not make an Indian master of the woods. The prevailing view of Indian travelers omitted how often they got lost, fell off log bridges, built rafts that sank, tumbled into rivers, lost or swamped canoes, and chased wayward horses. But such incompetence, clumsiness, or bad luck never dampened the enthusiasm among both European colonists and American Indians for making natives out to be nature's children.[113]

The stereotype's construction had profound implications. From there it was easy to conclude that "the woods" (as Europeans defined them) were the Indian's special province. Colonists judging him "everywhere at home in the woods" implicitly made the native out to be an alien being, consigned him to an alien land, and marked Europeans' distance from that realm. True, the occasional colonist might by long experience come to "know the woods like a savage." True, during the Seven Years' War some British officers, desperate for woodsmen and tired of trying to "coax that damned Tanny Race" into doing His Majesty's bidding, wondered if "it would be easier to make Indians of our White men." But colonists with more frontier experience insisted that this was impossible. "I cannot conceive the best white men to be equal to them in the Woods," George Washington wrote when invited to comment on the army's idea. David Zeisberger, who knew Indians far better than did young Washington, agreed that in the forest "[n]o European is equal to them."[114]

Instead of seeking (and finding) resemblance, travelers of all sorts focused on what divided them. Colonists were rubes who could never learn the woods' ways, Indians superstitious supermen born to perform spectacular feats on the road. From the characterization—or caricature—of Indians it was but a short step to the idea that they were not *super*human but *sub*human, ruled by instinct rather than education, more akin to the bear or fox than to a European. When one of those British officers reported that west of the Susquehanna River the land was "impenetrable almost to any thing humane save the Indians (if they be allowed the Appellation)," he was merely using the accepted idiom of travel culture.[115]

"Another Person Altogether"
Healing the Wounds of the Woods

Perhaps the most telling measure of the distance between prevailing colonial and Indian views on the traveler is how, at the end of his long sojourn, they treated a woods ranger's trauma. Both sides knew that those who ventured into the woods—however those woods were defined—ran the risk of being forever changed, of becoming figuratively what Onondagans in 1737 thought Weiser had become literally: "another person altogether."

But here the similarity ends. Pennsylvanians were decidedly ambivalent about people who ventured into the uncharted world that bounded the province. Such men were useful, their knowledge of the lands and peoples beyond the horizon indispensable. But these men could never fully be trusted, for those alien lands and peoples marked a man's soul. At the end of the colonial period J. Hector St. John de Crèvecoeur, well acquainted with the Susquehanna country's "great woods" and its "men of the woods," captured popular notions of what he called "the effects which follow by living in the woods." "It is with men as it is with the plants and animals that grow and live in the forests," Crèvecoeur wrote; "they are entirely different from those that live in the plains." Hunting makes colonists "ferocious, gloomy, and unsociable," and "[e]ating of wild meat . . . tends to alter their temper," leaving them "no better than carnivorous animals of a superior rank." Such folk are "bad people . . . who have degenerated" into "the most hideous parts of our society," the Frenchman insisted, developing "a strange sort of lawless profligacy, the impressions of which are indelible." In the minds of respectable colonists, then, the go-between was forever tainted by his time in "the immensity of these woods."[116]

Natives, too, were convinced that people came out of the forest changed, but rather than fear or despise them Indians worked to restore them, to erase what Crèvecoeur and other colonists thought indelible. The antidote for the poisons of the woods was the At the Woods' Edge Ceremony. Kin to the Iroquois Condolence ritual in both spirit and structure, the Woods' Edge not only summarized but also cured the afflictions brought on by a journey.[117] The go-between stepping out of the woods was, Indians believed, like the grief-stricken; his mind had been deranged by a terrible ordeal. To carry on, he had to shed the torments of the trail that clouded his perception and garbled his words. Ritually wiping clean the throat, ears, and eyes set things right, comforting the traveler as it did the bereaved. Then, and only then, when the travail of the woods had been countered and the wayfarer was whole again, was back in the clearing, could he set about the next phase of his work.

"He Was Too Proud to Obey a European"
The Squabble at Oscohu Creek

By the time a go-between got to this point—when he could get down to business—he had already tasted the difficulties of trying to connect one world to another. Travel through the woods had taught him that the vast distance between colonists and Indians was as much cultural as it was geographical. On the road, Indians discovered that Pennsylvanians could be clumsy companions and lousy hosts. Those colonists, meanwhile, seeing a native traveler gorge himself on their food (and, sometimes, their drink), were appalled by what looked like an uncontrollable appetite more suited to animals than to people. "Indians pulling meat like Beasts," wrote one disgusted Pennsylvanian, watching some Iroquois dine; "when the Victuals is dress'd they fall to like so many Wolves," exclaimed Post when Moses Tatamy, Isaac Stille, and other Christian Delaware messengers paused beside the path for a meal.[118]

At first glance a critique of table manners might not seem like much. In fact, however, these and other seemingly petty points of etiquette— where to camp, how to kindle a fire, which song to sing, what to carve on a tree—were the very stuff of the larger, cross-cultural indictments being issued during these years. Perhaps nowhere is the link people forged between the mundane and the meaningful more clear than on March 28, 1737, during the infamous Onondaga trip that Weiser and Shickellamy made, when deep snows, empty bellies, and arguments over which path to follow brought anger and alienation to the surface.[119]

Besides the German and Oneida go-betweens, the party consisted of Weiser's hired man, Stoffel Stump; Owis-gera, an Onondaga who had

wintered with Weiser; and Tawagarat, an Oneida warrior heading home
to Iroquoia from a foray against southern foes.[120] For breakfast that
morning the five men had eaten the last of their provisions. Then, for-
tified by sunshine, a warm south wind, and the hope of reaching the
Susquehanna River (and more food) before dark, they set forth. By
mid-morning the party came to a stream Iroquois "called *Oscohu,* (the
fierce)." How to cross? The Indians favored wading or building a raft.
Weiser refused (thinking the creek too deep and too swift) and proposed instead looking for quieter water downstream. At that, Weiser
wrote, "the Indians began to abuse Stoffel who they said was to blame,
that I had not followed their advice." When Weiser came to his man's
defense, the three natives turned on him, "called me a coward who
loved his life, but must die of hunger on this spot."

Weiser made the dispute into a cultural critique. "[I]t is true, we
Europeans love our lives, but also those of our fellow-creatures," he
replied; "the Indians, on the contrary loved their lives also, but often
murdered one another, which the Europeans did not do, and therefore
the Indians were cruel creatures, whose advice," Weiser concluded, at
last returning to the subject, "could not be followed in circumstances
like the present."

Shickellamy was unimpressed by this line of argument. "[H]e was the
guide," the Oneida insisted, "as being a person who had travelled the
route often, while I had never done so; he would cross there." But
Weiser's compass and the lay of the land convinced the colonist that a
better ford was nearby, and he was determined to find it, even though
the Indians went on ridiculing this "folly" and Tawagarat "said openly,
that he was too proud to obey a European." In the end the two Pennsylvanians hoisted their packs and left, Owis-gera followed, and (after
a moment's hesitation) so did Shickellamy. Only the "proud and obstinate" Tawagarat remained.

As it turned out, Weiser was right: quieter water was barely a mile
away. "My Indian companions thanked me for my good counsel," and—
to complete the triumph—"our obstinate *Tawagarat,* . . . very wet,"
later caught up, admitting, when Weiser "reproved him for his pride and
obstinacy," "that he had acted foolishly." Weiser had gambled his compass against Shickellamy's experience, and this time colonist and compass won. But Weiser lost, too. He had violated native custom, which
dictated that the most experienced command a traveling party.[121] He
had turned an argument about crossing a stream into a contest be-

tween cultures, condemning natives as "cruel creatures" and being told in turn that a European's opinion was worthless. Whether his Iroquois companions were really as grateful and as rueful as Weiser made them out to be is unclear. But we do know that a decade later one of Shickel-lamy's sons mentioned that as a traveling companion Weiser "was . . . not so good, he always quarreled!"[122]

Had Weiser been wrong, it seems unlikely that he would have recorded this little morality play for posterity. Yet neither his victory nor his moral are as important as what the episode reveals about travel's significance for understanding the colonial frontier. The squabble beside the Oscohu, like voyages into the woods, permits us to see what a go-between was up against. Quite apart from the wounds inflicted by the trail, that trail exposed how different Indians and Pennsylvanians were, how much they misunderstood, mistrusted, even hated one another. Highlighting the differences between peoples, journeys made clear how essential mediators were. At the same time, however, those crossings illustrated how difficult was the go-between's task. Not least of the difficulties was that some of the forces he struggled against— misunderstanding and mistrust bordering on hatred—lay in the heart and mind of the negotiator himself. Travel, which brought Indian and European together, cast in sharp relief how far apart they were.

CHAPTER IV

The Lessons of Brinksmanship:
Woodslore, 1728–1743

However difficult or perilous, most of a go-between's trips were on routine business—to prepare the way for a treaty, to make inquiries about this, to spread the word about that—not matters of life or death. In fact, disaster loomed just three times before war finally came to Pennsylvania in the mid-1750s. Jack Armstrong's fatal encounter with Mushemeelin was the third of those times. The first had come in 1728, sparked by rumors of a vast Indian conspiracy against British America, a clash between Shawnees and Pennsylvania farmers, and the murder of some unlucky Delawares by edgy colonists. The second erupted in the winter of 1742–1743 when an Iroquois war party's skirmish with Virginians threatened to ignite the frontier all the way from the Shenandoah Valley to Onondaga. John Bartram's trek to the Iroquois capital in the summer of 1743, a joyride for him, was, for his guides Shickellamy and Conrad Weiser, a peacekeeping mission.

Studying how negotiators handled the first two crises teaches valuable lessons in frontier brinksmanship—not the deadly modern game of threats and bluffs hurled while teetering on the edge of a precipice, but an earlier version, where people tried to pull their world back from the abyss. More, these episodes highlight how much the borderlands changed during the second quarter of the eighteenth century. In 1743 the place looked very different than it had just fifteen years before. Over that short span the principal axis linking Philadelphia with its native neighbors shifted from the lower to the upper Susquehanna Valley, from Conestoga to Shamokin at the Susquehanna Forks and, beyond, all the way to Iroquoia. At the same time, a new breed of go-between emerged. In 1728 no less than ten negotiators, all of them colonial fur traders, helped avert war. Fifteen years later that job went to just two men, neither of them traders: Shickellamy, the Oneida, and Conrad Weiser, the German colonist and adopted Mohawk who, like his Iroquois friend, arrived on the Pennsylvania frontier in the late 1720s. Each in his own right a gifted woodsman, together—and they usually *were* together—they possessed unmatched skill, subtlety, and power.

And yet however good all of these men were at their craft, however well they washed away the blood shed in 1728 and 1742, they never banished the frontier's doubt and discontent. They could rescue peace, but the harmony and union stressed in council speeches eluded them. Instead they faced a growing sense of disappointment, even disgust, conveyed by Indians in a tone so sharp that it made Civility's querulous comments to James Logan and Governor Keith in the early 1720s seem mild by comparison.

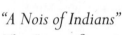

"A Nois of Indians"
The Crises of 1728

In 1728, for the first time, Penn's Woods came perilously close to frontier war. "[T]here is more danger of a misunderstanding with our Indians," James Logan delicately put it that May, "than I have ever known since I came into ye place" almost thirty years ago.[1] The situation was so volatile because so much went wrong at once. Go-betweens managed to head off disaster, but the resentment and fear that had brought on a crisis in the first place still lingered.

The first sign of trouble came in April from Ostonwakin, a village on the Susquehanna's West Branch (Map 4).[2] With the spring thaw, the old trader James Le Tort was getting ready for a trip across the mountains to do business with Miami Indians south of Lake Erie. Rumors wrecked his plans. First an "old Friend" of Le Tort's, a Delaware leader named Manawkyhickon, "discouraged him" with vague talk of enemies out there "who come to hunt not for Skins but for flesh and scalps."[3] Then another local, Madame Montour, pulled Le Tort aside with still more discouraging words. Consulted last fall, she had "seemed very much to approve" of his plans, Le Tort reported; in fact, she and her husband

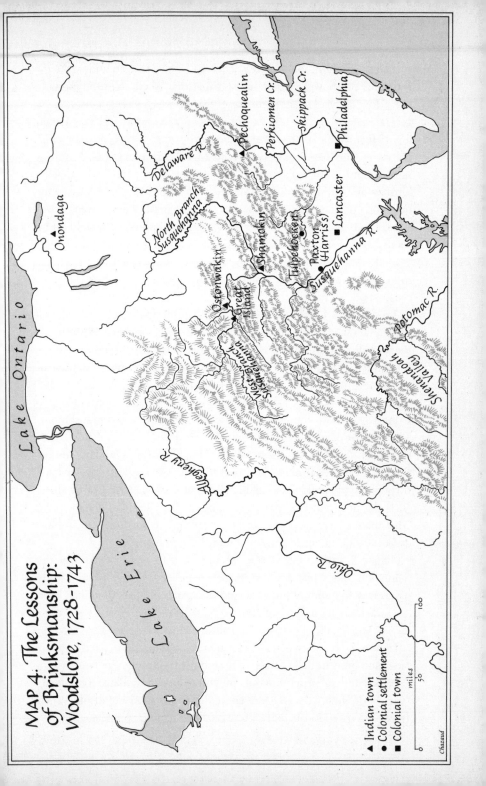

MAP 4. The Lessons of Brinksmanship: Woodslore, 1728-1743

Lake Ontario

Lake Erie

Onondaga ▲

North Branch Susquehanna

Delaware R.

Pechoquealin ▲

Perkiomen Cr.

Skippack Cr.

Philadelphia ■

Lancaster ■

Shamokin ▲

Tulpehocken ●

Paxton (Harris's) ●

Susquehanna R.

Ostonwakin ▲

Great Island ▲

West Branch Susquehanna

Allegheny R.

Potomac R.

Shenandoah Valley

Ohio R.

▲ Indian town
● Colonial settlement
■ Colonial town

miles
0   50   100

Chazaud

agreed to join him, looking "very cheerfull & desirous to undertake the Journey." But now Montour told Le Tort that "she could not goe with him," for "She had heard some news that he was a stranger to."

The story Montour told Le Tort was as convoluted as it was alarming. It featured a large wampum belt proposing war against Britain's colonists.[4] Le Tort's putative friend Manawkyhickon was, Montour said, behind it all. Furious that New Jersey authorities had hanged a kinsman for killing a colonist, Manawkyhickon had recently passed the belt along to some Cayuga friends of his, who in turn sent it west to Miamis. The belt asked whether these western people, too, "would lift up their Axes, and joyn with them against the Christians, to which they agreed." Learning of that agreement, Manawkyhickon had called in his men from the hunt, presumably to turn their sights from deer to colonists.[5]

Le Tort had heard enough. Grabbing John Scull, another colonial trader, he raced to Philadelphia, arriving in town on April 18. Officials there, still reeling from this report, were struck from a different direction two weeks later. Indians on the lower Susquehanna, longtime allies with one another and with Pennsylvania, were said to be "in a destracted Condition." Shawnees, having for some reason killed two Conestogas, now refused to hand over the culprits for punishment. The victims' kin, that report went, "resent [this] so hiley that . . . they threaten to cutt off the whole nation of the Shawnys." On May 1 almost twenty Conestoga men—"painted for the Warr, all armd"—passed through nearby colonial settlements to rendezvous with Conoy allies. "It is all our Opinions," wrote one anxious "borderer" to Philadelphia, "that the Governor's pressence pritty Speedily is absolutely nessessary at Conestogo to Settle Affares amongst the Indians."[6]

Those Susquehanna settlers would have to wait, because in the Schuylkill Valley just north of the capital rumor and fear had already given way to gunfire. Since the end of April, colonists there had been "so Alarmed by a Nois of Indians" that some had abandoned their farms. Vague talk of natives "Consulting Measures against us" took on a frightening reality when eleven native men showed up, paint on their faces and guns in their hands.[7] These must be "foreign Indians" with a "Spanish Indian" in command, petrified Pennsylvanians concluded, "very rude" fellows who harassed the locals for food and drink. When twenty of those locals, only a few of them armed, approached the intruders for a parley, the warriors' leader "brandished his Sword & commanded his Men to fire," wounding several and, colonists claimed, killing one.[8]

Indians told a different story. The warriors, they said, were neither foreign nor Spanish but friendly Shawnees from Pechoquealin on the Delaware River. Having heard rumors of an Indian raid on the province, they came to help colonists repel the invaders. Along the Schuylkill, the party, out of supplies, had politely asked people for food. Colonists, not Indians, had been rude. And colonists, not Indians, had started the shooting.[9]

Whoever fired first, "the Noise of the Skirmish" left "the Countrey in very great Disorder." Most colonists fled. Twenty of those remaining, hunkered down behind a mountain of wheat and flour at George Boone's mill, were sure that an all-out Indian attack was imminent; if reinforcements do not arrive soon, they warned, "we shall undoubtedly perish and our province [be] laid desolate and destroyed." Mingled with the fear was hatred and a thirst for vengeance. On May 10, figuring "from the Reports in the Countrey of the Indians having Killed some white men . . . [that] they might lawfully Kill any Indian whom they could find," several Pennsylvania men went looking for natives.[10]

They found some at the house of John Roberts, on Skippack Creek, a tributary of the Perkiomen, which in turn flowed into the Schuylkill. Roberts had been busy that day drafting a petition reporting Indian attacks to the governor and begging for help, then collecting seventy-seven names.[11] That done, he dispatched a rider to the capital and returned home to find his wife and son facing the very terror his petition anticipated: Indians. To be sure, this was not much of a war party. Tacocolie, a young Delaware man, was there with his pregnant wife Quilee (Hannah) and an older woman, along with two girls (one of them crippled) and a boy.[12] These Indians, with a cabin nearby, were known in the neighborhood, but Roberts still feared the worst. They had a bow and an alarming number of arrows; there sat the boy, in Roberts's own house, making more shafts. The Pennsylvanian sent his son to fetch help.

Young Roberts went to Walter Winter, who was also having a busy day. Hearing (incorrectly, it turned out) that Indians had killed two colonists and wounded three more, he "went about the Neighborhood" inviting people to make a stand at his house, then went back home to fortify the dwelling. As Winter battened down the windows, Roberts's son arrived to say "that his father was in Danger of being killed." Winter—grabbing his gun, his brother John, and his father-in-law, Morgan Herbert—set out for the Roberts place.

Now it was Tacocolie, with the women and girls at a woodpile near the front door, who became alarmed. Here came three armed colonists, closing fast; there stood Roberts in the doorway with a weapon. The Delaware got to his feet and picked up his bow. Stepping backward, he pulled an arrow from his quiver; the Winter brothers opened fire. Walter's shot hit Tacocolie in the chest; John's killed one of the women; then he raced up and, with his musket, "knocked another Indian Woman's Brains out." While Roberts buried an axe in the head of one of John's victims, the two brothers took off after the fleeing girls. Walter caught one and hauled her to the house; John pursued the other, clubbed her with his gun until she fell, then headed back. By the time he got there Tacocolie, mortally wounded, had pulled himself up and gone "staggering into a swamp near the house."[13]

The next morning the Winter brothers finished their business. Thinking twice about having let that wounded girl get away, they followed her to the Delaware cabin and ordered her to Walter's house. Then they dragged the women's bodies out of the road and covered them with leaves. Finally, with the two girls in tow, they headed for George Boone's stronghold at the mill, where they expected "to receive some Reward" for their labors.

Unfortunately for them, the Winters were thirty years ahead of their time. In 1758, Pennsylvanians who murdered three Indians and wounded two more would indeed have been rewarded for a good day's work. In 1728, however, the two men were going to jail, part of the scramble to keep all these sparks—not just the Delaware killings but Miamis and Manawkyhickon, Conestogas confronting one band of Shawnees and colonists another—from igniting a conflagration.

The easiest sparks to put out were those, like the Winters, in Pennsylvania's inhabited parts. On May 10 Governor Patrick Gordon rode north with "divers Gentlemen" and "used several Methods to quiet the Country," among them distributing ammunition and interviewing the colonist supposedly slain by those Shawnees. Next the governor's party brought the full weight of provincial authority to bear on the Winters, including a hue and cry, depositions, a coroner's inquest, and medical treatment for the wounded girls. Back in Philadelphia, Gordon issued a proclamation commanding Pennsylvanians to "treat . . . Indians with the same civil Regard that they would an English Subject." To demonstrate what happened to those who indulged in "that unbecoming Practice of expressing or Shewing their weak unhandsome fears," the province prosecuted, then hanged, John and Walter Winter.[14]

Gordon could do all this without leaving the familiar confines of Anglo-American ways; the rest of the business demanded different methods and different men. Despite the Susquehanna borderers' plea for the governor's presence, he could do little there without go-betweens, men who knew their job just as well as a coroner, jailer, or judge knew his. Guided by the experts and by old hands on the provincial council like James Logan, Gordon sent urgent messages into the Indian countries.[15] James Le Tort, John Scull, Scull's brother Nicholas, Anthony Zadowski, John Smith, Nicholas and John Schonhoven—these men set their fur trade business aside in order to bear speeches requesting more information about the rumors, condoling with Delawares over Tacocolie and the others, and at once reprimanding and conciliating the Pechoquealin Shawnees. And to "as many of those Indians, as I could find messengers to reach," Gordon added, went reminders of William Penn's friendship and invitations to a council devoted to renewing that friendship.

The soothing messages, with the customary presents "to confirm" them, set peoples back on the path toward peace. From one Susquehanna River town came a reply that began sternly by telling Gordon "to warn the back Inhabts Not to be so Ready to attack the Indians," then concluded with assurances that "We Remember very well the League between William Pen and the Indians." Meanwhile Sassoonan, now living with his people at Shamokin, pleaded ignorance of that mysterious war belt but promised to find out more about the rumors of conspiracy. A week later, after hearing of Tacocolie and Quilee, the Delaware headman sent a second friendly speech. "If we had not Rec'd this Letter from our Brother, we Should have been in some fear of Danger," Sassoonan said, "but now our doubts are over." Soon "we shall meet . . . and discourse together in Love," he concluded, accepting the invitation to parley.[16]

Two treaty councils subdued the noise. The first, in late May, took Gordon and thirty other Philadelphians to Conestoga (the last time provincial officials would deign to treat there), where they met with Conestogas, Conoys, Shawnees, and Delawares from the lower Susquehanna. The second, which convened in early June, brought Gordon, his council, and "a vast Audience that filled the [Quaker Meeting] House & all its Galleries" to see Sassoonan and his Delaware band.[17]

"[M]utual civilities" ruled both congresses. Colonists and Indians resurrected William Penn, fondled the links in the chain of friendship he and natives had forged, and pledged to remain "as one People, that Eat, as it were, with one Mouth, & are one Body & one Heart." As surely as the wheels of British law ground the Winter brothers to dust, so the wheels of frontier diplomacy buried Tacocolie, Quilee, and the others.[18]

With Sassoonan's farewell on June 5, silence ruled the long summer days. By fall, however, whispers about war resumed. Some thought the summer's very silence was sinister. What had happened to an Iroquois delegation, expected in the capital in early June? Why no visit, and no word, from Shamokin or Conestoga, when last spring Indians there had promised to resume talks in Philadelphia in two months? And what about those Shawnees at Pechoquealin, who were to meet the governor to settle their differences? Had James Le Tort and Madame Montour been right after all?[19]

Philadelphians had reason to ponder these questions anew on August 24, when word reached the provincial council that two colonial traders from up the Delaware were drinking at a tavern in town. Traders drinking was hardly news, but what Coarse Froom and John Schonhoven told the other patrons, "of some Disturbances amongst the Indians" up that way, certainly was. Soon the two stood before the governor—a bit unsteadily, as it turned out, for they had to be sent away to sober up. Two days later they were back to tell their story. When an Indian "from Sasquehannah" had arrived at Pechoquealin with a mysterious message, they said, the Shawnees there had left, abandoning houses and corn. Convinced that "some Mischief was on Foot," the two had then scurried off to Philadelphia.[20]

Worse news followed a few days later. Another town of Shawnees, this one on the Susquehanna's West Branch, had turned on colonial traders there, it was said, hanging one Timothy Higgins from the rafters and promising to do the same to the rest.[21] At this, panic again swept the borderlands. "[T]he Peaple in our Parts," wrote Anthony Zadowski from Pennsylvania's northern frontier on August 27, "is freed that thereis som Miscif hacin by the Indians." Nor were jittery farmers the only ones alarmed. Montour herself, Zadowski went on in his fractured prose, had "told me to not to go to Indians this fall un till by beter understanding bytwin Christians & Indians, for theris a great dissatisfaction a mongs them." As if all this were not bad enough, rumor had it that Shamokin, like Pechoquealin, was now a ghost town.[22]

Once again the province dispatched negotiators with instructions to check out "that Story about . . . the Miamis," find and question the Pechoquealin leader Kakowatchy, look into the hanging, and "inform yourselves of every thing else that may give Light into these affairs." And once again, the news was good. Higgins, after a narrow escape, was alive.[23] Indians at Conestoga were stockpiling skins to give the governor at a treaty in Philadelphia soon. And upstream at the Susquehanna Forks, Shamokin, anything but deserted, was busy with its own preparations for a visit to the provincial capital.

That treaty council, which opened on October 10, laid to rest lingering fears.[24] Speaking for Conestogas and Shawnees as well as his own Delawares, Sassoonan followed the well-worn rhetorical path, a route marked by fond memories of Penn and pledges of abiding friendship. "[A]ll the Indians think no more of that matter," he said of the "small Misunderstanding" at the Roberts farm; to prove it, the natives "express'd their Satisfaction by a harmonious Sound peculiar to them, in which they all joyned."

The harmony echoing through the Philadelphia Courthouse that fall day is testimony to negotiators' skill, and to a continued willingness on all sides to settle disputes with words rather than weapons. Confronted by a crisis of unprecedented proportions, Indians and colonists knew how to winnow truth from rumor, cover the dead, console the living, and rekindle the fires of friendship. Yet, as before, treaty talk could not muffle dissonance.

Some of the discord can be heard in the noise of colonial borderers that spring. Despite official efforts to demonize the Winter brothers—branding them, in speeches to both Indians and colonists, "furious wicked men"—in fact the two were not much different from the hundreds of Pennsylvanians who gathered to watch them die.[25] The Winters and their accomplices were alone in acting on the belief that they might "Kill any Indian they could find," but the idea itself was popular. Untold numbers of colonists believed every rumor of suddenly savage natives, signed petitions begging for help against those imagined bar-

baric hordes, and made Shawnee friends into foreign foes. This bundle of assumptions—all Indians are the same, all are enemies in disguise—was by no means as powerful or as universal as it would later become; if it had been, the three Delawares would not have been the only victims and the Winters would not have gone to the gallows. Nonetheless, the killers reflected a climate of opinion poisoned by prejudice against Indians.

In Indian country, too, people were in the habit of drawing a line between colonist and native. In the spring Sassoonan turned rumors of Manawkyhickon, Miamis, and others attacking Pennsylvania into "a wear between the white pepele and the Indians"; similarly, that fall Montour made a complex calculus of stories into a simple equation of trouble "bytwin the Christians & Indians."[26]

One source of native alienation was land, for during the 1720s the colonial encroachment on Indian territory that Civility and others had long been complaining about continued apace. So did official indifference to natives' plight. Asked in 1727 to stop their people from settling above Paxtang, provincial authorities refused, saying that "as the young People grow up they will spread of Course." Natives in the Susquehanna Valley who "behold all their Lands invaded by swarms of Strangers," James Logan observed at the time, will "suffer no manner of survey to be made there on any accot whatsoever."[27] Even Sassoonan's moving meditations on "Love & Peace" at those 1728 treaties included, as counterpoint, his shock at Pennsylvania's invasion of the Delawares' Tulpehocken lands. "[H]e could not himself believe the Christians had settled on them," the Delaware headman said, "till he came & with his own Eyes saw the Houses and Fields they had made there." Shawnees, meanwhile, expressed their own disgust with provincial expansion by starting an exodus from the Delaware and lower Susquehanna that took them first to the Susquehanna's upper reaches and finally over the mountains to Ohio.[28]

As Shawnees and Delawares retreated, Conestogas stayed put, but they were no happier with the course of events. True, at a Philadelphia council in the spring of 1729 the friendly rhetoric scaled new heights of hyperbole as Tawenna, an aged Conestoga leader who had shaken hands with William Penn, resurrected the Founder once more. *William Penn said, William Penn further said, William Penn told the Indians, William Penn often told them*—on and on Tawenna went. It was, the Conestoga concluded, "as if William Penn himself were alive."

But once Tawenna sat down, Pennsylvania's old ally Civility stood and, using a short speech against selling rum to Indians, once again measured the distance he saw between colonist and Indian. His "Concern[,] he said, was not so much for fear of any Accident [due to drunkenness] among the Indians themselves, for if one Indian should kill another they have many ways of making up such an Affair." With colonists, though, it was different. "[H]is Uneasiness proceeded," the Conestoga go-between went on, "from an Apprehension lest a Christian should be ill used by any Indian intoxicated with that Liquor."[29] The distinction was clear: natives—even from different nations—had "many ways" of reconciliation; natives and colonists did not. In fact, as events of the past year proved, negotiators could settle disputes between newcomers and Indians. But removing a more visceral feeling that prompted colonists to lump all Delawares, Iroquois, Shawnees, and the rest into one menacing mass while natives spoke of "the white pepele and the Indians"—that was something else again.

〰〰〰

"White People Are All of One Colour and as One Body"
Skirmishes

The swirling current of rumors and councils, fear and bloodshed in 1728 also heralded dramatic change on the frontier. Conestoga went from *de facto* Indian capital to quiet backwater, while Shamokin rose from obscurity to become, by 1742, the place where "the Indians have their Rendevous."[30] Civility, since 1710 a prominent frontier figure, sank into insignificance, his place taken by Shickellamy. A mere observer at Sassoonan's June 1728 Philadelphia treaty, this Oneida's importance was soon clear. His "Services had been & may yet further be of great advantage to this Government," provincial authorities concluded after talking further with him that fall.[31]

Those officials proved prophetic. In the years to come Shickellamy—with Conrad Weiser, James Logan in Philadelphia, and men in Iroquoia—was the architect of a new age. Pennsylvania leaders were keen to simplify Indian affairs, especially after the dizzying round of talks in 1728. Conestogas, Conoys, several different Delaware and Shawnee bands—it was too confusing. At the same time, Iroquois wanted to tighten lines of authority on their southern frontier. Thus a historic congruence came about. At major treaties in 1732, 1736, and 1742, Onondaga and Philadelphia became fast friends in order to promote trade and assert control over the peoples between them.[32]

The first shock to the new system Shickellamy, Weiser, and their peoples had erected came early one morning in January 1743 at a Shawnee settlement on the banks of the Susquehanna's West Branch.[33] Snug in his storehouse there, the fur trader Thomas McKee and his servant were rudely awakened by Indians who burst in to say that "they had heard the Dead Hollow, & were much surprized at it." Then McKee heard it, too, a chilling *Que, Que, Que* to announce that those approaching town had suffered some terrible loss.[34] The cry came from an island—Big Island, it was called, or Great Island—across from the village. As the two colonists piled into a canoe and paddled out to learn more, Shawnees on the riverbank shouted over the stream: *What is the matter?* "[T]he White Men had kill'd some of their Men," came the reply.

Reaching the island, McKee found ten Iroquois warriors, exhausted and famished after three weeks' march in the dead of winter. The trader greeted them warmly "according to the usual Way, saying How do you do my Friends?" He got a chilly response: "they shook their Heads and made no Answer." The band crossed to town and headed straight for the council house, McKee right behind. There, they told their story.[35]

That story began the previous fall, when twenty-one Onondagas and seven Oneidas, led by an Onondaga named Jonnhaty, left Iroquoia and headed south. Like generations of Iroquois men before them, they were bound for Catawba country on the southern piedmont. Like their forebears, too, these "Boys" and "Elders" carried with them bitter enmity fueled by raids back and forth. Our "Warr with the Catabaws . . . will last to the End of the World," Six Nations leaders promised colonists, "for they molest Us and speak Contemptuously of Us, which our Warriours will not bear."[36] Jonnhaty's warriors were no exception: steeped in memories of taunts and bloodshed, they hoped that their deeds—along with scalps or prisoners—would even the score and solace grieving kin back home.

At the outset the journey was routine. The band stashed its canoes at John Harris's, as usual, and—again, as usual—looked up a magistrate to get a paper ensuring safe passage, and the occasional meal, through Pennsylvania. Across the Potomac, though, things began to go wrong. The Iroquois could find no official to "renew" the passport. With deer scarce and farmers unwilling to provide food, the travelers killed some hogs and cattle.[37]

Pushing down the Shenandoah Valley, the party met ever greater resistance from the locals until one day it found itself with an impromptu escort. First one colonist joined them, then another and another; when warriors "stopped every now and then" to go "on one side of the Road to make Water," the Virginians "told the Indians to make hast[e] and come along." Along to where? At day's end the Iroquois found out: they reached "a big House" crammed with people, who invited the Indians inside. Some of the older warriors went; the rest waited in the yard, watching "more & more white People gathering." Inside, the Iroquois produced their Pennsylvania pass, only to be "told . . . they must not go any farther."

Sensing trouble, Indians in the yard called to their friends to get out. Out, instead, came a colonist, "Sword on his side, to bring the others in." Those others refused; the party's leaders emerged from the house; the man drew his sword; the Iroquois, with "a field Cry," snatched up their weapons. Jonnhaty quickly stepped in. "[B]e quiet till they were hurt . . . ," he told his men, "let the white People begin Violence." Picking up their bundles, the warriors quickly left, traveling all night to put as much distance as possible between them and that house.

For two days the Iroquois, camped in the hills, debated their next step. It had been a close call, but squabbles with colonists living beside the warpath were nothing new; the band would press on. Back to the main road they went, on the morning of December 18. Behind them on that highway came "a great Talk, & Noise of Horses." A couple of shots rang out, potshots at two Indian boys bringing up the rear. Then the "tramling of the Horses" stopped and a "Great number of white Men"—some forty altogether—dismounted.

Jonnhaty still hoped for the best. After all, he and his warriors "did not come to fight white Men, but the Cawtabaws." The Virginians carried a white flag, and he knew "that a white Colour was allways a token of Peace with the white Men." Maybe that volley a moment ago had only been to frighten them. The Iroquois set down their bundles, but obeyed his command to wait "till they should see what the White Men would do." What those white men did was open fire, killing two and wounding several more. "Fight for Life!" Jonnhaty cried as, firing his own gun in reply, he grabbed his tomahawk and led his men straight into the Virginians' ranks.

It was over fast, the Iroquois speaker at that Shawnee council house concluded. Colonists fled at once, in their ears Iroquois taunts daring them to stand their ground. Eight Virginians and four Indians lay dead; several more on both sides were wounded. The next day Jonnhaty and a dozen men headed west with the wounded on a roundabout route home. These ten were to make straight for Iroquoia with the bad news. But be careful, Jonnhaty had warned; "revenge nothing & be of good be-haviour as forme[r]ly if the[y] be not attacked." Remember, the war cap-tain told them, "there were different Sorts of white People." Some were still friends of the Six Nations.

At this point in the story Thomas McKee scrambled to his feet to en-dorse Jonnhaty's sentiments: colonists are not alike. The killings "are no ways owing to the People of Pennsylvania," he argued. "We . . . are not answerable for what the People of another Province may imprudently do. I therefore hope," he concluded, "that you will observe your Treaty of Peace with Pennsylvania and suffer me to remain Safe among You." But one Shawnee disagreed with McKee's attempt to distinguish Penn-sylvanians from Virginians, saying "that the white People are all of one Colour and as one Body, and in Case of Warr would assist one another."

Increasingly uneasy, McKee tried a different approach. Pulling aside his closest acquaintance in town, an elderly Shawnee, the trader took him into the store, handed him some tobacco, and urged "him to press to the Indians in Council" what McKee had said: remember your friend-ship with Pennsylvania; do not kill me. Soon the man returned to say that the council assented, "tho' it seem'd disagreeable to some of the Shawna's."

Another of the townsfolk was less sanguine about McKee's future. This informant, "a white Woman who had been taken Prisoner by the Indians in their Carolina Warr's," told the trader to leave at once.[38] The council had actually agreed to let the Shawnees decide, and those Shawnees were, even now, slipping out of town to seal his fate in secret. Run, or you are sure to be killed. McKee ran.

Virginians, meanwhile, were spreading their own story, a tale markedly different from the one McKee heard. This Iroquois war party, Virginia colonists said, had "appeared in a hostile manner among us killing and carrying off horses &ca." When colonists approached them to talk, flying a white flag of truce, the warriors called out "[']Oh Friends, are you there, have We found You?['] & on that," one Virginian reported, "fir'd on Our Flagg." Quickly over? The firefight had lasted forty-five minutes. Colonial cowards? The Virginians fought bravely, and Indians, not colonists, had fled the field.[39]

Whatever story they heard (and believed), Indians and colonists alike saw at once its ominous portent.[40] At Shamokin, Sassoonan talked of "this Dangerous Time," while in Philadelphia Governor George Thomas, at "this Critical Juncture," knew that conflict between Virginia and the Six Nations could "force Us into the War[,] too."[41] There was more to worry about than angry Iroquois or vengeful Virginians. In the lands between the two lived peoples who, acting upon their fear and hatred of each other, might widen the breach beyond repair. Pennsylvanians believed that Shawnees—"rough and . . . ungovernable," "turbulent & cruel"—were troublemakers.[42]

Pennsylvania's frontier folk were also a threat to peace. "[T]his accident had render'd the Inhabitants on the other side of Sasquehannah extremely uneasy, & Jealous of all Indians," Thomas fretted as he wondered how to "quiet their Mind."[43] By spring the sense of dread even struck susceptible souls east of the Susquehanna. Hearing wild talk "that the Indians . . . were come to a Resolution to cut off all the white People," some Pennsylvanians forgot their crops and cattle in search of refuge from the impending Armageddon.[44]

Iroquois warriors limping home with a story of colonial perfidy that was, to many native listeners, all too believable; Virginia borderers spreading a different account east to the coast and up into Pennsylvania that, again, fit widespread assumptions about Indian savagery—there was plenty of reason to fear frontier war. But those pressing for peace—from Williamsburg and Philadelphia to Shamokin and Onondaga—had considerable resources at their disposal. To "prevent the flame from spreading Wider," these colonies and nations set in motion diplomatic machinery honed over the past fifteen years. Trouble will ensue "if things are not prudently managed," Thomas warned as he sent McKee to consult Conrad Weiser at Tulpehocken; Weiser must go to Shamokin, "and there Concert Measures with Schick Calamy."[45]

Those measures started with two councils at Shamokin. At the first, on February 4, twenty-five men from the Susquehanna nations (including Shawnees) gathered to hear Weiser offer Pennsylvania's mediation and dispatch Shickellamy to Onondaga with this proposal. The second, convened after the Oneida go-between's return two months later, conveyed the Iroquois' willingness to make up their differences with Virginia.[46]

A promising start, but only that. Since Virginia had shed first blood, the Oneida explained, that province must visit Onondaga to set things right. "[I]f the Virginians would not come to do that," wrote Weiser, "he (Shikellimo) believed there would be a War."[47] Virginia officials, no more eager to see the Iroquois capital than Governor Keith had been in 1722, declined the invitation; but they did send Weiser in their stead, along with £100 worth of presents. In early July the colonist (as *Assaryquoa,* the Iroquois name for Virginia) and Shickellamy (personifying *Onas,* Penn's province, the mediator), collected John Bartram, Lewis Evans, and the Oneida's son, Tachnechdorus, and pointed their horses north.[48]

They reached the outskirts of Onondaga on the afternoon of July 21. Before them the settlement stretched for two or three miles along a creek running through what Bartram thought a "charming vale." Scattered among the tall grass and the plots of ripening corn, peas, and squash were forty houses, some standing alone, others in clusters of four or five. The inhabitants directed the travelers to the largest of these buildings, a bark house eighty feet long and seventeen across. Down its center ran a public passageway that connected the "apartments," each with a fireplace in that center aisle and a smokehole in the roof above.

The delegation settled in two rooms at one end of this house. Then, spreading rush mats on the low platforms in each room, their Onondaga hosts served corn mush and dried eels. Next came Canasatego and several other leading townsmen to offer a welcome "with a grave chearful complaisance, according to their custom." Filling a pipe with "Philadelphia Tobacco," the group spent the rest of the day smoking and having "some further discourse on things" that were, to Weiser anyway, "of no Consequence."

That night, as the new arrivals settled in and the fire burned low, they had a welcome of a different sort when a False Face paid a call. The man belonged to an Iroquois medicine society with important ritual and curative powers; he and others in the Company of Faces treated the sick and exorcised evil spirits.[49] Had he now come to do the same for these visitors, fresh from the woods? Slipping in at the far end of the long-house, the intruder announced his approach by throwing back his head and making what Bartram heard as "a hideous noise like the braying of an ass." The naturalist thought this creature's appearance no less hideous. Though entirely "disguised in as odd a dress as *Indian* folly could invent," it was the face that stood out. The wooden mask, painted black, boasted a nose several inches long; beneath was a crooked grin sporting enormous teeth; glittering in the firelight were brass eyes; atop it all dangled "long tresses" of buffalo hair and ropes made from corn husks. Shaking a rattle and pounding a staff on the dirt floor, the "comical fellow" proceeded to "hobble" with "antick postures." "[W]hen he had tired himself, which"—Bartram wrote drily—"was sometime after he had well tired us," the Face disappeared into the night.

Next morning, Shickellamy and Weiser continued the round of talks with Onondagas essential to "put us in the Way" toward a successful council. As delegations from the other Iroquois nations drifted in, the two ambassadors visited and were visited in turn, talking and joking about "the Occurrences of our Journey and General News." They sat as their hosts sang songs of welcome, raised cups of rum in toasts to *Assaryquoa, Onas,* and "the wise Counsellors of the united Nations," and ate their fill from kettles passed around. One day the two listened as Jonnhaty told his story to the Onondaga council; the next they joined eighteen of those councilors at a feast given by the war captain. One morning the two met Canasatego "in the Bushes to have a private Discourse . . . a little way distant from the Town" in order to "beg his Advice how to speak to everything when the Council should be met"; that afternoon they were summoned to meet with Onondaga leaders in the first of several planning sessions.

The full council of the Iroquois League, when it finally convened in the townhouse at midday on July 30, had a stately pace and an impressive majesty. What Weiser called "a deal of Ceremonies" took up the afternoon. Two grave Iroquois speakers strode slowly up and down the passage; a third sat "in the middle," singing "in a graceful tone." Together these men rekindled the council fire. One "rehearsed the beginning of the Union of the five Nations, [and] Praised their Grandfathers' Wisdom in establishing the Union or Alliance, by which they became a formidable Body." Then another rose to perform the At the Woods'

Edge Ceremony for their visitors. In answer, on behalf of those guests an Oneida, wampum string in hand, "repeated all that was said . . . , added more in Praise of their wise Fathers and of the happy union, [and] repeated all the Names of those Ancient Chiefs that establish'd it." At the end of the afternoon, amid the usual *Yo-hahs* of assent, the proceedings adjourned for a meal of corn soup.

The next day it was Weiser's turn. The Pennsylvanian, having enlisted Canasatego to "speak for me [that is, for Virginia] in Open Council," would hand the Onondaga a string or belt and whisper a reminder of each point; Canasatego would take it from there. The Onondaga loved being the center of attention. About sixty then, his height, along with a barrel chest and "brawny limbs," still made him an imposing figure.[50] Speaking as Virginia, he proceeded to remove the hatchet from the Six Nations' head, "to bury all that unhappy accident under the Ground, and to Lay a heavy stone upon it to keep it under for Ever." *Assaryquoa* offers condolences to the grieving kin, he went on, banishing clouds and repairing "the Chain of Friendship." After women brought in another meal—several steaming kettles of hominy and bread—an Iroquois rose to respond for his people, each point confirmed by the customary *Yo-hah.*

Their main business done, at dusk the sixty men broke up for boiled "cakes" and squash, then returned to their lodgings. The following morning the council gathered one last time, to thank *Onas* for his mediation and *Assaryquoa* for this "Kind visit." Then, "according to the Ancient Custom of that Fire," Weiser wrote, "a Song of Friendship and Joy was sung by the Chiefs, after this the Council Fire on their side was put out. I with the same Ceremonee," the colonist concluded, "put out the fire on behalf of Assaryquoa & Onas."

The grand council at Onondaga in the summer of 1743, like the Jack Armstrong affair that would begin that very fall, shows how well Conrad Weiser and Shickellamy could "Concert Measures."[51] With help from Thomas, Canasatego, and other like-minded men, the Pennsylvanian and the Oneida buried an incident that could have buried them—and everyone else on the frontier as well. The protocol and patience, the wampum and tobacco, the geographical range and cultural reach evident here point to a thorough mastery of diplomacy.

Both Pennsylvania and the Iroquois reaped the rewards of that mastery. Penn's province now aspired to rival New York, the Six Nations' oldest and closest friends in British America, in having a hand in Iroquois affairs.[52] Better still, it had Iroquois help in removing Delawares from their homeland. "Cousins," said Canasatego to Delawares at a Philadelphia council in July 1742, Conrad Weiser at his side, "Let this Belt of Wampum serve to Chastize You" for protesting Pennsylvania's encroachment and chicanery. "You ought to be taken by the Hair of the Head and shak'd severely till you recover your Senses and become Sober; you don't know what Ground you stand on, nor what you are doing; Our Brother Onas' Case is very just and plain. . . . [W]e charge You to remove instantly" to Wyoming or Shamokin, the Onondaga speaker went on, at Pennsylvania's prompting, before banishing Delaware protesters from the council chamber.[53]

At the same time, Pennsylvania's favor made the Iroquois so powerful in the Susquehanna country that they now felt free to boss peoples there around. "[T]ie your Tongues," they scolded Delawares. "You believe too many Lies, and are too forward in action," said a wampum belt sent to Shawnees. "You shall not pretend to Revenge our People that have been killed in Virginia." Six Nations spokesmen even boasted that "We are the Chief of all the Indians."[54]

Such bold talk and bolder action, and the alliance that supported them, rested upon Jonnhaty's assumption, the morning after that battle beside the Shenandoah, that *there were different Sorts of white People.* Some, as Thomas McKee was so quick to agree, were friends with Iroquois even if some were not; but, went this line of thought, there was no barrier between Indians and colonists. The notion of a permeable frontier, which allowed Iroquois and Pennsylvanians to make common cause against Shawnees and Delawares, gave negotiators like Weiser and Shickellamy the room they needed to maneuver, to pursue the grand intercultural alliances dreamed up in Onondaga and Philadelphia.

~~~~~

"We Are Indians"
Lingering Doubts

What continued to give those go-betweens trouble was the fact that Jonnhaty and McKee were a minority. Many Pennsylvania colonists were quick to assume the worst of Indians, and to assume it of all Indians alike. And strange as it may seem, those frontier farmers packing their bags or checking their muskets had kindred spirits in the Shawnees at Great Island, who insisted that all "white People" were the same.

But there, for most people, kinship ended, in the shared belief in a barrier between Indian and colonist. Indeed, for all their squabbles and differences, the various native peoples in touch with Penn's province increasingly found themselves in agreement on their colonial neighbors. Shawnees—watching their lands beside the Susquehanna and Delaware become Pennsylvania, leading that western exodus, declining Philadelphia's repeated invitations to return—might have been the most vocal in their objections.[55] European colonists are "like ye Doves," an elderly Shawnee man named Neshanockeow scoffed in 1745, "where one Comes & sits a whole Flock fly after him." John Sergeant, a missionary visiting them on the Susquehanna earlier that year, met stiff resistance. Many walked out on him; those who stayed "gave no serious attention at all to what I said. When I had done, they presently fell to talking, and reproaching Christianity, and shew'd an utter aversion to it."[56]

Yet despite Pennsylvania's attempt to dismiss Shawnees as "ye most mischievious of all our Indians," they were not the only ones embittered.[57] Delawares knew those flocks better than Neshanockeow did, for they bore the brunt of Pennsylvania's population increase—from 20,000 at William Penn's departure in 1701 to 100,000 by 1740—and the colony's determination to acquire more territory.[58] Sassoonan's unhappiness in 1728 at the loss of Tulpehocken was nothing compared to resentment over the so-called "Walking Purchase" of 1737, when William Penn's children Thomas and John grabbed a vast stretch of the Delaware Valley. Brandishing a copy of a "lost" 1686 land sale agreement, the proprietors had gotten Delawares to go along with the idea of relinquishing as much land as a man could walk in a day and a half, then—ignoring protests by Delaware observers—sent seasoned runners down a prepared trail to cover as much ground in that span as they could. And Delawares soon discovered that even this addition was not enough. Thomas Penn "keeps begging & plagueing us to Give Him some Land . . . ," they complained in 1740; "he Wearies us Out of Our Lives."[59]

Nor were Shawnees the only Indians giving missionaries a bad time.

"[T]hese poor heathens are extremely attached to the customs, traditions, and fabulous notions of their fathers," a discouraged David Brainerd wrote after touring the Susquehanna Valley in the fall of 1744. At one town en route "two or three . . . suspected that I had some ill design upon them, and urged that the white people had abused them and taken their lands from them, and therefore they had no reason to think that they were now concerned for their happiness." The others that day were friendlier, but, Brainerd admitted on his return, for the most part resistance in Indian country was heavy. They say " 'twas not the same God made them who made the white people, but another who commanded them to live by hunting, etc., and not conform to the customs of the white people."[60]

Even Pennsylvania's new friends the Six Nations—most of them still far removed from colonial farmers and land speculators—were wary. Remember that Shickellamy—a man who devoted his life to getting along with Europeans, a man who at Onondaga that summer of 1743 had personified Penn's province—joined the chorus of objections to David Brainerd, telling the missionary that "We are Indians, and don't wish to be transformed into white men." And Canasatego—*Assaryquoa* that August day at Onondaga in 1743—remarked, the year before, "our different Way of living from the White People."[61]

Other Iroquois also sounded like Shawnees or Delawares, complaining that colonists came "like Flocks of Birds" to settle Indian lands, even wondering whether the Winters had really been executed. "We have often heard of your hanging up those two persons," said a skeptical Canasatego at that Philadelphia council in July 1742, "but as none of Our Indians saw the Men Dye, many believe they were not hanged but transported to some other Colony." At Lancaster two years later, a Cayuga named Gachadow issued a more far-reaching indictment of colonists. "The World at the first was made on the other side of the Great water different from what it is on this side," Gachadow remarked, "as may be known from the different Colour of Our Skin and of Our Flesh. . . . You have your Laws and Customs and so have we."[62]

Such sensibilities penetrated everyday life on the frontier. Consider, for example, the sleeping arrangements at that Onondaga council house in July 1743. Weiser was Virginia, his friend and traveling companion Shickellamy, Pennsylvania; the others—Tachnechdorus, Bartram, Evans—were merely tagging along. Yet rather than place *Onas*

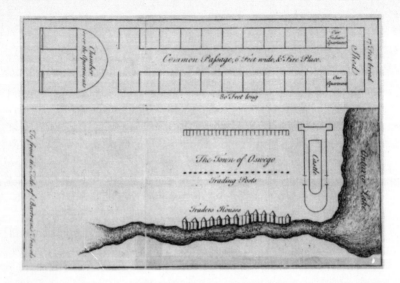

Figure 9. Sketch of the Town of Oswego and an Iroquois Longhouse, by John Bartram, shows the sleeping arrangements at Onondaga in the summer of 1743.

From John Bartram, *Observations on the Inhabitants, Climate, Soil, Rivers, Productions, Animals, and other Matters Worthy of Notice. Made by John Bartram, In his Travels form Pensilvania to Onondago, Oswego and the Lake Ontario, in Canada* . . . (London, 1751), frontispiece. Courtesy of the Library Company of Philadelphia.

with *Assaryquoa,* their aides opposite, the travelers' hosts divided the party differently, placing *Our Apartment* (as Bartram labeled it) opposite *Our Indians Apartment* (Figure 9). No one thought this worth comment; the very silence speaks of the gulf that left drowsy Indians on one side of a fire, weary colonists on the other.

CHAPTER V

"A Good Correspondance":
Conversations

The killings along the Shenandoah in 1742, like Jack Armstrong's death beside the Juniata soon thereafter, helped make Shickellamy and Conrad Weiser famous. But the real foundation of their partnership, and of the peace that their partnership nurtured, was a less spectacular routine of visits to one another. At Weiser's Tulpehocken home, at Shickellamy's Shamokin lodge, and at farmhouses, hunting cabins, and mills in between, the Oneida and the German met to smoke a pipe and "talke a great deal." Matters large and small came up, from a mysterious black wampum belt making the rounds to a Delaware's stolen peltry, from battles over the mountains to the clash of armies and empires beyond the seas. One winter night in 1746, when the two "sat down to discourse" by the headman's fire, was typical: over dinner the Iroquois asked "what news accured among the white people"; the Pennsylvanian, answering, went on and "asked what news accured among the Indians."[1]

Such quiet chats, through many seasons and many years, were the essence of what everyone from Weiser to Shawnee headmen to William Penn himself called "a Kind Correspondents" or "a Good Correspondance" between peoples.[2] To be sure, not every encounter between colonist and Indian was really "Correspondance." Pennsylvania traders who headed out in search of customers or Indians who trooped into a colonial settlement to peddle their wares; Moravians setting up a model farm in Indian country or coaxing natives to live in a model town on Bethlehem's outskirts; a colonial farmer who fed a passing war party or let an Indian family camp in his field—these people needed no go-between to write the script and direct the actors.

But those contacts did require the congenial climate that a negotiator helped sustain. As the calamities in the late 1720s and early 1740s attest, that climate was prone to sudden squalls. Rumors of war put colonists or Indians to flight. Missionaries, too, carefully scouted Shamokin, Onondaga, and Philadelphia for signs of trouble before sending the Lord's servants to live among natives. And colonial settlers only appreciated how much their lives had depended on what Iroquois called "frequent Opportunities of conferring and discoursing with their Brethren" when after 1754, conversation having stopped, peace disappeared beneath a torrent of blood and fire.[3]

The conversations that kept trouble at bay for so long were not as formal as a treaty conference, but they were indeed formal. The man doing the talking was a "Public Person" conducting "publick Negotiations"; message in hand, he was to "travel that Road between us and you, . . . [in order to] speak our Minds & your Minds to each other truly & freely."[4] Part of the assignment was, as native metaphor had it, to "clear . . . every Grub, Stump & Log" in the road between peoples, "that it may be straight, smooth & free for us and you."[5] Peace, like a road, required constant upkeep. Just as thoroughfares could succumb to fallen trees, overgrown bushes, and tall grass, so friendship was prey to the chaos and darkness that accompanied all human endeavors. Calling the work road maintenance may seem to belittle it; but what clearing metaphorical trails lacked in glamour it more than made up for in importance.

Keeping paths open was easier said than done. That evening at Shickellamy's house in 1746 was in fact made possible by a remarkable series of negotiations that got people past their linguistic and cultural differences. Like travel, talk was difficult, dangerous, thankless—and largely forgotten. But eavesdropping on the murmur of conversation, like following go-betweens into the woods, can offer a new angle of vision on the frontier experience, can reinforce the combination of concord and discord that recruitment and travel uncovered. On the one hand, negotiators, prodded by a general consensus on the need for regular contact, developed an eclectic yet powerful set of tools—pieces of paper and strings of wampum, along with linguistic dexterity and a knack for improvising—that got messages across. On the other hand, however, those beads and those pages also pick up, in the lower registers, a deepening unease and distrust. By midcentury, wampum and writing, made marvelously complementary in go-betweens' hands, became increasingly contentious as it appeared that people did not always speak (or write) "truly and freely." While negotiators became more conversant with channels of communication, the woods' static became more pronounced until, after 1750, frontier war ended Penn's "Kind Correspondence."

≈≈≈≈

"A Good Deal of News Going Backwards and Forwards"
Topics of Conversation

Indians and colonists always found plenty to talk about. The hottest topics, of course, were Sawantaeny, Armstrong, and other casualties of frontier friction. As at Conestoga in the 1710s, clashes were common wherever and whenever Pennsylvanians became the natives' neighbors. Indians killed a colonist's hogs, beat him up, stole his horse. Pennsylvanians assaulted an Indian woman, took apples from an Indian orchard, barged onto Indian land. Provincial fur traders toted too much rum to Indian towns; natives broke into a trader's storehouse and made off with some of that rum.[6] When a Delaware smashed a colonist's windows, the victim went after him "with a piece of Iron." Retaliating was proper, Indian leaders allowed, but "the white Man shou'd have beat him with his Arm only, it was too much to strike him with Iron."[7]

Although a mediator was often called upon to work out such moral calculations, he devoted most of his time to more routine matters. Distant Indian nations dispatched messengers to Penn's Woods in order to strike up a conversation. Other tribes, friends already, sent emissaries to arrange a treaty—or, sometimes, to postpone one, in which case an envoy would visit Philadelphia to apologize and explain, "lest the Delay should be misinterpreted or taken ill."[8] From that city, meanwhile, officials launched messages into Indian country "to establish & improve an amicable Correspondence." They reaffirmed ties to nearby groups. They kept in touch with Shawnee and Delaware emigrants to Ohio, assuring them that Penn's people still considered them friends, "tho' att Such a far Distance." They put out feelers—first north into Iroquoia, later toward the Great Lakes—to make new friends.[9]

The bulk of a negotiator's conversation was the swapping of information that Weiser and Shickellamy raised to an art form. When Teedyuscung observed in 1758 that "[t]here is a Good Deal of News going backwards and forwards," he could have been talking of 1738 or 1718 as well. Ever since William Penn's day, Pennsylvanians and their Indian neighbors had pledged to "be as . . . one Eye & Ear; . . . what the one saw the other should see, and what the one heard the other should hear."[10] When one of the Penns died or a new governor arrived, when the colony signed a treaty with other native nations or sent surveyors across the Susquehanna River, provincial officials dispatched someone to broadcast the news. Similarly, when natives learned of defections to the French or Iroquois plans to visit Delawares, they let Philadelphia know.[11]

Part of a negotiator's job was not just to carry those messages but also to gather information. Natives would show up "to hear what was doing," and a colonist in Indian country "would be glad to hear what News was passing among their several Tribes."[12] Some go-betweens had what amounted to standing orders to keep eyes and ears open. In 1694 the province, at once valuing and mistrusting Jacques Le Tort, ordered the French trader to "acquaint the governmt with all matters hee can hear of or observe concerning the Natives & the enemies of the countrie." A generation later, during the dark days of 1728, another nervous colonial official reminded Madame Montour of her pledge "to be industrious in procuring all the certain Intelligence she can, of all affairs transacted amongst the Indians that relate to ye Peace of this Province, & transmitt an acct of them to me."[13] Collecting and spreading news acquired the force of habit.

"No Confidence Can Be Placed Any Where" Interference

Pack up and head out, listen in and report back—the art of intercultural converse sounds simple, but it was in fact a dauntingly complex transaction. The first and most basic obstacle was language; a simple hello, not to mention a chat, required people to remove the language barrier. With Indians insisting that formal talks be in their tongue, that

chore usually fell to colonists.[14] Natives believed that having an interpreter gave them "more dignity," one Pennsylvanian explained, just as
use of "proper grammatical language" lent "their words . . . greater
weight and effect . . . , while some are afraid of committing mistakes
when speaking in an idiom not their own." Capturing and conveying an
Indian talk's finer points demanded great skill. "Particularly when they
have a joke to pass, a hint to give, or a shrewd remark to make, they
wish it to have all the advantages of a good translation, and that their wit
may not be spoiled by a foreign accent, improper expression, or awk-
ward delivery."[15]

The trick was finding a good translator, for Indian languages were
notoriously hard to learn.[16] A student of Iroquois discovered "that they
have various modes of speech and phrases peculiar to each age and
sex"—a hungry man announced his hunger with one word, a hungry
child with another—"which they strictly observe." Similarly, Delaware
had ten terms for *bear,* depending on the animal's age and sex, and *to
eat* varied according to whether the food required chewing. Those trying to figure out such nuances had to cope with the fact that some native speakers habitually dropped syllables, much depended on the right
accent, and Indians sometimes were reluctant teachers. To acquire what
one native called "an Indian *ear*" was a long and difficult apprentice-
ship.[17]

Colonists developing that ear had to contend with a discourse rid-
dled with "Perticular Iddoms or Diction" that "were very Peculiar,"
patterns of speech "adorned with noble images, strong metaphors,
and . . . allegory." In this highly figurative world of words *a day* could
mean *a year.* Kinfolk (brother and sister, father and uncle), anatomical
features (eyes and ears, mouths and hearts), landscape (paths and
roads, trees and stumps), and the heavens (sunshine and clouds, darkness and light) had expansive metaphorical meanings that left novices
"at a loss."[18]

The sense of being lost got worse if the language gap required more
than one translator. Even toward the end of the colonial era, makeshift
arrangements could be found. An August 1761 meeting in Philadelphia
heard Seneca George speak Seneca to Kanak't (Last Night), a Conoy,
who converted the words to Delaware so that Isaac Stille could, finally,
bear them across to waiting colonists. "When we met at Easton [earlier
this month]," Seneca George said at that talk in the provincial capital,

"we did not fully understand one another, we are therefore come here now, that we may understand each other more clearly." With Kanak't and Stille at his side, poised to haul his words over two linguistic spans, the Seneca's confidence seems misplaced.[19]

It did not help that Indians were known for obfuscation. Raised in a culture that discouraged open confrontation—"[a] person might be among them 30 years and even longer," wrote Conrad Weiser, "and not once see two sober Indians dispute or quarrel; when one of them has a deadly hatred to another, they endeavor to smother their anger"— natives often resorted to indirection to avoid unpleasantness.[20] They can "express themselves with great clearness and precision" when they want to, one observer noted, but they were also masters of the "art of dissembling." "If they intend to speak in an obscure manner, they can speak so cleverly and with so much circumstance that even Indians must puzzle out the true sense of their allusions."[21]

Communication problems were compounded by the rumors that flourished in the frontier's volatile atmosphere. Colonists picked up "various and Contradictory" stories from Indian country; natives might get good news from Penn's people, then bad news, then good once again.[22] The French, Pennsylvanians heard, are massing on the frontier. No, Indians had been told, they are sailing up the Delaware. The Iroquois are about to sweep down on the province and its native friends. Virginia is poised to invade the Susquehanna Valley.[23] Unnamed war parties are about to strike. Pennsylvania is plotting "to cutt off the Indians" by sending them poison blankets or luring them to Philadelphia in order to enslave them.[24] Rumors ran rampant, keeping everyone on edge.

The best (or worst) stories had a chilling specificity. Those French fur traders send mysterious letters, wrapped in blue linen, to "strange Indians." A Conestoga man being dragged off by other strangers yells to his wife that everyone should "be upon their Guard." A wampum belt, on its face a red tomahawk, is going from one village to the next.[25] Indians, just back to Conestoga from a trip southward, have brought in "several p[ar]ts of women's attire, viz: a Petticoat, White silk hood, Lace, &c."; another party has returned with scalps of a suspiciously light hue.[26]

"Ugly talk" like this did "a World of Mischief." Natives are "easily alarmed . . . by plausible storys," colonists fretted; ultimately it mattered little whether a tale were true, for "Indian Fears" about an impending conflict can "have as bad consequences as if they were in actual War." Colonists, too, felt "the Effect of fear," as the Winter brothers, or those families that rumors of war drove off the farm in 1743, could attest.[27]

So pernicious were "flying reports" that everyone tried to weaken the power of news traveling "under the Ground." William Penn's 1701 treaty with Susquehanna Indians sought to counter "evil minded persons and sowers of sedition" who went around spreading "Unkind or disadvantageous reports." Thereafter, colonists and natives repeatedly urged one another to ignore "Idle Tales or Lies" and the "Chirping" of the "bad Birds" perched "in almost every Bush."[28]

But which tales were idle? Which birds sang false? Jack Armstrong's killing was at first but a whisper, after all, and Sawantaeny's fate reached Philadelphia as "an imperfect relation." How to distinguish them from a tale about Indians stockpiling snowshoes for a winter raid on Penn's province? ("Shickellamy laughed at that" one.) From the story about torchbearing Indians creeping toward a farmstead on a nighttime raid? (The lights turned out to be fireflies.)[29] This was the hard part. "[N]o confidence can be placed any where," sighed Richard Peters as he sorted through conflicting reports from the interior; "the Indians tell so many Stories & the Traders are so sens[e]less & credulous." At a Susquehanna Indian town in 1760, an exasperated Christian Frederick Post heard so many wild tales that he finally stopped bothering to record them in his journal, "as the Indians have their own peculiar Policy in relating one Thing at the same Time thinking & acting quite the reverse."[30]

Indians were not the only ones given to spinning yarns. As Canasatego and other Iroquois came through Pennsylvania en route to Philadelphia one summer, "We enquir'd who" had murdered the Onondaga's nephew. But colonists, Canasatego went on, "told so many odd and different Stories that the People who gave the Accounts seem'd to us Like Drunken Men, and we could not tell what to believe. Indians, it is true, are apt sometimes to speak untruths," Canasatego admitted, "but white People . . . can utter falsehood fully as readily as Indians." The only way to cope with rumor and gossip was to send someone out (or call someone in) to "sift" stories, "to enquire and find out the Truth of the matter, and of every other thing that passes." Enter the go-between, "our true Corespondent."[31]

"Right Understanding of One Another"
Getting Through

"In Form"
The Basics of Conversational Etiquette

Those trying to converse amid rumor mongers and frontier frictions had powerful assistance, for an accepted code governed correct communication between peoples. Indians and colonists alike expected to be spoken to "in form," in a "regular manner." If protocol were ignored, Indians would say that "heretofore they had only heard from the English as a Noise in the Woods unintelligible"—and might even insist that they had heard nothing at all. Colonists, too, dismissed messages improperly sent as "only a transient discourse."[32]

"[R]ight understanding of one Another" meant not only finding "some suitable Person in whom we can place a Confidence" but also conforming to Indian custom. This, in turn, meant striking a passive pose that left the locals to invite you here and there, telling you where to wait and when to leave. On approaching his destination the wise messenger went along with the custom of firing guns in salute, and he learned to wait as a delegation of important men came out to greet him, to smoke a friendly pipe with him, and to escort him into town amid more gunfire. Similarly, a Delaware or Iroquois emissary approaching a colonial city was often "received . . . according to the Forms in use with Indians."[33]

Once a traveler was in the village, the Condolence began. Even if one side had already condoled the other immediately on hearing about the death of an important person—each time Shickellamy lost a son, Pennsylvania sent a gift to dry his tears, and in the spring of 1749 Weiser headed to Shamokin yet again, this time to console the Oneida's children at the death of their father—no message got through until hearts were healed "according to old Custom."[34] Indians insisted that "they cou'd not see the Road [to Philadelphia] nor hear what the Governor . . . had to say to them till that Ceremony had been done."[35] With tears dried and broken hearts mended, conversation could commence.

To pursue those talks, go-betweens surmounted the language barrier. It helped that, whatever the native tongue used in formal discourse, more and more Indians picked up some English—enough, at least, that they might serve as a check on a translator's accuracy. Watch what you say around the Iroquois here, a negotiator would warn a colonist visiting an Indian camp during a treaty; "most of them understand English."[36] English speakers were common in the Ohio country, and even Shickellamy knew some English. "[L]ye still *John,*" the Oneida "called out" to John Bartram when that False Face paid them a call in Onondaga. "I never heard him speak so much plain *English* before," the astonished naturalist remarked.[37] Neither did anyone else, apparently; no other colonist so much as mentioned the Oneida's knowing English. But Bartram was not the only colonist surprised when familiar words came from foreign mouths. "[T]hey mostly all Spake English," a Pennsylvanian said of Delaware warriors who captured him in 1758, and "one spoke as good English as I can."[38]

Colonial mediators, meanwhile, were not only more fluent in the Indian languages, they also had a surer grasp of native metaphor. So comfortable was one woodsman that, filling Pennsylvania officials in on Shawnee politics, he lapsed into Indian phrasing: "they have had a Tast of the Friench," he wrote, "and finde them Sweet in the Mouth and bitter in the Heart." Having heard this sort of talk for so long, those officials had come to know "the meaning of these Indian Expressions" well enough that translators bothered less with the usual parenthetical explanation of, say, "a clear & open road . . . (by this meaning a friendly communication)."[39] Thus Indians and colonists, driven by a powerful urge to communicate, enrolled in a vast, diffuse, and unnoticed educational experiment. But learning to let Indians lead and picking up the jargon was only the first course in the curriculum of the woods.

"Without Wampum Nothing Is to Be Done"
The Language of Beads

Tradition has it that Hiawatha, when he helped found the Great League by convincing the Iroquois nations to unite, was the first to place shell beads on a string.[40] Ever since that distant day, these seashells—harvested on the beaches of Long Island Sound, then drilled to make beads before being placed on strings or woven into belts—had great spiritual power in Indian America. Offered to propitiate the dead and other beings, wampum linked the visible and invisible worlds; passed to the living to patch up differences or ease the minds of the bereaved, it mended the torn social fabric of a town or clan; arranged in patterns and kept to recall formal conversations, it connected past to present.[41]

Use of wampum reached beyond clan or town to embrace strangers; it became a filament connecting disparate peoples across Indian country. Though Hiawatha's Iroquois heirs might claim pride of invention, many native groups considered shells "potent medicine."[42] The Shawnees' insistence on speaking (and being spoken to) with six strings of wampum is divinely ordained, their headmen once informed Pennsylvania; "when God spoke first to us . . . he gave six things [strings] and told us we must believe what he said" (Figure 10). Ohio Indian leaders, though "new beginners" in sending "Messengers to Indian Towns & Nations," already knew enough about diplomacy "to get Wampum to do the Business."[43] So vital was wampum as a medium of communication that no frontier negotiator could hope to succeed unless he knew the language of beads.

In diplomacy, wampum worked its magic in various ways. Indian messengers would say that it served to "confirm" or "enforce" their words, it guaranteed that "we speak truth" and ensured that a speech would "have Credit with you," would "have its full Effect on" the listener's "Mind."[44] Natives might even have thought strings and belts more powerful still, so powerful that the shells themselves held the message. Thus an Iroquois or Delaware council spoke words directly into a string or belt as we would into a tape recorder; then a messenger, reaching his destination, merely turned the beads on and became their mouthpiece. So animated, a belt took on a mind and life of its own. The wampum, Indian envoys might say, "has been leading us by the arm." One Iroquois go-between even talked of how "this day a Belt of Wampum (black) came to Shamokin from Oneida from the Six Nations," as if it had floated down the Susquehanna on its own.[45]

The delicate beads, then, carried heavy freight in formal conversation. "Without Wampum," one colonist observed, "Nothing is to be done Amongst the Indians."[46] The number of beads needed to conduct diplomacy was staggering. Some messengers had just a string or two in a pocket or pouch, but others crammed a bag or "casket" with ten, twenty, even thirty or more belts, each bearing part of a talk, each containing anywhere from several hundred to ten thousand beads that, woven into a belt, might be a foot wide and six feet long.[47] "It is amazing to think what a Quantity of Wampum this Journey will take in

Strings & Belts," Richard Peters grumbled as he prepared to dispatch messengers into the Indian countries. Demand at midcentury was so great that Philadelphia merchants asked contacts in New York City for 100,000 beads, and a "wampum maker"—a Delaware or Philadelphia woman, James Sympson in New York, or one of the Montour women on the Pennsylvania frontier—was kept busy.[48]

Wampum's value as a communications medium stemmed in part from its versatility. Just as it had many uses within a town, so between peoples one string might mark a messenger's status while another sanctioned part of a speech and—carefully stored in a "Counsel Bagg," then regularly pulled out for rehearsal of its message—kept words alive far into the future.[49] Better still, wampum could take many forms. A large belt or long string meant something important. White shells denoted peace, "black" (actually purple) ones war, though words of war also came in as scalps tied to a white belt, red paint splashed across it, or a hatchet woven into its face.[50]

Other patterns, their message less self-evident, nonetheless helped wampum be read and reread (Figures 11–12). Friendship might appear as people holding hands or as a row of dark beads running down a white belt to connect nations, themselves depicted as squares or diamonds, hands or human figures.[51] Some belts told a more specific tale. One, sent from Iroquoia to Susquehanna Indians in 1722 to urge that they dump rather than drink rum, bore a small circle for the keg and a hatchet denoting its destruction. Senecas wove one that had six human figures, five of them branded with two hearts, to say that Senecas alone, with but one heart, were true to the English. A belt Teedyuscung spoke on in 1756 was equally elaborate: an armed man posted at each end, with lines leading to an empty square in the middle, told of natives' determination to keep their country free of both British and French armies pressing upon it.[52]

However clear the message, making belts talk was an art. Pulling them out, a messenger would set them "in order on the Table," then pick up each one in turn and hold it while speaking its words. Wampum virtuosos had a certain flair. During the war an Onondaga messenger named Ogaghradarisha, to mark how far up the Susquehanna his people wanted Pennsylvania to build a fort, left a wampum belt folded in half to designate the road to Shamokin; then, at the right moment, he opened it full length to stretch, metaphorically, all the way upriver past Wyoming. Sometimes an Indian made a point of *"turning . . .* the

Figure 10. Wampum Strings.
Go-betweens used such strings as credentials
or for less important parts of their messages.
Courtesy of the University of Pennsylvania
Museum (negative #S4-142742).

Figure 11. The Penn or Great Treaty Wampum Belt.
Given to the Historical Society of Pennsylvania by a descendant
of William Penn, this belt is said to represent the friendship the
Founder forged with the Delaware Indians at the legendary
treaty of Shackamaxon in 1682 or 1683. Courtesy of the
Historical Society of Pennsylvania.

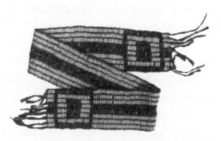

Figure 12. "Path" Wampum Belt.
Iroquois belt of unknown date, perhaps depicting
friendship (the long double row of beads)
between peoples (the squares at each end).
Courtesy of the University of Pennsylvania
Museum (negative #NC35-12972).

belt" when halfway through his talk, by which, one impressed colonist remarked, "it may be as well known . . . how far the speaker has advanced in his speech, as with us on taking a glance at the pages of a book or pamphlet while reading." Having finished, a messenger would then return the belt or string to the table, tie it to a stick, drape it over a pole laid across the rafters of a longhouse, or pass it to his listeners.[53]

If an envoy bearing an unpopular message tried to hand over the belt, his hostile audience kept it "talking" in equally dramatic fashion. Indians might refuse to touch a belt if they opposed its words. When one party of "war messengers" trying to recruit more men draped a belt over the shoulder or thigh of a headman, the recipient, "after shaking it off without touching it with his hands, . . . with a stick, threw it after them, as if he threw a snake or a toad out of his way." Peace belts might get the same cold treatment, as natives using tobacco pipes or sticks "throwed them on one side."[54]

Figures of speech so rich in expressive possibility and so thoroughly embedded in native life were bound to sweep colonists into their embrace. Pennsylvania was born too late for the frenzied days when wampum was money in New England and New Netherland, but Indian use of belts and strings in early conversations with the English along the Delaware quickly taught the newcomers its importance. The colony soon started dispatching messengers with the beads as a "Credential," and in 1700 William Penn himself was handing wampum to visiting Iroquois "in token of amitie & friendship wt ym."[55]

So thoroughly steeped in wampum culture did provincial leaders become that when Satcheecho returned in August 1722 from his second trip to Onondaga on the Sawantaeny business, Governor William Keith pronounced himself "surprised to see you bring no Credentials with you," and later returned to his disappointment that the Cayuga emissary had "brought no Belt or any other Token to confirm" the Iroquois reply. Thereafter, provincial officials felt confident enough to set Indians straight on wampum protocol. Some of these native visitors "were so hard put to it for an Excuse to come down" for a council, sneered Richard Peters in 1761, "that they laid before the Governor a Belt given for the Confirmation of ye peace three years ago as [if it were] a Belt given to invite them to a Treaty. In this," Peters concluded smugly, "they were set right."[56]

Colonists on the frontier, too, knew the spell wampum cast. Pennsylvania troops raiding an Indian village in 1756 systematically de-

stroyed houses and burned crops, but they knew enough to bring the
town's "Council Belts" back to Philadelphia. Whether the looters took
the wampum because of its spiritual and historical significance to
Indians—knowing its loss would be a blow to native morale—or because it would fetch a high price in a capital always needing more shells,
they appreciated beads' importance.[57]

By the close of the colonial era, Pennsylvanians had grown so attached to the new medium that they sent wampum belts to Iroquoia explaining the Stamp Act crisis. From this confidence came a desire to
experiment with form; some Pennsylvania belts bore decidedly non-
native designs as colonists added touches of their own. Instead of
hands or diamonds, belts might display the Penn family crest or a
provincial fort. Instead of paths or hearts, they sported dates or initials
immortalizing everyone from King George *(G.R.)* and Teedyuscung
(D.K., for Delaware King) to a provincial army officer *(W.C.,* for
William Clapham).[58]

Whatever their design and their message, shells were a go-between's
stock in trade. He advised wampum makers on the size, color, and pattern of belts, kept beads on hand just in case, and, before setting out
with a message, packed hundreds, even thousands, of the shells among
the "nessecarys . . . to Facilitate the Success of his Journey." To run
short or run out was to court disaster. Weiser fretted that one emissary
bound for the Indian countries "was without wampum for accidents,"
and in February 1760 Teedyuscung, preparing for another trip, complained "that he has not got Wampum enough" to carry Pennsylvania's
words of peace.[59]

Making their way through the Susquehanna Valley with Teedyuscung
and those words of peace that June, Christian Frederick Post, John
Hays, Isaac Stille, and Moses Tatamy met just the misfortune Weiser had
dreaded and the Delaware leader had predicted: they ran low on beads.
To Post's relief, local Indians, testifying to their desire for an end to war,
"Laid Down A Blanket and Preaclemed A Publick colection[,] and for
Joy the Wemen and Girels and children throd in wampom till There
Wase 14 fathem for to helpe For strings on our Jorney." That women
and children tossed beads onto the blanket suggests how each finished
string or belt represented large segments of a community, including not
just the messenger delivering it or the council sending it but also those
who obtained and strung the shells. For Post and the rest that day, it
meant the chance to resume "our old Buisness of Belt makeing," which

had already occupied much of their time during three days of bad weather on the road from Philadelphia.[60]

"A Letter . . . Is Considered a Very Important Thing"
The Power of Pen and Paper

While the others in that 1760 embassy continued "to Make Ready Belts and Strings and Speeches," Post sat down to write out those speeches "in a Large Hand that Isaac Still might Read them" at Indian councils farther west. A few days later, as the emissaries went on with their preparations for a push deeper into Indian country, the Nanticoke headman of a nearby village sent them "a Letter and Belt and string and Very Agreeable Speeches." At the time, no one thought either Post's scribbling or that Nanticoke message remarkable, for by then envoys routinely had paper in one pocket and wampum—tagged and numbered to correspond to particular written speeches—in the other.[61] While Pennsylvanians learned beadwork, they taught natives how writing, too, encouraged conversation.

Some Indians refused to go along, sending messages on wampum and insisting that "This is my Letter, Being I don't understand writing." But many embraced the new way of talking.[62] Like colonists learning about wampum, natives proved quick studies, and in Lasse Cocke's day Indian messengers joined their colonial counterparts to negotiate the borderlands with both letters and strings.[63] In 1715, Sassoonan, trying to dam the river of rum drowning his people, asked the governor for written permission to "stave all the rum that came amongst them." When that campaign failed and Shickellamy launched another Susquehanna temperance crusade, he made sure, before confronting provincial liquor dealers, to bring along a copy of the Pennsylvania law against selling alcohol to Indians.[64] Together the Oneida and the Delaware went after other colonial miscreants with writing, in 1733 sending a letter to John Harris that warned him off Indian land.[65] Similarly, warriors and ambassadors traveling through Pennsylvania, like Jonnhaty's band in 1742, made a point of getting passports from local magistrates in order to head off trouble with colonial settlers.

Jonnhaty and the rest demanded a document not just because it carried weight among colonists; in Indian country, too, the black scratches on paper took on an aura of authority. "A letter," wrote David Zeisberger, "especially if it is sealed, is considered a very important thing" among Indians; one that arrived in Onondaga generated such excitement that "[t]he whole town was full of it," and on hearing it read aloud natives "Suck'd in every paragraph." With writing acquiring talismanic power, Indian raiders who during the war lugged off French, German, and English Bibles from frontier settlements might have acted on impulses akin to their Pennsylvania counterparts who stole a town's council wampum: keenly aware of the objects' potency, they sought to capture it for themselves.[66]

Warriors hauling Bibles out of a burning farmhouse, townsfolk enraptured by a letter—these suggest the respect Indians had for the written word. Some scholars, reading that respect as awe, have posited an unbridgeable gulf between colonial and Indian media.[67] Turning page upon page of merchants' account books, hefting the stacks of correspondence and council minutes European colonists bequeathed us, one can glimpse a vast chasm between a European world built on writing and a native American universe confined to word of mouth. But the frontier was not so simple. Its means of expression had no obvious divide between literate and oral, but rather a spectrum—anchored at one end by thoroughgoing mastery of a curriculum of books and paper, at the other by immersion in oral culture—with negotiators, like almost everyone else, arrayed at various points between.[68]

The complexity and the confusion about where people stood arises not just because some Indian mediators like Isaac Stille could read and write while some colonists could not, but because of the frontier's eclectic jumble of skills and media. Many literate Pennsylvania go-betweens were far from accomplished authors; indeed, in penmanship, grammar, and spelling, some of their letters resemble the few surviving Indian writings. At the bottom of one colonist's report from Indian territory in 1738, a different hand advised: "This being wrote in the Woods by some Indian [i.e., colonial] trader only, we must be content with the sense of it." The arrogance here is unmistakable, but so is the frustration. It is hard not to sympathize with colonial officials forced to puzzle out the meaning in letters addressed "To the farist his Magesteis Commanden Offeverses," or doggedly deciphering a messenger's journal, written "So gud as I coud du in dies critical teim" when he "hed no fridom to reid as I Pliest I onley most stiell mey teym bey neyt it med hef bin rod a gud del mor."[69]

Doubtless most readers were delighted that such informants refrained from adding "a gud del mor." The people penning such fractured prose were in some ways closer to most Indians than to most colonists in their preferred forms of expression. While some fur traders kept meticulous records of every skin bought and every gun sold, others, as steeped in oral culture as their native customers, relied on memory. Around 1800 Alexander Lowry, an old Susquehanna trader summoned to court for a long overdue debt to a merchant, showed up at the hearing with neither papers nor account book. The authorities were about to call off the proceedings until he could produce the necessary documents; but then Lowry recited full "details of the payment of money, or other transactions, between the parties, and named the Spring or log where they occurred, in the western wilderness, through a period of forty years, all of which" the astonished creditor, consulting his ledger, pronounced correct. One of Lowry's contemporaries in the trade, John Hart, surprised another audience by reading a hatchet native callers had left for him, along with a sketch depicting a sunrise, the moon, and a man with a belt of scalps around his middle and seven lines above his head. Not only did Hart get the picture, he left a reply by drawing a heart shape and a pipe.[70]

Hart and other woodsmen who had learned to speak in pictures would have scoffed at the notion that natives could neither read nor write. Indian country was littered with evidence to the contrary. Beside the path stood those "archives," those "Indian histories" where natives chronicled their adventures taking deer and scalps, while at home in the village a "Jurnal" recounting a man's exploits sat on his bed (Figure 13). All of these depictions are "as intelligible to them," one colonist admitted, "as a written account is to us."[71]

For an Indian handy with picture-writing, pen and ink in some ways was no radical departure. Men who once had issued threats by "Marcking on a Board Certain Indian figures" began to put, in "a little Book," "the Picture and Marks of an Indian Warriour with his Gun and Spear."[72] Other natives cushioned the shock of the new by directing it into customary channels, drawing parallels between marks made on paper and figures made from shells (Figures 14–16). Like wampum, paper brought an author into direct contact with his audience, however many miles actually separated them. "[W]e look on" the belts you sent "as if we had seen your Kings in Person," Cherokees assured the Six Nations in 1758, just as in a letter Indians would say that "We now Speak to you, and we speak as in your presence, even face to face."[73]

Like belts and strings, too, papers went into a council bag for safekeeping. At first natives thought the object itself more important than

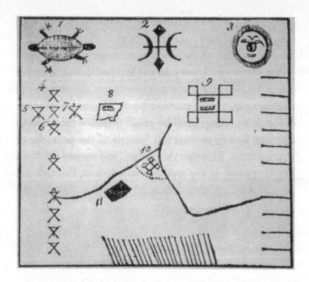

Figure 13. Warmarks by a Delaware, Wingimund, c. 1760s.

As read by another Delaware warrior and a colonial fur trader,
Wingimund's sketch told "the history of his whole warfare. The rude
resemblance of a Turtle on the left hand is the emblem by which his
Tribe or Nation is known. The Cross and the two Halfmoons are the
Characters by which he is personally distinguished among his nation.
That figure on the right hand is the Sun. Those strokes under it signify
the number of men he had with him when he made this mark, their
leaning to the left signifies that they have their backs towards the Sun
and are bound to the Northward. Those marks on the Lefthand under
the Turtle signify the number of scalps and prisoners he has taken and
of what sex. Those marked thus X are scalps, those $\hat{X}$ men prisoners
and those marked thus $\hat{X}$ women prisoners. The rough sketches of
Forts in the middle are what he has helped to attack," including Fort
Pitt and Detroit. *The Journal of Nicholas Cresswell, 1774–1777* (London,
1925), 110–111. Courtesy of the Newberry Library, Chicago.

the scratches on its surface, for some Indians kept a document even
after "it was so defaced that" a colonist "could not read any more of it
than a word here and there." Puzzled looks from Pennsylvanians unable
to make out the faded ink taught natives to shield the pages from wear
and tear. At Shamokin in 1748, Shickellamy brought out an old letter
of recommendation from the governor of Pennsylvania and listened,
"much pleas.d," as a colonist read it aloud.[74]

Paper so carefully preserved took its place beside wampum in the conversation between cultures. Headmen who got a letter inviting them to meet with Pennsylvania would keep it, sometimes for years, so that when they finally did come in they could return it to their host as they would an "invitation string" of wampum. That done, the visitor might pull out an old letter or treaty and pass it around as proof "that we have always been your fast Friends" or, clutching it in his hand, "speak on it" as he would a belt of beads.[75] Shawnees once went farther still, hauling out an old "Certificate of the renewal of our Friendship" and trying to get colonial officials to sign the document "afresh" as an endorsement of continued good relations. The startled governor and councilors declined the honor, but the request itself, with an Indian pushing a quill pen into a reluctant colonial hand, suggests how far native peoples had gone in making this medium their own.[76]

"Make Such a Speech . . . As You Think Proper"
Improvisational Arts

Wampum and writing helped keep clear the paths between peoples. They could become more useful still when the men carrying them were given a free hand in recasting them, for negotiation often required a mediator to change words, to change course, as circumstances warranted. While Indian councils tended to keep their intermediaries on a short leash—"we are only messengers, and cannot say much," envoys from Indian country would explain; if something "has not been given us in Charge by our Council," we can "have nothing to say to that"—colonial councils were less strict.[77] A novice might get detailed directions, but experienced hands like Weiser, Croghan, and Montour had considerable leeway in deciding how best to get a message across. Take this money, buy some presents, "and make such a Speech or Letter . . . as you think proper," Peters told Weiser when Shickellamy's children needed attention.[78] Formal business like invitations to treaties might generate instructions, and sometimes the draft of a speech, but even so it was left up to a go-between to "put this [message] into such a Dress, as will be most agreable to the People it is carried to," to make sure that "if any Expression be omitted necessary and usual on such occasions, . . . supply it."[79]

Indian emissaries recruited by Pennsylvania enjoyed similar freedom. In November 1755 Governor Robert Hunter Morris apologized to Scarouyady and Montour for even giving them detailed directions, since "You so well understand what you are going about . . . [that] there

COMBINING COLONIAL AND INDIAN SYMBOL SYSTEMS

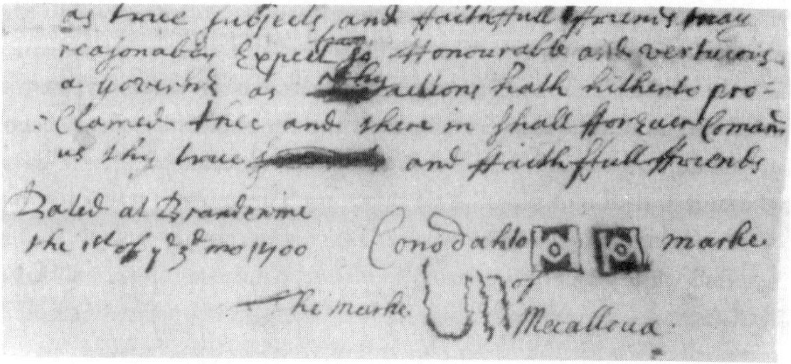

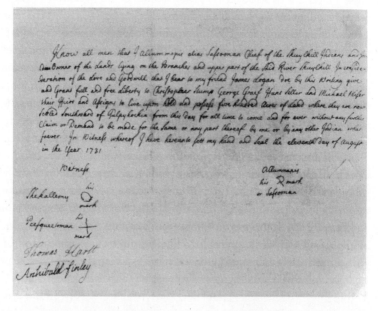

Figure 14. Marks of Conodahto and Meealloua on their letter to William Penn
in 1700 regarding Sylvester Garland's misbehavior.

Courtesy of the Historical Society of Pennsylvania.

Figure 15. Marks of Sassoonan, Shickellamy, and
Pisquetomen on a 1731 deed of sale.

Courtesy of the Historical Society of Pennsylvania.

Figure 16. Mark of Wiggoneekeenah, Delaware Indian, on a 1725
land deed to the Pennsylvania fur trader Edmond Cartlidge.
Courtesy of the Historical Society of Pennsylvania.

was little occasion for it." Six months later Morris dispatched Newcastle and other Indian messengers to enemy towns on the Susquehanna River with wampum, a speech, and instructions to "adopt the several articles to Indian Customs, retaining the Spirit and Substance of them."[80]

Invited to improvise, the negotiator had a better chance of carrying on conversation even on the most delicate and inflammatory topics. Newcastle, before embarking on that embassy to the enemy in the spring of 1756, had promised provincial officials that he and his companions "do Remember very well the words the Governor hath put in our mouths, and will deliver them faithfully." On reaching enemy territory, though, they quickly changed their minds. We were "Obliged to go of[f] a little from the Governor's Instructions," they admitted on their return to Philadelphia: the speech we delivered on your behalf said nothing about repatriating colonists the enemy had taken—a cardinal point in the provincial council chamber—because "some particular Friends among the Indians" there deemed it too early to discuss such matters.[81]

No messengers departed farther from the script provincial authorities handed them than another party bound for the upper Susquehanna a few years later. In September 1761 a colonist had killed a Delaware; soon the dead man's brother, Tenohwangogue, had recruited two other warriors and was heading toward Pennsylvania, "in . . . a furious temper," to take his revenge. At one Susquehanna Valley town en route, Moravian Delawares, learning of Tenohwangogue's mission, plied the three with 22,500 black wampum beads, convinced them to await a response from Philadelphia, and dispatched two villagers, Tongocone and Secomus, to the capital with the bad news.[82]

Grasping at once the gravity of the situation, Governor James Hamilton consulted his advisers, then drew up a reply and sent the two Delawares back, in the company of the Quakers Isaac Zane and Isaac Greenleaf. On the way north, the party picked up Isaac Stille and Teedyuscung, along with two more Moravian Delawares.

The Delaware envoys were so worried about the warriors awaiting them that the devout "Tongocone said it would be well for us to employ our hearts in constant prayer to our Maker to soften & turn the minds of those wicked men with whom we were going to do business." That business would not be easy, especially since Pennsylvania had sent ill-chosen words. When, en route, Zane rehearsed the governor's message, Tongocone "after a short pause . . . said it would not answer the end proposed"; the colonists had to promise to consider revisions before the Delawares would agree to proceed with the mission.[83]

Two days later the party paused to go over the message again; time had not improved it. The governor cleared eyes and ears at the outset, true, and at the end he offered perfunctory condolences.[84] But in between was a long, stern lecture: the alleged killer will be tried and justice done, but he pleads self defense, insisting that the Indian, armed with a scalping knife, was about to slaughter his family. Tenohwangogue is "much too hasty, and greatly in the wrong" to think of vengeance; go home, the message ordered, "and think no more of satisfying an unjust revenge on persons in no wise guilty of, or accessory to the death of your Relation."

The Delawares, on hearing Zane and Greenleaf read this, must have started praying harder. There are "but six words in it that would be usefull . . . ," Tongocone fumed; "if we were to read it as it was to them[,] they would go out of the house before it was half done." Give me your wampum, he instructed the colonists, "& then he could tell better what to say."

The Delawares' revision, unveiled two days later, bore little resemblance to the original. Gone was all that talk about the crime and the accused, trial and justice, self defense and going home. In its place was the cadence of condolence, couched in the soothing metaphor and repetition designed to comfort the bereaved: *Now Brother, . . . Now Brother, . . . Come Brother listen to me, . . . Come brother listen to me. . . . I will clap my hands to your eyes, because the tears are always filling up your eyes. Now brother I wipe the tears from your eyes.* It is impossible to say whether the governor's speech would have been the disaster Tongocone predicted. But the words he and the other Delaware go-betweens substituted— along with 10,000 more wampum beads, and a new shirt, coat, and hat—did persuade the bereaved man "to go home in quiet, & Contented and set my self down in peace."[85]

Was jettisoning a speech unusual? Or was Zane just more candid than other mediators because his journal was never intended for a provincial official's eyes?[86] We are left to wonder how many other messages carefully drafted in Philadelphia were quietly set aside or reconfigured in the woods. But with Zane, Tongocone, Stille, and the others, we glimpse some of a go-between's conversational gambits. Literally and figuratively making it up as they went along, some fashioned belts while others scribbled revised messages, some calculated the correct length of a string while others prayed. However earnestly they sought divine guidance, go-betweens relied more on accumulated wisdom and wiles, dexterity with shells and quills, to get a message across—and, more, to carry correspondence forward.

"Nothing but Nonsense"
Conversation Garbled and Stifled

"I Have Informed the Indians of What I Thought Was Proper"
The Craft of Editing

The general desire to promote trade and avoid war pushed peoples in and around Penn's Woods to find frequencies on which they could get through to one another. Building on that impulse, go-betweens gifted in languages, versed in the ways of wampum and writing, and able to think on their feet proved to be brilliant conversationalists with a dramatic impact on the frontier. When Isaac Zane, at the end of his 1761 mission, noted how "chearfulness appear'd in every countenance, & the affair which before this appear'd so dubious had now another face," he caught the sense of relief a go-between could deliver.[87] Getting the governor's letter "has Eas'd our minds," Delaware leaders had said in 1728. Another message from Philadelphia after the Virginia-Iroquois skirmish in 1742 had a similar soothing effect: "When . . . Conrad arriv'd with your Message, the Clouds were dispell'd, the Darkness ceased, and we now see as clearly and as well as ever."[88]

Minds eased, frowns erased, clouds lifted, darkness banished—the transformations suggest something of negotiators' power. But the work was neither as easy nor as successful as these dramatic contrasts suggest. Intercultural communication was plagued by ignorance and folly, fraud and mistrust, cupidity and arrogance; indeed, as time wore on, the interference got worse rather than better. A closer look reveals that not even Shickellamy and Weiser were as devoted to truth as they appeared; if these two putative paragons fell short of the ideal, imagine how far short others fell. All were human: they made mistakes, both honest and dishonest, and their agendas clashed as often as coincided. Even when interests did coincide, conversation lagged because colonists and Indi-

ans remained far apart on issues as fundamental as what part of a speech was most important, and which medium—paper or wampum—should have primacy.

The best place to begin exploring conversation's darker side is just where things looked brightest—the fireside chats Shickellamy had with Conrad Weiser. However open and free the Pennsylvanian's reports made these exchanges sound, in fact he never told his Indian friend all "the news" that "accured among the white people"; at one colloquy in the summer of 1747, for example, Weiser only "informed the Indians of what I thought was proper both from Europe & America," meaning by *proper* whatever put Britain and its dominions in the most favorable light.

At the same time, however, Weiser's superiors expected him to "demand from" Shickellamy and other headmen, "by virtue of the Treaties subsisting between this Province and the Indians, all that they know or have heard." Did colonists really expect complete candor? Weiser's asides in his reports—"This is what Shikelamy . . . assures to be true"; "he says we may depend upon the truth thereof"; "I dare say the man is true & Honest"—suggest doubt, as does colonial skepticism of "Indian stories." Certainly Pennsylvanians asking the Oneida "to open himself freely . . . , to tell his whole knowledge . . . and his thoughts" never got their wish; Shickellamy shaded the truth in ways that served Iroquois interests, and his own.[89]

The shading began with the Oneida's arrival at the Susquehanna Forks in 1728, when he asserted that "He is Sett over the Shawanah Indians" by the Six Nations, who "have," Pennsylvanians were led to believe, "an absolute Authority over all our Indians, & may command them as they please." The claim was far from the truth—Shawnees, Delawares, Conestogas, and the others had for years done pretty much as they wished—but Shickellamy made it his business to bring rhetoric closer to reality by weakening any rivals.[90]

His first target was the obstreperous Shawnee and fur trader, Peter Chartier, a man of influence among Susquehanna Shawnees. Neither Chartier nor his people accepted Iroquois claims of hegemony, and Chartier went out of his way to mock Shickellamy's pretensions to authority. In 1733 the Oneida, using as his excuse a Pennsylvania-Iroquois treaty article requiring "that if either they or we heard any ill News, Care should be taken to make it known to each other," came to the cap-

ital to proclaim Chartier a "wicked and prowd" fellow, a rum monger who flouted colonial law and flirted with the French. "[H]is Behaviour is such as gives just Apprehensions," Shickellamy declared ominously, that "some Mischiefs may happen if he is not called away from these parts." Called away or not, Chartier was soon gone for good: disgusted with Pennsylvania's land schemes, tired of Iroquois overseers, he spent more and more of his time west of the mountains.[91]

With one rival out of the way, Shickellamy turned on Sassoonan, the Delaware leader at Shamokin, who had a similar independent streak. In the late 1720s Sassoonan, not Shickellamy, had spoken at councils in Philadelphia, and during the early 1730s the two men worked together. But after 1740, as age and illness sapped the Delaware headman's strength, Shickellamy—again under the auspices of treaty agreements with Pennsylvania calling for regular exchange of news—set out to undermine the old man's authority. That Delaware is near death, the Oneida announced; he is out of his head; he has been on a binge for years, selling his people's council wampum to keep rum flowing into his cup; he is so unfit for formal meetings that "whenever a council fire was kindled he p——d into it." The province should appoint someone to rule in his place, since—another lie—he "has no Successor of [among] his Relations." It was no coincidence that during these years Sassoonan's nephews Pisquetomen, Shingas, and Tamaqua (Beaver), along with many other Delawares weary of Iroquois arrogance and interference, followed Shawnees down the westward trails toward the Ohio.[92]

Whatever Sassoonan's Delawares or Chartier's Shawnees thought of the "news" Shickellamy spread about them, Pennsylvania was happy to accept it as true in order to further the colony's ambition to rule or remove its native neighbors. Only when those disgruntled emigrants to Ohio began to speak with an independent voice in the late 1740s was Shickellamy's skewed version of the truth fully exposed, for only then did Onondaga's agenda come to clash with Pennsylvania's. Appalled that the axis of alliance running, through him, from Philadelphia to Onondaga was in danger of being replaced by a new chain of friendship stretching west from the provincial capital, Shickellamy stepped up his disinformation campaign by frantically concocting stories. "[T]he Journey to Ohio wou'd avail but little," he told Weiser in March 1748 on learning that his Tulpehocken confidant was soon to head west to be-

friend peoples out there; those groups cannot speak for themselves, because they are "altogether subject to the Six Nations." Stalling Weiser by claiming that Onondaga would soon send a delegation to Philadelphia "to treat about some Business of Consequence," Shickellamy looked the fool when no Iroquois showed up. By the end of August the string had run out, the fiction of Iroquois rule was exposed. The Oneida's old comrade was at Logstown on the Ohio River to raise the Union Jack, joining Indians in a toast to King George and new friends. "He is not alltogether pleased with my Journey to Ohio," Weiser reported, in something of an understatement. The diplomatic scaffolding that Shickellamy's conversations put up over the past two decades had come crashing down.[93]

"They Ought Not Thus to Treat"
Lost in Transmission

Weiser and Shickellamy were as attuned to one another as any two men in the border country, yet their talks fell far short of the treaty rhetoric about honest exchange. With them, however, we have only begun to plumb the depths of deceit, to glimpse how much words went astray as they crossed the frontier.

Many obstacles stood in the way of conversation. Sickness or bad weather might stop an envoy, as did a hunting or trading expedition and—among Indian messengers—a bad dream.[94] So did drink. The Pennsylvania fur traders in August 1728 who paused to slake their thirst (and spill their news) at a Philadelphia tavern had kindred spirits a generation later in Teedyuscung, who bartered his wampum for liquor, and Andrew Montour, who, having lost his dispatches, was (coincidentally?) held in Carlisle on a tavern debt.[95]

Sometimes Pennsylvania traders, perfectly sober, found good reason to fail as messengers. Charles Poke and Thomas Hill neglected to carry a belt from Allegheny Indians to Philadelphia, since that wampum told provincial officials how these two traders had "abused" the very people who now sent them east to turn themselves in! A request for more English goods sent by Ohio leaders in the 1740s met a similar oblivion, perhaps because the men toting (and burying) that plea wanted to keep the trade to themselves.[96]

Indians were surprised when a message given to men like Hill and Poke never got to its destination; Pennsylvania authorities were not.

Philadelphia officials eager to befriend Ohio peoples in order to expand trade and fend off the French had a hard time laying down secure lines of communication over the mountains. They bewailed the penchant of Shawnees there to send speeches "by Indian [i.e., colonial] Traders, some of which have been delivered & some not." These men are "thrusting themselves into the Carriage of Messages," one governor stormed, but they are "too partial, ignorant, and too much concerned for their own Interest" to be trusted. The council instructed one envoy to tell Indians that this is "not a becoming manner of addressing the Government"; next time, another official ordered, natives must "observe a greater Regularity in the publick Transactions."[97]

Emissaries Pennsylvania chose could be every bit as bad, Indians responded, clods "who either don't remember or designedly alter your meaning . . . ; take care," they scolded, "to choose faithful and proper people." Native frustration ran deep. "You have frequently sent us Messages by straggling Indians . . . ," a Cayuga named Tokahaio complained, "upon whom there is no dependence. They sometimes lose the Belts & Messages, and sometimes drink them away, but if they happen to meet us, they are nothing but Nonsense."[98]

Mishandling wampum was as common, and as annoying, as sending the wrong man. Though colonists became conversant with beads, wampum remained a foreign language in which they often made mistakes. One group of Pennsylvania envoys had to confess that they had "intirely forgot to bring any with us from Philadelphia," while others tried to talk peace holding a black belt or delivered important speeches "on small Belts and trifling little Strings." Some embarrassed colonists got off with "a general Laugh" at their ineptitude; some had to sit through a lecture. You have lost "Several of our Strong Belts" given to you before, Tokahaio said in 1758. Moreover, the English, "when they speak to us, they do it with a Shorter Belt or String than that which we spoke to them with. . . . They ought not thus to treat with Indians on Council Affairs."[99]

Three years later Tokahaio, back in Pennsylvania, was no happier. In his hand were wampum belts Philadelphia had sent to Onondaga. Oneidas had brought the wampum safely through to us, he said, but the beads are mute. Beyond saying vaguely that the belts "were about the Governor's Business, they brought no Speeches with them . . . ," the Cayuga concluded testily, handing them back to colonists; "you may know their meaning; we do not." Nor was this an isolated mishap.

Shortly before Tokahaio arrived, several Nanticokes had visited Philadelphia with another silent belt. It came a year ago, they explained, but all it said was that Pennsylvania's governor invited us to the capital; it did not say why. The Indians then accused the governor of handing wampum to a passing Indian, who gave it to another, "& so it goes thro' many hands, . . . but the last man knows not what was intended to be said . . . with the Belt. We think that whatever it is," the Nanticokes concluded, "that it could not have come from the Governor's heart."[100]

This variation of the children's game of Telephone—where a message gets distorted as it travels from one person to the next—suggests how intercultural conversation could go awry. It also suggests that colonists, despite Tokahaio's indictment, were not the only clumsy ones. Oneidas bearing shells from Philadelphia that they could not read; Teedyuscung swapping a belt for a bottle; Ohioans misplacing some of their strings—Indians were not always masters of the conversational arts either.[101]

Even a sober and skilled emissary found wampum hard to handle. However long a belt was, however elaborate its design, it was not a letter that could simply be picked up and deciphered by anyone familiar with the medium. A negotiator using wampum had to tie in his mind a particular speech with a particular belt's size, color, and pattern; if not, the beads were struck dumb. Surely, then, written documents were an improvement—an open book, as it were, to any educated eye? A belt wore obscure symbols; a page—any page—bore letters, words, sentences, all awaiting a trained glance to unveil its secrets.

But a document only looked more reliable. As Indians learned through painful experience, much depended on who did the writing; some scribes penned "loose Letters." In 1739 Shawnees visiting the capital found this out when provincial officials accused them, "from your own Letters," of favoring the French. There must be some mistake, the Indians replied; that letter "was not wrote agreeable to their Minds, nor as they designed." What happened is that "being merry over a Cup of good Liquor at Alleghenny, they then said they would write to you, their Brothers [in Philadelphia], which two white Men who were in Company undertook to do." Only now do we discover that those two, for reasons of their own, "so wrote what they themselves thought proper."[102]

In 1753 other Pennsylvania traders, living up to their worst reputa-

tion, strayed even farther from native intentions by slipping into an in-
nocuous letter, marked by headmen, a paragraph in which Indians supposedly agreed to sell their lands on the Ohio River's east side to pay
off trade debts. The governor and council, though always happy to buy
more territory, were so amazed by this extraordinary proposal and so
distrustful of the traders who penned it that they wondered if the Indians had been "in a sober, thoughtful mood" when their scruffy amanu-
enses took it down. Sure enough, inquiries confirmed that natives had
said no such thing.[103]

By midcentury the Ohio country, where Pennsylvania's ambitions
clashed with those of Virginia, France, and assorted Indian nations,
was particularly fertile soil for such chicanery. First came the debate
over Britain building a fort there. Thomas Penn (long since returned to
England to stay) and his loyalists in Philadelphia considered a stronghold
"a mark of Possession" that would counter both French and Virginians;
for their part, George Croghan and his fellow fur traders longed for the
protection a garrison could provide. Thus in January 1751 Croghan
arrived in the provincial capital to announce that Ohio Indians at
Logstown "are of opinion that their Brothers the English ought *to have
a fort on this River* to secure the Trade." Sent back that spring only to
"sound the Indians in a private manner that he might know their Sentiments" about this venture, the trader surprised everyone by returning with the natives' formal request for "a Strong House." Governor
James Hamilton was pleased; the Quaker-dominated assembly, opposed both to war and to spending money, was not. Imagine, then, its
delight when Andrew Montour, who had been at Croghan's side
throughout the Ohio visit, came in to deny that Indians had said any
such thing.[104]

Who was lying? It is as hard to tell now as it was then. Croghan, publicly humiliated, fought hard to clear his name (he even persuaded
Montour to change his story), but matters never got sorted out. Wherever truth lay, this chapter in the cross-cultural concourse reveals how
tangled the lines of communication were becoming as the number of
players on the frontier stage grew and the stakes mounted.

Conrad Weiser, who had visited the assembly with Montour to hear
the *métis* embarrass Croghan, soon found out how unpredictable a fellow Montour was, and how unfathomable the politics of the Ohio country. At Logstown in 1752, Montour pressed Indian leaders to accept the

expansive interpretation of an Iroquois land sale that Virginia and Weiser had obtained at Lancaster in 1744, a reading that would have given Ohio to the Old Dominion. But at another council Montour, reversing himself, insisted that "the Indians never Sold nor released it [the territory beyond the mountains;] If they did they were imposed upon by the Interpreter"—none other than the now "very angry" Weiser himself. Once again truth is elusive, and once again it is less important than what the dispute reveals about confusion in formal conversations.[105]

A return visit to the banks of the Ohio in December 1758 finds truth more evident and some go-betweens' efforts to evade it more obvious. Croghan and Montour, having long since patched up their differences, stood with General John Forbes's army on the ruins of Fort Duquesne at the Forks of the Ohio, just captured from the French. It was a pivotal moment in American history. British success in taking the stronghold owed much to their messengers' ability to convince Ohio Indians that, upon ousting the French, the British army would obey the natives' demand to leave Ohio. Believing that promise, natives sat out the contest and the French fell.[106] Now, meeting the triumphant Forbes, Ohio leaders repeated, several times, their insistence "that he should go back over the mountains." Forbes did turn around: desperately ill, he headed east to die. But he left behind Colonel Henry Bouquet and two hundred troops to build a stronghold, to be christened Fort Pitt. Now Bouquet, unhappy with the Indians' insistence on his retreat, wanted them to "alter their mind."

When native leaders refused, Croghan and Montour stepped in. As traders and, more recently, Crown Indian agents, both were keen to see the soldiers stay. First they simply refused to "tell Colonel *Bouquet* the *Indians'* answer." Then Croghan insisted that, in private talks with Bouquet, the headmen had indeed changed their minds about the troops. When Christian Frederick Post, who was also there, expressed doubts about that story, "Mr. Croghn grew very angry" and said any other account of Indian wishes "was a d——d lie." The Ohio natives, informed of Croghan's version, "said, Mr. *Croghn* and *Henry Montour* had not spoke and acted honestly and uprightly." Honest or not, Montour and Croghan—and Bouquet—got their wish: the army stayed. Ohio leaders learned the hard way that among a go-between's tricks was making *no* mean *yes* and *yes, no.*[107]

"It Is So Difficult for Us to Understand Each Other"
Lost in Translation

Croghan and Montour, caught by Post that winter day, offer the best example of how a negotiator could put words in someone's mouth. With Post's help, it is easy to see where, and why, something got lost in translation. But without a Post standing by at every conversation to point out where an interpreter strayed, it is harder to tell how much of what Croghan called "Indian Form" and Weiser termed "Indian Phrases" fell by the way.[108] It is clear, however, that even an interpreter committed to accurate translation had a difficult time getting messages through the cultural and linguistic interference, through the profound difference in agendas and customs.

Just a month after the Ohio Indians' meeting with Bouquet, one of the native leaders at that council, a Delaware named Custaloga, gave a French officer his version of the conversation.[109] It bore little resemblance to Bouquet's. While both accounts of the talks mentioned trade, peace, and return of colonial captives, they painted Bouquet and Britain in very different colors. Bouquet had himself boasting that "the English are . . . the most powerfull People on this Continent," insisting that the two hundred soldiers had to stay to protect traders, agreeing that the Indians must soon return their prisoners, and instructing natives to drive out all of the remaining French.

Custaloga's Bouquet was a more contrite fellow. "I . . . [am] going to be quite different from what you have seen and experienced of me up to the present," he allegedly promised. "It is," this Bouquet admitted, "unreasonable that we have come to stain your lands with blood . . . , we should have respected your lands." But fear not: we will leave soon, for "The King himself . . . forbids us to cross to the other side of the [Ohio] river, and orders us even to come away from it." Two hundred soldiers in a fort? No, only "a trading house here without a stockade." Drive away your French friend? "I shall be delighted to be door to door with him." Prisoners? Keep those "you have adopted as your relatives." But perhaps you might surrender the older ones, "who would be in the way, or of very little use to you." It is almost as if Custaloga and Bouquet were remembering different conversations.

This was hardly the first time transmission was garbled. In 1743 Oneidas told New York officials that, though the treaty minutes said nothing about it, during the council at Onondaga Virginia had actually admitted that colonists were to blame for the skirmish with Jonnhaty's men. And in 1756 the Onondaga envoy Ogaghradarisha, recalling his visit to Pennsylvania to request a colonial fort at Shamokin and propose another above Wyoming, had the governor say *"That as he found by woeful experience, that making purchases of Lands was the cause of much blood having been shed,* he was determined to buy no more."[110]

The line between true and false is harder to draw in these cases than it was with Post at the Ohio Forks. Did Custaloga consciously change Bouquet's words? Or was the Delaware offering an accurate (if not verbatim) account of the treaty, based on his own design or on a slanted interpretation by Andrew Montour? Ogaghradarisha's message begs the same questions. Was he putting words in the governor's mouth? Perhaps the fault lay in Weiser's interpretation that day, or in the gap between Weiser's Mohawk and Ogaghradarisha's Onondaga. Or maybe Ogaghradarisha mistook Pennsylvania's reluctance to accept at once his invitation to build a fort above Wyoming, so deep in Iroquois territory, as a policy statement against ever again buying native land. At this remove, one can only pose the questions; the rest is a guessing game. But it is no idle pastime. Pondering it, we approach the heart of translation's mystery, where words become malleable and imprecise, prey to the skills, schemes, and memories of those doing the talking.

Even in the best of times, interpretation is not an exact science. The equation that manufactures sentences from sounds has a host of variables, from the setting and audience to the translator's ability and sobriety or his agenda and attention span, not to mention the means of recording his work for future reference. The colonial era was not the best of times, even if an interpreter intended only the most faithful rendering of a speaker's words. Go-betweens were often tired, afraid, drunk, or bored—and sometimes all four at once. Their linguistic gifts ranged from fluency to ignorance, such as that exhibited by the Delaware Joseph Peepy, a regular translator in the last two decades of the colonial period who, near the end of his career, was said to speak only broken English. Moreover, fluency, so difficult to attain, was also easy to lose. In 1754 Weiser asked to be relieved of his duties "as a principal Interpreter" because "he is no longer Master of that Fluency he formerly had, and finding himself at a Loss for proper Terms to express himself is frequently obliged to make Use of Circumlocution." With rusty or inept translators, one colonist lamented how much of a native's eloquence was reduced to dross by an interpreter able to distill only "the sense" of it.[111]

It seems likely, then, that many an Indian speaker would have been disappointed to learn how much of his wisdom and wit were "spoiled" by a lousy accent, poor choice of words, and clumsy delivery. While we cannot measure the full extent of this impediment to understanding, we can identify elements of native speechmaking that, if not altogether abandoned by interpreters and scribes, at least received less emphasis, and therefore made less impact, than native American orators intended.

The first is repetition. Rehearsal of key words and phrases is vitally important to oral cultures intent on retaining their knowledge.[112] To natives like Tongocone and the other Delawares condoling Tenohwangogue in 1761, intoning phrases over and over again was, like regular renewal of friendship at councils, the very lifeblood of conversation. Colonists saw words differently. Like a treaty that stood for all time once it was written down and marked or signed by the right people, so a phrase, once spoken and inscribed, had no need to reappear. Only colonial inconsistency in translating and recording Indian speeches—with some interpreters and scribes more prone to include everything—exposes the gap, providing occasional glimpses of what must have been a consistent Indian reiteration:[113]

- The Delaware leader Sassoonan, 1715 (interpreter and scribe unknown): *added to the same effect, . . . further added, . . . added, . . . Continued in the same strain, . . . repeated the same.*
- Sassoonan again, 1740 (scribe unknown, interpreter "Thomas Freeman, an Indian"): *now we are come down; we are come into your House . . . . [W]e are glad now we are come; and my Uncles the Mingoes, came along with Us from Alleghany . . . . I tell you again that our Friends, the Mingoes, came along with Us, and are come into your House.*
- Ohio Delawares, 1758 (Christian Frederick Post, translator and scribe): *You have talked of that Peace and Friendship which we had formerly with you . . . . [A]lways remember that Friendship which we had formerly . . . . [O]ur good Friendship and Peace we had formerly . . . . . [T]hat Friendship we formerly had . . . . [T]hat Friendship with you we formerly*

had . . . . *[T]he Peace and Friendship we had Formerly . . . . [T]he Friendship which we had formerly amongst our Fathers and Grandfathers . . . . That
Friendship . . . which was formerly between us . . . . [T]hat Peace and Friendship which we formerly had with you.*

- An Oneida named Saghughsuniunt (Thomas King), 1762 (interpreter uncertain, scribe Richard Peters?): *call your Soldiers away from
Shamokin. . . . [T]ake away your Soldiers. . . . I must tell you again these Soldiers must go away from Shamokin Fort. . . . [T]here is no occasion for Soldiers to live there any longer. . . . [W]e must press you to take away your
Soldiers from Shamokin.*

Having skimmed these lines, the reader may now, perhaps, be readier to forgive colonial translators and scribes who usually saved their
breath and their ink, even if that meant altering the rhythms and accents
of native discourse.

A second strand of speech only occasionally found its way into the
record due to colonial delicacy, not colonial boredom. A native
speaker's use of the body as metaphor usually enraptured colonial au-
ditors, accustomed as they were to thinking in terms of a *body politic*.
Thus interpreters conveyed—and scribes recorded—metaphors from
head to foot. But amid all the body parts, private parts are conspicu-
ously absent from surviving accounts of speeches; they come up just
enough to suggest that colonists routinely bowdlerized Indian talks.

Much of this discourse centered on insults about turning men into
women. Why fight Catawbas? Because, a Cayuga said (through Weiser),
those southern Indians "sent us word that . . . they were men and double men for they had two P——s; that they could make Women of Us."
During the war with colonists another Iroquois explained that Delawares attacking Pennsylvania had boasted that "We are Men" and shall
keep fighting; do not try to stop us, "lest we cut off your private Parts
and make Women of you."[114]

Two other references to private parts confirm the suspicion that
colonists, not Indians, were responsible for keeping such talk to a min-
imum. The Pennsylvanian John Hays, with Christian Post at a council
on the Susquehanna in 1760, noted in his diary that one native stood to
complain about British exchange rates for furs. Prices are so high, the
Indian argued, that *he got but 6 fills of a Measure for a ribboned Stroud, and
it was so little that his Cock could Not Go in it, and he had But A little one.*

Significantly, polishing his grammar and spelling for the final report on their mission, Hays omitted this speech altogether.[115]

Conrad Weiser, translating for the Seneca go-between Newcastle, went in the opposite direction in his report, not away from the explicit but toward it. Newcastle says, the Pennsylvanian explained, that the Iroquois sent a message to Delawares that included talk of how those Delawares

> have Suffered the string that tied your petticoat to be cut loose by the French, and you lay with them, & so became a common Bawd, . . . and as you have thrown off the Cover of your modesty and become stark naked, . . . We now give you a little Prick and put it into your private Parts, and so let it grow there till you shall be a compleat man.

The speech has attracted scholarly attention for the light it sheds on Iroquois talk of Delawares as women. But its significance also lies in how Weiser handled it. Before repeating Newcastle's message, the negotiator was at pains to say that the image was not his, but the Seneca's: I only "took down in words . . . the literal Interpretation of what Newcastle said." Weiser's skittish way with those words makes one wonder how often he and others censored an Indian speech before it ever reached colonists' tender ears.[116]

Perhaps, given all the obstacles in the way—differences in language and emphasis, a metaphorical wilderness, the temptation to censor or edit speeches—we should be surprised that native voices from colonial times come through as clearly as they do. But at the time, Indians and colonists alike were frustrated by the enduring language barrier between them. In 1748 one Indian woman befriending Moravians at Shamokin broke down and wept because she "could not understand & Speake with" them better. Leaders on both sides knew the feeling. Governor William Keith, talking to Conestogas in 1722, was aware that "many words that we send to them [the Iroquois] & they send to us may be lost by the way & never told, because the English Interpreters do not understand the Indian Language so well as you." Though in the next generation interpreters were probably more skilled, the barrier remained. "I am sorry it is so difficult for us to understand each other . . . ," said Saghughsuniunt at Easton in 1762, staring across the linguistic gulf at colonial leaders. "[A]s we do not easily understand one another, we are obliged to deliver you the Substance in short of what we have to say, which makes it tedious." But tedium or merely getting the gist of it was, in some sense, not the worst thing happening to the good correspondence. More ominous still, Indian and colonist were coming to understand one another only too well.[117]

"This Faithfull Kind of Evidence . . . Must Be the Rule"
Writing Triumphant

The farther one goes in exploring frontier conversation, the darker the prospect appears. People lied; they made up letters and mishandled wampum; their incompetence or chicanery meant that countless words were "lost by the way & never told." Even writing and wampum, complementary as they could be in capable hands, ended up in contention as Indians came to fear the power of the pen and colonists insisted more shrilly on paper's primacy.

Contention between the two media was always there, in the weight each side accorded them. Where Indians considered written documents supplementary, colonists thought the opposite. "They were glad," Iroquois told Pennsylvania in 1722, "the Govr. sent them a Letter for that was like two tongues, and *confirmed* what the Messenger said to them." Two decades later Governor Thomas let slip the prevailing colonial view when he informed Shawnees that "I send you this not only under the Seal of our Government, but for *a further Confirmation* have added four Strings of Wampum."[118]

Like any literate people, colonists thought reliance on the spoken word a mistake. Speech, they insisted, is transitory and intangible; it lingers in the air for a heartbeat, then dies there, to be followed either by silence or by other evanescent sounds in the flow of thoughts expressed.[119] But putting those thoughts down on paper is, it seemed to Europeans, a different matter. Here, they believed, words make an indelible mark, become tangible objects that, years hence, can resurrect the talk of men long dead. Here, on the page, lies truth, a record of deeds, of wisdom, just waiting to be revived in order to enlighten generations to come. And here, in the ink, the message comes through clearly to sustain "Kind Correspondents."

Or so European colonists wished to believe. However close colonial and Indian modes of communication might look, however adept Pennsylvanians became with shell beads or Indians with writing, colonists nonetheless thought that literacy, civilization's hallmark, set them off from their native neighbors.[120] A spectrum of communicative forms there indeed was, but at its center lay, to the European (and, in the end, to the Indian) way of thinking, a divide separating peoples that could read and write from those that could not. While literacy is indeed a tool of communication, it is also "a mode of *ex*communication," a weapon that literally wrote off groups.[121]

On the Pennsylvania frontier these forces and ideas found expression in a war of words, wampum, and writing. Colonists conveyed to Indians a serene confidence in a document's accurate reflection of reality. "[N]o body," James Logan was said to have assured skeptical Delawares, "dared to write any thing wrong, for if any one writes any thing out of his own Head, We hang Him."[122] If Logan were right, many a Pennsylvanian (including Logan himself) would have ended his days at the end of a rope. None did; but however far from the truth, Logan's claim captures the arrogance of the literate.

His superior, Thomas Penn, agreed that paper must have the final say. "I doubt not," the proprietor told Conestogas in 1735, "but you will believe with me that the most proper Method for this [renewal of friendship between peoples] is to read over to you here, since you cannot read yourselves, the principal of those Writings," the agreements and land cessions from years past. At Lancaster nine years later Virginia commissioners arguing a point with the Iroquois added their voice to the colonial chorus of praise for paper. Consult our earlier treaty with you, the Virginians said; it "being in Writing is more certain than your Memory. That is the way the white people have of preserving Transactions of every kind," the commissioners explained, "and transmitting them down to their Children's Children for ever; and all Disputes among them are settled by this faithfull kind of Evidence, and must be the Rule between the Great King and you."[123]

Some Indians sounded awed, even cowed, by a document's power to carry thoughts across space or time. When I die I am going to hell, one aged Delaware solemnly told a missionary. "Ask'd . . . how he came to belive so, Said he I have liv'd with white People, (who can reed & Know many things from God), & they all Say so." In formal discourse, too, Indians might genuflect before the paper altar Penn and Logan erected for them. If we "make any Blunders, or have forgot any part of the Speech," Saghughsuniunt told Pennsylvania's governor in 1757, please "excuse" it, "as they cou'd not write, therefore, were obliged to keep every thing in their Memory."[124]

These two may have been putting colonists on, for alongside such obeisance were louder, more common Indian expressions of confidence in their own ways of recording and recalling things. In Philadelphia an Iroquois named Kanickhungo insisted that writing was not the only way to make the past live. "We who are now here are old Men," he said to Thomas Penn, James Logan, and a crowd of colonists in October 1736, "who have the Direction of Affairs in our own Nations, & as we are old, it may be thought that the Memory of these things may be lost with us, who have not like you the Art of preserving it, by committing all Transactions to writing"; not so, Kanickhungo continued, for "we nevertheless have Methods of transmitting from Father to Son an account of all these things, whereby you will find the Remembrance of them is faithfully preserved."[125]

Natives defending their own method of seeing that "succeeding Generations are made acquainted with what has passed" also came to doubt writing's capacity for capturing and conveying truth. Growing familiarity with the literate cosmos bred distrust. One reason Susquehanna Shawnees took such a dislike to Count Zinzendorf in 1742 was the Moravian's habit of holing up in a tent with his books and papers; it looked to Indians like sorcery, with the writings a tool of that malevolent craft. Around this time Canasatego, too, sounded the alarm. Waxing nostalgic for the days when Indians had the continent to themselves, the Onondaga told colonial leaders that "We are now . . . lyable to many . . . Inconveniences since the English came among Us, and particularly from the Pen and Ink work that is going on at the Table [pointing to the Secretarys]" scratching away there.[126]

In the years to come, suspicions of that work grew, pushed by traders' "loose Letters," by how documents, so fixed in appearance, could be so easily misread, by deeds whose boundaries on the page diverged from native memory of an agreement. Paper's power to pluck territory from Indian hands seemed particularly sinister.[127] "They say," remarked Post, "that they have been robbed of the lands by the writing of the whites." Indians leveled the charge time and again. "[W]hen You have gott a writing [confirming a land sale] from us," Delawares complained, "you lock it up in ye. Chest & no body Knows what you have bought or what you paid for it." We have "an Uneasiness on our Minds . . . concerning our Land," an Iroquois speaker told colonists in 1754. Our elders deny ever having sold it, yet now "We understand that there are Writings for all our Lands."[128]

During the war, fear of a literate world became so acute in the Indian countries that someone pulling out a book might have it knocked from his grasp or stolen. "I Durst Not Reead But sum times When they were in A Good Umer," wrote one colonial envoy, "and Not Long at A tim." Do not even let Indians know that you have books with you, another advised.[129]

Though reading was provocative, writing was worse. In the early 1760s Post warned colonists venturing into the Ohio country that "Indians are very suspicious of those white people whom they see engaged in reading and writing, especially the latter; believing that it concerns them or their territory." The go-between spoke from hard experience. During delicate wartime negotiations, he and his companions had drawn suspicious looks every time they picked up a pen. "[W]hat had they to write there?" the "very jealous" natives demanded.[130]

Jealousy was compounded by natives' growing dependence on books and papers. Like a headman holding an old piece of paper or an Iroquois warrior with a passport tucked away in his pack, Indians knew and used literacy's power. At the same time, however, they could not unlock all of its secrets, could neither abandon it nor fully embrace and exploit it. The result, among illiterate messengers, was occasional embarrassment and perpetual uneasiness. In the late 1750s the Ohio Delaware Tamaqua went from village to village, papers in hand, speaking words of peace, only to be told by some fur traders that what he carried was not a peace treaty but a land agreement.[131] Tamaqua's brother Pisquetomen knew the feeling. He once strode grandly into the provincial council chamber to lay belts and strings on the table, then faltered when it turned out that the accompanying paper he handed the governor did not, in fact, contain "the Substance" of that wampum; someone had given him the wrong document. Pressed to go ahead and "deliver what they had to say from their Memory," he and his companions declined; "he depended upon that Paper to Assist his Memory in what he had to say," Pisquetomen replied, "he could not do without it."[132]

He could not do without it—yet he could not even read it. The dilemma preoccupied and infuriated natives. No colonist saw this more clearly than Post, when Ohio leaders summoned him so that they could dictate a letter. "The jealousy natural to the *Indians* is not to be described," the messenger remarked; "for though they wanted me to write for them, they were afraid I would, at the same time, give other information, and this perplexed them."[133]

Indians thus perplexed came up with a variety of ways to master or counter writing's power. Some learned to read and write. "[T]hey had

Writers among themselves," Teedyuscung, thinking of Isaac Stille and Joseph Peepy, reminded provincial officials. But literate natives were rare, even at the end of the colonial era, so other groups adopted an educated colonist. In 1761 an Onondaga named Jenochiaada sent a messenger to Pennsylvania to say (on a wampum string) that "When I receive a Letter from you I cannot understand it, which I think very hard." Was the solution to insist on wampum, then? Not for Jenochiaada. "[W]e ought to have somebody living among us," he went on, "who can understand and interpret your Messages & the Letters you send to us." His candidate was "my [adopted] Child, James Sherlock"; please give him "your leave . . . [to] live amongst us."[134]

Ironically, even Indians who accepted the triumph of writing were often rebuffed when they wanted to learn its mysteries for themselves. Colonial officials, far from welcoming such overtures, sought to shore up the barrier between bookish people and everyone else.[135] When Oneidas in 1753 asked David Zeisberger to write a letter to Conrad Weiser, the Moravian refused, "adding, that if they had any message to send to Weiser, they should do it by means of a belt, which was a much better and surer way than by letter." Similarly, when Teedyuscung nine years later wished aloud that the peace just made among the Indians at Lancaster had been written down and "signed by all of us [headmen] . . . , that we might have it always to shew to our Children and Grand Children," Pennsylvania's governor "reminded him that it was not the Custom for Indians to sign writings to one another." The natives' ambivalence about writing was matched by colonial ambivalence about their having it.[136]

By then Teedyuscung was accustomed to British officials deflecting his tentative forays into the written universe. Since 1757, pressed by Moses Tatamy and Isaac Stille, he had struggled to get a clerk of his own in order to ensure an accurate account of his conversations with colonists. The contest began innocently enough at a treaty in July 1757 when the Delaware, pleading a faulty memory and a desire to "have things done regularly," asked for "a Copy of all the Proceedings." To this, provincial leaders agreed readily enough.[137]

But Teedyuscung's other request created a stir. I also want, he said, speaking (of course) on a wampum string, "a Clerk to take Minutes along with the Governor's Clerk." This was a rather different matter: handing over a copy of the minutes the governor's man takes is one thing, two clerks—and therefore two versions of the same speech—

quite another. Governor William Denny, counseled by Croghan and Weiser, refused. "No Indian Chief, before you, ever demanded to have a Clerk," Denny replied, "and none has ever been appointed for Indians in former Treaties."[138]

Resistance only confirmed Delaware suspicions about writing. "[H]e looked on it both unjust and unkind," Teedyuscung said, "to attempt . . . by this refusal to lead him on Blindfold and in the Dark." In the end the Indians got their wish, and Charles Thomson, headmaster of a Quaker school in Philadelphia, took a seat at the scribe's table. Croghan, in charge of keeping the minutes, was furious. "As to his having a Clerk or not having one I think it is a matter of little consequence," the old trader fumed, "but the having a Clerk was not the thing." That second scribe thrust an illegitimate voice (and pen) into official business; to Croghan, that was the crux of the matter.[139]

And yet in a larger sense the secretary was indeed "the thing," because he was a teacher that could guide illiterate Indians through the forbidden recesses of the written world, a world colonial leaders wanted to keep to themselves. Looking ahead, Croghan feared worse to come. Will Thomson now sit with Indians to help draft a speech, then read it in council as colonists did? Teedyuscung, no fool, proceeded along precisely those lines, asking Thomson, a distraught Croghan reported, "to read it off as a lawyer would put in a plea at the bar." This is "very extraordinary and the most unprecedented procedure ever known at an Indian treaty," the Pennsylvanian spluttered. He managed to talk the Delaware out of it this time, but what next? Sitting over in England, Thomas Penn knew. They will not stop at getting copies of treaties or their own clerk, Penn warned. Soon any disgruntled Indian—knowing that, as that Delaware had put it, documents are "in ye. Chest" under lock and key—will demand to see our land records. Forbid it, the proprietor ordered: "if they make a charge, they should make that charge good from the evidence they have, and not be allowed to search into the Cabinets of any Persons for Causes of Complaint."[140]

Some Indians, listening to squabbles over clerks, came to believe that there was another way, a better way, to embrace the strange new world of books while rejecting its colonial authors and authorities. In an effort to steal writing's spell for themselves, natives began to compose books of their own. "[H]e would Read Like Mad ofe it in the Morning," remarked one colonist after watching an Indian with a "Book of Pickters." Spiritual leaders began using texts to inspire others. One

Delaware "had drawn, as he pretended, by the direction of the great Spirit, a kind of map on a piece of deer skin, somewhat dressed like parchment, which he called 'the great Book or Writing.' . . . This map he held before him while preaching, frequently pointing to particular marks and spots upon it, and giving explanations as he went along." Increasingly, Indians making and reading such books counseled "total Seperation from" European colonists.[141]

It had come to this, then, William Penn's "Kind Correspondence." Indians rejected a colonial symbol system that they had come to read as a tool of oppression, turning to competing books, and competing visions, as an antidote to poison pens. Other natives sought to play the game by the newcomers' rules, only to be forbidden by colonists who, insisting that Truth lay on the face of their papers, also insisted on remaining Truth's sole custodian. The conversational aids—wampum and freedom, paper and words—had spawned mistrust and contempt, had driven a wedge between Indians and colonists that went deeper than a message lost or gone astray, deeper than rumor, ignorance, or incompetence, to touch the frontier's very heart.

———※———

"If We Had Been More Conversant"
Correspondence Ceases

After 1750, peoples in and around Penn's Woods were doing more than talking, more, even, than wrangling about clerks and copies, about whose books spoke truth, about where wisdom resided and deceit lurked: they were killing each other with terrible fury. Frontier war— known ever since as the Seven Years' War or the French and Indian War—erupted because a combination of new conditions and old unhappiness proved more than even the most gifted conversationalist could handle. With so many voices clamoring to be heard, conversation lapsed into cacophony, and finally into war cries and terrified shrieks.[142]

Gone, by 1750, were the days when Conrad Weiser and Shickellamy could manage most of the business between Pennsylvania and its Indian neighbors; the frontier was becoming too vast, the number of peoples involved too large, the lines of communication too long, for that. The Delaware, Shawnee, and Iroquois emigration into the Ohio country had altered the diplomatic landscape. While these groups kept up their trade and their talk of friendship with Pennsylvania, many of them—especially Shawnees and Delawares—also remembered all too well how Penn's people had driven them away. Mingled with fond memories of amity that, one Pennsylvania governor hoped, "remain stamp'd on your Minds, never to be forgott," were unhappy recollections of land fraud and trade abuse along the Delaware and the Lehigh, the Tulpehocken and the Susquehanna. It did not help that Indians, according to Croghan and many others who knew them, were "Jealous and Revengefull[,] Never forgett & seldom forgive where they think they are Ingered."[143]

And now colonists—not just Pennsylvanians but Virginians, with their newly-formed cadre of land speculators called the Ohio Company— were casting a hungry eye beyond the mountains, too, sending out surveyors to prepare, in secret, the way for further European settlement. "I took an Opportunity to set my Compass privately . . . ," wrote their agent, Christopher Gist, in November 1750, "for I understood it was dangerous to let a Compass be seen among these Indians." Memories of past misdeeds were so keen that shortly before war broke out, Indians at a town beside the Allegheny River "found a Rat & Kill'd it, at which ye antiants of them seem'd Concearned," saying "that ye French or English should get that Land from them, ye same prediction being made by their Grandfathers' on finding a Rat on Delaware before ye White People Came there." No wonder France, sending troops and traders into the Ohio at midcentury in order to check the English advance that threatened to cut French Canada off from French Louisiana, convinced natives that the British were up to no good.[144]

Complicating the frontier further, to the north sat William Johnson, his influence among the Iroquois growing steadily, while the Iroquois themselves kept trying to make good their claims to suzerainty over the increasingly populous and independent Ohio peoples. Even Pennsylvania was becoming a more complicated place to do Indian business. Proprietary officials sought money for arms and other gifts to counter the French and keep natives loyal; Quaker-dominated assemblies, which controlled the purse, refused. "As these [Indian] Affairs take up more time, and give more trouble to a Government, than almost all other Business put to gether," sighed Governor James Hamilton during one "dangerous Season" in November 1753, "it is a pity they afford so little Satisfaction in transacting them." A few months later a weary Conrad Weiser, listening to the hubbub, longed for the day when "I Shall not trouble my head any longer" about "Indian affairs. . . . [T]here is now So many Cookes in that Kitchen that the brothe is allready Spoiled."[145]

As late as 1750, Richard Peters had boasted to his superior, proprietor Thomas Penn, of Weiser's being so thoroughly in command that "I verily believe it is in his power to turn the Indian Councils which way he pleases." Hyperbole, of course; no one ever had that much say. Yet Peters captured the look of the Pennsylvania frontier in the recent past. Beginning in the late 1740s, however, as things started to fall apart for Weiser and for the world he knew, Pennsylvania's Indian agent began talking retirement. Indians pestered him with land and trade complaints, yet Philadelphia did nothing. "I shall be sick of Indian Affairs," the German colonist had warned Peters in June 1747, "If no medium is found to do them Justice."[146]

To make things worse, the colony's diplomatic opening to the Ohio country left Weiser overburdened and out of his depth. He was a Six Nations man, a veteran of the trail running from Philadelphia through Tulpehocken and Shamokin to Onondaga; the western paths and peoples lay beyond his ken. "I should think meselve happy if I had nothing to do in public affairs, and could turn farmer entirely," a frustrated Weiser wrote after meeting some Ohio folk in Lancaster during the summer of 1748. Then, that fall, Shickellamy died, robbing the colony of its closest Indian ally and Weiser of his best guide. The Pennsylvania agent who had handled the Shenandoah Valley and Armstrong messes was a different man from the one who, early in 1754, admitted that "I Can not force things to go as I will, but must Submit to accidents. . . . I am perplects with Indians affairs, and Can not say Such or Such is best."[147]

Nor was Weiser alone in his perplexity. Onondaga and Ohio, Quakers and proprietary men, Pennsylvania and Virginia, not to mention France and Britain—with so many contending forces, events were spinning out of any go-between's control. The surest proof of negotiators' impotence was that though they saw war coming, none could prevent it. Beginning in the late 1740s, Scarouyady, Croghan, Weiser, and Montour all warned Pennsylvania authorities that if no one answered the French offensive in the Ohio with guns and other gifts, even with troops and forts, those French would secure a foothold west of the mountains and turn Indians there against Pennsylvania in particular and Britain in general.[148] Quaker reluctance to finance war and British reluctance to provoke an incident worked against taking a hard line. So did squabbles among the go-betweens themselves about how to proceed. Weiser and Croghan have a "difference of Opinion" about which nations out there should get presents, a disgusted Hamilton wrote in 1750; this, the governor observed, arose "between Two persons who are suppos'd to understand Indian Affairs the best."[149] And that was before Croghan fought Montour about building forts, and Montour quarreled with Weiser about which land Indians had relinquished. All these squabbles left negotiators less able to sustain the conversation.

Disputes between negotiators, between governor and assembly, between Pennsylvania and New York, between Pennsylvania and Virginia, between Ohio nations and the Iroquois, between France and Britain—in the end all of these spelled a breakdown in correspondence, a breakdown more sinister than loose letters and mislaid wampum, misapprehension and mistranslation. Some thought the communications media specifically to blame. One native messenger said that Susquehanna Indians had joined the war in 1755 because Teedyuscung lacked wampum to send Pennsylvania word of their continuing allegiance. Teedyuscung himself, meanwhile, blamed writing for the bloodshed: "Somebody must have wrote wrong," he explained, "and that makes the Land all Bloody." But Scarouyady argued that the wave of fury and fear broke over Pennsylvania's frontier because of a longer, more pronounced failure of the conversation common for more than two generations. Pennsylvanians "had been too negligent of Cultivating . . . Friendship with the Indians . . . ," the Oneida scolded an audience in Philadelphia in the spring of 1756; conflict might have been avoided "If we had been more Conversant with each other."[150]

CHAPTER VI

In the Woods:
Woodslore, 1755–1758

"Heavy Storms"
Frontier War

In Shamokin, the heart of the Pennsylvania frontier at midcentury, the summer of 1755 passed much like any other (Map 5).[1] The Delaware, Iroquois, and Tutelo inhabitants went about their business, planting the river flats and hunting the uplands. A late frost that blasted young crops broke the routine, as did a sudden rise in the river that stole canoes from the banks, drunk Indians whose cries shattered the night, and an elderly Conoy's funeral. Near that burial ground on the outskirts of town sat the house and smithy of the Moravian mission, a mission now ten years old.[2] The three German men living there were also creatures of habit, tending their corn, mowing their meadow, speaking fractured Delaware to Indians (who might reply in broken German), savoring news or visitors from Bethlehem.[3]

Over the course of the summer a motley array of other visitors trooped to that town, and to that house and shop: a Pennsylvania fur trader and two Indians from out Allegheny way; a lone Englishman from above Wyoming; a Conoy bound for Lancaster; a German shoemaker from the nearest colonial settlement on the river's east side, a morning's ride over the hills; a Delaware family, back over those same hills after a shopping trip to Tulpehocken; Germans or Swiss from new farms on Penn's Creek, across the Susquehanna. So crowded did the Moravians' place get that one evening the missionaries turned away several Delawares because the house already held two colonists and seven Iroquois.[4]

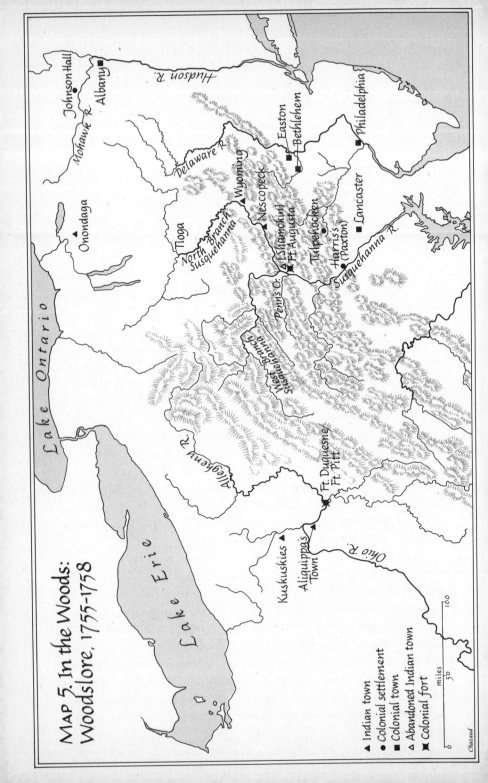

MAP 5. In the Woods:
Woodslore, 1755-1758

▲ Indian town
● Colonial settlement
■ Colonial town
△ Abandoned Indian town
■ Colonial fort

miles
0   50   100

Chazaud

Lake Ontario
Lake Erie

Hudson R.
Mohawk R.
Johnson Hall
Albany
Delaware R.
Easton
Bethlehem
Philadelphia
Onondaga
Wyoming
Nescopeck
Tioga
North Branch Susquehanna
Shamokin
Ft. Augusta
Tulpehocken
Lancaster
Harris's (Paxton)
Susquehanna R.
Penn's C.
West Branch Susquehanna
Allegheny R.
Ft. Duquesne
Ft. Pitt
Kuskuskies
Aliquippa's Town
Ohio R.

This everyday concourse, long common on the Pennsylvania frontier, would soon be brought to an abrupt end by "noise" and "heavy Storms" that started beyond the western mountains.[5] If those at the Susquehanna Forks worried about the French triumph over George Washington to the west in 1754—and, the next spring, General Edward Braddock's campaign to redeem Britain's fortunes—the missionaries' journal made no mention of it.[6] The "terrible news" of Braddock's defeat on July 9, which had colonists elsewhere in the Pennsylvania borderlands fleeing eastward and those staying behind "in a dismal fear," did not much disturb the peoples in and around Shamokin.[7]

But war came to town soon enough. In early October, a Delaware, saying that "French Indians" were near, advised the Moravians to flee. The missionaries, trusting in their god and their Shamokin friends, ignored the warning, but it was not long before they had reason to think again. On October 16 came word that enemy Indians had attacked the Penn's Creek people; as if to confirm the news, several warriors brought bloody weapons to the smith for repair. Close behind them came the Moravians' old friend, Tachnechdorus (John Shickellamy), "very anxious," to ask: *Now are you worried? Now do you want to leave here?*[8]

They were, and they did. Before dawn on October 24, the Germans slipped into the stream of colonists pouring back across the hills.[9] The *lingua franca* of this human torrent was fear: get out, they chorused, "leave the dead on the lands"; one man, tempted to go back to collect a few things, *"remembered Lot's Wife"* and scurried on. At the colonial settlement nearest Shamokin, "everything [was] in the worst fear and terror, and most had already fled." Farther along were ragged families, "cumeing away in a hurry Some allmost naked," who counted themselves lucky to have lost everything but their lives.[10]

Had they known about Penn's Creek in more detail, the refugees would have picked up their already frantic pace.[11] It had been every colonist's worst nightmare. One morning eight Indians showed up at Jean Jacques Le Roy's farm, dispatched him with tomahawks, then captured his son and daughter, along with another girl staying there. After looting and torching the house, the warriors shoved the father's body, feet first, halfway into the flames, leaving two hatchets in his head as their calling card. Then two of the Indians went on to the Leininger place nearby. That family—the father, his grown son, and two daughters were at home—suspected nothing as the visitors asked for rum and, told there was none, settled for tobacco. "We are Alleghany Indians, and your enemies," they suddenly shouted after smoking a pipe. "You must all die!" In no time they slew the men and carried the girls into the trees.[12]

The killing went on all day. That evening more warriors came back to camp "with six fresh and bloody scalps, which they threw at the feet of the poor captives, saying that they had a good hunt that day." The next day's hunt yielded another nine scalps and five more prisoners. Then, with ten captives in tow and fifteen scalps dangling from their belts, the raiders melted back into the forest. Terrified survivors returning to bury the victims found a silent land of blackened houses and butchered corpses.[13]

Once word of the devastation spread, the terror spread, too. Even the Tulpehocken Valley, forty miles from the Susquehanna, was "in such alarm as if they had already been killed." One family there, on being reassured that the enemy was still a ways off, rejoiced "that they could go to sleep in peace one more night."[14]

Peace would not last much longer, however: Indians invaded Tulpehocken on November 15. Many families fled toward Reading and safety; one, the Kobels, did not make it. With eight children under fourteen, including a newborn, the family was slow as father, mother, and eldest son each carried one of the younger ones. A war party of seven or eight men caught up with them in Abraham Sneider's cornfield, shot the father, and knocked the mother to the ground. Recovering her senses, the woman sat on a stump and began to nurse her infant while the warriors herded the other children "together and spoke to them in High Dutch [*Hoch Deutsch,* or High German], *be still we wont hurt you.*" A moment later one buried his hatchet in the mother's skull and, planting a foot on her neck, "tore off the Scalp." At this the children scattered, but their captors were too quick. One boy fell beside his mother; another child made it into Sneider's house before being caught, killed, and scalped; a girl reached a neighbor's garden before meeting the same fate. Racing to the rescue, neighbors came upon "Indians sitting on the [other four] Children scalping." All four were scalped alive; two lived to tell about it. With the infant (found, still breathing, beneath its mother's corpse), these two were all that remained of the Kobels.[15]

The killings, and all those still to come, were at once a legacy of negotiators and a repudiation of that legacy. Taught by decades of peaceful contact that go-betweens helped nurture, colonists and Indians had come to know one another well, well enough to share a pipe at Leininger's house, well enough that warriors spoke German to their German victims in Sneider's field. But the bloodshed that followed the pipe and the German seemed likely to put an end to the long conversation.

Certainly few Pennsylvanians were interested any longer in communication with Indians beyond what issued from the muzzle of a gun. Even before the Penn's Creek massacre, many colonists, convinced that all natives favored the French, were "malicious against our Indians," Weiser fretted; "they curse & damn em to their Faces." Come fall, reports of deeds by "these Bloody & Cruel Savages" only deepened the hatred. Shaken survivors, "the murder Shout" and "the last shrieks of their dying neighbours" still ringing in their ears, told horror stories that blurred the line between real and imagined atrocities: one war party attacked a young woman's funeral, tore open the casket, and scalped the corpse; others decapitated women and drank the blood of children "like Water." Who among colonists knew which gruesome tales were true, and which were the product of hatred, a deranged mind, a vivid imagination? At this point, though, who among colonists cared? Unable (or unwilling) to read the raids as anything but senseless savagery, blind and deaf to the messages of vengeance, anger, and power that Indians broadcast with tomahawks and taunts, frontier folk were ready to believe the worst.[16]

Not just the angry Ohio warriors carrying out the initial raids but Susquehanna Indians, too—neutral, at first—eventually came to believe that the time for talk with colonists had passed. Rumors tore through Susquehanna Valley communities in the early days of the war, telling that Pennsylvanians were about to retaliate against any Indians they could find. Blaming us for the attacks, natives there told one another, colonists have imprisoned 232 Delawares and now plan to invade Wyoming. Once there, "they intended to . . . bind the Indians, & carry them to Philad[elphi]a, and if any resisted, they would cut his Head off." So great was the fear that a Delaware seeing some Pennsylvanians at Shamokin on October 24 asked nervously, "What are the English come here for?" "To kill us I suppose," was his companion's prompt reply.[17]

Still, amid the shouts and shrieks were whispers of peace. Some colonists prayed that "Providential Interposition" would somehow "Change ye hearts & restore ye Sight," but most knew that peace demanded human, not divine, intervention. Fortunately, on both sides were men still determined to find a way out of the woods. "I cannot give over our Indians as yet," Weiser wrote on October 31. "They themselves are in fear both of French and English[,] Our People charging them to their Faces with Falshood."[18] At John Harris's nearby, meanwhile, Tohashwughtonionty (the Belt of Wampum or the Old Belt), Seneca George, and fifty or sixty more natives, most of them Ohio Iroquois, were Britain's steadfast friends. Even Ohio Delaware war parties, dragging Pennsylvanians off in 1755, paused to talk about ways to open peace negotiations.[19] From such frail hopes and small beginnings, peoples waged peace in the seasons to come. All of the usual problems of frontier negotiation—recruiting trusted, capable men; coming safe through the woods; carrying on a coherent conversation—would be infinitely more difficult, and more dangerous, in time of war.

The best way to appreciate just how difficult and dangerous is to chronicle three crucial campaigns in the battle for peace. The first, which fell to Scarouyady and Andrew Montour during the winter of 1755–1756, was to ensure that the Six Nations remained loyal to the British. The next, the following summer of 1756, sought to bring Pennsylvania's nearest foes, the Delawares and others on the North Branch of the Susquehanna, back into the fold, a task shared by the Iroquois Newcastle and Jagrea. The last (and hardest), winning back the Ohio peoples who had started the war, was undertaken in the summer and fall of 1758 by the Delaware Pisquetomen and the Moravian Christian Frederick Post.

Study of these three initiatives reveals that the famous councils at Easton and Lancaster—which stretched from 1756 to 1762 and forged, at last, a tenuous peace—were only the final steps on a long and perilous path. Convening those treaties required that negotiators convince colonists and Indians to approach one another without a gun or hatchet in hand. Through skill, tenacity, and luck, go-betweens managed that much; persuading those peoples to forget what the guns and hatchets had wrought was another matter.[20]

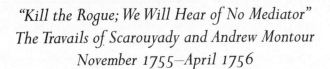

"Kill the Rogue; We Will Hear of No Mediator"
The Travails of Scarouyady and Andrew Montour
November 1755–April 1756

At Shamokin early on the morning of October 25, John Harris and Thomas McKee, with some forty other colonists, were hastily getting ready to leave town. It had been a grim journey and a long night. Several days before, upon hearing of the Indian raid at Penn's Creek, these "Paxton people" had headed upstream to scout the enemy and visit Shamokin, where they hoped "to know the minds of the Indians and their opinion of these times."[21] The horsemen had arrived in town at dusk on October 24, only to find Shamokin hard to read. On the one hand, McKee and Harris saw some familiar faces and were "seemingly well received." On the other, among the familiar faces were "a great number of strange Indians, . . . all painted Black" for war. Worse still, during the night Harris's men overheard Delawares plotting against them, talk followed by "the War Song" and then by four natives paddling off into the darkness. No wonder the colonists were keen to depart that morning. But then, as the visitors mounted up, Andrew Montour and Scarouyady stepped forward with some advice: the enemy, knowing that your favorite route home is on the Susquehanna's west bank, has laid a trap for you there; go down this side of the river instead.[22]

At the fork in the river road just outside Shamokin the colonists debated what to do.[23] The question framing the discussion was simple: could Montour and Scarouyady be trusted? Some in the party said yes. Montour, they remembered, had served Britain's American colonies for years, work that earned him a French bounty on his capture (or his scalp). Scarouyady, lacking the dubious distinction of a price on his head, was no less loyal, as the pistol, saddle, beaver hat, and ruffled shirt that grateful British officials had given him attested.[24] This Oneida had befriended James Logan years ago; since 1747, when he led the first Ohio delegation to Pennsylvania, he had demonstrated his attachment to the British time and time again. "[A] very hearty Friend of the English . . . ," Richard Peters observed in January 1755; "a brave and stout Man [who] has an Aversion to the French." Both the Oneida and the *métis* were with Washington, then with Braddock. Undaunted by those debacles, just a month ago the two had led a war party of Indians and Pennsylvanians against the French. Montour and Scarouyady, some Paxton men argued, have proven loyal too many times to be doubted now. Heed their warning; ride down this bank.[25]

Others disagreed. Scarouyady, to be sure, had no known record of crimes against the English save a fondness for rum and a sharp tongue. But he was an Indian, and all Indians were suspect now. Suspect, too, was this "French Andrew," this "Monsieur Montour" who, John Harris claimed, "knew many days of the Enemy's being on their March against us before he informed me."[26] And just now, when Montour had come forward with his warning, he was "painted as the rest," surely a sinister sign. Though admitting "'tis hard to tell," colonists urging the western route insisted that the advice be ignored; Montour was "an Enemy in his heart."[27]

The skeptics won. The men forded the river, and at Penn's Creek rode into an ambush. The Indians' first volley killed four and, amid the enemy's "shooting and hideous hollowing," sparked debate of another sort as "Some Cried let us fly others Stand your ground."[28] Most galloped off at once, flinging their guns into the river. The rest ducked into the trees and returned fire while making for the Susquehanna. Harris, abandoning his wounded horse midstream, swam the rest of the way; several of his companions drowned trying to cross.[29]

Imagine what Scarouyady and Montour must have thought when Thomas McKee, his hand shattered by a ball, scurried back to Shamokin and admitted that colonists, seeing Montour painted, had taken the *métis* at face value.[30] If ever the two go-betweens were to give up on Pennsylvania, now seemed the time. After all, everyone else in Shamokin was, however reluctantly, turning against the province. Kinfolk to the west had been working to draw these and other Susquehanna peoples away from Pennsylvania, sending a hatchet and English scalps, bringing encouraging words from the French, promising "Delawares that if they would assist them they would repossess them of their native Country and bring the [Pennsylvania] people under their Command."[31] Still, even after the raid on Penn's Creek, the town at the Forks had stood firm, assuring Pennsylvania that "if the white people will come up to Shamokin and assist[,] they will stand the French and fight them. They . . . want to see their Brethren's faces, and well armed." John Harris's men had brought the faces, and the arms, but then they, like every other colonist in the vicinity, retreated with alarming speed. At last Shamokin's people felt that they had no choice but to follow the enemy Indians' instructions and move upriver to Nescopeck, Wyoming, and other towns, towns that now throbbed with the war dances of native men ritually preparing themselves for raids on the province.[32]

But Scarouyady and Montour, with a few others, chose a different path out of Shamokin. Just before midnight on October 31 they showed up at John Harris's house, now a makeshift fort with loopholes in its walls.[33] If Harris wondered why these men remained true to Pennsylvania, he did not ask. Some have seen Weiser's steady hand here, but there may have been little choice. Their wives and children were at Harris's; could they collect them and return safely to the Indian countries?[34] Even if they got out of the province, after so many years serving the British could they change sides, could Montour elude bounty hunters or Scarouyady shed his fancy English clothes? It is impossible to recover the calculations that led them to head down the Susquehanna instead of up it; like Harris, we know only that they did.[35]

The welcome at Harris's that night must have been lukewarm, for many colonists still thought the two were with the French. The next day "divers p'sons" gathered news from Scarouyady and Montour; given the crowd, the fresh loopholes, and the lingering suspicions, this looked more like an interrogation than a chat.[36] In any case, Montour and a "Very Tired" Scarouyady soon broke free, bound for Philadelphia. A week later, Weiser in tow, they stood in the provincial council chamber, determined at "this dangerous time" to "have in plain Terms how things shall be."[37]

My words are for the "People of this Province," the Oneida told Governor Morris and the council that morning. In the afternoon the assembly, city officials, "and citizens" joined Morris and his council in the State House to hear Scarouyady, "with great Force and Energy, and with apparent Grief and Concern," offer the province one last chance to keep its native neighbors. Susquehanna Indians hate the French and will fight, he told the crowd, but they need Pennsylvania's help. "I must now know if you will stand by us," Scarouyady went on; "to be plain, if you will fight or not." If not, he said, throwing wampum belts on the table, "we will go somewhere else for protection and take care of ourselves."[38]

For several long days Scarouyady and Montour waited for an answer. Then, on November 12, Morris finally told them the truth: Pennsylvania can do nothing now. The assembly refuses to raise money for defense unless revenue from proprietary lands is included, the governor explained, but I have strict orders from the Penns to forbid taxes on those holdings. The Oneida heard the news "with amazement," and in private "spoke with great Contempt on our Measures." But in public he "still offered his own Services, and desired the Governor not to be cast down, but take time and enter cooly into the Consideration of what could be done, in which he would give his assistance heartily."[39] Even if Susquehanna Indians join the enemy, Pennsylvania is not alone. The Iroquois are still neutral, and it was to the Iroquois that Montour and Scarouyady decided to go. As Pennsylvania ambassadors, they would travel up the Susquehanna to sound the depths of disaffection there; once in Iroquoia, they would ask the Six Nations' help. On November 14 the emissaries set off, armed with instructions, a score of wampum strings and belts, and Morris's sensible (if silly) advice to "avoid going into places where they may be in danger of being hurt."[40]

It turned out that there were no such safe places. At Tulpehocken the envoys, escorted by Weiser, waded into an elemental sea of anger and hate. Indian raiders had just been there, leaving corpses strewn about and survivors furiously demanding a bounty on all Indian scalps, "be they Friends or Enemies." Lining the road were the spiritual heirs of John and Walter Winter a generation before, several hundred armed men who were "enraged against all the Indians, & would kill them without Distinction." The go-betweens rode a gauntlet of shouts and shaken fists, guns brandished and faces contorted with rage. "[W]hy must we be killed by the Indians and we not kill them!" colonists cried. "[W]hy are our Hands so tied?" Struggling through the maelstrom, Weiser and his two charges "parted in Love and Friendship."[41]

Love and friendship were just as scarce on the Susquehanna, however. At Wyoming, when Scarouyady asked some warriors to postpone their raid on Pennsylvania until his return from Iroquoia, "they with a Stick pushed aside the Belt in a contemptuous Manner, and muttering . . . in an angry Tone." The wampum fared no better at the Wyoming council. "They would not so much as touch his Belts he laid before them," one observer reported. "They throwed them on one side with their Pipes, and gave him ill Language." Worse, "whilst he was consulting with the eldest of them in the evening, the rest cried out of doors, let us kill the Rogue; we will hear of no Mediator, much less of a Master; hold your Tongue and be gone, or you shall live no longer."

It had been a close call. "I have but just escaped with life," the shaken Oneida reported from Iroquoia in early January.[42]

The welcome was warm in Iroquoia, and the Six Nations council held at William Johnson's in February reassuring. We did not start this war, the Iroquois sent word south to Pennsylvania; we oppose it; we will help. On March 21 Scarouyady and Montour—accompanied by several Indians and Daniel Claus, now one of Johnson's assistants— were back in Philadelphia, where they met up with Seneca George and other loyalists who had wintered near Harris's.[43]

While the news was "joyful," the envoys found the capital as frustrating as it had been in November.[44] "[T]he common People to a Man . . . insult us wherever we go," Scarouyady complained, yet while harassing its Indian friends, the colony—even after finally passing a defense bill—had done little about attacking its Indian foes. "We are amazed to find you still sitting with your Hands between your Knees," the Oneida scolded.[45]

Delays did nothing to improve his mood. "Fatigue and fresh Fish of which the Indians are fond threw them into pleuratick Disorders" and killed one. The Condolence took time away from negotiations, as did Morris, who—perhaps weary that "Indians adhere so closely to their Tedious Ceremonies"—was often out of town. Perhaps expressing his frustration, Scarouyady went on a drinking binge that took up two more days.[46]

The conversations in the capital ended up broadcasting mixed signals back to Indian country. On the one hand, the Indians lobbied hard for war, punctuating their words with a war dance in the State House. The province went along, declaring war on April 14 and setting bounties on Indian scalps.[47] On the other hand, scarcely was the dance done and war declared than Scarouyady, Montour, and the rest of the delegation held talks with Quakers that sent the opposite signal. At Quaker leader Israel Pemberton's crowded house on April 23, the Oneida accepted a white peace belt, and with it the Friends' "offer to stand as Mediators" for Pennsylvania and its foes. War and peace belts would go out in the same wampum bag.[48]

By then, Scarouyady and the others were more than ready to leave. As early as April 5 they had already "resolved to quitt this Government and live among their friends the Six Nations."[49] The delay and confusion of the next three weeks did nothing to change their minds; neither did rewards for their services and promises of captains' commissions if only they would stay on. The go-betweens tried to make a graceful exit. We leave Pennsylvania in order to help her, they assured worried colonial officials; we will represent you in Iroquoia, and there recruit warriors for a Susquehanna campaign. In fact, however, Scarouyady and Montour were giving up on the province for good.[50]

If the aged Oneida had any doubts about his decision to abandon Pennsylvania, they vanished on April 26, the day after he, Montour, Seneca George, and the rest of the party left Philadelphia, when Morris sent someone after them to ask about two young colonists who had gone with the Indians. One, formally adopted, "belonged to their family," Scarouyady replied; the other had come "of his own Inclination." Then, "in his fretting way," the Oneida launched a stinging rebuke of his erstwhile Pennsylvania friends. This, he said, is your answer to my suggestion that you send young men to live among the Indians "to get acquainted w[i]th their Language & Customs." I "must perceive now fully," he told Morris, "that the white people look'd at them [Indians] as Dogs, and would not trust their Children to their Care, whereby they could discover the little Confidence and Love they had to them."[51]

It was a profound change of heart. Just nine months earlier, furious with arrogant British incompetents like Braddock, Scarouyady had linked Indians to colonists in a common American heritage. "[D]on't let those that come from over the great Seas be concerned any more" in this war, he had instructed the Pennsylvania council; "they are unfit to fight in the Woods. Let us go ourselves, we that came out of this Ground, We may be assured to conquer the French." Now, thoroughly alienated from their fellow Americans, neither Scarouyady nor Montour would ever return to help Pennsylvania.[52]

"The Good Work So Fortunately Begun"
The Travails of Newcastle and Jagrea,
April–November, 1756

Early on April 26, the morning after Scarouyady, Montour, and their company left Philadelphia for Iroquoia, Conrad Weiser and three Indians showed up at Governor Morris's door. The three—Newcastle (Kos Showweyha, Kanuksusy), Jagrea (Sata Karoyis), and William Lacquis—

were the men Scarouyady had chosen to carry the Quakers' peace offering to the Susquehanna country. Morris assumed that the emissaries
had come to say their good-byes, since escorts and passports were already arranged. He was in for a surprise. "Scarroyady never consulted
us before hand," the three announced, "and took upon him in too
peremptory a Manner to order us to go. . . . [H]e had no Right to do
this: we are not his Vassals, nor to be treated in so haughty a Manner;
and, therefore, . . . we will not carry any of Scarroyady's Messages."[53]

On this sour note, the second of Pennsylvania's three peace initiatives
got under way. With Scarouyady's departure, hope for an end to the
hostilities came to rest on the trio he had pointed to at Israel Pemberton's on April 23, and who now stood so unhappily before Morris.[54]
Newcastle, Jagrea, and Lacquis were to succeed where Scarouyady and
Montour had failed: coaxing Susquehanna peoples onto the road toward
peace.

The three were in some ways obvious choices to be "Pennsylvania
Messengers." Lacquis, a Jersey Delaware, would be living proof that,
despite all the rumors, colonists had not killed every Indian among
them.[55] Newcastle and Jagrea were Ohio men known for their allegiance to the province. A Seneca war leader and son of "Queen"
Aliquippa who earned his English name because of that alleged meeting with William Penn at the town beside the Delaware, in 1747 Newcastle had resurfaced in Penn's Woods with Scarouyady's Ohio
delegation. Since then he had followed the same hard road of other
Ohio peoples loyal to the British, through Washington's defeat at Great
Meadows and Braddock's killing field to refugee camps at George
Croghan's and, during the winter of 1755–1756, John Harris's.[56] The
Mohawk Jagrea was a younger but also useful man; Scarouyady's son-
in-law, he, too, had borne messages across the mountains. So respected
were these Ohioans that in January 1756, when Indians designated two
Pennsylvanians as go-betweens, they named the two *Jagrea* and *Kos
Showweyha*.[57]

On the other hand, however, Scarouyady's choice that day at Pemberton's must have puzzled some people. None of the three knew the
way to the North Branch; none claimed to be a speaker versed in the
ways of wampum and words.[58] Lacquis was so unimportant that on
the list of natives gathered at Pemberton's he was lumped, last, with
"Severall Indian Women." Colonists who did know the Delaware
thought him undependable, "impudent & mischievous in his Nature." If

no one castigated Lacquis's two companions so harshly, some did doubt their judgment. Newcastle occasionally drank too much, as did "drunken Zigrea," but worse was their tendency, drunk or sober, to panic. In January 1756, the Indian loyalists wintering at Harris's heard that some colonists were coming to kill them. Most stayed put, trusting Weiser to head off trouble, but Jagrea and Newcastle fled, and that night "Newcastle got . . . light headed." Thinking "every Person . . . an Enemy," the Seneca disappeared for several days. In Bethlehem six months later it was Jagrea who, angry at some slight, stormed off into the darkness.[59]

Whatever their handicaps in temperament and experience, once Morris and Weiser convinced them to proceed, Newcastle and his companions set out to silence the Susquehanna's noise. During the next six months, Newcastle made three trips north on Pennsylvania's behalf. The first, in May, took him, with Jagrea and Lacquis, to the North Branch of the Susquehanna to hunt for signs of peace. Finding those hopeful signs—peoples there were starving and haunted by rumors of an imminent colonial invasion—the three brought back "very good news."[60] To further what Jagrea called "the good Work so fortunately begun," Newcastle returned to the Susquehanna in July— accompanied this time by John Pumpshire and two other Jersey Delawares (Jagrea and Lacquis having dropped out)—in order to invite the Indians to a treaty. By July 20 he was in Philadelphia again, again saying that "in General Matters look well": the Delaware leader Teedyuscung was at that very moment in Easton, ready to talk about ending hostilities.[61] Then, after that council, the first in a long series that would bring peace to Pennsylvania, Newcastle headed north once more, this time by wagon and boat through colonial settlements to Iroquoia, in order "to enquire into the Character and Credentials of Teedyuscung," the colony's new friend, that volatile Delaware peacemaker.[62] In mid-October the Seneca was back in the Pennsylvania capital yet again. It was to be his last stop. He died there in early November, on the eve of the colony's second treaty with the Susquehanna peoples he had coaxed toward the council fire.

Though it cost him his life, Newcastle's negotiation was an extraordinary achievement. Twice venturing into enemy territory on the Susquehanna where, just months before, Scarouyady and Montour had been "very often in Danger of losing both our Messages and our Lives," Newcastle emerged not only with his life but with people inclined toward peace. So great was the peril that in April Scarouyady, who knew better than anyone what awaited in the Susquehanna country, had wondered aloud whether Newcastle and the others would "have their throats cut."[63]

Certainly Newcastle, casting his eyes northward, had expected the worst. From Bethlehem on May 2 he and his companions sent a "last Declaration" back to Morris that was a contingency plan for disaster.[64] If we do not return in thirty-five days, assume we are killed or captured. If we do get through but our return is blocked by "either the white People, or the bad Indians," we will take the following detour. If the person carrying our flag and passport is killed "and the others . . . forced, to run for their Life," we will devise the following alternate signs. Newcastle was not light-headed this time. The party's guide, a Christian Delaware named Memenwoot (Augustus), was no less afraid. Having agreed to go, "he called his Wife, Mother-in-Law, and two Sons together, and Declared to them his Last Will."[65]

It was not clear who posed the greatest threat, "the white People, or the bad Indians." Another Augustus, the Moravian leader Augustus Spangenberg, "thought them [the messengers] all in greater Dangers of being hurt" on the frontier above Bethlehem "than any where Else in all the Province," "for People in our Parts are more allarmed at the Sight of an Indian, and more eager after their Blood, then lower down in the Province." On one journey Newcastle, even with a Pennsylvania passport and an English flag to shield him from colonial outrage, had to hole up in a Bethlehem house for three weeks while New Jersey militia hunted Indian scalps to the north.[66]

Sidestepping would-be colonial killers, upon crossing the frontier the emissaries still faced "bad Indians." As Newcastle and his companions approached one Susquehanna town on their first expedition that May, they were almost done in by the sort of rumor Lacquis was sent to quell. The English have killed all but two of the Indians living among them, this variation of the invasion story went; they had spared Augustus only because he promised "to lead on the white People against the Indians." And who was the first of the travelers to come within view of the town? None other than their guide, Augustus! The townsfolk, their worst fears apparently realized, assumed that a colonial army marched right behind him.[67]

Newcastle cleared this up, but—among some Delawares, at least—resentment of him endured. At the Easton treaty in July Teedyuscung

pulled the Seneca aside to tell him of rumors that Delaware conjurers were planning to kill him. Newcastle—drunk this time, not
light-headed—went to the governor to wail "that the Delawares had bewitched him and he should dye soon." While the befuddled Morris was
trying to calm the man, Teedyuscung "bolted into the Room, fell into
a violent Passion with New Castle, . . . and desired he might not be re-
garded in any thing he should say on such a foolish subject, exclaiming,
He bewitched! the Governor was too wise to hearken to such silly Stories," then roared out again. However silly the tale might seem, that
night Newcastle fell ill and, "To the surprise of every Body" (except, one
assumes, the victim), lay near death.[68]

Three days later the patient had recovered with (or in spite of) the
help of a colonial doctor, but in Philadelphia that fall his luck finally ran
out. Colonists diagnosed the malady as smallpox; perhaps the Seneca
thought Delaware conjurers had found him. In any case, on the afternoon of November 6, the day Pennsylvania's new governor, William
Denny, left for Easton and another round of peace talks with Teedyuscung, "a vast Train" followed the old Seneca's casket to the Quaker burial ground where—at his request—he was laid to rest among Friends.[69]

That funeral cortege winding through Philadelphia streets to fulfill
Newcastle's last wish suggests that this Indian, at least, kept his attach-
ment to Pennsylvania. "[H]e was," mourned Richard Peters after the
Seneca's death, "faithful, sensible and industrious."[70] But a colonial eu-
logy, like a Quaker burial, can be deceptive. Newcastle was close to
Friends because, the previous April at Pemberton's house, they had
presented themselves as the only true heirs of the great William Penn.
But conversations in Philadelphia over the next six months made the
Seneca fret and fume about Penn's people as much as Scarouyady ever
did, for it turned out that the problem with Pennsylvania went beyond
its diseases or angry frontiersmen to the obtuseness and incompetence
of its leaders. "[I]t behoves you to use Dispatch," the ambassadors advised the governor and council upon returning from that first visit to
the Susquehanna, "and send us back quickly with your answers, least,
as Times are dangerous, any thing may intervene." Listening politely,
provincial authorities let many things intervene. Morris, at John Harris's, blandly invited the messengers there for a chat. No, came the
curt reply: that was "a Place of Blood" unfit for words of peace.[71]

Once everyone gathered in the capital near the end of May, though,
more problems surfaced. As he bade the Seneca farewell a month be-

fore, Governor Morris had promised to bring Newcastle's niece, Cana-dahawaby, to town in order to await the messengers' return. Now, find-ing her not yet in Philadelphia, Newcastle "was so much disgusted . . . that he . . . declined returning to" the Susquehanna.[72] Even as Morris placated the Seneca emissary and dispatched someone to fetch the girl, Pennsylvania officials ignored the advice to hurry. They awaited further word from Onondaga; they proclaimed a ceasefire; they tried to collect more Jersey Indians to take Lacquis's place as proof that colonists had spared local natives. Not until June 8—with Newcastle warning that Susquehanna Indians would think Pennsylvania had murdered the mes-sengers if they stayed any longer—did the colony send him back.[73]

On his return from that second trip in July, Newcastle again found Philadelphia infuriating. "[T]he times are very Precarious," he said "in a very Serious manner" on July 20; "not a moment is to be lost." Yet the colony dithered. "The [Delaware] Forks is believed to be the place of Meeting," he replied testily when Morris wondered where to hold the treaty. Since Teedyuscung awaits you there, "what need of any Alter-ation? let it be there; tarry not but Hasten to him."[74]

Newcastle's third and final visit to Philadelphia that fall went no bet-ter. He brought word that the Six Nations thought Teedyuscung at best a blowhard and at worst a fraud. Not only was the Delaware man un-predictable, not only did he possess nowhere near the authority he claimed, he had a tenuous commitment to peace, having led war par-ties against Pennsylvania and visited a French fort.[75] But though the Seneca negotiator had "much to say" to Philadelphia officials that Oc-tober, no one wanted to listen; it was too late to halt the peace talks he had set in motion. Teedyuscung was already on his way to Easton for an-other council. Even if he did not speak for all of the Indians, he still spoke for some, and he spoke of peace at a time when other natives were still making Pennsylvania a "waist Land." The meeting with him must go ahead.[76]

It would go ahead without Newcastle, who fell ill while waiting—again!—for colonial officials. We can only speculate on the Seneca's thoughts as he lay dying, but they were probably akin to Scarouyady's the previous spring: Pennsylvanians were dilatory and contentious; they listened to that impostor Teedyuscung; they broke promises; they ignored his repeated requests, that fall, "to be sent into the Coun-try" away from the capital, its people, its maladies. "He has not been well used," a rueful Richard Peters admitted soon after the Seneca's arrival in October.[77] Newcastle died before he could fret and flee as Scarouyady had; but he died, it seems clear, doubting the word, and the wisdom, of the people with whom he had cast his lot, and for whom he had risked his life.

"Their Faces Were Quite Distorted with Rage"
The Travails of Pisquetomen and Post,
June–November, 1758

At Wyoming early on the morning of June 28, 1758, a Pennsylvanian joined some Indians for breakfast beside a fire. The hosts were the Delaware leader Pisquetomen and a handful of other "Indians from Allegheny"; their guest was the Moravian missionary and provincial messenger Christian Frederick Post. The men sat amid a cluster of log cabins, with a garden and fenced field nearby, a sign of provincial favor that colonial workers had built for Teedyuscung's people just a month before.[78] With his plate of bear and turkey Post got a grilling and a lecture. The Allegheny Indians "asked me many Questions . . . ," he wrote, and "complained strongly that they never had heard any Satisfactory Account of . . . any [peace] Treaties that had been held, nor received any Belts 'till now lately." "[T]he English were not in fault," Post protested, "for they had often sent the Messages, Belts and Invitations to them that they might come down and speak together." We do want peace; trust me; come to Philadelphia; you will see. The next day the Moravian led the Delaware toward the capital, and toward peace.

The two seemed an unlikely pair. Newcastle and Jagrea, like Scarouyady and Montour, had known one another before embarking on their missions; they drew from the same wellsprings of experience. Pisquetomen and Post followed very different paths to Wyoming. Pisquetomen, nephew of Sassoonan, was known for his towering rages and strings of English curses, Post for his serenity and sweet disposition. Pisquetomen hated Pennsylvania colonists for driving his people from Tulpehocken to Shamokin and then over the mountains; Post loved Indians, loved them so much indeed that he had twice married among them.[79] Not only were these two men an odd couple; they were improbable peacemakers. Pisquetomen, who had led the raid on Penn's

Creek in October 1755, was hardly the sort of messenger colonists were likely to embrace. Post, with no prior experience as a negotiator, was a missionary and therefore automatically suspect in Indian country.

On the other hand, the Delaware warrior and the German missionary were neither wholly incompatible nor utterly ill-equipped to negotiate. Both were Susquehanna men, Post having lived at Wyoming for several years, Pisquetomen at Shamokin. Both knew English as well as Delaware. Both had connections on the far side of the cultural divide: Pisquetomen is "known to many here" from his years with Sassoonan, officials in Philadelphia remarked when he arrived in July; later, in the Ohio country, Post often crossed paths with old friends from his Susquehanna days. Such experience made them both culturally flexible enough that Pisquetomen "sometimes Calls himself a Quaker," while Post, in turn, said he was the Delawares' "own flesh and blood."[80]

Even weaknesses could become strengths. Pisquetomen might have been the man who sank a hatchet into Jean Jacques Le Roy's head and opened fire on John Harris; but if such a renowned war leader came seeking peace, perhaps peace was indeed possible. At the same time, Post's very inexperience as a go-between was an advantage of sorts, for it left him untainted by the colonial chicanery Indians resented so bitterly. If the two seemed an odd couple, they nonetheless had qualities that would be useful on the journey that lay before them.[81]

That journey would not be easy. Almost two more years of sorrow and terror stood between Newcastle's last trip and Post's first. Just that spring, Ohio war parties again preyed on Pennsylvania, then headed home with fresh scalps dangling from their belts and bound prisoners stumbling along behind.[82] Indians had their own reasons to be afraid, for behind the warriors, too, was an army under General John Forbes, an army bound (as Braddock's had been in 1755) for the French stronghold, Fort Duquesne, at the Forks of the Ohio, an army so large that Indian scouts spent an entire day trying to find the end of its line of march. As usual, rumors fed the fear. Many colonists thought that Indian treaty talk was a charade, that the white wampum belts hid bloody scalping knives. Natives, more frightened still, heard "every Day new accounts and Stories of the bad Designs the English had against the Indians."[83]

Still, there was hope, for some people beside both the Delaware River and the Ohio yearned for an end to war. Many Indians—short of food, wracked by disease, poorly supplied by the French, shaken by a

Pennsylvania raid over the mountains in the fall of 1756—peered and probed eastward, searching for signals of peace.[84] Meanwhile Pennsylvania had, as Post said at Wyoming, been sending just those signals. The problem was that the Six Nations and Teedyuscung, both keen to claim authority in the Ohio country, tended to bury messages that did not bear their stamp, while the French played on native fears about the silence from the east so shrewdly that those natives "could not believe that [Pennsylvania] would make Peace with them."[85] It was to break these sound barriers that Post had headed into Indian country, just as Pisquetomen had come east to learn "what is true and what is false." Knowing opportunity when it sat down next to him, the Moravian abandoned his mission and joined the Delaware's.[86]

From that chance encounter in Wyoming came this unlikely, historic partnership. Between late June and late November 1758 the German and the Delaware—accompanied by various other colonists and Indians—traveled hundreds of miles together to calm the heavy storms that, for four long years, had battered the frontier. To Philadelphia they went in July, to hear talk of peace from the governor himself.[87] By mid-August, bearing soft words and white wampum from *Onas,* they were at the Ohio Indian town of Kuskuskies to turn people of the region away from war. Back east the two ambassadors came five weeks later with the encouraging news that Ohio Indians did indeed want peace negotiations to go forward. Then, after a month of meetings in Pennsylvania, it was over the mountains to Kuskuskies once more, with speeches that persuaded Ohio Indians to sit out Forbes's impending assault on Fort Duquesne. On November 24 Post and his companions took down the French flag flying over the Kuskuskies council house and hoisted Britain's colors in its stead. The next day word reached town that, the French having withdrawn, "the *English* had the field." Post and Pisquetomen, with help from colonial and native comrades, had saved Forbes from Braddock's fate.[88]

The roundabout route from Wyoming in June to Kuskuskies in November was fraught with peril, both for the negotiators themselves and for their mission. Where their predecessors—Scarouyady and Montour, Newcastle and Jagrea—had met the same dangers at the same time, the risk for Pisquetomen and Post alternated from one to the other depending on where they were. In the Ohio country Post, by his mere presence (and what that presence stood for), faced terrible danger on his grueling round of meals, dances, and councils. At one village two warriors "were very surly. When I went to shake hands with one of them, he gave me his little finger; the other withdrew his hand entirely." At another the townsfolk "surrounded me," Post wrote, "with drawn knives in their hands, in such a manner, that I could hardly get along. . . . Their faces were quite distorted with rage, and they went so far as to say, I should not live long."[89]

The French did what they could to make this prediction come true. Placing a bounty on Post's scalp helped. So did having an officer dog his steps as the emissary went from Kuskuskies to other towns, preaching peace; more officers joined the threatening crowd when the diplomatic itinerary took the Pennsylvanian to an island in the very shadow of Fort Duquesne. Instructed "not to stir from the fire," the obliging Post "stuck constantly as close to the fire, as if I had been chained there."[90]

Having slipped the clutches of the French, Post still faced a Delaware named Essoweyoualand (Shamokin Daniel), one of his companions on the trip from Pennsylvania. While the missionary had hugged the fireside, Essoweyoualand—already unhappy with the colony's failure to pay him adequately for an earlier mission—spent three days in the fort being courted by the French and came back, Post observed, "quite changed." "The English are fools," Daniel suddenly said, turning on Post, "and so are you." "Do not believe him," the Delaware interrupted when Post talked of peace, "he tells nothing but idle lying stories. . . . G—d d—n you for a fool."[91]

Post survived these brushes with death to see Philadelphia again, but just as he broke free of danger, his companion Pisquetomen was at risk. Heading, as the Delaware put it, "through the fire" of frontier settlements, Pisquetomen and the other native negotiators were sometimes scorched, as Post had been in Ohio. One morning, the Moravian wrote, "some of the *Irish* people, knowing some of the *Indians,* in a rash manner exclaimed against them, and we had some difficulty to get them off clear." Not even General Forbes's headquarters offered sanctuary; soon after the party made camp there en route west in the fall, "some of the officers came, and spoke very rashly to our *Indians,* in respect to their conduct to our people."[92]

Like Post, Pisquetomen got in trouble merely by showing his face; the wounds of his raids were still fresh. But both men, each in his own way, also made matters worse. Post infuriated natives by scribbling too much in a notebook and talking too much with the Indians' captives. Moreover, the speeches he brought kept mentioning Teedyuscung and those colonial prisoners, topics so out of order—Ohioans wanted to hear from the governor, not that Delaware, and thought it premature to talk about redeeming captives—that Indians wondered if Pennsylvanians "wanted brains." Pisquetomen, too, occasionally seemed to be short on brains. When those British officers "spoke very rashly," the Delaware—no Post—"answered as rashly, and said, 'they did not understand such usage; . . . if we [the English] had a mind to war, they knew how to help themselves; and they were not afraid of us.' "[93]

But just as each go-between got into trouble, so each helped protect the other from that trouble, protection that was formal and explicit. "Boys, hearken," Pisquetomen's brother Tamaqua announced on first seeing Post at Kuskuskies; "we sat here without ever expecting again to see our brethren the *English;* but now one of them is brought before you, that you may see your brethren, the *English,* with your own eyes." *Is brought before you:* as Pisquetomen carried the words and wampum, so the Delaware toted Post himself, "in my bosom," for safekeeping. Thereafter Tamaqua, Pisquetomen, and Post's other Ohio sponsors shielded him from angry natives, scheming French, and the duplicitous Daniel.[94]

In Pennsylvania it was Pisquetomen, not Post, who had to be rescued from angry natives. A militia escort saw the Delaware and his Indian companions safely to Philadelphia and, in early October, on to the treaty council at Easton. Leaving that town and treaty later in the month, Pisquetomen took Post by the hand to formally "put ourselves under your protection to bring us safe through [Pennsylvania], and to secure us from all danger."[95]

Bring the Indians safe through Post did, just as they had done for him. But no chaperone could shield emissaries from the sorts of delays that had so plagued missions throughout the war years. After Post, in late August, had cheated the French, stood up to Essoweyoualand, and made it back to Kuskuskies, he had to wait there while the Indians debated an answer to Pennsylvania's peace offering. Their council was bitterly divided. Even the Moravian's friends remained skeptical. Here is Post, "with good news and fine speeches"; but here, too, are Forbes's soldiers, "now . . . standing *before our doors.*" Would these troops fight the French, then retire back across the mountains? Post said yes; others (including other colonists), no. Surely the English will drive the French out, then turn on the Indians "to destroy us, and take our lands." Discussion went on so long that Post's patience wore thin. "It is a troublesome cross and heavy yoke to draw this people," he confided to his diary. "They can punish and squeeze a body's heart to the utmost."[96]

Pisquetomen could have said the same after spending more than two weeks in the thick of another large and fractious council, this one at Easton in October. As one colonial participant wrote, "the success of all we have done or can do [about peace] is now near a Crisis," yet the congress dragged on.[97] Here the problem was not whether to make peace—everyone favored it—but the sheer size of the gathering and the number of agendas being pursued. While several hundred Indians from thirteen nations met with colonists from New Jersey and Pennsylvania, and while those colonists squabbled with Indians and with one another over everything from who should speak first to who had bought land, enemy war parties struck nearby. Peace must have seemed as far away there as it had at Kuskuskies. Like Post earlier that fall, Pisquetomen chafed to be on his way.[98]

At last Pennsylvania's reply was ready, full of good talk about peace and assurances that, once the French were removed, the British would stay out of Ohio. Late on the afternoon of October 22, a month since arriving on the provincial frontier, the emissaries sat down with Governor William Denny to take their leave. Setting a bottle of wine on the table and taking a string of wampum in hand, the governor once again "put under Pisquatomans Care" the men heading west to pave the way for Forbes's army. And little more than a month after that, Pisquetomen and those men had helped colonists accomplish their mission of moving Indians away from the French and toward peace.[99]

Traveling a difficult and dangerous road, talking late into the night, roasting meat over a fire, looking out for one another, the obscure Moravian missionary and the renowned Delaware leader managed to bridge the chasm of blood and fear between Pennsylvania and the Ohio country.[100] But their union of interest and intercultural skills proved short-lived. Indeed, their differences were more pronounced than ever after their partnership dissolved, for while Post went back with Forbes across the mountains, the army—breaking the promises Post, Pennsylvania, and Forbes had made to Ohio Indians—did not.

Pisquetomen had always dreaded this outcome, had feared that the plot of dispossession played out along the Delaware and the Susquehanna would someday cross the mountains. "[W]e have great reason to believe you intend to drive us away, and settle the country," he and other Delawares told Post at Kuskuskies on September 1, 1758; "or else, why do you come to fight in the land that God has given us?" Time and again, Post denied that colonists had designs on the Ohio country and promised that, after driving out the French, British troops would withdraw; time and again, Pisquetomen expressed doubts. On the second trip to Kuskuskies in November, an exasperated Post wrote, "*Pesquitomen* began to argue" about lands yet again, asking "whether the *English* thought to settle the country? We are always jealous," the Delaware went on, "the *English* will take the land from us." The following summer, with a British fort and settlement now at the Forks, Pisquetomen again "put it closely to" a Pennsylvanian there "what ye English . . . meant by coming here with a great army." Like his predecessors, that colonist insisted that the troops were there only temporarily; once the French were "subdued, ye army would be called away home."[101]

That day never came, and it is possible to read in Pisquetomen a growing disillusionment with his Pennsylvania brethren, a disillusionment deeper than anything Scarouyady or Newcastle had felt in 1756. Discussing Britain's territorial ambitions with Post at Kuskuskies that day in September 1758, the man who sometimes said he was a Quaker joined Tamaqua and the others to draw a line between "the white people" (whom "God has given . . . the tame creatures") and "the *Indians*" (whom "God has given the deer, and other wild creatures"). The distinction made, it became an indictment of colonial ways. "[W]e know there are always a great number of people [colonists] that want to get rich; they never have enough; look, we do not want to be rich, and take away that which others have."[102]

Nothing those colonists did in the months and years to come would have erased Pisquetomen's doubts about them. If the disappointed Delaware did not pick up his weapon and head back to Penn's Creek, neither did he continue the push for peace. In the spring of 1759 two Pennsylvania women, survivors of Penn's Creek who managed to escape a long captivity, claimed that Pisquetomen "does not appear to them to be hearty for ye English, but to be false hearted." Hearty or not, Pisquetomen dropped out of the shuttle diplomacy. He did not join his brothers Tamaqua and Shingas when they carried Pennsylvania's message deeper into Indian country, nor did he go with them for further talks in the colony itself.[103]

Post was similarly disenchanted. In 1760 this man, who had risked his life in the cause of peace, thought everlasting war a more likely prospect. "[F]or my part," he wrote, "I can never see t[h]rough how a peace can be settled with the Indians. To root theym out or to subdue theym I think it is impossible for this time, for theire is not one who rightly knows there Country and theare lurking holes." Still, he hoped for conquest, believing that it would "Open a Door" for missionary work. Deriding "their Stupid & Tragical way of Worship," thinking them "Voide of Reason," Post hardly sounded like Indians' "flesh and blood" anymore.[104]

No wonder that, when the Moravian did resume mission work in the Ohio country, he found it tough going. "What makes us afraid when you build a house among us," Delawares at a village called Tuscorawas replied in November 1760 when the Moravian asked for land to start a mission, is that "may be some other people will say 'we will build there,' and so one and then another will come, and they do not love our people." Post wanted to bring in assistants—"I alone cannot come through, and I must have somebody with me, brother," he explained— but Indians resisted. "Take thyself a wife who will attend thee," they proposed. Though he had twice married native women, this time Post demurred. "Your women are not good," he replied, "they look too much upon other men besides; they wish to have everyone whom they see, they are not contented with one & this is not pleasing to our Maker." Disagreeing—"brother we know some women that will stay with one man"—Indians still held out against additional colonists in their territory, proposing instead that Post "buy . . . a neger that works for you." Only when the Moravian threatened to go elsewhere with his mission, only when he actually "call'd for his Horse to be gone," did natives finally relent; "bring you someone along," they said grudgingly, "that may live with you."[105]

Post's triumph was short-lived, for resentment still ran high. Initially willing to let him "Clear as much Land as he would," by the spring of 1762 "they had limited him to a Garden Spot abo[u]t a quarter of an Acre." En route with the missionary to the Lancaster treaty that summer, Delawares said several times that they intended to "Deliver Frederick Post to ye Governor & tell him to keep him at home." By fall the "Old Man," back at Tuscorawas, discovered that enemies had wrecked his garden and given him "small hope of being Alowed to Plant anything" at all "next Spring." Like Pisquetomen, like Scarouyady and Montour, like Newcastle, Post had come up against, had personified, the limits of peacemaking.[106]

"They Would Let No Whit Man Go Throw Thire Contry"
The Limits of Peacemaking

Neutralizing Ohio, mollifying Teedyuscung, securing Onondaga—these were remarkable accomplishments, testimony to the mediators' skill, tenacity, and courage. In a way, the wartime negotiations were the go-betweens' finest hour. Working against great odds, they managed to resurrect something like peace. It helped that Post and the others could tap a common stock of happier memories. "[M]y wish," Pennsylvania told Ohio Delawares through Post, "is that we may join close together in that old brotherly love and friendship, which our grandfathers had." Not only that, the provincial speech continued, but "We look upon you as our countrymen, that sprung out of the same ground with us." Those Delawares, drafting their reply, picked up the thread "of that Peace and Friendship which we had formerly with you."[107]

Yet if the old words still had power, negotiation was forever different. On the one hand, nothing much had changed, from trails and wampum to factions and delays. On the other hand, however, everything had changed. The transformation was akin to the contrast between a photograph and its negative: before the mid-1750s, the envoy had worked in a world at peace, however serious a particular crisis; after that killing season commenced, he moved in a world at war.

Amid all the killing, symptoms of a deeper malaise—blind hatred—became more pervasive, making peace work that much harder. The faces full of rage that every Indian messenger met in Pennsylvania had as their counterpart the taunts and abuse heaped on Post in Ohio. Nor did the truce he and Pisquetomen cobbled together late in 1758 change anyone's mind. "Drub them Trounce them &c are the favourite themes" here, reported a colonist from one Pennsylvania frontier town in February 1759, "supposing they are now at [our] Mercy." In Indian country, too, "there was no Peace." "A Dark Spirit prevails here, with which the People seem to be possess'd," Post and John Hays reported from the upper Susquehanna in the spring of 1760. Natives are convinced that "it was intended by the English to drive them all out & possess themselves of their Land." That fall Moses Tatamy and Isaac Stille, back from the Ohio, brought more bad news. "They say they have taken a vast deal of Pains to promote the good work of Peace," wrote one colonist who spoke with them, "and have had very rugged Work in some Places, occasioned by the Jealousies which the proceedings of the English occasions."[108]

Lines between Indian and colonist, long obscured or overlooked, were being drawn more starkly now. One sign of the change was that natives expected to hear colonial messages only from colonists. "[I]t would be of great consequence to them . . . ," Pisquetomen had told Post over breakfast in Wyoming, "to hear the Governor's mind from their [colonists'] own Mouths." We have decided, they informed the governor's "mouth," Post, that fall, "not to give any credit to any message, sent from the English by *Indians*." Hearing Philadelphia's words from a Delaware or Iroquois messenger was no longer enough; white speeches had to come from white men. Gone were the days—not so long ago—when at Onondaga Shickellamy could personify Pennsylvania or Canasatego, Virginia.[109]

On their ride up the Susquehanna Valley in 1760, Post and Hays collided with the new paradigm. Bearing words of peace from governor and Crown, the Pennsylvanians headed out with Moses Tatamy, Isaac Stille, Teedyuscung, and other Delawares, bound for an Indian council beyond the mountains. The two colonists never got there. From the Iroquois came stern messages instructing Hays and Post to go no farther, for "it is agree'd on by the 5 Nations, that White Men shall not travel this Way." When the colonists stayed put, hoping for a change of heart, more messengers came. "[T]hey Would Let No whit man Go throw thire contry by Sum old A Greement A Mongst them Selves For feer of Spies to See the Land." If you stay here, the warning said, you "might possibly be roasted alive." At last, Post and Hays pointed their mounts toward home, while Stille, Tatamy, Teedyuscung and the other Delawares—skin color and kindred their passport—pushed deeper into Indian country.[110]

For all the hatred and death, neither Post, turning back, nor Tatamy, forging ahead, completely lost hope in peace. There was still talk of a grand treaty to remove all bitterness from hearts so long stricken with grief. Both sides knew the power of a council, knew that Pisquetomen and Post had only brokered a ceasefire; peace required that Ohio leaders visit Pennsylvania.[111] "Now, Brother," one Ohio Delaware had sent word to Philadelphia in September 1758, "I let you know that you shall soon see me by your council fire, and then I shall hear from you myself, the plain truth, in every respect." In reply, the province sent with Post and Pisquetomen a white wampum belt bearing a human figure at each end and a line running down the middle. "[B]y this Belt I make a Road for you," the wampum said, "and invite you to come to Philadelphia to your first Old Council Fire."[112]

"Soon" ended up being four years—peace was formally and finally concluded at Lancaster in August 1762—but the importance of those "Invitation Messages," and of the treaty councils they set up, cannot be denied. No matter how skilled the negotiators, no matter how good the messages, no matter how large the wampum belts, a gathering of leaders was always vital, never more so than now. Colonists hate Indians, who in turn "still breathe Threatnings & Slaughter"; only a treaty, invoking old formulas of friendship, had any hope of healing these wounds.

CHAPTER VII

"A Sort of Confusion": Treaties

As the peacemakers knew, ultimately all paths led to a clearing, all conversations to a council. What Iroquois called *Caligh Wanorum* ("Matters of great Consequence") required that the "old and wise People" on both sides meet "in a National way by Treaties." When it came to forging or refurbishing the chain of friendship—and, when that chain broke in the mid-1750s, trying to mend it—mere messengers would not do. Indians were "glad . . . we are come to see the Faces of all our [Pennsylvania] Brethren," especially those of "[t]he Govr & all his great people." Colonists, too, wanted to meet "the Chief Rulers of their [Indian] Towns & Nations."[1]

In some ways, treaty councils changed markedly over the course of the colonial era.[2] Early congresses tended to be small and (according to the surviving record, at least) inarticulate affairs. Convened in Philadelphia or Conestoga, they drew two or three dozen people, and scribes barely sketched the negotiations. After 1720, as Pennsylvania's expansion brought it into closer contact with other Indians and other provinces, assemblies took place farther afield, at Lancaster or Easton on the colony's frontier, at Albany or Johnson Hall in New York—even, in 1768, at Fort Stanwix on the Mohawk River. These later gatherings were more crowded: the band of one hundred Iroquois visiting Philadelphia in 1736 seemed huge to Pennsylvanians accustomed to smaller delegations, but thereafter a treaty would attract five or ten (or, at Fort Stanwix, thirty) times that many natives, along with scores and sometimes hundreds of colonists. With bigger crowds came fuller written accounts of the speeches and rituals that made up council architecture.[3]

On the surface, then, the small gatherings along the Delaware in the colony's early years bear little resemblance to the throngs beside the Mohawk some eighty years later. Yet for all the obvious differences between Shackamaxon and Stanwix, they were variations on a theme. Most treaties took place in colonial territory but adhered to native protocol. All brought "Great Ones" together.[4] And all devoted most of their time to a few key issues: peace and war, trade and land.

These grand affairs have been famous from Conrad Weiser's day to our own. Benjamin Franklin, seeing money in the eloquent speeches and exotic ceremonies, printed the proceedings of thirteen councils and shipped hundreds of copies to eager buyers in England. More recently, scholars have found the treaty minutes an evidential mother lode that yields rich literary and ethnographic lore as well as a colorful chapter in American diplomatic history.[5] The endless fascination is easy to understand. Councils are compelling theater, a lively stage on which the peoples of early America acted out the contest for the continent. It helps, too, that thanks to Franklin and other printers, the official minutes of these congresses are readily available.

But those minutes offer a distorted view. What made it onto the printed page was the result of decisions by colonists who took down the words spoken during a session, then "settled" the minutes at the end of the day, and later spent time "correcting" and "revising" those notes for publication. Thus omissions, deletions, and distortions—some intentional, some not—inevitably crept into the famous published accounts.[6] Superintendent of Indian Affairs William Johnson admitted that secretaries routinely "softened" Indians' "animated" speeches. "Savages . . . have the most extravagant notions of Freedom, property, and independence," Johnson observed; since "they endeavour to maintain their own importance by the most forcible expressions, . . . their words for fear of offence have been often Glossed over before they were committed to Writing."[7] But not even the most scrupulous scribe could capture every nuance of a treaty session. A speaker's posture or gesture, listeners' frowns or muttered asides—on these and much more besides, the renowned treaty records are virtually silent.[8]

No less misleading is the attention to formal sessions. Indians, and some colonists, knew that "the Transactions at the publick Conferences . . . Is a very small part of" what went on. Talks in the bushes were essential, especially since natives believed that friendship between peoples lay not in the text but in the context, not in some piece of paper drawn up at the end but in a harmonious feeling nurtured over days or weeks. The colonial record keeper, his gaze fixed on final results, missed much of what happened during that long stretch of time.[9]

Revisiting treaties with the go-between messes up the simplified, sanitized view of these extraordinary occasions (Figure 17). A negotiator knew treaty culture better than anyone, knew it from the council ground at midday to an Indian camp late at night to a governor's chambers at sunup, knew it as high pageantry and (sometimes) low comedy, short tempers and frayed nerves, perilous moments when people forgot, rewrote, or discarded the script and magical moments when those people found something like communion. Through a mediator's eyes, the logistical and cultural difficulties, the "sort of Confusion" of a congress, loom large.[10] Yet watching him work also reveals how shrewd management and sheer luck got peoples past these difficulties.

The intermediary, too, exposes the treaty's ultimate failure to achieve its oft-stated purpose of sustaining friendship from generation to generation. The growing numbers attending, the richer elaboration of protocol, the improved agility of go-betweens—none of this checked

Figure 17. Conference at Johnson Hall, by E. L. Henry, c. 1900.
Henry's depiction of a meeting at Sir William Johnson's house reflects the orderly, tidy treaty accounts "settled" by colonial scribes more than the "sort of confusion" common to councils. Courtesy of the Albany Institute of History and Art.

colonial expansion or erased bitter memories of past crimes. On the contrary: far from simply being a casualty of disaffection, councils—where colonists acquired land, often by shady means—actually helped pave the way for the European invasion of the interior while at the same time adding to the stock of unhappy memories. By the end of the colonial period, both Pennsylvania and the Indians on its borders, thoroughly disillusioned by what treaties had wrought, were ready to give up on them altogether.

And give up, too, on the men managing those treaties. But lingering with those men a little longer, after the council's decline had commenced, has still another sad lesson to teach: go-betweens themselves were one reason friendship and understanding eluded the conclaves. The attitudes, impulses, and visions that divided colonist from Indian can be found in the very men bringing those peoples together at the council fire. Far from being part of the solution to stormy relations between native and newcomer, the go-between turned out to be part of the problem.

✦

"A Great Concourse of People"
The Treaty as Spectacle

The first thing to strike any visitor at a treaty site was the human carnival there.[11] The sheer number of people packed into the houses, taverns, council chambers, and streets beggared belief. Many were curious colonists. While Indian traders and messengers were a common sight in Pennsylvania towns, the council was a special occasion that tempted many Pennsylvanians to drop what they were doing in order to take a look. "A great concourse of people followed" Indians into town, and thereafter a "tumult . . . every day gathered" to gawk at them in the streets or watch them eat. Opening and closing ceremonies, along with other "extraordinary Days," could draw "many People . . . out of ye Country," but any formal session might attract "a vast Audience."[12]

A similar curiosity enticed those Indians to a treaty. Philadelphia's paved streets and brick houses, its enormous ships and bustling markets were novelties to natives who, despite the fear of disease, wanted to see the sights for themselves. A congress was also a chance to get European goods. Especially during wartime, when ordinary channels of exchange shut down, necessity brought people to councils. "Some," one Mohawk observed, came in "from a true Love of Peace with their Brethren the English, and some for want of every thing, especially Victuals." They left not only with food and stories to tell those back home but also with needles and thread, scarlet coats and beaver hats, brass kettles and tobacco pipes, blankets and hoes, mittens and fish hooks, scissors and mirrors.[13]

No less important in bringing Indians to a conference was their political custom of consensus. Where a few Pennsylvanians—the governor, his council, and perhaps some commissioners appointed by the assembly—could do business for the province, natives needed more. By their very presence, large numbers of people, including young warriors and women, sanctioned agreements. The scores of men and women, who usually came to Pennsylvania with "a great many small children" in tow, made an Indian camp at a treaty, with its huts of boards, poles, or branches perched on the outskirts of Lancaster or Philadelphia, look more like a town than a delegation.[14]

With so many peoples about, the treaty ground was a visual feast. Colonists ranged in appearance from the powdered wig and laced cuffs of a governor or councilor to the moccasins and leggings of a fur trader, from the sober garb of Quakers to the work clothes of farmers and tradesmen—with, during the war, the colors of provincial troops and the redcoats of British regulars added to the mix. Indian dress was no less eye-catching. Conestogas and other natives living amid colonial settlements wore clothes that resembled their neighbors', while Indians from remoter towns might walk the streets either "dressed in a remarkable plain manner, with a broad Flat Hat, like a Q[uake]r" or sporting laced hats and colorful coats trimmed with gold or silver, outfits given them by grateful colonial officials. Even if many natives seemed, to colonists, "poorly dressed" in ragged matchcoats or dirty shirts, they still cut imposing figures with their scalp locks, body tattoos, and facial paint.[15]

This treat for the eye was accompanied by an assault on the ear. Indians already thinking that colonists talked too loud, and too much, must have been taken aback by the din of a colonial street.[16] But for Pennsylvanians, too, a treaty sounded different. Everyday noises—the rattle of a passing wagon, the jangling of a horse's equipage, the clang and clatter of a blacksmith at work—grew louder as a fleet of wagons hauling supplies or tired Indians rolled into town, as a score of horses bearing the governor and his entourage arrived, as Indians brought guns, hatchets, and knives to the smithy for repair.[17] To these sounds a congress added the song of natives announcing their arrival, the rattle of wampum they wore around neck and arm, the clank of the men's silver gorgets, the tinkle of the bells and thimbles women wore on their ankles—and sometimes, deep into the night, the thump of a drum beneath the sharp cries of dancers.[18] Those dancers and women, those blacksmiths and wagoners made a cacophony of another sort whenever they opened their mouths to speak. German, Shawnee, Oneida, Gaelic, Delaware, English—these tongues and more filled the air, mingling there with the accents of a Delaware speaking German or a Cayuga trying out his English, not to mention a colonist attempting Shawnee or Seneca.

There were plenty of chances to chat, for during treaties Pennsylvanians constantly made their way to the Indian camp. Provisioners with sacks of meal or barrels of beer might run into Quakers on their way to talk religion with natives. Amid those bent on satisfying the hunger of bellies or souls were the curious who sauntered out "to View the Indians &ca." These tourists poked their heads into cabin doorways or shook hands with headmen, chatted with Madame Montour or tossed coins to children. At dusk the sightseers would gather to watch young Indian men dance in a circle around elderly drummers seated beside a campfire. The natives' "dark-color'd Bodies, half naked, seen only by the gloomy Light of the Bonfire," the "frantic" hops, the relentless drums, the "Indian song," the "terrible shriek and halloo," the "horrid Yellings"—all this, Benjamin Franklin wrote after one council, "form'd a Scene the most resembling our Ideas of Hell that could well be imagin'd."[19]

Sometimes the dancers came to the town rather than the town going to the dancers. At Lancaster one June evening in 1744 a band of warriors—tomahawks in their hands, feathers atop their heads, faces painted "in a frightful manner"—came "hollooing and shrieking" through the streets to the governor's lodging, danced there "to a horrid noise" while "flourishing their weapons," then moved on to do an encore down the way. Most encounters in a colonial village were less dramatic. Natives stopped by a tavern for a drink or a meal, dropped in on a Quaker meeting, bought a horse, swapped some pelts.[20]

The round of casual contacts was punctuated by more formal occasions when native and colonial leaders sat down together to eat. Some of these dinners included less than ten Indians, others three hundred. Sometimes the provincial hosts "mixed them Indian and English beside one another"; sometimes natives sat at tables near their Pennsylvania counterparts, with the negotiator hovering between. Even a meal where a china bowl shattered and Iroquois made off with the glasses could be counted a success, for it helped people get acquainted outside the confines of a council session.[21]

The setting for those council sessions varied. In Philadelphia the Courthouse and Quaker Meeting House saw many treaties during the first half of the century before being supplanted by the even more impressive State House (Figures 18–19). At Lancaster the county courthouse, a two-story brick edifice topped by a cupola, supposedly could hold more than eight hundred people. Elsewhere diplomats had humbler surroundings: at Albany Indians sat in the street; Easton had a "Booth," a "large Shed," or a "publick Bower"; and at Fort Stanwix in 1768 colonists erected a "large Arbour."[22]

However different the theater, the arrangement of props and actors on the stage was much the same. On one side sat provincial officials, flanked by their attendants and advisers. Before them was a table for the scribe, where wampum belts could be placed and documents arranged. Across the way, on boards, benches, or steps, were the Indians—headmen in front, warriors, women, and children behind or milling about within earshot. In the middle stood the interpreter, poised to translate the speeches (Figure 20).[23]

The stage directions, like the actors' marks, had a common template. While a colonial leader stood to read his speech, clutching pages of prepared remarks, Indian orators had a different protocol. Wampum in hand, pacing up and down, pausing to make a fist or stamp a foot for emphasis, the native's cadence was slow, his voice loud, his accent and tone altered for public discourse. Indian or colonist, after each sentence or paragraph the speaker would pause to let the interpreter go to work.[24]

At last, with the treaty business concluded, there were hands to clasp and toasts to make, gifts to pass out and farewells to say. Then, a week or (more often) a month after the first arrivals began drifting in, the conference would break up, the delegates would head home, and life, for the locals, would resume its customary rhythms.

Figure 18. Philadelphia Courthouse and Quaker Meeting House.
These two buildings on High Street were sites of many Indian treaties
in the first four decades of the eighteenth century. John F. Watson, *Annals of
Philadelphia and Pennsylvania, In the Olden Time; Being A Collection of Memoirs,
Anecdotes, and Incidents of the City and Its Inhabitants, and of the Earliest Settlements
of the Inland Part of Pennsylvania, From the Days of the Founders,* vol. I (Philadelphia,
1845), facing p. 351. Courtesy of the Library Company of Philadelphia.

Figure 19. The State House in Philadelphia, 1778, engraved
from a detail in a painting by Charles Willson Peale.
Later known as Independence Hall, this building hosted many important treaty
councils in the late colonial era. Native delegations stayed either in the sheds or on
the second story of the East Wing. Courtesy of the American Philosophical Society.

Figure 20. The Indians Giving a Talk to Colonel Bouquet . . . in Octr. 1764.
Engraving from a sketch by Benjamin West, in [William Smith], *An Historical Account of the Expedition Against the Ohio Indians, in the year MDCCLXIV under the Command of Henry Bouquet, Esq.* (London, 1766). The shed and fire, the scribe and Indian holding a wampum belt suggest something of the setting for treaty councils, though here, as before, no translator is included. Courtesy of the Rosenbach Museum and Library.

"4 Weecks Spent Disagreable"
A Treaty's Trials

For Indian and colonial spectators trudging back home, the council was great entertainment, a welcome break from routine. The negotiator saw things differently. To him, a treaty was such trouble that he must have yearned for the simple challenge of an icy path or a frontier murder. Many would have nodded glumly at Weiser's terse assessment of one congress: "4 weecks Spent disagreable."[25] Understanding those weeks requires a look at what made them such unhappy occasions.

Simply getting everyone in the same place at the same time was like herding cats. Though colonial officials sometimes kept Indians waiting, usually it was colonists who suffered "great anxiety" and "great Impatience" as days passed with no sign of the expected ambassadors.[26] Pleas that a delegation pick up its pace fell on deaf ears, for Indians intent on cultivating harmony would not be rushed.[27] Someone died: pause to ritually cover the dead and console the living. Someone else had a vision: halt to ponder its meaning. Then, too, at Shamokin and other native towns en route travelers would stop for days "to Settle their affairs with" the locals and visit kinfolk. They are "in no Hurry at all," one frazzled go-between escorting them sighed.[28]

In some ways the only thing worse than an Indian delegation not arriving was one arriving, for these guests taxed conductors' patience and provisioners' resources. "I declare," wrote Weiser one August day, looking out a window at 250 Indians camped in his yard, "I wish I had gone out of the way into a neighbouring province, I am altogether tired of Indians, my patience with their behaviour is wore out" (Figure 21). It was a "great burden," Christian Frederick Post agreed while guiding Ohio Indians to Lancaster through blistering heat in 1762. "I got much tired by furnishing these people with provisions, Waggons and horses."[29]

The frustration stemmed from the difficulty of managing such a crowd—sometimes hot, sometimes soaked, sometimes sick, or old, or lame, always tired and hungry. "[N]othing is Secure" between here and the capital if the Indians are not fed, warned Weiser from Tulpehocken; "everything about my house was destroyed" already, and famished delegations had a habit of swarming onto farms to pick apples, butcher cows, pluck chickens, and harvest corn, while their dogs feasted on mutton.[30]

Hungry natives were bad enough; drunk ones were worse. Delegations that moved at a snail's pace stopped dead once Indians, having gotten ahold of some liquor despite their escort's best efforts, enjoyed (and then recovered from) a "frolick." Rum also increased the chances of trouble with the locals, trouble more serious than some missing

Figure 21. Conrad Weiser's House in Tulpehocken, built c. 1730.
Here Weiser met with Shickellamy or other go-betweens and hosted many Indian
delegations, which camped in his yard on their way to and from Philadelphia. Courtesy of
the Conrad Weiser Homestead, Pennsylvania Historical and Museum Commission, 1998.

poultry or livestock. In 1749, for example, a drunk Nanticoke in a party bound for Philadelphia tomahawked one colonist and threatened another with a knife before being beaten up by friends of the victim.[31]

Negotiators beset by a hungry or thirsty horde of natives found getting provincial officials to the treaty site much easier. With colonial leaders, however, problems began on their arrival, for they proved a cranky, demanding bunch. Are there enough beds, linens, tablecloths, and kitchen furniture? Barbers, washerwomen, and cooks? To keep savagery at bay, some gentlemen shipped wagonloads of such essentials as kegs of rum, beer, and wine, along with boxes of lemons and limes, sugar and tobacco, coffee and tea; some even brought their own beds.[32] But these amenities did not satisfy men accustomed to Philadelphia's finest. Besides Easton's "very indifferent" wine and Lancaster's lack of a backgammon table, the chorus of complaint included "unclean Beds" and "nauseous eggs and bacon," "sorry rum" and "Bad Beef," a "very nasty Table Cloath" and "a Laxative Disorder Occasioned by drinking the Limestone Water."[33]

Trying as it was to cater to balky native headmen and sullen colonial officials, this was only the beginning of a go-between's troubles. A more severe trial was that the very men ostensibly in charge of a treaty might be amateurs or fools—or both. A provincial delegate was out of his element, and not just because of lousy food and lumpy beds. At home in Anglo-American ways and accustomed to giving orders, at a meeting with Indians he had to follow instructions from lowly colonists (or even lower Indians) who told him to do and say odd things. Most novices, calculating the cost of failure, grudgingly went along; but some almost wrecked a treaty with their arrogance and ignorance.

None were more ignorant or arrogant than William Denny, governor of Pennsylvania for three years during the war. Denny, a military man, was a terrible politician and a worse diplomat.[34] He had, his many critics claimed, three moods: "a little peevish," "peevish," and "excessively peevish." During the Easton council of October 1758, with the fate of John Forbes's army in the balance, Denny was at his worst. In his first chat with Indians, he "indiscreetly . . . used some threatening expressions against them."[35] As the talks wore on, the governor's meager supply of patience ran out. When Indians were slow to gather for a session, Denny "swore and stampt said he was ill used," then abruptly left town. Colonists watching this "scandalous" and "shocking" outburst declared him "unfit for business." Indians agreed. At dinner the next day Iroquois headmen "ridiculd him," asking Weiser "to go with them to search him to see if he was a man or woman."[36]

Denny was not the only man at Easton that fall who angered Iroquois and exasperated negotiators: Teedyuscung matched him in peevishness. When, at one session, a Seneca named Tagashata rose to speak, the Delaware, rum bottle in hand, staggered in "very drunk." Setting the bottle beneath the table (where a colonist discreetly tipped it over to prevent any more drinking), Teedyuscung called the Iroquois "fools" and proclaimed himself "King of all the nations and of all the world." In English, he "swore . . . prodigiously"; "in Indian" he told natives, among other things, "that the way to be well used by them [colonists] was to make war on them and cut their throats." When Tagashata finally went ahead with his speech, Teedyuscung interrupted several times more before running out to grab a wampum belt and returning to insist that he be heard. No one suggested a check of his breeches, but Teedyuscung, like Denny, could wreak havoc with efforts to sustain an atmosphere of decorum and consensus.[37]

Cleaning up after incompetents was one of a negotiator's messier chores. More common, and more difficult to handle, were fundamental differences in expectations about a treaty's proper tempo. Here again, while Indian diplomats sometimes asked colonists to hurry up, more often it was those colonists who waited.[38] The conflict was rooted in a clash of cultures. Pennsylvanians with their eyes on results like a land sale wanted to proceed quickly and directly toward those ends; Indians, with less tangible aims, preferred a more circuitous route. There was, natives believed, "a fit time" to hear important words, "for then the Heart is soft, and they would go into the Heart and not be lost." Preparing hearts took time.[39] A delegation must not be of troubled mind or battered body: hence Indians, on finally reaching a council ground, took several days to rest, eat, cover the graves of those who had died since the last gathering, and dry the tears of those who still mourned. "[U]ntil that [Condolence Ceremony] was done," Iroquois explained, "they were like Children . . . who cannot Act in publick Affairs."[40] That task accomplished, native ambassadors then convened private councils among themselves to hear all parties and reach a consensus before the treaty began. Once formal talks got under way, further delays were inevitable, since answers to speeches demanded the same deliberation. "Publick Business," Tagashata explained at Easton, "requires great Consideration."[41]

William Denny was not the only British official with an urge to stamp and swear at what he considered "delitory forms of business" crammed with "trifling Ceremony" and "long and tedious speeches." "We Go on Slowly, & too much so," grumbled one colonist waiting for native leaders, "owing to the long Councils . . . among the Indians."[42] Desperate to speed things up, provincial leaders made mistakes that added to a mediator's woes. They neglected the Condolence. They interrupted, spoke out of turn, and skipped from one topic to another. They answered Indian speeches "immediately out of hand" instead of pausing to ponder a proper reply, raised "Main Business" outside council sessions, and, like Denny, scurried away in unseemly haste.[43]

Even those trying to get it right could make a mess of things. In 1753, Pennsylvania treaty commissioners knew enough to order a shipment of goods for the Condolence Ceremony, but when that shipment was late they insulted Indians by asking if a mere list of the items would do for now. Nine years later a governor dutifully performed the expected Condolence, but he did so for the wrong dead man, "wch gave the Ind[ia]ns some Surprize."[44]

Surprise often gave way to annoyance and then to anger at colonial bumbling. Asking Indians to hurry up earned the cold reply that "they were unacquainted with Hours, but would give Notice when they were ready." Answering their speeches too quickly "altogether displeas'd" them. Looking "in haste to go home" elicited requests to "be patient, & stay." The accumulation of errors was more than some Indians could bear. "[I]t was plain," said the Cayuga Tokahaio "in a very warm speech" at Easton in 1758, "the *English* either did not understand *Indian* Affairs, or else did not act and speak with that Sincerity and in the Manner they ought. . . . If the *English* knew no better how to manage *Indian* Affairs, they should not call them together."[45]

Go-betweens trying to synchronize colonial and Indian tempos also had to cope with the squabbles that, plaguing both sides, often slowed the pace. Among British colonial authorities, disputes got worse over time, because Pennsylvanians increasingly had to sit next to men from other provinces. Colonies brought to a treaty so many different agendas—one might seek land, another peace, another warriors—that they debated whether to draft one speech to Indians, or several.[46] That settled, other issues would emerge. Should Pennsylvania's Quaker commissioners be allowed to keep their hats on? Should we just "walk in and *take Places as we thot Proper*" or follow protocol? If protocol, how to determine precedence? Royal colonies first, proprietaries second? The oldest? The one "Longest in attending the Treaty" with these natives? The government spending the most money? Or perhaps geography should determine the order, but if so, where to start, north or south?[47] At Albany in 1745 delegates from Massachusetts and New York brought contention into the open when they had a violent argument on the street in full view and hearing of the Iroquois—and did so, one observer remarked, "just at the time when the Indians delivered a belt recommending our Union as it would be our Strength."[48]

A decade later, with union as elusive as ever, the Crown tried to simplify things by creating a superintendent of Indian affairs for the Northern Department and appointing William Johnson to be the King's man on the frontier. But provincial authorities, especially Pennsylvania's, proved unwilling to surrender their ties to the tribes; hence, adding Johnson (and Croghan, his deputy) only compounded the confusion. When the superintendent finally visited Pennsylvania in 1762 for a treaty conference in Easton, he was roughly handled by Quaker leaders who, convinced that he was helping cheat Delawares of land, denounced him in open council. Sir William stormed out, crying that he "would do nothing more in such a Mob and such treatment he never had met before."[49]

Johnson was only getting a taste of the wrangling that Pennsylvania treaties had featured for years. Since the war's beginning, Quakers had assumed a prominent role in frontier diplomacy, sending messages, giving presents, and attending treaties. This challenge to proprietary Indian policy was a new battleground in an older campaign. Friends, and the provincial assembly they dominated, had been at odds on a number of fronts with the proprietor Thomas Penn and his appointees for a decade before the war.[50] The start of Indian raids gave both sides fresh ammunition and their contest fresh urgency, not least because it threw Quakers on the defensive, branded as soft on Indians and slow to defend the frontier. Friends responded with deeper involvement in Indian affairs, arguing that the real cause of the conflict was abuse of natives by the proprietors and their minions.

With stakes high and contestants articulate, what Conrad Weiser called "a paper war" broke out that has continued to this day.[51] Like most political and scholarly debates where lines are so sharply drawn, the truth lies somewhere in between. Friends were indeed animated by high principles that included seeing justice done displaced Delawares, but in this case justice coincided with the economic interests of Quaker merchants involved in the fur trade and the political interests of proprietary opponents. Those proprietary men did indeed have much to answer for and something to hide, but they were genuinely appalled that Quakers wanted a say in foreign policy, especially when that say involved telling Indians to trust neither provincial nor Crown officials.[52]

For go-betweens trying to run a treaty, the dispute had disastrous consequences, for it gave the council ground all the decorum of a schoolyard. It became a world of taunts and epithets—"Impudent Scoundrel," "turbulent Creature," "pitiful dog," "violent unmannerly brute," "rascal and villain"—of lookouts and spies, of winks and whispers, of back rooms and staircases, of hallways and alleys, of rumors and muttering, of clandestine meetings at midnight or dawn. Distinguished (and sometimes elderly and portly) men forgot their dignity to scurry along a back path or duck behind a house, to poke their heads into open windows or doorways, to threaten, fist clenched, to "knock . . .

down" an opponent or "hit him a slap in the chops." "O, Mischief is going on," John Pumpshire cried when he saw the Quaker leader Israel Pemberton tug Moses Tatamy by the sleeve and lead him behind a house for a chat. "Israel is Wicked." Whether Pumpshire's assessment of Pemberton was correct, his assertion that "Mischief is going on" captures the contention pervading treaties between 1756 and 1762.[53]

Indians, seeing the squabbles, wondered if "there were more Onasses than one." Yet natives were not immune to "quarrle[s]" or "high words."[54] Their disagreements seem fewer and quieter because they neglected to record every debate for posterity. Occasionally a colonist would note that Indians gathered at the far end of a room "were very warm and earnest in their Debates, and seem'd to differ much in Opinion." More often the only signs of disagreement were the messages of postponement go-betweens brought to impatient colonists, explaining that the headmen were still in council. The larger and more diverse the Indian delegation, the more likely the disputes and delays. At Easton in 1758, George Croghan, taking stock of the thirteen nations gathered for the treaty, fretted that "the Indians are Much Divided and Jelious of Each other."[55]

Indians mired in endless, sometimes heated private talks, colonists shaking fists at each other, Johnson storming out—all this guaranteed the negotiator long days and fitful nights. But during the war years these squabbles paled next to the growing hatred between Indians and colonists, hatred that, born of the bloodshed, threatened to tear apart peace councils.

No treaty had ever been the soul of serenity, of course. Indian delegations long had gotten drunk, staggered down the street, and sometimes taken merchandise from any shopkeeper unwise enough to display his wares outside. A go-between was always alert for signs of trouble. At Lancaster in 1744, Weiser cautioned Virginians visiting the natives' camp "not to talk much of the Indians, nor laugh at their dress, or make any remarks on their behaviour; . . . it would be very much resented by them," he explained, "and might cause some differences betwixt the white people and them."[56]

Still, not until the war did treaties become explosive. Colonists who now "crowded so close upon the Indians that they could hardly get air" came not out of curiosity; they were looking for trouble. No wonder many Indians approaching a treaty site thought it looked more like a trap than a place where a council fire blazed: the English awaiting you there will slit your throats, warned rumors and dreams, or poison your water.[57]

Some townsfolk were eager to do all this, and worse, if given a chance, for Pennsylvanians reeling from Indian raids were suspicious of natives talking peace. It did not help that the first peacemakers, Teedyuscung and his band at Easton in July 1756, were a belligerent bunch: he paraded about in a French coat while Delaware women wore shirts "made of Dutch Table Cloaths, which, it is supposed they took from the People they murdered on our Frontiers." Nor did it help when, at the next Easton council that fall, a young man named Henry Hess, having escaped from captivity, was able to point out, among the Delawares in town to talk peace, the very men who had killed, stripped, and scalped his father.[58]

Lancaster the following spring of 1757 was equally volatile. Colonists nearby, furious that enemy war parties were still slaughtering people even as Pennsylvania leaders shook hands with Indians in the courthouse, decided to send provincial peacemakers a message. Before dawn on May 18 they drove a wagon bearing four bodies—one a pregnant woman, all of them "scalped and butchered in a most horrid Manner"—through town, parked it at the front door of the courthouse, and demanded that Governor Denny come out and see what peace had wrought. When Denny declined the invitation, "some of the more clamorous talked publickly of dragging him out & shooting both him & the [treaty] Comm[issioner]:s bye the Corpses."[59]

These three councils were calm, however, compared with the congress held at Easton two months after the Lancaster proceedings ended. Weiser, reaching town on July 14, found it full of men from New Jersey who "had agreed and Signed to Come to Easton to Cutt off the Indians that are now there." After arresting one troublemaker and jailing another, he reported that "The common People behave very ill, in asking the Indians unbecoming Questions, and using ill Language." A bad situation got worse at dusk on July 17 when a woman raced into town "as if distracted" to say that Indians had slain her family on their farm just two miles away. By the time scouts returned to report a false alarm, Easton was in an uproar. "The cry of the common People, of which the Town was full, was very great against the Indians," Weiser wrote.[60]

The mediator "had the good Luck to pacify both the white People and the Indians" this time, but the situation remained dangerous. Two weeks later natives became so angry at colonial delays that "some of ye Young Indians blackt themselves as for War and loaded their Guns." On the outskirts of town one of Teedyuscung's sons, painted like the other warriors, drew a bead on James Hamilton, the former governor, before someone wrestled the gun out of the young man's hands.[61]

Blackened warriors, bloody corpses, frightened farmers racing in to report another raid—all created an atmosphere more likely to prolong than end conflict. But if such scenes were exceptional, if they were a product of war, they are only the most extreme form of every treaty ground's clash and clamor. With a mismatched and ill-tempered horde of people bringing different expectations and assumptions, it is a wonder the negotiator managed to get anything done at all. But he did.

<hr>

"Dexterous Management"
Sorting out the Confusion

During treaties the go-between's day was an endless round of chores. One morning he was in some Pennsylvania official's quarters for a consultation; that night he might stay up late to draft a speech. In between, problems sought him out. We are low on wampum. The governor has gone fishing. The Indians are drunk. Teedyuscung wants us to fetch his mother-in-law, but she is out gathering huckleberries somewhere. What shall we do? "[E]very Hour of the day gave me Some new trouble," grumbled Weiser.[62]

Crises great and small took a toll. At one treaty Croghan went off "in a Passion," and Montour stalked out of a meeting "in great wrath." Weiser, who also abandoned a council, railed against governors for being slow to greet Indians and carped at Quakers for being too quick to do so, snubbed Canasatego by refusing to shake hands and "gave Deedjoskon the slip in the Dark" in order to sleep in peace. I am "much fatigued in mind and body," he wrote Governor Denny after one treaty. "These irregular people I had to deal with have tired me sufficiently." The Indian agent did not say so, but among those irregulars was Denny himself.[63]

Weiser often wished he were somewhere else, but never more than one fall day in 1736, standing on the riverbank at Shamokin. He had come to greet an Iroquois delegation headed to a treaty in Philadelphia. Now, bearing down on him came eighteen vessels packed with more than one hundred Iroquois, many "of them people of authority and the very Chiefs." Weiser, recognizing only a few faces, was close to panic. "All the rest," he fretted, "are Strangers to me." As the fleet, white flag flying, drew near shore, "I was troubled in my mind," Weiser admitted, "did not know what to say or what to doe."[64]

Drawing on his experience, his instincts, and his Shamokin friends, Weiser overcame this case of nerves. There, and at treaties over the next quarter of a century, he proved able to get both sides "put in the proper method" to council together. With a handful of other go-betweens, he won acclaim for "dexterous management," for "peculiar address to manage the Indians," for having "a great deal of skill and caution."[65]

So much of this management occurred in the shadows that it remains hidden. Were the Six Nations at Lancaster unhappy with the "bales and boxes" of merchandise they were to receive for signing a release to land claims in Maryland? Then they went "down into the courthouse, to consult among themselves, . . . with their interpreter" (Weiser), and came back satisfied. Did, two days later, a few headmen still balk? Weiser somehow persuaded them to change their minds. Were Ohio Indian leaders reluctant to let colonists settle west of the mountains? Andrew Montour met "with his Brethren, the other Sachems, in private," and promptly returned with their consent.[66]

But if these chats left few traces in the records,[67] enough of the negotiator's handiwork remains to reveal some of the secrets of his success. The main secret was convincing recalcitrant and befuddled colonists to follow Indian custom. When a delegation arrives, speak "in their own way, with three small strings of Wampum in hand," and follow "the usual Ceremonies . . . towards them."[68] When Indians "dreamed yt they shoud meet with some disaster" and "their Doctor advised a Kegg of Rum to prevent it," honor the request, however odd it seems. When they hand over some game and a colonist "damn'd them & sayd they brought it [only] to get ten times as much Victuals" in return, tell him he would be wiser to accept it graciously and then "throw it out of the back door to the Dogs than not to receive it." Such customs might seem "only Ceremonies and meer triffling"; they are neither, so listen politely, write it all down, and accept proffered belts, even if the council's official opening is days away: "all should be set right" later.[69]

The next step was to learn more about whom one was dealing with.

It is unclear how Indians collected information, but their "usual Method" of taking a few days' rest after arriving to chat "about News and other Occurrences" doubtless helped them assess their colonial counterparts.[70] Those colonists, meanwhile, were systematically gathering intelligence. "Sitting down w[i]th some of the Chiefs," the go-between would compile "a List of a good many names," including "the whole number of all Sorts women &c of each nation." Counting heads and taking names was no easy task. "I Counted them meselves," a weary mediator boasted of one contingent numbering 260 souls.[71]

Sizing up headmen and finding out their "Condition and Disposition" was harder still. Scarouyady, busy at one council "sounding them [some Wyandots from Ohio] as to their Affection for the English," asked the governor "not to be uneasy if it should take some time to do it." And Weiser, meeting Teedyuscung for the first time, asked that the treaty be postponed. I am "a Stranger to Teedyuscung," he explained, "and it would take up some time, at least a Day, to be rightly informed of his Temper and Expectations."[72]

Scarouyady's *sounding,* with its sense of probing murky depths to get some idea of what lies below the surface, captures the work of negotiators during a council's early going. "It is not in my power to sound the Indians so as to know their real Intentions," admitted Richard Peters during one treaty. But, knowing that go-betweens had powers he lacked, he put them to work "finding out even the most latent design in" an Indian camp.[73]

Sounding helped a negotiator chart a course through the council's unpredictable waters. It also brought to light Indian wishes that were exhausting to satisfy but dangerous to ignore. Hatchets, guns, knives, and a hand vise need mending. Sagechsadon and Tocahagen want new tobacco pipes, two other natives branding irons. Onicknaqua admires the hats in a shop, and Coxagensucha hopes for a kettle. Copy down Madame Montour's remedy for a fever, and hold on to Lappachpitton's money, "left . . . in my hand [for safekeeping] when he was drunk." Nor were influential people the only ones deserving attention. Knowing Indians' devotion to their children, an experienced mediator made sure that one child received a hatchet he coveted and others got "small money" or some "Cakes peaches [and] Apples."[74]

Having made it through the preliminaries, a go-between could turn to the formal treaty business. He sat down with British colonial officials

"to read over Council Speeches and to do Business for them, and to settle the Belts," then hurried off "to advise with" Indians as they "asked
his Opinion of divers Matters." That done, he sorted out who should
speak first, when to hand out gifts, and what to do with this pipe or that
wampum belt.[75]

However carefully scripted the words and wampum, the negotiator
had to expect things to go wrong during their delivery, leaving a council ground "dark and confused." Occasionally something got lost in
translation. When Teedyuscung concluded a speech by repeating "the
Delaware word 'Whish Shiksy,' . . . with Great Earnestness and in a very
Pathetick Tone," Weiser, who knew that the Mohawk equivalent, *Jago*,
carried "a very extensive and forcible sense," asked for clarification. If
"the real meaning of the Indians" remained obscure, if natives still
"seemed very much at a Loss about the Governor's Speech," the intermediary would meet privately to clarify things. Wampum that went
wrong got the same treatment. John Pumpshire, handing over a thoroughly alarming belt of black beads at the first peace talks, was quick
to explain that this did not mean war: note the white spots, Pumpshire
said; these are "the ten nations that came with Teedyuscung" to end the
conflict.[76]

Some surprises required less clarity, not more. When Virginia commissioners at Lancaster in 1744, speaking of "the Indians with great
Contempt" and "determin'd to" take "an high Hand," interrupted
Weiser's translation of the Iroquois' opening speech to say that Weiser
was deliberately misinterpreting to favor the Six Nations, the go-
between adjourned the proceedings for a private conference of
colonists to put Virginia in its place. If an Iroquois, "with apparent
warmth and resentment in his face and manner," gave a speech that
was too explosive for public council, the negotiator refused to interpret
it, insisting it come out in private.[77]

As these delicate moments suggest, a go-between had to be able to
think on his feet, had to know when to be firm and when to back off.
A governor who refused to greet the Indians on their arrival must be
branded a man who "does not act the part of a well wisher to his
Majestys people and interest, at this Critical Times." A Mohawk who
interrupted translation of a colonial address to make his own "bold and
rude Speech" must be interrupted in turn and told "to forbear and hold
his Tongue."[78]

Yet the knack of knowing when to speak or act with force was knowing, too, just how far to go. That note questioning a governor's patrio-
tism must be followed by an apology that attributed the outburst to
excessive enthusiasm for the country's cause. That "bold and rude" Mohawk could only be challenged after careful reading of the other Indian
faces left the go-between "well assured that the Majority of the Indian
Council were not pleas'd" with the speech, either.[79]

The negotiator's navigation through a treaty's treacherous shoals was
aided immeasurably by parallels in native and European diplomatic
conduct that helped offset the profound differences in their ways of
doing business. Beyond the basic assumption that treaties were a good
idea, from William Penn forward, colonists bewildered by native protocol at least appreciated the natives' imposing presence and inspired
performance. The Indians "have manifested themselves to be Judicious
prudent men," Pennsylvanians remarked, with "as much Finess . . . as
might be expected at Versailles." Even British soldiers with little love
for natives were impressed. "I wish you had been here to hear their
Speeches," wrote one officer after formal talks. "I was amazed to See So
much of true understanding, dignity, and Strength of argument."[80]

Both sides also thought ritual essential to frame and sanction public
occasions, and both considered food, drink, and tobacco vital in that enterprise. The menu of "a handsome Indian Dinner" at Shickellamy's
lodge in Shamokin might bear little resemblance to the "great variety
of dishes" served in the Lancaster courthouse, but a feast's place in the
proceedings was much the same. A governor might have found it odd
to puff on a long, feathered calumet while Indians sang and shook gourd
rattles, but smoking a sociable pipe certainly was nothing new. Similarly, while colonists' rum, wine, or punch replaced natives' traditional
berry juice as a ritual potion, and while toasts were imported to Indian
country, "a friendly Glass" at the end of each council session was "according to the Indian custom."[81]

Kindred cries of assent furthered the sense of common experience.
Indians customarily signaled the end of each proposal with a "Shout of
Approbation." Someone would begin, slowly calling out *U——huy;*
then, "with one Voice, in exact Time," those assembled (or each tribe
in turn) answered with a drawn out *Ió* that rose, fell, and rose again
until—still "at once, in exact Time"—they "stop at the Height." The
colonial ear heard this many ways—"Yohah" and "*U——huy,*" "ho-

ho" and "Yoheigh-heigh," *"woh! wugh!"* and "Yohay," "Ka-ha-lah" and "Io-hau"—but all agreed that Indians performed it "with great order, and the utmost ceremony and decorum."[82]

Colonists came to respond with Britain's customary three "huzzas." At Lancaster in 1744 this cry "a good deal surprised [some Iroquois], they having never heard the like noise." But as governor, councilors, and even bystanders chimed in, natives came to accept, indeed to expect, this colonial cry. "The Indians desired that if their Answer was approved," wrote a Pennsylvanian during a treaty in Albany, "the Govr would Shew that approbation in the English manner—on which the Govr [of] New York Stood up Said he was Satisfyed and now who were So might also Stand and then[?] they gave three An Zoy's." So close was the correspondence that after one session "Gentlemen and Indians present gave three shouts" in unison.[83]

Orchestrating shouts and presiding over dinners, filling pipes and glasses, go-betweens at a treaty further promoted fellowship by getting colonists and Indians to strike chords of common memory. When during the war Scarouyady and Post played up a sense of kinship between natives and Pennsylvanians, they echoed an idea with deep roots in diplomatic discourse, as the two sides talked of being "one Flesh and Blood," "one People" who "spring out of the same Spot of Ground" and "are, therefore, . . . Countrymen."[84]

Such harmonious notes still resonated across the frontier because William Penn lived on in Indian country, despite the years and the bloodshed. "[W]hat [Penn] said to the Indians is fresh in our minds and memory," Teedyuscung assured colonists during the war. Two decades later, some elderly Indians still were "able to relate how peaceably and agreeably the whites and Indians dwelt together, as if they had been one people." Frequent rehearsals kept memory alive. To the end of the colonial era and beyond, natives convened "in some shady spot as nearly as possible similar to those where they used to meet their brother *Mi-quan*" to go over, once more, the ancient words.[85]

Negotiators' dogged pursuit of comity, combined with congruent customs, seductive memories of a shared past, and a desire to find ways to get along, conjured many extraordinary moments of consonance when diffidence and difference gave way to fellow feeling and a shared humanity. One Indian on an Easton street "dressed . . . like a Q[uake]r, . . . askt . . . if he was a Qr, . . . smiling, answered Yes, Yes, I

a Quaker now." One evening in the Lancaster courthouse some years before, another native, "a young Indian" who had joined a party held by
colonial officials and their aides, "danced a jig . . . in a most surprising
manner" with one Philadelphian while two Germans sawed away at "harp
and fiddle." Later that same evening, the colonial "younger persons raised
their jollity by dancing in the Indian dress, and after their manner."[86]

Young gentlemen prancing about in native garb, one Indian posing as
a Quaker and another dancing with a Philadelphian—at such times a
treaty met, even exceeded, the hopes of those assembled. Here the
woods were left behind. Here Indian and colonist "may see one another Face to Face."[87] Here, by the council fire, peoples from different
worlds, guided by go-betweens, found ways to get along, to make new
friends or keep old ones, to sell land or promote trade, to pursue war
or make peace. It was a remarkable achievement.

※

"I Am of a Quite Different Nature from You"
Indian Disenchantment with Treaties

It was also, ultimately, an empty achievement. Moving speeches and
bright flashes of concord cannot hide treaties' failure truly to unite
colonists and Indians in the face of European colonial expansion and a
Christian cosmology sanctioning, even sanctifying, the woods' demise.
Looking back across the years from the arbor in the shadow of Fort
Stanwix at almost a century of treaties between Penn's province and its
Indian neighbors, it is clear that these gatherings had, at best, an ambiguous legacy. Intended to bring people together, treaties ended up
driving them apart. Intended to promote harmony, in the end they
produced dissonance. And while councils did spawn understanding,
that understanding ended in hatred. Natives saw the treaties' harsh
truth before colonists did, but by the 1760s both sides, deeply disillusioned, turned away from treaties—and away, too, from the men who
managed them.

Read in a different light, even the most beguiling episodes of fellow
feeling take on a gloomier look. After all, that Indian in Quaker dress
who announced "Yes, Yes, I a Quaker now," went on to say "but when
I go away I—Indian again." And the gentlemen at Lancaster, clad in an

Indian get-up and doing their version of an Iroquois dance, were hardly going native. Nor did a shared meal make colonists embrace Indians' humanity. On the contrary: one provincial leader breaking bread with Iroquois left the table convinced that his dinner companions were even more savage than he had thought. The banquet, "served up in very good order," quickly degenerated because Indians had no manners. They "fed lustily, drank heartily, and were very greasy before they finished their dinner," this observer sneered, "for, by the bye, they made no use of their forks." Even yelling in unison marked the limits of convergence. The sheer variety of colonial efforts to convey the precise sound Indians made—one auditor even admitted that it was "an articulate sonorous noise which I cannot describe in Letters"—proves that, as another said, the *Yo-hah* was "very difficult for a white man to imitate well."[88]

Powerful memories of William Penn's ways and words, of a common birthright along the Delaware, too, can play tricks on the imagination. There was no eliding the hard fact that by the 1760s Indians holding these memorial services for the Founder were beside the Muskingum River, hundreds of miles west of their putative brethren in Penn's Woods. Moreover, competing with the happy memories was a growing accumulation of unhappy ones, a dead weight of past wrongs that strangled and stifled concordance. Post could bring to Ohio in the fall of 1758 Pennsylvania's assurances "that all past offences shall be forgotten, and never more talked of, by us, our children and grand children hereafter," but he also knew that the odds were against amnesia. Pisquetomen himself, having only just escaped the clutches of vengeful colonists, could attest to that. His experience only confirmed Indians' conviction that "they have done so much mischief to the white people that they think it impossible they should be forgiven." In coming to such a conclusion, Indians were merely assuming that a Pennsylvanian's memory was as keen as their own. Abuse "is not brought so easy out of their minds," Post admitted; "they keep it to their graves, and leave the seed of it in their children and grand children's minds."[89]

Treaties devoted to inducing an epidemic of amnesia in the Indian countries also had to contend with a colonial land rush that added to the litany of native grievances. With Pennsylvania's population jumping from 100,000 in 1740 to twice that in 1760, squabbles and resentments plaguing the lower Susquehanna Valley during the 1710s played out again and again to the west and north. Pennsylvania hunters invaded the forests to compete with Indians for what game was left. Close behind came surveyors reckoning latitude, noting "exceeding good Meadows" and "very good Land," checking riverbanks for mill sites. Prospectors poked around, too, pestering natives for word of rocks with glittering flecks or veins, then chipping samples for analysis back in Philadelphia. Hunter, farmer, miner—by the middle of the eighteenth century colonial men were dreaming of the day when each of them "would have two hundred acres of rich land on the Ohio."[90]

A colonist's dream was a native's nightmare. "[A]ll Indians," observed George Croghan, "hate to Live on any Land that they Cant Call thire own." With each passing year, that fate crept closer to the nations bordering Penn's Woods, so close that by 1750 "the very sight of an Instrument [for surveying] would raise their Jealousy." Behind alarm about colonial invasion lurked a more far-reaching fear of colonial power. These strangers, natives thought, have even changed America's weather, for "since the Europeans came into their country they have had to suffer heavy snow, cold, and torrential rains, as well as severe and terrible thunderstorms, all of which were allegedly unknown to them before the arrival of the strangers." The strangers' power actually reached beyond this world to touch the next. "[T]he white people had blocked up the road [to heaven] for the Indians . . . ," natives said; now we are "obliged to make a long circuit to come to God."[91]

The native response to this ominous turn of events was not surrender but stiffer resolve. Voices stressing difference grew louder. "[Y]ou know I am not as you are," the Oneida headman Saghughsuniunt (Thomas King) reminded colonial leaders at the Lancaster council in August 1762. "I am of a quite different Nature from you." Any native going against that "nature" ran into trouble. He "wants to make English Men of the Indians," Susquehanna people explained when asked why they despised Teedyuscung. The very idea of becoming English could be as amusing as it was frightening. In 1759, when Ohio headmen mistook a message from Pennsylvania for a proposal "that their young people and ours should be married together," they "Laughed at the Letter."[92]

Even Pennsylvania's most steadfast friends were turning their backs on the province. In 1767 Seneca George began enticing to Iroquoia those Nanticokes and Delawares still living on ancestral lands in Maryland and New Jersey "so that they may all settle together on the Six Nation lands, and be out of trouble, and danger from the White People."

What trouble? What danger? Colonial neighbors, Seneca George explained, "having got all their [the Indians'] lands, and [by] them means become rich, are now very cross to them & forget their former Obligations."[93]

Treaty tradition fell victim to this deepening Indian disillusionment with the colonial world. But treaties were not just a casualty of these changes; they—and the men who made them—were also a cause. True, the protocol and politics worked well enough when colonial and native agendas coincided. The early Delaware land sales, the overtures from Iroquoia after 1720 and from the Ohio country in the 1740s—councils dealing with these and other shared goals were amicable enough. But when Indian and colonial ends clashed, councils contributed to the climate of distrust because Pennsylvanians seemed intent on achieving their goals at any cost. "I request thee," wrote James Logan to Weiser on the eve of one congress, "to exert thy Self and to Suffer no difficulties to abate thy Courage but beat it through against all and over all opposition."[94] *Beat it through:* Logan captured colonists' grim determination to bend treaty councils to their will.

Many of a go-between's tools for promoting concord could also become weapons for chicanery and coercion. Liquor, for example, was an accepted, even essential, part of diplomatic culture, nurturing good will. But in large doses it befuddled native minds, enabling colonists to soften up the opposition. At Lancaster during the delicate moment in 1744 when the Iroquois were to sign a release of land claims in Virginia, one colonist noted how "We were obliged to put about the glass pretty briskly." During the war years drink became a major weapon in the Quakers' battle with proprietary forces. Each side accused the other of plying natives with liquor to win their affection or—worse—to so stupefy them that they could say nothing at all.[95]

The same was true of gifts. Everyone agreed that, like liquor, presents were an essential feature of frontier diplomacy, a lubricant of social relations, a tangible sign of favor. "Whoever is acquainted with the Nature of an Indian knows that they have their Hands and Eyes open, to receive at all Times," Weiser explained; "be the Thing ever so just, that is required of them, they want some Present before they consent to it." Surely no one would deny Sagechsadon a tobacco pipe, Onicknaqua a hat, or those children their pennies and fruit?[96]

But at other times, especially when a land sale was involved, "Private Presents" became bribes. In 1754 Weiser wrote Richard Peters that the surest way to buy more Indian territory was to "fall in with some greedy [Iroquois] fellows for Money that will undertake to bring things about to Our wishes." In May the go-between sent three of Shickel-lamy's sons north to prepare the way, promising them that, besides being "well paid" for the trip, they would receive a £10 annual pension. One of their assignments on reaching Iroquoia was to enlist the aid of Gagradodon, a Cayuga headman, to serve as adviser on land matters in exchange for one hundred "pieces of Spanish."[97] And so it went: forty dollars to Iroquois leaders the day they signed a deed, two hundred pieces of eight at a treaty's close, £600 to Delawares "after Teedyuscung had publickly declared" the proprietaries innocent of "the high Charges of Forgery & fraud"—payoffs were as routine as kegs.[98]

More generally, councils provided colonists with abundant oppor-tunities to bend Indians to the British will. At treaties in the 1730s John and Thomas Penn joined James Logan to bully Delawares into surrendering more land. Refuse, Logan was said to have warned, and "you'll make the big Trees and Logs, and great Logs and Stones tum-ble down into our Road."[99] Legerdemain with documents, already part of ordinary diplomatic conversation, easily translated to the council grounds. Just as provincial officials, often with help from Weiser or other negotiators, rearranged names on maps of the Delaware and Susquehanna Valleys to fool Indian delegations about the amount of territory being sold,[100] so they drew up the deeds in language that was deliberately vague. At Lancaster in 1744, for example, the Iroquois thought they were relinquishing rights only to the Shenandoah Valley; Virginians took the key phrase—"all the lands within the said colony as it is now or hereafter may be peopled and bounded"—to mean all the way to their Crown charter's western limits, the Pacific Ocean.[101] Again and again, natives fell victim to an expansive reading of treaty terms, as colonists laid claim to territory that was, Iroquois and other nations insisted, "not according to the Bargain," that ran counter to what natives at a congress had "expressly said and stipulated," that went "against the Indians mind."[102]

Sleight of hand and pen like this usually left a trail in the record; council speeches, which did not, were even easier to manipulate. The very improvised obfuscations that could promote harmony—confining contentious speeches to private talks, for example—could also be use-ful in placing, or keeping, Indians in the dark about colonial intentions.

If the Pennsylvania proprietaries' defense against charges of land fraud took several hours to deliver in English, the translator gave, in Delaware, only a brief synopsis of "what they had been doing." The same censorship might also soften, if not silence, Indian opposition to further European intrusion. If an Iroquois launched into a fifteen-minute tirade against a proposed colonial road into Indian country, a speech "with so much Earnestness" that "many [natives] seemed amazed while he was speaking," the interpreter shared with his English audience "but a small part" of the whole.[103]

The dexterity of Weiser and other go-betweens in Pennsylvania's service opened the American interior to colonial expansion, but the price in lives lost and blood spilled was high. Another casualty of council duplicity was natives' faith in treaty culture. When colonists under cover of fake maps or vague treaty agreements moved up the Susquehanna and the Delaware or past the Shenandoah, natives were going to catch on to what councils had done. You people "used many arts and much cunning, to talk the Indians and their chiefs out of their lands," said one disgusted Cayuga in 1750, and Teedyuscung often complained that Pennsylvania "held Treaties under the Bushes," "in a Corner," "in the dark," or "by Candle light."[104]

But it was the council's ends, not just its means, that caused estrangement. Delawares, Iroquois, Shawnees, and others discovered that while they considered a treaty sustenance for a relationship between peoples, colonists thought of it primarily as an engine of empire. Whatever other purposes a congress served, in the colonial mind land lay at its foundation. Fort Stanwix, with its hordes of hungry speculators, its secret deals, its surrender of vast tracts of America, is only the most famous (or infamous) example of this territorial imperative. True, in some ways Shackamaxon and Fort Stanwix were not just miles and years apart but far apart, too, in temper: one glowed with the light of Penn's yearning for a new chapter in human relations and native readiness to share that dream; the other reflected a different age, an age of wild speculation and shrewd manipulation of treaty protocol in order to feed an insatiable appetite. Yet both Shackamaxon and Stanwix were concerned with the transfer of America from native to European hands, as were all of the conferences between.[105]

The result was a reversal in which side sought councils. Where Conestogas and other natives early in the century had dragged reluctant colonists to regular treaties, after midcentury Indians were the reluctant ones. Why does the governor want to see us, suspicious Ohio leaders asked Post as he escorted them to Lancaster for a congress in 1762. "[I]f this was the Intention of the Govr to speak about Land," they insisted, "we would not go further, but turn back again directly." Land "was not the Governors chief matter," Post replied evasively, but to his journal he confided his hope that "somebody can help those people out of their Dream and jealously, before their reasons run to far."[106]

"[J]ealously," of course, was fully justified. Treaties had been the means of acquiring Indian country. As if that were not bad enough, councils did not even give natives the promised peace in return. "[T]he English have killed more of us since the Peace has been made than they did in the first War," said Indians in 1763, and in 1770 an Iroquois told William Johnson that "It is now worse than it was before" the Fort Stanwix council. "[Y]ou then told us as you had done before, that we should pass our time in peace, and travel in Security, that Trade should Flourish, . . . and that care should be taken to prevent any Person from imposing on us. . . . Brother . . . ," he concluded, "we do not see it."[107] Treaties went on; their guiding spirit guttered out.

———✵———

"The Exorbitant Presents and Great Servility . . . Paid to Indians"
Colonists Abandon Councils

Many colonists, too, were losing faith in the culture of diplomacy, though not for the same reasons. Willing enough to accept these conventions when they promoted trade, kept peace, bought land, and broke the routine, Pennsylvanians changed their minds once war began. Tales of Indian cruelty, spread by word of mouth and by provincial newspapers, made it harder to think kindly of natives. That raids went on even during peace talks convinced many that Indian killers and Indian peacemakers were one and the same. Too many remembered the coats and cloaks Teedyuscung's band wore at Easton. Too many heard Henry Hess describe what those Delawares, now in town, had done to his father. And Hess had plenty of company. "[T]he Captain of the Gang" that captured Thomas Baird "told him he was at one of the Indian Treaties with this Government, and shewed him a Medal he received there." My Delaware captors told me, another escaped prisoner reported, that "they had been lately at Philad[elphi]a, that they would Treat with the English as long as they could get Presents, and Scalp and Captivate [the English] as long as the French would reward 'em for 'em," even scoffing "that they lov'd their white Brethren so well that they wanted a few of 'em to hoe Corn for them."[108]

Infuriated by the taunts, the attacks, and the tales, Pennsylvanians' anger against Indians, against colonial officials, and against councils burned ever hotter. Borderers, recalling "former Treaties," were outraged by "the exorbitant presents and great Servility therein paid to Indians." The great Lancaster congress of 1762, where Ohio natives finally made peace with the province, looked to many frontier folk like the height of official folly: there, amid talk of peace and trade, "not only was the Blood of our many murdered Brethren tamely covered, but our poor unhappy captivated Friends [were] abandoned to Slavery among the Savages."[109]

The spirit of Lancaster, and indeed of all the treaties before it, died little more than a year later, when the "Contagion" of Indian hating turned its feverish gaze toward Conestoga.[110] The place was a tempting target. Things there had changed since Civility's day, when it had been a major native settlement colonists considered "far back in the Woods." By 1740 Pennsylvania farmers had surrounded the Indian town, now home to two or three score Indians led by an elderly man named Sheehays. Son of Conodahto, the headman who had confronted Sylvester Garland and treated with the Founder so long ago, Sheehays had been at councils since the 1710s.[111] Now, on the several hundred acres reserved for them by the proprietaries, he and the other Conestogas scratched out a meager existence. They grew corn on some of the land and rented out the rest. Occasional supplies of flour, clothing, and other goods from the government helped keep cold or hunger at bay, as did the hogs women tended and what deer men could find on the two nearby farms that still permitted them to hunt. Like those hunters, native weavers relied on ancient skills, peddling baskets and brooms to neighboring colonists. If these resources did not suffice, some fell to begging at the door of those same neighbors.[112]

A hard, precarious, sometimes humiliating life, no doubt, but it gave

Conestogas a niche in Pennsylvania society; dressing like ordinary farmers, they "in a Manner were become white People." Indian children, some of them named after "favourite [colonial] neighbors," played with Pennsylvania friends, and Indian peddlers "often spent the night by the kitchen fire of the farms round about."[113]

The frontier war that erupted in the mid-1750s imperiled this small native island in a vast colonial sea. When enemy raiders hit the Paxton settlements nearby, shaken survivors began to turn on these Conestogas. Indians there grew "affraid to go any distance to sell their wares, as people began to threaten them with what was likely to be their fate." That fate, apparently, linked their lands and their lives. "[T]he Dutch & other people frighten ye Indians," a Conestoga complained in 1758, "saying in their Talk with one another wch is over our Land . . . yt the Indians will be killed."[114]

The Conestoga those colonists wanted most to kill was Will Sock (Toshetaquah), though it had not always been so.[115] In the war's early days, Pennsylvanians had been glad to call this man *friend*. In the summer of 1756 he had gone up to the Susquehanna Forks with the first frightened provincial troops dispatched to build Fort Augusta there. The next winter, having come from the Ohio country on British business, he and another Conestoga returned to the stronghold those soldiers had built at the Forks, in his pocket a passport from the governor and instructions from George Croghan, deputy superintendent of Indian affairs. Leaving the garrison to carry another message west, the two got an impressive send-off: "3 platoons of 12 men" fired a salute, followed by "3 roughs of all the Drums, 3 huzas, & one Great gun."[116]

The cannon's echoes had scarcely died away before whispers about Will Sock began to be heard. He had visited enemy towns and carried a French flag. He had killed one colonist, held another captive, and "had green white scalps" of still others. "I believe," wrote one frightened Pennsylvanian who crossed paths with him, "that he had murder in his heart."[117]

Sock's heart remains hard to read. It is clear that the mask of deference so many Settlement Indians wore for protection fitted him badly; he tended to "demand" things of colonists, and sometimes refused to answer their questions. It is clear, too, that he tried to persuade his people to move up the Susquehanna into Indian country. But it is less clear that his plans included joining Pennsylvania's foes. What mattered was what colonists thought, and most thought Sock a treacherous killer, his home town the enemy's lair.

These suspicions might have subsided had war not come back to Pennsylvania in the spring of 1763. Once again the bloodshed began over the mountains, among native peoples who, alarmed by the British army's failure to withdraw from Ohio, read as a hostile act Britain's refusal to continue the flow of gifts that marked friendship.[118] And once again a war that started far away soon swept eastward. "[T]his Township is Breaking up . . . ," John Harris exclaimed from Paxton in mid-July, "there is Such a General Pannick & Confusion Prevailing among the whole Countrey." As before, war parties tore through the frontier valleys, leaving fear and anguish in their wake. As before, colonists' ears rang with lurid tales of mutilated bodies and fresh scalps. As before, men left their farms to patrol the mountain passes, peering into the gathering dusk of a summer evening, waiting for hell to show its face.[119]

At Paxton those scouts, tired of waiting, decided to carry the fight to the enemy. In late August, 110 Paxton men headed up the Susquehanna's West Branch. Just above the Forks an enemy war party surprised them, roaring over a hilltop "naked[,] painted black, running like so many Furies" to slay four men and wound six more. The rest, reeling, made their way downriver in the dark, the wounded "groaning & crying enough to make ones heart ach[e]."[120]

Heartache returned in October, when Paxtonians again marched up the Susquehanna, this time following the North Branch to Wyoming, where a fledgling settlement of Connecticut folk had staked a claim to the land by virtue of their original charter's expansive terms and a fraudulent purchase from some Iroquois. Whether the troops went to oust these squatters or kill Indians (or both) is unclear. What they found, though, was those New Englanders, nine men and one woman, "most cruelly butchered; the Woman was roasted, and had two Hinges in her Hands—supposed to be put in red hot; and several of the Men had Awls thrust in their Eyes, and Spears, Arrows, Pitchforks, &c. sticking in their Bodies."[121]

The hinges and awls bore a customary Indian message of anger and revenge—anger at Connecticut's invasion, revenge for the mysterious fire, arranged if not actually kindled by Connecticut men, that had killed Teedyuscung and destroyed the Delaware town there the previous spring.[122] But, as before, Paxton's defenders did not get that message. They took away from Wyoming only a deepening hatred of savages and a determination to even the score.

The return of chaos in 1763 revived suspicions of what John Harris called the "Basket & Broommaking Bandittey" living among colonists; these people looked innocent enough, but they were "in Reality our most dangerous Enemies."[123] On November 30, Conestogas, sensing this ominous shift, sent a message to the new governor, John Penn, grandson of the Founder. Marked by Sheehays and two other men, the letter included a string of wampum "to welcome you into this Country." "[W]e were settled at this place by an Agreement of Peace and Amity established between your Grandfather & ours," they reminded him. Not only that, but because "we have always lived in Peace and Quietness with our Brethren & Neighbours round us during the last & present Indian Wars," we count on your "favour and protection."[124]

Sheehays had a way with the old words, insisting three years earlier that "old William Penn had a particular regard for the Conestogo Indians; he loved, indeed, all the Indians, but there was a singular love between him and . . . the Conestogo Indians."[125] By the winter of 1763, however, the time-honored rhetoric had lost its power to protect natives. Before daybreak on December 14, some fifty mounted colonists approached the sleeping cabins at Conestoga. It was bitterly cold, the snow deep and more coming down. In short order everyone—Sheehays and his son Ess-canesh, along with two other men and two women—was dead, the houses plundered and ablaze, the Paxton men—tomahawks bloody, "coats cover'd with snow and sleet"—homeward bound.[126]

Their business was not done. Fourteen other Conestogas—three couples, along with five boys and three girls—had been scattered about, peddling their wares, on that fatal morning. Within days, local officials rounded these survivors up and deposited them in Lancaster's workhouse until the province figured out what to do with them.[127]

Neither that sturdy building nor Lancaster's citizens offered much protection when, late in the afternoon of December 27, the Paxton men rode into town to finish the job. Careful planning made quick work of it. Twelve stayed outside to hold off any locals foolish enough to interfere (none did); three broke down the workhouse door, then five more stormed through it to cover the jailers, while the rest, shouting, rushed past and went for the Indians. In fifteen minutes, as curious townsfolk streamed toward the commotion, the gang was out and away.

"Hooping & Hallowing," they circled the county courthouse, firing their guns into the air, then rode off down the icy streets.

Behind them was carnage. In the workhouse yard "lay the whole of them, men, women and children, spread about . . . ; shot—scalped—hacked—and cut to pieces." Against one wall splattered with blood and brains sprawled an Indian man whose remains were as grisly as anything his killers might have seen at Wyoming. Shot in the chest, hands and feet chopped off, "his head was blown to atoms" when someone jammed a musket in his mouth and pulled the trigger. Near the rear door sprawled two children, perhaps three years old, skulls split and scalps gone. Beneath them was Kanianquas (Molly) and her husband, Will Sock.[128]

Tellers of this tale usually follow the Paxton Boys out of town: a month later, now several hundred strong, these borderers marched on Philadelphia to pursue their anti-Indian, anti-treaty campaign; met on the capital's outskirts by Benjamin Franklin and other provincial leaders, the frontiersmen presented their grievances and withdrew, heading thence not toward prison or the gallows (none were ever arrested, much less tried and convicted), but into the printing presses and history books, as contemporary politicians and later scholars tried to make sense of their deeds.[129] But we ought instead to pause a moment at that workhouse, its walls wet with gore, or to linger a few miles away, beside the smoldering ruins and fresh graves out by Conestoga Creek.[130] Though they hardly looked it that snowy December, these were treaty grounds. At Conestoga, Sheehays had reminded Pennsylvanians in 1758, "a fire was kindled . . . that had burnt a long while"—had burned, in fact, since William Penn's visit to the place in 1700. Lancaster's council fire was younger, started only in 1744, but it, too, had blazed brightly, lighting the way not only for Conestogas and Pennsylvanians but for Delawares and Marylanders, Iroquois and Virginians, Shawnees and Wyandots. The courthouse around which the Paxton men rode in triumph had seen many treaty councils. In that building Indians and colonists had dined and danced together; down those streets young Iroquois men had sped, yelling and prancing, to act out their martial exploits for a colonial audience. Now both Conestoga and Lancaster had seen meetings of a different sort. Now they sat, bloody ground, mute repudiation of council culture and all that it stood for.[131]

Colonists sorting through the smoldering ruins at Conestoga that bitter day, where "the dead bodies lay among the rubbish of their burnt cabbins like half consum'd logs," came upon a bag that had somehow escaped the flames. Inside were two wampum belts and six ancient documents. The longest (and probably the oldest) of these papers was the treaty Conestogas and other Indians had made with William Penn in the City of Brotherly Love in 1701 when the two sides pledged "that they shall forever hereafter be as one Head & One Heart, & live in true Friendship & Amity as one People." In closing, Penn had promised, "for himself, his heirs and Successors, yt he and they will at all times shew themselves true Friends & Brothers to all & every one of ye Said Indians."[132]

"No Indian Treaties Shall Be Held"
The Go-betweens' Decline

It is easy to lose sight of the go-betweens while tracking the hurricane that blew across the frontier and left, in its wake, a landscape forever altered. Musket and scalping knife now competed with wampum belt and peace pipe. Pennsylvania leaders, ever more convinced that all Indians were "faithless Barbarians," vowed that "all the letters, & Belts, &ca they can bring"—a negotiator's very stock in trade—would not change their minds about natives' true colors. And most colonists had had enough of Indian councils. "[A]ll the Country," wrote one Pennsylvanian from Paxton in February 1764, "now seems determined that no Indian Treaties shall be held."[133]

No wonder that, in this new age, go-betweens were quieter. Thomas McKee and Conrad Weiser, Moses Tatamy and Isaac Stille, George Croghan and Andrew Montour—for a generation these and a handful of other men had loomed large in the life of the frontier. Now they began to leave the stage one way or another, eclipsed by the bloody course of events. During the late 1750s John Pumpshire (Cawkeeponen), the Jersey Delaware who in 1756 had gone with Newcastle to Wyoming and then guided Teedyuscung at Easton, sank from sight. Then, in the summer of 1760 Weiser died. "We . . . are at a great loss, and sit in darkness, as well as you, by the death of Conrad Weiser," said Seneca George, condoling Pennsylvania, "as since his Death we cannot so well understand one another."[134]

Darkness soon deepened. That fall Moses Tatamy followed Weiser into the grave, and as the decade wore on, many other prominent mediators went into semi-retirement. Isaac Stille, after a long sojourn through the heart of the continent, returned to live quietly on a Friend's estate near Philadelphia, his days spent impressing neighbors with his marksmanship and peddling traps or ladles. Another Delaware, Joseph Peepy (Weholelahund), who had worked with Stille many times, took a different path. Enlisting in the Christian campaign to win Indian souls, he shuttled back and forth between New Jersey, Moravian Indian towns above Wyoming, and the Ohio country, where he translated for missionaries spreading their good news. In his early days out there Peepy might have crossed paths with another of Stille's old traveling companions, Christian Frederick Post, who was resuming his mission work in Ohio. But that "feald" turned out to be so "thick with torns & briers groen up" that in 1764, full of "sorri & greaf," the Moravian left to try his luck on the Mosquito Coast.[135]

Even old hands still active in diplomacy kept a lower profile during the 1760s. Thomas McKee did less Indian business. His superior in the Indian Department, George Croghan, though his powerful voice was still heard, found fewer occasions to speak up and fewer listeners when he did. Another Croghan deputy, Andrew Montour, spent most of his time over the Alleghenies or up in Iroquoia, only occasionally returning to his old Susquehanna haunts.[136]

Treaties and talks went on, of course, as anyone stopping by Fort Stanwix in the fall of 1768—or Fort Pitt at many other times—could see.[137] But the men who had so long managed Pennsylvania's relations with its native neighbors were less in demand than ever before, less often consulted and less often heeded. Architects of accommodation, they now seemed out of touch with the times.

Weiser, McKee, and Croghan had fallen out of touch because people thought them soft on Indians. As the line between native and European hardened, they seemed to straddle the cultural divide in ways that made colonists uncomfortable. Weiser was *Tarachiawagon;* McKee, Croghan, and Post had native wives; Croghan went farther still, getting named to the Ohio Iroquois council, called "one of our People" by Indians there, and supposedly asserting "that he was not an Englishman, but an Indian."[138]

All three would suffer for these connections to the Indian countries.

Soon after war broke out, some of Weiser's own neighbors threatened to shoot him, thinking he was "a Traitor of the Country who held with the Indians." The old agent—helped by friends who pulled him away from one window, where he was too good a target—emerged unscathed, but he never was free from the sort of "mad man" so common in those days. Shortly before his death, Weiser was in Reading to put up copies of a proclamation condemning recent killings of some friendly Indians when "Some one Gentleman was not pleased with them[,] Justified that Murder very much."[139]

Poor Thomas McKee lived long enough to face a whole army of such gentlemen when he condemned the Conestoga slaughter. McKee had known those Indians well—when they needed someone to look after their affairs, it was to McKee that they usually turned—and knew, too, that they were innocent. Their death, he thundered, is "a most detestable Murder, . . . not only contrary to the Laws of Government but Christianity, and every thing that ought to distinguish us from Savages." The old trader's candor cost him. "I dare not move a Step from my house," he wrote in June 1765, eighteen months after the killings. "[M]y Family are in the greatest consternation, being in imminent danger of having our House set on fire, or bodily hurt done us, as I have often been threatened by the Rioters."[140]

George Croghan, too, went against the grain. He condemned the Conestogas' killers and criticized the military for taking a high hand with Indians, ignoring his warnings that to cut off gifts was tantamount to declaring war. Moreover, at a time when few of his fellow colonists had anything good to say about natives, Croghan, "fully preswaded of the Justice & Lagality of the Indians Title [to land] as an Independent p[e]ople," asserted that "Justice, Honour and our own interest" required colonists to treat these nations "with propriety and address."[141]

In fact, those thinking these three negotiators soft on Indians need not have worried. The three were closer kin to Paxton people and British officers than it looked. During the war, all three, far from wavering in their allegiance, led the fight against Pennsylvania's Indian enemies.[142] And while both McKee and Croghan condemned the Conestoga massacres, neither opposed the idea of massacring natives. McKee, sympathetic to Conestogas, was no apologist for Indians; he just thought that the Paxton Boys had slaughtered the wrong ones. "I should have thought the People who have thus behaved" so brutally at

Conestoga and Lancaster "more excusable if they had cut off in Philada [the Moravian Indians] maintain'd [there] at the Public Expence, as there is some Reason to believe that some of these have acted against us."[143] McKee had no objection to killing women and children, as long as he thought they were the right ones.

George Croghan, meanwhile, opposed both the slaughter of Conestogas and the plans to do the same to Moravian Indians cowering on that island in the Delaware near Philadelphia. Instead, Croghan argued, make such killing a part of a larger strategy. "[A]ll Indians have A Greatt Regard fer Each other," he wrote on learning of the renewed attacks in 1763, and many natives still live among colonists. Lock these people up, he urged, then tell our foes that if raids continue we will slay the hostages.[144]

Croghan's cold-blooded calculations were a logical extension of his disdain for Indians. Once a treaty was over and Indians out of earshot, the trader and agent routinely spoke not of coexistence but of conquest, not of admiration but contempt. Of news he obtained from a native in 1754, he wrote: "this Indian, I think, is to be believ'd, if there Can be any Creadett given to what an Indian Sayes." French people he met "are a More Savidge people than ye Indians if there Can be any pople so." Croghan always favored peace, because gifts and councils were cheaper than troops and forts. But he had no doubt that colonists could, if need be, defeat the Indians and "reduce them to a State of servitude." Even as he urged that colonial authorities seek natives' "love and affection," he also knew that ultimately "there is no way to make them happy but by fear."[145]

Conrad Weiser was of the same mind. Long considered among those colonists most sympathetic to Indians, in fact Weiser often spoke of them with disgust. A Frenchman he saw is "now an Indian in appearance, if not worse." While natives have "some Religion," at bottom they are "barbarians" and "heathen" who worship "idols."[146] Weiser himself was a spiritual wanderer—his quest for meaning took him from Lutheran and Reformed congregations to Conrad Beissel's Ephrata mystics to Moravians and finally back to the Lutherans—but he never considered Indian spirituality, even though that faith seems no more silly than, say, Beissel's, said to include the belief "that the elimination of human waste was not a necessary function of the body."[147]

More revealing still of Weiser's real view of Indians, and of the life among them he had led, is his insistence that his children not follow in his footsteps and become go-betweens. Provincial officials pressuring him to train a successor found him "obstinately determined that none of his Children should learn Indian." These officials only persuaded him to have his son Sammy taught by his own Mohawk family "with ye greatest difficulty," and even then Weiser, for reasons he kept to himself, was quick to call the tutorials a failure and bring Sammy home.[148]

If even Weiser, McKee, and Croghan drew such sharp lines between colonists and Indians yet still were branded Indian lovers, there was no hope that Christian Delaware go-betweens would ever escape the stain of savagery to be accepted as Pennsylvanians and brethren in the faith. The first to discover this hard truth was Moses Tatamy. Friend of Count Zinzendorf and David Brainerd, of Israel Pemberton and Conrad Weiser, Tatamy toward the end of his life grew deeply disenchanted as he learned more about the colonial world. Certainly the Walking Purchase colored his view; two decades later he was still stewing about "ye Running Walk," that "Fraud and great Fraud."[149] But there was more to his unhappiness than that. Walking Purchase or no, Tatamy had taken his stamp from a European template. When the province drove Delawares out of the Forks, Tatamy, with several others, had even sought permission to stay among his erstwhile Pennsylvania friends.

This brought him up against the limits of colonial tolerance. "[H]aving embraced the Christian Religion and attained some small Degree of Knowledge therein," these Delawares told Governor George Thomas, "they are desirous of living under the same Laws with the English, and praying that some place might be allotted them where they may live in the Enjoyment of the same Religion & Laws with them [colonists]." This had been William Penn's dream; but Penn was dead, and Thomas unmoved. Instead of simply rejecting the petition, in November 1742 Thomas summoned Tatamy and another Delaware to the provincial council chamber, "interrogated" them "concerning their Knowledge of Christianity," then announced that "it appeared they had very little if any at all."[150]

Thanks to David Brainerd, Tatamy soon underwent an arduous, thoroughgoing conversion. By 1745 the Delaware was, Brainerd rejoiced, "a new man," so transformed that he "appear'd like another Man to his Neighbours."[151] But not new and different enough for most of those neighbors. Christian devotion, fancy clothes, a life patterned on European ways—none sufficed to end officials' contempt for such "prating, busy and ignorant Indians," or to prevent Tatamy's own son being murdered merely for being an Indian. Near the end of his life Tatamy was a changed man. Once patient with the haughty Zinzendorf, he now berated the humble Post. Once keen to push his fellow Indians toward colonial ways, he now, some said, warned natives that "it was intended by the English to drive them all out & possess themselves of their Land." Once remarkably sober, in 1760 he was prone to "Druncken Fitts."[152]

Isaac Stille and Joseph Peepy drank, too, as their colonial aspirations ended in alienation akin to Tatamy's, but they ultimately took their disenchantment farther. While never publicly humiliated or shot at, neither did these two Delawares ever win full colonial respect or trust. Post doubted Stille's loyalty in the fall of 1758, and on another mission two years later a colonist thought that "he play'd ye: Janus." No one ever questioned Peepy's loyalty, but the missionaries dismissed him as "ignorant" and "considerable flighty." Tired, perhaps, of being patronized, the "Aged" Peepy joined fifty Indian families to leave their old homes near Penn's Woods and seek a new life in Ohio.[153]

Soon thereafter Isaac Stille also gathered up what Delawares he could find among colonists and headed west. Peepy had kept his reasons for abandoning his homeland to himself; Stille had more to say. Though one who knew him during those last years in Pennsylvania remembered him as "always remarkable pleasant" and insisted that the Delaware "always appeared happy & reconciled to his Lot," in fact Stille was an angry man. Britain's failure to return back over the mountains after taking Fort Duquesne still rankled. Isaac himself had borne the army's promise west with Pisquetomen and Post that perilous fall of 1758, arguing fiercely for it in those decisive days. When Britain broke its word, "his honourable feelings were hurt beyond expression," so hurt that he disappeared into the western wilds for several years.[154]

Then in 1775, having long since returned to live among colonists, Stille "thought it his duty to remove all the remains of his Tribe to a fine vacant part of the Country that [he] had passed through" during that sojourn. Perhaps his last job as interpreter for the province, when Iroquois kin of the dead Conestogas came to Philadelphia in the spring of 1775 seeking compensation, reminded Stille of Indians' bleak future in Pennsylvania, prompting him to turn his gaze westward. He said only that he led the exodus "in order to keep them away from War & Rum." At last, wearing clothes donated by neighboring whites, on their backs heavy bundles held on by "broad Straps across their Foreheads," in October 1775 Stille's band of forty—women on one side, men on the other, two women on horseback between the lines, in front Isaac himself in feathered cap—left Penn's Woods for the last time.[155]

But none of these Indian or European men—not Stille or Tatamy, not Weiser or Croghan—embodied the frontier's possibilities, the meeting and merging of cultures, better than Andrew Montour (Oughsara); and none were as disillusioned or as adrift as he. Montour spent his life keeping up his credentials as both an Indian and a European. In March 1762, he and his son John planned to set up a trading post near Shamokin, arguing "that being Indians, they had a Right to settle anywhere upon Indian Lands." In the years to come, Montour connected in other ways to Indian country. He briefly moved back to his original West Branch home, claiming tracts where Montour villages once had stood. When those lands went to creditors, Montour settled on the south side of the Ohio River a few miles below Pittsburgh—land that he called not Montoursville but Oughsaragoh (place of Oughsara).[156]

At the same time, Montour was also adopting more trappings of European colonial culture, trappings that went well beyond the "Silver Laced hatt" and other finery he continued to fancy. He took his mother's last name, but his son took his. Moving farther still away from the matrilineal habits of thought he had known in his youth, in the mid-1750s he arranged for his children to be "independent of the Mother," sending them to school in Philadelphia and Williamsburg.[157]

Trying to be both Indian and European, Montour ended up being neither. The life that he made for himself, the path he traveled, turned out to be a dead end, not an avenue to some new social order. There was no place in between, there were no words to describe the sort of person he was, and precious few people like him in English America.

A closer look reveals that, in this final generation of negotiators on the colonial frontier, even among men so bicultural, so flexible, so skilled at crossing the cultural divide, there were limits to how much they wanted to get along, how close they wished to come, one to another. There was, after all, a deep fissure between Indian and colonial worlds. Far from obliterating that fault line, except for Andrew Montour, the go-betweens in fact personified it and perpetuated it. If they were unable to see past their differences in order to embrace their similarities, no wonder the treaty culture they orchestrated ended up as it did.

~~~~~

"Will Not It Be Impossible . . . to Live Together?" The Land Speaks

So much of the negotiators' distance and alienation lies in subtle signs hard to decipher. Tatamy spoke of his grief and anger through the bottle in his hand, Peepy and Stille, finally, spoke with their feet. Post and McKee, Weiser and Croghan left more of their private thoughts; Montour left none. But for all of these men, literate and nonliterate, the clearest expression of these feelings can be found in the very land affairs that were so central to treaty history. Watching them pursue their dreams, sketching the lineaments of those dreams on territory in and around Penn's Woods, we can best see their legacy.

No provincial go-between was immune to the land fever that afflicted British America; none could resist the temptation to play on the Indians' trust to acquire more. Thomas McKee arranged private gifts of prime real estate from his Indian friends. Post, though he never sought land for himself, was so captivated by the Indian countries he passed through that his account of his second journey with Pisquetomen in 1758—here is "a rich fine bottom land well timbered," there "a large tract of fine land"—makes him sound more like a land speculator than a messenger or missionary.[158]

But no one was more enamored of Indian lands than George Croghan, who crammed his travel journals with glowing descriptions of "the face of the country." Even when, on one trip, Indians tomahawked, captured, and carried him off, the fur trader was still noting how the land through which the war party dragged him was the "best pasture in the World." For Croghan the question was not *whether* more of this territory would come into colonial hands, but only "*when* ye. back Lands is Purchest of the ye. Indians." At the 1768 Fort Stanwix sweepstakes and land lottery, he was among the biggest winners, making off with more than 100,000 acres.[159]

If Conrad Weiser's appetite for land was no match for Croghan's, nonetheless he, too, constantly pressed Indians to surrender more territory. Beginning his life in Pennsylvania as a squatter on the Delawares' Tulpehocken domain, he went on to a career that earned him substantial grants from friendly Indians and grateful proprietors. From 1742 onwards, he chipped steadily away at Iroquois resistance, but land fever really infected him after his first visit to Ohio in 1748. "[H]e talks in raptures about the Soil and Waters" there, remarked Richard Peters.[160] Indeed, the man could scarcely contain himself. "[I]t [is] a tousand pity that Such a large and good Country Should be unsetled," Weiser mused, ignoring the Indian nations there, "or fall into the hands of the French." While looking toward the day when "the land will fall at last into the English hands," Weiser redoubled his efforts in Iroquoia "to bring the Indians into an humour to sell the Lands," hoping that he would have "the Satisfaction to make another Stout purchase of the Indians for the Honourable the proprietors."[161]

In the course of this long campaign, Weiser's strategies included bribery, secret deals, and—taking his cue from personal experience— unleashing squatters. "[O]ur people Should be let loose to Set upon any part of the Indian lands," he wrote in February 1754, "upon giveing Sec[urity] for their Complying with the proprietary terms after pu[rchase;] the Indians would Come in and demand Consideration . . . and what Can they Say, the people of pensilvania are their [Breth]ren according to the treatys Subsisting." Shortly after the Pennsylvania agent's death, Tachnechdorus (John Shickellamy) called him "one of the greatest thieves in the World for Lands."[162]

Swept up in the land rush, Weiser did not envision, did not work toward, did not even want a world in which Indians and colonists were one heart and one body, in which half of him truly belonged to the Iroquois. Quite the contrary: a mingling of European and Indian was his worst fear, one he conjured up for Richard Peters when the proprietary secretary fretted that squatters on Indian land might cause a war. "Mr Weiser apprehends a worse Effect," Peters reported, "that is that they will [instead] become tributary to the Indians and pay them yearly Sums for their Lycence to be there." This was already the custom in some parts of the frontier, Weiser warned in 1749; if it spreads, "the Proprietors will not only have all the abandoned People of the Province to deal with but the Indians too and . . . *they will mutually support each other* and do a vast deal of Mischief."[163]

For all their rhetoric about being one people with the newcomers, Indians shared Weiser's fear of mixing and mingling. Iroquois policy had long been to settle bands of refugee Indians on the Six Nations' frontiers, making them buffers protecting Iroquoia from colonial neighbors.[164] Meanwhile some of those refugees, trusting neither colonists nor Iroquois, were pursuing their own goal of a land base. Delaware go-betweens led the fight. However akin to a colonist they might seem, they spoke in their land deals of a separate destiny.

Establishing a secure home on the Susquehanna was an old dream among Delawares pushed out of their ancestral lands. "[I]f I mistake not," James Logan fretted in 1736, "Allumapis [Sassoonan] (or his People whether he be living or not) design to get some grant [from the Six Nations] for the Land above the Hills" on Pennsylvania's northern frontier. Two decades later Tatamy, Peepy, Stille, and Pumpshire carried on the effort to make this dream come true. Using Teedyuscung as spokesman when convenient, these Delawares mustered all of their negotiating skill to press Pennsylvania and Iroquois leaders alike for a grant of territory they could call their own.[165]

Their goal, a permanent barrier between them and their provincial neighbors, was the clearest expression of their vision of a separate future. The best way to restore peace and right past wrongs is to give Delawares a Susquehanna homeland, Moses Tatamy and John Pumpshire told Weiser as the three go-betweens rode along the road from Easton to the frontier after a treaty in November 1756. "Both these Indians were desirous, or rather insisted upon," wrote Weiser, "that I should use my Endeavours with the Governor and People of Pennsylvania, to lay out a large Tract of Land on Sasquehannah, and secure it so to their Posterity that none of them could sell and nobody buy it." Do this, Tatamy and Pumpshire promised, and "the Delawares would, for the most part, if not all, come and live on it, and be reconciled to the People and Government of Pennsylvania for ever."[166]

Weiser favored the plan; other Pennsylvanians did not. This is not our land to give, provincial authorities replied; it belongs to the Six Nations. At Easton in October 1758, when Teedyuscung pressed those Iroquois for a deed to some Susquehanna territory, they "went away angry," saying "what are we Englis[h] now to give Deeds to Indians"? But Delawares did not give up. They sketched a map of the land they had in mind. They got the Pennsylvania assembly to support, in principle, "certain Boundaries fixed between them and the People of this Province." They extracted from Quakers a promise to buy the lands in question if the Iroquois ever agreed to sell.[167]

At Philadelphia in August 1761 the negotiators tried yet again.[168] Draw up a deed to Wyoming in the name of Isaac Stille and Joseph

Peepy, a Conoy named Kanak't (Last Night) advised Pennsylvania officials (with Stille interpreting)—"not for themselves," he hastened to add, "but for the Delawares." We will then get the Iroquois to sign it. The governor gave the usual answer about this being none of Pennsylvania's business, and less than two years later, this dream, this attempt to write onto the landscape the Delaware go-betweens' desire to keep colonists (and the Iroquois) at arm's length, went up in flames when Connecticut schemers burned down the Delaware village at Wyoming.[169] But the dream's failure is perhaps less important than its dogged pursuit, and what that pursuit reveals about the inner feelings, the abiding declarations of independence, animating Tatamy, Peepy, Pumpshire, and Stille.

Weiser and Croghan dreamed of the day when Indians were out of the way, Tatamy and Pumpshire of the time when Wyoming was the Delaware capital. Andrew Montour, judging from his land dealings at midcentury, had a different idea. Inchoate, never stated outright, Montour's hopes, his vision of the future, can be traced in the speculative schemes he hatched downstream a ways from Wyoming. In those negotiations, Montour's hand can be seen clearly—and clearly puts him at odds with most native Americans and most European colonists of his day, including his fellow go-betweens.

Montour's land speculation first surfaced in 1748, when he left Ohio after a short stay and brought his family back to the Susquehanna—and back, he thought, forever. "Andrew Montour has pitched upon a place in the Proprietor's mannor, at Canatqueany [Conodoguinet Creek, across the Susquehanna River from John Harris's]," reported Weiser that August. "He Expects that the Government shall build him a house there, and furnish his family with necessarys."[170] Inadvertently or not, Montour had touched a sore spot in Pennsylvania's history with its native neighbors. In 1731 the province, trying to lure disaffected Shawnees back over the mountains from the Ohio, had set aside land along the Conodoguinet in the proprietaries' name "in order to accommodate the Shawaana Indians or such others as may think fit to settle there."[171] The Shawnees never came back, but—apparently considering himself one of those "others"—Montour did. Believing "the Land to belong Still to the Indians . . . ," he explained, "he only Soposd he Might Live there for his Life." He even hired a colonist to build him a house, promising payment from Philadelphia. From Philadelphia instead came, in 1750, word that Montour was in trouble. The news made him "very uneasy[,] Expecting to be putt in Jale for the money he owed" the builder.[172]

Montour managed to stay out of jail, but his first attempt to live on a patch of native ground amid European colonists was a fiasco. He did not give up on the idea, however. A year later he had set his sights on some land farther up the Susquehanna, and this time Montour visited both Onondaga and Philadelphia to get approval. The Iroquois apparently were noncommittal; Pennsylvanians, whom he lobbied "earnestly and repeatedly," were more ready to listen.[173] In April 1752 the governor, seeing here an opportunity to keep squatters out of Indian country and the colony out of trouble, issued Montour a commission "to go and live . . . over the Kittochtinny Hills . . . , in order that you may by your personal Care and Vigilance preserve those Lands ['not purchased of the Indians'] from being settled as well as warn off all who have presumed to go there."[174]

Paper in hand, a delighted Montour moved to Sherman's Creek, just south of the Juniata River.[175] Once there, however, he began to depart dramatically from his instructions, sketching on the land his vision of the region's future and his own place in that future. Instead of driving out European colonial settlers already there and warning off others on their way, Montour actually began to recruit these people, inviting them into the valley and setting them up as his tenants.[176] "[H]e aims of haveing a large piece of ground over the hills and a good Number of Setlers on it to pay Contribution to him," Weiser wrote to Richard Peters.[177] Drawing from his experiences in the Susquehanna Valley—his home village "a promiscuous Indian population," his wives Delaware and Conoy, his neighbors Shawnees, Germans, Tutelos, and Irish—Montour apparently envisioned a place that brought different peoples together, a place where a man like him felt at home.[178]

Peters and Weiser were determined to stop him. They were in a contest with Montour, a contest not just for land but for the power to determine what sort of society was to be born on the Susquehanna—and, perhaps, beyond it. Would it resemble the Delaware Valley, now virtually empty of Indians? Or would it be something new, forged by various refugee and emigrant groups—European and Indian—from the common Susquehanna experience of the past generation and led by men like Montour?

The answer to these questions came at Albany in July 1754 when Weiser and Peters purchased from the Six Nations the land beneath Montour's feet. Pennsylvania won in part because the Iroquois were as unhappy with Montour's plan as Weiser and Peters were. In the past, Iroquois sales of land had served to keep European colonists at bay. Their view of the future was closer to Weiser's and Stille's than to Montour's: America was to be a land of lines dividing Indians from Europeans, not a place where lines blurred and peoples came together.

Just how important this speculative venture was to Montour, just how great a blow the Albany purchase was, became abundantly clear when he next crossed paths with Weiser, at John Harris's in the early fall of 1754. Weiser, headed west, persuaded Montour to go along; the Pennsylvania interpreter soon had reason to regret issuing that invitation. "[W]hen he meet me at John Harris'," Weiser reported, "he called for so much punch that himself . . . and other Indians got drunk, the same at Tobias Hendricks [on the road west]. I bought 2 quarts of Rum there to use on our Journey, but he drunk most all the first day."

The liquor unleashed a torrent of rage. Montour "Cursed and swore . . . , damned me more than hundred times . . . ," Weiser continued. "He is vexed at the new purchase. Told me I cheated the Indians. He says he will now kill any white men that will pretend to settle on his Creek. . . . I left him drunk . . . ," Weiser concluded; "on one legg he had a stocking and no shoe, on the other a shoe and no stocking. . . . He swore terrible when he saw me mount my horse."[179]

The image of that drunk and disheveled figure hurling abuse at Weiser's retreating back exposes how badly Montour had misread the realities of the colonial frontier. Only after Montour had made it his life's ambition to become the leading citizen of the territory between the woods and the inhabited parts, only then did he discover that he had pitched his camp, had pitched his life, in a no-man's land.

Though many go-betweens crossed the cultural divide between Indians and Europeans, few, it turned out, really felt at home on the far side. Croghan, Weiser, the Oneidas Shickellamy and Scarouyady, even, for all their colonial mimicry, Tatamy and Stille—these and the rest were anchored on one side of the frontier or the other, however much they went back and forth. Like Thomas Gist, a frontiersman Wyandots in 1758 captured, stripped, shaved, painted, and adopted, European colonists in the Indian countries were only "acting the part of an Indian." "I could do [this acting] very well," Gist boasted after he—"determined to be what I really was"—made good his escape.[180]

Gist, like Weiser and Croghan, like Shickellamy and Scarouyady, like Tatamy and Stille, knew what he really was. Did Montour? Here the answer is less clear; it is as hard to read the man now as it was 250 years ago. What can be said is that Montour was never able to borrow or to fashion a vocabulary that would define him as neither Indian nor European but something new, something else altogether. Lacking that working vocabulary, Montour was lost—and all but alone, with no critical mass of people like himself sufficient to weave new social patterns from the frayed edges of the old. "Will not it be impossible for Indians and White people to live together?" asked Richard Peters, even as he tried to keep those frayed margins from unraveling further. "Will not there be an eternal Intercourse of Rum and a perpetual Scene of quarreling?"[181] Three centuries after William Penn, two centuries after Andrew Montour, a century after Wounded Knee, the questions linger.[182]

The Killing of Young Seneca George, 1769

"You Have Killed One of Us"
The Murder

The 1760s witnessed not only the disappearance of Andrew Montour and the other go-betweens of the Pennsylvania frontier, but also the disenchantment of the treaty regime those mediators had done so much to construct. Chicanery at Fort Stanwix epitomizing the council ground's poisoned atmosphere; random murders making a mockery of the peaceful words exchanged at those gatherings; Paxton Boys, not Thomas McKee or Conrad Weiser, now the most prominent border folk—these and other features of frontier life spelled the end of the conversation William Penn had struck up with native peoples in 1682. For a time, the borderlands' Indian and European inhabitants were poised between a common past and a divided future; old habits of thought, old patterns of discourse, old rituals of comity died hard. But die those old ways did: by the close of the colonial era, Penn's peaceable kingdom probably had fewer native Americans living within its borders than any other British province. A good place to glimpse the passing of one era and the dawn of another is on a stretch of the Susquehanna near the old haunts of Jack Armstrong and Shickellamy, of Thomas McKee and Andrew Montour.

Early in the summer of 1769 several Indians left the town of Otsiningo on the Susquehanna's North Branch and headed down that river on a fishing trip (Map 6). At home the weather had been hot, the hunting poor, the people ill "and . . . in Distress." Past the junction of the river's North and West branches the men went; some twenty miles

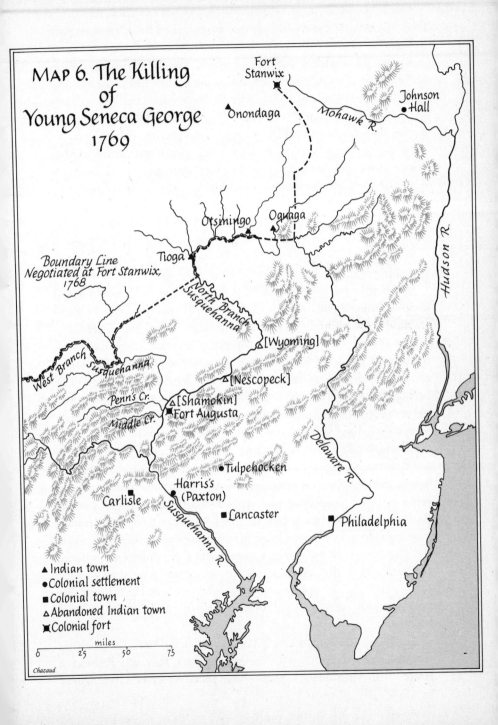

MAP 6. The Killing
of
Young Seneca George
1769

Fort Stanwix

Johnson Hall

Onondaga

Mohawk R.

Otsiningo

Owaga

Tioga

Boundary Line
Negotiated at Fort Stanwix,
1768

North Branch Susquehanna

Hudson R.

△[Wyoming]

West Branch Susquehanna

△[Nescopeck]

Penns Cr.

△[Shamokin]
Fort Augusta

Middle Cr.

Delaware R.

•Tulpehocken

Harris's
(Paxton)

•Carlisle

•Lancaster

Susquehanna R.

■Philadelphia

▲ Indian town
● Colonial settlement
■ Colonial town
△ Abandoned Indian town
✕ Colonial fort

miles
0   25   50   75

Chazaud

farther down, on the west bank, they stopped and built "an open Bark Cabbin."[1]

It turned out that the fishermen had fled one sort of distress only to find another. However good the fishing there, they had chosen a poor spot, for the wounds of Indian war still festered on the Pennsylvania frontier. Just upstream was Penn's Creek, the scene of two Indian raids during that terrible October in 1755. A wedge driven into a tree to mark where enemy warriors had ambushed John Harris's men was but one of many "sad memorials" littering the landscape. The skeletons of makeshift forts and the charred remains of farmsteads offered mute testimony to those dark days, as did the loopholes—and bullet holes—that pockmarked what houses still stood. Nearby might be graves, or the hoops on which warriors had dried the scalps of their victims. A few of those victims survived—scarred for life, sometimes prone to fits—as gruesome reminders of what Indians had wrought.

Not that frontier folk needed much reminding. Who could forget seeing a father butchered, a son dragged off into the forest, a sister stolen and, redeemed years later, never quite right again? Grisly accounts of real, exaggerated, or imaginary atrocities kept memories fresh. "[A]ll the people in these back Settlements . . . ," wrote one traveler after a tour of the frontier, "are very taleful of the Indian War."[2] Feelings ran so high that the man who murdered a native American was, like the Paxton Boys, applauded more often than arrested. It was open season on Indians.[3]

As fate would have it, Indian hating was particularly virulent where the fishermen pitched camp that June. Just downstream was Middle Creek, infamous because eighteen months earlier one Frederick Stump had murdered and scalped six natives there, then stuffed the corpses through a hole in the ice to hide the deed. Next day, to cover his tracks, Stump and his servant, John Ironcutter, had hurried up the creek to find and slay the rest of that party, a woman and three children. Captured and imprisoned, the two were freed by frontiersmen fed up with what they considered the colony's coddling of Indians and convinced that provincial officials were about to drag the suspects off to Philadelphia for trial.[4]

The Indians putting up that hut on the riverbank knew the frontier's troubled past. En route down the Susquehanna, they, too, had seen a land shrouded in sadness. Wyoming was "soiled with Blood" by killings.[5]

Farther along lay the blackened remains of Nescopeck and Shamokin, set ablaze soon after the first raids at Penn's Creek. And next to Shamokin's ruins stood Fort Augusta, empty of soldiers now these four years past.

Yet while that stronghold stood deserted, everywhere else the Susquehanna Valley was alive with colonists blazing trees and clearing land in the race for the territories opened up the previous fall by the Treaty of Fort Stanwix. "I am Tould the woods is full of land Hunters already," wrote one Susquehanna speculator less than a month after the council beside the Mohawk River adjourned.[6] And Penn's Creek? Middle Creek? These names, or their native cognates, the travelers from Otsiningo would have heard before. Some of their parents, longtime friends of Pennsylvania, had been on that part of the Susquehanna in the fall of 1755, and some of Stump's victims were from up the North Branch. His deed, and his escape, made as big a stir in the Indian countries as it did among colonists.[7]

Still, for all the unhappy memories, there seemed little cause for alarm that summer. The Indian nations were officially at peace with the English, the visitors knew, and they themselves had come to catch fish, not scalp Pennsylvanians. Certainly they showed no concern when, one evening in early July, a canoe full of colonists approached the shore. Fishermen like us, the Indians thought as they watched from their cabin, noting the fire glowing in the craft to lure prey toward the surface.[8] Then, without warning, the man in the stern pointed something at the group on shore—a gun, it looked like, not a paddle or pole—and before anyone could move he fired. One Indian fell, "shot thro the body." He died without uttering a word.

The dead man's companions had plenty to say. "You have killed one of us," they cried, at which the canoeists dumped their fire over the side and took off downriver. The Indians, wise to white ways, took off, too, not in pursuit of that canoe but in search of a colonist with authority. Near the Forks they found a magistrate named Turbutt Francis, told him their story, and—certain they would recognize the killer if they saw him again—urged Francis to launch a manhunt. Eventually the search party made its way down the west bank to Caspar Reid's place, a one-room inn where, some nights, twenty tired souls fought assorted dogs and cats for sleeping space on the dirt floor. There the Indians spied the canoe and identified Caspar's brother, Peter, as the gunman. Francis promptly seized the suspect and deposited him in the Lancaster jail, then sent word upriver to inform the victim's kin of the tragedy and invite them to a Condolence Ceremony. That done, he hurried off to the capital with the news.[9]

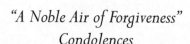

"A Noble Air of Forgiveness"
Condolences

Francis arrived in Philadelphia on July 17 to find colonial leaders already fretting about the frontier. At Wyoming, Connecticut colonists were digging in, staking their colonial charter rights against Pennsylvania's. Farther west there was the new boundary line agreed upon at the Fort Stanwix council to worry about. Who would survey it that fall? How could Pennsylvania invite Indian observers along and not end up feeding a whole tribe?[10]

And now this murder. The accused was locked up, true, but everyone knew that when a Pennsylvanian who killed an Indian was jailed, "Rescues succeed arrests" with such alarming frequency that Peter Reid might go the way of Stump and Ironcutter. Even if provincial authorities managed to keep the suspect in custody long enough to try him, a conviction was impossible since "there is none but [Indians (testimony?)] which will not be allowed." The situation looked grim. "[T]his is a matter of the utmost Consequence," wrote a Pennsylvania councilor to William Johnson on July 20, asking that the superintendent spread the sad news—but "in the most favorable light"—across Iroquoia. If the natives are not mollified, Indian war loomed again.[11]

It did nothing to improve prospects for peace that Peter Reid had not shot just any native; he had killed "a Young Indian of a Family distinguished for their unalterable Attachment to the English." The head of that family was Seneca George (Osternados).[12] War captain, master of the Condolence (it was he who dried Pennsylvania's tears after the death of Conrad Weiser), perhaps also a medicine man, this "Indian of Note" had first caught the attention of the English in the Ohio country some two decades before and then, around 1750, had moved to Otsiningo on the North Branch of the Susquehanna.[13] For the rest of that decade, the Seneca's English allegiance largely set the course of his life. With Scarouyady and other loyalists, he took shelter at George

Croghan's after the French victory at Great Meadows in July 1754. During the bleak winter of 1755–1756, when it seemed that all of Indian America was raiding Pennsylvania, Osternados joined the handful of other old men who, with their families, hunkered down at John Harris's to ride out the storm.[14] Thereafter he went back and forth across the region—off to the frontier to fight Britain's enemies, to Philadelphia and Johnson Hall for talks, to Lancaster and Easton for treaties, home to Otsiningo, then back to Philadelphia and Harris's—on missions of war and peace.

Though he roamed far and wide, the source of Seneca George's stature was Otsiningo. It was there that he had become a go-between who, like Scarouyady and Shickellamy, began as someone sent by the Six Nations to look after foreign Indian peoples living on the Iroquoian frontier. Otsiningo, "the [southern] door to the Six Nations," was a refugee haven in the mid-eighteenth century, not so much a town as a cluster of settlements inhabited by Nanticokes, Conoys, Tuscaroras, Mohicans, and Shawnees, as well as a smattering of Iroquois. Osternados spoke to Onondaga, to Pennsylvania, and to William Johnson on behalf of the peoples there (and sometimes for all those along the Susquehanna from Wyoming north), peoples he called "my Children."[15]

While looking after his fictive offspring, Seneca George was also making plans for his own son (known to colonists only as "young Seneca George") to succeed him. "I . . . hope the Governor will look upon my Son," he said proudly as he presented the lad during talks at the Pennsylvania State House in 1761, "whom I shall Commission to supply my place after my death." The boy, the aged Seneca's only surviving child, was perhaps ten at the time.[16] Before the decade was out, that dream would be dashed on the Susquehanna shore. His son was dead and, like someone lost in the woods, the grief-stricken father was "covered with darkness."[17]

The person Pennsylvania put in charge of bringing light to banish the Seneca man's darkness was Colonel Turbutt Francis. Though only twenty-nine years old that summer, Francis was no novice when it came to Indians. At nineteen he had scouted with warriors against the French, and five years later he had joined British forces attacking Ohio Indians. Home in Pennsylvania after the war, his position as a frontier magistrate ensured that Indians would call on him about squabbles with settlers well before the friends of Young Seneca George sought him out.[18]

These and other encounters with natives prompted Francis to consider a career in Indian affairs. What he lacked in experience, he made up for in ambition and connections. Member of a prominent Philadelphia family, young Francis had the chief justice of Pennsylvania and the attorney general of New York writing letters on his behalf, and he lined up no less than General Thomas Gage and Governor John Penn to do the same. During the 1760s, Francis, spending these assets freely, launched a campaign to enlist William Johnson as his patron. The young Pennsylvanian busied himself traveling between Johnson Hall and Philadelphia, hoping to enter, permanently, the superintendent's orbit. Aiming high, he set his sights on replacing George Croghan as deputy superintendent. Whenever he heard a rumor that the old fur trader was resigning his Crown office, Francis would write to Johnson—or have others write on his behalf—to put his name forward. The campaign never won him the post, but it did win the disappointed Francis letters from Johnson pledging "the Continuance of my Esteem."[19]

Whether Francis had Seneca George's esteem is less certain. The two had first met in the spring of 1756 when "Tubby" Francis, not yet sixteen, having gotten the family maid pregnant, "ran away with Nunngatootha [Scarouyady] and the rest of the Indians"—among them, Seneca George—then leaving Philadelphia for New York. Tubby told the Iroquois that he wanted to live with them; he told his friends that he was off to join the army. Whatever his real intentions, those friends caught up to him in New Jersey and hauled him home.[20]

Francis never did move in with Indians, but three years later he realized his ambition to join the army. Whatever colonists thought of the young Pennsylvanian's military exploits, it is unlikely Indians were impressed. At one point Francis and some of his men got lost in the woods. At another, he fathered a son with a sister of Silver Heels (Aroas), a Seneca messenger Osternados knew well. The ambitious officer, having convinced her to let him raise the child, then abandoned the scheme—and the boy, who ended up among Indians near Montreal, living with neither parent.[21]

None of these escapades would have won Turbutt Francis the sort of name he yearned to make for himself in Indian country. Aware of that, perhaps, Francis might have hoped that this Condolence council was his chance to prove himself as a go-between. In early August he left the capital and retraced his steps to the Susquehanna junction. In his pocket he carried the governor's speech. Behind him came packhorses piled with presents: black cloth, "dark Coloured" silk handkerchiefs, a dozen shirts, four pairs of shoes and buckles, three kegs of rum, plus paint, tobacco, and brass kettles. Flour and corn to feed the Indians would be picked up en route to supplement the two barrels of pork shipped with the gifts.[22] Armed with the words and the merchandise needed to dry Seneca George's tears, Colonel Francis approached Fort Augusta to await the Indians.

To Francis, that fort must have been a pleasant sight. Its palisades and blockhouses, barracks and magazine, officers' quarters and commandant's house symbolized his colony's success in turning back the savage foe and imposing a new order on the frontier. The fifty-three Indians approaching the Forks from the other direction on the morning of August 19 would have seen things differently. Though some of them had been among Pennsylvania's Indian loyalists who asked in 1756 that the fort be built, once the war was over colonists had broken promises to return the Forks to natives. Rather than becoming a trading post or disappearing altogether, Augusta was instead a magnet for "vast Numbers" of the intruders, people bent on creating a "very considerable Settlement" with no place for Indians.[23]

Turning that day from the colonial fort and all the new faces, the delegation made for the site of old Shamokin just to the north, ground rich in memory and meaning for the Iroquois, Delawares, Nanticokes, and Conoys who climbed out of their canoes and set up camp there that Saturday morning. It was here that Conrad Weiser had lost his nerve in 1736 when another embassy from the north approached the shore. It was here that a painted Andrew Montour had tried to convince John Harris and his men to slip the trap set for them in October 1755. Weiser and Montour were gone now, of course—one to the grave, the other beyond the mountains. But still on the site were tangible signs of Shamokin's central place in the Susquehanna peoples' history: here was Montour's Island, there the ruins of the house Weiser had built for Shickellamy, nearby the site of the Moravian mission and smithy.

No one had much time to dwell on the past; opening ceremonies were to take place in the fort that very afternoon. Before long, the Indians had arranged themselves on one side of the garrison's central courtyard. In front sat Seneca George, an Onondaga named Genquant, and Last Night (Kanak't), the Conoy headman;[24] behind them, standing or sitting, were "22 more Warriors, and Young Men." Opposite were some fifty colonists from the vicinity and, seated at a table, Colonel Francis, a scribe, and local dignitaries. Somewhere in between stood Isaac Stille, up from Philadelphia, poised to convert from Delaware to English Last Night's translation of the Seneca's words.

Things got off to a rocky start. Osternados opened by recounting how it happened that an invitation to him had brought more than fifty Indians to the council. "[Y]ou could not expect me to come alone," he concluded testily. Pennsylvania had been eager to keep down the costs of this council, and now, somehow, it had let its disappointment with the size of the delegation show.[25]

Seneca George's mood did not improve as the afternoon wore on. "[Y]ou . . . very well know what the Custom is when the Governor meets his Brethren at any place where he appoints a Council Fire . . . ," the Iroquois lectured Francis. "[W]e desire you will give us something to eat, for this," he repeated, "is always the Custom when We meet the Governor at a Council Fire." When Pennsylvania's magistrate stood to reply, "Seneca George got up and desired Colonel Francis would not speak then, it being better to consider what had been said to him till Monday."[26]

Francis had bungled the preliminaries; he did better at the main event that Monday. String of wampum in hand, he outlined the colony's efforts to see that justice was done. With strouds he then buried the body, with handkerchiefs dried the Indians' tears, and with a wampum belt scraped away "all the Blood that has lain on the Ground or may have stained the Bushes." Having ensured that "no uneasiness . . . remain[s] in your Minds," Francis brought out the presents, "a Token of our Affection for you and to comfort your Hearts."[27]

When the conference reconvened on Wednesday, Seneca George, who "seemed oppressed with Grief," asked Last Night to deliver the Indians' answer, assuring colonists that "His Words and mine are one." This elderly, corpulent Conoy was, like Seneca George, a leader at Otsiningo. Traveling here and there to treaties, the two men had become such close friends that in 1761 the Seneca had announced that if he died he would leave his son in the Conoy's care.[28]

So Last Night, too, had been touched by this killing. Now he stood to answer for his comrade "on this good Day." The words followed an old, faded script fashioned by Last Night's ancestors and John Penn's grandfather. Speaking directly to Governor Penn through Francis, the

Conoy expressed his pleasure at seeing the "Stain" wiped "from the Face of the Earth." Now Indians and colonists must "hold fast that good Friendship whereof our Grandfathers laid fast Foundations when you came first into this Country. . . . We had in old Time," the Conoy went on, "a very firm Peace, and you and I used always then to speak to one another." This conversation must continue, "this our antient friendship" must endure.

Having stayed on the old rhetorical paths, Last Night now turned to more personal matters. At the Fort Stanwix council last fall William Johnson had killed one of my steers to feed the Indians, and he never paid me for it. Will Colonel Francis? And speaking of food, supply us with provisions for the journey home. Last Night, for one, was eager to begin that return trip. Unable, perhaps, to resist an allusion to the Pennsylvanian's own sexual history, the Conoy headman explained that his urge to get back to Otsiningo was, in fact, the colonel's fault. "I was in hopes you would have sent me a *Squaw* to keep me warm at Night," he chided Francis. "Perhaps you have one to keep you warm, but as you did not send me one, I must go home to my own as fast as I can."

"I have really none here," protested Francis after Last Night had finished. "We keep all ours in Philadelphia, and we are as desirous to get home as you are." Then, promising the Indians rum, flour, and ammunition for the trip home, Francis sat down amid "great Cheerfulness and many Signs of Approbation by the Indians."

On this happy note the conference seemed ready to break up. But one more person seated at the table with Francis had something to say. This was Frederick Weiser, one of Conrad Weiser's children. Though he had not followed in his father's footsteps and become a go-between, Frederick was no stranger to Indians. In 1745, just seventeen years old, he had helped drive packhorses to Shamokin, the first stop on Conrad Weiser's trip to Onondaga that year. A decade later, in October 1755, he and his younger brother Peter had sped from Tulpehocken to Penn's Creek to rescue their cousin and his family in the days after the Indian attack there. And less than a month after that, another rescue mission had failed when Frederick, on patrol near Tulpehocken, arrived too late. Coming on the body of the Kobel woman killed and scalped by those German-speaking Indians in Sneider's cornfield, he turned her over "to see who she might have been," only to find beneath her an infant, still breathing. The following summer death struck even closer to home when Indians killed and scalped Frederick's young cousin and namesake.[29]

Now, his Indian adventures past—though doubtless not forgotten—Frederick Weiser was back at Shamokin, back this time as Conrad Weiser's oldest surviving son, to speak to Seneca George.[30] "Myself and the Children of Conrad have had great Grief and many Tears for the unhappy Death of your Son," his speech began, "and our Tears have run down our Cheeks in greater abundance because a Cousin of ours, the Sister's Son of our Father Conrad, has been suspected of doing the Mischief." Frederick had come to assure Seneca George that the Weisers would not stand in the way of the trial, to ask that the Indians "not entertain in your hearts any ill will against any of the Family or Children of your old Friend and Brother Conrad Weiser, on account of this one man," and to give the grieving Seneca a "small Present . . . to wipe all Tears from your eyes."

Seneca George was stunned; he had not known that the killer and his old friend were kin.[31] For several minutes he sat, "in a deep silence, with his eyes fixed on the Ground; and Tears visibly flowing from them." Perhaps he thought back to the good country he had left for Otsiningo. Of how, until the French wars, he had "got [his] living very well" in his new home on the Susquehanna. Of how years of service to Britain in those campaigns had left him "very poor, and [how he] had not for all [his] trouble so much as a Knife, a Kettle, or any Cloaths." Of how impoverishment of a different sort had struck in 1758 when another son had died of smallpox in Philadelphia. Of how, just two years ago, he had worked to get Indians out of the colonial inhabited parts because of "danger from the White People."[32] Certainly he thought of Conrad Weiser, "my Brother and Friend," dead nine summers now. And of his own son, who had just followed Conrad into the ground, put there by one of Weiser's own people—a sister's child, no less, by Iroquois reckoning closer kin to Conrad than was Frederick himself.

At last, Seneca George rose to speak. He fondly remembered Conrad Weiser. He mourned his son, whose death, "now that I am old, . . . hath almost entirely cut away my Heart." Nonetheless, Osternados promised Frederick Weiser, "this matter shall be remembered no more against his Family to their Hurt." As he spoke, the Seneca had been walking slowly across the council ground toward the colonists; now he was near their table. Running up to it, he grasped Weiser's hand and said, "I have no ill-will to you Mr. Weiser. None to you Colonel Francis," the Seneca went on, shaking the magistrate's hand in turn. "Nor any to you . . . , nor any to you . . . ," he repeated, grasping hands as he went down the table. Then he turned to the assembled colonists, spread his arms wide, and announced, "nor have I any ill-will to any of you my Brethren the English."

Now it was the colonists' turn to be stunned, and to weep. *"This is Noble,"* cried some at the table as Seneca George approached, hand outstretched. "[H]is *action* and behaviour were surprizingly great," one Pennsylvanian exclaimed, struck by the "manly Spirit of Forgiveness and Reconciliation" that the Indian conveyed "by his Looks, Gesture, and whole Action." Indeed, so moving was it that, as Seneca George talked of his loss, his speech was "understood even before interpreted, by the tone and manner in which it was delivered." And then, when "he sprang forward with a noble air of Forgiveness," his words again "stood in need of no Interpretation."

It was a transcendent moment in the long history of Penn's Woods. Here, as never before, native and colonist seemed to truly see one another, seemed to truly speak and hear. Ancient healing rituals, old words of comfort, powerful memories of union—all set the stage for a meeting of minds and hearts. The go-between was, at last, superfluous. Isaac Stille and Last Night could not keep up, and this time they did not need to.

But any transcendence was temporary. Powerful images of colonists scrambling to their feet to clasp the old Seneca's hand, of an Indian opening his arms to embrace and forgive all the English, cannot obscure the gestures' ultimate futility. Osternados had enabled those gathered at the fort to forget, for an instant, what had brought them there. But even if Francis and Weiser wiped clean the blood and dried the tears, more blood—and more tears—would follow soon enough. The times when tears of sympathy replaced tears of anguish, when soft words and warm handshakes replaced war cries and scalping knives, were few and fleeting indeed.

Perhaps even that moment of communion was itself illusory. Did colonists really understand what Osternados said as he approached the table, or were they merely investing him with sentiments they felt he should have? "[N]ever was there a more striking Example of true Oratory," they asserted; Seneca George had found the means "to express the strong and natural Feelings of the Soul."[33] But whose soul?

During these decades Europeans in America were beginning to think of Indians not as people to be feared or converted but specimens to be pitied or studied. In Pennsylvania, with hatred and land hunger driving native peoples west, they were on the verge of vanishing altogether from the everyday scene. As Indians retreated, their relics and remains became souvenirs. Wooden spoons crafted by Delaware hands found a place in a "cabinet of curiosities"; an Indian pot held shoe polish; Indian skulls unearthed by workmen digging a canal became "vessels out of which the cats were fed."[34]

A central component of this tectonic shift in the natives' place in American life, this change from Indians as neighbors to Indians as exotica, was the cult of white admiration for the eloquence of a dying race, a taste acquired in the late eighteenth century that lives on today in the popularity of laments attributed to Chief Joseph or Chief Seattle. The most famous early example of this rhetoric of defeat and despair would appear five years after Seneca George met Turbutt Francis at Fort Augusta, spoken—so the story goes—by another Susquehanna Iroquois, Shickellamy's son Soyechtowa (James Logan). In "a morsel of eloquence . . . so admired, that it flew through all the public papers of the continent" before Thomas Jefferson immortalized it in his *Notes on the State of Virginia,* Logan, recalling his "love for the whites" before colonists murdered his family, lamented that now "[t]here runs not a drop of my blood in the veins of any living creature. . . . Who is there to mourn for Logan?—Not one."[35] But already in the late summer of 1769, Europeans in America had an ear for what they believed to be the last words of a doomed people, and Seneca George's speech enjoyed brief renown. "You have doubtless seen an Acco[un]t published in pensilvania and Reprinted in New York of the Famous Congress between old Seneca George and Colo Francis," wrote one Philadelphian to Sir William Johnson.[36]

Well before publication of their "Famous Congress" captivated readers in provincial capitals, Turbutt Francis and Seneca George, each in his own way, demonstrated just how transitory, how illusory, how empty, had been their handshake at the fort. Within days of the council's close, Francis—declaring that "such an other piece of work I wish never to be engaged in"—was gone, headed not back to Philadelphia but up the Susquehanna's North Branch to scout, on the sly, some salt springs near the Indian town of Oquaga.[37] Caught trespassing on Iroquois territory, he beat a hasty retreat, only to resume his relentless campaign to acquire land, this time up the West Branch, and this time more successfully. "Tubby is a great speculator, and as enterprising as speculative," wrote one friend.[38]

Seneca George, bound not for Oquaga but for Otsiningo, had taken the same route up the North Branch from the Forks. He never made it home. Near Wyoming his canoe hit rough water and the Seneca went under. In Philadelphia it was reported that he had fallen out; Indians apparently thought he had jumped. Perhaps his woods had claimed him at last.[39]

Acknowledgments

During the decade or so that I have been traipsing along behind the go-betweens, I frequently lost my way and ended up in various sorts of woods. Many individuals and institutions helped rescue me from the thickets of intractable evidence, conceptual confusion, and sloppy prose into which I blundered. While grateful for their help in extricating me, I alone, of course, am to blame for getting myself into trouble in the first place, and for whatever darkness and noise lingers in the preceding pages.

Generous financial assistance from many quarters helped me on my literal and figurative travels. A Summer Research Stipend from the Library Company of Philadelphia and the Historical Society of Pennsylvania got the project under way; further trips to archives were funded by the American Historical Association's Michael Kraus Research Grant and a Summer Stipend from the National Endowment for the Humanities. The NEH also awarded me a Fellowship for College Teachers, which I was able to combine with grants from the American Council of Learned Societies and the John Simon Guggenheim Memorial Foundation in order to obtain a year's leave from teaching. From the project's first forays to its finishing touches, Vassar College has been extraordinarily generous in supporting my research, both with annual funding and paid leaves. No less generous, albeit in a different way, have been the archivists and librarians at Vassar, the Library Company of Philadelphia, the Historical Society of Pennsylvania, the American Philosophical Society, Haverford College, Swarthmore College, the Chester County Archives, the Chester County Historical Society, the York

County Archives, the Lancaster County Historical Society, and the Northumberland County Historical Society.

When, from time to time, I wanted to escape the archive or library in order to try out some of my ideas, I found many willing listeners and thoughtful critics. Michael Zuckerman hosted a lively seminar of scholars in Philadelphia; Charles Cohen did the same at an Early American History Colloquium at the University of Wisconsin, Madison, as did Bernard Bailyn at Harvard University's Charles Warren Center for Studies in American History. Natalie Davis invited me to talk about woodslore to a joint session in Princeton of the Shelby Cullom Davis Center for Historical Studies and the Philadelphia Center for Early American Studies, then Stephen Aron invited me back to Princeton so that I could learn more from the historians there. Further suggestions came from visits to the University of Kansas, Lehigh University, Muhlenberg College, and the Center for Early Modern History at the University of Minnesota.

So engaging did I find the scholars at Minnesota that I began inviting myself back for longer visits to that center and school in my native state. For many summers, and during the year's leave from Vassar when most of this book was written, the early Americanists at Minnesota adopted me and, on several occasions in their Colonial History Workshop, patiently aided my efforts to fathom the woods. I am especially grateful to Lucy Simler, John Howe, and Jean O'Brien for making those longer stays both possible and enjoyable.

Jean O'Brien was one of several people who graciously read an earlier—and substantially longer—version of the manuscript, offering copious comments and insights. Joining her in that herculean task were Clyde Griffen, Peter Mancall, Michael McConnell, and Laurel Thatcher Ulrich, all of whom gave me many helpful suggestions. In addition, early in my travels through the woods Richard White offered valuable guidance. Near journey's end, Karim Tiro helped me find and procure illustrations, while David Oestreicher, Bruce L. Pearson, and Hanni Woodbury patiently answered a bewildered stranger's queries about Indian words. From beginning to end, my editor, Steve Forman, has had faith in the project even when I did not, and patience when mine ran out; he always saw, often more clearly than I, where this was going and how it might get there.

Here at Vassar, many have nurtured this work and its author over the years. Anthony S. Wohl always offered encouragement and wise counsel, especially at one crucial moment. Leslie Offutt and Miriam Cohen have, in countless ways, enriched my personal and professional life. Robert DeMaria, Jr., at once humbled and inspired me with his humane approach to life and learning and his vast knowledge of the early modern Atlantic world.

Farther afield, and for an even longer span of time, Douglas Greenberg has been an indispensable guide. As I began thinking about the woods, he offered astute comments on the route I envisioned, helping me chart, and then steer, a steady course. No less steady was his serene confidence that I could follow that course to my destination. Doug also had an uncanny knack for knowing just when to say *give yourself a break* and when to ask, all innocence and incredulity: *but surely you must be almost done by* now?

As the book's dedication suggests, early in this project's life I found myself in woods of a different, darker sort. For helping me through those passages, I am grateful to more kin, friends, and colleagues than can be named here, but three I must acknowledge. My eldest son, Davy, a bright spirit throughout these years, has lighted my way with his infectious enthusiasms, his droll sense of humor, and his devotion to hapless baseball teams. More recently my youngest, Will, the amiable hurricane, came along to add his own joyful noise to my days (and many of my nights). Through it all my wife, Linda, has been gracious enough to share life's pathway with me. One could wish for no better traveling companion; she has sustained me, and our sons, with her infinite compassion, her quiet courage, and her indomitable spirit.

Poughkeepsie, New York   JHM
June 1998

Abbreviations

AIQ   *American Indian Quarterly*

APS   American Philosophical Society

Arch. Md.   William Hand Browne et al., eds., *Archives of Maryland,* 72 volumes (Baltimore, Md., 1883–)

Barber   "Miss Rhoda Barber's Journal of Settlement at Wrights Ferry on Susquehanna River," HSP

Bartram, Observations   John Bartram, *Observations on the Inhabitants, Climate, Soil, Rivers, Productions, Animals, and other Matters Worthy of Notice. Made by John Bartram, In his Travels from Pensilvania to Onondago, Oswego and the Lake Ontario, in Canada . . .* (London, 1751)

Cammerhoff   John W. Jordan, trans., "Bishop J. C. F. Cammerhoff's Narrative of a Journey to Shamokin, Penna., in the Winter of 1748," *PMHB,* XXIX (1905), 160–179

CCA   Chester County Archives, West Chester, Pennsylvania

CCW   Correspondence of Conrad Weiser, in Papers of Conrad Weiser, HSP

Chew   "Benjamin Chew's Journal of a Journey to Easton, 1758," in Julian P. Boyd, ed., *Indian Treaties Printed by Benjamin Franklin, 1732–1762* (Philadelphia, 1938), 312–318

Claus, Memoirs   "Memoirs of Daniel Claus, pertaining to his Descent and how he came to America with a concise account of his Adventures and Services," *Iroq. Ind.,* Reel 36

Croghan 1750–65   "A Selection of George Croghan's Letters and Journals Relating to Tours into the Western Country—November 16, 1750–November, 1765," in Reuben Gold Thwaites, ed., *Early*

Western Travels, 1748–1846, vol. I (Cleveland, Ohio, 1904), 45–173

CVSP   William P. Palmer, ed., *Calendar of Virginia State Papers And Other Manuscripts, 1652–1781, Preserved in the Capitol at Richmond,* vol. I (Richmond, Va., 1875)

DHNY   E. B. O'Callaghan, ed., *The Documentary History of the State of New-York . . . ,* 4 vols. (Albany, N.Y., 1849–1851)

DRCNY   E. B. O'Callaghan and B. Fernow, eds., *Documents Relative to the Colonial History of the State of New-York . . . ,* 15 vols. (Albany, N.Y., 1856–1887)

DSP   Eugene Du Simitiere Papers, LCP

EC   Frank M. Etting Collection, HSP

EJCCV   H. R. McIlwaine, ed., *Executive Journals of the Council of Colonial Virginia,* 6 vols. (Richmond, Va., 1925–1966)

Evans   Charles Evans, *American Bibliography: A Chronological Dictionary of All Books, Pamphlets, and Periodical Publications Printed in the United States of America . . . ,* 15 vols. (Chicago, 1903–1959), cited by item number

FA   Philadelphia Yearly Meeting, Indian Committee Records, Friendly Association for Regaining & Preserving Peace with the Indians by Pacific Measures, vols. AA1–AA5, Quaker Collection, Haverford College

GCP   George Croghan Papers, Cadwalader Collection, HSP, cited by box and file numbers

Gist   "Christopher Gist's First and Second Journals, September 11, 1750–March 29, 1752 . . . ," in Lois Mulkearn, ed., *George Mercer Papers Relating to the Ohio Company of Virginia* (Pittsburgh, Pa., 1954)

Hanna,   Charles A. Hanna, *The Wilderness Trail; or, The Ventures and Adventures of the Pennsylvania Traders on the Allegheny Path . . . ,* 2
Wilderness Trail   vols. (New York, 1911)

Hays   William A. Hunter, ed., "John Hays' Diary and Journal of 1760," *Pennsylvania Archaeologist,* XXIV (1954), 63–83

Heckewelder,   John Heckewelder, *History, Manners, and Customs of the Indian
History   Nations, Who Once Inhabited Pennsylvania and The Neighboring States,* rev. ed. (Philadelphia, 1881)

HP   Timothy Horsfield Papers, APS

HSP	Historical Society of Pennsylvania
Iroq. Ind.	Francis Jennings et al., eds., *Iroquois Indians: A Documentary History of the Six Nations and their League,* microfilm edition, 50 reels (Woodbridge, Conn., 1985)
JAH	*Journal of American History*
Jennings, *Ambiguous Iroquois Empire*	Francis Jennings, *The Ambiguous Iroquois Empire: The Covenant Chain Confederation of Indian Tribes with English Colonies From Its Beginnings to the Lancaster Treaty of 1744* (New York, 1984)
Jennings, *Empire of Fortune*	Francis Jennings, *Empire of Fortune: Crowns, Colonies, and Tribes in the Seven Years War in America* (New York, 1988)
JLLB	James Logan Letterbooks, LP
Journals of Claus and Weiser	Helga Dobler and William A. Starna, trans. and eds., *The Journals of Christian Daniel Claus and Conrad Weiser: A Journey to Onondaga, 1750,* in *Transactions of the American Philosophical Society,* LXXXIV, Part 2 (Philadelphia, 1994)
Kenny 1758–59	John W. Jordan, ed., "James Kenny's 'Journal to Ye Westward,' 1758–59," *PMHB,* XXXVII (1913), 395–449
Kenny 1761–63	John W. Jordan, ed., "The Journal of James Kenny, 1761–1763," *PMHB,* XXXVII (1913), 1–47, 152–201
LC	James Logan Correspondence, APS
LCP	Library Company of Philadelphia
Logstown Treaty	"The Treaty of Logg's Town, 1752. Commission, Instructions, &c., Journal of Virginia Commissioners, and Text of Treaty," *VMHB,* XIII (1905–1906), 143–174
Loskiel, *History*	George Henry Loskiel, *History of the Mission of the United Brethren Among the Indians in North America* (London, 1794)
LP	James Logan Papers, HSP, cited (where needed) by box and folder number
Marshe	"Witham Marshe's Journal of the Treaty held With the Six Nations by the Commissioners of Maryland, And Other Provinces, At Lancaster, in Pennsylvania, June, 1744," *Collections of the Massachusetts Historical Society, For the Year MDCCC,* 1st ser., VII, 171–201
MCA	Moravian Church Archives: Records of the Moravian Mission Among the Indians of North America (microfilm, 40 reels, cited by reel, box, folder, and item number)
McConnell, *A Country Between*	Michael N. McConnell, *A Country Between: The Upper Ohio Valley and Its Peoples, 1724–1774* (Lincoln, Neb., 1992)

MJNY   William M. Beauchamp, ed., *Moravian Journals Relating to
                  Central New York, 1745–1766* (Syracuse, N.Y., 1916)

MPCP   *Minutes of the Provincial Council of Pennsylvania, From the
                  Organization to the Termination of the Proprietary Government,* 10
                  vols. (Harrisburg, Pa., 1851–1852)

MVHR   *Mississippi Valley Historical Review*

PA   *Pennsylvania Archives,* 9 series, 138 vols. (Harrisburg and
                  Philadelphia, Pa., 1852–1949), cited by series and volume
                  number

Pemberton 1762   "Journal of James Pemberton at the Lancaster Treaty, 1762,"
                  in Julian P. Boyd, ed., *Indian Treaties Printed by Benjamin Franklin,
                  1732–1762* (Philadelphia, 1938), 319–322

PG   *Pennsylvania Gazette*

PGW   William W. Abbott et al., eds., *The Papers of George Washington.
                  Colonial Series,* 10 vols. to date (Charlottesville, 1983–   )

PHB   S. K. Stevens et al., eds., *The Papers of Henry Bouquet,* 6 vols.
                  (Harrisburg, Pa., 1972–1994); or S. K. Stevens et al., eds., *The
                  Papers of Col. Henry Bouquet,* 19 vols. (Harrisburg, Pa.,
                  1940–1943)

PMHB   *Pennsylvania Magazine of History and Biography*

PMIA   Penn Manuscripts, Indian Affairs, HSP

PMOC   Penn Manuscripts, Official Correspondence, HSP (and
                  microfilm)

Post 1758   "Two Journals of Western Tours, By Charles [*sic*] Frederick
                  Post: One, To the Neighborhood of Fort DuQuesne
                  (July–September, 1758); The Other, To the Ohio (October,
                  1758–January, 1759)," in Reuben Gold Thwaites, ed., *Early
                  Western Travels, 1748–1846,* vol. I (Cleveland, Ohio, 1904),
                  175–291

Post 1760   "Journal of Mr Christn. Fred Post, in Company with
                  Teedyuscung, Mr John Hays, Isaac Still, & Moses Tattamy, to
                  the great Council of the different Indian Nations, 1760," HSP

PPEC   Pemberton Papers, EC, numbers 28 and 29, cited as vols. I
                  and II

PPHSP   Pemberton Papers, HSP, cited by box and file number

PPM   Penn-Physick Manuscripts, HSP

Procs. APS   *Proceedings of the American Philosophical Society*

PSF   Papers of the Shippen Family, HSP

PWJ   James Sullivan et al., eds., *The Papers of Sir William Johnson*, 14 vols. (Albany, N.Y., 1921–1965)

PWP   Richard S. Dunn et al., eds., *The Papers of William Penn*, 5 vols. (Philadelphia, 1981–1986)

Richter, *Ordeal* Daniel K. Richter, *The Ordeal of the Longhouse: The Peoples of the Iroquois League in the Era of European Colonization* (Chapel Hill, N.C., 1992)

RPCEC   Records of the Provincial Council in the Pennsylvania State Archives, Executive Correspondence (microfilm, Harrisburg, Pa.), cited by reel and item numbers

RPLB, 1737–1750 Richard Peters Letterbook, 1737–1750, RPP

RPP   Richard Peters Papers, HSP

SCP   Julian Boyd and Robert Taylor, eds., *The Susquehannah Company Papers*, 11 vols. (Wilkes-Barre, Pa., and Ithaca, N.Y., 1930–1971)

Smith, *Account* James Smith, *An Account of the Remarkable Occurrences in the Life and Travels of Col. James Smith During His Captivity with the Indians, In the Years 1755, '56, '57, '58, and '59* (Cincinnati, Ohio, 1907)

Spangenberg John W. Jordan, ed., "Spangenberg's Notes of Travel to Onondaga in 1745," *PMHB*, II (1878), 424–432, III (1879), 56–64

[Thomson],   [Charles Thomson], *An Enquiry Into the Causes of the Alienation*
 Enquiry   *of the Delaware and Shawanese Indians from the British Interest, And Into the Measures taken for Recovering their Friendship* . . . (London, 1759)

VMHB   *Virginia Magazine of History and Biography*

Wallace,   Anthony F. C. Wallace, *King of the Delawares: Teedyuscung,*
 Teedyuscung *1700–1763* (Salem, N.H., 1984 [orig. pub. 1949])

Wallace, *Weiser* Paul A. W. Wallace, *Conrad Weiser, 1696–1760: Friend of Colonist and Mohawk* (Philadelphia, 1945)

Weiser 1737   Hiester H. Muhlenberg, trans., "Narrative of a Journey, Made in the Year 1737, by Conrad Weiser, Indian Agent and Provincial Interpreter, from Tulpehocken in the Province of Pennsylvania to Onondago . . . ," *Collections of the Historical Society of Pennsylvania*, I (Philadelphia, 1853), 6–33

Weiser 1745   "Journal of Conrad Weiser at the Albany Treaty of 1745," in Julian P. Boyd, ed., *Indian Treaties Printed by Benjamin Franklin, 1732–1762* (Philadelphia, 1938), 309–311

Weiser 1748   "Conrad Weiser's Journal of a Tour to the Ohio, August 11–October 2, 1748," in Reuben Gold Thwaites, ed., *Early Western Travels, 1748–1846*, vol. I (Cleveland, Ohio, 1904), 21–44

Weiser 1751   "A Journal of the proceedings of Conrad Weiser in his Journey to Albany with a Message from the Governor of pensilvania to the Six Nations of Indians, 1751," DSP, 966.F.27

Weiser, "Notes"   Abraham H. Cassell, comp., Helen Bell, trans., "Notes on the Iroquois and Delaware Indians. Communications from Conrad Weiser to Christopher Saur, Which Appeared in the Years 1746–1749 in His Newspaper Printed at Germantown, Entitled 'The High German Pennsylvania Historical Writer, Or a Collection of Important Events from the Kingdom of Nature and the Church' And from His (Saur's) Almanacs," *PMHB*, I (1877), 163–167, 319–323, II (1878), 407–410

Weiser, "Observations"   Conrad Weiser, "Observations made on the Pamphlet, intituled, an Inquiry into the Causes of the Alienation of the Delaware and Shawano Indians from the British Intrest. by Conrad Weiser. Chiefly on Land Affairs," MCA, 30/225/6/6

White, *Middle Ground*   Richard White, *The Middle Ground: Indians, Empires, and Republics in the Great Lakes Region, 1650–1815* (New York, 1991)

WMQ   *William and Mary Quarterly*

Zane 1758   Joseph H. Coates, ed., "Journal of Isaac Zane to Wyoming, 1758," *PMHB*, XXX (1906), 417–426

Zane 1761   "The Journal of Isaac Zane in Company with Isaac Greenleaf with the Governers Message to the Monse Indians," FA, V

Zeisberger, *Diaries*   Archer Butler Hulbert and William Nathaniel Schwarze, eds., "The Moravian Records, Volume Two. The Diaries of Zeisberger Relating to the First Missions in the Ohio Basin," *Ohio Archaeological and Historical Publications*, XXI, no. 1 (January 1912)

Zeisberger, *History*   Archer Butler Hulbert and William Nathaniel Schwarze, eds., "David Zeisberger's History of North American Indians," *Ohio Archaeological and Historical Publications*, XIX (1910)

Portions of this work have previously appeared in other forms in " 'The Cast of His Countenance': Reading Andrew Montour," in Ronald Hoffman, Mechal Sobel, and

Fredrika J. Teute, eds., *Through a Glass Darkly: Reflections on Personal Identity in Early America* (Chapel Hill, N.C., 1997), 13–39; and "Shamokin, 'the very seat of the Prince of darkness': Unsettling the Early American Frontier," in Andrew R. L. Cayton and Fredrika J. Teute, eds., *Contact Points: American Frontiers from the Mohawk Valley to the Mississippi, 1750–1830* (Chapel Hill, N.C., 1998), 16–59.

Notes

Introduction

1. Events surrounding this meeting can be followed in McConnell, *A Country Between*, ch. 4. For "Indian country" or "the Indian countries," see *MPCP*, IV, 760, V, 119, 122, 424 (colonists using the phrase), VII, 6, IX, 87 (Indians using the phrase); for "english ground," David McClure, *Diary of David McClure, Doctor of Divinity, 1748–1820,* ed. Franklin B. Dexter (New York, 1899), 100.

2. Norman O. Brown, *Hermes the Thief: The Evolution of a Myth,* 2d ed. (New York, 1969); Vincent Crapanzano, "Hermes' Dilemma: The Masking of Subversion in Ethnographic Description," in James Clifford and George E. Marcus, eds., *Writing Culture: The Poetics and Politics of Ethnography* (Berkeley, Calif., 1986), 51–53; Jerry H. Bentley, *Old World Encounters: Cross-Cultural Contacts and Exchanges in Pre-Modern Times* (New York, 1993); Philip D. Curtin, *Cross-Cultural Trade in World History* (Cambridge, Eng., 1984).

3. *MPCP,* V, 352. For wampum's full meaning and significance, see ch. V.

4. *Ibid.,* VII, 140 ("dangerous places"; for singing and pacing, see IV, 663). *DRCNY,* V, 373 (accidents; for rumors, Logstown Treaty, 155; *MPCP,* VII, 315). *MPCP,* IV, 180 (mouth and throat), VI, 152 (eyes), VII, 140 (ears).

The specific elements in recorded At the Woods' Edge ceremonies differed, probably reflecting variation over time and between peoples as well as the vagaries of colonial recordkeeping. The earliest surviving version, in 1645, is reprinted in Francis Jennings et al., eds., *The History and Culture of Iroquois Diplomacy: An Interdisciplinary Guide to the Treaties of the Six Nations and Their League* (Syracuse, N.Y., 1985), 128, 137–138.

For scholarship on this ritual, see Horatio Hale, ed., *The Iroquois Book of Rites* (Toronto, 1963 [orig. pub. 1883]), 117–121; William M. Beauchamp, *Civil, Religious and Mourning Councils and Ceremonies of Adoption of the New York*

Indians, New York State Museum, *Bulletin,* no. 113 (Albany, N.Y., 1975 [orig. pub. 1907]), 355–359, 365, 386; J. N. B. Hewitt, "The Requickening Address of the Iroquois Condolence Council," *Journal of the Washington Academy of Sciences,* XXXIV (1944), 65; William N. Fenton, "Structure, Continuity, and Change in the Process of Iroquois Treaty Making," in Jennings et al., eds., *History and Culture of Iroquois Diplomacy,* 28; Mary A. Druke, "Iroquois Treaties: Common Forms, Varying Interpretations," *ibid.,* 93; Michael K. Foster, "Another Look at the Function of Wampum in Iroquois-White Councils," *ibid.,* 105–107; George R. Hamell, "The Iroquois and the World's Rim: Speculations on Color, Culture, and Contact," *AIQ,* XVI (1992), 451–469; idem, "Mythical Realities and European Contact in the Northeast during the Sixteenth and Seventeenth Centuries," *Man in the Northeast,* no. 33 (1987), 63–87; John Arthur Gibson, *Concerning the League: The Iroquois League Tradition as Dictated in Onondaga,* ed. and trans. Hanni Woodbury, Reg Henry, and Harry Webster, Algonquian and Iroquoian Linguistics, Memoir 9 (Winnipeg, 1992); Matthew Dennis, *Cultivating a Landscape of Peace: Iroquois-European Encounters in Seventeenth-Century America* (Ithaca, N.Y., 1993), ch. 3. Spelling of the rite varies, even in a single volume (Jennings et al., eds., *History and Culture of Iroquois Diplomacy,* 28, 93, 106, 124).

The importance of boundary crossing in human societies is set forth in Arnold van Gennep, *The Rites of Passage,* trans. Monika B. Vizedom and Gabrielle L. Caffee (London, 1960 [orig. pub. 1908]), esp. ch. 2.

5. J. N. B. Hewitt, "Legend of the Founding of the Iroquois League," *American Anthropologist,* V (1892), 137–138; Gibson, *Concerning the League,* xix–xx.

6. *MPCP,* II, 388 (Shawnees), VII, 315 ("Custom"), 650, VIII, 150 (expecting it). For Delawares performing it for other Indians, see Post 1758, 270; Zeisberger, *History,* 150–151.

7. *MPCP,* IV, 80 ("own way"), VII, 206 ("usual addresses"), VIII, 150 (Denny). Other examples are *ibid.,* 157, 175, 724–725, 733–734, V, 532, VII, 650, 708, 711; *PA,* 1st, II, 726. And see Timothy J. Shannon, "The Crossroads of Empire: The Albany Congress of 1754 and the British Atlantic Community" (Ph.D. diss., Northwestern University, 1993), 282–291.

8. Simon Schama, *Landscape and Memory* (New York, 1995), Part I.

9. William Bradford, *Of Plymouth Plantation, 1620–1647,* ed. Samuel Eliot Morison (New York, 1952), 62.

10. Of the vast literature on European and American understandings of wilderness, I have particularly profited from Schama, *Landscape and Memory;* Clarence J. Glacken, *Traces on the Rhodian Shore: Nature and Culture in Western Thought from Ancient Times to the End of the Eighteenth Century* (Berkeley, Calif., 1967); Robert Pogue Harrison, *Forests: The Shadow of Civilization* (Chicago, 1992); Roderick Nash, *Wilderness and the American Mind* (New

Haven, Conn., 1967); Max Oelschlaeger, *The Idea of Wilderness: From Prehistory to the Age of Ecology* (New Haven, Conn., 1991); Richard Slotkin, *Regeneration through Violence: The Mythology of the American Frontier, 1600–1860* (Middletown, Conn., 1973); Keith Thomas, *Man and the Natural World: A History of Modern Sensibility* (New York, 1983); Frederick Turner, *Beyond Geography: The Western Spirit Against the Wilderness* (New York, 1980); George H. Williams, *Wilderness and Paradise in Christian Thought: The Biblical Experience of the Desert in the History of Christianity and the Paradise Theme in the Theological Idea of the University* (New York, 1962).

11. Albert Cook Myers, ed., *Narratives of Early Pennsylvania, West New Jersey, and Delaware, 1630–1707* (New York, 1912), 226–229. See also *PA,* 1st, I, 68.

12. Markham and German colonist quoted in Joseph Kelley, *Pennsylvania: The Colonial Years, 1681–1776* (Garden City, N.Y., 1980), 42, 71; *MPCP,* III, 581 (John Penn; see also 129, 275; Myers, ed., *Narratives of Early Pennsylvania,* 383, 397).

13. Adolph B. Benson, ed., *The America of 1750: Peter Kalm's Travels in North America. The English Version of 1770* (New York, 1937), 48; "Governor Thomas Pownall's Description of the Streets and the Main Roads About Philadelphia," *PMHB,* XVIII (1894), 213–214; Benjamin Franklin, *Autobiography and Other Writings,* ed. Kenneth Silverman (New York, 1986), 41.

14. Williams, *Wilderness and Paradise,* 4; Nash, *Wilderness and the American Mind,* 1–6; William Cronon, ed., *Uncommon Ground: Rethinking the Human Place in Nature* (New York, 1995).

15. *MPCP,* III, 132. Though "Penn's Woods" officially meant all of the territory granted William Penn, I use it as a synonym for "the inhabited parts," the lands colonists controlled.

16. *PA,* 1st, I, 304 ("Large Intriestt"). Weiser 1737, 7; *MPCP,* V, 213 (Weiser). Croghan saw the landscape the same way (*PA,* 1st, II, 118; *MPCP,* VI, 218; Croghan to Richard Peters, 23 Nov. 1754, GCP, 5/19. For Evans, see Lawrence Henry Gipson, ed., *Lewis Evans. To Which is Added Evans'* A Brief Account of Pennsylvania (Philadelphia, 1939), 149. See also Thomas Pownall, "The Face of the Country," in *A Topographical Description of the Dominions of the United States of America . . . ,* ed. Lois Mulkearn (Pittsburgh, Pa., 1949), 23–24, 30.

17. Gipson, ed., *Evans,* 149; James Fenimore Cooper, *The Pathfinder, or The Inland Sea* (Albany, N.Y., 1981 [orig. pub. 1839, rev. ed. 1851]), 8–9; Francis Parkman, *The Conspiracy of Pontiac and the Indian War After the Conquest of Canada* (Lincoln, Neb., 1994), I, 147.

18. For forest diplomacy, see George S. Snyderman, "The Function of Wampum," *Procs. APS,* XCVIII (1954), 478; William N. Fenton, *American Indian and White Relations to 1830: Needs and Opportunities for Study* (Chapel Hill,

N.C., 1957), 4, 22; Yasuhide Kawashima, "Forest Diplomats: The Role of Interpreters in Indian-White Relations on the Early American Frontier," *AIQ*, XIII (1989), 1–14.

19. Cammerhoff, 177; *MPCP*, IV, 684; VIII, 133 ("Woods"); VI, 341 ("Wilderness"); Wallace, *Weiser*, 91; Shamokin Diary, 6 Mar. 1748, MCA, 6/121/4/1; *MPCP*, VI, 341, VIII, 133 ("Bushes"); Eben Norton Horsford, ed., *Zeisberger's Indian Dictionary . . . Printed from the Original Manuscript in Harvard College Library* (Cambridge, Mass., 1887), 78, 231 (Delaware and Iroquois; see also Daniel G. Brinton, ed., *A Lenâpé–English Dictionary* [Philadelphia, 1888], 26, 139–140).

Studies of this distinction are largely limited to the Iroquois: Beauchamp, *Councils and Ceremonies,* 352–359, 365, 386, 393–397, 421; Gibson, *Concerning the League,* xix–xx, xxxii, xxxvi, xxxviii, xl, 542, 597–600, 607–618; Anthony F. C. Wallace, "The Modal Personality Structure of the Tuscarora Indians As Revealed by the Rorschach Test," Bureau of American Ethnology, Smithsonian Institution, *Bulletin* 150 (Washington, D.C., 1952), 24–28; idem, *The Death and Rebirth of the Seneca* (New York, 1970), 24, 37–38, 67, 91–100; Hazel W. Hertzberg, *The Great Tree and the Longhouse: The Culture of the Iroquois* (New York, 1966), 23–24; Elisabeth Tooker, "Women in Iroquois Society," in Michael K. Foster et al., eds., *Extending the Rafters: Interdisciplinary Approaches to Iroquoian Studies* (Albany, N.Y., 1984), 119; Richter, *Ordeal of the Longhouse,* 23–24, 31–32; Dennis, *Cultivating a Landscape,* 26–41; Dean Snow, *The Iroquois* (Cambridge, Mass., 1994), 39, 54–55; Hamell, "The Iroquois and the World's Rim," *AIQ*, XVI (1992), 451–469; idem, "Mythical Realities," *Man in the Northeast,* no. 33 (1987), 63–87. The way neighboring Indians embraced the At the Woods' Edge Ceremony suggests a similar cosmology. For Delawares, see Zeisberger, *History,* 127; William W. Newcomb, Jr., *The Culture and Acculturation of the Delaware Indians,* University of Michigan, Museum of Anthropology, Anthropology Papers, 10 (Ann Arbor, Mich., 1956), 61; Herbert C. Kraft, *The Lenape: Archaeology, History, and Ethnohistory* (Newark, N.J., 1986), ch. 6; Jay Miller, "A Strucon Model of Delaware Culture and the Position of Mediators," *American Ethnologist,* VI (1979), 797–798. Other natives with similar views are discussed in Joel W. Martin, *Sacred Revolt: The Muskogees' Struggle for a New World* (Boston, 1991), 143–144; Gregory Evans Dowd, *A Spirited Resistance: The North American Indian Struggle for Unity, 1745–1815* (Baltimore, Md., 1992), ch. I.

20. Arthur C. Parker, *Seneca Myths and Folk Tales,* Buffalo Historical Society, *Publications,* XXVII (1923), 289.

21. Horatio Hale, "A Lawgiver of the Stone Age," in Elisabeth Tooker, ed., *An Iroquois Source Book,* I (New York, 1985), 330 (quotation). Time and again, Iroquois tales collected a century ago begin with the characters living on the outskirts of a town or in the woods as they embark on their adventures.

Parker, *Seneca Myths;* idem, "Fundamental Factors in Seneca Folk Lore," New York State Museum, *Bulletin* (1924), 62; William M. Beauchamp, ed., *Iroquois Folk Lore Gathered from the Six Nations of New York* (Syracuse, N.Y., 1922); Harriet Maxwell Converse, *Myths and Legends of the New York State Iroquois,* ed. Arthur Caswell Parker (Albany, N.Y., 1974 [orig. pub. 1908]); J. N. B. Hewitt, "Iroquoian Cosmology," Part I, *Twenty-First Annual Report of the Bureau of American Ethnology . . . , 1899–1900* (Washington, D.C., 1903), 127–339; Hewitt and Jeremiah Curtin, eds., "Seneca Fiction, Legends, and Myths," *Thirty-Second Annual Report of the Bureau of American Ethnology . . . , 1910–1911* (Washington, D.C., 1918); Jeremiah Curtin, *Seneca Indian Myths* (New York, 1923). For Delaware tales, see John Bierhorst, *Mythology of the Lenape: Guide and Texts* (Tucson, Ariz., 1995), 92–93, 95, 99–100, 102–105.

22. Joseph-Francois Lafitau, *Customs of the American Indians Compared with the Customs of Primitive Times,* trans. and ed. William N. Fenton and Elizabeth L. Moore, 2 vols. (Toronto, 1974–1975), II, 260.

23. Claus, Memoirs, 18. And see Bartram, *Observations,* 63; Jay Miller, "*Kwulakan:* The Delaware Side of Their Movement West," *Pennsylvania Archaeologist,* XLV (1975), 45–46.

24. *MPCP,* IV, 651, 684 (Shamokin), V, 475 (Onondaga; see also IV, 664–666).

25. Slotkin (*Regeneration through Violence,* 55) also notes the parallels.

26. White, *Middle Ground.* For work suggesting the limits to a middle ground, especially on the Anglo-American frontier, see Daniel K. Richter, "Whose Indian History?" *WMQ,* 3d ser., L (1993), 390; Virginia DeJohn Anderson, "King Philip's Herds: Indians, Colonists, and the Problem of Livestock in Early New England," *ibid.,* LI (1994), 601–624; Martin H. Quitt, "Trade and Acculturation at Jamestown, 1607–1609: The Limits of Understanding," *ibid.,* LII (1995), 227–258.

27. Michael K. Foster, "When Words Become Deeds: An Analysis of Three Iroquois Longhouse Speech Events," *Explorations in the Ethnography of Speaking,* ed. Richard Bauman and Joel Sherzer, 2d ed. (Cambridge, Eng., 1989), 366–367. Karim Tiro helped clarify my thinking on this issue.

28. Karen Ordahl Kupperman, ed., *Captain John Smith: A Select Edition of his Writings* (Chapel Hill, N.C., 1988), 17; J. Hector St. John de Crèvecoeur, *Letters from an American Farmer and Sketches of Eighteenth-Century America,* ed. Albert E. Stone (New York, 1981), 71, 82.

29. McClure, *Diary,* 56; Nathaniel Holland to Israel Pemberton, 16 Apr. 1761, FA, IV, 95 ("Indian ground"); *MPCP,* VIII, 196 (Indian calls it "the English Country"); *PA,* 1st, II, 759 ("well vers'd").

30. *PA,* 1st, II, 385; also 289 ("Woodboys").

31. Peters to Weiser, 24 Jan. 1750/51, CCW, I, 24 ("cannot do"); *PGW,* I, 124 (Washington); *PHB,* V, 294 ("Anchor"); Peters to Weiser, 18 June 1746, RPP, II, 59 ("Treasure").

32. Ann Uhry Abrams, "Benjamin West's Documentation of Colonial History: *William Penn's Treaty with the Indians," The Art Bulletin,* LXIV (1982), 70, and figs. 13–15; Abrams, *The Valiant Hero: Benjamin West and Grand-Style History Painting,* New Directions in American Art (Washington, D.C., 1985), 194; J. William Frost, "William Penn's Experiment in the Wilderness: Promise and Legend," *PMHB,* CVII (1983), 600–602.

33. Scholars differ over whether this treaty actually took place. Jennings, *Ambiguous Iroquois Empire,* 245–248; C. A. Weslager, *The Delaware Indians: A History* (New Brunswick, N.J., 1972), 167. For nineteenth-century treatments, see Thomas J. Clarkson, *Memoirs of the Public and Private Life of William Penn,* rev. ed. (London, 1849), 124–126; M. L. Weems, *The Life of William Penn, the Settler of Pennsylvania, the Founder of Philadelphia . . .* (Philadelphia, 1836), 144–148, 156–157; John F. Watson, "The Indian Treaty, For The Lands Now the Site of Philadelphia and the Adjacent Country," HSP, *Memoirs,* III, Part 2 (1836), 129–140; Peter S. Du Ponceau and J. Francis Fisher, "A Memoir on the History of the Celebrated Treaty made by William Penn with the Indians under the Elm Tree at Shackamaxon, in the Year 1682," *ibid.,* 141–204; "Presentation to the Historical Society of Pennsylvania of the Belt of Wampum Delivered by the Indians to William Penn, at the Great Treaty under the Elm Tree, in 1682," *ibid.,* VI (1858), 205–281; Frederick D. Stone, "Penn's Treaty with the Indians: Did it Take Place in 1682 or 1683?" *PMHB,* VI (1882), 217–238.

   Other treatments of the painting are Ellen Starr Brinton, "Benjamin West's Painting of Penn's Treaty with the Indians," *Bulletin of the Friends' Historical Association,* XXX (1941), 99–189; Charles Coleman Sellers and Anthony N. B. Garvan, *Symbols of Peace: William Penn's Treaty with the Indians* (Philadelphia, 1976); Robert C. Alberts, *Benjamin West: A Biography* (Boston, 1978); Beth Fowkes Tobin, "Native Land and Foreign Desire: *William Penn's Treaty with the Indians," American Indian Culture and Research Journal,* XIX (1995), 87–119. The painting's ethnographic accuracy has recently been praised by J. C. H. King, "Woodlands Artifacts from the Studio of Benjamin West, 1738–1820," *American Indian Art Magazine,* XVII (1991), 34–47, and Arthur Einhorn and Thomas S. Abler, "Bonnets, Plumes, and Headbands in West's Painting of Penn's Treaty," *ibid.,* XXI (1996), 44–53.

34. Sellers and Garvan, *Symbols of Peace,* Preface and Acknowledgments; Alberts, *West,* 111.

35. Brinton, "West's Painting," *Bull. Friends' Hist. Assoc.,* XXX (1941), 100, 128–133; Sellers and Garvan, *Symbols of Peace,* plates 5, 9–12, 14, 15; Alberts, *West,* 110–111. It also found its way, in the 1820s, into the nation's capitol, when Nicholas Gevelot carved it into the stone above the north door of the Rotunda. Intriguingly and almost uniquely, Gevelot—perhaps

because he was himself a foreigner in the early republic—included an interpreter in his tableau. Few followed his lead, preferring instead the image composed by West. Vivien Green Fryd, *Art and Empire: The Politics of Ethnicity in the United States Capitol, 1815–1860* (New Haven, Conn., 1992), 18, 28–32, 36, 40. For the significance of a painting that depicts another encounter and does include the translator, see David Murray, *Forked Tongues: Speech, Writing, and Representation in North American Indian Texts* (Bloomington, Ind., 1991), 1.

36. Alice Ford, *Edward Hicks: His Life and Art* (New York, 1985), 54.

37. Ford, *Hicks;* idem, *Edward Hicks: Painter of the Peaceable Kingdom* (Philadelphia, 1952); Williams, *Wilderness and Paradise,* 115–116.

38. For example, Joseph S. Walton, *Conrad Weiser and the Indian Policy of Colonial Pennsylvania* (Philadelphia, 1900); Albert T. Volwiler, *George Croghan and the Westward Movement, 1741–1782* (Cleveland, Ohio, 1926); Lily Lee Nixon, *James Burd, Frontier Defender, 1726–1793* (Philadelphia, 1941); Kenneth P. Bailey, *Thomas Cresap: Maryland Frontiersman* (Boston, 1944); Wallace, *Weiser;* Sewell Elias Slick, *William Trent and the West* (Harrisburg, Pa., 1947); Nicholas B. Wainwright, *George Croghan, Wilderness Diplomat* (Chapel Hill, N.C., 1959); Alfred Procter James, *George Mercer of the Ohio Company: A Study in Frustration* (Pittsburgh, Pa., 1963); Robert Grant Crist, *George Croghan of Pennsboro* (Harrisburg, Pa., 1965); Howard Lewin, "A Frontier Diplomat: Andrew Montour," *Pennsylvania History,* XXXIII (1966), 153–186; Kenneth P. Bailey, *Christopher Gist: Colonial Frontiersman, Explorer, and Indian Agent* (Hamden, Conn., 1976); Walter T. Champion, Jr., "Christian Frederick Post and the Winning of the West," *PMHB,* CIV (1980), 308–325. An exceptionally sensitive study of a Delaware figure is Wallace, *Teedyuscung.*

Recently, shorter, more sophisticated biographies have begun to appear. See David G. Sweet and Gary B. Nash, eds., *Struggle and Survival in Colonial America* (Berkeley, Calif., 1981); Frances Karttunen, *Between Worlds: Interpreters, Guides, and Survivors* (New Brunswick, N.J., 1994); Margaret Connell Szasz, ed., *Between Indian and White Worlds: The Cultural Broker* (Norman, Okla., 1994); Robert S. Grumet, ed., *Northeastern Indian Lives, 1632–1816* (Amherst, Mass., 1996); Colin G. Calloway, "Simon Girty: Interpreter and Intermediary," in James A. Clifton, ed., *Being and Becoming Indian: Biographical Studies of North American Frontiers* (Chicago, 1989), 38–58; Alan Taylor, "Captain Hendrick Aupaumut: The Dilemmas of an Intercultural Broker," *Ethnohistory,* XLIII (1996), 431–457.

Recent works that do look for patterns include J. Frederick Fausz, "Middlemen in Peace and War: Virginia's Earliest Indian Interpreters, 1608–1632," *VMHB,* XCV (1987), 41–64; Patricia Galloway, "Talking with Indians: Interpreters and Diplomacy in French Louisiana," in Winthrop D.

Jordan and Sheila L. Skemp, eds., *Race and Family in the Colonial South* (Jackson, Miss., 1987), 109–129; Nancy L. Hagedorn, " 'A Friend to Go Between Them': The Interpreter as Cultural Broker During Anglo-Iroquois Councils, 1740–1770," *Ethnohistory*, XXXV (1988), 60–80; idem, "Brokers of Understanding: Interpreters as Agents of Cultural Exchange in Colonial New York," *New York History*, LXXVI (1995), 379–408; Daniel K. Richter, "Cultural Brokers and Intercultural Politics: New York–Iroquois Relations, 1664–1701," *JAH*, LXXV (1988), 41–67; Kawashima, "Forest Diplomats," *AIQ*, XIII (1989), 1–14.

39. The literature on Indian diplomacy is vast. Besides works cited above, see Richard Aquila, *The Iroquois Restoration: Iroquois Diplomacy on the Colonial Frontier, 1701–1754* (Detroit, Mich., 1983); Jennings, *Empire of Fortune;* Daniel K. Richter and James H. Merrell, eds., *Beyond the Covenant Chain: The Iroquois and Their Neighbors in Indian North America, 1600–1800* (Syracuse, N.Y., 1987).

40. *Arch. Md.,* IX, 71 (Denny); *PHB*, III, 108 ("drudgery"). For "Indian Business," see *MPCP*, VI, 284, VII, 226; Logstown Treaty, 165, 167.

41. I have profited from more general work on interpretation, especially Murray, *Forked Tongues;* Eric Cheyfitz, *The Poetics of Imperialism: Translation and Colonization from the Tempest to Tarzan* (New York, 1991); Stephen J. Greenblatt, *Learning to Curse: Essays in Early Modern Culture* (New York, 1990); idem, *Marvelous Possessions: The Wonder of the New World* (Chicago, 1991).

42. *MPCP,* V, 455 ("publick Character"; also VI, 444), III, 500, V, 73, VII, 65, VIII, 87 ("Publick Business"), 659 ("charged"). Richard Peters, Diary, 10 Oct. 1758, RPP ("State affairs"). (I thank Christopher Cecil for help in transcribing Peters's difficult handwriting.) The opposite were "private Men" (Peters to the Proprietaries, 26 Nov. 1753, PMOC, VI, 133; Spangenberg to the Governor, 23 May 1756, MCA, 34/317/2/7). Parker, *Seneca Myths and Tales,* 120 (Hatondas).

43. *MPCP,* IV, 581.

44. Horsford, ed., *Zeisberger's Indian Dictionary,* 65, 105 (Iroquois and Delaware words for "emissary" and "interpreter"). *PHB*, ser. 21649, I, 81 (Croghan). *Oxford English Dictionary,* 2d ed., *s.v.,* "negotiate." I do not, however, call these people *brokers* or *cultural brokers,* a term popular for a generation or more (Szasz, Introduction, in her *Between Indian and White Worlds*). The term is too vague and elastic: it can be construed to embrace anyone and everyone who had dealings of some sort with another culture. I thank Daniel K. Richter for helping me think through the nomenclature.

45. *PWP,* II, 120, 129. The story of the seventeenth-century Delaware Valley, and of Penn's relations with the Indians, can be found in Carl Bridenbaugh, "The Old and New Societies of the Delaware Valley in the Seventeenth Century," *PMHB*, C (1976), 143–172; Carol Hoffecker et al., eds., *New*

Sweden in America (Newark, Del., 1995), Part II; Francis Jennings, "Brother Miquon: Good Lord!" in Richard S. Dunn and Mary Maples Dunn, eds., *The World of William Penn* (Philadelphia, 1986), 195–214; C. A. Weslager, *Dutch Explorers, Traders and Settlers in the Delaware Valley, 1609–1674* (Philadelphia, 1961).

46. *MPCP*, II, 600 ("Joyn'd"), IV, 581 ("equal Parts"). The (mis)printed version of the first speech has it: "the Indians makes themselves as half Indians." I correct it here. For Weiser's names, see Wallace, *Weiser*, 32, 194.

47. Szasz, ed., *Between Indian and White Worlds;* Karttunen, *Between Worlds;* Grumet, ed., *Northeastern Indian Lives.*

48. Frederick Turner calls these "luminous items" (*Beyond Geography,* xii); Stephen Greenblatt terms them "representative anecdotes" (*Marvelous Possessions,* 2–3; *Learning to Curse,* 5).

49. *PHB*, ser. 21653, 133.

50. *MPCP*, VI, 205; the rest of this exchange is at 194, 340.

Prologue: The Killing of Jack Armstrong, 1744

1. Unless otherwise noted, the following account is reconstructed from *MPCP*, IV, 675–685, 742–747; *PA*, 1st, I, 643–652. The originals, with some variation (mostly in spelling and punctuation), are in RPCEC, B2, 368, 370–378. The provincial assembly's discussions are in *PA*, 8th, IV, 2918–2920, 2922–2924, 2940–2941, 3019, 3044, 3058.

   For other treatments of the incident (which largely reprint the documents), see U. J. Jones, *History of the Early Settlement of the Juniata Valley . . . ,* 2d ed. (Harrisburg, Pa., 1940 [orig. pub. 1889]), 125–134, 384–386; G. S. Rowe, *Embattled Bench: The Pennsylvania Supreme Court and the Forging of a Democratic Society, 1684–1809* (Newark, Del., 1994), 88–89; Hanna, *Wilderness Trail,* II, 349–351; William Brewster, *The Pennsylvania and New York Frontier, 1700–1763* (Philadelphia, 1954), 21–22; Wallace, *Weiser,* ch. 22. I follow Wallace on the spelling of the Delaware's name, which colonists spelled many ways.

2. The probable route can be followed in Paul A. W. Wallace, *Indian Paths of Pennsylvania* (Harrisburg, Pa., 1965), 77. The name of one of the companions is confused in the record: Mushemeelin called him Billy (*PA,* 1st, I, 646; *PG,* 10 May 1744), while Weiser and Shickellamy used Jemmey or a variation (*MPCP,* IV, 682, 684).

3. For earlier examples of killings, see *MPCP,* III, 285–287, 313–314; *PA,* 1st, I, 254. For attacks, see *PA,* 1st, I, 227, 232, 254, 265; *MPCP,* IV, 446–447. For "Jack's Narrows" and its function as a reminder, see *PA,* 1st, I, 751,

758–759, II, 136; Robert Greenhalgh Albion and Leonidas Dodson, eds., *Philip Vickers Fithian: Journal, 1775–1776* . . . (Princeton, N.J., 1934), 115; Wallace, *Weiser,* 175; Wallace, *Indian Paths,* 51, 77; Hanna, *Wilderness Trail,* I, 207 (a photograph of the Narrows is in *ibid.,* facing 253). More than a century later, locals still marked the site with a ghost story and a poem (Jones, *Juniata Valley,* 386–392).

4. For context, see Wallace, *Weiser,* 175, 184. For Delawares and Shawnees, see Jennings, *Ambiguous Iroquois Empire,* chs. 15–17. Formal notice of the war reached Philadelphia in June (Wallace, *Weiser,* 184). For worries about the Six Nations coming, *PA,* 1st, I, 649; Richard Hockley to Thomas Penn, 16 June 1744, PMOC, IV, 7. There were widespread fears in the region that spring about "the dreaded French war." Carl Bridenbaugh, ed., *Gentleman's Progress: The* Itinerarium *of Dr. Alexander Hamilton, 1744* (Chapel Hill, N.C., 1948), 7, 15, 20, 24–25, 30.

5. Conrad Weiser's Account of His Journey to Shamokin, 2 May 1744, RPCEC, B2, 377.

6. Jemmey's "whole Story" might have told of his suspicion that John killed one of the men, since the rest of the passage talked of securing the "Murderers"—John and Mushemeelin.

7. This may have been a common threat among Indians. In 1747 Ohio Indians telling Pennsylvania about their war against the French spoke of setting kettles over a fire so "that the French Men's Heads might soon be boil'd" (*MPCP,* V, 147).

8. For Berry's, Wallace, *Weiser,* 138. This is Shickellamy's version of John's release. Another had it that Shickellamy's sons lost their nerve: afraid of resentment against their father for handing over a "Young Man who was in great Esteem with them [Delawares]," they let him go. Mushemeelin had a third explanation, but he either kept it to himself or never convinced a colonist to write it down.

9. I have combined the Lancaster account (*PA,* 1st, I, 646–647) with one given some two weeks later from the Philadelphia prison (*PG,* 10 May 1744). These differ in some respects, but their central points—that Mushemeelin killed Armstrong and Arnold in self defense, and John murdered Smith—are the same.

10. For the government's demand, see also Peters to Weiser, 26 Apr. 1744, LC, IV, 100: if the other two men are not turned over, "all Commerce and Confidence is at an end with the Indians."

11. Since Montour spoke English, Weiser must have taken the further step for the sake of the Iroquois present.

12. *Translation of a German Letter, Wrote by Conrad Weiser* . . . (Philadelphia, 1 Evans 8062), 6–7.

13. Weiser, Account of His Journey, 2 May 1744, RPCEC, B2, 377.

14. Treaty at Lancaster, 1744, in Julian P. Boyd, ed., *Indian Treaties Printed by Benjamin Franklin, 1736–1762* (Philadelphia, 1938), 57–58, 67, 68.

15. Wallace, *Weiser,* 206, 238.

16. *Ibid.,* 183, 206; *PG,* 8, 15 Nov. 1744. Weiser was in Philadelphia eighteen days for the trial (Indian Charges, 1744, CCW, I, 11). Though Gov. Thomas talked as if the trial were to follow precedent, in fact the province had to scramble to solve the question of jurisdiction: the crime had taken place beyond the colonial inhabited parts. Therefore on 19 October the colony passed "An Act for the Speedy Trial of Capital Offences Committed by Any Indian or Indians in the Remote Parts of the Province." The statute included "all capital offenses which have been or hereafter shall be committed" by Indians "within the bounds of this province in places remote from inhabitants" (*Statutes at Large of Pennsylvania, 1682–1809,* 17 vols. [Harrisburg, Pa., 1896–1915], V, 5–6). For the assembly's discussion, see *PA,* 8th, IV, 3019–3020.

17. David Brainerd, Journal, 1745, APS, 30; Shamokin Diary, 7–8 Jan. 1748, MCA, 6/121/4/1. And see Barry C. Kent, *Susquehanna's Indians,* Anthropological Series, no. 6 (Harrisburg, Pa., 1989), 100; Kent et al., "A Map of 18th Century Indian Towns in Pennsylvania," *Pennsylvania Archaeologist,* LI (1981), 11.

18. *MPCP,* IV, 681.

19. Benjamin Franklin's *Pennsylvania Gazette* still had doubts, reporting in November that "Yesterday, Mushemelon, the Indian, who murdered Armstrong the Trader, and *one* of his Men, was executed here" (*PG,* 15 Nov. 1744, emphasis added).

I: Paths to the Woods

1. Wallace, *Weiser,* chs. 1–5; James H. Merrell, "Shickellamy, 'a Person of Consequence,' " in Robert S. Grumet, ed., *Northeastern Indian Lives, 1632–1816* (Amherst, Mass., 1996), 227–257; Nancy Hagedorn, " 'Faithful, Knowing, and Prudent': Andrew Montour as Interpreter and Cultural Broker, 1740–1772," in Margaret Connell Szasz, ed., *Between Indian and White Worlds: The Cultural Broker* (Norman, Okla., 1994), 44–60; James H. Merrell, " 'The Cast of His Countenance': Reading Andrew Montour," in Ronald Hoffman, Mechal Sobel, and Fredrika J. Teute, eds., *Through A Glass Darkly: Reflections on Personal Identity in Early America* (Chapel Hill, N.C., 1997), 13–39. For Montour's answering a French greeting in English, see William C. Reichel, ed., *Memorials of the Moravian Church,* I (Philadelphia, 1870), 96.

2. *MPCP,* IV, 636.

3. Weiser 1737, 8; Marshe, 189–190.

4. Reichel, ed., *Memorials,* I, 99; *PA,* 2d, VII, 261. Peters to the Proprietor, 7 Feb. 1753, PMOC, VI, 5.

5. Frederick S. Weiser, ed., *John Frederich Weisers Buch containing The Autobiography of John Conrad Weiser (1696–1760)* (Hanover, Pa., 1976). An exception is Claus, Memoirs. Isaac Stille, a Delaware go-between from 1755 to 1775, was said to have written his memoirs, since lost (John F. Watson, *Annals of Philadelphia and Pennsylvania, In the Olden Time . . . ,* 2 vols., 2d ed. [Philadelphia, 1845], II, 171–172).

6. John H. Carter, "Shikellamy, The Indian Vice King at Shamokin," *Proceedings and Addresses of the Northumberland County Historical Society,* III (1931), 53.

7. *MPCP,* IV, 88.

8. *Ibid.* ("true good Man"); Indian Affairs—Conversations at Pembertons, April 1756, in a box labeled "Indians (transferred from Society Collections)," HSP ("hearty & sincere").

9. Council at Philadelphia, 25 and 28 Jan. 1722/3, DSP, 966.F.6. Satcheecho was a Cayuga by birth.

10. *PA,* 8th, V, 3873–3874; *MPCP,* VII, 296.

11. James H. Merrell, *The Indians' New World: Catawbas and their Neighbors from European Contact through the Era of Removal* (Chapel Hill, N.C., 1989), ch. IV; idem, " 'The Customes of Our Countrey': Indians and Colonists in Early America," in Bernard Bailyn and Philip D. Morgan, eds., *Strangers Within the Realm: Cultural Margins of the First British Empire* (Chapel Hill, N.C., 1991), 137–142.

12. *MPCP,* IV, 662 (Nanticokes; for another example, see Israel Pemberton to Isaac Zane, 5 June 1758, FA, I, 527; *MPCP,* VIII, 124–125; *PWJ,* II, 858–859; *PA,* 1st, III, 404, 428). *MPCP,* VII, 67 (Iroquois to Delaware towns). DRCNY, VII, 579 ("always expect"). See also Marshe, 180; Heckewelder, *History,* 311–312; Thomas Brainerd, *The Life of John Brainerd, The Brother of David Brainerd, And His Successor as Missionary to the Indians of New Jersey* (Philadelphia, 1865), 233n.

Of the leading colonial go-betweens in this theater only Christopher Gist, a Virginian active in the Ohio country during the 1750s, was less than skilled in an Indian language. "He knows but little of their language it is true," George Washington admitted when recommending him, "but is well acquainted with their manners and customs—especially of the southern Indians" (*PGW,* IV, 172).

13. *MPCP,* III, 132–133. Virginia records mention only that an interpreter was present at the meetings, without saying who this person was or how the governor obtained him (*EJCCV,* III, 552–554). Eleven years later, casting about for Shawnee go-betweens he thought qualified, Logan was still looking for fluency first, for "one . . . who can speak some English (if such can

be procured)." Logan to James Wright, 24 1ober 1732, JLLB, 1716–1743, 308.

14. *DRCNY,* VIII, 115–116.

15. Zeisberger, *History,* 96 ("endurance"; "sensible and reliable"; "high regard"), 143 ("public speaking"). Joseph-Francois Lafitau, *Customs of the American Indians Compared with the Customs of Primitive Times,* trans. and ed. William N. Fenton and Elizabeth L. Moore, 2 vols. (Toronto, 1974–1977), II, 173 ("old men"); Heckewelder (*History,* 108–109) stressed the differing levels of importance. Augustus Spangenberg to the Governor and to William Logan, 2 May 1756, MCA, 34/317/2/5, and Northampton County, Miscellaneous Manuscripts, Bethlehem and Vicinity, 1741–1849, 39, HSP ("Family"); *MPCP,* VII, 49 (Scarouyady).

16. *PA,* 1st, I, 230 ("stiff"), II, 725 ("haughty"). For native attitudes, Post 1758, 230; Smith, *Account,* 47; *PWJ,* XI, 228–229.

17. *PWJ,* IX, 205 ("Manageing"; see also 439, II, 828, XI, 128, 212; *MPCP,* VI, 381; *PGW,* IV, 141). *MPCP,* IV, 576–577 ("Skill"; see also IX, 453; *PWJ,* III, 663). Peters to the Proprietaries, 26 Dec. 1756, Richard Peters Letters to Proprietaries of Pennsylvania, 1755–1757, Simon Gratz Collection, Case 2, Box 33-a, 125, HSP ("Talents"); Peters to Gen. Monckton, 29 Aug. 1760, *Collections of the Massachusetts Historical Society,* 4th ser., IX (1871), 306 ("Disposition"); *MPCP,* VII, 432 ("Ear"); Weiser, "Observations," 6 ("Light"); *Journals of Claus and Weiser,* 32 (joke).

18. Conrad Weiser, "An Account of the first Confederacy of the *Six Nations . . . ,*" *The American Magazine,* Dec. 1744, 669 ("Genius"). *PA,* 2d, VI, 664 ("opinion").

19. *DHNY,* II, 946–947. Also *PWJ,* VIII, 1129–1130.

20. *PWJ,* XI, 841–842 ("mystery"). Hays, 77 ("Indien Life").

21. *MPCP,* V, 350 (firing guns). Heckewelder, *History,* 270–275; Kenny 1761–63, 46; Samuel Evans, "Lowrey Family," Lancaster County [Pa.] Historical Society, 46 (funeral). Deposition of George Croghan, 16 Oct. 1776, GCP, 6/30 (council). Gist, 17, 23, 121–122 (dance). David McClure, *Diary of David McClure, Doctor of Divinity, 1748–1820,* ed. Franklin B. Dexter (New York, 1899), 53; Bartram, *Observations,* 15; RPLB, 1737–1750, 381; Kenneth P. Bailey, ed., *The Ohio Company Papers, 1753–1817 . . .* (Arcata, Calif., 1947), 139; *PA,* 1st, III, 437, 460; *PWJ,* XII, 1097–1098 (liaisons with Indian women). *MPCP,* VI, 195, 616 (war party). Evans, "Lowrey Family," 28; *PA,* 1st, I, 254–255; Kenny 1761–63, 178 (hunting). *MPCP,* II, 385 (torture). *PA,* 1st, I, 254–255, 425; Kenny 1758–59, 438 (drinking). *MPCP,* III, 285 (singing and dancing; I have corrected a misprint that has it *signing*).

22. Weiser, ed., *Autobiography,* 23 ("very cruel"). *PWJ,* VIII, 65 ("whole Winter").

23. Albert Cook Myers, ed., *Narratives of Early Pennsylvania, West New Jersey, and Delaware, 1630–1707* (New York, 1912), 230, 400; *PWP,* II, 448–454, IV,

564–565. The language Penn learned was the local jargon (Ives Goddard, "The Delaware Jargon," in Carol E. Hoffecker et al., eds., *New Sweden in America* [Newark, Del., 1995], 138).

24. Joseph E. Illick, *Colonial Pennsylvania: A History* (New York, 1976), 44, 63.

25. For Cocke, see ch. II. For Farmer, see Albright G. Zimmerman, "The Indian Trade of Colonial Pennsylvania" (Ph.D. diss., University of Delaware, 1966), 48–49, 59, 85, 152; Jennings, *Ambiguous Iroquois Empire,* 255; idem, "Miquon's Passing: Indian-European Relations in Colonial Pennsylvania, 1674 to 1755" (Ph.D. diss., University of Pennsylvania, 1965), 124, 138, 285; *MPCP,* III, 157 ("Gent"), 316, 318 ("Esquire"). For French, see Jennings, *Ambiguous Iroquois Empire,* 259–260, 269, 279; *MPCP,* III, 338.

26. *MPCP,* II, 300 ("virtuous Conversation"; see also *PA,* 8th, I, 653, 667). *PGW,* II, 120 ("Sense and Character").

27. A possible exception, when Logan and his party had "their Chief abode" with Shawnees (though perhaps with Martin Chartier, a trader living among those Indians), is in *MPCP,* II, 246.

28. RPLB, 1737–1750, 307 (emphasis added). Later salutes to Peters's skills, like Weiser's remark, were more flattery than fact (*MPCP,* VI, 269, VIII, 172).

29. *PHB,* I, 405 ("curse"); *PWJ,* XI, 212 ("Manner of Managing"). *PHB,* ser. 21648, I, 149 ("faint Idea").

30. *MPCP,* VI, 589. Barry C. Kent (*Susquehanna's Indians,* Anthropological Series, no. 6 [Harrisburg, Pa., 1989], 60–61) wonders if Newcastle's family lived among Conestogas in Penn's day before moving west with other Susquehanna River migrants.

31. *PGW,* I, 135; *MPCP,* VII, 6.

32. Logstown Treaty, 165 (Croghan). *MPCP,* IV, 88; Wallace, *Weiser,* 194–195 (Weiser).

33. *Ibid.,* VIII, 436. *PA,* 1st, I, 254–255. The Indians here were referring specifically to traders, but the sentiment carried over to negotiators.

34. *MPCP,* VI, 193 ("assist"; see also VIII, 632, 638–639). *PWJ,* I, 637 ("trust"; see also *MPCP,* VII, 158). "Andrew Montour's Conversation with the Secretary," 20 Feb. 1759, Indian and Military Affairs of Colonial Pennsylvania, 1737–1775, 702, APS ("all know"); *MPCP,* VIII, 754 ("everywhere known"; see also 734–735; *MJNY,* 33).

35. Instructions to Thomas Smallman, [1763?], GCP, 5/28 ("Sober"); *MPCP,* VIII, 774 ("quiet"); Zane 1761, 19 Oct. ("well disposed"). Minutes of the Easton Treaty, 29 July 1756, Friends Historical Association, Mss., I, Haverford College Library, in *Iroq. Ind.,* Reel 19 ("Sound hearts"); *MPCP,* IV, 88 ("faithfull and honest"). And see 581, VIII, 46.

36. Weiser, "Notes," 408. Weiser's concern that Indians think him honest is in Wallace, *Weiser,* 143, 292–293. And see "Private Intelligence or Rather Observations on Ind. Politicks by Frederick Post," PMIA, IV, 50.

37. Easton Treaty, 29 July 1756, in *Iroq. Ind.*, Reel 19 ("strong heads"). *PWJ*, XI, 841 ("thick Scull"). Weiser, "Notes," 408 ("courageous"). *MPCP*, VI, 459–460 ("foolish"); Post 1758, 212–213 ("drunk"). Loskiel, *History*, Part II, 119 (Shickellamy); Clarence Walworth Alvord and Clarence Edwin Carter, eds., *The New Regime, 1765–1767, Collections of the Illinois State Historical Library*, XI (Springfield, Ill., 1916), 316 (Croghan).

38. Hays, 75, 81. Also Post 1760, 17 June.

39. Loskiel, *History*, Part II, 91–92, 119; John H. Carter, "The Moravians at Shamokin," *Procs. Northumberland Co. Hist. Soc.*, IX (1937), 66 (Mack). Shamokin Diary, 6 Jan., 25 Feb., 1, 23 Mar., 2, 8, 11 Apr. 1748, MCA, 6/121/4/1 (Harris). The story of women in the trade remains to be told.

40. *PWJ*, X, 849 ("Dale to say"); Thomas Chalkley, *Journal, or Historical Account, of the Life, Travels, and Christian Experiences, of . . . Thomas Chalkley . . .*, in *A Collection of the Works of Thomas Chalkley* (Philadelphia, 1749, Evans 6297), 49–50 (speaking in council); C. Hale Sipe, *The Indian Chiefs of Pennsylvania* (Harrisburg, Pa., 1927), 203, 255–258 (Aliquippa). For women's roles, see Anthony F. C. Wallace, *The Death and Rebirth of the Seneca* (New York, 1970), Part I; idem, "Women, Land, and Society: Three Aspects of Aboriginal Delaware Life," *Pennsylvania Archaeologist*, XVII (1947), 1–37; idem, "Some Psychological Characteristics of the Delaware Indians During the 17th and 18th Centuries," *ibid.*, XX (1950), 33–39; Robert Steven Grumet, "Sunksquaws, Shamans, and Tradeswomen: Middle Atlantic Coastal Algonkian Women During the 17th and 18th Centuries," in Mona Etienne and Eleanor Leacock, eds., *Women and Colonization: Anthropological Perspectives* (New York, 1979), 43–62; Nancy Shoemaker, ed., *Negotiators of Change: Historical Perspectives on Native American Women* (New York, 1995).

41. Alison Duncan Hirsch, "*Métis* Women and the Struggle to Survive on the Middle Ground: Madame Montour and Her Family" (unpub. ms., 1995). I am grateful to Professor Hirsch for sharing her work with me.

42. For the rare exceptions, see *MPCP*, V, 643–644; Post 1760, 16 May (messengers). Chee-na-wan (Peggy), a Conestoga, once translated at a meeting that her father, the headman Sheehays, had with two provincial leaders. *MPCP*, VIII, 457, IX, 89, 104–105; [Benjamin Franklin], *A Narrative of the Late Massacres . . .*, in Leonard W. Labaree et al., eds., *The Papers of Benjamin Franklin*, 32 vols. to date (New Haven, Conn., 1959–   ), XI, 49.

43. *MPCP*, V, 655–656 (Harris). *PA*, 1st, I, 231–232; James Logan to A. Cornish, 18 May 1732, Logan Letterbook, 1731–1732, 59, Maria Dickinson Logan Papers, HSP (Cornish). The location of the house is noted in *MPCP*, III, 309. For other women occasionally interpreting at more formal council sessions, see *MPCP*, II, 121–122, 141, III, 167, 189.

44. *MPCP*, III, 271 ("Interpretess"), 337 ("Mistress"). *PA*, 2d, VII, 156 ("well treated"); Marshe, 189–191. Her position in New York is noted in Hanna,

Wilderness Trail, I, 199, n.1. For her prominence in Pennsylvania, see *MPCP,* III, 295–296, 334, 337; *PA,* 1st, I, 211, 227–229; Wallace, *Weiser,* 139; Weiser 1737, 8; Reichel, ed., *Memorials,* I, 96–98; Shamokin Diary, 16–19, 26 Sept., 17 Oct., 3 Nov. 1745, MCA, 28/217/12b/1.

45. *PA,* 2d, VII, 156 (quotation); Marshe, 189–191.

46. *PA,* 1st, I, 231–232. Laurel Thatcher Ulrich, *Good Wives: Image and Reality in the Lives of Women in Northern New England, 1650–1750* (New York, 1982), ch. 2.

47. One missionary trying to collect an audience for a sermon glimpsed this gender gap. The Indian women, he found, "supposing the affair we were upon was of a public nature belonging only to the men . . . , could not readily be persuaded to come and hear." Brainerd to Ebenezer Pemberton, 5 Nov. 1744, in Jonathan Edwards, *The Life of David Brainerd,* ed. Norman Pettit, The Works of Jonathan Edwards, VII (New Haven, Conn., 1985), 579.

48. *PA,* 1st, II, 681–682 (Newcastle). *DRCNY,* VII, 259 ("foolish"); *PWJ,* IX, 865 ("old woman"). And see *PA,* 1st, III, 417, 418; Zeisberger, *History,* 116, 124–125.

Such talk carried even heavier meaning because Delawares, as a people, were sometimes called "women." Scholars disagree about the title's significance. Some see it as a denigration, a way of forbidding this people from participation in diplomatic discussion. Others argue that it was an honorific, giving Delawares a special role, akin to that of women in a town, as peacemakers. The statements about women included here, however, are so derogatory that they are not open to much debate. For discussion of Delawares as women, see C. A. Weslager, *The Delaware Indians: A History* (New Brunswick, N.J., 1972), 180–181; Jennings, *Ambiguous Iroquois Empire,* 45–46, 161–162; idem, " 'Pennsylvania Indians' and the Iroquois," in Daniel K. Richter and James H. Merrell, eds., *Beyond the Covenant Chain: The Iroquois and Their Neighbors in Indian North America, 1600–1800* (Syracuse, N.Y., 1987), 79–80; Jay Miller, "The Delaware as Women: A Symbolic Solution," *American Ethnologist,* I (1974), 507–514; "Moses Titamy's Accot. of Indian Complaints &ca.," n.d., FA, I, 65.

49. *MPCP,* III, 572–573, 578.

50. *Ibid.,* II, 548.

51. *Ibid.,* IV, 733.

52. Claus, Memoirs, 4–8, 13–17. The journey is in *Journals of Claus and Weiser.*

53. Wallace, *Weiser,* ch. 3; Weiser, *Autobiography,* 15, 17.

54. J. Frederick Fausz, "Middlemen in Peace and War: Virginia's Earliest Indian Interpreters, 1608–1632," *VMHB,* XCV (1987), 41–64; Patricia Galloway, "Talking with Indians: Interpreters and Diplomacy in French Louisiana," in

Winthrop D. Jordan and Sheila L. Skemp, eds., *Race and Family in the Colonial South* (Jackson, Miss., 1987), 109–129.

55. *MPCP,* IV, 733; the invitation is on 730. In this light his sanguine assessment of finding another *Tarachiawagon* looks more like an attempt to politely decline Virginia's invitation than a realistic survey of possible candidates. And see Logstown Treaty, 151–152, 172–173. Later some Iroquois were persuaded to send children to New England for schooling. James Axtell, "Dr. Wheelock's Little Red School," in idem, *The European and the Indian: Essays in the Ethnohistory of Colonial North America* (New York, 1981), 87–109.

56. *PA,* 1st, II, 646.

57. *MPCP,* VIII, 756, 770. For more on Kisheta, consult *PHB,* II, 241, 305–306, 355, 448, 458, 648. If, as some believe, Kisheta was Ogaghradarisha, an elderly Onondaga, the child might have been sent to Philadelphia in 1756 (*MPCP,* VII, 157–158, 301).

58. *MPCP,* V, 518, 543, 546; Weiser 1751, 10 July; *PA,* 8th, V, 3809; Claus, *Memoirs,* 13–15; Peters to Weiser, 3 Jan. and 11 July 1752, RPP, III, 53, 57; Wallace, *Weiser,* 323, 332, 337–339. For the later assessments, *PA,* 1st, IV, 41; *MPCP,* VIII, 631–632, 638.

59. *MPCP,* III, 153.

60. Jacqueline Peterson, "Prelude to Red River: A Social Portrait of the Great Lakes Métis," *Ethnohistory,* XXV (1978), 41–67; Jennifer S. H. Brown, *Strangers in Blood: Fur Trade Company Families in Indian Country* (Vancouver, 1980); Peterson and Brown, *The New Peoples: Being and Becoming Métis in North America* (Lincoln, Neb., 1985); Dennis F. K. Madill, "Riel, Red River, and Beyond: New Developments in Métis History," in Colin G. Calloway, ed., *New Directions in American Indian History* (Norman, Okla., 1988), 49–78.

61. Sylvester K. Stevens and Donald H. Kent, eds., *Wilderness Chronicles of Northwestern Pennsylvania* (Harrisburg, Pa., 1941), 19 ("influence"). *PA,* 1st, I, 425 ("one of us"; see also Treaty between Pennsylvania and Indians, Philadelphia, 6 Oct. 1732, DSP, in *Iroq. Ind.,* Reel 10). *PA,* 1st, I, 328 ("Stands firm"). For Chartier, William A. Hunter, *Peter Chartier: Knave of the Wild Frontier,* Cumberland County Historical Society, Historical Papers, IX, no. 4 (1973); Jennings, *Ambiguous Iroquois Empire,* 269–270; White, *Middle Ground,* 189–193.

62. Stevens and Kent, eds., *Wilderness Chronicles,* 19 ("esteemed"). *PA,* 1st, I, 330, 394, 425; *MPCP,* III, 459; *CVSP,* I, 231.

63. Stevens and Kent, eds., *Wilderness Chronicles,* 19.

64. Jennings, *Ambiguous Iroquois Empire,* 269–270; White, *Middle Ground,* 189–192; *MPCP,* IV, 757–758; Deposition of Peter Tostee, James Dinnen, and George Croghan, 14 May 1745, RPP, II, 32; Hanna, *Wilderness Trail,* I, 311–312.

65. Weiser to Peters[?], 24 Jan. 1745/6, DSP, 966.F.24 ("wicked," "cowart"); *MPCP,* IV, 757–758, V, 2 ("capable"), 5 ("treacherous"). White, *Middle Ground,* 191 *(francois métis).*

66. A good summary of Montour's public career is Howard Lewin, "A Frontier Diplomat: Andrew Montour," *Pennsylvania History,* XXXIII (1966), 153–186.

67. *MPCP,* V, 290; *PA,* 1st, II, 12 (Weiser, 1748). *MPCP,* VI, 151, 160 (Weiser, Indian and white). For Montour as Indian, see *ibid.,* 588, VII, 64; *Arch. Md.,* VI, 342; for Peters's views, see Peters, Diary, 30 Sept., 1, 26 Oct. 1758, RPP. For Montour as white, see Reichel, ed., *Memorials,* I, 102; *PWJ,* III, 301.

68. Echnizera is in *MPCP,* VII, 491; Treaty of Logstown, 165. For Oughsara, Hanna, *Wilderness Trail,* I, 245.

69. Reichel, ed., *Memorials,* I, 95–96.

70. An excellent discussion of how frontier peoples used clothing as social markers is Timothy J. Shannon, "Dressing for Success on the Mohawk Frontier: Hendrick, William Johnson, and the Indian Fashion," *WMQ,* 3d ser., LIII (1996), 13–42.

71. *PWJ,* IX, 494; *PA,* 1st, III, 42 (commission). Peters to Weiser, 6 Feb. 1753, CCW, I, 38 (wampum). *Arch. Md.,* VI, 139 ("useful"); *CVSP,* I, 245 ("Character"). For his importance to Ohio Indians, see *MPCP,* V, 54, 455, 497, 540, 683; *CVSP,* I, 245–247; Richard Peters to the Proprietors, 11 Sept. 1753, PMOC, VI, 105. For his being a member of the Iroquois council, see Logstown Treaty, 165; Peters to Weiser, 6 Feb. 1753, CCW, I, 38; Peters to the Proprietor, 7 Feb. 1753, PMOC, VI, 5; *MPCP,* V, 540, 607, 683.

72. James H. Merrell, " 'Their Very Bones Shall Fight': The Catawba-Iroquois Wars," in Richter and Merrell, eds., *Beyond the Covenant Chain,* 124, 128 (father); *PA,* 2d, VII, 156 (uncle); *MPCP,* III, 295 (aunt), VII, 95–96 (Delaware). There is considerable uncertainty about Montour's second wife. Some have said she was an Oneida (Hagedorn, "Montour," in Szasz, ed., *Between Indian and White Worlds,* 48), and indeed she was clearly connected to the Oneidas (*PWJ,* IX, 661–662, 871, X, 481). But she also knew Conoy (633–634) and was identified by Montour himself as a kinswoman of a Conoy chief (Peters, Diary, 25 Oct. 1758, RPP).

73. *MPCP,* V, 290.

74. Peters to the Proprietor, 6 Nov. 1753, PMOC, VI, 115; Lewin, "Montour," *Pa. History,* XXXIII (1966), 158; RPLB, 1737–1750, 365; Peters, Diary, 13 Oct. 1758, RPP (Peters's views). Weiser to Peters, Feb. [?] 1753, CCW, I, 17 ("pride"); Weiser to [?], [1753–1754], *ibid.,* II, 25 ("Impudent," "Sorry"); *PA,* 1st, II, 12 ("hard to please"). *PWJ,* III, 778 ("cannot Trust"). *MJNY,* 175 (Iroquois).

75. *PA,* 1st, I, 750.

76. *MPCP,* IV, 653, *PWJ,* III, 940 ("Consequence"); *PA,* 1st, I, 750. The ritual is in Logstown Treaty, 165. For wampum, see ch. V.

77. *MPCP*, V, 615; and see Epilogue.

78. Weiser to Logan, 2 Sept. 1736, LP, 10/59 ("greatest right"). Civility, the Conestoga go-between, also had Oneida ties. Born a Susquehannock (Conestoga), he was adopted by Oneidas, then at some point returned to his homeland on the lower Susquehanna (*MPCP*, III, 133, 572). It might also be significant that he and other mediators still had kin living in Iroquoia: *MPCP*, II, 204 (Shawydoohungh), IV, 53 (Civility); *MJNY*, 62 (Shickellamy).

   A number of Indian go-betweens did have foreign language skills. Pisquetomen, like Shawydoohungh, spoke English and served as an interpreter. Many others knew another Indian language—Newcastle spoke Shawnee, Civility Delaware—suggesting that they, through trade, marriage, or diplomacy, already had extensive experience with another people.

79. Civility, variously described as a headman, may be an exception to this rule.

80. Weiser to Logan, 16 Sept. 1736, LP, 10/62; Weiser to Logan, 25 Sept. 1736, LC, IV, 61. See Richter, *Ordeal of the Longhouse*, 46–47, 274–275. *MPCP*, VIII, 124.

81. Morris to [?], French and Indian War, 1756, Case 15, Box 18, Gratz Coll., HSP ("low"); Thomas Lee to Weiser, 11 Dec. 1748, RPP, II, 115 ("lyes"); Peters, quoted in Zimmerman, "Indian Trade," 174 ("worthless"); *MPCP*, V, 630 ("Wretches"; see also 749).

82. *MPCP*, III, 137 ("insolent"); Marshe, 184 ("impudent"); Logan to the Penns, 6 mo. 1731, JLLB, III [1721–1732], 343 ("abusive"); Logan to Isaac Taylor, 4 Nov. 1719, Taylor Papers, Correspondence, 1683–1723, doc. 2931, HSP ("talk high"). Edward Shippen to Daniel Lowry, 12 Feb. 1752, Edward Shippen Letterbook, 1751–1752, PSF, Small Books, no. 10 ("laughing"); Smith, *Account*, 110 ("burlesque"); *PA*, 1st, I, 505 ("Oaths"). The "Oaths and Imprecations" in this instance were from Thomas Cresap, who in the 1730s lived on the Susquehanna River on lands contested by Maryland and Pennsylvania. Cresap, a trader, got his goods from Philadelphia merchants. PSF, XXVII, Bills and Receipts, 1721–1754, 90 *et passim;* David Magaw to Edward Shippen, 25 Jan. 1745/6, *ibid.,* I; Edward Shippen to James Burd, 19 Dec. 1752, Edward Shippen Letterbook, 1751–1752, PSF.

   They were also, often, in debt. Davison, the Indians' "Ears," was thrown in jail for debt (*MPCP*, VII, 60), and Croghan often kept away from Philadelphia to avoid his creditors (*PA*, 1st, II, 484; *MPCP*, VI, 743–744; Nicholas B. Wainwright, *George Croghan, Wilderness Diplomat* [Chapel Hill, N.C., 1959], index, *Croghan, George, debts*).

83. *PA*, 1st, II, 690 ("ignorant"); *PHB*, II, 182 ("observant"). *PWJ*, VII, 1040 ("Ideas"; see also IX, 43; *DRCNY*, VI, 540–541).

84. *Arch. Md.,* VIII, 342 ("sweet profits," referring to the fur trade on the Pennsylvania border). Shamokin Diary, 26 Jan. 1748, MCA, 6/121/4/1 ("eagerness").

85. *PA,* 1st, I, 304–306.

86. Samuel Hopkins, *Historical Memoirs, Relating to the Housatunnuck Indians* . . . (Boston, 1753, Evans 7023), 90 ("vile Sort"); *MPCP,* III, 156 (Swindel). *MPCP,* II, 471 (matchcoats), 511 ("waylay"), 554 (corn), V, 318–319 (stones); 87–88, 229, 232, 237; Samuel Blunston to the Proprietor, 25 Aug. 1735, Lancaster County, Miscellaneous Papers, 1724–1772, 19, HSP (gun).

87. Hopkins, *Historical Memoirs,* 90–91 ("debauch"; see also Zeisberger, *Diaries,* 98–99); Smith, *Account,* 74–75 ("Oonasahroona").

88. *MPCP,* III, 46–47, V, 676.

89. Petition of James Le Tort, [1724?], Indian Traders file, Indian Box 2, CCA ("Infancy"). For landlords, see Account of Indian Debts Due James Le Tort, 8ber 1704, LP, 11/4; William A. Hunter, ed., "Traders on the Ohio: 1730," *Western Pennsylvania Historical Magazine,* XXXV (1952), 35, 92; Bailey, ed., *Ohio Co. Papers,* 129 (also 52, 112). McClure, *Diary,* 53 ("successful trade"). Bartram, *Observations,* 15 (Shamokin). For other liaisons, consult RPLB, 1737–1750, 381; *PWJ,* VII, 182, IX, 456 (might not have been an Indian woman, but a colonial woman raised by Indians; see Cammerhoff, 169); Bailey, ed., *Ohio Co. Papers,* 139; *PA,* 1st, III, 437, 460; *PWJ,* XII, 1097–1098.

90. On Indians taking English names, Post 1758, 253, n.96; *PWJ,* XI, 723; Minutes of Conferences held at Fort Pitt, 26 Apr. 1768, in *Iroq. Ind.,* Reel 29 (Le Tort); *MPCP,* VIII, 489; Bailey, ed., *Ohio Co. Papers,* 41, 46, 51, 55 *et passim* (McKee). *MPCP,* II, 556 (Bizaillon allowed); *PA,* 1st, I, 341, 425 (Cartlidge); RPLB, 1737–1750, 381 (McKee).

91. Gist, 10.

92. RPLB, 1737–1750, 323 (1748); Edward Shippen to William Allen, 18 Dec. 1758, PSF, III (1758); Kenny 1761–63, 186 (1763).

93. *MPCP,* VII, 354–355 ("surprized"). Quoted in Wallace, *Weiser,* 335–336 ("illiterate"); Peters to the Proprietors, 26 June 1756, Peters Letters to Proprietaries, 1755–1757, 66, Gratz Coll., HSP ("vile Rascal").

94. *MPCP,* V, 122 ("acquainted"). McKee to [?], 14 Aug. 1754, Berks and Montgomery Counties, Miscellaneous Manuscripts, 1693–1869, 181, HSP ("Cups"); *PWJ,* VII, 315 (ammunition, "reserved"), X, 597 ("sulky").

95. For Le Tort, see Logan to Edward Farmer, 20 Mar. 1703, JLLB, 1702–1726. His trip is in *MPCP,* II, 101–102; Edward Armstrong, ed., and Deborah Logan, comp., *Correspondence Between William Penn and James Logan, Secretary of the Province of Pennsylvania, and Others, 1700–1750,* 2 vols., HSP, *Memoirs,* IX–X (1870–1872), I, 197. For Cartlidge, see Logan to Edward Shippen, 3 Sept. 1730, LP, 1/98; Memorandum, 14 11 mo. 1731/2, *ibid.,* 2/18; Logan to Edmond Cartlidge, 15 Apr. 1732, to Samuel Blunston, 23 May 1732, to Samuel Storke, 21 June 1723 [*sic:* 1732], Logan Letterbook, 1731–1732, 50b, 60, 68, Maria Dickinson Logan Pprs., HSP; Logan to John

Wright, 24 Dec. 1732, Logan to Edmond Cartlidge, 24 Dec. 1732, JLLB, 1716–1743, 308–309.

96. *PA*, 8th, I, 653 (assembly). Chalkley, *Journal*, 50 (Conestoga).

97. Brainerd to Ebenezer Pemberton, 5 Nov. 1744, in Edwards, *Life of Brainerd*, ed. Pettit, 578.

98. For Sergeant, see James Axtell, *The Invasion Within: The Contest of Cultures in Colonial North America* (New York, 1985), 196–200; Hopkins, *Historical Memoirs*. For David Brainerd, consult Edwards, *Life of Brainerd*, ed. Pettit, 293–295, 320–332, 419–426, 578–579, 581–583. For David's brother, John, see Brainerd, *John Brainerd*, 230–250.

Background on Moravians can be found in Paul A. W. Wallace, ed., *The Travels of John Heckewelder in Frontier America* (Pittsburgh, Pa., 1958), Introduction; Gillian Lindt Gollin, *Moravians in Two Worlds: A Study of Changing Communities* (New York, 1967); Beverly Prior Smaby, *The Transformation of Moravian Bethlehem: From Communal Mission to Family Economy* (Philadelphia, 1988), ch. 1. For the missions, see Carter, "Moravians at Shamokin," *Procs. Northumberland Co. Hist. Soc.*, IX (1937), 52–72; Elma E. Gray, *Wilderness Christians: The Moravian Mission to the Delaware Indians* (Ithaca, N.Y., 1956); Wallace, *Weiser*, chs. 15, 17; John R. Weinlick, *Count Zinzendorf* (New York, 1956), 174–177; Earl P. Olmstead, *Blackcoats Among the Delaware: David Zeisberger on the Ohio Frontier* (Kent, Ohio, 1991).

99. *DRCNY*, VII, 970; *PWJ*, V, 531 (English missionaries). Shamokin Diary, 29–30 Sept., 1, 6 Oct. 1745, MCA, 28/217/12B/1 (harvesting corn); *ibid.*, 14 Oct. (beans); 27 Mar. 1748, 6/121/4/1 ("ready to assist"); *MJNY*, 174, 184–185, 189–190, 201 (planting); Cammerhoff, 173 (Macks). Also *MJNY*, 171, 203, 206; White, *Middle Ground*, 328.

100. *MJNY*, 229 ("separate"; see also 162, 181, 192; Shamokin Diary, 3 Nov. 1745, MCA, 28/217/12b/1). Erminie Wheeler-Voegelin, ed., "Heckewelder to du Ponceau," *Ethnohistory*, VI (1959), 76–77 (Mack and Zeisberger); Edmund De Schweinitz, *The Life and Times of David Zeisberger, The Western Pioneer and Apostle of the Indians* (Philadelphia, 1870), 133–134; Spangenberg, 57; *MJNY*, 25, 97, 109; John W. Jordan, ed., "Rev. John Martin Mack's Narrative of a Visit to Onondaga in 1752," *PMHB*, XXIX (1905), 346, 353; Post to Peter Boehler, 30 Nov. 1760, MCA, 28/219/7/21; Wallace, ed., *Travels of Heckewelder*, 42. Post's name is in *MPCP*, VIII, 690.

101. See ch. II.

102. *PA*, 1st, III, 579 ("future harvest"), 703; Post to Peters, 2 Feb. 1760, MCA, 28/219/7/14.

103. Meeting between Gov. Hamilton and Brothers Joseph, Herman, and Rogers, 17 June 1752, MCA, 34/317/1/3 ("Maxim"). Reichel, ed., *Memorials*, I, 87; *MJNY*, 175, 179. David Zeisberger occasionally read or wrote a

letter or carried a message, but this was unusual before 1770 (*MJNY,* 224; *DHNY,* IV, 310; *PA,* 1st, IV, 74–75, 78; *MPCP,* VIII, 698). He also attended some 1750s treaties in an unofficial capacity (De Schweinitz, *Zeisberger,* 242, 245–246, 251).

104. Meeting with Hamilton, 17 June 1752, MCA, 34/317/1/3; "State of the Case respecting the Brethren's going among the five Nations, humbly laid before his Honour the Governour," 18 June 1752, *ibid.,* 34/317/1/4. *MPCP,* V, 575–576. De Schweinitz, *Zeisberger,* 123–130, 177–178, 223; *PA,* 8th, VI, 5482–5483.

105. Shamokin Diary, 25–26 Jan., 16 Mar. 1748, MCA, 6/121/4/1 (friendly encounters). Quoted in Carter, "Moravians at Shamokin," *Procs. Northumberland Co. Hist. Soc.,* IX (1937), 67; *MJNY,* 142, 144. See also Edwards, *Life of Brainerd,* ed. Pettit, 580; Brainerd, *John Brainerd,* 234, 237, 239.

106. Edwards, *Life of Brainerd,* ed. Pettit, 323.

107. Brainerd's visit to the Susquehanna is recounted in *ibid.,* 324–331, 420–425 ("devil now reigns" on 324). Shamokin Diary, 12 Oct. 1745, MCA, 28/217/12B/1 ("Ridiculed"), 2 Apr. 1748, 6/121/4/1 ("Evill things"; see Jordan, ed., "Mack's Narrative," *PMHB,* XXIX [1905], 346–349; *Journals of Claus and Weiser,* 13–14). *PWJ,* VIII, 8 ("steal their Lands"). For a summary of Indian opposition, *PWJ,* VII, 596–602.

108. For drink and noise, see *MJNY,* 186, 188; Martin Mack, Journey to Wyoming, 11 Apr. 1745, MCA, 28/217/12/3; Shamokin Diary, 17–18 Sept. 1745, 28/217/12B/1 ("Beasts"; see also 16, 19 Oct., 2 Nov. 1745); 20, 23 ("Swaring Bitterly") Feb., 17–18 Mar. 1748, 6/121/4/1. "Constant danger" quoted in Carter, "Moravians at Shamokin," *Procs. Northumberland Co. Hist. Soc.,* IX (1937), 64 (see also 72).

109. Shamokin Diary, 20 ("Deceit"), 25 Sept., 24 Oct. 1745, MCA, 28/217/12B/1 (Brainerd); Reichel, ed., *Memorials,* I, 91, 93.

110. *MJNY,* 35 ("my own people"), 51 ("not at home"), 61 ("especially glad"), 136, 193–194; Shamokin Diary, 17 Oct. 1745, MCA, 28/217/12B/1.

111. *PA,* 1st, IV, 90; *MPCP,* VI, 360, VIII, 730; Indians—Treaty at Easton, July 1756, in "Indians (transferred from Society Collections)," HSP.

112. Merrell, "Customes of Our Countrey," in Bailyn and Morgan, eds., *Strangers within the Realm,* 119–120; Edward McM. Larrabee, "Recurrent Themes and Sequences in North American Indian-European Culture Contact," *Transactions of the American Philosophical Society,* new ser., LXVI, Part 7 (1976); Gregory Evans Dowd, *The Indians of New Jersey* (Trenton, N.J., 1992); Weslager, *Delaware Indians,* ch. 12; Wallace, *Teedyuscung,* chs. 1–2.

113. William A. Hunter, "Moses (Tunda) Tatamy, Delaware Indian Diplomat," in Herbert C. Kraft, ed., *A Delaware Indian Symposium,* Anthropological Series, no. 4 (Harrisburg, Pa., 1974), 72; Brainerd, *John Brainerd,* 243–244, 248; Wallace, *Teedyuscung,* 18–19.

114. A detailed account of Moses Tatamy's conversion experience is in Brainerd, *Journal,* 1745, APS, 1–7. See Richard W. Pointer, " 'Poor Indians' and the 'Poor in Spirit': The Indian Impact on David Brainerd," *New England Quarterly,* LXVII (1994), 403–426; Jane T. Merritt, "Dreaming of the Savior's Blood: Moravians and the Indian Great Awakening in Pennsylvania," *WMQ,* 3d ser., LIV (1997), 723–746.

115. Edwards, *Life of Brainerd,* ed. Pettit, 332 ("what a difference"). Brainerd, *Journal,* 1745, APS, 1–2 ("well fitted"), 6 ("deportment"); John Woolman, *The Journal of John Woolman* (Boston, 1909 [orig. pub. 1871]), 184 ("conduct"). Brainerd, *John Brainerd,* 248 ("method of living"). Loskiel, *History,* Part II, 24 ("housekeeping").

116. For hunting, John Carson to Gov. Denny, 21 Jan., 24 Apr. 1758, RPCEC, B8, 1742, 1862; Joseph Shippen, Jr., to Edward Shippen, 20 Mar. 1758, PSF, III; Fort Augusta, Ledger A, 27, 45, Gratz Coll., Case 17, Box 20, HSP (Chilloway, who also wore earrings [U. J. Jones, *History of the Early Settlement of the Juniata Valley* . . . (Harrisburg, Pa., 1940 [orig. pub. 1889]), 324]). Charles Beatty, *The Journal of a Two Months Tour; With a View of Promoting Religion Among the Frontier Inhabitants of Pensylvania, And of Introducing Christianity Among the Indians to the Westward of the Alegh-geny Mountains* . . . (London, 1768), 36, 38–39 (Peepy).

For clothes, John Pumpshire to Israel Pemberton, 23 Oct. 1756, FA, I, 199; Account, 20 May 1758, *ibid.,* 481; Pemberton, Account, 1756, *ibid.,* III, 439; Account, 24–26 Apr. 1760, *ibid., 455* (also Bible, treaty); Account, 7 Apr. 1761, *ibid.,* IV, 83; Reichel, ed., *Memorials,* I, 236; Job Chilloway Account, 20 July 1762, James Burd, Account Book, 1753–1763, APS. For portmanteau, see *MPCP,* VIII, 496.

For Indians reading and writing, see *MPCP,* VII, 189 (for the author, see John Pumpshire to the commander of Fort Allen, 1 July 1756 [copy], and Timothy Horsfield to William Parsons, 7 July 1756, HP, I, 155, 177; Peters to Weiser, 11 July 1756, RPP, IV, 66); John Pumpshire to Israel Pemberton, 23 Oct. 1756, FA, I, 199; Petition to Israel Pemberton, 8 Mar. 1758, *ibid.,* 427; Stephen Calvins [*sic*] to Isaac Stille, 30 Aug. 1760, *ibid.,* IV, 11; Watson, *Annals of Philadelphia,* I, 171; Post 1758, 252–253, 261; *PA,* 1st, III, 739.

117. Benjamin Lightfoot to Israel Pemberton, 7 Sept. 1760, FA, IV, 19 (tea). Account, 1 5 mo. 1762, *ibid.,* 367; Watson, *Annals of Philadelphia,* II, 171–172; Preston to Watson, 5 Aug. 1828, Watson's Annals (ms. notes), II, 558, HSP; Hunter, "Tatamy," in Kraft, ed., *Delaware Symposium,* 82; Brainerd, *John Brainerd,* 278, 280 (children in colonial schools).

Enlistments are in Geo. Reynolds to William Edwards, 14 July 1756, HP, I, 221; "Jersey Indians Listed with Capt Johnson," n.d., LP, 11/65; Brainerd, *John Brainerd,* 314, 316. For attorneys, see *PA,* 1st, I, 630–631, 641–642, III, 341–346 (quotation on 346).

118. Reichel, ed., *Memorials,* I, 102 ("an eye on him"); Loskiel, *History,* Part II, 24 ("listened").

119. Governor's Directions to William Logan, [June 1756], LP, 11/64 ("disposition"; see *MPCP,* VII, 144). Loskiel, *History,* Part II, 24; Reichel, ed., *Memorials,* I, 26–27; *MPCP,* VIII, 150 (Tatamy). *PWJ,* XII, 305 (Peepy; see also Zane 1761, 16–19 October).

120. Zane 1761, 15 October.

121. "Unstable" quoted in Wallace, *Teedyuscung,* 40. For Teedyuscung's behavior, see *ibid.,* esp. 2, 14–18, 41–43, 52; Minutes of the Friendly Association, 1755–1757, 23, HSP.

122. Peters to Penn, 22 Nov. 1756, PMOC, VIII, 201 ("sort of People," "Riffraff"); RPLB, 1737–1750, 157–158 ("Rascalls"); Peters to the Proprietor, 14 Feb. 1757, Peters Letters to the Proprietaries, 1755–1757, 140, Gratz Coll., HSP ("straggling"). Weiser, "Observations"; *PA,* 1st, IV, 40. See also *PWJ,* VII, 598.

123. Peters to Penn (extract), 4 Aug. 1756, PMIA, II, 99 (Teedyuscung). *PWJ,* II, 788 ("unacquainted"; see also V, 420).

124. "All those Inds. who from their situation and our endeavors are become in some measure Civilized have hitherto derived no advantages from it," noted William Johnson in explaining why "Uncivilized Indians" resist missionaries, "that on the Contrary they are poor, abject, full of Avarice, Hypocrisy, & in short have imbibed all our Vices, without any of our Good Qualities" (*PWJ,* VII, 597). *Ibid.,* 599 ("deportment"; see also Zane 1761, 17 and 19 October).

125. Edwards, *Life of Brainerd,* ed. Pettit, 426; Shamokin Diary, 5–6 June 1749, MCA, 6/121/5/2. Onondagas even had different words for "Indians," "Christian People–Europeans," and "Christian People–Indians." See Eben Norton Horsford, ed., *Zeisberger's Indian Dictionary . . . Printed from the Original Manuscript in Harvard College Library* (Cambridge, Mass., 1887), 102, 141.

126. Other examples of colonial women taken captive are in *MPCP,* IV, 633; Gist, 14. For the fortunes of captives, see James Axtell, "The White Indians of Colonial America," in *The European and the Indian: Essays in the Ethnohistory of Colonial North America* (New York, 1981), 168–206; Alden T. Vaughan and Daniel K. Richter, "Crossing the Cultural Divide: Indians and New Englanders," *Proceedings of the American Antiquarian Society,* XC (1980), 23–99; White, *Middle Ground,* 326–327; June Namias, *White Captives: Gender and Ethnicity on the American Frontier* (Chapel Hill, N.C., 1993); John Demos, *The Unredeemed Captive: A Family Story from Early America* (New York, 1994). Matthew C. Ward ("Fighting the 'Old Women': Indian Strategy on the Virginia and Pennsylvania Frontier," *VMHB,* CIII [1995], 316) offers a conservative estimate of 1,000 people taken captive. Deserters were fewer, and got

less attention. See *MPCP*, VIII, 486, 488, 493–494, 617–618, 758; *PWJ*, XI, 224.

127. *PWJ*, XI, 169 ("deep Attachment"); *PHB*, V, 318 ("just the same"), VI, 515.

128. *PA*, 1st, III, 478–479 (Burke; see also 437, 460; *MPCP*, VIII, 143, 147). For questioning, see Examination of Lawrence Burke, 9 July 1758, RPCEC, B9, 1960; *PWJ*, XI, 224–225, 241; *PHB*, ser. 21650, I, 100–103, 112, 116, 119.

129. *PWJ*, IX, 591, 779. Jonathan Ryal, a German who left the Oswego garrison in 1759 to live among the Nanticokes and Conoys, was "a Good Man" who "had been sent of [*sic*] Errands by them" (*MPCP*, VIII, 493). In January 1768 Gersham Hicks, "formerly a Prisoner with the Indians," carried a message to Indians (*MPCP*, IX, 444, 453–454, 480), apparently having shed some of the mistrust he generated earlier.

130. Peters to Weiser, 28 July 1757, CCW, II, 133; *PHB*, II, 344 (Burke). Nathaniel Holland to Israel Pemberton, 21 8 mo. 1760, FA, IV, 3; *SCP*, II, 168; *PWJ*, X, 533, XI, 439, 451, 460, 598 (Owens). McClure, *Diary*, 55; White, *Middle Ground*, 329 (Nickels).

131. *MPCP*, VIII, 758.

132. *PA*, 8th, VI, 5361, VII, 5894–5895 (redeemed captives forgetting). For captives fleeing, see Nathaniel Holland to Israel Pemberton, 27 Mar. 1759, FA, III, 51; Report, Aug. 1761, *ibid.*, V, 15; Hays, 79; Zeisberger, *Diaries*, 47–48, 59.

133. Smith, *Account*, 106–107. See also *PA*, 8th, VII, 5509–5510.

134. *PA*, 1st, III, 478 ("King & Country"); Israel Pemberton to Forbes, 4 7 mo. 1758, FA, II, 95 (Burke; see also *PHB*, II, 381). Holland to Pemberton, 12 Sept. 1760, FA, IV, 27 (Owens). *PHB*, ser. 21650, I, 112; VI, 522–526 (Hicks a "Notorious Villain"), 541 ("attached").

　　Owens was proof of how desperate a man could get. He showed up from the Indian countries in June 1764 with five scalps, including, it was said, those of his Indian wife and family, whom he had killed as they slept. But even this failed to convince colonists of his loyalty. "As he was always much attached to Indians, I fancy he began to fear he was unsafe amongst them, & killed them rather [to?] make his peace with ye English than from any dislike either to them, or their principles" (*PWJ*, XI, 224–225, 241).

135. "Complete mess," quoted in Wallace, *Weiser*, 141. *MPCP*, III, 286 (Burt).

136. *MJNY*, 178 ("wander"). Go-betweens called their enterprise "errands" in *Translation of a German Letter, wrote by Conrad Weiser* . . . (Philadelphia, 1757, Evans 8062), 6; *MPCP*, VI, 196.

137. Reichel, ed., *Memorials*, I, 79 (Weiser); *MPCP*, III, 153.

138. For Post wanting a salary, see Peters to Post, 24 Jan. 1760, MCA, 28/219/8/7; Kenny 1761–63, 194–195. *MPCP*, II, 555 (1711), IV, 653 ("rewarded"; see also VII, 630–631; *PA*, 1st, II, 218; *PGW*, I, 97, 101, 106).

PA, 8th, VI, 4655 ("for Services"). Newcastle's Charges, 1756, Northampton Co., Misc. Mss., Bethlehem and Vicinity, 29, HSP; "Indian Charges from ye Arrival of . . . Thos. Penn to his departure," PMIA, I, 46 (Weiser).

139. Thomas Lee to Weiser, 30 Aug. 1744, *The Lee Family Papers, 1742–1795,* ed. Paul P. Hoffman (Charlottesville, Va., 1966), microfilm, Reel 1.

140. *MPCP,* III, 382; "Journal of Daniels Journey to the Allegheny," PPEC, II, 29; *PA,* 1st, III, 469, 627; "My Certificate to ye Assembly in behalf of Edm. Cartlidge, Aug. 1736," LP, 10/117. For Weiser waiting, see *PA,* 8th, IV, 3357; Peters to Thomas Penn, 18 Mar. 1758, Lardner Family Papers, HSP; Weiser to Peters, 16 Dec. 1758, CCW, II, 141.

141. *MPCP,* VI, 344, 359–360.

142. *PWJ,* III, 940 ("Mercenary motive"). *MPCP,* IX, 775 (horse; see also VIII, 490, 756–757, 770; Post 1760, 17 June; Account, 8 May 1758, FA, II, 238–239.

143. *PA,* 1st, I, 661 (Shickellamy's first house); 2d, VII, 262; Indian Charges paid Conrad Weiser, 12 Dec. 1759, PPM, XI, 113 (second house); Wallace, *Teedyuscung,* ch. 14.

144. One of the Indians' complaints about Teedyuscung was his lack of generosity with goods obtained from colonists. Samuel Foulke to Israel Pemberton, 26 July 1758, FA, II, 151.

145. Israel Pemberton to Isaac Zane, 5 June 1758, FA, I, 527 (Osternados). *MPCP,* VII, 87; William Logan to the Governor, 6 May 1757, LP, 11/48 (Scarouyady). Post 1758, 236 (Pisquetomen).

146. *PA,* 1st, II, 725 ("raw bon'd"), 727 ("Force of Liquor"; see also 724; Wallace, *Teedyuscung,* chs. 8, 10, 15). Zane 1758, 417–426 (sober); Zane 1761, 15 Oct. ("coat Pockets").

147. For tavern debts, Wallace, *Weiser,* 339–340; Lewin, "Montour," *Pa. History,* XXXIII (1966), 158; Penn Manuscripts, Accounts, II, 5, doc. 80a, 10, doc. 85b, HSP; *PWJ,* X, 148. Kenny 1758–59, 429 ("laugh"). *PWJ,* III, 4 (Croghan; see also 874).

148. Toasts, GCP, 8/14 (see also Croghan's Bill of Entertainment, 19 Mar. 1768, *ibid.*); "copiously" is quoted in Robert Grant Crist, *George Croghan of Pennsboro* (Harrisburg, Pa., 1965), 7. Kenny 1758–59, 438 (Teedyuscung fight).

149. Peter C. Mancall, *Deadly Medicine: Indians and Alcohol in Early America* (Ithaca, N.Y., 1995).

150. Some—including Pisquetomen, Croghan, and Scarouyady—retired from public business until they recovered from a binge; others, such as Teedyuscung and John Davison, drew criticism because they made the mistake of staggering on instead of holing up.

151. Post 1758, 283–285; PHB, V, 330 (Croghan). "An Account of the Captivity of Hugh Gibson Among the Delaware Indians . . . ," 1756–1759, *Coll. Mass. Hist. Soc.,* 3d ser., VI (1837), 144–146, 153 (Pisquetomen). *PA,* 1st, II, 645

(Scarouyady); *MPCP,* III, 501 (Chartier), 504 ("Ill will"), IV, 650 (curt with Weiser). Peters to the Proprietaries, 16 Mar. 1752, PMOC, V, 217 ("imperiousness"); Reichel, ed., *Memorials,* I, 107 ("impatience"; also *Journals of Claus and Weiser,* 43, 46); Bartram, *Observations,* 66–67 ("vexation").

152. Peters to the Proprietors, 14 Dec. 1752, PMOC, V, 311; *PA,* 1st, II, 144. "Public performances" is David Brainerd's phrase (Brainerd, Journal, 1745, APS, 6). Wallace, *Teedyuscung,* 19. *DRCNY,* VI, 795–796 (Weiser).

153. *MPCP,* III, 46 (Civility), IV, 88 ("equally divided"; see also 581; RPLB, 1737–1750, 273). Kenny 1758–59, 433 (Pisquetomen); [Thomson], *Enquiry,* 173; Chew, 314 (Croghan).

154. *MPCP,* IV, 88 (emphasis added).

155. James Lynch, "The Iroquois Confederacy, and the Adoption and Administration of Non-Iroquoian Individuals and Groups Prior to 1756," *Man in the Northeast,* no. 30 (Fall 1985), 84–88.

156. Hays, 75.

157. *Ibid.,* 68, 74–75, 78.

158. *Ibid.,* 78, 81 (emphasis added). "[T]hey Eat it With out Salt," the disgusted and astonished Hays noted, "For [throw?] it up Lik Mad." This apparently was a ritual purgative.

159. *DHNY,* IV, 430 (Johnson). Weiser, "Account," *American Magazine,* Dec. 1744, 667.

160. Bartram, *Observations,* 59; *MPCP,* IV, 661–663, 778 ("engaged"); VI, 112 ("private Councellor"; see also *Journals of Claus and Weiser,* 17–18, 44); Weiser 1751, 10 July ("no European"; see also *MPCP,* V, 541–542).

161. Spangenberg, 428.

162. Delaware Indians to the Governor, 3 Jan. 1740/41, PMIA, IV, 30 (1741); *MPCP,* VIII, 48 (Teedyuscung); Petition to Israel Pemberton, 8 Mar. 1758, FA, I, 427.

II: Finding Friends, 1699–1723

1. *PWP,* II, 243, n.1, 337. For "Esq.," see *MPCP,* I, 326, 372. His biography is in Peter Stebbins Craig, *The 1693 Census of the Swedes on the Delaware: Family Histories of the Swedish Lutheran Church Members Residing in Pennsylvania, Delaware, West New Jersey and Cecil County, Maryland, 1683–1693,* Studies in Swedish American Genealogy, 3 (Winter Park, Fla., 1993), 29, 162–163.

2. For land sales, *PWP,* II, 242–243, 261–267, and map, 491; *PA,* 1st, I, 42–43, 48–49, 62–64, 67, 92–93, 95, 124–125. His house is noted in C. A. Weslager, *The Delaware Indians: A History* (New Brunswick, N.J., 1972), 161.

Other scholars place his "home plantation" after 1678 at Passyunk (Craig, *1693 Census,* 29).

3. *MPCP,* I, 147, 340, 372, 435–436, 447–448, II, 557 ("was living"); *PWP,* II, 242–243, III, 106–107, 187–188, 451–453.

4. This excludes Penn's early approaches to the Iroquois, in which, during these years, the proprietor's reach far exceeded his grasp. See Gary B. Nash, "The Quest for the Susquehanna Valley: New York, Pennsylvania, and the Seventeenth-Century Fur Trade," *New York History,* XLVIII (1967), 3–27; Jennings, *Ambiguous Iroquois Empire,* ch. 12; idem, " 'Pennsylvania Indians' and the Iroquois," in Daniel K. Richter and James H. Merrell, eds., *Beyond the Covenant Chain: The Iroquois and Their Neighbors in Indian North America, 1600–1800* (Syracuse, N.Y., 1987), 80–84.

5. For the movement of these groups into Pennsylvania, see Hanna, *Wilderness Trail;* Barry C. Kent, *Susquehanna's Indians,* Anthropological Series, no. 6 (Harrisburg, Pa., 1989); Paul A. W. Wallace, *Indians in Pennsylvania,* rev. ed., William A. Hunter (Harrisburg, Pa., 1986); Francis Jennings, "Susquehannock," in William C. Sturtevant, series ed., *Handbook of North American Indians,* XV, Bruce G. Trigger, volume ed., *The Northeast* (Washington, D.C., 1978), 366–367; Peter C. Mancall, *Valley of Opportunity: Economic Culture along the Upper Susquehanna, 1700–1800* (Ithaca, N.Y., 1991), ch. 2.

6. This story is from "Petition of Conodahto and Meealloua," 1 3 mo. 1700, LP, 11/2. It has been published in *PWP,* III, 599–602, and Alden Vaughan, gen. ed., *Early American Indian Documents: Treaties and Laws, 1607–1789,* Donald H. Kent, vol. ed., *Pennsylvania and Delaware Treaties, 1629–1739* (Washington, D.C., 1979), I, 97–98.

7. *PA,* 1st, XII, 280.

8. In fact, since the woman was from Carolina and the "Savinnos" were probably emigrants from the southern river that would bear their name, it is possible that these "Naked Indians" were not Miamis from the Great Lakes region who had been attacking Susquehanna River towns (*PWP,* III, 602 n.3), but some southern nation that had raided Meealloua's people along the Savannah.

9. *PWP,* III, 602; *MPCP,* II, 470. Garland, mentioned in Pennsylvania records as early as 1693, might have been related to Susanna and John Garland, who in the early 1670s received licenses from New York officials to trade on the Delaware River. *MPCP,* I, 376; Albright G. Zimmerman, "The Indian Trade of Colonial Pennsylvania" (Ph.D. diss., University of Delaware, 1966), 25–26, 29; Hanna, *Wilderness Trail,* I, 77. The document he carried might be *PA,* 1st, XII, 280.

10. For colonial readings of Indians' failure to plant or their abandonment of planted fields as trouble brewing, see *MPCP,* II, 510, 603, III, 329.

11. He continued in the fur trade for another fifteen years and occasionally brought provincial authorities information about developments in the Indian countries. His later career is in *MPCP*, II, 33, 45, 48, 70–71, 510; Hanna, *Wilderness Trail*, I, 42, 152, 171, 172; James Logan, Account Book, 1712–1720, 47, 54, 151, 154, LP; Logan to John Askew, 16 6 mo. 1715, JLLB, 1712–1715, 299.

12. Unless otherwise noted, this account is derived from *MPCP*, II, 385–390. My spelling of *Bizaillon* is from a signature around this time by Michael's brother Pierre (or Peter). John Parker Account Book [1700–1752], Ms. 33830, n.p., Chester County Historical Society, West Chester, Pa.

13. *MPCP*, II, 244–247. For laws, see *ibid.*, 18–19, 221–222, 247, 300; *Statutes at Large of Pennsylvania, 1682–1809*, 17 vols. (Harrisburg, Pa., 1896–1915), II, 229–231.

14. Shawydoohungh is in *MPCP*, II, 15, 18, 26, 387, 469, 510, 533, 537, 553, 555, 565–566, 574, 607; *PWP*, IV, 55, n.14, 99, n.5; Edward Armstrong, ed., and Deborah Logan, comp., *Correspondence Between William Penn and James Logan, Secretary of the Province of Pennsylvania, and Others, 1700–1750*, 2 vols., HSP, *Memoirs*, IX–X (1870–1872), I, 125, 148, 179, 197–198; Proceedings of the Council at Conestoga, 31 July 1710, PMIA, I, 34; Thomas and Mary Davies, Account, 1703, PPM, IX, 3. The last mention of "Harry" I have found was dated 14 September 1715.

15. Hanna, *Wilderness Trail*, I, chs. 4–5; David H. Landis, "Conoy Indian Town and Peter Bezaillion," *Papers of the Lancaster County Historical Society*, XXXVII (1933), 113–136; Evelyn A. Benson, "The Huguenot LeTorts: First Christian Family on the Conestoga," *Journal of the Lancaster County Historical Society*, LXV (1961), 92–105; Francis Jennings, "The Indian Trade of the Susquehanna Valley," *Procs. APS*, CX (1966), 411–413, 417–418; Lucy L. Rankin, "Pierre Bezaillion," *Susquehanna: Monthly Magazine*, IX, no. 6 (June 1984), 30–31; Francess G. Halpenny, ed., *Dictionary of Canadian Biography*, III (Toronto, 1974), 65–66 (Bizaillon). Zimmerman, "Indian Trade," 49–52, 56–57; *Arch. Md.*, VIII, 342–350, 458–467, 486–487, 517–518, 524, XXIII, 428–429 (Chartier).

16. *Arch. Md.*, VIII, 345 ("used the Woods"). Leon de Valinger, Jr., ed., *Court Records of Kent County, Delaware*, American Legal Records, VIII (Washington, D.C., 1959), 313 ("admitted"; Bizaillon's first wife, who may have been an Indian, could speak Onondaga. See *MPCP*, II, 141). *Arch. Md.*, VIII, 346, 486, 517 (Chartier).

In the late 1680s Jacques Le Tort, and perhaps also Pierre Bizaillon, traveled from the Schuylkill to the Ohio and from there up the Mississippi to a "great yellow River" (Benson, "LeTorts," *Jnl. Lanc. Co. Hist. Soc.*, LXV [1961], 99). His son would follow in those footsteps, making several journeys deep into the interior (Logan to Isaac Taylor, 23 Feb. 1724, Taylor Papers, Correspondence, 1723–1750, doc. 3000, HSP).

17. Will of Pierre Bizaillon, 9 Jan. 1741/2, Inventory 805, CCA (Bizaillon; see also James Logan, Receipt Book, 1702–1709, 11, LP; Parker, Account Book, Chester County Hist. Soc.). *Arch. Md.,* VIII, 345 ("Spie"), 347 ("not right"); de Valinger, ed., *Court Recs. of Kent County,* 313 ("Allien"); Hanna, *Wilderness Trail,* I, 165 ("private correspondence"); *MPCP,* I, 396 ("strange Indians"), 436 ("obscure places"), II, 18–19 ("very dangerous"), 471 ("suspicious words"). For watching and following, see *MPCP,* I, 334, II, 182, 474; *Arch. Md.,* XX, 406, 470. For interrogation, see *MPCP,* I, 396–397, 435–436, II, 100–101, 131; Logan to Edward Farmer, 20 Mar. 1703, JLLB, 1702–1726; Armstrong, ed., *Corr. Penn and Logan,* I, 197, 224–225. For imprisonment, see *Arch. Md.,* VIII, 347, 350, 354, 383; *MPCP,* II, 18–19, 163, 170–171, 539; James Le Tort's Petition and Account of Indian Debts, 8ber 1704, LP, 11/4.

18. *MPCP,* II, 385. Godin's only other appearances in the records came three years earlier, when he brought word of Indian unrest and was accused of stealing another trader's goods (*ibid.,* 138, 141, 168, 181–183).

19. Kent, *Susquehanna's Indians,* 88–89; George P. Donehoo, *A History of the Indian Villages and Place Names in Pennsylvania, with Numerous Historical Notes and References* (Harrisburg, Pa., 1928), 146–148. This is the first mention of this Indian settlement in the records. Its headman was probably Sassoonan, said to be living there before 1709.

20. Gary B. Nash, *Quakers and Politics: Pennsylvania, 1681–1726* (Princeton, N.J., 1968), 256–260. Evans was born in 1678.

21. In 1763 a letter dated 28 September 1708 from the provincial council to the Conestogas turned up in the effects of Conestoga Indians killed by the so-called Paxton Boys (see ch. VII). Written by James Logan, it was (according to colonists who saw and summarized it in 1763) "a Request to the Indians to apprehend Nichole Godin, on suspicions of several treasonable Practices against the Government" (*MPCP,* IX, 102). I have not been able to determine whether this letter was misread or misdated in 1763, or if in 1708 Godin was once again free and leading provincial authorities on a merry chase.

22. The distance is noted in *MPCP,* III, 155. The date of this encounter was probably the first week in February 1722 (John Cartlidge was back at his house on Conestoga Creek by 17 February [Cartlidge to Isaac Taylor, 17 Feb. 1721/2, Taylor Pprs., Corr., 1682–1723, doc. 2975, HSP]). I have reconstructed it from *MPCP,* III, 148–152, and Depositions of Jonathan Swindel and William Wilkins, Society Miscellaneous Collections, Indians, 1682–1900, Box 11c, Folder 2, HSP. The crucial testimony of the two

servants, omitted from the official version, was discovered by Francis Jennings. For his treatment of the episode, see "Miquon's Passing: Indian-European Relations in Colonial Pennsylvania, 1674 to 1755" (Ph.D. diss., University of Pennsylvania, 1965), 197–206; *Ambiguous Iroquois Empire,* 290–293. (Another account, dealt with below, is so obviously a fabrication aimed at exonerating the Cartlidges that I ignore it here.)

The variation in these accounts is considerable, especially in how threatening Sawantaeny was and how violent was the Cartlidges' response. My version is based on areas of general agreement, and details from one or two accounts that strike me as likely to be true. I rely especially on Wilkins's deposition. Unlike Swindel, Wilkins testified when his master was not nearby; he was less bent on excusing the colonists, though it must be noted that he remained John Cartlidge's servant, and later Edmond Cartlidge's client, after the Sawantaeny affair was over.

23. Strangely, the servants said that the guide was either a Tuscarora named Charles or one "Jathcote." The weight of the evidence, and the Conoys' familiarity with the Potomac region (their territory before 1700), favors Ayaquachan.

24. According to Wilkins and Swindel; Indian witnesses made no mention either of fist or face, saying only that Sawantaeny "asked" or "demanded" more rum, "pressing" Cartlidge for it.

25. It was a good question. Swindel claimed that the gun indeed was loaded—he saw powder in the pan, and the ramrod, later inserted into the muzzle, stood out far enough to suggest powder and ball; Wilkins was less certain, saying he only saw two or three grains of powder in the pan.

26. Colonists disputed this assessment of Sawantaeny's condition, made by Acquittanachke, arguing that the Seneca was not that badly hurt. There was, to be sure, a lot of blood, but according to Wilkins Sawantaeny felt well enough to get up and take both him and Edmond Cartlidge "by the hand to be friends with them" again. Both servants swore that when they peeked into the cabin one last time before departing they found the injured Indian asleep—I "heard him Snore," Wilkins insisted. The Cartlidge brothers later doubted that the Seneca was even dead. In any case, they claimed, "what they did . . . in their own Defence and for preservation of their own lives," "what was done on their part by reason of the amazing Surprize they were in," could not have killed him (*MPCP,* III, 156).

27. *Ibid.,* 150, 168, 189. For the Senecas' place in Pennsylvania's thinking at this time, see Jennings, *Ambiguous Iroquois Empire,* 291.

28. County Tax Lists, 1718–1721, C-1 through C-3, CCA.

29. *MPCP,* III, 78, 103 ("good Friend"; also 120, 125). For the location of his house, see Taylor Pprs., Lancaster County Surveys, doc. 2389, HSP. He

had a 300-acre farm and nearly 100 horses and cattle (Inventory of John Cartlidge's Estate, 10 Dec. 1723 [*sic*—probably 1722, as he died around 23 November of that year], CCA). Besides this farm, Cartlidge owned another 1500 acres on "Shickasolonge" (Taylor Pprs., Lancaster Co. Surveys, doc. 2723, HSP). From 1718 to 1721, Cartlidge was among the largest tax-payers in Conestoga Township (County Tax Lists, 1718–1721, C-1 through C-3, CCA). Further biographical information on him is in Zimmerman, "Indian Trade," 153–158. For his interpreting, see *MPCP,* III, 45–49, 78–81, 92–98, 114, 123–130.

30. *MPCP,* III, 48. "Serviceable" is James Logan's term (Logan to Simon Clement, 22 Nov. 1722, PMOC, I, 119).

31. I use the name colonists commonly employed. The first mention of him is at a council in June 1710 (*MPCP,* II, 511), where he was called "the Seneques Kings," but *Seneca* was a common English shorthand for Iroquois. Colonists in later years termed him "a War Captain & Chief," or "the present Chief or Captain" of the Conestogas (II, 553, III, 45). His work as an interpreter can be found in III, 45, 80, 138, 148, 163, 189, 216. And see Hanna, *Wilderness Trail,* I, 80–81; C. Hale Sipe, *The Indian Chiefs of Pennsylvania* (Harrisburg, Pa., 1927), 79–87.

32. Council held at Philadelphia, 15 7ber 1718, LP, 11/7; *MPCP,* III, 103 (1720; also 97).

33. *Ibid.,* 153; Depositions of Richard Salter, Jr., and George Rescarrick, 10 Mar. 1721/2, DSP, 966.F.2.

34. Jennings makes a persuasive case for Gov. Keith's eagerness to attack James Logan through Logan's men on the Susquehanna, the Cartlidges. Without denying the importance of political warfare in the provincial capital, it is also clear that Keith had other reasons to seek a settlement more genuine than the one the Cartlidges had constructed.

35. Logan to Gov. Hunter, 4 June 1719, JLLB, 1702–1726 ("animated"); *MPCP,* III, 121. The history of Iroquois-Pennsylvania relations during these years is told in Jennings, *Ambiguous Iroquois Empire,* Part 3; idem, " 'Pennsylvania Indians' and the Iroquois," in Richter and Merrell, eds., *Beyond the Covenant Chain,* 82–87; Richard Aquila, *The Iroquois Restoration: Iroquois Diplomacy on the Colonial Frontier, 1701–1754* (Detroit, Mich., 1983), ch. 6; Richter, *Ordeal of the Longhouse,* 241–244, 268–270, 273–276.

36. Norris, quoted in Zimmerman, "Indian Trade," 156 ("Murmur"). *MPCP,* II, 467, 469, 511–512, III, 77–81 (French). For Logan, see *MPCP,* II, 15–16, 244–247, III, 92; Logan to John Askew, 3, 19 3 mo. 1715, JLLB, 1712–1715, 285, 290; Logan to Isaac Taylor, 26 2 mo. 1718, Taylor Pprs., Corr., doc. 2875, HSP; Jennings, *Ambiguous Iroquois Empire,* chs. 13–17; Zimmerman, "Indian Trade," chs. 4–5.

37. *MPCP,* II, 469, 531, III, 19, 92, 123. *PA,* 2d, VII, 73 ("just Interpretation").

38. *MPCP,* III, 93, 102, 148, 181, 188–189, 197, 219; Council with the Indians at Conestoga, 6–7 Apr. 1722, DSP, 966.F.4; *PA,* 2d, VII, 73.

39. *MPCP,* II, 574, 607, III, 46 ("voice & mind"; also 80, 94, 216).

40. For colonists failing to realize that Indians expected condolences to open conferences, see *ibid.,* II, 533, III, 92.

41. For these months, see *ibid.,* III, 155–221. Jennings argues that the two never saw a jail cell, but the evidence suggests otherwise, even if they were not incarcerated the entire time (about six months) their case was before Indian and colonial authorities. See also Council at Conestoga, 6–7 Apr. 1722, DSP, 966.F.4.

42. *MPCP,* III, 164, 189.

43. *Ibid.,* 164.

44. *Ibid.,* 168 ("busie"). That autumn John Cartlidge died of a fever he had contracted in Philadelphia; he had been in the capital to collect another message from the government to Conestoga, a clear indication that he was back in everyone's good graces (Logan to Simon Clement, 22 Nov. 1722, PMOC, I, 119; Council at Philadelphia, 28 Jan. 1722/3, DSP, 966.F.6).

45. *MPCP,* III, 217, 220.

46. For fur trade figures, see Stephen H. Cutcliffe, "Colonial Indian Policy as a Measure of Rising Imperialism: New York and Pennsylvania, 1700–1755," *Western Pennsylvania Historical Magazine,* LXIV (1981), 240–242; Eric Hinderaker, *Elusive Empires: Constructing Colonialism in the Ohio Valley, 1673–1800* (New York, 1997), 24.

47. *MPCP,* II, 15, 244, III, 79. See also *ibid.,* II, 388, 474, 553, 555, 574, 599–601, III, 47, 93–94, 123–124; Council at Philadelphia, 15 7ber 1718, LP, 11/7; Council at Conestoga, 6–7 Apr. 1722, DSP, 966.F.4. Evans did not use it in 1707, but by Keith's day it was commonplace. Whether this represents a shift in sentiment or merely better note-taking is unclear.

48. Francis Jennings, "Brother Miquon: Good Lord!" in Richard S. Dunn and Mary Maples Dunn, eds., *The World of William Penn* (Philadelphia, 1986), 195–214; Thomas J. Sugrue, "The Peopling and Depeopling of Early Pennsylvania: Indians and Colonists, 1680–1720," *PMHB,* CXVI (1992), 3–31. He genuinely wanted Indian and colonist to "live friendly together," to avoid "all occasions of Heart burnings and mischief," but he also had doubts, doubts he expressed by adding that they should get along "as much as in us lieth" (*MPCP,* I, 28).

49. *MPCP,* II, 16–17.

50. *Ibid.,* III, 123.

51. *Ibid.,* II, 600–601 ("wholly ignorant"; and see 554–556, 608, III, 125); II, 556, 602, 608 (Pennsylvania response). Another reflection of differing values was the colonial habit of calculating the market value of the skins and furs Indians brought as gifts (554–555, 559, 574, 601, III, 47, 274–275).

52. The province claimed these lands by virtue of William Penn's 1683 purchase of the lower Susquehanna from Governor Thomas Dongan of New York, who bought the land in turn from Iroquois claiming right of conquest over the native Susquehannocks (Jennings, *Ambiguous Iroquois Empire,* 226–230). An excellent overview of European settlement in this region and the Indians' response is Jennings, "Indian Trade," *Procs. APS,* CX (1966), 421–424.

53. James Steel to Isaac Taylor, 24 7ber 1714, Taylor Pprs., Corr., doc. 2827, HSP (mill); John Cartlidge to James Logan, 8 Apr. 1717, LP, 1/79 (smithy); *PA,* 6th, XIV, 259 (road). For survey work, Taylor Pprs., Lanc. Co. Surveys, docs. 2860, 2875, 2915, 2919, 2920, 2931, HSP.

54. Colonists' complaints are in Logan to P. Bizaillon, 28 Oct. 1713, JLLB, 1712–1715, 157; *MPCP,* III, 221 (quotations; see also 100, 137, 154; Council at Conestoga, 6–7 Apr. 1722, DSP, 966.F.4). For Indian complaints, see *MPCP,* II, 471, 554, III, 218 (quotation; also 48, 97, 137).

55. To be sure, governors and councils occasionally ordered troublesome colonists removed, fences built, and boundaries marked (*MPCP,* II, 555–556, III, 49, 137–138).

56. For Logan, see Jennings, *Ambiguous Iroquois Empire,* esp. 265–268; idem, "Indian Trade," *Procs. APS,* CX (1966), 414–424. For Keith, Council at Conestoga, 6–7 Apr. 1722, DSP, 966. F.4 (emphasis added; see also *MPCP,* III, 184–185). Keith's adventures with those western lands are in Jennings, *Ambiguous Iroquois Empire,* 291–294; Logan to Simon Clement, 12 Apr. 1722, PMOC, I, 107; to "Esteemed Friend," 22 9ber 1722, *ibid.,* 119; to Henry Gouldney, 7 3 mo. 1723, *ibid.,* 125.

57. *MPCP,* II, 403–405 (see also *PWP,* IV, 674–675; Cartlidge to Isaac Taylor, 17 Feb. 1721/2, Taylor Pprs., Corr., doc. 2975, HSP).

58. County Tax Lists, 1718, C-1, 1719/20, C-2, CCA; "Inventory of Martin Chartier's Estate," *Publications of the Lancaster County Historical Society,* XXIX (1925), 130–133.

59. "They look upon themselves but like Children," Civility allegedly said, "Rather to be Directed by this Governmt. than Fit to offer any thing more on this head" (*MPCP,* III, 46, 78). The topic was whether Indians should go off to war against southern enemies. Civility and other speakers could be obsequious when it suited them at other times, too (*ibid.,* 80, 94; Council at Conestoga, 6–7 Apr. 1722, DSP, 966.F.4).

60. Council at Conestoga, 6–7 Apr. 1722, DSP, 966.F.4 (Keith). *MPCP,* III, 92, 95 (Logan). For other lectures, consult *ibid.,* 24, 78–79, 92–93, 95–97, 127–128.

61. *MPCP,* III, 93 ("one Body"; emphasis added), 217 ("discerning"). Also Council at Conestoga, 6–7 Apr. 1722, DSP, 966.F.4.

62. *MPCP,* III, 94; Council at Conestoga, 6–7 Apr. 1722, DSP, 966.F.4.

63. "I hope you and your Children will never forget it," the governor replied at the next council, and Civility changed his tone, explaining that according to Penn "after three Generations were passed, and the People gone who heard his words, he desired that the writing which he left with them might be read to the fourth Generation" (*MPCP*, III, 181, 217). In 1735 Civility again mentioned it for William Penn's son, Thomas, at a Philadelphia treaty. The proprietor promptly hauled out the 1701 agreement, had it read aloud and interpreted to the assembled Conestoga, Conoy, and Shawnee Indians, then pointedly said: "You . . . see that the great Treaty of Friendship then made, was not for three Generations only but forever, that is as long as the Sun & Moon shall endure, or Water to flow in the Rivers, which is the Language that has always been used on these Occasions" (*ibid.*, 599–604).

64. Not surprisingly, colonial authorities disagreed. Council at Conestoga, 6–7 Apr. 1722, DSP, 966.F.4.

65. *MPCP*, II, 244 (Logan), 474 ("very welcome"), 531 (1711). For invitations, see 469, 511. For Indians showing up without an invitation, see 470, 474, III, 45. Indian views on treaties are in William N. Fenton, "Structure, Continuity, and Change in the Process of Iroquois Treaty Making," in Francis Jennings et al., eds., *The History and Culture of Iroquois Diplomacy: An Interdisciplinary Guide to the Treaties of the Six Nations and Their League* (Syracuse, N.Y., 1985), 6; Michael K. Foster, "Another Look at the Function of Wampum in Iroquois-White Councils," *ibid.*, 110.

66. *MPCP*, III, 218.

67. *Ibid.*, 167.

68. *Ibid.*, 121, II, 395.

69. Armstrong, ed., *Corr. Penn and Logan*, I, 43; Jennings, *Ambiguous Iroquois Empire*, 237–238; Kent, *Susquehanna's Indians*, 60–61. Legend has Penn visiting Indians, sitting on the ground with them, dancing with them, and hosting Indian dances in his garden (Weslager, *Delaware Indians*, ch. 8).

III: Passages through the Woods

1. *MPCP*, III, 191 (Keith; the quotation heading the chapter is *ibid.*, 449). For Montour's travels, see *ibid.*, V, 607–608, 634–637, 660, 668, 677, 683, 712, 730, 757; H. R. McIlwaine, ed., *Journals of the House of Burgesses of Virginia, 1752–1758* (Richmond, Va., 1909), 515–516, 520; Lois Mulkearn, ed., *George Mercer Papers Relating to the Ohio Company of Virginia* (Pittsburgh, Pa., 1954), 78–79; *MJNY*, 174–175; [Bernhard A. Grube], "A Missionary's Tour to Shamokin and the West Branch of the Susquehanna, 1753," *PMHB*, XXXIX (1915), 443.

2. Conrad Weiser and William Parsons, "An Accot. of Provision &ca. taken on Our Journey to Wyoming," 5 Oct. 1738, Indian Walk Manuscripts, Swarthmore College Library.

3. Indians left few accounts of their adventures on the road beyond the formulas of the At the Woods' Edge Ceremony. The colonial go-between, when he wrote anything at all, generally included what his superiors wanted to read: what happened once he reached his destination. Many of the richest travel accounts are from missionaries, who included trials on the road as part of their larger spiritual journey. Though few missionaries became go-betweens, their accounts generally correspond with those of other colonists who left records, including Bartram, Weiser, Croghan, Christopher Gist, and John Hays.

   The dearth of information on Indian messengers traveling among colonial settlements has led to my sometimes including accounts of larger parties of Indians, such as diplomatic delegations. Those delegations, more numerous, may have increased pressure on colonial resources and made colonists less hospitable as a result. Still, including these bigger collections of travelers offers clues to an emissary's journeys through Pennsylvania.

   Few scholars have examined the culture of travel. Exceptions are Paul A. W. Wallace, *Indian Paths of Pennsylvania* (Harrisburg, Pa., 1965), Introduction; James Axtell, *The Invasion Within: The Contest of Cultures in Colonial North America* (New York, 1985), 72–74; Helen C. Rountree, "The Powhatans and Other Woodland Indians as Travelers," in Rountree, ed., *Powhatan Foreign Relations, 1500–1722* (Charlottesville, Va., 1993), 21–52; Peter C. Mancall, *Valley of Opportunity: Economic Culture along the Upper Susquehanna, 1700–1800* (Ithaca, N.Y., 1991), chs. 1–2.

4. Even so, hints of difficulties crept into Bartram's account (*Observations*, 28, 34, 35, 64, 67, 69).

5. Weiser 1737, 10–11, 18, 19; Wallace, *Weiser*, 82.

6. *MPCP*, IV, 660–661 (Weiser). Post 1760, 27 June.

7. Weiser to Gov. Hamilton, 30 June 1750, CCW, I, 27. For the importance Indians attached to such main thoroughfares, see *MPCP*, VIII, 615; Post 1760, 17 June; Wallace, *Weiser*, 91; Zeisberger, *Diaries*, 14. An exception to this was Christian Frederick Post's journeys to the Ohio in 1758, when his Indian companions steered clear of the main paths to elude French-allied Indians opposed to his mission.

8. Croghan 1750–65, 124–125 ("clear Woods"; also 135; Smith, *Account*, 21; Gist, 24; *MJNY*, 160, 168; David McClure, *Diary of David McClure, Doctor of Divinity, 1748–1820,* ed. Franklin B. Dexter [New York, 1899], 49, 58–59). Lancaster County, Petition to Gov. John Penn, Mar. 1769, RPCEC, B11, 2741 ("Great Road").

9. For Indian trails, see *MPCP,* V, 122, VI, 302, VII, 445–446; *PA,* 1st, II, 192; J. W. Early, trans., "Frederick A. C. Muhlenberg's Report of His First Trip to Shamokin . . . ," *Lutheran Church Review,* XXV (1906), 538; *MJNY,* 169; *PA,* 8th, V, 3678–3679; John Woolman, *The Journal of John Woolman* (Boston, 1909 [orig. pub. 1871]), 207. Joseph Shippen to William Shippen, Jr., 13 Jan. 1755, Joseph Shippen Letterbook, 1754–1755, PSF ("Horror"). *Journals of Claus and Weiser,* 37 (Claus; see also Woolman, *Journal,* 207).

10. For bogs, see Post 1758, 227, 229; *MPCP,* V, 472; Spangenberg, 56; *MJNY,* 36, 44, 68, 169; Weiser 1737, 18; *Journals of Claus and Weiser,* 39; Hays, 67; Eben Norton Horsford, ed., *Zeisberger's Indian Dictionary . . . Printed from the Original Manuscript in Harvard College Library* (Cambridge, Mass., 1887), 189. Spangenberg, 56 (trees; see also *MJNY,* 36, 39, 68, 218–219, 227, 237; *DHNY,* III, 1041; Woolman, *Journal,* 198, 207).

11. *MJNY,* 237.

12. For colonists getting lost, see *Journals of Claus and Weiser,* 23; Travel Diary, 20 Oct. 1748, MCA, 30/225/2/1. For Indians, *MJNY,* 159, 168 (quotations). Horsford, ed., *Zeisberger's Indian Dictionary,* 67, 124, 223. See also Post 1758, 192–193; Zeisberger, *Diaries,* 11–12; Bartram, *Observations,* 66; Hays, 74.

13. Wallace, *Weiser,* 70 ("Endess hills"); Lawrence Henry Gipson, *Lewis Evans. To Which is Added Evans'* A Brief Account of Pennsylvania (Philadelphia, 1939), 96 ("Steep ascents"). Shamokin Diary, 4 Nov. 1745, MCA, 28/217/12B/1 (hands and knees). William C. Reichel, ed., *Memorials of the Moravian Church,* I (Philadelphia, 1870), 84–85 (train; see also "Extracts from Mr. Lewis Evans' Journal, 1743," in Thomas Pownall, *A Topographical Description of the Dominions of the United States of America . . . ,* ed. Lois Mulkearn (Pittsburgh, Pa., 1949), 169; Early, trans., "Muhlenberg's Report," *Lutheran Church Rev.,* XXV (1906), 536–538). Post 1760, 10 May ("tremble"). For horses, see Hays, 82; Post 1758, 228, 245; Zeisberger, *Diaries,* 36; Gist, 29.

14. Weiser 1737, 9 (quotation), 10 (6 or 7 crossings); Hays, 79 (5); *MJNY,* 36 (30); John W. Jordan, trans., "Rev. John Ettwein's Notes of Travel from the North Branch of the Susquehanna to the Beaver River, Pennsylvania, 1772," *PMHB,* XXV (1901), 209 (36). And see Bartram, *Observations,* 35. For fording, see Reichel, ed., *Memorials,* I, 93, 94; Cammerhoff, 170; Kenny 1758–59, 407; Kenny 1761–63, 4.

15. Post 1758, 247–248, 281; Gist, 18, 30, 39. In 1737 Weiser's party built one in ninety minutes (Weiser 1737, 12–13).

16. Post 1758, 282; Weiser 1737, 7 (also 8, 14).

17. Weiser 1737, 11.

18. For colonists using canoes, see Adolph B. Benson, ed., *The America of 1750. Peter Kalm's Travels in North America. The English Version of 1770* (New York, 1937), 85, 108; Military Letter-Books of Joseph Shippen, 1756–1758, 3,

PSF. Experienced colonists preferred batteaux for transporting goods and large numbers of people (*PA*, 1st, III, 627). *MJNY*, 26 ("glide"), 167 ("pleasant"; see also Bartram, *Observations,* 65–66). Wallace (*Indian Paths,* 2) disagrees about the canoe's popularity.

19. Memorandum, 2 7ber 1732, PSF, XXVII, Bills and Receipts, 1721–1754, 26; also *Arch. Md.,* VIII, 10–11; Weiser 1737, 21; *MJNY,* 72; Zeisberger, *Diaries,* 13, 42. For the frequency of "Canoe Place," see Wallace, *Indian Paths,* 135. For fleets, see *PA,* 2d, II, 662; "Military Letters of Captain Joseph Shippen of the Provincial Service, 1756–1758," *PMHB,* XXXVI (1912), 415–416; Weiser to James Logan, 16 Sept. 1736, LP, 10/62; Burd to William Allen, 28 June 1762, PSF, V; *MJNY,* 160.

20. Zeisberger, *History,* 23 (quickly). Howard H. Peckham, ed., "Thomas Gist's Indian Captivity, 1758–1759," *PMHB,* LXXX (1956), 296; *MJNY,* 99 (birch). Weiser 1737, 21 (chestnut). Wallace, *Indian Paths,* 2; Zeisberger, *History,* 51; Benson, ed., *America of 1750,* 363–365 (elm). *MJNY,* 25–26 (bark). Dugout canoes were increasingly popular (Zeisberger, *History,* 23) as Indians acquired sharp tools (Benson, ed., *America of 1750,* 229–230). It is often hard to tell what kind of bark Indians were using. Zeisberger, *History,* 23; Peckham, ed., "Gist's Captivity," *PMHB,* LXXX (1956), 296 (repairs easy). Zeisberger, *History,* 23; Memorandum, 2 7ber 1732, PSF, XXVII, Bills and Receipts, 1721–1754, 26 (heavy loads). For additional general accounts of their construction and use, see Joseph-Francois Lafitau, *Customs of the American Indians Compared with the Customs of Primitive Times,* trans. and ed. William N. Fenton and Elizabeth L. Moore, 2 vols. (Toronto, 1974–1977), II, 124–126; Richard Smith, *A Tour of Four Great Rivers: The Hudson, Mohawk, Susquehanna and Delaware in 1769* . . . (Port Washington, N.Y., 1964), 48, 50, 58; Lewis Henry Morgan, *League of the Ho-Dé-No-Sau-Nee, or Iroquois* (New York, 1962 [orig. pub. 1851]), 367–369; William N. Fenton and Ernest Stanley Dodge, "An Elm Bark Canoe in the Peabody Museum of Salem," *The American Neptune,* IX (1949), 185–206.

21. For downstream, see CW to [?], n.d., CCW, II, 27. See also *PA,* 1st, III, 507; "John Jennings 'Journal From Fort Pitt to Fort Chartres in the Illinois Country,' March–April, 1766," *PMHB,* XXXI (1907), 150. For upstream, *MJNY,* 156 (quotation), 162. For Indian sailors, see Fenton and Dodge, "Elm Bark Canoe," *American Neptune,* IX (1949), 200.

22. Weiser 1737, 21; *MJNY,* 179–180; Benson, ed., *America of 1750,* 364; *Arch. Md.,* VIII, 10; RPLB, 1737–1750, 28.

23. Benson, ed., *America of 1750,* 365; Zeisberger, *History,* 23; *MJNY,* 223; [Grube], "Missionary's Tour," *PMHB,* XXXIX (1915), 442; *PWJ,* IX, 779; Paul A. W. Wallace, ed., *The Travels of John Heckewelder in Frontier America* (Pittsburgh, Pa., 1958), 97.

24. Peckham, ed., "Gist's Captivity," *PMHB*, LXXX (1956), 296 ("brown paper"). *MJNY*, 30, 102, 181, 183; Weiser 1737, 21 (repairs). Horsford, ed., *Zeisberger's Indian Dictionary*, 198, 222.

25. Though portages connected the principal river systems, claims that canoeists could "go whither they will" and "get almost anywhere by water" were exaggerated (Zeisberger, *History,* 23, 41). For the portages, see Jennings, *Ambiguous Iroquois Empire,* 76, map 5.

26. As colonists came to see the wisdom of walking when in Indian country (*MJNY,* 57), so Indians began to use horses. "Harry the Interpreter" (Shawydoohungh), who had a horse by 1715, was the first of many native go-betweens to ride across the frontier (Logan, Account Book, 1712–1720, LP, 85, 126). See also Indian Charges, 17 Dec. 1742, PPM, X, 22; *PA,* 1st, III, 718; Reichel, ed., *Memorials,* I, 235; Newcastle's Charges, 1756, Northampton Co., Miscellaneous Manuscripts, Bethlehem and Vicinity, 1741–1849, 29, HSP; Smith, *Account,* 32, 36, 42; Bartram, *Observations,* 21; John Langdale to Israel Pemberton, 18 3 mo. 1761, Roberts Collection, Haverford College Library.

27. The rule of thumb on grass is in Logan to James Coutts, 6 3 mo. 1704, JLLB, 1702–1726; *PA,* 1st, I, 672; *MPCP,* IV, 757, VI, 35; Peters to the Proprietaries, 17 Feb. 1749, 5 May 1750, PMOC, IV, 195, V, 2; Post 1760, 11 May. For buying corn, Gist, 13; Account of Expenses of Conrad Weiser & his Son to Shamokin and Wyoming, April 1754, PPM, XI, 52; Post 1758, 280. For exceptions, see Gist, 15–16; Smith, *Account,* 40–41. For strays, see Reichel, ed., *Memorials,* I, 94, 95, 98; Spangenberg, 426, 56, 58, 59; Cammerhoff, 171; *MJNY,* 34–36; Post 1758, 190, 225, 241–242, 279, 287, 289; Woolman, *Journal,* 192–193; Kenny 1758–59, 409, 411–415; Post 1760, 11, 17, 18 May, 19, 24 June; Croghan 1750–65, 124; *PA,* 1st, IV, 94–97; Jordan, trans., "Ettwein's Notes of Travel," *PMHB,* XXV (1901), 208–209; McClure, *Diary,* 13, 58; Weiser 1748, 44, n.43.

28. Jonathan Edwards, *The Life of David Brainerd,* ed. Norman Pettit, The Works of Jonathan Edwards, vol. VII (New Haven, Conn., 1985), 582 (leg broken), 294 (poison); Spangenberg, 58 (drowned). Jordan, trans., "Ettwein's Notes of Travel," *PMHB,* XXV (1901), 210, 213; *SCP,* I, 287 (snake). Post 1758, 188–189, 234; Bartram, *Observations,* 74; *MPCP,* V, 472 (lame; "24 hours"). Post 1758, 228, 285, 287; Weiser 1748, 25, n.19, 44, n.43; *Journals of Claus and Weiser,* 39; Kenny 1758–59, 416, 418; Account of Weiser, Apr. 1754, PPM, XI, 52; *PA,* 1st, IV, 95 (exhausted).

29. For traveling in winter, see *MPCP,* II, 403–404, III, 544–545, IV, 643, VI, 697–699, VII, 12–13, 65–67; Journal by Capt. Joseph Shippen at Fort Augusta, 1757–1758, 15 Feb. 1758, Small Books, no. 6, PSF; Wallace, *Weiser,* 353; Wallace, *Teedyuscung,* 169.

30. Kenneth P. Bailey, ed., *The Ohio Company Papers, 1753–1817* . . . (Arcata, Calif., 1947), 28 ("impassible"). Gottlieb Mittelberger, *Journey to Pennsylvania,* ed. and trans. Oscar Handlin and John Clive (Cambridge, Mass., 1960), 78 ("cold spells"). Snow fell as early as October and as late as June (*MJNY,* 194, 225–227), and deep snow might remain in April (Martin Mack, Journey to Wyoming, 7–9 Apr. 1745, MCA, 28/217/12/3).

31. Weiser 1737, 10 (also 7–9).

32. Weiser to Peters, 15 Mar. 1754, CCW, I, 44.

33. Cammerhoff, 164 (traders). Indians turning back are noted in *PA,* 2d, II, 652–653; Nathaniel Holland to Israel Pemberton, 16 Apr. 1761, FA, IV, 95. Many other Indians simply refused even to dispatch messengers when winter approached, promising instead to come in the spring (*MPCP,* II, 246, 471). Other envoys chose to overwinter in Indian towns on the lower Susquehanna rather than head across the mountains (*MPCP,* V, 212, 222).

34. Weiser 1737, 7–9, 14 (quotation); Post 1758, 241, 244, 282, 285, 287, 289, 290, 291; Croghan 1750–65, 124; Gist, 8–9, 11, 13, 15, 28–30, 32, 34–36, 38; Cammerhoff, 165, 166, 178–179; Zeisberger, *Diaries,* 17; *PA,* 2d, II, 642; Smith, *Account,* 90, 93. For Zeisberger's phrases on snow, cold, and "Raw weather," see Horsford, ed., *Zeisberger's Indian Dictionary,* 24, 66, 79, 97, 155, 177.

35. Post 1758, 291; Kenny 1761–63, 31, 32; Peters, Diary, 1755 [*sic*], 8 Jan. 1756, RPP (solid ice). Kenny 1758–59, 399, 401; Cammerhoff, 162 (ice too thin). Horsford, ed., *Zeisberger's Indian Dictionary,* 195 ("how thick"). Cammerhoff, 163, 166–168; Weiser 1737, 7; Croghan to [?], 10 Feb. 1761, GCP, 5/23; *MPCP,* VI, 782.

36. Weiser 1737, 15. One colonial fur trader died crossing a stream like this (*ibid.,* 8; also Wallace, ed., *Travels of Heckewelder,* 38). For the noise, Cammerhoff, 166; Kenny 1758–59, 399.

37. *PA,* 1st, IV, 93, 95; *MJNY,* 63, 65–66, 81. Weiser in his later years postponed trips to avoid hot weather (*MPCP,* VI, 150; *PA,* 1st, III, 218). For rains, see Post 1758, 227; *PA,* 1st, III, 735–736, 738, 740; *MJNY,* 68; Hays, 67, 70, 72; Post 1760, 18 May, 23, 24, 26–28 June; Jordan, trans., "Ettwein's Notes of Travel," *PMHB,* XXV (1901), 209, 211; Zeisberger, *Diaries,* 10–11; Spangenberg, 63; Horsford, ed., *Zeisberger's Indian Dictionary,* 136, 154, 181, 227.

38. *MJNY,* 26 ("rocks"; see also 29, 31, 32, 101–102; Smith, *Account,* 96–99; Paul A. W. Wallace, *Indians in Pennsylvania,* rev. ed., William A. Hunter [Harrisburg, Pa., 1986], 41; idem, *Indian Paths,* 2). *MJNY,* 83; *PA,* 1st, III, 504; Richard Peters, "An Account of the Quakers and their Conduct at Easton," 29 July 1757, MCA, 34/317/3/4a; Post 1760, 10, 22 May, 24–27, 29 June (fording).

39. *PA,* 1st, II, 41 ("Gnats"). Hays, 70 ("Misquiteis"), 82 ("Nates"). Jordan, trans., "Ettwein's Notes of Travel," *PMHB,* XXV (1901), 215 *("ponkis").* Post 1760, 24, 26, 27 June; Bartram, *Observations,* 12, 34. For sleeping, see Spangenberg, 62; "An Account of the Famine Among the Indians of the North and West Branch of the Susquehanna, in the Summer of 1748," *PMHB,* XVI (1892), 430; *MJNY,* 73; Post 1758, 189; Kenny 1761–63, 6; *PA,* 1st, IV, 93. For being troubled by various insects over the course of a single summer's trip, see *MJNY,* 63, 68, 73, 81, 82, 87, 98.

40. Zeisberger, *History,* 22 ("game"; and see Horsford, ed., *Zeisberger's Indian Dictionary,* 145: "A Country Where ev'ry Thing is in great Plenty"). *MJNY,* 27–31, 67, 86–87. Croghan 1750–65, 130–131 (see also 132–133, 140, 143, 151; Gist, *passim*). Bartram, *Observations,* 64 (also *MJNY,* 38).

41. Weiser 1737, 13–14. *MJNY,* 160 ("suffered"; also 165, 173, 176, 178). *Ibid.,* 179 (Nanticokes). For hungry Indian travelers, see Message of John Shickellamy to Gov. Hamilton, 7 Aug. 1760, PMIA, III, 90; *PA,* 1st, II, 9; Post 1758, 282, n.108.

42. Weiser 1737, 8, 13, 17–18 (emphasis added). And see *MPCP,* III, 152, 164, 189, V, 517, VII, 491, 512, 515; *PA,* 1st, I, 213, II, 23; Horsford, ed., *Zeisberger's Indian Dictionary,* 66, 98, 141.

43. "Account of Famine," *PMHB,* XVI (1892), 431; *MJNY,* 86, 98–99, 173; *PA,* 1st, I, 758. *PA,* 1st, II, 41 (Weiser; also Wallace, *Weiser,* 134).

44. *MPCP,* IX, 616 ("divide it"). *MJNY,* 31, 32, 102, 160; Bartram, *Observations,* 33; Spangenberg, 63, 64; Post 1758, 249.

45. Bartram, *Observations,* 16 ("punctually"), 24 (double portion; and see 64–65). The philosophy behind this is in Heckewelder, *History,* 101–102. See also Smith, *Account,* 43–44; Mack, Journey to Wyoming, 16 Apr. 1745, MCA, 28/217/12/3; Martin Mack, Journal, 1 Sept. 1755, *ibid.,* 28/217/12B/4; Weiser, "Notes," 323; *MJNY,* 43, 83, 86 *et passim;* [Grube], "Tour," *PMHB,* XXXIX (1915), 442, 444; "Account of Famine," *PMHB,* XVI (1892), 430–432; *MPCP,* VII, 357; McClure, *Diary,* 77. Examples of where Indians failed to automatically offer food (many of these have colonists "buying," which in some cases may simply be their failure to understand reciprocal gift-giving) are in *MJNY,* 157; Hays, 70; Post 1760, 16 and 29 May, 12 June; Gist, 33; [Grube], "Tour," *PMHB,* XXXIX (1915), 443–444; Cammerhoff, 173.

46. Beverley W. Bond, Jr., ed., "The Captivity of Charles Stuart, 1755–1757," *MVHR,* XIII (1926–1927), 62. See also *MJNY,* 212; *PA,* 1st, III, 548.

47. Smith, *Account,* 7, 31, 69; *Journals of Claus and Weiser,* 41.

48. Hays, 73; Weiser 1737, 14; Heckewelder, *History,* 196 (quotations); Zeisberger, *History,* 86. For foods colonists served Indians, see Reichel, ed., *Memorials,* I, 189–366; Account of Indian Charges, PMIA, I, 46; Weiser, In-

dian Expences, 1744, RPP, II, 16; Indian Expences, 1749, CCW, I, 21. Toward the end of the colonial era Indians occasionally were offering colonial travelers more familiar fare such as pork, tea, coffee, and butter and milk (*MJNY,* 64–65, 85, 89; Hays, 74, 77–78).

49. *PA,* 1st, IV, 93 (salted meat); *PWJ,* XIII, 191, 205 (lice); Heckewelder, *History,* 196 (entrails). Smith, *Account,* 7, 31, 69 (colonist adjusting to meat without bread or salt). *MJNY,* 71 ("Asseroni"). The translation is in Richter, *Ordeal of the Longhouse,* 353–354. Some colonists translated this as "enemies and strangers" (Reichel, ed., *Memorials,* I, 19).

50. Weiser to Logan, 16 Sept. 1736, LP, 10/62.

51. Claus, Memoirs, 12. And see Bartram, *Observations,* 16.

52. Post 1758, 192, 227 (wet), 229 (pebbles), 232, 248; Zeisberger, *Diaries,* 17 (rocky ground); Weiser 1737, 14 (standing).

53. Kenny 1758–59, 407; Smith, *Account,* 62–65.

54. Peckham, ed., "Gist's Captivity," *PMHB,* LXXX (1956), 297; Smith, *Account,* 27–28.

55. Invoice of Indian Goods, April 1748, LP, 11/34; Accounts, 31 May 1758, FA, III, 431 (hammock). Reichel, ed., *Memorials,* I, 82, 85, 106; Spangenberg, 425, 426; Post 1758, 248; *PA,* 1st, III, 736; Post 1760, 3, 7 May, 6 June; Kenny 1761–63, 20; Zane 1761, 16 Oct.; Wallace, ed., *Travels of Heckewelder,* 41; McClure, *Diary,* 55 (tents). For Indian tents, see Smith, *Account,* 53, 57; Zeisberger, *Diaries,* 36.

56. For posts, sticks, and stakes, see Zeisberger, *History,* 22; Bartram, *Observations,* 20–21, 35, 38 (coat); Weiser, "Notes," 319–320; Jordan, trans., "Ettwein's Notes of Travel," *PMHB,* XXV (1901), 214. Weiser 1737, 18; *MJNY,* 27–32, 36–38, 61, 66, 68, 82; Benson, ed., *America of 1750,* 353–354, 591; *PA,* 1st, IV, 431; Smith, *Tour of Four Rivers,* 39, 41 (bark). Weiser 1737, 10 (branches). Post 1758, 285; Zeisberger, *Diaries,* 47 (skins). Early, trans., "Muhlenberg's Report," *Lutheran Church Rev.,* XXV (1906), 536–537 ("wretched hut"); Arthur C. Parker, *Seneca Myths and Folk Tales,* Buffalo Historical Society, *Publications,* XXVII (1923), 278, 283 (trail lodges). For abandoned dwellings, see Spangenberg, 63; Gist, 8, 9; Mack, Journey to Wyoming, 6, 8 Apr. 1745, MCA, 28/217/12/3; *MJNY,* 100, 102; Bartram, *Observations,* 13. Some lodges became landmarks (compare Gist, 8–9, and *PA,* 1st, II, 135).

57. Cammerhoff, 177; *MPCP,* IV, 662; Bartram, *Observations,* 31; Spangenberg, 58; *MJNY,* 141, 218; Post 1758, 194, n.28 (visitors' houses). *Journals of Claus and Weiser,* 14 (quotation); *MPCP,* V, 475; Wallace, *Weiser,* 313 (Pennsylvania house in Onondaga). John W. Jordan, ed., "Rev. John Martin Mack's Narrative of a Visit to Onondaga in 1752," *PMHB,* XXIX (1905), 351; *Journals of Claus and Weiser,* 45 (chief's house). Weiser 1737, 8, 13, 15; *MPCP,* V, 475; Zeisberger, *Diaries,* 39, 49 (families). A summary is in Zeisberger, *History,* 93.

58. Wallace, *Weiser,* 141 (1742; see also 313; Gist, 23–24; *Journals of Claus and Weiser,* 13–14). Spangenberg, 58 (1745).

59. This contradicts the claim of one colonist, a newcomer to Indian affairs, that natives "will not, on any occasion whatsoever, dwell, or even stay, in houses built by white people" (Marshe, 179). For examples of Indians lodging with colonists, see "Indian Charges from ye Arrival of . . . Thos. Penn to his departure," PMIA, I, 46; Indian Charges, 1741, *ibid.,* 48; Esther Hanson, Indian Account, 7 10 mo. 1734, PPM, IX, 12; "Sums Paid by Richard Peters on Accot. of the Indians," *ibid.,* X, 42; Peters to Weiser, 10 June 1742, RPP, I, 85; RPLB, 1737–1750, 41; *MJNY,* 175 (in Philadelphia). Andrew Burnaby, *Travels through the Middle Settlements of North-America. In the Years 1759 and 1760 . . . ,* 2d ed. (Ithaca, N.Y., 1960 [orig. pub. 1775]), 54; John F. Watson, *Annals of Philadelphia and Pennsylvania, In the Olden Time . . . ,* 2d ed., 2 vols. (Philadelphia, 1845), II, 163 (apartments in the State House). Richard Peters, Diary, 1 and 6 Oct. 1758, RPP (tavern in Easton). *PA,* 1st, II, 681–682, III, 66; Reichel, ed., *Memorials,* I, 230–231n., 265n., 269n., 270n.; Capt. Nicholas Widerhold to [?], 6 Aug. 1756, HP, II, 253 (forts). Wallace, *Weiser,* 133; *MJNY,* 175; *MPCP,* VII, 6 (quotation).

60. For Indians turning back, see *MPCP,* VIII, 98, and below, ch. V. The Moravian dream is in Travel Diary, 12 Oct. 1748, MCA, 30/225/2/1. See also "An Account of the Captivity of Hugh Gibson Among the Delaware Indians . . . , 1756–1759, *Collections of the Massachusetts Historical Society,* 3d ser., VI (1837), 148, where a captive's dream, having come true, impressed his native captors. Indian dreaming on the trail bears further scrutiny. Iroquois later recalled building "trail lodges" in answer to dreams (Parker, *Seneca Myths and Folktales,* 283), while colonists reported that war parties often resorted to conjury or divination to determine the best course to follow (*PHB,* II, 401–402; *Journals of Claus and Weiser,* 41–42).

61. For example, Spangenberg; Cammerhoff; Travel Diary, Oct. 1748, MCA, 30/225/2/1; Reichel, ed., *Memorials,* I, 80 n. (colonists corrupt the Indian word *Tolheo* to *The Hole*), 82; Gist, 38; *MJNY,* 168; "Account of the Voyage on the Beautiful River made in 1749, under the Direction of Monsieur de Celoron, by Father Bonnecamps," in Reuben Gold Thwaites, ed., *The Jesuit Relations and Allied Documents: Travels and Explorations of the Jesuit Missionaries in New France, 1610–1791,* LXIX (Cleveland, Ohio, 1900), 173–175.

62. Cammerhoff, 167 (see also *DHNY,* III, 1042); Smith, *Account,* 96–99 (prayer). Jordan, ed., "Mack's Narrative," *PMHB,* XXIX (1905), 350 (see also 349, 357); *MJNY,* 61, 82, 102, 180; Wallace, ed., *Travels of Heckewelder,* 39 (song). Bartram, *Observations,* 29 (Indian melody; see also 38). Colonial fur traders were also known to sing songs (Samuel Evans, "Lowrey Family," Lancaster County [Pa.] Historical Society, 41–42).

James Smith, traveling with a slave named Jamie, whiled away the days recuperating from an injury by composing a tune that began: "Six weeks I've in the desart been With one mulatto lad, Excepting this poor stupid slave, No company I had." Whatever pleasure Smith derived from his lyric, we can imagine that young Jamie, who had been nursing the injured man all those weeks, must have tired of hearing it "frequently sung" (Smith, *Account,* 117–118).

63. *MPCP,* IV, 653 ("Fellow travellers"). For curing, see Benson, ed., *America of 1750,* 106; Weiser 1737, 21; Gist, 9, 27. Milton W. Hamilton, ed., "Guy Johnson's Opinions on the American Indian," *PMHB,* LXXVII (1953), 318; Zeisberger, *History,* 116 (talk).

64. Post 1758, 240, 248, 256; Weiser 1737, 17. And see *MJNY,* 27, 34, 35, 40, 45, 80–81, 184, 190–191; Jordan, ed., "Mack's Narrative," *PMHB,* XXIX (1905), 345.

65. *PA,* 1st, III, 223; *MJNY,* 61, 101; *PHB,* II, 582, 662. Donald Jackson, ed., *The Diaries of George Washington,* I (Charlottesville, Va., 1976), 154; Post 1758, 245, 248 ("Indian walking Dress").

66. Travel Diary, 10 Oct. 1748, MCA, 30/225/2/1.

67. Weiser to Logan, 25 Sept. 1736, LC, IV, 61.

68. *MPCP,* VII, 157, 158; Lawrence H. Leder, ed., *The Livingston Indian Records, 1666–1723* (Gettysburg, Pa., 1956), 69–70; Loskiel, *History,* Part I, 30. For colonial examples, see *MPCP,* V, 348–349; Weiser 1748, 44, n.43; Gist; Jordan, trans., "Ettwein's Notes of Travel," *PMHB,* XXV (1901), 210.

69. *Translation of a German Letter, Wrote by Conrad Weiser* . . . (Philadelphia, 1757, Evans 8062), 2; *PGW,* IV, 241.

70. Robert Lettis Hooper to Mr. Wharton, 25 May 1770, Indian Records Collection, Papers Relating to Indian Losses, 27, HSP ("everything"). Edward Shippen to "Dear Children," 31 Dec. 1753, Edward Shippen Letterbook, 1753–1756, 66, APS ("Sugar &c."). For colonists' baggage, see Weiser and Parsons, Account of Provision, 5 Oct. 1738, Indian Walk Mss., Swarthmore College Library; Account of Weiser, Apr. 1754, PPM, XI, 52; "An Account of my Journey to Onantago . . . 1745," CCW, I, 12; Invoice of Indian Goods, Apr. 1758, LP, 11/34; Claus, Memoirs, 12; *MPCP,* V, 294; Thomas Brainerd, *The Life of John Brainerd, The Brother of David Brainerd, And His Successor as Missionary to the Indians of New Jersey* (Philadelphia, 1865), 231.

71. *MPCP,* IV, 631–632, 644; VII, 68; Reichel, ed., *Memorials,* I, 279; Zeisberger, *History,* 22, 24, 115–116; E. Saller to Mr. Taffe, n.d., Burd-Shippen Papers, Letters, APS; Nicholas Wetterholt, Journal, 1763, 9 Oct., Northampton Co., Misc. Mss., Bethlehem and Vicinity, 91, HSP; *PA,* 1st, III, 211; Weiser 1737, 10; Heckewelder, *History,* 195; Bartram, *Observations,* 71.

72. Weiser, *German Letter,* 5–6 (see also Smith, *Account,* 90–95). Zeisberger, *History,* 120.

73. William Denny to Spangenberg, 2 Dec. 1756 (extract), HP, II, 343 ("troublesome"); George Reynolds to William Parsons, 12 Aug. 1756, *ibid.*, 261 ("unruly"). See also Horsfield to Franklin, Fox, &c., 29 Nov. 1756, *ibid.*, 316–317; *PWP*, IV, 156; Logan to "Honoured Friend," 10 July 1727, JLLB, 1716–1743, 136–137; Nicholas Wetterholt to Timothy Horsfield, 13 Sept. 1763, Northampton Co., Misc. Mss., Bethlehem and Vicinity, 117, HSP.

74. Peters to Weiser, 10 June 1742, RPP, I, 85 ("by themselves"; see also Post 1758, 238, 240–241). William Parsons[?] to William Edmonds, 8 Aug. 1756, Northampton Co., Misc. Mss., 1727–1758, 217, HSP; Geo. Reynolds to William Parsons, 12 Aug. 1756, HP, II, 261 ("Good Distance of[f]"); *PA*, 1st, III, 6, 318 ("somewhat used").

   The very lengths to which Indians loyal to Britain went in January 1756 to confirm William Blythe as their man in Carlisle suggest difficulties in getting ordinary Pennsylvanians to play host. Natives chose Blythe because they "had been at a Loss for some proper House to come to." Tired, perhaps, of being turned away from one place after another, they went through the formality of appointing Blythe, complete with an Indian name, "in order to direct any of their Brethren, the Indians at their several Towns, whose House to enquire for when they come to see their Brethren of Pennsylvania" (*MPCP*, VII, 6). Similarly, in 1762 Iroquois asked that John Harris "may be supplied with provisions & other necessaries for our Chiefs & old Men, as they pass to and fro about the good work of peace. We know John Harris" (*ibid.*, VIII, 772).

75. "Journal of Captain Thomas Morris, . . . Detroit, September 25, 1764," in Reuben Gold Thwaites, ed., *Early Western Travels, 1748–1846* (Cleveland, Ohio, 1904), I, 311 ("credible"). See also *MPCP*, VI, 399; *DHNY*, II, 913; *PHB*, II, 307; William Parsons to Weiser, 26 Mar. 1757, CCW, II, 47; Speech of John Shickellamy, 7 Aug. 1760, FA, III, 503. The feast-and-famine regimen that Indians followed away from home made them disinclined to accept the idea of "rations"; at the end of their first day out they might cook and eat all of the meat provided them rather than save some for later in the trip (*PA*, 1st, IV, 94).

76. Weiser to Peters, 6 Aug. 1749, DSP, 966.F.26a ("questions"; the original has "is it"; I correct it here for clarity's sake). See also *MPCP*, IV, 93–94 ("admire"), VI, 140–141, 146, 150, 161, 218–219; *PA*, 1st, II, 211–212, 2d, II, 690 ("angry"). *MPCP*, VII, 71 (caused war). "When we did live among you," one Delaware recalled, "if any of us killd a little pig we were put int[o] Jail & made to pay a great deel, & if we went into any Orchard to take an apple of[f] the Ground or a Peach that must otherwise rot, they call'd us yellow Dogs & whip'd us wth the horse whip till they most kill'd us" (Post, Report on a Conference with Ohio Indians, Sept. 1758, RPCEC, B9, 2005).

77. Bartram, *Observations*, 24.

78. *MJNY*, 27–29, 37, 47, 143; McClure, *Diary*, 58. And see ch. IV.

79. *MPCP,* V, 478 ("Spirits"). For colonists falling ill, see II, 470, III, 184 ("fatigue"), V, 348, 350, 355; *MJNY,* 70, 103, 104; Weiser 1737, 16, 21; Gist, 8–10, 27; *PA,* 1st, IV, 93, 95; McClure, *Diary,* 59. Logan to Allumapees, 12 June 1731, JLLB, III [1721–1732], 176 ("out of ye way"). David Zeisberger's vocabulary included how to warn, in Onondaga, "It is said the small pox is there." Horsford, ed., *Zeisberger's Indian Dictionary,* 147.

80. *PA,* 1st, I, 551. See also *ibid.,* 394; Logan to "Neecoconer & Cacowackecko Chiefs of ye Shawnese Indians," 12[?] July 1739, Alverthorpe Letterbook, C, 46, LP. For the deaths in 1732, see *MPCP,* III, 459–463; *PA,* 1st, I, 394; Treaty between Pennsylvania and Indians, Philadelphia, 30 Sept.–7 Oct. 1732, DSP, in *Iroq. Ind.,* Reel 10; Logan to James Wright, 24 1ober 1732, Logan to Edmond Cartlidge, 24 1ober 1732, JLLB, 1716–1743, 308–309.

81. *MPCP,* V, 298; Peters to the Proprietaries, 27 July 1748, PMOC, IV, 137. Also *MPCP,* VII, 465–466; *PA,* 1st, II, 9, 11; *Journals of Claus and Weiser,* 19. For the Oneidas' 1749 losses, see *MPCP,* V, 478; *MJNY,* 50, 92.

82. *PA,* 1st, III, 67. For other Indians dying among colonists, see Reichel, ed., *Memorials,* I, 284, 285, 350, and n.; *MPCP,* IV, 585, VI, 153–154; "James Dunlap Receipt—Brotherton," GCP, 3/16; Horsfield to Franklin, Fox, &c., 29 Nov. 1756, 21 Jan. 1757, HP, II, 316, 351.

  Indian thoughts on the death of loved ones far away are at once obscure and contradictory. Shawnees, upon learning that one of their own had been "bury'd . . . so handsomely" by colonists in Philadelphia, were grateful, "for had He died in the Woods his Bones wou'd have been scattered and perhaps devour'd by wild Beasts" (*PA,* 1st, I, 394). Nanticokes from Wyoming, on the other hand, apparently thinking that "the Woods" included colonial settlements, risked their lives in 1757 to return to Lancaster in the midst of a war in order "to remove the bones of their friends that had deceased there during the treaty, to their own town for burial" (Reichel, ed., *Memorials,* I, 341).

83. *MPCP,* III, 608, V, 473–474; *PWJ,* XI, 444. Tribal custom did not guarantee an ambassador's safety. While Indians insisted that "we always treat Messengers or Peace makers kindly in the hottest of War . . . ," in fact "[i]f the sentiment for continuing war prevails in the council, then woe to the ambassadors! The law of nations does not protect them at all" (Wallace, *Weiser,* 92; Lafitau, *Customs,* II, 174). Post 1758, 200, 204, 212–215, 254; Hays, 68, 75, 79–81; Croghan, 1750–65, 138–139; *PA,* 1st, III, 737, 740; Morris, "Journal," in Thwaites, ed., *Early Western Travels,* I, 304, 307–308, 312–317 (treating envoys roughly). Heckewelder suggested that Indians' failure to respect messengers was due to European colonial influence (*History,* 181–184).

84. *PA,* 1st, IV, 60 (also II, 383).

85. Journal of Joseph Shippen, Building of Fort Augusta, 1756, 2 July, Small

Books, no. 4, PSF (see also 20 July); William A. Hunter, ed., "Thomas Barton and the Forbes Expedition," *PMHB,* XCV (1971), 481.

86. *PA,* 1st, III, 692, 720–721, 2d, II, 600–603, 612–613 (passports). For other markings, see *MPCP,* VII, 34; *PA,* 1st, II, 668, 682, III, 487, 2d, II, 601–602, 613, 652, 658, 661–662, 665; *PHB,* II, 136, 173, 215, 667; *PGW,* V, 270; *PWJ,* XI, 213; [Lt. Dodge?] to Horsfield, [Aug. 1763], Northampton Co., Misc. Mss., Bethlehem and Vicinity, 95, HSP; Spangenberg to the Governor, 2 May 1756, MCA, 34/317/2/5; Peters to Weiser, 28 July 1758, CCW, II, 133; Meeting with Newcastle and Company, 25 June 1756, Records of the Moravian Mission, box 323, folder 2, item 3, in *Iroq. Ind.,* Reel 19; Joseph Shippen, Orderly Book, 13, 20 July 1758, Small Books, no. 8, PSF.

87. Edward Shippen to Joseph Shippen, 19 June 1756, Correspondence of Edward and Joseph Shippen, 1750–1758, Shippen Papers, APS ("duty to destroy"; see also *MPCP,* VI, 495). *PA,* 1st, II, 634 ("often insulted"; also 647). For close calls and concerns about colonists' attacks, see *PA,* 1st, II, 383, 505, 634, 647, IV, 95, 98; Post 1758, 238; Spangenberg to Israel Pemberton, 2 May 1756, FA, I, 135.

88. Reichel, ed., *Memorials,* I, 304–305, 312, 332, 334–338, 349; William Masters et al. to [?], 26 July 1757, Emitt Collections, 236, Rare Books and Mss., New York Public Library, in *Iroq. Ind.,* Reel 21; *PA,* 1st, III, 209, 247, 251–252; "Indian Intelligence" [1756–1757], HP, II, 328. For William Tatamy as messenger, see *MPCP,* VII, 670, 671, 674. For other examples of killings, see *MPCP,* IX, 45; *PA,* 1st, IV, 65; *PWJ,* X, 318; Proprietaries' Account with Richard Peters, 20 Sept. 1758, PPM, XI, 105.

89. McClure, *Diary,* 90, 92; Zeisberger, *Diaries,* 34–35; "Antiquities," DSP, 1412.Q.22b (graves). Bartram, *Observations,* 19 ("footsteps"), 70–72 (towns). *Ibid.,* 32–33; *MJNY,* 37; Spangenberg, 58–59 (conjurers' huts and posts). *MJNY,* 41 (markings, "archives"; see also 46, 100; Zeisberger, *History,* 114; Zinzendorf Diary, 27 Sept. 1742, MCA, 6/121/1/1; Spangenberg, 58; Woolman, *Journal,* 190–191; McClure, *Diary,* 90; *DHNY,* IV, 436; Robert Greenhalgh Albion and Leonidas Dodson, eds., *Philip Vickers Fithian: Journal, 1775–1776* . . . [Princeton, N.J., 1934], 82, 84; Reichel, ed., *Memorials,* I, 82; Travel Diary, 4 Oct. 1748, MCA, 30/225/2/1; Wallace, *Indian Paths,* 7–10; *DHNY,* I, 7–10).

90. Heckewelder, *History,* 198–200; Bartram, *Observations,* 27; Weiser 1737, 11 (see also Spangenberg, 56–57).

91. Smith, *Account,* 84–85; Weiser, "Notes," 319; Zeisberger, *History,* 131; Jordan, trans., "Ettwein's Notes of Travel," *PMHB,* XXV (1901), 214–215; Reichel, ed., *Memorials,* I, 94; Weiser 1737, 10. For *Otkon,* see Lafitau, *Customs,* I, 236, 238.

92. Bartram, *Observations,* 56.

93. Weiser, "Notes," 319–320.

94. Bartram, *Observations,* 68, 70; Wallace, ed., *Travels of Heckewelder,* 110. *Ponkis:* Jordan, trans., "Ettwein's Notes of Travel," *PMHB,* XXV (1901), 215.

95. Quoted in Wallace, *Weiser,* 199. See also Weiser 1737, 10–11; Smith, *Account,* 96–99.

96. See Greg Dening, *Islands and Beaches: Discourse on a Silent Land: Marquesas 1774–1880* (Chicago, 1983).

97. Benson, ed., *America of 1750,* 54–55 (ferryman). For faded signatures, see Records of Donegal Presbytery, vol. I (A), 1732–1735, 5 (typescript), Presbyterian Historical Society, Philadelphia; William Parsons to Weiser, 31 Oct. 1755, Lancaster County, Miscellaneous Papers, 1724–1772, 105, HSP; Reichel, ed., *Memorials,* I, 82; Travel Diary, 4 Oct. 1748, MCA, 30/225/2/1; Zeisberger, *Diaries,* 34–35; Zeisberger, *History,* 89.

98. Jay Miller, "*Kwulakan:* The Delaware Side of Their Movement West," *Pennsylvania Archaeologist,* XLV (1975), 45–46. *MPCP,* IV, 705, VI, 341, 779 (Conodoguinet). The province had specifically set aside this land for Shawnees (who declined repeated invitations to return to it), but Indians seemed to consider it a more general native reserve, perhaps a place not yet tainted by colonial settlement. Thomas Penn to Tobias Hendricks, 6 May 1736, and Ed Smart to Thomas Penn, 14 Nov. 1736, Penn Mss., Additional Miscellaneous Letters, I, 41, 43, HSP; Barry C. Kent, *Susquehanna's Indians,* Anthropological Series, no. 6 (Harrisburg, Pa., 1989), 70, 87–89; George P. Donehoo, *A History of the Indian Villages and Place Names in Pennsylvania, with Numerous Historical Notes and References* (Harrisburg, Pa., 1928), 42–44; Croghan to Peters, 8 Sept. 1750, PPM, XI, 15. Benson, ed., *America of 1750,* 176 (hunters' memories).

99. The best scholarship on this process considers other parts of English colonial America. Jon Butler, *Awash in a Sea of Faith: Christianizing the American People* (Cambridge, Mass., 1990); David Hall, *Worlds of Wonder, Days of Judgment: Popular Religious Belief in Early New England* (New York, 1989); Mechal Sobel, *The World They Made Together: Black and White Values in Eighteenth-Century Virginia* (Princeton, N.J., 1987), chs. 7–8.

100. Zane 1758, 425 (referring to an instance on the Susquehanna when both Indians and colonists were "pondering the Mistary" of a sign).

101. Post 1760, 10 May; Bartram, *Observations,* 74. For other colonists noting this, see Weiser 1737, 7; Cammerhoff, 165; Travel Diary, 3, 20 Oct. 1748, MCA, 30/225/2/1.

102. *PG,* 5 Dec. 1755 (Tatamy calls it "inhabited parts"); *PA,* 1st, II, 115, 229; *CVSP,* I, 232.

103. *PA,* 8th, V, 3679, talking of "Mensurations." For colonists occasionally going by time, see *PA,* 1st, II, 131; Mittelberger, *Journey,* 62, 75, 90. For Indians sometimes reporting miles, see *MPCP,* VII, 64–69, 158.

104. Post 1760, 15 May, 16 June.

105. Deposition of John Craig, 30 Mar. 1756, PMIA, II, 78. Reichel, ed., *Memorials,* I, 232–233, 235–236, 301; Newcastle's Charges, 1756, Northampton County, Misc. Mss., Bethlehem and Vicinity, 29, 31, HSP (Indians heavily laden). Post 1758, 245 (colonists traveling light).

106. Post 1760, 15 May ("behave"; the words are Teedyuscung's). C. A. Weslager, *The Delaware Indian Westward Migration. With the Texts of Two Manuscripts (1821–22) Responding to General Lewis Cass's Inquiries About Lenape Culture and Language* (Wallingford, Pa., 1978), 95, 118; Vernon Kinietz and Erminie W. Voegelin, eds., *Shawnee Traditions: C. C. Trowbridge's Account,* Occasional Contributions from the Museum of Anthropology of the University of Michigan, no. 9 (Ann Arbor, Mich., 1939), 48; Journal of Shippen, Building of Fort Augusta, 1756, 5 and 7 July, 30 Aug., PSF; Edward Shippen to Gov. James Hamilton (draft), 1 Sept. 1763, Burd-Shippen Pprs., Letters, APS; McClure, *Diary,* 12; Weiser 1737, 9.

107. Heckewelder, *History,* 191. And see *MPCP,* VII, 80.

108. Reichel, ed., *Memorials,* I, 103, 105–107; Wallace, *Weiser,* 141. A delightful account of Zinzendorf's misadventures is in *ibid.,* ch. 17.

109. Bartram, *Observations,* 37, 56, 68, 70 (also Smith, *Account,* 96–99); Weiser, "Notes," 319.

110. Lafitau, *Customs,* II, 130; Zeisberger, *History,* 21. See also *ibid.,* 96; Ruth Springer and Louise Wallman, eds., "Two Swedish Pastors Describe Philadelphia, 1700 and 1702," *PMHB,* LXXXIV (1960), 217; Michael F. Metcalf, trans. and ed., "Letters from the Delaware II: The Reverend Andreas Sandel, June 17, 1702," *Swedish-American Historical Quarterly,* XXXIX (1988), 59.

111. Heckewelder, *History,* 178–180, 309 ("laughter"); Lafitau, *Customs,* II, 140 ("glance").

112. Heckewelder, *History,* 307–308 (first two quotations); *MJNY,* 171 ("details"). See also *ibid.,* 38, 40, 80, 86; Lafitau, *Customs,* I, 321, II, 130, 140; Baron de Lahontan [Louis-Armand de Lom d'Arce], *New Voyages to North-America,* ed. Reuben Gold Thwaites, 2 vols. (Chicago, 1903 [orig. pub. 1703]), II, 427; Peters to the Proprietaries, 27 July 1748, PMOC, IV, 137.

113. Hamilton, ed., "Guy Johnson's Opinions," *PMHB,* LXXVII (1953), 318; Weiser 1737, 10, 13, 14; *MJNY,* 194, 223.

114. *PHB,* II, 206, 215, 222; Zeisberger, *History,* 21.

115. Alfred Proctor James, ed., *The Writings of General John Forbes Relating to His Service in North America* (Menasha, Wisc., 1938), 141.

116. J. Hector St. John de Crèvecoeur, *Letters from an American Farmer and Sketches of Eighteenth-Century America,* ed. Albert E. Stone (New York, 1981), 72–73, 76–78. For his visit to the Susquehanna Valley, see *ibid.,* 353–380; H. L. Bourdin and S. T. Williams, eds., "Crèvecoeur on the Susquehanna,

1774–1776," *Yale Review,* XIV (1925), 552–584. See also John Hales, "The Landscape of Tragedy: Crèvecoeur's 'Susquehanna,' " *Early American Literature,* XX (1985), 39–63.

117. Horatio Hale, ed., *The Iroquois Book of Rites* (Toronto, 1963 [orig. pub. 1883]); Mathew Dennis, *Cultivating a Landscape of Peace: Iroquois-European Encounters in Seventeenth-Century America* (Ithaca, N.Y., 1993), ch. 3.

118. Peters, Diary, 24 Oct. 1758, RPP. Post 1760, 23 May.

119. Weiser 1737, 11–13.

120. A *Tawyia-kaarat* was listed among the "Anayint" (Oneida) Indians at a 1742 council in Philadelphia (*MPCP,* IV, 584).

121. Heckewelder, *History,* 104, 165–168. Zeisberger advised travelers to "accommodate oneself to the Indians, for admonition or remonstrance easily offends them and makes them act in a very contrary manner" (*History,* 120). It is significant that Shickellamy, in the end, went with Weiser rather than staying with Tawagarat. This may suggest a shift in the balance of power in the woods from Indian to colonial; or it may have been the result of Shickellamy's having been appointed by the proprietor himself as Weiser's guide (and protector?), making him responsible for the German's well being. (I am grateful to William Jordan for these insights.)

On a later trip in the woods Weiser got into a similar fight, except that this time he played Shickellamy's part (the expert and guide) and Count Zinzendorf, Weiser's. Once again, the point of dispute was the route and itinerary; once again, harsh words were exchanged. And once again, Weiser, as guide, gave in, as Shickellamy had (Wallace, *Weiser,* 142).

122. John W. Jordan, trans., Bishop Cammerhoff's Letters to Zinzendorf, 1747–1749, Letter X, 10–16 Feb. 1748, 155, HSP. Weiser also had a "disagreement of tempers" with Lewis Evans that precluded their taking a second journey together. Peters to the Proprietaries, 16 Feb. 1749, PMOC, IV, 189.

IV: The Lessons of Brinksmanship, 1728–1743

1. Logan to John Penn, 15 May 1728, JLLB, 1716–1743, 172 (and PMOC, II, 9).

2. The village is called "Chenastry" in this account; but see George P. Donehoo, *A History of the Indian Villages and Place Names in Pennsylvania, with Numerous Historical Notes and References* (Harrisburg, Pa., 1928), 24, 140–143. Unless otherwise noted, the following paragraphs are from *MPCP,* III, 295–298.

3. These enemies are "white heads" in the published council minutes, most likely a misreading of "flat heads," or southern Indians (especially Creeks and Catawbas).

4. One place the story gets muddled is in the belt's origins. Manawkyhickon had accepted the belt from a Delaware woman whose son had been murdered by Shawnees; she hoped that "her Tears might be wiped away" by killing some Shawnees. The Delaware leader, apparently, recast the belt's message to target colonists rather than (or as well as?) Shawnees.

5. For Manawkyhickon and New Jersey, see Wallace, *Teedyuscung*, 197–200. The possibility of a general conspiracy against British colonists is suggested by Jennings, *Ambiguous Iroquois Empire*, 300–308. Others doubt this was more than rumor. Richter, *Ordeal of the Longhouse*, 378, n.33.

6. *PA*, 1st, I, 213, 217.

7. *Ibid.*, 209–210. Other copies of this petition are in *PA*, 6th, XIV, 262–263; RPCEC, B1, 60.

8. *MPCP*, III, 302–304; *PA*, 1st, I, 223.

9. *MPCP*, III, 309; *PA*, 1st, I, 216.

10. *MPCP*, III, 303–304; *PA*, 1st, I, 213–214, 217–218.

11. Samuel Whitaker Pennypacker, "Bebber's Township and the Dutch Patroons of Pennsylvania," *PMHB*, XXXII (1907), 11. Elsewhere it is Cucussea, Chester County (*PA*, 1st, I, 221). Details of this incident are in *PA*, 1st, I, 215–216, 218–220. The petition is in *ibid.*, 213–214, which reproduces (omitting some signatures) RPCEC, B1, 64. Forty-four of the names are in Roberts's hand.

12. Gov. Gordon once called Tacocolie old (*PA*, 1st, I, 217), and once young (*MPCP*, III, 306). James Logan, who mentioned that the woman was "big with Child," called the Delaware man young (Logan to John Penn, 15 May 1728, JLLB, 1716–1743, 173). The woman's name is in J. Smith Futhey and Gilbert Cope, *History of Chester Country, Pennsylvania, with Genealogical and Biographical Sketches* (Evansville, Ind., 1974 [orig. pub. 1881]), 407. I am grateful to Laurie A. Rofini for this last reference.

13. The fate of the boy in the house is unknown.

14. *MPCP*, III, 303–308; *PA*, 1st, I, 217–221. The Winters were hanged on 3 July 1728 (Futhey and Cope, *History of Chester County*, 407). Herbert spent the summer in jail, but was released by the end of August (*MPCP*, III, 326–327; *PA*, 1st, I, 225–226; Gordon to the Proprietaries, 11 July 1728, PMOC, II, 19). Unlike John and Edmond Cartlidge six years before, the condemned men apparently lacked powerful friends in the capital who might have saved them.

15. *MPCP*, III, 304–306, 309; *PA*, 1st, I, 210–211, 214–217, 220–224.

16. *PA*, 1st, I, 214–216, 224.

17. *MPCP*, III, 309–326; Francis Jennings, "Incident at Tulpehocken," *Pennsylvania History*, XXXV (1968), 335–355. The Indian delegation also included Shickellamy (the Oneida's first appearance in the diplomatic arena) and a solitary Shawnee.

18. *MPCP*, III, 310, 314, 318. The only exception to the civility was Sassoonan's complaint about land, treated below. At the Conestoga council, no one mentioned the dispute between Shawnees and Conestogas; both nations were represented there, perhaps indicating that they had already made up their differences. Nor, at Philadelphia, was there any mention of the war belt or the Miamis.

19. *MPCP*, III, 306, 330; *PA*, 1st, I, 216, 217, 223, 230, 242.

20. *MPCP*, III, 329.

21. *PA*, 1st, I, 227. The town's probable location is noted in Hanna, *Wilderness Trail*, I, 194; Donehoo, *Place Names*, 103.

22. *PA*, 1st, I, 227, 229.

23. *Ibid.*, 227–229, 232.

24. *MPCP*, III, 333–337. The death of Civility's only child postponed the treaty with Conestogas until the following spring. No one reported questioning Kakowatchy or learning why Shawnees had abandoned Pechoquealin.

25. For the crowd at the execution, see *MPCP*, IV, 574. Official descriptions of them are in *ibid.*, III, 308, 312, 317.

26. *PA*, 1st, I, 214, 227.

27. *MPCP*, III, 271–277; *PA*, 1st, I, 205–206 (1727). Logan to John Penn, 18 Oct. 1728, 13 6 mo. 1729, PMOC, II, 33, 83 (see also same to same, 6 Dec. 1727, I, 311).

28. *MPCP*, III, 322 (Sassoonan; and see Jennings, "Incident at Tulpehocken," *Pa. History*, XXXV [1968], 335–355). Jennings, *Ambiguous Iroquois Empire*, 306–307; McConnell, *A Country Between*, chs. 1–2 (exodus).

29. *MPCP*, III, 363–364.

30. William C. Reichel, ed., *Memorials of the Moravian Church*, I (Philadelphia, 1870), 133.

31. *MPCP*, III, 337; James H. Merrell, "Shickellamy, 'a Person of Consequence,' " in Robert S. Grumet, ed., *Northeastern Indian Lives, 1632–1816* (Amherst, Mass., 1996), 227–257 (Shickellamy). As early as 1728, Pennsylvania only reluctantly turned to Civility when it needed a go-between, and even then provincial officials asked local magistrates to go with him in order to keep an eye on him. "It were to be wished he were more to be depended on. . . . He is the best however that at present is to be mett with to undertake it, and we must endeavor to make the best of him" (*PA*, 1st, I, 230). Two years later Civility was complaining that Conestogas now "see how little our Counsels is Minded" (*ibid.*, 272), and in 1736 James Logan lumped him among native

leaders thought to be "weak and too often knavish" (Logan to Weiser, 18 Oct. 1736, LP, 2/58).

32. See Richter, *Ordeal of the Longhouse,* 241–244, 273–276; McConnell, *A Country Between,* 55–58; Jennings, *Ambiguous Iroquois Empire,* chs. 15–17; Wallace, *Weiser,* chs. 6, 11, 16; idem, *Indians in Pennsylvania,* rev. ed., William A. Hunter (Harrisburg, Pa., 1986), chs. 16–17. For Logan's view of the developments, see Logan to [Clarke?], 12 Nov. 1740, LC, IV, 20.

33. McKee's story is in *MPCP,* IV, 630–633. Other treatments of these incidents are Wallace, *Weiser,* chs. 18–20; Jennings, *Ambiguous Iroquois Empire,* 354–355.

34. The sound is described in Wallace, *Weiser,* 145.

35. I have reconstructed the Iroquois story from three principal accounts. The first is the one McKee set down in his deposition, some twelve days after hearing it at the Shawnee town from a leader of the ten Iroquois warriors—but not Jonnhaty (*MPCP,* IV, 631–632; also *PG,* 27 Jan. 1743). The second is Conrad Weiser's, heard at Shamokin on 4 February, from "one who calls Shikellimo his Grandfather" and who was at the scene (*MPCP,* IV, 644–646; an almost identical manuscript version is in "The Report of Conrad Weiser . . . of his Journeys to Shamokin on the Affairs of Virginia & Maryland," 21 Apr. 1743, FA, I, 41, 43). The third is an account, in Weiser's hand, similar to the second, endorsed "Memorandum" and "Skirmish in Virginia by Jonnhaty" (CCW, I, 33). The similarity between the second and third versions suggests that the third is a draft of the second. However, there are differences between them, and it is curious that Weiser would call the narrator a grandson of Shickellamy in one account and Jonnhaty in another without connecting the two. If they were indeed one and the same, Jonnhaty must have been a fictive grandson; it is unlikely that in 1743 Shickellamy would have had a grandson old enough to be a war captain. To further confuse the issue, at Onondaga on 24 July Weiser wrote that he saw Jonnhaty and heard his story, as if meeting the man and hearing it for the first time, and promised to take the account down in writing before he left town (*MPCP,* IV, 662). Could the "Memorandum" be the fulfillment of that promise? In any case, there is enough correspondence among the three accounts to allow a single telling of the Indians' version of what took place. For additional reports, see Peter Wraxall, *An Abridgement of the Indian Affairs Contained in Four Folio Volumes, Transacted In the Colony of New York, From the Year 1678 to the Year 1751,* ed. Charles Howard McIlwain (Cambridge, Mass., 1915), 230–231; *DRCNY,* VI, 230–242.

36. *MPCP,* IV, 668. For the causes and character of this conflict, consult Daniel K. Richter, "War and Culture: The Iroquois Experience," *WMQ,* 3d Ser., XL (1983), 528–559; James H. Merrell, " 'Their Very Bones Shall Fight': The

Catawba-Iroquois Wars," in Daniel K. Richter and James H. Merrell, eds., *Beyond the Covenant Chain: The Iroquois and Their Neighbors in Indian North America, 1600–1800* (Syracuse, N.Y., 1987), 115–133.

37. They later admitted to taking "one Cask Syder" and to killing "one Hog, one Calf, and one Horse" (*DRCNY,* VI, 239).

38. Some have speculated that this woman became McKee's wife (Hanna, *Wilderness Trail,* I, 210). Later in the decade McKee did have a wife from among the Shawnees, and she might have been of European origin, but reports vary. RPLB, 1737–1750, 381; Cammerhoff, 169; *PWJ,* IX, 456.

39. *DRCNY,* VI, 230–231 ("hostile manner"). See also *MPCP,* IV, 635–636; *EJCCV,* V, 112–113; *Iroq. Ind.,* Reel 11, 18 Dec. 1742, 18 Dec. 1742–8 Feb. 1743, 23 Dec. 1742 ("Our Flagg"), 14 Feb., 27 Apr. 1743; *PG,* 27 Jan., 31 Mar. 1743; The Draper Manuscript Collection, Virginia Papers, Series ZZ (microfilm, Madison, Wisc.), Reel 121, v. 4, 1–4; *South Carolina Gazette,* 7 Mar. 1743. I am grateful to Turk McClesky for alerting me to the Draper Manuscripts and the newspaper reports. His account of this episode is in "Across the First Divide: Frontiers of Settlement and Culture in Augusta County, Virginia, 1738–1770" (Ph.D. diss., College of William and Mary, 1990), 249–252.

   That day in the Shenandoah Valley, recalling a boundary drawn between the Six Nations and Virginia some two decades before, each party believed that the other had no right even to be there. The Iroquois understood that no Virginians were to cross the first line of western hills; Virginians insisted that the line lay one range farther west. *MPCP,* IV, 717–718; Jennings, *Ambiguous Iroquois Empire,* 279–281, 294–295, and map 11.

40. Officials in Virginia—and in New York, when they heard—believed the colonists' version. In Pennsylvania there was less certainty. Thomas doubted "the Indian side of the Story," yet at the same time he wrote to Virginia's Gov. William Gooch that "if the Inhabitants of the back parts of Virginia have no more Truth and Honesty than some of ours, I should make no Scruple to prefer an Iroquois' Testimony to their's." After hearing Col. Patton tell his version in person, in 1744, Thomas "seem'd satisfy'd that the Indians were the first Aggressors." For his part, Conrad Weiser, on meeting Jonnhaty and hearing his story, pronounced the war captain "a very thoughtful and honest Man." For New York, see *DRCNY,* VI, 231, 236, 238–239; for Pennsylvania, *MPCP,* IV, 635–636, 653, 662; R. Alonzo Brock, ed., "Journal of William Black, 1744 . . . ," *PMHB,* I (1877), 413; *PA,* 1st, I, 662–663.

41. *MPCP,* IV, 636 ("force Us"), 643 (Sassoonan), 653 ("Juncture"). And see 634, 649; *DRCNY,* VI, 237, 241.

42. Logan to George Clarke, 4 Aug. 1737 ("rough"), Logan to Gooch, 11 May 1737 ("cruel"), LC, IV. See also *PA,* 1st, I, 230.

43. *MPCP*, IV, 634. This was no idle fear: the Winter brothers haunted the province yet. "I am not without Apprehensions," the governor wrote, "of their falling upon some of the Indians as they did once before" (*ibid.,* 636).

44. *Ibid.,* 655–656. Richard Hockley to Thomas Penn[?], 20 June 1743, PMOC, III, 259. Meanwhile local natives, perhaps recalling Tacocolie and Quilee, collected all "the Straggling Indians . . . into their Towns upon Account of the late Skirmish in Virginia" (*MPCP*, IV, 657).

45. *Ibid.,* 634, 636.

46. *Ibid.,* 641–651.

47. *Ibid.,* 650.

48. The description of their visit is from *ibid.,* 660–669; Bartram, *Observations,* 40–46, 56–63.

49. Anthony F. C. Wallace, *The Death and Rebirth of the Seneca* (New York, 1970), 37, 53–54, 78–93; William N. Fenton, *The False Faces of the Iroquois* (Norman, Okla., 1987). And see *Journals of Claus and Weiser,* 47.

50. Marshe, 179.

51. As in the Armstrong affair, they set aside the matter of truth, or who fired first. The issue did come up at the Onondaga council, but only briefly. To Virginia's attempt to sidestep the question of blame—"I will not Dispute with you about it," Canasatego had said on the colony's behalf—the Iroquois were sure that "you have by this Time full Satisfactions from your own People besides what You had from Us, that your People had begun Hostilities." But in the interests of peace and harmony the Iroquois were quick to agree that "an evil spirit was the promoter of the late unhappy Skirmish." Virginia lore had it that one of the colonists—"one of those madmen who so often disgrace partys of Militia by their disobedience to orders"—did indeed fire on an Indian straggler (Draper Mss., 4ZZ2-3).

52. Gov. Gooch actually apologized to George Clarke, his New York counterpart, for even mentioning the incident to him in the first place, as if Clarke's colony had not dominated Iroquois-English affairs for generations (*EJCCV,* V, 130).

53. *MPCP*, IV, 579–580. For Pennsylvania's prompting, see 575–576.

54. *Ibid.,* 649–650.

55. *PA,* 1st, I, 299–306, 327–328, 394–395, 425, 549–553.

56. Shamokin Diary, 31 Oct. 1745, MCA, 28/217/12B/1, 6 Mar. 1748, 6/121/4/1 (Neshanockeow). Samuel Hopkins, *Historical Memoirs, Relating to the Housatunnuck Indians . . .* (Boston, 1753, Evans 7023), 90.

57. Logan to Thomas, 19 June 1742, Alverthorpe Letterbook, D, 156, LP.

58. Peter C. Mancall, *Valley of Opportunity: Economic Culture along the Upper Susquehanna, 1700–1800* (Ithaca, N.Y., 1991), 73.

59. Delaware Indians "To Mr. Jeremiah Langhorne & all Magistrates in Pennsylvania," 21 Nov. 1740, PMIA, I, 30. For the Walking Purchase, see Jennings, *Ambiguous Iroquois Empire,* ch. 17; Wallace, *Teedyuscung,* ch. 2.

60. David Brainerd to Ebenezer Pemberton, 5 Nov. 1744, in Jonathan Edwards, *The Life of David Brainerd,* ed. Norman Pettit, The Works of Jonathan Edwards, vol. VII (New Haven, Conn., 1985), 578, 580.

61. Spangenberg, 428; *MPCP,* IV, 581.

62. *MPCP,* IV, 574 ("transported"), 713 ("Flocks"; also 570, 572), 720 (Gachadow).

V: Conversations

1. *PA,* 1st, I, 671 ("talke"); Weiser to Peters[?], 24 Jan. 1745/6, DSP, 966.F.24 ("discourse"; see also *MPCP,* V, 136–139, 162, 167, 212, 222–223; *PA,* 1st, I, 750–751, 756–769; Weiser to [?], 15 Apr. 1746, CCW, I, 14).

2. Weiser to Peters, 27 Oct. 1754, quoted in Wallace, *Weiser,* 372. See also "Sentements of Ohio," n.d., CCW, II, 27; *PA,* 1st, I, 551; Albert Cook Myers, ed., *William Penn: His Own Account of the Lenni Lenape or Delaware Indians, 1683* (Moylan, Pa., 1937), 87.

3. *MPCP,* III, 440.

4. *Ibid.,* 449 (also 440, 446, IV, 642); VI, 444 ("Public Person"); Post, "An Observation or Two made in my several Conversations with Indians . . ." [19 Jan. 1759], RPCEC, B9, 2075.

5. *MPCP,* III, 449 ("Grub").

6. *Ibid.,* I, 180 (hogs), IV, 413, 419–420 (assault), VI, 420, IX, 426 (land), VIII, 401 (horses); *PA,* 1st, I, 295 (woman and apples), 239–240, 271–272 (land). Indian complaints about liquor are legion. See *MPCP,* II, 33, 45, 48, 511, III, 46–48, V, 167, 676; *PA,* 1st, I, 327–328, 394–395, 425, 549–552. For natives stealing rum, see *MPCP,* I, 187–188; Gary B. Nash, ed., "The First Decade in Pennsylvania: Letters of William Markham and Thomas Holme to William Penn," *PMHB,* XC (1966), 333; *PWP,* II, 106–108; *PA,* 1st, I, 455.

7. "Minutes of what pass'd between the Proprietor & the Delaware Indians, 9th June 1733," PMIA, I, 37.

8. *PA,* 1st, I, 737, 741–743; *MPCP,* III, 507 (distant nations). For friends, see 512 (quotation; also 578; *PA,* 1st, I, 233–234, 551).

9. *PA,* 1st, I, 341 ("Distance"; and see 302–304, 327–330), 347 ("amicable"); 454, 551–552 (feelers).

10. *MPCP,* II, 553 ("Ear"), VIII, 34 (Teedyuscung). See also II, 554, 574, III, 598, IV, 568, VIII, 46, 508; *PA,* 1st, I, 211, 241–242; Speech of John Shickellamy, 7 Aug. 1760, FA, III, 503.

11. *MPCP*, III, 209–212, V, 73, 84, 98; *PA*, 1st, I, 229; Wallace, *Weiser*, 373 (word from Philadelphia). *MPCP*, IV, 747, V, 137, 167, 212, 222 (word from Indian country).

12. *PHB*, II, 198; Howard H. Peckham, ed., *George Croghan's Journal of His Trip to Detroit in 1767* . . . (Ann Arbor, Mich., 1939), 34.

13. *MPCP*, I, 436; *PA*, 1st, I, 211. "As I am settled . . . at Cheningo [Otsiningo, on the Susquehanna's North Branch]," Seneca George (Osternados) promised Pennsylvania officials in 1761, "I shall be able to give the Governor an account of any thing that is transacted in the Council of the Six Nations" (*MPCP*, VIII, 656).

14. Marshe, 180; Heckewelder, *History*, 311–312; *PA*, 2d, VI, 650.

15. Heckewelder, *History*, 311–312.

16. Some was probably pidgin, but it is doubtful that pidgin sufficed for formal talks. Ives Goddard, "The Delaware Jargon," in Carol E. Hoffecker et al., eds., *New Sweden in America* (Newark, Del., 1995), 137–149.

17. *DHNY*, IV, 435 (Iroquois); Zeisberger, *History*, 144; Heckewelder, *History*, xliii, 320. Some colonists believed that Indians were reluctant teachers (Cammerhoff, 172), but others found Delawares "mightly pleas'd that I have preferr'd thier [sic] Tongue in learning most of it so I can converse a little with them" (Kenny 1761–63, 169). Heckewelder said that Indians were glad to teach their language, but could be reluctant to answer too many questions, improperly posed (*History*, 320–322).

18. Beverly McAnear, ed., "Personal Accounts of the Albany Congress of 1754," *MVHR*, XXXIX (1953), 731 ("Diction"); *DHNY*, IV, 435 ("allegory"); *PA*, 1st, III, 467 ("at a loss").

19. *MPCP*, VIII, 655–656. See also III, 199; Cammerhoff, 174; Pemberton 1762, 319; Journal of Joseph Shippen, Building of Fort Augusta, 1756, 11 Oct., Small Books, no. 4, PSF.

20. Weiser, "Notes," 322. William Penn himself noted that "they are great Concealers of their own resentments" (*PWP*, II, 449). And see Anthony F. C. Wallace, *The Death and Rebirth of the Seneca* (New York, 1970), Part I.

21. Zeisberger, *History*, 143 (also Heckewelder, *History*, 150).

22. *MPCP*, VIII, 305 (also 310), 709. Gregory Dowd properly sees rumors as products of uncertainty and anxiety, or sometimes calculated attempts to discover the mood and intentions of the other side, noting that their frequency and nature vary over time ("The Panic of 1751: The Significance of Rumors on the South Carolina-Cherokee Frontier," *WMQ*, 3d ser., LIII [1996], 526–560). Rumors on the Pennsylvania frontier were a fairly constant phenomenon, while more frequent and more alarming at some times than others (and especially during the war years of the late 1750s).

23. *MPCP*, I, 299–301, 396–397, 435–436, II, 471 (French attacks), 474–475 (by sea); 145, 204, 509–510; Logan to Col. Burnet, 18 Apr. 1728, JLLB,

III [1721–1732], 202; *PWP,* III, 451–455 (other attacks). *MPCP,* III, 500–501, 504; *MJNY,* 204 (Virginia).

24. *MPCP,* III, 501. Meeting between Gov. Hamilton and Brothers Joseph, Herman, and Rogers, 17 June 1752, MCA, 34/317/1/3. For other fears of attack, see *MPCP,* I, 157–158, 396, 448–449, II, 71, 245; Narrative of John Budd, 4 July 1694, in Penn Letters and Ancient Documents, 274, APS; Nash, ed., "First Decade," *PMHB,* XC (1966), 333.

25. *MPCP,* I, 397, II, 509–510; *PWP,* III, 452.

26. *MPCP,* II, 70–71 (clothing), 562–563, III, 500–503, 511–512, 564–565, 604–607; *PA,* 1st, I, 439 (scalps).

27. *MPCP,* II, 510 ("talk"), V, 286–287 ("actual War"), 656 ("Effect"); *Arch. Md.,* VI, 437 ("Mischief," "alarmed").

28. Edward Armstrong, ed., and Deborah Logan, comp., *Correspondence Between William Penn and James Logan, Secretary of the Province of Pennsylvania, and Others, 1700–1750,* 2 vols., HSP, *Memoirs,* IX–X (1870–1872), I, 179 ("reports"); *MPCP,* II, 16 ("sowers"), III, 501 ("Ground"; see also VI, 152), IV, 433 ("Idle"), 444, VIII, 35, 46 ("Chirping"); *PA,* 1st, I, 232; Kenny 1761–63, 155. Similar admonitions, from both Indians and colonists, are in *MPCP,* II, 245–246, 387, 471, 474–475, 516. For provincial laws against rumors, see *Statutes at Large of Pennsylvania, 1682–1809,* 17 vols. (Harrisburg, Pa., 1896–1915), II, 229, 366, III, 61.

29. *MPCP,* III, 146 ("imperfect"); V, 2; Weiser to Peters[?], 24 Jan. 1745/6, DSP, 966.F.24; Wallace, Weiser, 233 (snowshoes); Nash, ed., "First Decade," *PMHB,* XC (1966), 333 (fireflies).

30. Peters to "Hond Sir," 5 July 1753, PMOC, VI, 73 (see also James Hamilton to Thomas Penn, 30 Apr. 1751, V, 135; *PA,* 1st, I, 762). Post 1760, 23 May. But Post believed that messengers were held to a different, higher standard. Indians, like colonists, sometimes lie, Post observed, but not, he insisted, in "publick Negotiations." Natives consider a messenger to be a truth teller, not only in formal speeches but "also the Words in Conversation" of a more casual sort. Colonial go-betweens, the missionary went on, too often forget this; their wild promises, when unfulfilled, foster among the natives nothing but "Bitterness & Revenge. . . . The Lyes of our Traders," the missionary concluded, "often expose us to the Hatred of the Indians. But the Lyes of our Messengers will always expose us to danger from the Indians." Post, "An Observation or Two," [19 Jan. 1759], RPCEC, B9, 2075.

31. *MPCP,* V, 401 (Canasatego), VI, 152 ("enquire"), VIII, 115 ("sift"); *PA,* 1st, II, 23.

32. *MPCP,* VI, 613; VII, 48 ("in form"; also IV, 657); Peters to "Hond Sir," 5 July 1753, PMOC, VI, 73 ("regular"). "Journal of Daniels Journey to the Allegheny," PPEC, II, 29 ("Noise"). Heckewelder, *History,* 109. James Hamilton to Weiser, 27 Apr. 1751, RPP, III, 38 ("transient").

33. *MPCP,* VIII, 639 ("understanding"), IV, 568 ("suitable"). *PA,* 1st, III, 505–507; Hays, *passim* (passive). *MPCP,* II, 386, V, 349–350, 530, VI, 151 (firing). VII, 137, VIII, 150 (colonial city). An experienced go-between took Indian advice (see V, 167) and sent a runner ahead to announce his impending arrival. A man who gave no warning simply walked in, while locals piled out of houses and greeted him informally as he made his way to the headman's house (*PA,* 1st, II, 491; *MPCP,* VIII, 143–144).

34. *MPCP,* VI, 152 ("Custom"). For Shickellamy, *PA,* 1st, I, 241–242, 665–666, 673, II, 23; Indian Charges, 1744, CCW, I, 11. And see Croghan to Peters, 16 Oct. 1754, GCP, 5/19; Croghan to Maj. Gen. Monckton, 3 Oct. 1761, *ibid.,* 5/23.

35. *MPCP,* V, 474, VI, 152, 180 (quotation), VII, 47, 68.

36. Marshe, 180. See also *PA,* 1st, II, 724, III, 107.

37. Bartram, *Observations,* 43. Kenny 1761–63, 12, 18, 21, 154; Smith, *Account,* 6, 8, 10, 15, 20, 22–23, 25 (Ohio country).

38. *PA,* 1st, III, 397.

39. George Miranda Report, n.d., Provincial Council Papers, N.D. file, HSP ("Sweet"). *MPCP,* II, 600 ("friendly"), III, 319 ("Expressions"). When in doubt, colonists would ask Indians to elaborate, also furthering the educational process (VII, 209, VIII, 88).

40. Lynn Ceci, "The Value of Wampum among the New York Iroquois: A Case Study in Artifact Analysis," *Journal of Anthropological Research,* XXXVIII (1982), 102–103.

41. Lewis Henry Morgan, *League of the Ho-Dé-No-Sau-Nee, or Iroquois* (New York, 1962 [orig. pub. 1851]), 116, 120–121; William M. Beauchamp, "Wampum and Shell Articles Used by the New York Indians," New York State Museum, *Bulletin,* no. 41, VIII (Albany, N.Y., 1901 [repr. ed. New York, 1978]), 319–480; idem, "Wampum Used in Council and as Currency," *The American Antiquarian and Oriental Journal,* XX (1898), 1–13; Frank G. Speck, "The Functions of Wampum among the Eastern Algonkian," *Memoirs of the American Anthropological Association,* VI (1919), 3–74; Wilbur R. Jacobs, "Wampum, The Protocol of Indian Diplomacy," *WMQ ,* 3d ser., VI (1949), 596–604; George S. Snyderman, "The Function of Wampum," *Procs. APS,* XCVII (1954), 469–494; Ceci, "Native Wampum as a Peripheral Resource in the Seventeenth-Century World System," in Laurence M. Hauptman and James D. Wherry, eds., *The Pequots in Southern New England: The Fall and Rise of an American Indian Nation* (Norman, Okla., 1990), 48–63; Michael K. Foster, "Another Look at the Function of Wampum in Iroquois-White Councils," in Francis Jennings et al., eds., *The History and Culture of Iroquois Diplomacy: An Interdisciplinary Guide to the Treaties of the Six Nations and Their League* (Syracuse, N.Y., 1985), 99–114; Christopher L. Miller and George R. Hamell, "A New Perspective on Indian-White Contact: Cul-

tural Symbols and Colonial Trade," *JAH,* LXXIII (1986), 311–328; Richter, *Ordeal of the Longhouse,* 32, 47–49, 84–85, 276–277. A modern meditation on wampum's meaning that appeared after this section was written is Jerry Martin, *Shell Game: A True Account of Beads and Money in North America* (San Francisco, 1996). For colonial treatments of the subject, see Joseph-Francois Lafitau, *Customs of the American Indians Compared with the Customs of Primitive Times,* trans. and ed. William N. Fenton and Elizabeth L. Moore, 2 vols. (Toronto, 1974–1975), I, 310–312; Loskiel, *History,* Part I, 26–28; Heck-ewelder, *History,* 109–110.

42. Frank G. Speck, *A Study of the Delaware Indian Big House Ceremony,* 2 vols. (Harrisburg, Pa., 1931), II, 64.

43. *MPCP,* V, 358, 569–570.

44. *MPCP,* V, 537 ("Mind"), 615, VII, 156 ("confirm"); VIII, 470 ("enforce"); *PA,* 1st, I, 737 ("truth"); Seneca George to Gov. Denny, 25 June 1758, RPCEC, B9, 1947 ("Credit").

45. Foster, "Another Look at Wampum," in Jennings et al., eds., *History and Culture of Iroquois Diplomacy,* esp. 104–106; *MPCP,* VI, 615 ("this day").

46. Information regarding Teedyuscung delivered to Spangenberg from a Dela-ware Indian (Augustus), 30 July 1756, PMIA, II, 98 (and see *DHNY,* II, 625). The claim of nothing ever being done is somewhat overstated. As Mary Druke has noted ("Iroquois Treaties: Common Forms, Varying Inter-pretations," in Jennings et al., eds., *History and Culture of Iroquois Diplomacy,* 88–90), Indians sometimes substituted deerskins or sticks for beads, and sometimes went ahead without any item at all. The *process* of speaking on something was as crucial as having a tangible marker of that speech. My own findings confirm this, while suggesting that substitutes declined over time, and that Indians usually noted it when they spoke without wampum.

47. *MPCP,* II, 387 (20 belts), 546–549 (32), VI, 194–198 (10); Proceedings of the Council at Conestoga, 31 July 1710, PMIA, I, 34, in *Iroq. Ind.,* Reel 7 (26 belts, 2 strings, 31 sticks). For the number of beads, see *Journals of Claus and Weiser,* 12–13; *PA,* 1st, II, 17, III, 555; *Collections of the Illinois Historical Society Library,* XI, 21; Peters, Diary, 2–4, 6, 7, 9, 15, 22, 25 Oct. 1758, RPP. *MPCP,* VIII, 508 (pocket). Account of the Easton Treaty, June 1762, Friendly Association Mss., Swarthmore College Library (pouch). *PWJ,* II, 860–861 (casket or chest).

48. Peters to the Proprietaries, 15 Nov. 1755, Richard Peters Letters to the Pro-prietaries of Pennsylvania, 1755–1757, 17, Simon Gratz Collection, Case 2, Box 33-a, HSP ("amazing"). Israel Pemberton to Geo. Browne, 22 May 1758, FA, I, 494; Peters to Weiser, 13 7ber 1758, CCW, II, 135 (100,000). Edward Shippen to Joseph Shippen, 19 June 1751, PSF, I (Sympson, "a wampum maker"; it is unclear whether Sympson drilled the wampum or

was among those who wove it into belts). Peters to Croghan, 23 Apr. 1755, RPCEC, B5, 801 (Philadelphia woman). Peters, Diary, 6–7 Oct. 1758, RPP (Montour). For women, see Israel Pemberton to Christian Frederick Post, 6 5 mo. 1760, Pemberton Papers, Folder 2, Haverford College Library; *MPCP,* VII, 216–218; Beauchamp, "Wampum in Council," *American Antiquarian and Oriental Jnl.,* XX (1898), 9.

49. *PA,* 1st, I, 762 ("Bagg"); Heckewelder, *History,* 186. Sassoonan allegedly selling wampum from the council bag was a sort of sacrilege, especially since his other name, Alumapees, meant "preserver of the records" (Francis Jennings, "The Delaware Interregnum," *PMHB,* LXXXIX [1965], 174).

50. *PA,* 1st, I, 741–742; *MPCP,* VI, 195, 686 (hatchets), VII, 66 (scalps). Those agreeing with a message could also "add Strength to" a belt by tying a string to it. Conference at Israel Pemberton's, 23 Apr. 1756, LP, 11/41; Minutes of a Conference at Easton, 12 Oct. 1758, RPCEC, B9, 2024; *MPCP,* VI, 685–686, IX, 47; Nathaniel Holland to Israel Pemberton, 16 Oct. 1760, FA, IV, 43.

51. *MPCP,* V, 673 (human figures). Foster, "Another Look at Wampum," in Jennings et al., eds., *History and Culture of Iroquois Diplomacy,* 108–109; Post 1758, 264 (path). Post 1758, 270–271; *MPCP,* IX, 329 (diamonds). *MPCP,* V, 673, VII, 701, VIII, 158, 747 (figures). *MPCP,* IX, 330 (squares). *MPCP,* II, 246; Journal by Capt. Joseph Shippen at Fort Augusta, 1757–1758, 15 Feb. 1758, Small Books, no. 6, PSF (hands).

52. *MPCP,* III, 154 (1722); *PWJ,* XI, 371 (Senecas); Indians—Treaty at Easton, 28 July 1756, in a box labeled "Indians (transferred from Society Collections)," HSP (Teedyuscung).

53. Conference at Armstrong's, 10 June 1756, Between Col. William Clapham and Ogaghradarisha, PMIA, II, 92. Heckewelder, *History, 108 ("turning"). MPCP,* II, 387 (hang belts or strings on a line), 471 (board), VIII, 174, 179 (in order); Wallace, *Weiser,* 91 (stick); Bartram, *Observations,* 60 (pole).

54. Heckewelder, *History,* 109–110 ("snake"). *MPCP,* VII, 49, 65–66 ("throwed"). See also VI, 197–198; Post 1758, 256; Kenny 1761–63, 24; Peters to the Proprietors, 26 Oct. 1749, PMOC, IV, 245.

55. *MPCP,* I, 586 ("amitie"), II, 141, 145, 204 ("Credential"), 387, 461; Logan Account Book, 1712–1720, 99, 112, 115, 169, LP. Marshall Becker ("Lenape Land Sales, Treaties, and Wampum Belts," *PMHB,* CVIII [1984], 354) doubts that early land cessions "involved the use of formal belts or strings of wampum." However, Indians were using belts to confirm their speeches with Pennsylvania from a very early day, and Lasse Cock's 1682 charges for work on the Proprietor's behalf included money for wampum. Thomas Budd, *Good Order Established in Pennsilvania & New-Jersey, in America, Being a true Account of the Country* . . . (Philadelphia, 1685), 28–29; *MPCP,* I,

447–448; *PWP,* II, 243. The story of wampum in New England is told in Neal Salisbury, *Manitou and Providence: Indians, Europeans, and the Making of New England, 1500–1643* (New York, 1982), 147–152; Ceci, "Wampum as a Peripheral Resource," in Hauptman and Wherry, eds., *Pequots,* 48–63; Lois Scozzari, "The Significance of Wampum to Seventeenth-Century Indians in New England," *Connecticut Review,* XVII (1995), 59–69.

56. *MPCP,* III, 191–192, 198 (Keith). Richard Peters to Monckton, 15 Aug. 1761, *Collections of the Massachusetts Historical Society,* 4th ser., IX (1871), 440. Other observers argued that Indians handling those belts were indeed observing proper protocol (Israel Pemberton to Mary Pemberton, 5 Aug. 1761, FA, IV, 153–158). See Peters to Penn, 18 Feb. 1756 (copy), PMOC, VIII, 41; Post 1760, 27, 29 May.

57. Peters to Thomas Penn, 30 Oct. 1756, PMOC, VIII, 185.

58. *PWJ,* V, 201; XII, 75 (Stamp Act). Julian P. Boyd, "Indian Affairs in Pennsylvania, 1736–1762," in idem, ed., *Indian Treaties Printed by Benjamin Franklin, 1736–1762* (Philadelphia, 1938), xxvi (Penn family); Journal of Shippen, Building of Fort Augusta, 1756, 28 July, PSF (Clapham, forts); *MPCP,* VII, 701 *(G.R., D.K.).* For *G.R.* on Indian belts, *MPCP,* VII, 522; "Substance of a Conversation with Gray Eyes, a Delaware Indian Messenger," 24 May 1761, FA, IV, 123. Indians delivered lettered belts as early as 1654 (Beauchamp, "Wampum and Shell Articles," New York State Mus., *Bulletin,* no. 41, VIII [1901], 390; idem, "Wampum in Council," *American Antiquarian and Oriental Jnl.,* XX [1898], 6). In addition, initials in rings, bottles, pipes, and coins were familiar enough in Susquehanna Valley towns. Barry C. Kent, *Susquehanna's Indians,* Anthropological Series, no. 6 (Harrisburg, Pa., 1989), 209–210, 223, 225, 269, 276, 279.

59. Croghan to Gage, 22 Mar. 1765, GCP, 5/27 ("nessecarys"). For advising, Peters to Croghan, 23 Apr. 1755, RPCEC, B5, 801. For string on hand, *MPCP,* VI, 150–151, VIII, 468. Weiser to Peters, 28 Jan. 1754, CCW, I, 43 ("accidents"); *PA,* 1st, III, 701 ("Wampum enough").

60. Hays, 79, 66–67. See also 69–70, 76, 78; Post 1760, 6, 13–14, 16 May, 11–12 June. For wampum having the sanction of many people, see Richter, *Ordeal of the Longhouse,* 47–48.

61. *PA,* 1st, III, 737; Hays, 68–69; Post 1760, 30–31 May (1760). For combining, see *MPCP,* III, 459, VI, 150, VII, 147, VIII, 212; Post 1758, 243; *PA,* 1st, I, 229–230, II, 193–194, III, 556; *CVSP,* I, 231; Kenneth P. Bailey, ed., *The Ohio Company Papers, 1753–1817* . . . (Arcata, Calif., 1947), 21; Instructions to Post and Thomson, 7 June 1758, MCA, 28/219/8/2; Joseph Shippen, Jr., to John Jacob Schmick, 28 Jan. 1768, Joseph Shippen, Jr., Letterbook, 1763–1773, 28, APS.

62. *CVSP,* I, 232 ("don't understand"; see also Weiser to Logan, 16 Sept. 1736, LP, 10/62; *MJNY,* 95; *MPCP,* III, 362). Examples of Indians sending letters

and strings are in *MPCP,* III, 103, 504–505, IV, 656–658, V, 568–570, 691–692; *PA,* 1st, IV, 60–61. Sources suggest that some Indians dispensed with beads altogether in favor of letters, but this may be colonial scribes' decision to omit what they considered the less important wampum.

63. Peter Wraxall, *An Abridgement of the Indian Affairs Contained in Four Folio Volumes, Transacted In the Colony of New York, From the Year 1678 to the Year 1751,* ed. Charles Howard McIlwain (Cambridge, Mass., 1915), 33; Albert Cook Myers, ed., *Narratives of Early Pennsylvania, West New Jersey, and Delaware, 1630–1707* (New York, 1912), 173; Logan Account Book, 1712–1720, 217, LP; *MPCP,* III, 154, 609; Council at Philadelphia, 25 and 28 Jan. 1722/3, DSP, 966.F.6.

64. *MPCP,* II, 604 (also III, 276, 581); *PA,* 1st, I, 455 (and see 425).

65. *MPCP,* III, 503.

66. Zeisberger, *History,* 145 ("very important"); *MJNY,* 212 ("whole town"); *PWJ,* IX, 407 ("Suck'd in"). *PA,* 2d, VII, 430; Smith, *Account,* 24; Kenny 1761–63, 178. They probably also knew what account books were, judging by the number of colonial fur traders whose books Indians took or destroyed during the war (Bailey, ed., *Ohio Co. Papers,* 121, 134, 138–139, 159).

67. The two major articles on Indian responses to literacy in eastern North America reflect the two prevailing strains of thought about literacy and orality in the abundant literature on the subject. James Axtell, positing a gulf between native and newcomer, chronicles the wonder and awe with which Indians greeted books and paper; more recently, Peter Wogan has stressed a continuum in media of communication, and examined how readily Indians understood, and incorporated, European ways. My own view, here and later in the chapter, tries to suggest that both are right: a continuum there was, but both Indians and colonists also detected a divide. Axtell, "The Power of Print in the Eastern Woodlands," in idem, *After Columbus: Essays in the Ethnohistory of Colonial North America* (New York, 1988), ch. IX; Wogan, "Perceptions of European Literacy in Early Contact Situations," *Ethnohistory,* XLI (1994), 407–429. For other work on native contacts, see Jill Lepore, "Dead Men Tell No Tales: John Sassamon and the Fatal Consequences of Literacy," *American Quarterly,* XLVI (1994), 479–512; Jane Merritt, "The Power of Language: Cultural Meanings and the Colonial Encounter on the Pennsylvania Frontier" (unpub. ms., 1994; I am grateful to Professor Merritt for sharing her work with me); David Murray, *Forked Tongues: Speech, Writing, and Representation in North American Indian Texts* (Bloomington, Ind., 1991), ch. 2.

My thinking on literacy and orality has been shaped by the following: Keith H. Basso, "The Ethnography of Writing," in Richard Bauman and Joel Sherzer, eds., *Explorations in the Ethnography of Speaking,* 2d ed. (New York, 1989), 425–432; Michael K. Foster, "When Words Become Deeds: An Analysis of Three Iroquois Longhouse Speech Events," *ibid.,* 354–367; Wallace Chafe and Deborah Tannen, "The Relations Between Written and Spoken Language," *Annual Review of Anthropology*, XVI (1987), 383–407; Robert DeMaria, Jr., and Rachel Kitzinger, eds., *Transformations of the Word* (special issue of *Language and Communication: An Interdisciplinary Journal*, IX [1989]); Ruth Finnegan, *Literacy and Orality: Studies in the Technology of Communication* (London, 1988); Albertine Gaur, *A History of Writing*, rev. ed. (London, 1987); I. J. Gelb, *The Study of Writing*, 2d ed. (Chicago, 1963); Jack Goody, *The Domestication of the Savage Mind* (Cambridge, Eng., 1977); idem, *The Interface Between the Written and the Oral* (New York, 1987); idem, ed., *Literacy in Traditional Societies* (Cambridge, Eng., 1968); Michael Harbsmeier, "Writing and the Other: Travellers' Literacy, or Towards an Archaeology of Orality," in Karen Schousboe and Morgens Trolle Larsen, eds., *Literacy and Society* (Copenhagen, 1989), 197–228; Eric A. Havelock, *The Muse Learns to Write: Reflections on Orality and Literacy from Antiquity to the Present* (New Haven, Conn., 1986); Nicholas Hudson, *Writing and European Thought, 1600–1830* (New York, 1994); Harold A. Innis, *The Bias of Communication* (Toronto, 1951); Walter D. Mignolo, "Literacy and Colonization: The New World Experience," in René Jara and Nicholas Spadaccini, eds., *1492–1992: Rediscovering Colonial Writing* (Minneapolis, Minn., 1989), 51–96 (I am grateful to Karen Stolley for alerting me to this work); Walter J. Ong, *Orality and Literacy: The Technologizing of the Word* (New York, 1982); Brian V. Street, *Literacy in Theory and Practice*, Cambridge Studies in Oral and Literate Culture (London, 1984); Deborah Tannen, ed., *Spoken and Written Language: Exploring Orality and Literacy*, Advances in Discourse Processes, IX (Norwood, N.J., 1982).

68. Harvey J. Graff, *The Legacies of Literacy: Continuities and Contradictions in Western Culture and Society* (Bloomington, Ind., 1987), 5.

69. Newcheconner to Logan, 9 Apr. 1738, LP, 11/29 ("the sense"). *PGW*, I, 105 ("farist"); Post to the Governor, 26 Sept. 1758, MCA, 28/219/9/7 ("critical teim"). For other examples of Post's prose, see *PA*, 1st, III, 742–744; Post 1758, 183–184. For woodsmen with varying levels of literacy, see *PA*, 1st, IV, 61; letters to Edward Shippen of 1 Oct. 1735 (George Miranda), 5 Aug. 1742 (George Gabriel), 26 June 1742 (Benjamin Moore), PSF, I. Even some of Weiser's prose was, Richard Peters wrote, "ill formd and ill spelld" (Peters to the Proprietors, 24 Oct. 1748, PMOC, IV, 163), and one British officer considered Croghan illiterate (Wallace, *Weiser*, 336).

70. Samuel Evans, "Lowrey Family," Lancaster County [Pa.] Historical Society, 47–48 (Lowry); U. J. Jones, *History of the Early Settlement of the Juniata Valley . . .*, 2d ed. (Harrisburg, Pa., 1940 [orig. pub. 1889]), 185–186 (Hart).

71. John Woolman, *The Journal of John Woolman* (Boston, 1909 [orig. pub. 1871]), 190–191 ("histories"); Hays, 77 ("Jurnal"); Loskiel, *History*, Part I, 25 ("intelligible"). And see Baron de Lahontan [Louis-Armand de Lom d'Arce],

New Voyages to North-America, ed. Reuben Gold Thwaites, 2 vols. (Chicago, 1903 [orig. pub. 1703]), II, 510–514; Lafitau, *Customs,* II, 36–37; Gist, 28; Heckewelder, *History,* 130–131; Nicholas Cresswell, *The Journal of Nicholas Cresswell, 1774–1777* (London, 1925), 110–111. The most famous of all Indian picture-writing, the Walam Olum of the Delawares, has been convincingly proved a fraud by David M. Oestreicher, "Unmasking the *Walam Olum:* A 19th-Century Hoax," Archaeological Society of New Jersey, *Bulletin,* no. 49 (1994), 1–44.

Even as I see the distinction, I am not persuaded by those positing a vast difference between pictographic and chirographic communication. (Gelb, *Writing,* 29, 35–36; Ong, *Orality and Literacy,* 84, 86; Jack Goody and Ian Watt, "The Consequences of Literacy," in Goody, ed., *Literacy in Traditional Societies,* 27, 30, 34–35, 38; Murray, *Forked Tongues,* ch. 2).

72. Timothy Horsfield to Gov. Hamilton, 5 Sept. 1761, HP, II, 445; Edward Shippen to Hamilton, 29 Oct. 1763, Correspondence of Edward and Joseph Shippen, 1750–1778, Shippen Papers, APS. Diplomats, too, could write: at Onondaga in 1754 a Nanticoke's speech on the evils of liquor was "accentuated by a letter, written on wood with black paint" (*MJNY,* 199–200).

73. *PWJ,* II, 861, VII, 348. On wampum having this quality, see Foster, "Another Look at Wampum," in Jennings et al., eds., *History and Culture of Iroquois Diplomacy,* 107.

74. Zeisberger, *History,* 93–94; Edmund De Schweinitz, *The Life and Times of David Zeisberger, The Western Pioneer and Apostle of the Indians* (Philadelphia, 1870), 217; *MPCP,* IX, 102 (council bag). Depositions, 1725, LP, 11/12 ("defaced"). Shamokin Diary, 28 Feb. 1748, MCA, 6/121/4/1 (Shickellamy; see also *Journals of Claus and Weiser,* 43). For other examples of documents being saved, see *MPCP,* III, 94, IV, 433, V, 316, VIII, 668–669; *PWJ,* XI, 463; *PHB,* VI, 96.

75. *MPCP,* III, 334, IV, 433 (invitation; for invitation strings of wampum being handled in this way, see III, 437); III, 599, VII, 7–9 (Conestogas pulling out documents; for the documents, see ch. VII). For speaking on paper, see Council with the Indians at Conestoga, 6 Apr. 1722, DSP, 966.F.4. Civility, speaking for Conoys in July 1720, said that Conoys "have no Writing to shew their League of Friendship as the others have, and therefore desire they may be favoured with one lest if they should transgress by Reason of Rum, . . . they may be cast off and forgotten that ever they were in Friendship with us" (*MPCP,* III, 94).

76. *MPCP,* V, 316. Shawnees at a different council again pulled out "an old Treaty" and "several Letters from Mr. Logan—and one or two from you" (Peters to Thomas Penn [copy], 18 Feb. 1756, PMOC, VIII, 41).

77. Post 1758, 239 (also 245); *MPCP,* V, 439 (also VI, 277–278, VIII, 417, IX, 541–542; *Arch. Md.,* XXIII, 427; Minutes of the Easton Treaty, 28 July 1756,

Friends Historical Association, Mss., I, Haverford College Library, in *Iroq. Ind.*, Reel 19).

78. Peters to Weiser, 13 Apr. 1751, RPP, III, 35. And see William Logan to Weiser, 21 Oct. 1747, *ibid.*, II, 84; James Logan to Weiser, 28 Jan. 1742/3, Alverthorpe Letterbook, E, 174, LP; same to same, 18 Oct. 1736, LP, 2/58; *MPCP*, I, 187–188, V, 288–293, 449, 518–522, 570, 733, VI, 146–149, 154, 186–187; *PA*, 1st, II, 203.

79. Thomas to Weiser, 26 Feb. 1741/2, RPP, I, 73 ("Dress"); *MPCP*, V, 449, 570. See also *PA*, 1st, II, 203.

80. *MPCP*, VI, 697–699 (quotation on 699), VII, 148 ("Spirit").

81. *Ibid.*, VII, 108–109, 119, 138–139, 200–201. Examples of having a free hand are in *PA*, 1st, I, 671–672; *MPCP*, IV, 779, VI, 147–149, 154, VIII, 471; *PWJ*, X, 566.

82. For these, and for the background on this encounter, see "Papunehay & o[the]rs at Quehaloosing" to the Governor, 16 Sept. 1761, FA, IV, 191; Friendly Association Trustees to the Governor on a proposed Message to the Munsee Indians, Oct. 1761, *ibid.*, 203; Papoonan to the Governor[?], 2 Oct. 1761, *ibid.*, 223; "The Governor's Answer to Papounham and the Indians at Wighalousing," 10 Oct. 1761, *ibid.*, 236.

83. Zane 1761, 14 Oct.

84. "A Message from the Governor to the Chief of the Munsey Indians at Ossuntsing. Or to the Three Munsey Indians now at Wyoming . . . ," 12 Oct. 1761, FA, IV, 231.

85. Zane 1761, 17–19 Oct. Another example of Indians advising colonists to revise a speech drafted in Philadelphia is Post 1760, 12 May, 1 June.

86. It is significant, though, that the governor also consulted Quakers before drafting the speech, and that he followed the Quakers' advice; Zane, in his journal, was by no means vindicating the Friends' wisdom, which Tongocone rejected along with the governor's.

87. Zane 1761, 19 Oct.

88. *PA*, 1st, I, 224; *MPCP*, IV, 651.

89. *MPCP*, III, 502 ("freely"), V, 86 ("assures"), 88 ("demand," "proper"); *PA*, 1st, I, 232 ("stories"), 748–749 ("Treaties"), 757 ("depend"), 758 ("Honest").

90. *PA*, 1st, I, 228; *MPCP*, III, 330–331; Gov. Patrick Gordon to "Gentlemen," 15 1ober [Dec.] 1731, PMOC, II, 221 (1728). Francis Jennings, " 'Pennsylvania' Indians and the Iroquois," in Daniel K. Richter and James H. Merrell, eds., *Beyond the Covenant Chain: The Iroquois and Their Neighbors in Indian North America, 1600–1800* (Syracuse, N.Y., 1987), ch. 5 (realities).

91. *MPCP*, III, 500–501. Weiser to Peters[?], 24 Jan. 1745/6, DSP, 966.F.24.

92. *MPCP*, IV, 681, V, 88; *PA*, 1st, I, 762; Cammerhoff, 175–176; Spangenberg, 430; John H. Carter, "The Moravians at Shamokin," *Proceedings of the Northumberland County Historical Society*, IX (1937), 65; Peters to the Pro-

prietors, 11 May 1748, PMOC, IV, 93; John W. Jordan, trans., Bishop Cammerhoff's Letters to Zinzendorf, 1747–1749, IV, 22–24 May 1747, 24,
HSP ("council fire"). See Francis Jennings, "The Delaware Interrregnum,"
PMHB, LXXXIX (1965), 174–198. One visitor in 1745 said that, although
ill, Sassoonan still had the respect of his people (Spangenberg, 430–431).

93. *MPCP*, V, 212, 222; *PA*, 1st, II, 8. See James H. Merrell, "Shickellamy, 'a Person of Consequence,' " in Robert S. Grumet, ed., *Northeastern Indian Lives,
1632–1816* (Amherst, Mass., 1996), 248–249; Wallace, *Weiser,* ch. 32.

94. *PA*, 2d, II, 653; *MPCP*, VIII, 98. For snow, see *MPCP*, VIII, 87, 92; *PA*, 2d, II,
650–654. Post 1758, 186; *MPCP*, V, 486, 599–600; R. A. Brock, ed., *The Official Records of Robert Dinwiddie, Lieutenant-Governor of the Colony of Virginia,
1751–1758 . . .* , 2 vols., Virginia Historical Society, *Collections,* new ser.,
III–IV (Richmond, Va., 1883), I, 22, 398 (illness). Weiser to Col. Gale,
[Spring 1743], RPP, II, 5 (hunting).

95. *MPCP*, III, 329 (1728); Minutes of an Indian Treaty at Pittsburgh, 18 Aug.
1760, Recs. Mor. Miss., Box 323, Folder 7, Item 1, in *Iroq. Ind.*, Reel 23
(Teedyuscung); *PWJ*, X, 148 (Montour). See also Post 1758, 185, 236; *PA*,
1st, III, 420; Israel Pemberton to Christian Frederick Post, 6 5 mo. 1760,
Pemberton Pprs., Haverford College Library; Nathaniel Holland to [Israel
Pemberton], 16 Oct. 1760, FA, IV, 431.

96. *PA*, 1st, I, 425 (Poke and Hill); Weiser 1748, 43, n.42; *MPCP*, V, 438 (Ohio).

97. *MPCP*, V, 293, 633, 636.

98. *DRCNY*, VII, 259 ("proper"); *MPCP*, VIII, 644 ("Nonsense"; see also 656).

99. Edward Shippen to the Governor, 26 Nov. 1757, Edward Shippen Letterbook, 1753–1761, 170, APS ("forgot"; also Logstown Treaty, 156); Israel
Pemberton to Mary Pemberton, 11 May 1757, PPHSP, XII, 18 (black
wampum); [Thomson], *Enquiry,* 105–106, 181 ("trifling," "small Belts");
PWJ, XII, 242–243 (laugh); *MPCP*, VIII, 212 (Tokahaio).

100. *MPCP*, VIII, 615 (Nanticokes), 634 (Tokahaio; the governor [640] denied
having sent them). See also IX, 87–88; "Rough Draft of Message to ye
Onondago Council," 14 May 1761, FA, IV, 107–112.

101. *MPCP*, V, 677.

102. *Ibid.*, 293 ("loose Letters"), IV, 343 (Shawnees).

103. *Ibid.*, V, 691–695, 703 ("mood"), 734; Peters to Proprietaries, 26 Nov.
1753, PMOC, VI, 133; George Croghan to "Your Honour," 3 Feb. 1754,
ibid., 155; *PA*, 1st, II, 119. During the 1750s British colonists accused the
French of duping Indians by "reading" putative English messages plotting the
conquest of Indian country (*PWJ*, II, 512; Post 1758, 252–253; *PA*, 2d, VI,
568).

104. *MPCP*, V, 514 ("sound"), 538 ("Strong House"). See Nicholas B. Wainwright,
George Croghan, Wilderness Diplomat (Chapel Hill, N.C., 1959), 35, 41–44;
McConnell, *A Country Between,* 93–95.

105. Logstown Treaty, 171–172; Peters to Weiser, 6 Feb. 1753, CCW, I, 38; Weiser to [?], [1753–1754], CCW, II, 25; Peters to the Proprietor, 6 Nov. 1753, PMOC, VI, 115; Wallace, *Weiser*, 348.

106. See ch. VI.

107. Post 1758, 282–285. See David L. Ghere, "Mistranslations and Misinformation: Diplomacy on the Maine Frontier, 1725 to 1775," *American Indian Culture and Research Journal*, VIII (1984), 3–26.

108. *MPCP*, VII, 683; Weiser, "Observations." See David Murray, *Forked Tongues*, ch. 3.

109. *PHB*, II, 621–626. For Custaloga, see McConnell, *A Country Between*, 102, 105, 108. Another account of the Bouquet conference is in *PA*, 1st, III, 571–574.

110. Minutes of the New York Commissioners of Indian Affairs, 14 Aug. 1743, in *Iroq. Ind.*, Reel 11 (Oneidas). *DRCNY*, VII, 197 (1756). For additional remarks on this meeting, see *MPCP*, VII, 156–160, 170–172, 182, 184; *PA*, 2d, VI, 521–522; *PWJ*, II, 488–491, 521–522. Another example is 439–440, IX, 347–383; *MPCP*, VII, 41–42, 46–47, 67, 69, 71, 106.

111. David McClure, *Diary of David McClure, Doctor of Divinity, 1748–1820*, ed. Franklin B. Dexter (New York, 1899), 59 (Peepy); *MPCP*, VI, 49 (Weiser); Cadwallader Colden, *The History of the Five Indian Nations Depending on the Province of New-York in America* (Ithaca, N.Y., 1958 [orig. pub. 1727 and 1747]), xi ("sense").

112. My thinking here owes much to Ong, *Orality and Literacy*, ch. 3.

113. *MPCP*, II, 600, IV, 433–434, VIII, 188, 753. Compare Sassoonan's speeches at IV, 307–308, 643, 680.

114. *Ibid.*, IV, 721, VII, 522.

115. Hays, 81. The interpreter was probably Post, Isaac Stille, or Moses Tatamy. Hays's prose here is so fractured and cluttered by marginalia that, for clarity's sake, I have cleaned it up. The original reads, with marginal additions in brackets: "he Got But 6 fulls of A Misher [for a Ribond Stroud] and it was so litel that his Kock could Not Go in it and [he had But A litel one] Said he had But A Litel one [kock] Neither."

116. *MPCP*, VII, 217–218.

117. Shamokin Diary, 16 Jan. 1748, MCA, 6/121/4/1 (Indian woman); *MPCP*, III, 169 (Keith), VIII, 743 (King).

118. *Ibid.*, III, 189 (emphasis added); Gov. George Thomas to the Shawnees, 16 Aug. 1742, RPP, I, 93 (emphasis added).

119. This and the following paragraph owe a great debt to Ong, *Literacy and Orality*, especially ch. 3.

120. Stephen J. Greenblatt, *Marvelous Possessions: The Wonder of the New World* (Chicago, 1991), 9–10; Harbsmeier, "Writing and the Other," in Schousboe and Larsen, eds., *Literacy and Society*, 199–203; Goody, *Interface*.

121. Harbsmeier, "Writing and the Other," in Schousboe and Larsen, eds., *Literacy and Society,* 203 (emphasis added).

122. *PWJ,* III, 767.

123. *MPCP,* III, 599 (1735), IV, 718 (1744).

124. Shamokin Diary, 21 Feb. 1748, MCA, 6/121/4/1 (aged Delaware); *MPCP,* VII, 521 (King). On Indian awe, on writing as sacred, see Loskiel, *History,* Part I, 23–24.

125. *MPCP,* IV, 84 (see also II, 574).

126. Wallace, *Weiser,* 141 (Zinzendorf); *MPCP,* IV, 708 (Canasatego).

127. See Goody, *Interface,* xv; Hudson, *Writing and European Thought,* 162–163; Claude Lévi-Strauss, *Tristes Tropiques,* trans. John Weightman and Doreen Weightman (New York, 1974), 296–300.

128. Wallace, ed., *Travels of Heckewelder,* 64 (Post); Moses Tatamy, Declaration, [1757], FA, I, 405–408 (Delawares); *MPCP,* VI, 74 (Iroquois).

129. Hays, 80 (knocked; "Durst Not Reead"); Smith, *Account,* 28 (stolen, though he also noted—3, 24, 39—that Indians sometimes let him read); Wallace, ed., *Travels of Heckewelder,* 64 (hide books).

130. Wallace, ed., *Travels of Heckewelder,* 64 ("suspicious"; see also Post to Israel Pemberton, 8 Aug. 1761, FA, IV, 167). Post 1758, 252 (see also 226–227, 247; "Journal of Captain Thomas Morris, Detroit, September 25, 1764," in Reuben Gold Thwaites, ed., *Early Western Travels, 1748–1846* [Cleveland, Ohio, 1904], I, 322).

131. *PA,* 1st, IV, 96. Andrew Montour was once so unwilling to trust his wampum that he asked Virginians if the message he bore from Onondaga to Williamsburg could be "set down in paper, to assist his memory and prevent mistakes." H. R. McIlwaine, ed., *Journals of the House of Burgesses of Virginia, 1752–1758* (Richmond, Va., 1909), Appendix, 515. Other examples are *MPCP,* VII, 137, 199; Peters to Thomas Penn[?], 1 June 1756, PMOC, VIII, 95. In July 1756 Teedyuscung and Kos Showweyha (Newcastle) sent a message to the governor, and insisted, "for to remember the Words accompanying this String," that colonists "wrote them Down from the Kings mouth" ("At Timothy Horsfields," 18 July 1756, FA, I, 147).

132. *MPCP,* VIII, 174.

133. Post 1758, 201.

134. *PA,* 1st, III, 343 (Teedyuscung). *MPCP,* VIII, 630, 632, 638–639 (1761). And see Meeting with Killbuck, 10 5 mo. 1771, FA, IV, 419; his official visit is in *MPCP,* IX, 735–742.

135. Jane Merritt and I have, independently, come to this conclusion, and come to it using the same examples. Merritt, "The Power of Language," 26–27.

136. *MJNY,* 179 (Zeisberger); *MPCP,* IX, 8 (Teedyuscung).

137. *MPCP,* VII, 652–655. For the clerk fight, see Jennings, *Empire of Fortune,* 342–345; Theodore Thayer, *Israel Pemberton, King of the Quakers* (Philadel-

phia, 1943), 140. The debate can be found in *MPCP,* VII, 648–665, 689–690, VIII, 30–31, 47, 50; Charles Thomson to the Governor, 23 Aug. 1756, Charles Thomson, Correspondence, Gratz Collection, HSP; *PA,* 2d, VI, 570–571; *DRCNY,* VII, 322–323; Charles Thomson to William Franklin, 13 Mar. 1758, Papers of Benjamin Franklin, B:F85, v. 488, f.122, APS; Peters to Penn, 19 Mar. 1758, Lardner Family Papers, HSP; *PWJ,* III, 766, 771–773.

138. *MPCP,* VII, 664. Colonial officials often tried to monopolize secretarial duties to prevent conflicting accounts or (their enemies claimed) to keep the truth hidden behind a screen of misrepresentation and omissions. *PWJ,* IX, 743–744; Thomas Walker and Andrew Lewis to Lord Botetourt, 14 Dec. 1768, encl. in Botetourt to [?], 24 Dec. 1768, in *Iroq. Ind.,* Reel 29.

   Croghan and Weiser were convinced that Quaker foes of the proprietors were behind this demand, that Israel Pemberton and other Friends had put Teedyuscung up to it as a means of turning the Delawares into a weapon for flaying the proprietors' men (see ch. VII for this dispute). Certainly Friends favored the move (*MPCP,* VII, 656–657), but it was probably not their idea. Moses Tatamy said that he had suggested it some time before, when Teedyuscung and other leaders were complaining about how paper always seemed to favor colonists. Play their game, Tatamy advised; get a scribe of your own to keep the English honest. "Moses Titamy's Accot. of Indian Complaints &ca.," n.d., and Tatamy, Declaration, [1757], FA, I, 65, 405–408. See also Papers of the Friendly Association, 23 June 1762, Swarthmore College Library, where Stille insisted, again, that Teedyuscung's desire for a clerk and papers came from the Delawares themselves, and from Teedyuscung's fear that "there was Some people wanting to blind him."

139. *MPCP,* VII, 656 (Teedyuscung); *PA,* 2d, VI, 570–571 (Croghan).

140. *PA,* 2d, VI, 570–571; Penn to Peters, 14 Nov. 1757, RPP, IV, 122.

141. Hays, 76–77 ("Read Like Mad"); Heckewelder, *History,* 291–293 ("great Book"). Kenny 1761–63, 171, 173, 175 ("Seperation"); Zeisberger, *Diaries,* 25.

142. The literature on the coming of the war is vast. The most detailed account (though one that neglects the Indians' point of view) is Lawrence Henry Gipson, *The British Empire Before the American Revolution,* 15 vols. (New York, 1958–1970). More recent treatments that pay greater attention to Indians include Stephen F. Auth, *The Ten Years' War: Indian-White Relations in Pennsylvania, 1755–1765* (New York, 1989), ch. 2; Jennings, *Empire of Fortune,* Part One; Donald H. Kent, *The French Invasion of Western Pennsylvania, 1753* (Harrisburg, Pa., 1954); McConnell, *A Country Between,* chs. 1–6; White, *Middle Ground,* chs. 5–6; Eric Hinderaker, *Elusive Empires: Constructing Colonialism in*

the Ohio Valley, *1673–1800* (New York, 1997), 41–45, and ch. 4. The fullest, if outdated, account of the attacks on Pennsylvania can be found in C. Hale Sipe, *The Indian Wars of Pennsylvania* . . . (Harrisburg, Pa., 1929), chs. 7–10.

Indian explanations for their actions, which usually focused on land grievances, can be found in *MPCP,* VII, 51–52, 70–71, 431–432, VIII, 197–198; *PA,* 1st, II, 776–778, III, 45, 46, 57, 548–550; Beverley W. Bond, Jr., "The Captivity of Charles Stuart, 1755–57," *MVHR,* XIII (1926–1927), 64–65; "Journal of Daniels Journey," PPEC, II, 29; "Titamy's Accot.," FA, I, 65; Peters, Diary, 16 Jan. 1756, 2, 9, 12 Oct. 1758, RPP; [Thomson], *Enquiry,* 81–82; Chew, 315–317; William West to [?], 12 Jan. 1756, PMOC, VIII, 13.

143. *MPCP,* III, 311 ("stamp'd"). Croghan to Franklin (copy), 2 Oct. 1767, GCP, 5/29 ("Jealous"; see also Croghan to Gen. Monckton, 26 July 1761, GCP, 5/23; *PWJ,* III, 964–965; *PHB,* VI, 137–138).

144. Gist, 9–10; Kenny 1761–63, 45.

145. Hamilton to the Proprietary, 26 Nov. 1753, PMOC, VI, 139 ("a pity"); *MPCP,* V, 696 ("dangerous Season"); Weiser to Peters, 28 Jan. 1754, CCW, I, 43 ("Cookes").

146. Peters to Penn, 28 Sept. 1750, PMOC, V, 57 ("pleases"). *PA,* 1st, I, 751 ("sick"; see also 758–759, 761–762, II, 15, 23–24; *MPCP,* V, 87–88).

147. *PA,* 1st, II, 12 ("happy"); Weiser to Peters, 7 Feb. 1754, Berks and Montgomery Counties, Miscellaneous Manuscripts, 1693–1869, 55, HSP ("perplects"). In November 1747, he wrote that "my Commission for the Transaction of Indian Affairs did not extend to Ohio" (*MPCP,* V, 138). For an example of the mistakes his ignorance caused, see Weiser 1748, 43, n.42.

148. For examples of the warnings, see *PA,* 1st, II, 144, 173–174, 2d, VI, 548–554 (Croghan); *MPCP,* VI, 46 (Montour); Wallace, *Weiser,* 372–373; Weiser to [?], [1753–1754], CCW, II, 25; *MPCP,* V, 147, VI, 589–590.

149. Hamilton to Thomas Penn, 18 Nov. 1750, PMOC, V, 89.

150. Information regarding Teedyuscung delivered to Spangenberg . . . from a Delaware Indian (Augustus), 30 July 1756, PMIA, II, 98 (wampum); *PWJ,* III, 767 ("wrote wrong"); Conference at Pemberton's, 19–23 Apr. 1756, LP, 11/41 (Scarouyady).

VI: In the Woods, 1755–1758

1. Events in Shamokin can be followed in Shamokin Diary, April–Sept. 1755, MCA, 6/121/7/1. At the end of this journal is a section entitled "Br. Rösler's Relation von sein u. seiner Brr. Philip Wesa, u. Marcus Kiefers

letzten Auffenthalt in Shomokin . . . Im Jahr 1755" (hereafter referred to as "Rösler's Relation"); Rösler offered general observations as well as a daily account of events from 11 through 30 Oct. 1755.

2. "Kurze Nachricht von meiner besuch reise nach Shomoko . . . ," 6 June 1755, MCA, 6/121/9/5 (frost); Shamokin Diary, 30 Aug. 1755 (canoes), 7–8, 14 Apr., 10–11 May, 15 July, 19 Sept. 1755 (drinking), 17–21 Aug. 1755 (burial), *ibid.,* 6/121/7/1. For the Moravians' location near a cemetery, see *ibid.,* 9 Sept. 1755. Their house and smithy were on a new site, constructed in 1753 (*ibid.,* 16 Apr., 29 May, 1, 2 June 1753, 6/121/6/1).

3. References to farm work can be found throughout the journal for these months. For cattle, see 13 June 1755; Johann Gattermeyer to Spangenberg, 30 Mar. 1755, *ibid.,* 6/121/8/11. The men there were Gottfried Rösler, Marcus Kiefer, and Philip Wesa. In the spring Gattermeyer was also in residence. Shamokin Diary, 11 Apr. 1755, *ibid.,* 6/121/7/1 (speaking German and Delaware). For letters and visitors from Bethlehem, see 18 Apr., 3–4, 26 June, 2, 9, 21, 25 Aug., 20 Sept. 1755.

4. *Ibid.,* 23 May (Allegheny visitors), 24 Apr. (English traveler), 22 Sept. 1755 (Conoy traveler). *Ibid.,* 18 June 1753, 6/121/6/1, 15, 28 June 1754, 6/121/6/2; "Kurze Nachricht," 3, 6 June 1755, MCA, 6/121/9/5 (shoemaker's name and location); Shamokin Diary, 12–13 Apr., 5, 14, 25 May, 14–15 June, 10, 21–22, 24 July 1755, *ibid.,* 6/121/7/1 (visits to and from him in 1755), 5 Aug. 1755 (Delawares to Tulpehocken; for other Indians visiting colonial towns and settlements, see 18 Apr., 7 May, 14, 19 July 1755). *Ibid.,* 2 May 1755 (visitors from across the river; other visits to and from these settlements are at *ibid.,* 20 Jan., 20 Apr., 5 May 1754, 6/121/6/2, 19, 22 Apr. 1755, 6/121/7/1). *Ibid.,* 15 May 1755 (turned Delawares away).

5. The terms are Scarouyady's (*MPCP,* VI, 685; and see VII, 8). The Susquehanna Forks was not entirely without tension that year. In February, one Jacob Beyerly arrived in town to announce that the proprietaries had granted him the land at the Forks and he intended to plant some forty families there come spring. He then wrote his name on the side of the Moravians' house, with the date and the message, in German, that *"forewarns every Body from this place"* (Weiser to Peters, 8 Mar. 1755, CCW, I, 50). In May, a colonial family built a house and planted crops very near Shamokin (Shamokin Diary, 2, 4, 12 May 1755, MCA, 6/121/7/1), and others were surreptitiously hunting land (2 July). Weiser, passing through, paused to talk privately about measuring out Shamokin itself (6 June), just as he had been having land in the vicinity surveyed that spring (Weiser to Peters, 8 Mar. 1755, CCW, I, 50, 11 Mar. 1755, RPP, IV, 7). That Indians were uneasy is clear from Shamokin diary entries for 2 May and 7 June 1755.

6. A visitor in early June reported hearing "nothing of the war" ("Kurze Nachricht," 6 June 1755, MCA, 6/121/9/5), but there were occasional hints (Shamokin Diary, 23 May, 22 June 1755, *ibid.*, 6/121/7/1).

7. *Ibid.*, 26 July 1755 ("news"); John Harris to Peters, 27 July 1755, RPP, IV, 34 (fleeing); Weiser to Peters, 31 July 1755, *ibid.*, 37 ("dismal"). And see *MPCP*, VI, 590, 601; *PA*, 1st, II, 385–386.

8. "Rösler's Relation," 16 Oct. 1755, MCA, 6/121/7/1.

9. The missionaries' actual itinerary was somewhat complicated. The first to leave was Rösler; it is his account on which I rely. His mission was to reach Tulpehocken, and from there send news of the attacks to Bethlehem and request advice; he was to return to Shamokin on 28 October. The day after Rösler departed, however, Tachnechdorus all but ordered the remaining two Germans out, so Philip Wesa left, catching up with Rösler in Tulpehocken on 26 October. The next morning, 27 October, Rösler started out on his promised return trip, but on the unanimous advice of refugees he met en route he finally turned around. Marcus Kiefer, meanwhile, packed up, burying what he could not carry. With the help of friendly Indians, Kiefer finally made his way back to Bethlehem, arriving there on 15 November.

10. "Rösler's Relation," 24 Oct. 1755, MCA, 6/121/7/1 ("fled"); Weiser to [?], 5 Jan. 1756, CCW, I, 63 ("naked").

11. The full story emerged only when some of those taken prisoner in the raid were repatriated. See, for example, *PA*, 1st, III, 633–634, 2d, VII, 427–438.

12. *PA*, 2d, VII, 429, 8th, V, 4144. And see *MPCP*, VI, 647.

13. *PA*, 2d, VII, 430. An infant, too young to take along, was another of the casualties (*MPCP*, VI, 645).

14. "Rösler's Relation," 28 Oct. 1755, MCA, 6/121/7/1.

15. This story is from *PA*, 1st, II, 503–504, 511–512; *MPCP*, VI, 703–704; Capt. Jacob Morgan, Deposition (copy), 16 Nov. 1755, DSP, 966.F.490, 43–44; *PG*, 20 Nov. 1755. There are variations in these accounts, such as the spelling of the family's name. Lists of colonists killed that autumn are in CCW, II, 89, 107, 109, 115, 119; *PG*, 18, 25 Dec. 1755; "Lists of Pennsylvania Settlers Murdered, Scalped and Taken Prisoners by the Indians, 1755–1756," *PMHB*, XXXII (1908), 309–319; Lt. Col. Armstrong to Peters, 25 Nov. 1757, PMOC, VIII, 285.

16. *MPCP*, VI, 495 ("damn"), 675–676 ("Shout," "shrieks"); Adam Hoops to Isaac Norris, 3 Nov. 1755, DSP, 966.F.49e, 27 ("Bloody"; also James Wright to "My Worthy Friend" [copy], 6 Nov. 1755, DSP, 966.F.49g, 31); *PA*, 1st, II, 462–463 ("like Water," decapitated); Thomas Barton to Peters, 22 Aug. 1756, Indian and Military Affairs of Colonial Pennsylvania, 1737–1775, 399, APS (corpse). For explanations of violence and its meaning, see Jennings, *Empire of Fortune*, 188; White, *Middle Ground*, 358–359; Matthew C.

Ward, "Fighting the 'Old Women': Indian Strategy on the Virginia and Pennsylvania Frontier, 1754–1758," *VMHB,* CIII (1995), 310–313; Frederic W. Gleach, *Powhatan's World and Colonial Virginia: A Conflict of Cultures* (Lincoln, Neb., 1997), 43–54.

17. *PA,* 1st, II, 484, 492 ("bind"); *PWJ,* IX, 335–336. *MPCP,* VI, 648 ("kill us"; also *PA,* 1st, II, 491).

18. James Pemberton to Hannah Pemberton, 4 8 mo. 1756, PPHSP, XII, 55b ("Providential"); James Pemberton to John Pemberton, 10 10 mo. 1757, *ibid.,* 157 ("Change"). Weiser to Morris, 31 Oct. 1755, DSP, 966.F.49, 11 ("fear"; and see Weiser to William Parsons, 1 Nov. 1755, HP, I, 35; *MPCP,* VI, 656; *PA,* 1st, II, 474, 8th, V, 4104; Hoops to Norris, 31 Oct. 1755, DSP, 966.F.49e, 26).

19. *MPCP,* VI, 613–615, 646 (Harris's); Beverley W. Bond, ed., "The Captivity of Charles Stuart, 1755–1757," *MVHR,* XIII (1926–1927), 64–65 (Ohio).

20. The best scholarly accounts of the peace process are Wallace, *Weiser,* Parts IV–V; Wallace, *Teedyuscung,* chs. 8–16; William A. Hunter, "Provincial Negotiations with the Western Indians, 1754–58," *Pennsylvania History,* XVIII (1951), 213–219; Stephen F. Auth, *The Ten Years' War: Indian-White Relations in Pennsylvania, 1755–1765* (New York, 1989); Jennings, *Empire of Fortune,* chs. 12, 15, 17, 19; White, *Middle Ground,* 248–256; McConnell, *A Country Between,* chs. 6–7.

21. *MPCP,* VI, 646 ("opinion"), 658 ("Paxton people"). The story of these events can be followed in *ibid.,* 645–701, and *PA,* 1st, II, 443–493.

22. *MPCP,* VI, 648 ("Song"), 657–658 ("received," "strange"; also 654). Accounts of that morning's conversation vary. Some say that Montour issued the warning (*ibid.,* 658), others that Scarouyady did (*PWJ,* IX, 334–335), still others simply that the colonists "were advised" to avoid the western shore (*MPCP,* VI, 648). Given the close cooperation of Montour and Scarouyady that fall, it seems likely that both were there, with Montour doing the talking (Scarouyady spoke no English).

23. No one recorded the details of the debate. I have reconstructed its likely character from other information, particularly from comments about Montour and Scarouyady offered by John Harris and other Paxton folk in the days following the discussion beside the Susquehanna.

24. *CVSP,* I, 249; Penn Manuscripts, Accounts, II, Doc. 100a, 26, HSP.

25. *MPCP,* VI, 287 (Peters). For their being with Washington and Braddock, see 130, 140, 151–152, 397–398, 470, 524, 589; *PA,* 8th, V, 3978, 4008; Proprietaries' Account with Richard Peters, 20 Sept. 1758, PPM, XI, 105; Penn Mss., Accounts, II, Doc. 100a, 26, HSP. For the September 1755 war party, see *MPCP,* VI, 613, 615–616; Shamokin Diary, 12 Sept. 1755, MCA, 6/121/7/1.

Scarouyady lacks an authoritative biography. An outdated account is C. Hale Sipe, *The Indian Chiefs of Pennsylvania* (Harrisburg, Pa., 1927), chs. 15–16. Born in Iroquoia, like Shickellamy he was sent by the Six Nations to keep an eye on the Shawnees, this time in the Ohio country. Settling at Logstown, like Shickellamy he translated that specific—and, given Shawnee independence, hopeless—task into a more general authority in the region. The first mention of him in the records is a mark he made on a letter to Pennsylvania dated 20 Apr. 1747 (Indians at Allegheny to "Brother of Philadelphia," RPCEC, B3, 455; *PA,* 1st, I, 737–738). On 11 November 1747, at a council with ten warriors from Ohio, "old Scaiohady" told provincial officials "that he was here in James Logan's time, a long while ago . . . ; that he was then employ'd in the Affairs of this Government" (*MPCP,* V, 147).

26. *MPCP,* V, 660 ("French Andrew"), VI, 343–344, 358–359 (Scarouyady), 654 ("March"); *PA,* 1st, III, 42 ("Monsieur Montour"). Moreover, the two had answered an invitation to Great Island on the West Branch, where six Delawares and four Shawnees from the Ohio talked of their plans (*PA,* 1st, II, 451–452; *MPCP,* VI, 672–673, 682–683; John Armstrong to Gov. Morris, 2 Nov. 1755, DSP, 966.F.49a, 20–21; Peters to the Proprietaries, 15 Nov. 1755, Richard Peters Letters to the Proprietaries of Pennsylvania, 1755–1757, Simon Gratz Collection, Case 2, Box 33-a, 15, HSP).

27. *MPCP,* VI, 658 ("painted"); *PA,* 1st, II, 458. And see Hoops to Norris, 31 Oct. 1755, DSP, 966.F.49e, 27. Two years earlier, Weiser had pronounced Montour "a French man in his heart" (Peters to the Proprietor, 6 Nov. 1753, PMOC, VI, 115).

28. Harris to Norris, 27 Oct. 1755, DSP, 966.F.49a, 21–22; Weiser to Parsons, 28 Oct. 1755, HP, I, 69.

29. Harris to Norris, 27 Oct. 1755, DSP, 966.F.49a, 21; *MPCP,* VI, 649, 655, VII, 154.

30. Weiser to Parsons, 28 Oct. 1755, HP, I, 69 (McKee). The Old Belt was said to be so "in a rage" that he "Cry'd like a Child" at the news (*MPCP,* VI, 655; Weiser to Morris, 30 Oct. 1755, DSP, 966.F.49a, 10). Whether he was angry at colonists or enemy Indians—or both—is unclear.

31. *MPCP,* VI, 654 (hatchet, scalps), 659 (promise), 682–683 (message). See also *ibid.,* 642, VII, 51; Richard Peters, Diary, 1755 [*sic*], 15 Jan. 1756, RPP.

32. *MPCP,* VI, 649–650 ("faces"; also 646, 654). For the Susquehanna peoples' thinking, see 752; "Moses Titamy's Accot. of Indian Complaints &ca.," n.d., FA, I, 65; Wallace, *Teedyuscung,* 72–83.

33. *MPCP,* VI, 655–656, 669. Word of their approach can be found in *ibid.,* 654–655; Harris to Franklin, 31 Oct. 1755, DSP, 966.F.49b, 22.

34. *PA,* 8th, V, 4093; *MPCP,* VI, 613–614. Wallace, *Weiser,* 409 (Weiser's role).

35. They would have known the fate of another British ally, Old Briton (La Demoiselle, Memeskia), an Ohio leader killed and eaten by French-allied Indians a few years before. Jennings, *Empire of Fortune,* 49; McConnell, *A Country Between,* 98–100; White, *Middle Ground,* 230–231.

36. Weiser to James Read, 1 Nov. 1755, DSP, 966.F.49a, 11; Hoops to Norris, 31 Oct. 1755, *ibid.,* 966.F.49e, 27; *MPCP,* VI, 686; *PA,* 1st, II, 562 (doubts). *PA,* 1st, II, 451–453 (meeting at Harris's). At least ten colonists were present (*MPCP,* VI, 669; William Buchanan to Croghan, 2 Nov. 1756, PSF, II).

37. Buchanan to Croghan, 2 Nov. 1756, PSF, II ("Tired"); *MPCP,* VI, 681–682; Wallace, *Weiser,* 406.

38. *MPCP,* VI, 683 ("People"), 685–686 ("be plain"); Wallace, *Weiser,* 407 ("Grief").

39. *MPCP,* VI, 692, 697, VII, 12, 65.

40. *Ibid.,* VI, 697–699 (instructions), VII, 68–69 (estimate of belts).

41. *PA,* 1st, II, 503–505.

42. *MPCP,* VII, 12 ("escaped"; also 65), 49 ("throwed"), 53 ("Rogue"), 65–66 ("muttering").

43. *Ibid.,* 1–7, 33–34, 46–61, 64 (back in Philadelphia). Just what sort of help the Iroquois offered was unclear. The official minutes of the council had them agreeing, reluctantly, to continue efforts to stop the Delawares; Pennsylvania should not strike back until mediation failed. Montour and Scarouyady told a different story, a tale of "private Councils" where the Oneida had convinced the Iroquois that "the English should fight, and never cease Hostilities until the Delawares were brought to make Peace and delivered over their Prisoners." Was Scarouyady carrying on his own campaign against the French? Assessing "the Character of Scarroyady" in January 1755, Richard Peters had warned Johnson about him. "He . . . wants without any good Reason to strike them [the French], and secretly purposes to animate the Six Nations to take Part in the War." Asked to invite the Six Nations to Winchester, Scarouyady chose for wampum a large black belt that looked to Peters like a war belt (*MPCP,* VI, 287–288). For the events at Johnson's, see *MPCP,* VII, 106; *PWJ,* II, 439–440. The treaty is in *PWJ,* IX, 331–339, 347–383; *MPCP,* VII, 41–42, 46–47, 67, 69, 71. Johnson was surprised and annoyed when Pennsylvania declared war in April (*PWJ,* II, 439–440, 447; *MPCP,* VII, 101–102, 113–114, 116–118; *PA,* 1st, II, 651–656). On the other hand, Pennsylvania argued that the Iroquois seemed decidedly reluctant to do anything at all: Johnson had to ask them several times (*PWJ,* IX, 452, 455, 475–478; *DRCNY,* VII, 118–119). Significantly, Senecas and Ohio Delawares were absent (*MPCP,* VII, 97, 99).

44. Thomas Balch, ed., *Letters and Papers Relating Chiefly to the Provincial History of Pennsylvania* . . . (Philadelphia, 1855), 52 ("joyful"). "[N]othing but Confusion reigns here," a disgusted Claus wrote (*PWJ,* II, 439).

45. *MPCP,* VII, 79 ("amazed"), 80 ("insult"; and Weiser to Thomas Penn, 28 Feb. 1756, PMOC, VIII, 61).

46. Peters to Penn, 25 Apr. 1756, PMOC, VIII, 75; *MPCP,* VII, 70; *PWJ,* II, 440 (illness). *MPCP,* VII, 64, 70, 87 (Scarouyady); *PWJ,* II, 442 (Morris).

47. *MPCP,* VII, 74–76, 79–80, 88–90, 105–107. The bounty is in *PA,* 1st, II, 619, 651–653.

48. The meeting, though unofficial, was not clandestine (*MPCP,* VII, 83–86, 103–104). Its minutes are in LP, 11/41, and FA, III, 530–533. A listing of other, variant copies is in Jennings, *Empire of Fortune,* 270, n.45. For Johnson's unhappiness with "these Opposite Belts," see *DHNY,* II, 722–723. Peters, perhaps to avoid criticism, claimed that the governor did not, in the end, send the Quakers' message but "sent ye Message in his own name." Still, the message seemed to speak both war and peace (Peters to Thomas Penn, 30 Apr. 1756, PMOC, VIII, 83). Scarouyady's opinion of this strange combination is unclear. "[T]ho' this may seem to Contradict what the Governor hath said to us," he remarked elliptically, "We don't mean but let that be as it is."

49. *PWJ,* II, 438. Scarouyady's joyous welcome above Tioga (*MPCP,* VII, 81, 90) might have been a factor in his decision.

50. *MPCP,* VII, 90; Peters to Penn, 25 Apr. 1756, PMOC, VIII, 75. *MPCP,* VII, 92, 94; *PA,* 1st, II, 627–628, 8th, V, 4362 (reward).

51. *PA,* 1st, II, 645–646; *MPCP,* VI, 689. The one formally adopted was Thomas Græme (*ibid.,* VII, 6). For the other, Turbutt Francis, see Epilogue.

52. *MPCP,* VI, 589 ("unfit"). Scarouyady died at Lancaster of smallpox in May 1757. He spent the last year of his life, except for this trip to the Lancaster treaty, in Iroquoia. (*MPCP,* VII, 507, 509, 512. James[?] Pemberton to Dr. J. Fothergill, 30 5 mo. 1757, PPEC, II, 23; William Logan to the Governor, 6 May 1757, LP, 11/48; Daniel Clark to James Burd, 21 May 1757, and John Harris to James Burd, n.d., PSF, II.) Montour lived for sixteen more years, and passed through the province many times. He also left some of his children in Philadelphia (*MPCP,* VII, 95–96). Henceforth, however, he moved in William Johnson's orbit, not Pennsylvania's.

53. *MPCP,* VII, 105; Weiser to Morris, 25 Apr. 1756, FA, I, 131.

54. Conference at Israel Pemberton's, 23 Apr. 1756, LP, 11/41. Peters to Weiser, 5 [sic 25?] Apr. 1756, RPP, IV, 52.

55. *MPCP,* VII, 138 ("Pennsylvania Messengers"). Morris asked him to say this explicitly (108), and the province later sought to get the same message across (145).

56. *Ibid.,* V, 145–151, 166, VI, 524, 588–589; *PGW,* I, 135, 140, n.20. See Sipe, *Indian Chiefs of Pennsylvania,* 258–266; McConnell, *A Country Between,* 16, 22–24, 30, 45, 110; William C. Reichel, ed., *Memorials of the Moravian Church,* I (Philadelphia, 1870), 232n.

57. *MPCP,* VI, 194, 198–199, 206, 494, 523–524, VII, 6; Wallace, *Weiser,* 387–391.

58. *MPCP,* VII, 137. Newcastle, apparently a speaker in 1747, said in 1756 that he was a soldier (Weiser to Morris, 25 Apr. 1756, FA, I, 131).

59. *PA,* 1st, II, 645 ("Nature"), 681–682 (Bethlehem); *MPCP,* VI, 681 ("drunken Zigrea"), VII, 33–35 ("light headed"). For Newcastle's drinking, Weiser to Morris, 25 Apr. 1756, FA, I, 131; *PA,* 1st, II, 727. So ill-suited did this threesome seem that one wonders if Scarouyady and Montour hoped that the Quaker peace initiative would fail. After all, the two had pressed Pennsylvania to declare war that April, even though the Six Nations' February treaty with William Johnson agreed on further negotiations. Moreover, standing there in the crowd at Pemberton's were many capable, experienced Indian go-betweens, including Seneca George and the Old Belt.

60. Spangenberg to [the Governor], 20 May 1756, MCA, 34/317/2/6 ("news"). Conditions on the Susquehanna that spring and summer are in Spangenberg to the Governor, 23 May 1756, *ibid.,* 34/317/2/7; *MPCP,* VII, 171, 242–243, 283–284; *PA,* 1st, II, 615–616, 634, 666, III, 44–46, 56–57; *PG,* 9 Sept. 1756; Memorandum of a Conversation with Indians, 31 May, 1 June 1756, RPCEC, B6, 1169–1170; Weiser to Parsons, 4 July 1756, HP, I, 173; Wallace, *Teedyuscung,* 87–89, 93–94.

61. *MPCP,* VII, 142 ("fortunately begun"), 198–200.

62. *Ibid.,* 222–225, 296; *DRCNY,* VII, 197; *PWJ,* IX, 526–527.

63. *MPCP,* VII, 65 ("Danger"); Conference at Pemberton's, 19–23 Apr. 1756, LP, 11/41 ("throats").

64. Spangenberg to the Governor, 2 May 1756, MCA, 34/317/2/5; *MPCP,* VII, 119. And see *PA,* 1st, II, 682–683, for similar contingency plans on the second trip.

65. *MPCP,* VII, 118–119 ("Last Will"). For Augustus, VIII, 132; *PA,* 1st, II, 636–637; Spangenberg to the Governor, 23 May 1756, MCA, 34/317/2/7; Spangenberg to William Logan, 2 May 1756, Northampton County, Miscellaneous Manuscripts, Bethlehem and Vicinity, 1741–1849, 39, HSP.

66. *MPCP,* VII, 119 ("allarmd"; also Spangenberg to Israel Pemberton, 2 May 1756, FA, I, 135). *MPCP,* VII, 163–165, 174–175; *PA,* 1st, II, 668, 670–671, 2d, II, 600–602; Wallace, *Teedyuscung,* 95.

67. Spangenberg to the Governor, 23 May 1756, MCA, 34/317/2/7.

68. *PA,* 1st, II, 727–728; Reichel, ed., *Memorials,* I, 256.

69. Peters to the Proprietors, 22 Nov. 1756, PMOC, VIII, 205; James Pemberton to Israel Pemberton, 12 Nov. 1756, PPHSP, XI, 144; Minutes of the Friendly Association, 1755–1757, 17, 34 (verso), HSP; *MPCP,* VII, 307, 337–338; *PG,* 4 Nov. 1756. The illness appeared while he was conferring with Weiser at Tulpehocken and worsened when he and Weiser returned to

Philadelphia on 29 October. The possibility that Newcastle might have thought Delawares were behind it is in Wallace, *Teedyuscung,* 114.

70. Peters to the Proprietors, 22 Nov. 1756, PMOC, VIII, 205. See also Peters to the Proprietaries, 14 June 1756, Peters Letters to the Proprietaries, 1755–1757, 59, Gratz Coll., HSP.

71. *MPCP,* VII, 142 ("Dispatch"); Spangenberg to [the Governor], 20 May 1756, MCA, 34/317/2/6 ("Blood").

72. *MPCP,* VII, 144. Her name is in *PA,* 1st, II, 684–685. It is unclear whether she was his daughter or his niece. Given Iroquois matrilineal practices, maternal uncles were closer than fathers.

73. *MPCP,* VII, 144–148, 175–176; Directions to William Logan, n.d., LP, 11/64; "Jersey Indians Listed with Capt Johnson," n.d., *ibid.,* 11/65; Conversation with Indians, 1 June 1756, RPCEC, B6, 1170. That Lacquis was unconvincing is clear from *MPCP,* VII, 141. Augustus, too, insisted that the rumors were false (Spangenberg to the Governor, 23 May 1756, MCA, 34/317/2/7).

74. *MPCP,* VII, 198–200.

75. *Ibid.,* 284, 296–298; *PA,* 1st, II, 729–730, III, 46, 56, 96–97. For unflattering assessments of the Delaware leader, consult Richard Peters, Memorandum of a Conversation with John Shickellamy, 8 Sept. 1756, RPCEC, B7, 1268; *MPCP,* VII, 244, 310. And see Wallace, *Teedyuscung,* chs. 6–7.

76. Peters[?] to Weiser[?], 18 Oct. 1756, LC, IV, 157 ("much to say"); *MPCP,* VII, 302–304 (attacks).

77. Peters[?] to Weiser[?], 18 Oct. 1756, LC, IV, 157.

78. *MPCP,* VIII, 143–145 (encounter). For the building project, Wallace, *Teedyuscung,* 184–189; Zane 1758, 417–426. *MPCP,* VIII, 33–35, 42–46, 54–55, 87–97, 114–115, 138, 151–152, 195, 200; *PA,* 1st, III, 490–491 (messages).

79. "An Account of the Captivity of Hugh Gibson Among the Delaware Indians . . . ," 1756–1759, *Collections of the Massachusetts Historical Society,* 3d ser., VI (1837), 145, 146, 153; Albert G. Rau, "Moravian Missions and Colonial Politics," *Moravian Historical Society Transactions,* XI (1936), 137–145.

80. *PA,* 1st, III, 462 ("known"); Post 1758, 193, 195 n.30 (Ohio). Kenny 1758–59, 433 ("Quaker"); Post 1758, 216 ("flesh and blood"; also 222; Post to Peter Boehler, 30 Nov. 1760, MCA, 28/219/7/21; *MPCP,* VIII, 690).

81. For Post, see Rau, "Moravian Missions," *Moravian Hist. Soc. Trans.,* XI (1936), 137–145; "Six Months on the Frontier of Northampton County, Penna., During the Indian War, October 1755–June 1756," *PMHB,* XXXIX (1915), 346–347; William A. Hunter, "Documented Subdivisions of the Delaware Indians," *Bulletin of the Archaeological Society of New Jersey,* XXXV (1978),

24. For Pisquetomen, see Wallace, *Teedyuscung,* 71, 191; Francis Jennings, "A Vanishing Indian: Francis Parkman Versus His Sources," *PMHB,* LXXXVII (1963), 306–323; idem, "The Delaware Interregnum," *PMHB,* LXXXIX (1965), 174–198; Michael N. McConnell, "Pisquetomen and Tamaqua: Mediating Peace in the Ohio," in Robert S. Grumet, ed., *Northeastern Indian Lives, 1632–1816* (Amherst, Mass., 1996), 273–294.

82. *PA,* 1st, III, 377, 396–397, 413, 414, 424–427, 504–515; *MPCP,* VIII, 84, 95, 99, 102, 114–115, 120, 127; Post 1758, 189–190.

83. *PA,* 1st, III, 506; Wallace, *Teedyuscung,* 172–174 (army). *MPCP,* VII, 282; *PA,* 1st, III, 397 (colonial rumors). *MPCP,* VIII, 124–127, 129, 134; *PA,* 1st, III, 405, 415, 428; Wallace, *Teedyuscung,* 184–190 (Indian rumors).

84. For Indians' reasons for seeking peace, see McConnell, *A Country Between,* 124–129. For talk of peace earlier, Walter T. Champion, "Christian Frederick Post and the Winning of the West," *PMHB,* CIV (1980), 317; Wallace, *Teedyuscung,* 168–170, 172; Hunter, "Provincial Negotiations," *Pa. Hist.,* XVIII (1951), 214. But some Indians denied ever sending peace feelers to Pennsylvania (Post 1758, 196).

85. *MPCP,* VIII, 144. Talk of messages not getting through was common: Champion, "Post," *PMHB,* CIV (1980), 316–317; *MPCP,* VIII, 144, 200; *PA,* 1st, III, 459–460; Jennings, *Empire of Fortune,* 281, 326, 386; Wallace, *Teedyuscung,* chs. 12–13.

86. *MPCP,* VIII, 129–139, 142–145; *PA,* 1st, III, 412–422.

87. Jennings, *Empire of Fortune,* 384–389; *MPCP,* VIII, 147–148; *PA,* 1st, III, 456–469.

88. Post 1758. See McConnell, *A Country Between,* 129–135; Jennings, *Empire of Fortune,* 385–403, 408–413; White, *Middle Ground,* 249–251; Auth, *Ten Years' War,* ch. 3.

89. Post 1758, 197, 200.

90. *Ibid.,* 204. For French machinations, see 202–204, 210, 223.

91. *Ibid.,* 209, 212 (and see 189, 213, 223–224, 232, 257–258; Nathaniel Holland to Israel Pemberton[?], 13 11 mo. 1758, FA, II, 298–299). Essoweyoualand's version mentions none of this, though he did admit to having stayed three days in Fort Duquesne ("Journal of Daniels Journey to the Allegheny," PPEC, II, 29).

92. Post 1758, 237–243.

93. *Ibid.,* 199 ("brains"), 226, 242–243 ("rashly"), 247.

94. *Ibid.,* 194 ("eyes"), 224–225, 252; *MPCP,* VIII, 187, 206; *PA,* 1st, III, 581 (Pisquetomen carried Post). The credit for recognizing Post's role belongs to Jennings ("Vanishing Indian," *PMHB,* LXXXVII [1963], 306–323).

95. Post 1758, 237.

96. *Ibid.,* 214–216, 221–222, 225.

97. Israel Pemberton to Charles Read, 10 Sept. 1758, FA, II, 232.

98. For the treaty, *MPCP,* VIII, 175–223, and ch. VII. Peters, Diary, 6 (enemy attacks), 19 (Pisquetomen) Oct. 1758, RPP.

99. *Ibid.,* 18 [*sic:* 15], 17, 22 ("Care") Oct. 1758; *MPCP,* VIII, 206–208. See McConnell, *A Country Between,* 132.

100. Post 1758, 190, 192.

101. *Ibid.,* 213–216, 221–222, 224, 240 (see also 256–258); Kenny 1758–59, 433.

102. Post 1758, 215. Their formal reply to Pennsylvania distinguished people by color: "you are of one nation and colour, in all the *English* governments," as opposed to "all the nations of my colour" (219).

103. *PA,* 1st, III, 634. He did talk that spring and summer of favoring peace (Kenny, 1758–59, 421, 427, 429), but he kept a captive as late as 1761 (Kenny 1761–63, 26). McConnell ("Pisquetomen and Tamaqua," in Grumet, ed., *Northeastern Indian Lives,* 287), citing *PA,* 1st, IV, 93—a reference to Beaver's eldest brother—thinks Pisquetomen tried to go to the Lancaster peace treaty in 1762. Perhaps; but one colonist said that Beaver's eldest brother was one "John" (Kenny, 1761–63, 168).

104. *PA,* 1st, III, 709 ("lurking holes"); Post to [?], 30 Oct. 1760, MCA, 28/219/7/16 ("Door"); Post 1760, 24 May ("Stupid"); Kenny 1761–63, 40 ("Voide").

105. Post to Boehler, 30 Nov. 1760, MCA, 28/219/7/21; Kenny 1761–63, 25. (I have cleaned up Post's very difficult prose and spelling for clarity's sake.) On his peace mission in 1758, Post found Indians already worried that a missionary would be the entering wedge for colonial farmers (Post 1758, 280).

106. James Kenny to Israel Pemberton, Jr., 19 5 mo. 1762, PPHSP, XV, 147 ("Clear"); Kenny 1761–63, 155 ("limmited"), 160 ("Deliver"; see also 165, 167), 170 ("hope"), 192 ("Old Man"). Post, defeated, talked of shifting his site to Cuyahoga (187) or going on a grand tour that would take him into Canada (193). See John Heckewelder, *A Narrative of the Mission of the United Brethren Among the Delaware and Mohegan Indians, From Its Commencement, In the Year 1740, To the Close of the Year 1808 . . .* (Philadelphia, 1820), 59–65.

107. Post 1758, 207 (Pennsylvania; also 205–206, 216), 218–220; *MPCP,* VIII, 188–189 (Delawares).

108. Benjamin Lightfoot to Israel Pemberton, 23 Feb. 1759, FA, II, 457 ("Drub"), 7 Sept. 1760, FA, IV, 19 (Tatamy and Stille); Post 1760, 3, 5, 20 June (also 27 May, and Nathaniel Holland to Israel Pemberton, 16 Apr. 1761, FA, IV, 95).

109. *MPCP,* VIII, 145 ("own Mouths"); Post 1758, 279–280 ("credit"). The two Allegheny men "expressed a great Desire that some White Man should go with them" (Charles Thomson to Susannah Wright, 20 July 1758, Miscel-

laneous Manuscripts, APS). See also *MPCP,* V, 633, VII, 165–166, VIII, 615–616; *PA,* 1st, III, 416, 507.

110. Post 1760, 27 May ("roasted alive"), 2 June ("agree'd"; also 2, 16, 17 June); Hays, 80 ("Spies"; also 68, 69, 71, 75, 77, 79).

111. Auth, *Ten Years' War,* 9, 106–107, and chs. 5–7; White, *Middle Ground,* 250; McConnell, *A Country Between,* chs. 6–8.

112. Post 1758, 221 ("Brother"; also 217); *MPCP,* VIII, 207–208 ("Road").

VII: Treaties

1. *MPCP,* III, 124 ("old and wise People"), IV, 433 ("Faces"), VIII, 119 *(Caligh Wanorum);* John Langdale to Israel Pemberton, 18 3 mo. 1761, Roberts Collection, Haverford College Library ("National way"); Pemberton 1762, 321 ("great people"); Weiser to Logan, 25 Sept. 1736, LC, IV, 61 ("Chief Rulers"; also Weiser to Logan, 16 Sept. 1736, LP, 10/62). In 1751 a Mohawk, seeing Weiser, pointedly "asked whether the Governor of pensilvania or any Commissioner was Come" (Weiser 1751, 30 June).

2. Attempts to distinguish treaties from other sorts of meetings have not yielded a clear definition of these gatherings. Indians and colonists certainly did not have consistent categories, though they did, on occasion, differentiate between "a Treaty" and "a private Bargain and [land] sale" ("Moses Tatamie's Accot. of Indian Claims, taken from his Mouth at Easton," [1757], EC, no. 32, Miscellaneous Manuscripts, 94), between a "publick Treaty" and "private Conferences," the latter being only a gathering of "the wise men and Counsellors on both sides" (*MPCP,* VIII, 30).

   Not surprisingly, then, scholars using colonial records have had difficulty defining a treaty. Marshall Becker, a student of the Delawares, asserts that "[i]n general, any formal meeting between a group of Lenape and representatives of the colonial government was called a 'treaty.' " These would include "meetings held only to discuss land sales as well as the conclaves held in order to sign transfer documents relating to these sales," along with meetings "to discuss and to attempt to resolve various issues" (Becker, "Lenape Land Sales, Treaties, and Wampum Belts," *PMHB,* CVIII [1984], 354). Writing of the Iroquois, William Fenton ("Structure, Continuity, and Change in the Process of Iroquois Treaty Making," in Francis Jennings et al., eds., *The History and Culture of Iroquois Diplomacy: An Interdisciplinary Guide to the Treaties of the Six Nations and Their League* [Syracuse, N.Y., 1985], 27) reports four types: (1) "talk in the bushes" as a means of setting an agenda; (2) "more formal meetings or conferences preliminary to a treaty"; (3) "fre-

quent councils for condoling someone, for showing new chiefs, for communication of 'news,' and polishing the Chain [of Friendship]"; (4) "large
conferences leading to a definite result—extending the Chain, fixing boundaries, land cessions, and formal alliances for peace and war—which are
documented by deed or written proceedings afterward published—are
what we know as Indian treaties. The latter were usually initiated by colonial officials and held at colonial or Crown expense. They form the body of
the Indian treaty literature surviving today." Mary Druke ("Iroquois Treaties:
Common Forms, Varying Interpretations," *ibid.*, 92), too, posits a four-
part scheme, but it does not conform precisely to Fenton's: "(1) invitations; (2) preliminary meetings between delegates of one nation or one
party to council negotiations; (3) major council transactions [or 'main in-
ternational council meetings,' *ibid.*, 94]; (4) ratification of a treaty and/or
reporting of delegates to the person or group to whom, or for whom, they
were responsible in the negotiations." Neither Druke nor Fenton offers examples that might fix these categories. Other scholars distinguish a "core"
of "solemn, fully ritualized treaty proceedings," "the main events," from
"other 'councils' or 'conferences,' " but caution that "the formal gradation
between such terms may be projections into the past of modern notions"
("Descriptive Treaty Calendar," *ibid.*, 157–158).

My own reading of council proceedings suggests that a certain studied
vagueness is indeed warranted, to allow for a spectrum of formal meetings
and for differing interpretations of the importance of various conclaves, but
that all parties clearly considered a large core set of encounters central to
their ongoing conversation. Among these encounters were: Albany, 1722
and 1754; Philadelphia, 1732, 1736, 1742, 1749; Lancaster, 1744, 1757,
1762; Easton, 1756, 1757, 1758, 1761, 1762. My analysis draws heavily
upon, but is not limited to, this constellation of councils. It excludes, for example, Weiser's visits to Onondaga in 1737, 1743, 1745, and 1750, since in
each case he was preparing the way for a treaty by dealing with a particular issue, not holding a treaty that reached conclusions on weighty matters.
But I have considered the famous Logstown treaties of 1748, 1751, and
1752, even though here, too, Weiser, Croghan, Montour, and others were
there, under instruction from provincial authorities, delivering gifts and
pursuing certain initiatives more than reaching agreements. Still, at Logstown many of the obstacles (delays, drink, and disagreements), settings (an
arbor), size (several hundred natives in attendance), and techniques (gathering intelligence and lists of names, holding private councils) resembled
those of treaty councils held over the mountains. *MPCP,* V, 348–358,
517–540; Logstown Treaty; Lois Mulkearn, ed., *George Mercer Papers Relating to the Ohio Company of Virginia* (Pittsburgh, Pa. 1954), 44–56 *et passim.* A

recent account of treaties that appeared after this chapter was written is Robert A. Williams, Jr., *Linking Arms Together: American Indian Treaty Visions of Law and Peace, 1600–1800* (New York, 1997).

3. Nancy Hagedorn ("Brokers of Understanding: Interpreters as Agents of Cultural Exchange in Colonial New York," *New York History,* LXXVI [1995], 379–408) argues that protocol became more fully developed between 1690 and 1740; hence the expanded minutes. I am inclined to agree, though I wonder if some of that greater articulation is a function of the scribes' realization of the importance of these rituals to Indians.

4. Thomas McKee to [?], 14 Aug. 1754, Berks and Montgomery Counties, Miscellaneous Manuscripts, 1693–1869, 181, HSP; *MPCP,* VIII, 488.

5. Lawrence C. Wroth, "The Indian Treaty as Literature," *Yale Review,* XVII (1928), 749–766; Carl Van Doren, "Introduction," in Julian P. Boyd, ed., *Indian Treaties Printed by Benjamin Franklin, 1732–1762* (Philadelphia, 1938); A. M. Drummond and Richard Moody, "Indian Treaties: The First American Dramas," *Quarterly Journal of Speech,* XXXIX (1953), 15–24. For diplomacy, see Michael K. Foster et al., eds., *Extending the Rafters: Interdisciplinary Approaches to Iroquoian Studies* (Albany, N.Y., 1984); Daniel K. Richter and James H. Merrell, eds., *Beyond the Covenant Chain: The Iroquois and Their Neighbors in Indian North America, 1600–1800* (Syracuse, N.Y., 1987); Jennings et al., eds., *History and Culture of Iroquois Diplomacy;* Steven V. Ireton, "Conflict Resolution and Indian Treaties on the American Indian Frontier, 1730–1768" (Ph.D. diss., University of California at Santa Barbara, 1988), esp. ch. VII; Dorothy V. Jones, *License for Empire: Colonialism by Treaty in Early America* (Chicago, 1982); Francis Paul Prucha, *American Indian Treaties: The History of a Political Anomaly* (Berkeley, Calif., 1994); Timothy J. Shannon, "The Crossroads of Empire: The Albany Congress of 1754 and the British Atlantic Community" (Ph.D. diss., Northwestern University, 1993).

6. For "settling ye Minutes," Peters, Diary, 8, 14, 16 Oct. 1758, RPP. For "correcting" and "revising," *ibid.,* 31 Oct., 1–4, 6 Nov. 1758. Also Peters, Diary, 2, 6 Sept. 1762, RPP. Some scholars have argued that there was "not too much expurgation" by scribes (Van Doren, "Introduction," in Boyd, ed., *Indian Treaties,* xviii); David Murray disagrees (*Forked Tongues: Speech, Writing, and Representation in North American Indian Texts* [Bloomington, Ind., 1991], ch. 3). A closer look erodes confidence in the accuracy of recorded minutes. During the war, Quaker observers often charged proprietary scribes with fraud. When talk turned to proprietary land affairs, for example, Quakers claimed that Richard Peters "threw down his Pen, and declared he would take no Minutes when the King [Teedyuscung] came to complain of the Proprietors" ([Thomson], *Enquiry,* 99–101; also 30–31). More often it was simply a matter of quiet editing. "The Minutes are calculated to skew[?], rather than give a true Acco.t of ye Proceedings," Israel Pemberton complained

after another council; "the Acknowledgemts ye Indians make of their attachments to & dependance on Friends . . . [are] carefully suppressed" (Israel Pemberton to Samuel Wily, 2 Dec. 1758, PPHSP, XIII, 14. Also Peters, Diary, 12 Oct. 1758, RPP; Account of the Easton Treaty, June 1762, Friendly Association Mss., Swarthmore College Library; *PA,* 8th, VI, 4502; Pemberton 1762, 321). "[T]hey were miserably[?] curtail'd & mangled," exclaimed another, upon comparing the official minutes with "ye Mem[ory] of several present" (James[?] Pemberton to John Fothergill, 2 8 mo. 1758, PPEC, II, 26). Charges of land fraud at Easton in 1762, Quakers claimed, gave the official recorder "a plain intention to Omit minuting this Matter & pass it over" (John Pemberton to Rachel Pemberton, 27 8 mo. 1762, PPHSP, XVI, 33; Pemberton 1762, 321). And *PA,* 8th, V, 4098–4099, 4146, 4169.

Then there were examples of unintentional failure to take good notes, or of editing or otherwise revising and distorting what was said, including omission of treaty rituals as too tedious. John Kinsey, Journal, 14 Oct. 1745, Swarthmore College Library (confused); Weiser 1751, 19 June, 2 July; Minutes of the Indian Treaty at Pittsburgh, 16 Aug. 1760, Recs. Mor. Miss., Box 323, Folder 7, Item 1, in *Iroq. Ind.,* Reel 23. On one occasion colonists agreed that an article of a treaty "shou'd not be spoke but was agreed to be true and shou'd be enter'd into the Minutes" (RPLB, 1737–1750, 252). For variations between different scribes, see *PWJ,* XI, 395, and compare *MPCP,* VII, 649–714, with *DRCNY,* VII, 280–321.

7. *DHNY,* II, 946. For the minutes of that council, see *DRCNY,* VIII, 111–137 (private meetings, 122–125). A variant transcription is in duplicate of a letter from Lord Botetourt to [?], 24 Dec. 1768, in *Iroq. Ind.,* Reel 29. For other remarks about taking minutes, consult Beverly McAnear, ed., "Personal Accounts of the Albany Congress of 1754," *MVHR,* XXXIX (1953), 741; Kinsey, Journal, 14 Oct. 1745, HSP; Weiser 1751, 19 June, 2 July; Minutes of Treaty at Pittsburgh, 16 Aug. 1760, Recs. Mor. Miss., 323/7/1, in *Iroq. Ind.,* Reel 23.

8. Druke, "Iroquois Treaties," in Jennings et al., eds., *History and Culture of Iroquois Diplomacy,* 87–88.

9. *PWJ,* VII, 852 ("small part"; also *DHNY,* IV, 397). Linguists have noted how oral and literate societies value different things in a conversation: the former focus on the link between speaker and audience, the latter on the content of what is said. For the distinction between *text* and *context,* see Deborah Tannen, ed., *Coherence in Spoken and Written Discourse,* Advances in Discourse Processes, XII (Norwood, N.J., 1984), xv, 2. For the importance of harmony, see Fenton, "Iroquois Treaty Making," in Jennings et al., eds., *History and Culture of Iroquois Diplomacy,* 6–7; Richter, *Ordeal of the Longhouse,* 40; Jane Merritt, "The Power of Language: Cultural Meanings and the Colonial Encounter on the Pennsylvania Frontier," 16–17 (unpub. ms., 1994). Both for-

mal treaty minutes and informal accounts of events behind the scenes are far richer after 1730 (and especially after 1750) than before. Examples of the poverty of records at earlier councils are *MPCP,* II, 15, 158–159, 251–252.

10. RPLB, 1737–1750, 251. Also [Thomson], *Enquiry,* 180; James Pemberton to Hannah Pemberton, 3 Aug. 1757, PPHSP, XII, 55a.

11. Brief treatments of the council scene can be found in Wallace, *Weiser,* 459–460, 476–478, 524–526; Jennings, *Empire of Fortune,* 397; Jerome H. Wood, *Conestoga Crossroads: Lancaster, Pennsylvania, 1730–1790* (Harrisburg, Pa., 1979), 71–74.

12. Marshe, 11 ("followed"), 20 (dine); William Plumsted to Richard Peters, 12 Feb. 1755, Penn Manuscripts, Accounts, II, 22, doc. 97b, HSP ("tumult"; also Claus, Memoirs); *PA,* 1st, III, 274 ("Days," "Country"); *MPCP,* III, 219, 318 ("vast Audience"), 447, 450, IV, 82, 432, 443, VII, 207.

13. *MPCP,* VII, 491 ("true Love"; also George Croghan to Israel Pemberton, 6 Apr. 1757, FA, I, 279; Indian Treaty Minutes, 24 Sept. 1771, RPCEC, B12, 2821–2822). For fear of disease, see ch. III, and *MJNY,* 92. But for every Indian saying he would never go to Philadelphia, many more reported that they had gone, despite whatever misgivings they had (*ibid.,* 48–50, 52–53, 60, 75, 87). Weiser, Account of Indian Charges, Oct. 1736, Penn Mss., Accounts, I, 33, doc. 25, HSP (Indians on board ship). For European wares obtained, see "A List of Indian goods fitt for Presents for the ohio Indians," n.d., GCP, 6/30; "Friends Goods," 11 mo. 1756, FA, I, 215; List of Goods to be Delivered the Indians by the Province, 11 mo. 1756, *ibid.,* 219; "Goods Belonging to the Friendly Association . . . ," 4–5 8 mo. 1757, *ibid.,* 387; "Division of Goods belonging to ye Frdly Associatn at Lancaster," *ibid.,* n.d., 411.

14. Marshe, 176 (quotation). For children at an Easton treaty, *PA,* 1st, III, 210, 218, 744–745; *MPCP,* VII, 649; List of Tribes at the Gap near Fort Allen, 27 July 1761, in "Indians, 1757–1769, and n.d.," in a box labeled "Indians (transferred from Society Collections)," HSP. And see *PWJ,* X, 515; Zeisberger, *Diaries,* 82. Marshe, 179; Message delivered to the Indians, 6 May 1757, LP, 11/49; Pemberton 1762, 320, 322; *MPCP,* VIII, 721–722, 728; Benjamin Franklin, *Autobiography and Other Writings,* ed. Kenneth Silverman (New York, 1986), 135 (huts).

15. Logstown Treaty, 155; Wallace, *Weiser,* 143–144; Gist, 20. *PA,* 1st, III, 276 ("Flat Hat"). Marshe, 180 ("poorly dressed," paint). Heckewelder, *History,* 205–207; Travel Diary, 16 Oct. 1748, MCA, 30/225/2/1 (tattoos). Ruth L. Springer and Louise Wallman, eds., "Two Swedish Pastors Describe Philadelphia, 1700 and 1702," *PMHB,* LXXXIV (1960), 216; *DHNY,* III, 1042–1043; *PA,* 1st, IV, 61, 67; Peters, Diary, 29 Sept. 1758, RPP (paint).

16. Heckewelder, *History,* 190.

17. "Account of Expences to Easton," June 1762, Penn Mss., Accounts, II, 50, doc. 123, HSP.

18. Marshe, 179; Kenny 1758–59, 422; *PWJ*, X, 852; *MPCP*, II, 599, IX, 259; Loskiel, *History*, Part II, 133 (singing); Logstown Treaty, 155 (wampum, breastplates); *PA*, 1st, I, 269 (arm and neck wampum belts); Heckewelder, *History*, 203; Barry C. Kent, *Susquehanna's Indians*, Anthropological Series, no. 6 (Harrisburg, Pa., 1989), 207–210 (bells, thimbles); Marshe, 182 (drums).

19. Peters to Weiser, 4 June 1744, RPP, II, 12 (provisioners). James Steel Letterbook, 1730–1741, 95, HSP; William C. Reichel, ed., *Memorials of the Moravian Church*, I (Philadelphia, 1870), 283–284, 298; *MPCP*, VI, 467 (provisions). For Quakers, see Pemberton 1762, 320–322; Friendly Association, Mss., 8 mo. 1761, Swarthmore College Library. McAnear, ed., "Accounts of Albany," *MVHR*, XXXIX (1953), 733 ("View"); Marshe, 181–182, 189–191 ("frantic," "song," "shriek"; and 179); Franklin, *Autobiography*, ed. Silverman, 135 ("Bodies," "Bonfire," "Yellings," "Hell"). Franklin was describing intoxicated Indians he saw at a council in Carlisle; doubtless the alcohol heightened the sense of chaos, but sober Indians could have a similar effect.

20. Marshe, 198 ("noise"); *MPCP*, VIII, 51 (tavern); Pemberton 1762, 320; John Pemberton to Rachel Pemberton, 22 and 24 8 mo. 1762, PPHSP, XVI, 26, 29b (meeting); *MPCP*, IX, 7 (horse); William Parsons to Peters, 10 Apr. 1757, RPP, IV, 88 (peltry). And see Logan to the Governor, 6 May 1757, LP, 11/48.

21. Peters to Penn (extract), 4 Aug. 1756, PMIA, II, 99 ("mixed"); Marshe, 193 (negotiator between). "Messieurs Penn and Peters Dr. to Robt Lottridge," 8 July 1754, PMIA, IV, 7; *MPCP*, VII, 705 (300). For similar occasions—some explicitly dinners, others, more vaguely, "entertainment"—see II, 9, III, 437, IV, 56, 92, 95, 563–564, 573, VII, 215; Marshe, 193; "Indian Charges," 5 July 1742, Penn Mss., Accounts, I, 55, doc. 47b, HSP; Minutes of the Treaty at Easton, 30 July 1756, FA, I, 155; Israel Pemberton to Mary Pemberton, 10 11 mo. 1756, PPHSP, XI, 140; Kenny, 1758–59, 429.

22. Russell F. Weigley, *Philadelphia: A 300-Year History* (New York, 1982), 12, 33, 100. Marshe, 176 (Lancaster). For Albany, "The Journal of Isaac Norris, During a Trip to Albany in 1745, And An Account of a Treaty held There in October of That Year," *PMHB*, XXVII (1903), 24–25; Kinsey, Journal, 12 Oct. 1745, HSP; William L. McDowell, ed., *Documents Relating to Indian Affairs, 1750–1754* (Columbia, S.C., 1958), 93 (street), 94 (tent). For Easton, see *PWJ*, III, 762–791; Peters to Lynford Lardner, 21 June 1762, PMOC, IV, 40 ("Bower"); Peters, Diary, 29 Sept. 1758, RPP; "Minutes of Council at Philadelphia . . . ; and an account of the visit to the Indians at the time of the treaty at Easton," in *Iroq. Ind.*, Reel 23, 11–16 July 1760–1761 (shed); *PA*, 1st, III, 249; Israel Pemberton to Mary Pemberton, 21 7 mo. 1757, PPHSP, XII, 46 (booth). *PWJ*, XII, 666 (Stanwix).

23. Loskiel (*History,* Part II, 134), described a meeting between Nanticokes, Shawnees, and Moravians. *MPCP,* IV, 433 (table). Minutes of the Friendly Assoc., 1755–1757, 20, HSP (benches).

24. For the difference, see Chew, 313; Zeisberger, *History,* 96, 142. Wallace, *Weiser,* 91 (loud and slow). Bartram, *Observations,* 58 (walking). Minutes of the Treaty at Easton, 28 July 1756, Friends Historical Association, Mss., I, Haverford College Library, in *Iroq. Ind.,* Reel 19 (closing fist).

25. Weiser to Burd, 3 Oct. 1757, PSF, III.

26. Easton Treaty, 28 July 1756, Friends Historical Assn., Mss., I, Haverford College Library, in *Iroq. Ind.,* Reel 19; *PA,* 1st, III, 32–33, 35; *MPCP,* VII, 465–500, 510–511 (Indians waiting). Peters to Weiser, 11 June 1744, RPP, II, 14 ("anxiety" and "Impatience"). In 1744 the Lancaster conference convened two months after Virginia and Maryland leaders thought it was scheduled to commence (they had miscalculated the number of moons that were to pass before Indians would set off). Gov. Thomas to Gooch and Bladen, 20 Jan. 1743/4, RPP, II, 2; "Journal of William Black, 1744 . . . ," ed. R. Alonzo Brock, *PMHB,* I (1877), 117–132, 233–249, 404–419, II (1878), 40–49. Twenty-four years later, Virginia commissioners to the Fort Stanwix treaty in 1768 were off by three months and several hundred miles (*PWJ,* VI, 297, 406, 423, 429, 436, XII, 608, 617–627). For other examples of colonists being kept waiting, see McAnear, ed., "Accounts of Albany," *MVHR,* XXXIX (1953), 735, 740; *MPCP,* IX, 250–257.

27. Weiser to Logan, 16 Sept. 1736, LP, 10/62.

28. *MPCP,* VII, 465–466 (death), IX, 252, 254 (vision). For stops, Weiser to Logan, 2, 16 Sept. 1736, LP, 10/58, 10/62; same to same, 25 Sept. 1736, Roberts Collection, Haverford College Library; Weiser, Indian Expences, 1744, RPP, II, 16; Weiser to Peters, 6 Aug. 1749, DSP, 966.F.26a ("no Hurry").

29. Weiser to Peters, 6 Aug. 1749, DSP, 966.F.26a (see also Logan to Weiser, 1 Nov. 1736, LP, 2/59); *PA,* 1st, IV, 96 (Post).

30. Weiser to Peters, 12 Aug. 1749, DSP, 966.F.26c ("Secure"). Same to same, 6 Aug. 1749, *ibid.,* 966.F.26a; Indian Expences, 1749, CCW, I, 21; Horsfield to the Governor, 3 Sept. 1761, HP, II, 441; *PA,* 8th, IV, 2938–2939, 3253–3254, 3257, 3261–3262, 3275, 3359, 3428, 3466, V, 4011, 4070, 4349, VI, 5362; *MPCP,* VIII, 770; Michael Gross, Account of Indian Expenses, Lancaster, July 1748, RPCEC, B2, 524; John Dunbar, ed., *The Paxton Papers* (The Hague, 1957), 198. The full story of Weiser's disastrous 1749 escort is told in Wallace, *Weiser,* ch. 34.

31. *PA,* 1st, IV, 97 ("frolick"); Indian Expences, 1749, CCW, I, 21. Weiser to Peters, 12 Aug. 1749, DSP, 966.F.26c (Nanticoke; also William Logan to the Governor, 6 May 1757, LP, 11/48).

32. *PA,* 1st, III, 208–209; "Account of Expences to Easton," June 1762, Penn Mss., Accounts, II, 50, doc. 123, HSP. Peters, Diary, 1755 [*sic*], 6 Jan. (barber), 7, 20 Jan. 1756 (washerwomen, servants), RPP; Israel Pemberton to Mary Pemberton, 5 Aug. 1761, FA, IV, 153–158 (cooks). Peters to William Parsons, 22 July 1756, HP, I, 239; Account "for Sundries sent up by a Waggon to Easton for the Use of the Governor and his Company," 14 June 1762, Penn Mss., Accounts, II, 49, doc. 122b, HSP. *PA,* 1st, III, 217, 516; Richard Peters to William Logan, 2 Oct. 1758, LP, 11/52; Minutes of the Friendly Assoc., 1755–1757, 18, HSP; Account, 10 Oct. 1758, FA, II, 267 (beds).

33. *PA,* 1st, I, 658 (backgammon), III, 516 (wine); Peters to the Proprietaries, 27 July 1748, PMOC, IV, 137 ("unclean Beds"); Marshe, 172 ("eggs and bacon," "sorry rum"); Peters, Diary, 31 Aug. 1762, RPP ("Beef," "Table Cloath"); William Logan to John Smith, 16 Jan. 1756, LCP, Yi2 7290, F250, in *Iroq. Ind.,* Reel 18 ("Laxative Disorder"). The Pembertons, who were Quakers, tended to be an exception to the gentlefolks' demands. Israel Pemberton to Mary Pemberton, 10 Nov. 1756, same to James Pemberton, 10 Nov. 1756, XI, 140, 141, Israel Pemberton to Mary Pemberton, 11 May 1757, XII, 18, same to same, 21 July 1757, 46, James Pemberton to Hannah Pemberton, 4 Aug. 1757, 56, PPHSP.

34. Nicholas B. Wainwright, "Governor William Denny in Pennsylvania," *PMHB,* LXXXI (1957), 170–198; Wallace, *Weiser,* 440, 459, 469; Peters, Diary, Sept.–Nov. 1758, RPP; Chew, 312, 313. Denny was not the only amateur. See also Virginia treaty commissioner Thomas Lee's behavior at Lancaster in 1744 (RPLB, 1737–1750, 249–252; Hamilton to Thomas Penn, 10 July 1750, PMOC, V, 27; *MPCP,* IV, 699), and New York Governor George Clinton at Albany treaties of 1745 (Weiser 1745, 309–311; Wallace, *Weiser,* 230–231) and 1751 (Weiser 1751, 10 July). In September 1755, after Braddock's defeat, George Croghan predicted that provincial officials' blundering would drive all Indians into the arms of the French by the following spring, "for they [officials] hate to be att any Expence or Truble Nor Do any of them understand Indian Affairs" (*PWJ,* II, 29–30).

35. Peters, Diary, 15, 21, 22, 23 Oct. 1758, RPP; Chew, 312 ("indiscreetly"), 315 (moods). And Peters to the Proprietors, 16 Sept., 30 Oct. 1756, Peters Letters to the Proprietaries, 1755–1757, 90, 107, Simon Gratz Collection, Case 2, Box 33-a, HSP; Peters to the Proprietors, 10 Jan. 1757, Penn Mss., Additional Miscellaneous Letters, I, 100, HSP; *PA,* 8th, VI, 4782–4783.

36. Peters, Diary, 23–24 Oct. 1758, RPP. Also Israel Pemberton to Charles Read, 10 Sept. 1758, Pemberton to Gen. John Forbes, 26 Oct. 1758, FA, II, 231, 275, 279.

37. Peters, Diary, 12 Oct. 1758, RPP; Chew, 314. The performance was no sur-

prise to anyone who had seen Teedyuscung at councils the past two years. His behavior at that first Easton treaty in July 1756 set the tone for treaties to come. Wallace, *Teedyuscung,* ch. VIII; *MPCP,* VII, 204–220; *PA, 1st,* II, 722–730.

38. McKee to [?], 28 July 1756, PSF, III; Peters, Diary, 18 Oct. 1758, RPP; Weiser 1751, 5 July; *PA, 1st,* II, 726, IV, 67; Minutes of a Conversation with Teedyuscung, 31 7 mo. 1757, FA, I, 379.

39. The "Heart is soft" were the words of Papoonhal, on hearing a spiritual message from Quakers (Some Remarks, 11–16 July 1760–1761, HM 8249, Huntington Library, in *Iroq. Ind.,* Reel 23). See Smith, *Account,* 91; *MPCP,* IV, 560.

40. *DRCNY,* VI, 99 ("like Children"). *MPCP,* VI, 275, VII, 465–466; Claus, Memoirs, 11–12; *PA, 1st,* I, 666 (Condolence). Natives would also pause in the middle of a treaty for Condolence and a funeral (*MPCP,* VIII, 213; Peters, Diary, 23 Oct. 1758, RPP).

41. Wallace, *Weiser,* 534–535; George S. Snyderman, "The Function of Wampum," *Procs. APS,* XCVIII (1954), 487 (private councils). *MPCP,* VIII, 180 (Tagashata).

42. David McClure, *Diary of David McClure, Doctor of Divinity, 1748–1820,* ed. Franklin B. Dexter (New York, 1899), 66 ("delitory"); Pemberton 1762, 319 ("trifling"); *MPCP,* VII, 53–54 ("long and tedious"); William Logan to John Smith, 17 Oct. 1758, LCP, Yi2 7291 F83, in *Iroq. Ind.,* Reel 22 ("long Councils"). Also *MPCP,* VI, 275; Albert Cook Myers, ed., *Narratives of Early Pennsylvania, West New Jersey, and Delaware, 1630–1707* (New York, 1912), 235; Shippen to Denny, 26 Nov. 1757, Edward Shippen Letterbook, 1753–1761, 170, verso, APS; Gooch to Thomas Lee, 14 June 1744, Paul P. Hoffman, ed., *The Lee Family Papers, 1742–1795* (microfilm, Charlottesville, Va., 1966), reel 1.

43. *MPCP,* II, 533; Minutes of the Friendly Assoc., 1755–1757, 22, verso, HSP (Condolence). Weiser 1745, 310–311 (interrupted, answered too soon, hurried away); *MPCP,* VIII, 205 (spoke out of turn); Pemberton 1762, 321 (skipped topics); Weiser 1745, 309; *MPCP,* IV, 560, 564 ("Main Business").

44. *MPCP,* V, 666; Pemberton 1762, 321–322.

45. *MPCP,* VIII, 180 ("Hours"; also III, 92, V, 673; Chew, 316), 757 ("stay"); Weiser 1745, 311 ("displeas'd"); [Thomson], *Enquiry,* 181 (Tokahaio). The official version of Tokahaio's speech was shorter, and less explicit in condemning Pennsylvania authorities (*MPCP,* VIII, 212).

46. Kinsey, Journal, 7 and 10 Oct. 1745, HSP; Norris, "Journal," *PMHB,* XXVII (1903), 25; *MPCP,* VI, 113–114; *DRCNY,* VI, 291–292, 302. Among the treaties when Pennsylvania and other colonies sat down together, see Albany in 1722 and 1754, Lancaster in 1744, and Easton in 1758 and 1762. Also Shannon, "Crossroads of Empire," 285–291.

47. Kinsey, Journal, 5, 10, and 12 Oct. 1745, HSP; Norris, "Journal," *PMHB,* XXVII (1903), 23 (hats). McAnear, ed., "Accounts of Albany," *MVHR,* XXXIX (1953), 731 ("walk in"), 732–733 (precedence); RPLB, 1737–1750, 253 (oldest).

48. Kinsey, Journal, 12 Oct. 1745, HSP.

49. Richard Hockley to Lynford Lardner, 23 June 1762, PMIA, IV, 39. And Peters to Lardner, 23 June 1762, *ibid.,* 41; Account of the Easton Treaty, June 1762, Friendly Association Mss., Swarthmore College Library; *PWJ,* III, 772–775, X, 300–301; Chew, 316.

50. James H. Hutson, *Pennsylvania Politics, 1746–1770: The Movement for Royal Government and Its Consequences* (Princeton, N.J., 1972), ch. 1; Jennings, *Empire of Fortune,* 83–95.

51. *PA,* 1st, III, 312 (Weiser). [Thomson], *Enquiry* (contemporary). Modern: Paul Wallace *(Weiser),* Anthony Wallace *(Teedyuscung),* and Theodore Thayer *(Israel Pemberton, King of the Quakers* [Philadelphia, 1943]; "The Friendly Association," *PMHB,* LXVII [1943], 356–376) tend to favor the proprietary side; Francis Jennings *(Empire of Fortune),* Stephen F. Auth *(The Ten Years' War: Indian-White Relations in Pennsylvania, 1755–1765* [New York, 1989]), and Robert Daiutolo, Jr. ("The Role of Quakers in Indian Affairs During the French and Indian War," *Quaker History,* LXXVII [1988], 1–30) favor Friends and Teedyuscung.

52. Gen. Forbes landed in the middle of the battle and provided a vivid account of its effects. Alfred Proctor James, ed., *Writings of General John Forbes Relating to His Service in North America* (Menasha, Wisc., 1938), 73, 76, 102; *PHB,* II, 383.

53. Peters, Diary, 19, 24 Oct. 1758, RPP; Peters to Monckton, 29 Aug. 1760, *Collections of the Massachusetts Historical Society,* 4th ser., IX (1871), 306; Chew, 313–318; Israel Pemberton to Fothergill, 2 8 mo. 1757, PPEC, II, 26; Charles Thomson to William Franklin, 12 Mar. 1758, Papers of Benjamin Franklin, B:F85, vol. 48, f. 122, APS; *PA,* 1st, III, 235–236, 249–250, 254–255, 274–276, 314; [Thomson], *Enquiry,* 176; Peters, "An Account of the Quakers and their Conduct at Easton," 19 July 1757, MCA, 34/317/3/4a; Minutes of the Friendly Assoc., 1755–1757, 13 verso, 19 verso, 20–21, 23, HSP; Weiser, Observations (Pumpshire).

54. Chew, 315 ("more Onasses"; also Indians—Treaty at Easton, 28 July 1756, in "Indians [transferred from Society Collections]," HSP; *MPCP,* VIII, 744–745); Weiser to Peters, 12 Aug. 1749, DSP, 966.F.26c ("quarrle[s]," "high words").

55. *MPCP,* VI, 115 ("differ much"); *PWJ,* III, 4 ("Jelious"; also Peters to William Logan, 2 Oct. 1758, LP, 11/52; Wallace, *Weiser,* 267).

56. Marshe, 180 ("remarks"; and see 182). Weiser to Logan, 16 Sept. 1736, LP, 10/62 (Indians taking goods). *MPCP,* I, 334, II, 603; Council Held at

Philadelphia, 15 7ber 1718, LP, 11/7; Logan to Weiser, 18 Oct. 1736, *ibid.,* 10/64; Logan to Lt. Gov. Geo. Clark, 17 Jan. 1737, LC, IV, 4–5 (drinking). Colonial efforts to stop it, through proclamations and the town crier, had little effect (*MPCP,* IV, 86, V, 397–398; *PA,* 1st, III, 236–237, 437–438, 519–520). After a council with the Iroquois in the capital in 1742, provincial leaders decided that Indian delegations brought "so much Trouble" to the capital that "We detrmin'd on all future Occasions to meet them upon Sasquahanna or at some other distant Place" (Thomas to Gooch, 20 Jan. 1743/4 [copy], RPP, II, 2).

57. *PA,* 1st, IV, 98 ("crowded"). For Indian fears, *MPCP,* VII, 285–286; Pemberton 1762, 319 (poisoning); Horsfield to Denny, 27 Oct. 1756, HP, II, 314; Israel Pemberton to Mary Pemberton, 10, 13 11 mo. 1756, and to John Pemberton[?], 10 11 mo. 1756, PPHSP, XI, 137, 140–144; Zeisberger, *Diaries,* 77, 79–80; *PA,* 1st, III, 5–6, 8, 33, 44–45, 109. The fears were compounded when a treaty site housed troops as well as negotiators (*ibid.,* 218, 221; James[?] Pemberton to Fothergill, 30 5 mo. 1757, PPEC, II, 23).

58. *PA,* 1st, II, 724–725; Wallace, *Teedyuscung,* 105; "Indian Intelligence," [1756–1757], HP, II, 324 (Teedyuscung). *PA,* 1st, III, 56 (Hess). Also Dunbar, ed., *Paxton Papers,* 196.

59. James[?] Pemberton to Fothergill, 30 5 mo. 1757, PPEC, II, 23; *PG,* 26 May, 7 July 1757; *PA,* 1st, III, 194 ("scalped"); Charles Thomson to William Franklin, May[?] 1757, Pprs. of Franklin, B:F85, vol. 48, f. 120, APS; Thomas Balch, ed., *Letters and Papers Relating Chiefly to the Provincial History of Pennsylvania* . . . (Philadelphia, 1855), 78.

60. Testimony of Mathew Lowry, 16 July 1757, CCW, II, 85 ("Signed"); *PA,* 1st, III, 212, 221–222. For similar problems with Jersey folk—including orders to stop all ferries and imprisoning some people—at Easton the previous November, see Minutes of the Friendly Assoc., 1755–1757, 18, 19 verso, 21, HSP.

61. *PA,* 1st, III, 275–276. See also James Pemberton to Hannah Pemberton, 3, 4 Aug. 1757, PPHSP, XII, 55a–b.

62. Minutes of the Treaty at Easton, 27 July 1756, FA, I, 155 (fishing); Peters, Diary, 12 (drunk, up late), 20 (morning) Oct. 1758, RPP; Reichel, ed., *Memorials,* I, 314, 314 n. (mother-in-law); Weiser to William Parsons, 13 Feb. 1756, HP, I, 103 (Weiser).

63. [Thomson], *Enquiry,* 178 (Croghan); Peters, Diary, 29 Sept. 1758, RPP (Montour); RPLB, 1737–1750, 377 (Weiser left council); Weiser 1745, 311; *PA,* 1st, III, 439 (governors); Weiser, Observations (Quakers); Weiser to Peters, 6 Aug. 1749, DSP, 966F.26a (refused to shake hands); *PA,* 1st, III, 66 (slept alone), 2d, VII, 269 (to Denny).

64. Weiser to Logan, 16 Sept. 1736, LP, 10/62.

65. Kinsey, Journal, 8 Oct. 1745, HSP ("method"; see also 12 Oct.). Marshe, 196 ("dexterous"); *PWJ*, III, 10–11 ("address"); Chew, 317 ("caution").

66. Marshe, 188, 195–196; *MPCP*, IV, 715–716 (Lancaster); Logstown Treaty, 171–172.

67. This is even more true of Indian go-betweens' activities at a treaty; little as we know about how Weiser or Croghan operated, we know far less about Moses Tatamy or John Pumpshire.

68. *MPCP*, IV, 80 ("own way"), VIII, 150 ("usual"; and *PA*, 1st, I, 649, III, 439; *PWJ*, VI, 400, IX, 531; Chew, 312; Peters, Diary, 6, 10 Oct. 1758, RPP).

69. Peters, Diary, 29–30 Sept., 3 Oct. 1758, RPP ("dreamed," "set right"); Weiser 1745, 311 ("damn'd"); *PA*, 1st, I, 649 ("triffling").

70. *MPCP*, IV, 560. Also II, 471, 474; Memorandum of a Conference at Carlisle, 27 Sept. 1753, Pprs. of Franklin, B:F85, vol. 50ii, f. 49, APS; *PA*, 1st, II, 722–723.

71. Logan to Weiser, 11 July 1742, RPP, I, 88 ("all Sorts"); Weiser to Peters, 12 Aug. 1749, DSP, 966.F.26c ("meselves"). And see List of Indians, 4 July 1758, RPCEC, B9, 1954; Peters to Weiser, 13 7ber 1758, CCW, II, 135; Account of the Indians at Easton, Oct. 1758, FA, II, 259–260; Logan to Weiser, 5 Sept. 1736, LP, 10/60.

72. *MPCP*, V, 669 ("Condition"), VI, 552 ("sounding"); *PA*, 1st, II, 726–727 (Weiser). And 2d, VI, 566–569; *MPCP*, V, 685–686, VII, 308–311.

73. Peters to William Logan, 2 Oct. 1758, LP, 11/52. The definition of *sound* in the *Oxford English Dictionary* lists both this sense and the nautical term. For its use, Peters to the Proprietors, 7 Aug., 26 Oct. 1749, and to Thomas Penn, 3 May 1753, PMOC, III, 233, IV, 247, VI, 43; Peters, Diary, 6–7 Oct. 1758, RPP; Chew, 317; *MPCP*, III, 438, IV, 653.

74. Indian Charges, 17 Dec. 1742, PPM, X, 22; Peters to Weiser, 28 Feb. 1741[/2], LC, IV, 70; Weiser, Indian Accounts, Sept.–Oct. 1758, *ibid.*, 158; Weiser, Indian Expences, 1744 RPP, II, 16; Wallace, *Weiser*, 196; "Account of Sums I paid to Indians," 22 Sept. 1757, Penn Mss., Accounts, II, 35, doc. 109, HSP; Marshe, 189.

75. Peters, Diary, 13 Oct. 1758, RPP ("read over"); McDowell, ed., *Docs. Relating to Indian Affairs,* 95 ("Opinion"); *MPCP*, IV, 87 (gifts), VI, 115 ("advise"), 364, VII, 216 (pipe and wampum), 206 (speak first). And V, 350, 531; RPLB, 1737–1750, 253, 377; Logstown Treaty, 164.

76. *MPCP*, VI, 209 ("Whish Shiksy"), VII, 677 ("confused"), 681–683 ("meaning"), 699 ("Loss"); see also Minutes of the Friendly Assoc., 1755–1757, 20 verso, 22 verso, HSP. *PA*, 1st, III, 216 (Pumpshire).

77. RPLB, 1737–1750, 249–252; *MPCP*, IV, 699 (Lancaster). Chew, 315 (Iroquois; also Peters, Diary, 13 Oct. 1758, RPP; *MPCP*, VIII, 189–190).

78. *PA,* 1st, III, 439 (governor); Weiser 1745, 309 (Mohawk; the official account makes no mention of this incident [*DRCNY,* VI, 293]). And see Weiser to Peters, 6 Aug. 1749, DSP, 966.F.26a, and postscript, 966.F.26b.

79. Weiser to Peters, 12 Aug. 1749, DSP, 966.F.26c; Weiser 1745, 309.

80. Israel Pemberton to Mary Pemberton, 28 May 1757, PPHSP, XII, 23; Langdale to Israel Pemberton, 18 3 mo. 1761, Roberts Coll., Haverford College Library; *PHB,* II, 102. Also *PWP,* II, 453; Marshe, 200; Wallace, *Weiser,* 191; Chew, 313.

81. *MPCP,* II, 599 (pipe), III, 658, IV, 95 ("Glass"), 563 ("custom"), 650 ("Indian Dinner"); Marshe, 193 ("dishes"). Memorandum of a Conference at Carlisle, 26 Sept. 1753, Pprs. of Franklin, B:F85, vol. 5oii, f. 49, APS. Bartram, *Observations,* 74–75; *MPCP,* IV, 662, 665, 780–782 (Indians dining). For tobacco and toasts at councils Indians hosted, see *MPCP,* V, 350–351, 660–669; Logstown Treaty, 154. For colonial toasts, *MPCP,* IV, 730–731, 736, VIII, 223; *PWJ,* IX, 847. Often pipe and glass went around together (Marshe, 181; *MPCP,* III, 209). For berry juice, Fenton, "Iroquois Treaty Making," in Jennings et al., eds., *History and Culture of Iroquois Diplomacy,* 25.

82. Weiser, "An Account of the first Confederacy of the *Six Nations . . . ,"The American Magazine,* Dec. 1744, 668 ("Height"); Croghan 1750–65, 64, n.27; McAnear, ed., "Accounts of Albany," *MVHR,* XXXIX (1953), 741; Marshe, 185; Bartram, *Observations,* 22; McClure, *Diary,* 63; *Journals of Claus and Weiser,* 44; Wallace, *Weiser,* 69.

83. Marshe, 195 ("noise"); Kinsey, Journal, 12 Oct. 1745, HSP ("An Zoy's"; *DRCNY,* VI, 300); *MPCP,* IV, 727 ("three shouts").

84. *Ibid.,* VI, 156–157, V, 354–355 (also 519; Post 1760, 13 May).

85. *MPCP,* VII, 317 ("fresh"; also IV, 657, VI, 156); Zeisberger, *History,* 27 ("relate"); Heckewelder, *History,* 186 ("shady spot").

86. *PA,* 1st, III, 276 ("Quaker"; and see Kenny 1758–59, 433–434); Marshe, 185–186 (Lancaster).

87. *MPCP,* VII, 669.

88. *PA,* 1st, III, 276 ("Indian again"); Marshe, 193 ("greasy"); *The Letters and Papers of Cadwallader Colden, Collections of the New-York Historical Society,* 1917, 131 ("sonorous"); Bartram, *Observations,* 22 ("difficult").

89. Examination of Lawrence Burke, 9 July 1758, RPCEC, B9, 1960 ("forgiven"; and *PA,* 1st, III, 549); Post 1758, 206, 231.

90. *MPCP,* IV, 434, 445; Nathaniel Holland to Israel Pemberton, 1 Jan. 1760, FA, III, 307; *PA,* 8th, VI, 5097, 5121 (hunters). For surveyors, see *SCP,* I, 284–288; Donna Bingham Munger, *Pennsylvania Land Records: A History and Guide for Research* (Wilmington, Del., 1991), 113; Peter C. Mancall, *Valley of Opportunity: Economic Culture Along the Upper Susquehanna, 1700–1800* (Ithaca, N.Y., 1991), ch. 1. Thomas Pownall, *A Topographical Description of the*

Dominions of the United States of America . . . , ed. Lois Mulkearn (Pittsburgh, Pa., 1949), 169; John Bartram to Cadwallader Colden, 25 Jan. 1745/6, Gratz Coll., Case 7, Box 21, HSP; Balch, ed., *Letters and Papers,* 191–192; "The Distance," untitled ms., n.d., GCP, 5/21 (prospectors). Kenny to Israel Pemberton, Jr., 19 5 mo. 1762, PPHSP, XV, 147; Balch, ed., *Letters and Papers,* 121–122 (dreams).

91. *PWJ,* II, 29 (Croghan); Peters to the Proprietaries, 30 Jan. 1750/1, 16 Mar. 1752, PMOC, V, 121, 217 (survey equipment); Gottlieb Mittelberger, *Journey to Pennsylvania,* ed. and trans. Oscar Handlin and John Clive (Cambridge, Mass., 1960), 78–79 (weather); Zeisberger, *History,* 133 ("road"). Also 122; *PA,* 1st, I, 761–762; *PWJ,* VI, 401.

92. *MPCP,* VIII, 120 (Teedyuscung), 742 (King); Samuel Lightfoot to Israel Pemberton, 19 7 mo. 1759, FA, III, 223 (Ohio; and see Post 1760, 19 May).

93. *PWJ,* XII, 258–259.

94. Logan to Weiser, 18 June 1744, Alverthorpe Letterbook, F, 215, LP.

95. Marshe, 195 ("briskly"). Chew, 317; *PA,* 1st, III, 544–545 (Quakers accused). [Thomson], *Enquiry,* 114, 118; Wallace, *Weiser,* 481; Israel Pemberton to Fothergill, 3 8 mo. 1757, PPEC, II, 27 (Quakers accusing).

96. Weiser, "Observations."

97. "Private Presents," 19 July 1757, Penn Mss., Accounts, II, 34, doc. 108a, HSP; "Private Presents Expected," 20 Aug. 1762, RPCEC, B10, 2436. Weiser to Peters, 15 Mar. 1754, CCW, I, 44 ("fall in"). Wallace, *Weiser,* 353–358; *MPCP,* VI, 112; Accounts of the Indian Purchase, 29 Aug. 1758, PPM, XI, 58 (Albany). In October 1754, Weiser paid to have a house built for the Shickellamys, along with horses to the three Shickellamy brothers and £17 in cash; the following spring, he reported giving cash to Shickellamys for the deed. Indian Charges Paid Conrad Weiser, 12 Dec. 1759, PPM, XI, 113. See also "Expences with the Indians of the Six united Nations in Albany, during the time of the Treaty . . . ," Penn Mss., Accounts, II, 12, doc. 87a, HSP.

98. Croghan, Account, 1758, RPP, V, 65; Peters, Diary, 26 Oct. 1758, RPP; Peters to the Proprietaries, 11 Sept. 1749, PMOC, IV, 239; Peters, Account, 3 Sept. 1762, PPM, XII, 13.

99. *PWJ,* III, 767. See Jennings, *Ambiguous Iroquois Empire,* chs. 16–17, App. B.

100. Wallace, *Teedyuscung,* 25–26; Wallace, *Weiser,* 98; Jennings, *Ambiguous Iroquois Empire,* 337; Peters to the Proprietaries, 11 Sept. 1749, PMOC, IV, 239.

101. Quoted in Jennings, *Empire of Fortune,* 10. Cayugas visiting Philadelphia in 1727 learned that an earlier treaty's written record on land differed dramatically from their memory of the agreement. Logan to "Honourd Frd.," 10 July 1727, PMOC, I, 283.

102. Weiser to Peters, 12 Oct. 1754, CCW, I, 47. See Jennings, *Empire of Fortune,* 103–104; Wallace, *Weiser,* ch. 41.; *MPCP,* VI, 119–123.

103. *PWJ,* III, 772 ("doing"; see also 769–771, 777–778; Account of the Easton Treaty, June 1762, Friendly Assoc., Mss., Swarthmore College Library; James[?] Pemberton to Fothergill, PPEC, II, 26). Pemberton 1762, 321 ("small part"; and *MPCP,* VI, 278–281).

104. *MJNY,* 45; Indians—Treaty at Easton, July 1756, in "Indians (transferred from Society Collections)," HSP; *PWJ,* III, 775, 781; *MPCP,* VII, 217.

105. For the Treaty of Fort Stanwix, see *DRCNY,* VIII, 111–134; Randolph Downes, *Council Fires on the Upper Ohio: A Narrative of Indian Affairs in the Upper Ohio Valley until 1795* (Pittsburgh, Pa., 1940), 141–145; Jack M. Sosin, *Whitehall and the Wilderness: The Middle West in British Colonial Policy, 1760–1775* (Lincoln, Neb., 1961), 172–193; *SCP,* III, Introduction; Ray A. Billington, "The Fort Stanwix Treaty of 1768," *New York History,* XXV (1944), 182–194; Nicholas B. Wainwright, *George Croghan, Wilderness Diplomat* (Chapel Hill, N.C., 1959), ch. 11; Peter Marshall, "Sir William Johnson and the Treaty of Fort Stanwix, 1768," *Journal of American Studies,* I (1967), 149–179; Ireton, "Conflict Resolution and Indian Treaties," ch. 3; Bernard Bailyn, *Voyagers to the West: A Passage in the Peopling of America on the Eve of Revolution* (New York, 1986), 568–582; McConnell, *A Country Between,* chs. 10–11; White, *Middle Ground,* 351–353; Mancall, *Valley of Opportunity,* 90–94.

106. *PA,* 1st, IV, 93 (also III, 709).

107. *MPCP,* IX, 78 (1763); *PA,* 1st, IV, 374 (1770). And see *PWJ,* VII, 226–227. A survey of the hatred is in Alden T. Vaughan, "Frontier Banditti and the Indians: The Paxton Boys' Legacy, 1763–1775," *Pennsylvania History,* LI (1984), 1–29.

108. *PG,* 11 May 1758 (Baird); *PA,* 1st, III, 391 ("hoe Corn"). Examples of colonial suspicion and alleged Indian boasting are in *MPCP,* VII, 243, 282, 284, 302–303, 358; *PA,* 1st, II, 720–721, III, 10–11, 36–37, 42–44, 211, 218, 397, 2d, II, 680–683; *PG,* 21, 28 Oct., 4, 11, 18 Nov. 1756, 5, 12, 26 May, 2 June, 14, 21 July, 4, 11 Aug. 1757, 19 Oct. 1758; Sebastian Zimmerman and Daniel Levan to Weiser, 6 Nov. 1756, RPCEC, B7, 1335; William Henry Egle, *History of the Counties of Dauphin and Lebanon in the Commonwealth of Pennsylvania: Biographical and Genealogical* (Philadelphia, 1883), 52–53; Weiser to [?], 6 June 1757, CCW, II, 73; "Indian Intelligence," [1756–1757], HP, II, 328.

109. *MPCP,* IX, 143. Similar sentiments later in the decade are *ibid.,* 462.

110. *PA,* 8th, VII, 5554. Other targets included Moravian Indians (Hindle, "The March of the Paxton Boys," *WMQ*, 3d ser., III [1946], 461–486).

111. For population estimates, see Kent, *Susquehanna's Indians,* 385. For colonial settlement, see Martin Hervin Brackbill, "The Manor of Conestoga in the Colonial Period," *Papers of the Lancaster County Historical Society,* XLII (1938), 27. Few of these Indians were Susquehannocks. Sheehays was said to be

Seneca, but his kin were Cayuga (Kent, *Susquehanna's Indians,* 68). In 1744 Weiser said that Oneidas had adopted Susquehannock survivors, and "When these had forgot their Language, they were sent back to Conestogo, where a few are now left, and speak the Onayder's Language" (Weiser, "Account," *American Magazine,* Dec. 1744, 666–667; also *MPCP,* IV, 585; *PA,* 1st, I, 657). A vocabulary taken in 1757 from one of them, Will Sock, was Seneca (Kent, *Susquehanna's Indians,* 62–63).

The age of Sheehays (also Sohaes, Seweese, Shahaise, Sohaise, Jo. Hays) is unclear. It has been said that he had met William Penn (David H. Landis, "Historical Address," *Historical Papers and Addresses of the Lancaster County Historical Society,* XXVIII [1924], 137), but that seems unlikely, for he never mentioned it, and would certainly have done so to colonial authorities in his efforts to keep their trust. For his kinship to Conodahto, see *MPCP,* III, 102. Spelling variations make it hard to tell when he began to attend treaties (*MPCP,* II, 553, 574, 606, III, 45, 102, 123). In 1756 he described himself as "an old man" who "must die soon" (VII, 8).

112. Brackbill, "Manor of Conestoga," *Pprs. Lanc. Co. Hist. Soc.,* XLII (1938), 17–46; Landis, "Address," *Hist. Pprs. and Addresses Lanc. Co. Hist. Soc.,* XXVIII (1924), 136; "Address of D. F. Magee, Esq.," *ibid.,* 139; Kent, *Susquehanna's Indians,* 66; *MPCP,* VII, 768, VIII, 113–114, 116–117, 122–123, 457, IX, 89; *PA,* 8th, V, 4202, 4204, 4351, VI, 4479–4480, 4495, 4874; John Carson to Gov. Denny, 24 Apr. 1758, RPCEC, B8, 1862; Barber; Thomas McKee, Account, 15 Feb. 1764, GCP, 1/19; Account, 10 1 mo. 1759, FA, II, 410–412.

113. *PWJ,* XI, 56–57 ("white People"). Barber; Leonard W. Labaree et al., eds., *The Papers of Benjamin Franklin,* 32 vols. to date (New Haven, Conn., 1959–ف), XI, 149 (children and peddlers). Rhoda Barber, born several years after 1763 and not writing her account until 1830, heard these Conestoga stories from her brothers and parents. Her recollections must be used with caution (her casualty count is wrong, for example). Nonetheless, her account is balanced (she noted that Conestogas were beggars) and cautious ("I do not vouch for the truth of this," she said of one story that was not from her family's firsthand experience). Moreover, it is clear that her brothers (ten and twelve years old in 1763) knew Indian children, for they mentioned one by name ("Christie," or in the colonial records "Chrisly" [*MPCP,* IX, 104]).

114. Barber ("threaten"; also *MPCP,* VII, 8, VIII, 117). Peters, Diary, 6 Oct. 1758, RPP ("Dutch"; and *MPCP,* VIII, 457). For some of the attacks, *PG,* 9 Sept. 1756, 26 May, 15, 22 Sept., 6, 13, 27 Oct. 1757. For colonists trying to get portions of the proprietary Manor of Conestoga for themselves, see Peters to Thomas Penn, 18 Feb., 26 June 1756, 27 Jan. 1757, PMOC, VIII, 41, 123, 227.

115. Vocabulary in the Mingo Tongue, 25 Jan. 1757, APS. Also Bill, also Soc, Sack, Sawk, and Tenseedaagua (*MPCP,* IX, 103).

116. Journal of Joseph Shippen, Building of Fort Augusta, 1756, 29 July, Small Books, no. 4, PSF; Charles Garroway to James Burd, 23 Jan. 1757, *ibid.,* II; *MPCP,* VII, 385, 403; *PA,* 2d, II, 650–651, 653–654; Passport, 8 Jan. 1757, RPCEC, B7, 1434; Vocabulary in the Mingo Tongue, 25 Jan. 1757, APS.

117. Court of Enquiry, Fort Augusta, 31 Jan. 1757, PSF, II; *MPCP,* VIII, 113, 118–121 (Senecas), 135; *PA,* 1st, III, 419–420 (flag), 433; Nathaniel Holland to Israel Pemberton, 13 Apr. 1758, FA, I, 463 (captive); D. Henderson to [?], 27 Dec. 1763, *ibid.,* IV, 37–39 (scalps); Zane 1758, 423–424 ("heart"). James Wright, long a provincial agent for Conestogas, insisted that he "does not believe that even one, no not Bill Sawk himself, (of whom many people have a very bad opinion) ever hurt a hair of one head of any Whiteman" (Edward Shippen to Joseph Shippen, 19 Dec. 1763, Correspondence of Edward and Joseph Shippen, 1750–1778, Shippen Papers, APS). Thomas McKee, who knew them even better than Wright did, also insisted that all of them, Sock included, were innocent (*PWJ,* XI, 56).

118. McConnell, *A Country Between,* ch. 8; White, *Middle Ground,* chs. 6–7; Gregory E. Dowd, *A Spirited Resistance: The North American Indian Struggle for Unity, 1745–1815* (Baltimore, Md., 1992), ch. 2.

119. *PHB,* VI, 312 (Harris; also Shippen to [Joseph Shippen], 21 July 1763, Corr. Edward and Joseph Shippen, 1750–1778, Shippen Pprs., APS). For attacks, see *PG,* summer and fall 1763; Narrative of Robert Robison, in Archibald Loudon, *A Selection of Some of the Most Interesting Narratives of Outrages, Committed by the Indians in their Wars with the White People,* II (Carlisle, Pa., 1811), 177–181; C. Hale Sipe, *The Indian Wars of Pennsylvania . . .* (Harrisburg, Pa., 1929), chs. 18–21, esp. 430–438, 453–454, 456–463. For patrols, Hubertis M. Cummings, "The Paxton Killings," *Journal of Presbyterian History,* XLIV (1966), 230–231; George W. Franz, *Paxton: A Study of Community Structure and Mobility in the Colonial Pennsylvania Backcountry* (New York, 1989), 46, 53, 56.

120. Edward Shippen to Gov. Hamilton, 1 Sept. 1763, Burd-Shippen Papers, Correspondence, APS. Also *PA,* 2d, VII, 469–470; Narrative of the Battle of Muncy and Short Account of the Battle of Muncy Hill, in Loudon, *Selection,* II, 184–188, 202–203; Sipe, *Indian Wars,* ch. 20; *PG,* 8 Sept. 1763.

121. *PG,* 27 Oct. 1763; also *PA,* 1st, IV, 127, 2d, VII, 475.

122. See Wallace, *Teedyuscung,* 263–264.

123. *PWJ,* IV, 417 ("Bandittey"); Dunbar, ed., *Paxton Papers,* 194 ("most dangerous"; and see *MPCP,* IX, 138–145). Franz (*Paxton,* Appendix A) calls into question putative accounts, in defense of the Paxton Boys, by several contemporaries, accounts that appear only in a newspaper article dated 1843.

124. *MPCP*, IX, 88–89. The printed version has it "your Grandfathers," but a copy in the Lancaster County Historical Society has it "your Grandfather," which, given the intended recipient, makes more sense. "Address of the Conestoga Indians to John Penn, Esq., Governor of Pennsylvania, sent by Captain Montour," Lancaster County [Pa.] Historical Society, Case 1, Section H, Folder 74. Colonists, too, saw trouble coming (Dunbar, ed., *Paxton Papers*, 22–24).

125. *MPCP*, VIII, 457.

126. Edward Shippen to Joseph Shippen, 19 Dec. 1763, 5 Jan. 1764, Corr. Edward and Joseph Shippen, 1750–1778, Shippen Pprs., APS; Barber; *MPCP*, IX, 89–99, 103; *PA*, 1st, IV, 147–149, 152, 2d, VII, 482; *PWJ*, XI, 55; Hindle, "March of the Paxton Boys," *WMQ*, 3d ser., III (1946), 461–486; Landis, "Address," *Hist. Pprs. and Addresses Lanc. Co. Hist. Soc.*, XXVIII (1924), 137; Cummings, "Paxton Killings," *Jnl. Presbyterian Hist.*, XLIV (1966), 233–235.

127. *MPCP*, IX, 103–104; Bausman, "Massacre of the Conestoga Indians," *Pprs. Lanc. Co. Hist. Soc.*, XVIII (1914), 179. The story below is from *MPCP*, IX, 100–114, 123–127; *PA*, 1st, IV, 151–156; Edward Shippen to Joseph Shippen, 19 Dec. 1763, 5 Jan. 1764, Corr. Edward and Joseph Shippen, 1750–1778, Shippen Pprs., APS; D. Henderson to Joseph Galloway, 27 Dec. 1763, Roberts Coll., Haverford College Library; Henderson to [?], 27 Dec. 1763, FA, IV, 379.

128. John Heckewelder, *A Narrative of the Mission of the United Brethren Among the Delaware and Mohegan Indians, From Its Commencement, In the Year 1740, To the Close of the Year 1808* . . . (Philadelphia, 1820), 78–80. It is hard to differentiate, in the accounts of the attack, the workhouse approved by the Assembly in 1763 from the prison, built in 1739, a two-story structure at the corner of King and Winter streets (Wood, *Conestoga Crossroads*, 10, 17, 66).

129. Hutson, *Pennsylvania Politics*, 84–113; Hindle, "March of the Paxton Boys," *WMQ*, 3d ser., III (1946), 461–486; James E. Crowley, "The Paxton Disturbance and Ideas of Order in Pennsylvania Politics," *Pennsylvania History*, XXXVII (1970), 317–339; Vaughan, "Frontier Banditti," *ibid.*, LI (1984), 1–29; James Kirby Martin, "The Return of the Paxton Boys and the Historical State of the Pennsylvania Frontier," *ibid.*, XXXVIII (1971), 117–133; Dunbar, ed., *Paxton Papers*, reprints 28 of the 63 pamphlets, including poems, plays, dialogues, and a farce.

130. For the land's fate, see Magee, "Address," *Hist. Pprs. and Addresses of Lanc. Co. Hist. Soc.*, XXVIII (1924), 139–144. A minister named Thomas Barton schemed to get the land for himself (*DHNY*, IV, 381–382; Barton to Peters, 2 June, 24 Aug. 1768, RPP, VI, 58, 62; *PWJ*, VII, 813; Barton to Edmund Physick, 18 Dec. 1770, Penn Mss., Additional Misc. Letters, II, 22, HSP).

131. *MPCP,* VIII, 122 ("burnt"); Heckewelder, *History,* 184. For Indians identify-
ing certain sites as polluted by bloodshed, see Spangenberg to [the Gover-
nor], 20 May 1756, MCA, 34/317/2/6; Benjamin Lightfoot to Israel
Pemberton, 7 Sept. 1760, FA, IV, 19; *MJNY,* 225.

132. Barber ("logs"); *MPCP,* II, 15–17, IX, 102; Henderson to [?], 27 Dec. 1763,
FA, IV, 379.

133. Burd to Shippen, 19 Jan. 1764, PSF, VI ("Barbarians"; see also Shippen to
Burd, 11, 25 Jan. 1764, PSF, VI; James Hamilton to Timothy Horsfield, 20
Sept. 1763, HP, II, 487). John Elder to Col. Shippen, 1 Feb. 1764, quoted
in Franz, *Paxton,* 77 ("determined"). "Savages will be Savages still," wrote Edward Shippen to Thomas Penn (20 Nov. 1759, PMOC, IX, 128); a decade
later another leading colonist, John Brainerd, discouraged with his mission
work in New Jersey, echoed Shippen's sentiments: "There is too much truth
in that common saying: 'Indians will be Indians' " (Brainerd to Eleazer
Wheelock, 22 June 1769, in Jonathan Edwards, *The Life of David Brainerd,* ed.
Norman Pettit, The Works of Jonathan Edwards, VII [New Haven, Conn.,
1985], 383).

134. *MPCP,* VIII, 631 (Seneca George). Pumpshire was at the treaty settling New
Jersey land affairs in February 1758 (*PA,* 1st, III, 342, 344, 346), and an account later that year mentioned him (*ibid.,* 8th, VI, 5058, 5061).

135. Wallace, *Weiser,* ch. 64; William A. Hunter, "Moses (Tunda) Tatamy, Dela-
ware Indian Diplomat," in Herbert C. Kraft, ed., *A Delaware Indian Symposium,* Anthropological Series, no. 4 (Harrisburg, Pa., 1974), 84 (Tatamy).
Hays, 63, n.3; John F. Watson, *Annals of Philadelphia and Pennsylvania, in the
Olden Time . . . ,* 2d ed., 2 vols. (Philadelphia, 1845), 171–172; Samuel Pre-
ston to John F. Watson, 5 Aug. 1828, 25 Jan. 1829, Watson's Annals (mss.),
II, 556–562, 574, HSP; Copy of a Message from Indians at Brotherton,
West Jersey, to the Ohio Indians, by Joseph Peepy, 6 Aug. 1767, FA, IV,
395–398; *MPCP,* IX, 611–612, 620, 694; X, 255–257 (Stille). For Peepy, see
PWJ, V, 570–571, XII, 305–306; Charles Beatty, *The Journal of a Two Months
Tour; With a View of Promoting Religion Among the Frontier Inhabitants of Pensylvania, And of Introducing Christianity Among the Indians to the Westward of the
Allegh-geny Mountains . . .* (London, 1768), 9, 25, 32–33, 36–39; Passport
for Joseph Peepy, 10 Mar. 1767, RPCEC, B11, 2652; Zeisberger, *Diaries,*
39–40; Catalogue of Baptised Indians, Ettwein Copy, MCA, 33/313/7,
nos. 620, 623, 634, 635, 680; *MPCP,* IX, 738; McClure, *Diary,* 46–47,
49–53, 56–59, 72–78, 81–82, 84, 86, 103. For his occasional service as a
diplomatic go-between, *MPCP,* X, 61–64; *PWJ,* VIII, 648, 674. For Post, see
Post to Israel Pemberton, 8 Aug., 16 Oct. 1761, 20 Nov. 1762, FA, IV, 167,
247 ("briers"), 339 ("sorri & greaf"); Reuben Gold Thwaites, ed., *Early
Western Travels, 1748–1846* (Cleveland, Ohio, 1904), I, 181–182.

136. Howard Lewin, "A Frontier Diplomat: Andrew Montour," *Pennsylvania History,* XXXIII (1966), 180–186; *PHB,* VI, 329; Narrative of Muncy, in Loudon, *Selection,* II, 185; Edward Shippen to James Hamilton, 29 Oct. 1763, Corr. Edward and Joseph Shippen, 1750–1778, Shippen Pprs., APS; Turbutt Francis to Richard Peters, 7 Mar. 1769, RPP, VI, 74.

137. Jones, *License for Empire.*

138. Logstown Treaty, 165 (council, "People"); Chew, 314; [Thomson], *Enquiry,* 173 (Croghan).

139. *PA,* 1st, II, 505 ("Traitor"), 511 (threaten); Weiser to Peters, 1 Mar. 1760, CCW, II, 171 ("Justified"). For the killing, *PA,* 1st, III, 705–707, 731–732, 2d, VII, 278. The proclamation is in *MPCP,* VIII, 456.

140. *PWJ,* XI, 56 ("detestable"), 760–761 ("consternation"). For his work with Conestogas, *MPCP,* VIII, 113, 117, 118, 768–769, IX, 89.

141. Croghan to Samuel Wharton, 2 Nov. 1771, GCP, 6/30; *DRCNY,* VII, 606. Wainwright, *Croghan,* chs. 9–14, makes clear that Croghan was still active in Indian councils, even with the various distractions. Some sense of Croghan's growing disenchantment can be seen in *PWJ,* III, 662–663, X, 134–135, 597–598; *PHB,* VI, 137–138, 169–170, 430–431. For gout, *PWJ,* VII, 388, 487. For his talk of retirement, *ibid.,* 528–529; *DHNY,* II, 838–839. For his refusal to offer advice, *PWJ,* VIII, 11, 57.

142. Wallace, *Weiser,* chs. 45–47; *PA,* 1st, II, 551, 553–555, 563–564 (McKee), 452, 462–463, 484; Wainwright, *Croghan,* esp. ch. 5 (Croghan).

143. *PWJ,* XI, 56.

144. *PHB,* ser. 21649, I, 166. Bouquet's reply is *ibid.,* 199.

145. *PA,* 1st, II, 173 ("Creadett"); *PWJ,* XI, 840 ("More Savidge"); *DRCNY,* VII, 606 ("reduce them," "fear").

146. *Translation of a German Letter, Wrote by Conrad Weiser* . . . (Philadelphia, 1757, Evans 8062), 2 ("some Religion"); Weiser 1737, 17, 18, 21.

147. Wallace, *Weiser,* chs. 7, 12–13 (quotation on 51). See also E. G. Alderfer, *The Ephrata Commune: An Early American Counterculture* (Pittsburgh, Pa., 1985).

148. Peters to Thomas Penn[?], 28 Sept. 1750, PMOC, V, 57 ("obstinately," "difficulty"). Also Peters to Thomas Penn, 17 Nov. 1750, 3 May 1753, Peters to the Proprietor, 6 Nov. 1753, *ibid.,* 87, VI, 47, 115; Penn to Peters, 31 Aug. 1748, RPP, II, 111; Weiser to the Governor, 22 Apr. 1751, CCW, I, 35; Peters to Weiser, 27 Apr. 1753, *ibid.,* 40.

149. Moses Tatamy, Declaration, [1757], FA, I, 405–408; "Tatamie's Accot. of Indian Claims," [1757], EC, no. 32, Misc. Mss., 94.

150. *MPCP,* IV, 624–625.

151. Brainerd, Diary, 1745, 1–7 (quotations on 3, 6), APS.

152. Peters to the Proprietor, 14 Feb. 1757, Peters Letters to the Proprietaries, 1755–1757, 144, Gratz Coll., HSP ("prating"). Post 1760, 8 May (fits), 20

(warning), 21 June (challenged Post). Testimony to his earlier sobriety is in *PG,* 4 Dec. 1755. For further mention of his drinking, Israel Pemberton to Christian Frederick Post, 6 5 mo. 1760, Pemberton Papers, Folder 2, Haverford College Library. Perhaps also reflecting his disengagement from colonial culture, Tatamy sold his land sometime before 14 February 1757 (Peters to the Proprietor, Peters Letters to the Proprietaries, 1755–1757, 143–144, Gratz Coll., HSP).

153. Albert G. Rau, "Moravian Missions and Colonial Politics," *Moravian Historical Society Transactions,* XI (1936), 143; Langdale to Israel Pemberton, 18 3 mo. 1761, Roberts Coll., Haverford College Library (Stille). In addition, Post in 1760 complained, cryptically, that Stille "behaved a little unmannerly" (Post 1760, 1 June). McClure, *Diary,* 46–47, 59; *PWJ,* V, 571; "Christian Indians of Wilusing and Shechecumunk to the Representatives of the Freemen of the Province of Pennsilvania," 16 May 1772, FA, IV, 459 (Peepy).

154. Preston to Watson, 5 Aug. 1828, Watson's Annals (mss.), II, 556–558, HSP. Stille disappears from provincial records between March 1763 and January 1769. On both of those occasions he requested land (100 acres the first time, 200 the second) as compensation for his services to the colony (*PA,* 8th, VI, 5420, 5423–5424, 5460, VII, 6333).

155. *MPCP,* X, 255–257; Preston to Watson, 5 Aug. 1828, 25 Jan. 1829, Watson's Annals (mss.), II, 562, 574, HSP. Some said he died on the Wabash (*ibid.,* 562), others that he died before crossing the Susquehanna en route west (Hays, 63, n.3).

156. Lt. Caleb Graydon to Col. James Burd, 10 Apr. 1762, PSF, V ("being Indians"). Hanna, *Wilderness Trail,* I, 245; J. F. Meginness, *Otzinachson; Or, A History of the West Branch Valley of the Susquehanna . . .* (Philadelphia, 1857), 38, 39, 139, 157; *PWJ,* VI, 596–597, VII, 335–336, 568, 575, 690. For his farm above the Shamokin site, *PA,* 2d, VII, 472; Narrative of Robison, in Loudon, *Selection,* II, 174; *PHB,* VI, 295.

157. "Mr. Mitchell's Receipt for Capt. Montour," 7 July 1762, GCP, 1/18; Croghan, Accounts, 1759, *ibid.,* 1/13; Finley's Account, 1760, *ibid.,* 1/14. Peters to Thomas Penn, 25 Apr. 1756, PMOC, VIII, 73; *MPCP,* VII, 95–96. Glimpses of the Montour children's lives in Philadelphia can be gained from accounts submitted to the assembly for their lodging, food, clothing, schooling, and medicine. At least one of these children, Debby Montour, remained in Philadelphia until 1766 (*PA,* 8th, V, 4093, 4183, VI, 4656–4657, 4859–4860, 5146, 5151, 5272, 5362–5363, VII, 5853, 5933, 5944, 5968, 6224–6226).

158. Thomas Penn to Richard Peters, 13 Feb. 1749[1750?], RPP, III, 4 (McKee). Post 1758, 244–246, 248–249, 281, 285. And see his remarks on the Susquehanna country during a trip in 1760 (Post 1760, 18 and 23 May).

159. Croghan 1750–65, 129, 130 ("face"), 140 ("pasture"), 143 *et passim.* "Crochans," 5 July 1754, GCP, 1/8 ("Purchest"; emphasis added). He was also working, in 1763, with Bouquet on lands and possible mines (*PHB,* VI, 170). For his land dealings, see Wainwright, *Croghan,* 255–258; Mancall, *Valley of Opportunity,* 97–98, 103–105; Alan Taylor, *William Cooper's Town: Power and Persuasion on the Frontier of the Early American Republic* (New York, 1995), 44–52.

160. Auth, *Ten Years' War,* 87; Wallace, *Weiser,* 25–26, 28–29, 31, 34–36, 170–171, 286, 351, 377–378; RPLB, 1737–1750, 148–149, 329 ("raptures").

161. Weiser to Peters, 28 Jan. 1754, CCW, I, 43 ("Stout purchase"); Weiser to [?], n.d., *ibid.,* II, 27 ("pity," "English hands"); Peters to the Proprietaries, 16 Feb. 1749, PMOC, IV, 189 ("humour"). For his campaign, see Peters to Penn[?], 10 Feb. 1749, RPP, III, 3; Penn to Peters, 13 Feb. 1749[/50?], *ibid.,* 4; Peters to Weiser, 19 Sept. 1751, *ibid.,* 47; Weiser to Peters, 8 May 1749, Feb. [?] 1753, CCW, I, 19, 17; RPLB, 1737–1750, 363, 375–381; *PA,* 2d, II, 588–589, 683–684; Peters to Weiser, 25 Dec. 1751[?], LC, IV, 154; Weiser to Peters, 10 Nov. 1753, *ibid.,* 155; Peters to "Sir," and to the Proprietors, 3 May, 21 Aug., 26 Nov. 1753, PMOC, VI, 47, 95, 133; Peters to the Proprietors, 21 Dec. 1754, Penn Mss., Additional Misc. Letters, I, 89, HSP; same to same, 1 June 1756, Peters Letters to the Proprietaries, 1755–1757, 50, 52, Gratz Coll., HSP.

162. Weiser to Peters, 7 Feb. 1754, Berks and Montgomery Cos., Misc. Mss., 55, HSP ("let loose"; and see RPLB, 1737–1750, 327). Holland to Israel Pemberton, 16 Apr. 1761, FA, IV, 95 ("thieves"). For Weiser's designs on Shamokin itself, see Shamokin Diary, 6 June 1755, MCA 6/121/7/1 (I am grateful to Beverly Smaby for help translating this passage).

163. RPLB, 1737–1750, 363 (emphasis added; and see 378).

164. Post, "An Observation or Two made in my several Conversations with Indians . . . ," [19 Jan. 1759], RPCEC, B9, 2075.

165. Logan to Weiser, 18 Oct. 1736, LP, 2/58 ("design"). "Tatamie's Accot. of Indian Claims," EC, no. 32, Misc. Mss., 94; Tatamy, Declaration, [1757], FA, I, 405–408. That the go-betweens were not Teedyuscung's pawns, and indeed on occasion operated independently of him, is suggested by: "Indian Intelligence," [1756–1757], HP, II, 324; *MPCP,* VII, 358, 431–433, VIII, 630–660, 708–709. The Delaware quest for a homeland on the Susquehanna in the 1750s is the central argument of Auth, *Ten Years' War.* And consult Wallace, *Teedyuscung,* ch. 14; William Peters to Thomas Penn, 17 Feb. 1758, PMOC, IX, 11.

166. *MPCP,* VII, 431–433. The printed version has it incorrectly as Joseph Tatamy (Hunter, "Tatamy," in Kraft, ed., *Delaware Indian Symposium,* 78, n.5).

167. *PA,* 8th, VI, 4623 ("certain Boundaries"), 4625; *MPCP,* VIII, 660–661; Peters, Diary, 20 Oct. 1758, RPP ("angry"); [Thomson], *Enquiry,* 183; Wallace,

Teedyuscung, 179; "Draught of Land Desired by the Delawares for a Settlement . . . ," RPCEC, B8, 1595; Israel Pemberton to Isaac Zane, 5 June 1758, FA, I, 527; *PWJ,* X, 553. They also persuaded the colony to build English houses for Indians at Wyoming (Wallace, *Teedyuscung,* 181–189).

168. *MPCP,* VIII, 655–661; Report of the Treaty, Aug. 1761, FA, IV, 139–150.

169. Wallace, *Teedyuscung,* chs. 17, 19 (land dispute). Wallace is certain that Connecticut's Susquehannah Company was behind the fire; and see Jennings, *Empire of Fortune,* 434–436.

170. *PA,* 1st, II, 12. See George P. Donehoo, *A History of the Indian Villages and Place Names in Pennsylvania, with Numerous Historical Notes and References* (Harrisburg, Pa., 1928), 42–44; *PA,* 3d, IV, no. 34; Barry C. Kent et al., "A Map of 18th Century Indian Towns in Pennsylvania," *Pennsylvania Archaeologist,* LI (1981), 4, fig. 2.

171. Quoted in Kent, *Susquehanna's Indians,* 88.

172. Croghan to Peters, 8 Sept. 1750, PPM, XI, 15. Also Thomas Penn to Peters, 21 Feb. 1755, RPP, IV, 4. Montour was, by colonial law, correct (Donehoo, *Indian Villages,* 42–43).

173. It is difficult to learn much about Montour's negotiations with the Iroquois; we only have colonial suspicions and fears about those conversations. Peters to Weiser, 19 Sept. 1751, RPP, III, 47; Weiser to Peters, Feb. [?] 1753, Peters to Weiser, 6 Feb. 1753, CCW, I, 17, 38; Peters to the Proprietors, 3 May 1753, PMOC, VI, 47; Wallace, *Weiser,* 355.

174. *MPCP,* V, 566–567. In the past the province had granted licenses permitting European colonists to settle on unpurchased Indian lands, though these were for specific tracts of land and did not come with the charge of keeping other settlers out. (Donna Bingham Munger, *Pennsylvania Land Records: A History and Guide for Research* [Wilmington, Del., 1991], 68–70.) Provincial efforts to oust squatters tended to backfire. In the 1740s Indians were furious when officials sent to remove colonists from Susquehanna lands started to survey those lands instead. "[T]hey are in League with the Trespassers," said native spokesmen, who insisted that "more effectual Methods may be used, and honester persons employ'd" (*MPCP,* IV, 570, 572). Whether these Indians considered Montour "more effectual" and "honester" is unclear.

175. Hanna, *Wilderness Trail,* I, 226–227; Paul A. W. Wallace, *Indian Paths of Pennsylvania* (Harrisburg, Pa., 1965), 49, 115.

176. Weiser to Peters, Feb.[?] 1753, CCW, I, 17; Peters to Weiser, 6 Feb. 1753, *ibid.,* 38; Peters to the Proprietors, 7 Feb., 3 May 1753, PMOC, VI, 5, 47; Weiser to Peters, 2 May 1754, PMIA, II, 9, quoted in Wallace, *Weiser,* 355. At one point Peters began to believe Montour's denial of these charges (Peters to the Proprietor, 6 Nov. 1753, PMOC, VI, 115). Weiser, however, re-

mained convinced that Montour was up to something (Weiser to Peters, 7 Feb. 1754, Berks and Montgomery Cos., Misc. Mss., 1693–1869, 55, HSP).

177. Weiser to Peters, Feb.[?] 1753, CCW, I, 17; Weiser to Peters, 7 Feb. 1754, Berks and Montgomery Cos., Misc. Mss., 55, HSP).

178. Reichel, ed., *Memorials,* I, 98.

179. *PA,* 2d, VII, 261.

180. Howard H. Peckham, ed., "Thomas Gist's Indian Captivity," *PMHB,* LXXX (1956), 302.

181. *PA,* 1st, II, 214. For an introduction to the successful construction of new identities elsewhere in North America, see Dennis F. K. Madill, "Riel, Red River, and Beyond: New Directions in Métis History," in Colin G. Calloway, ed., *New Directions in American Indian History* (Norman, Okla., 1988), 49–78.

182. With compliments to Edmund S. Morgan, *American Slavery, American Freedom: The Ordeal of Colonial Virginia* (New York, 1975), 387.

Epilogue: The Killing of Young Seneca George, 1769

1. *PWJ,* III, 63 ("Cabbin"), VII, 154; *MPCP,* IX, 605 ("Distress"). Richard Smith, *A Tour of Four Great Rivers: The Hudson, Mohawk, Susquehanna and Delaware in 1769* . . . (Port Washington, N.Y., 1964), 84 (hunger). *Ibid.,* 78; *PWJ,* VII, 53; Theodore G. Tappert and John W. Doberstein, trans., *The Journals of Henry Melchior Muhlenberg,* 3 vols. (Philadelphia, 1942–1958), II, 399 (heat).

2. Paul A. W. Wallace, *The Travels of John Heckewelder in Frontier America* (Pittsburgh, Pa., 1958), 38 ("sad memorials," blackened houses and barns, stories, all remarked on a trip through Pennsylvania farther west). J. F. Meginness, *Otzinachson; Or, A History of the West Branch Valley of the Susquehanna* . . . (Philadelphia, 1857), 65 (Harris ambush site marked). Post 1758, 189–190 (scalp hoops). *PA,* 8th, VII, 5749; Charles Rhoads Roberts et al., *History of Lehigh County, Pennsylvania, and a Genealogical and Biographical Record of Its Families,* 2 vols. (Allentown, Pa., 1914), II, 102–103 (grave), 104, 108 (scalping victims; scalped girls subject to fits). *PA,* 8th, V, 4374; "An Account of the Captivity of Richard Bard," in Archibald Loudon, *A Selection of Some of the Most Interesting Narratives of Outrages, Committed by the Indians in their Wars with the White People,* II (Carlisle, Pa., 1811), 75; *PG,* 20 Nov. 1755, 1 Apr. 1756, 14 July 1757 (other scalping survivors in Pennsylvania). J. W. Early, trans., "Frederick A. C. Muhlenberg's Report of His First Trip to Shamokin . . . ," *Lutheran Church Review,* XXV (1906), 535–536, 538 (fort ruin, stories, graves of Indians and colonists, burned farms). D. B. Brunner, *The Indians of Berks County* . . . (Reading, Pa., 1881), 23–24,

46–47; U. J. Jones, *History of the Early Settlement of the Juniata Valley . . . ,* 2d ed. (Harrisburg, Pa., 1940 [orig. pub. 1889]) (stories). Robert Greenhalgh Albion and Leonidas Dodson, eds., *Philip Vickers Fithian: Journal, 1775–1776 . . .* (Princeton, N.J., 1934), 154 ("taleful"; see also 164). Charles Beatty, *The Journal of a Two Months Tour; With a View of Promoting Religion Among the Frontier Inhabitants of Pensylvania, And of Introducing Christianity Among the Indians to the Westward of the Allegh-geny Mountains . . .* (London, 1768), 11–12 (stories, houses and fences burned, "marks of the ravages of the cruel and barbarous enemy" almost everywhere on the frontier west of the Susquehanna, 1766).

3. Officials' frustrations at their inability to bring colonists to justice are in John Penn to "Uncle," 12 Sept. 1766, PMOC, X, 82; John Penn to Thomas Penn, 30 Mar. 1768, *ibid.,* 132; James Hamilton to Thomas Penn, 23 May 1768, *ibid.,* 156; *PA,* 8th, VII, 6178; *DRCNY,* VII, 835–837, 852.

4. G. S. Rowe, "The Frederick Stump Affair, 1768, And Its Challenge to Legal Historians of Early Pennsylvania," *Pennsylvania History,* XLIX (1982), esp. 259–261. *MPCP,* IX, 414–415, 436–438, 441–467, 470, 484, 488, 490; *PA,* 8th, VII, 6108–6110, 6123–6125, 6129–6134; Deposition of William Blyth, 19 Jan. 1768, PMOC, X, 124; John Penn to Thomas Penn, 21 Jan., 8 Feb. 1768, *ibid.,* 126, 130; William Allen to Thomas Penn, 25 Feb. 1768, *ibid.,* 136; Edward Shippen to James Tilghman, 2 Feb. 1768, PSF, VI. For oral traditions, see Meginness, *Otzinachson,* 112–113, 115, 119.

5. *MJNY,* 225.

6. Jno Little to James Burd, 25 Nov. 1768, PSF, VI. For the land rush, which one scholar called among the greatest in history, see *SCP,* III, Introduction, esp. xiii; Donna Bingham Munger, *Pennsylvania Land Records: A History and Guide for Research* (Wilmington, Del., 1991), 80–81; Meginness, *Otzinachson,* 44–46. Pennsylvanians at Stanwix kept Indian runners standing by to race southward the moment the agreement was signed in order to get a jump on the competition (William Allen to Thomas Penn, 4 Dec. 1768, PMOC, X, 186).

7. For the victims' identity, *MPCP,* IX, 470. For the impact in Indian country, *ibid.,* 497–506; Loskiel, *History,* Part III, 25; *PWJ,* VI, 108, 111, 128–129; Croghan to Gage, 17 Feb. 1768, GCP, 5/30; *PA,* 8th, VII, 6143, 6184–6185.

8. *PWJ,* VII, 63. For fire fishing techniques, see William N. Fenton and Ernest Stanley Dodge, "An Elm Bark Canoe in the Peabody Museum of Salem," *The American Neptune,* IX (1949), 196.

9. *PWJ,* VII, 63. Oswald Seidensticker, "Frederick Augustus Conrad Muhlenberg, Speaker of the House of Representatives, in the First Congress, 1789," *PMHB,* XIII (1889), 186; Early, trans., "Muhlenberg's Report," *Lutheran Church Rev.,* XXV (1906), 540–542; Edward Shippen to James Burd, 14 July 1769, PSF, VII; *PA,* 8th, VII, 6433, 6446.

10. *MPCP,* IX, 585–589; William Brewster, *The Pennsylvania and New York Frontier, 1700–1763* (Philadelphia, 1954), 159; *PWJ,* VII, 75, 179.

11. *PWJ,* VII, 64.

12. *Ibid.,* 154 ("Attachment"). Conference at Israel Pemberton's, 23 Apr. 1756, LP, 11/41 (Osternados); He was also called Otsinados (Indians at Pemberton's, [Apr. 1756], FA, III, 535) and either Cadsedan-hiunt or Hatchin-Hatta (*MPCP,* V, 438).

13. The first references to him I have found are *MPCP,* V, 438, 440. *Ibid.,* VI, 160 ("chief"), IX, 615, 617 (war leader), VIII, 631–632 (Condolence; and see *PWJ,* XII, 59, 259); *PWJ,* II, 858–859 (medicine man); Minutes of the Friendly Association, 1755–1757, 41, HSP ("Indian of Note"). In addition, while he spoke no English, he was said to understand it some (*PWJ,* IX, 595; *MPCP,* VIII, 121). In 1761 he said that "[i]t is many years since I left my Country and settled myself at Susquehanna" (*ibid.,* 656).

14. *MPCP,* VI, 160, 613, VII, 3, 64.

15. *Ibid.,* IX, 611 ("Children"), 617 ("door"); *PWJ,* XII, 60–61. Dolores Elliott, "Otsiningo, An Example of an Eighteenth Century Settlement Pattern," *Current Perspectives in Northeastern Archaeology,* XVII (1977), 93–105. He was also a go-between in Iroquois relations with Indian peoples even farther from the Six Nations' southern "door," at least twice escorting Cherokee ambassadors, who called him "our elder Brother" (*PWJ,* II, 858–859, IX, 848; *MPCP,* VIII, 124–125; William Denny to William Johnson, 27 June 1758, PMOC, IX, 43).

16. *MPCP,* VIII, 656. The son's presence that day is suggested in "List of Goods presented to Last Night & his Companions," 31 Aug. 1761, FA, IV, 183. This child was the only one of the Seneca's children still alive in 1761. In 1758 Seneca George had had a daughter called Peggy, and that same year an Indian named Johnny, apparently a Mohawk, was said to be "the Son of the present Wife of Seneca George" (*PA,* 1st, IV, 476; Denny to Johnson, 27 June 1758, PMOC, IX, 43). For his possibly being a Mohawk, see Edward Shippen to Joseph Shippen, 28 May 1758, Correspondence of Edward and Joseph Shippen, 1750–1778, Shippen Papers, APS). This Johnny, who escorted Cherokees from Winchester to Philadelphia in June 1758, died in Philadelphia that very month (Seneca George to Gov. Denny, 25 June 1758, RPCEC, B9, 1947). "Young Seneca George" may have been the child who in October 1757 was said to have been in Philadelphia some time, ill with smallpox and now (presumably recovered?) in need of clothing and—"if He [Seneca George?] can be perswaded"—schooling (Minutes of the Friendly Assoc., 1755–1757, 41, verso, HSP. See also Accounts, 4 12 mo. 1758, FA, II, 410–412).

17. J. N. B. Hewitt, "The Requickening Address of the Iroquois Condolence Council," *Journal of the Washington Academy of Sciences,* XXXIV (1944), 73. For

the link in the Iroquois mind between grief and the woods, see also *ibid.,* 68; Horatio Hale, ed., *The Iroquois Book of Rites* (Toronto, 1963 [orig. pub., 1883], 117–121.

18. *PWJ,* X, 117, 122, 124, 171, XIII, 142; *PA,* 1st, IV, 176–178, 194, 210; W. A. Newman Dorland, "The Second Troop Philadelphia City Cavalry," *PMHB,* XLIX (1925), 82; James Tilghman to Thomas and Richard Penn, 14 Aug. 1766, PMOC, X, 53; John Penn to Thomas Penn, 12 Sept. 1766, *ibid.,* 82; Rowe, "Stump Affair," *Pa. History,* XLIX (1982), 282, n.7; Thomas Balch, ed., *Letters and Papers Relating Chiefly to the Provincial History of Pennsylvania . . .* (Philadelphia, 1855), xliv, 50.

19. *PWJ,* III, 901, IV, 255, V, 515, 525, VI, 518, 545, VIII, 292–293, 308, XII, 276–277.

20. *PA,* 1st, II, 645–646; Edward Shippen to Joseph Shippen, 1 Aug. 1756, PSF, II. Seneca George had been slated to stay behind in Philadelphia (*MPCP,* VII, 90), but went at least part way with Scarouyady's party (Account of John Ferguson, 14 June 1756, Richard Peters, Accounts, 1755–1760, Records of the Proprietary Government, RG-21, microfilm 0597, Reel 1, Pennsylvania State Archives; I am grateful to Jane Merritt for this reference).

21. *PWJ,* VIII, 235, X, 171. Exactly how much of Francis's story Seneca George knew is not clear. "You and I are Friends and know each other," the Seneca reminded Francis when he saw him at Fort Augusta that summer.

22. *MPCP,* IX, 604; *PA,* 8th, VII, 6398; John Harris to James Burd[?], 17 Aug. 1769, PSF, VII. The speech is *MPCP,* IX, 613–614.

23. *MPCP,* VIII, 752–754 (Indians' demand it revert to their control). *PA,* 1st, XII, 338–339, 8th, VII, 6382.

24. List of Indians, [1758?], FA, I, 563. Other variations include Kandt, Conniack, and Canahatch (*MPCP,* VIII, 176, 218, 730).

25. *PWJ,* VII, 64.

26. *MPCP,* IX, 611–620. Unless otherwise noted, all quotations of the council speeches are from this source. The next day Francis stumbled again by failing to invite the Indians to a church service held in the fort. Getting word of the plan, "Seneca George sent Notice that his People worshipped the same God with the English, and would attend Divine Service, which they did accordingly, with great Decency."

27. *PG,* 7 Sept. 1769.

28. *Ibid.; MPCP,* VIII, 656. In the official minutes, Seneca George said that Last Night spoke because the Conoy was a chief, and he was only a war captain. More likely it was because Seneca George was the one grieving, and the bereaved could not do business.

29. Wallace, *Weiser,* 219–220, 396, 398; P. C. Croll, *Conrad Weiser and His Memorial Park: A Little History in Three Parts* (Reading, Pa., 1926), 110–112. *PA,* 1st,

II, 503–504; *PG,* 20 Nov. 1755 (patrol; while on that patrol, Frederick also scalped an Indian corpse). "Lists of Pennsylvania Settlers Murdered, Scalped and Taken Prisoners by the Indians, 1755–1756," *PMHB,* XXXII (1908), 310; Conrad Weiser to William Parsons, 4 July 1756, HP, I, 173 (namesake).

30. It appears that Francis served as Weiser's speaker.

31. *PG,* 7 Sept. 1769.

32. *MPCP,* VIII, 656 ("very poor"); Seneca George to Gov. Denny, 25 June 1758, RPCEC, B9, 1947 (smallpox); *PWJ,* XII, 258–259 (1767).

33. *PG,* 7 Sept. 1769. The religious, mystical dimension to this event is reinforced by the Quaker John Woolman's report of preaching to Indians on the Susquehanna's North Branch in 1763 without an interpreter, "feeling 'his mind covered with the spirit of prayer' " (Edmund De Schweinitz, *The Life and Times of David Zeisberger, The Western Pioneer and Apostle of the Indians* [Philadelphia, 1870], 271; Woolman, *The Journal of John Woolman* [Boston, 1909 (orig. pub. 1871)], 201–202).

34. Adolph B. Benson, ed., *The America of 1750. Peter Kalm's Travels in North America. The English Version of 1770* (New York, 1937), 176, 172–173; Brunner, *Indians of Berks County,* 73.

35. Thomas Jefferson, *Notes on the State of Virginia,* ed. William Peden (Chapel Hill, N.C., 1955), 63, 227; Edward D. Seeber, "Critical Views on Logan's Speech," *Journal of American Folklore,* LX (1947), 130–146; Ray H. Sandefur, "Logan's Oration—How Authentic," *Quarterly Journal of Speech,* XLVI (1960), 289–296; James H. O'Donnell III, "Logan's Oration: A Case Study in Ethnographic Authentication," *ibid.,* LXV (1979), 150–156; David Murray, *Forked Tongues: Speech, Writing, and Representation in North American Indian Texts* (Bloomington, Ind., 1991), 35–36; Edward G. Gray, "The Making of Logan, The Mingo Orator," in Norman Fiering and Edward G. Gray, eds., *The Language Encounter in America* (New York, forthcoming). I am grateful to Professor Gray for sharing his work with me. And see Robert F. Berkhofer, Jr., *The White Man's Indian: Images of the American Indian from Columbus to the Present* (New York, 1978); Bernard W. Sheehan, *Seeds of Extinction: Jeffersonian Philanthropy and the American Indian* (Chapel Hill., N.C., 1973).

36. *PWJ,* VII, 274.

37. Francis to James Tilghman, 28 Aug. 1769, Society Collections, Francis, HSP. *PWJ,* VII, 226–227, 253–255, 292–293; Balch, ed., *Letters and Papers,* 224–225.

38. Quoted in Albion and Dodson, eds., *Fithian Journal,* 50, n.9. Francis, involved in land speculation from 1764 onward, became one of the largest landowners on the West Branch of the Susquehanna. *PA,* 3d, XXV, 135–138; *SCP,* III, xiv; Herbert C. Bell, *History of Northumberland County, Pennsylvania*

(Chicago, 1891), 83–84; Albion and Dodson, eds., *Fithian Journal,* 50. A sense of his enthusiasm can be gained from Turbutt Francis to Brother, 25 Feb. 1769, Society Colls., Francis, HSP; Turbutt Francis to Richard Peters, 7 Mar. 1769, RPP, VI, 74.

39. *PG,* 28 Sept. 1769. The possibility of suicide is based on Johnson's writing, cryptically, of "the fathers Misfortune, which I find some of the Indians are so unreasonable as to Censure us for" (*PWJ,* VII, 226; also in *PA,* 1st, IV, 349). The Superintendent had met, on 25 September, "3 Susquehanna Indians, Relations of the Man Murdered," and four more from Susquehanna on 5 October (*PWJ,* XII, 762).

Index